WAR AND PEACE IN AN
AGE OF TERRORISM

WAR AND PEACE IN AN AGE OF TERRORISM

A READER

Edited by

William M. Evan

The Wharton School and
School of Arts and Sciences
University of Pennsylvania

Boston ■ New York ■ San Francisco
Mexico City ■ Montreal ■ Toronto ■ London ■ Madrid ■ Munich ■ Paris
Hong Kong ■ Singapore ■ Tokyo ■ Cape Town ■ Sydney

Senior Series Editor: Jeff Lasser
Series Editorial Assistant: Heather McNally
Senior Marketing Manager: Kelly May
Composition and Prepress Buyer: Linda Cox
Manufacturing Buyer: JoAnne Sweeney
Cover Coordinator: Kristina Mose-Libon
Editorial-Production Coordinator: Mary Beth Finch
Editorial-Production Service: Omegatype Typography, Inc.
Electronic Composition: Omegatype Typography, Inc.

For related titles and support materials, visit our online catalog at www.ablongman.com.

Library of Congress Cataloging-in-Publication Data

War and peace in an age of terrorism : a reader / William M. Evan [compiler].
    p. cm.
    Includes bibliographical references and index.
    ISBN 0-205-42848-7
    1. War. 2. Peace. 3. Terrorism. I. Evan, William M.

JZ6385.W37 2006
303.6'6—dc22

        2004058705

Printed in the United States of America.

10 9 8 7 6 5 4 3 2 1   09 08 07 06 05 04

To Sarah

CONTENTS

PART FOUR   Theories of the Causes of War   87

■ Biological Theories

■ Economic Theories

■ Technological Theories

LIST OF TABLES

LIST OF FIGURES

PREFACE

Wars, in the nineteenth and twentieth centuries, were typically initiated and waged by state actors. World War I and World War II, the Korean War and the Vietnam War all exemplify the role of state actors as well as the scope and lethality of international wars. In the aftermath of World War II, the process of decolonization in Africa, Asia and the Middle East triggered a surge of civil wars. The failure of political and national movements to realize their aspirations gave rise to a phenomenon of terrorism by nonstate actors.

In the 1970s and 1980s, acts of terrorism became increasingly common: hijacking of airliners, kidnapping of diplomats, embassy takeovers and bombings. Terrorist organizations were identified and blacklisted. In the 1990s and in the beginning of the twenty-first century, terrorist organizations have emerged, some with amorphous identities and structures. Traditional terrorist tactics have given way to more ambitious objectives—the most daring and destructive attacks being the crimes against humanity committed on September 11, 2001.

The lexicon of current terrorism has also expanded to include bio-terrorism, chemical terrorism, radiological terrorism, cyber-terrorism, and potentially even nuclear terrorism. Threatening our individual, national and global security are terrorist organizations determined to steal poorly secured weapons of mass destruction and looking to recruit martyrs for suicide bombings.

The catastrophic events of September 11 ushered in the "War on Terrorism," an open-ended effort targeting principally non-state actors anywhere and everywhere in the world. Among the targets of this war are international terrorist networks, principally Al Qaeda—a radical Islamic fundamentalist movement credited with acts of terrorism in Afghanistan, Pakistan, Indonesia, Kenya, Tanzania and elsewhere.

The ominous risks of a nuclear terrorist attack are increasing according to Bruce Blair, president of the Center for Defense Information:

> I wouldn't be at all surprised if nuclear weapons are used over the next 15 or 20 years, first and foremost by a terrorist group that gets its hands on a Russian nuclear weapon or a Pakistani nuclear weapon.[1]

Are such terrorist networks supported and financed by state actors? If so, will these terrorist organizations, sometime in the future, come into possession of weapons of mass destruction that they may eventually unleash on their enemies? Will the terrorist networks increasingly escalate their acts of terror? These alarming threats define our new age of terrorism.

We would do well to heed the warning of Steven Weinberg, Nobel Laureate in particle physics:

> We face another danger, even greater than that from terrorists. For all the good relations between Russia and the US today, Russian nuclear forces are frozen in a cold-war configuration, one designed to respond to warning of an American attack within ten minutes by a massive nuclear counterattack, before a single nuclear weapon can reach Russia's land-based missiles or control centers. This puts not just a city or two but the entire US in danger of irreversible destruction by a mistake, a danger that will increase as Russia's capacities to detect an attack become more and more degraded. Much could be done to lessen this danger, such as seriously reducing nuclear arsenals on both sides and sharing information about missile launches, but this has not been a priority of any US administration.[2]

The international political community, as it is presently constituted, poses a great threat to humankind. The 191 nation-states of the United Nations, though formally committed to upholding Article 1 of the UN Charter to maintain international peace and security, nevertheless engage in an intense rivalry with one another in order to achieve the goal of national security. Pursuing this goal, these nation-states allocate substantial percentages of their resources to military preparedness in order to protect their territorial sovereignty. The unanticipated consequence of this ubiquitous policy is the emergence of a world of nation-states that arms itself to the teeth, thereby squandering precious resources that could otherwise be used for the improvement of the human condition.

In a world that has become irreversibly interdependent, with a constant flow across national borders of capital, goods, people, knowledge and ideas, one would think that the goal of all countries would be global security. Such an alternative policy would require strengthening multilateral institutions, whether it be the International Monetary Fund (IMF); the World Bank, the World Health Organization (WHO); the World Trade Organization (WTO); the International Atomic Energy Agency; the United Nations Educational, Scientific and Cultural Organization (UNESCO); the Food and Agricultural Association (FAO); and so on. By pursuing the goal of global security, leaders of nation-states would promote world peace and thereby also achieve national security.

Prior to the establishment of the United Nations, Mortimer J. Adler published a prescient book entitled *How to Think about War and Peace.*[3] In this book, Adler presents a careful and reasoned brief for replacing the existing system of sovereign nation-states with a world federation of limited but adequate power.

This book is divided into five parts. Part I consists of a historical overview of war. Part II presents alternative perspectives on the war on terrorism. Part III presents a comparison of religious and secular theories of just and unjust war. Part IV sets forth six theories of the causes of war. Part V deals with six theories and strategies for the resolution of conflicts and the prevention of war.

Three appendices, containing a wealth of information about world conflicts, conclude this book. Appendix I consists of a list of civil wars and international wars from 1945 to 1995. In Appendix II, 167 countries are ranked on several crucial indicators, such as military expenditures as a percent of GNP and arms exports and imports in millions of dollars. Finally, Appendix III lists the Nobel Peace Prize winners from 1901 to 2003. These exemplary individuals will hopefully inspire generations of readers of this book to pursue creative efforts for peace.

The overall purpose of this reader is to stimulate students and other readers to invent new ways of analyzing war, new ways of resolving conflicts and new strategies for preventing war—the scourge of mankind.

Notes

1. Quoted in Nicholas D. Kristof, "A Nuclear 9/11," *New York Times,* March 10, 2004, p. A27.

2. Steven Weinberg, "What Price Glory?," *New York Review of Books,* vol. L, No. 17, November 6, 2003, p. 60.

3. Mortimer J. Adler, *How to Think about War and Peace.* New York: Fordham University Press, 1944, 1971, 1995.

Acknowledgments

With the collapse of the Soviet Union in 1991 and the subsequent end of the Cold War, I decided to introduce a new course on war and peace, the purpose of which was to identify the forces promoting war in the developed and developing countries and the countervailing forces promoting peace. In the process of teaching this course I have accumulated many debts of gratitude to successive generations of my students.

I would like to single out the following students for many helpful evaluations of the course readings that I selected: Mark Ford, Ashley Johnson and Constantine Tujios. I also had the good fortune of having Sana Jaffrey as a student and as a research assistant; she provided invaluable and extensive editorial assistance.

I owe a very special debt of gratitude to my friend Frits Dambrink of the Reprographics Department of the Wharton School for his expertise in digitally editing the text of this book.

I would like to thank the following reviewers for their comments on the manuscript: James Berk, Texas A&M University; Martin Hebert, Haverford College; Kathleen Mass Weigert, Georgetown University; and Nigel J. Young, Colgate University.

I also wish to acknowledge my deep gratitude to Jeff Lasser of Allyn and Bacon, who, early on in our discussions, recognized the potential value of this book.

Finally, for her love, wisdom and encouragement through all the years we have shared, I am deeply grateful to my wife, Sarah Evan, to whom this book is dedicated.

—W. M. E.

WAR AND PEACE IN AN AGE OF TERRORISM

PART

Historical Overview

Is war a universal and inevitable attribute of human societies? Can war be prevented? Can war be eliminated? These are some of the overarching and provocative questions of this book.

We begin the historical overview of war in Part I with an essay by Will and Ariel Durant. They open their essay with two arresting propositions: "War is one of the constants of history, and has not diminished with civilization or democracy. In the last 3,421 years of recorded history only 268 have seen no war." They then present the contrasting views of war by a general and by a philosopher.

The second reading is an excerpt from the Chinese General Sun Tzu's *The Art of War,* written two and half thousand years ago. Sun Tzu's book has enjoyed a surprising popularity among students of the social sciences as well as students of business management. Using metaphorical language, Sun Tzu asserts that the art of war can be governed by five basic factors: moral law, heaven, earth, the commander, and method and discipline. He also presents a penetrating discussion of the uses of spies as a source of "knowledge of the enemy's dispositions."

The last reading in Part I is an excerpt from Van Creveld's recent book *The Art of War and Military Thoughts.* Van Creveld does not focus on the origins of war but rather on the origins of military thought. "Since war is among the oldest of human activities, and long antedates the invention of writing, presumably the earliest attempts to think it out have not survived and took the form of poems which were sung or recited on suitable occasions."

Between 1945 and 1991, the majority of writers on war, impressed with spectacular technological progress, focused their attention on how new weapons would be integrated into future wars. As the millennium drew to a close, two opposing views of war were articulated. The first, influenced by General von Clausewitz, contends that war will continue to be used as an instrument of policy in interstate conflicts, notwithstanding the proliferation of weapons of mass destruction and information warfare. The second school of thought, to which Van Creveld subscribes, believes that future wars will be waged primarily by nonstate actors, namely, organizations that do not own sovereign territory. It remains to be seen which of these two visions of future wars will be borne out by history.

Will Durant
Ariel Durant

The Lessons of History

War is one of the constants of history, and has not diminished with civilization or democracy. In the last 3,421 years of recorded history only 268 have seen no war. We have acknowledged war as at present the ultimate form of competition and natural selection in the human species. "*Polemos pater panton,*" said Heracleitus; war, or competition, is the father of all things, the potent source of ideas, inventions, institutions, and states. Peace is an unstable equilibrium, which can be preserved only by acknowledged supremacy or equal power.

The causes of war are the same as the causes of competition among individuals: acquisitiveness, pugnacity, and pride; the desire for food, land, materials, fuels, mastery. . . . The individual submits to restraints laid upon him by morals and laws, and agrees to replace combat with conference, because the state guarantees him basic protection in his life, property, and legal rights. The state itself acknowledges no substantial restraints, either because it is strong enough to defy any interference with its will or because there is no superstate to offer it basic protection, and no international law or moral code wielding effective force.

In the individual, pride gives added vigor in the competitions of life; in the state, nationalism gives added force in diplomacy and war. When the states of Europe freed themselves from papal overlordship and protection, each state encouraged nationalism as a supplement to its army and navy. If it foresaw conflict with any particular country it fomented, in its people, hatred of that country, and formulated catchwords to bring that hatred to a lethal point; meanwhile it stressed its love of peace. . . .

In the seventeenth and eighteenth centuries war was a contest of aristocracies rather than of peoples. In the twentieth century the improvement of communication, transport, weapons, and means of indoctrination made war a struggle of peoples, involving civilians as well as combatants, and winning victory through the wholesale destruction of property and life. One war can now destroy the labor of centuries in building cities, creating art, and developing habits of civilization. In apologetic consolation war now promotes science and technology, whose deadly inventions, if they are not forgotten in universal destitution and barbarism, may later enlarge the material achievements of peace.

In every century the generals and the rulers (with rare exceptions like Ashoka and Augustus) have smiled at the philosophers' timid dislike of war. In the military interpretation of history war is the final arbiter, and is accepted as natural and necessary by all but cowards and simpletons. What but the victory of Charles Martel at Tours (732) kept France and Spain from becoming Mohammedan? What would have happened to our classic heritage if it had not been protected by arms against Mongol and Tatar invasions? We laugh at generals who die in bed (forgetting that they are more valuable alive than dead), but we build statues to them when they turn back a Hitler or a Genghis Khan. It is pitiful (says the general) that so many young men die in battle, but more of them die in automobile accidents than in war, and many of them riot and rot for lack of discipline; they need an outlet for their combativeness, their adventurousness, their weariness with prosaic routine; if they must die

READING 1   The Lessons of History

sooner or later why not let them die for their country in the anesthesia of battle and the aura of glory? Even a philosopher, if he knows history, will admit that a long peace may fatally weaken the martial muscles of a nation. In the present inadequacy of international law and sentiment a nation must be ready at any moment to defend itself; and when its essential interests are involved it must be allowed to use any means it considers necessary to its survival. The Ten Commandments must be silent when self-preservation is at stake.

It is clear (continues the general) that the United States must assume today the task that Great Britain performed so well in the nineteenth century—the protection of Western civilization from external danger. Communist governments, armed with old birth rates and new weapons, have repeatedly proclaimed their resolve to destroy the economy and independence of non-Communist states. Young nations, longing for an Industrial Revolution to give them economic wealth and military power, are impressed by the rapid industrialization of Russia under governmental management; Western capitalism might be more productive in the end, but it seems slower in development; the new governors, eager to control the resources and manhood of their states, are a likely prey to Communist propaganda, infiltration, and subversion. Unless this spreading process is halted it is only a matter of time before nearly all Asia, Africa, and South America will be under Communist leadership, and Australia, New Zealand, North America, and Western Europe will be surrounded by enemies on every side. . . .

Should North America, now at the height of its power, accept such a future as inevitable, withdraw within its frontiers, and let itself be encircled by hostile states controlling its access to materials and markets, and compelling it, like any besieged people, to imitate its enemies and establish governmental dictatorship over every phase of its once free and stimulating life? Should the leaders of America consider only the reluctance of this epicurean generation to face so great

an issue, or should they consider also, what future generations of Americans would wish that these leaders had done? Is it not wiser to resist at once, to carry the war to the enemy, to fight on foreign soil, to sacrifice, if it need be, a hundred thousand American lives and perhaps a million noncombatants, but to leave America free to live its own life in security and freedom? Is not such a farsighted policy fully in accord with the lessons of history?

The philosopher answers: Yes, and the devastating results will be in accord with history, except that they will be multiplied in proportion to the increased number and mobility of the engaged forces, and the unparalleled destructiveness of the weapons used. There is something greater than history. Somewhere, sometime, in the name of humanity, we must challenge a thousand evil precedents, and dare to apply the Golden Rule to nations, as the Buddhist King Ashoka did (262 B.C.), or at least do what Augustus did when he bade Tiberius desist from further invasion of Germany (A.D. 9). Let us refuse, at whatever cost to ourselves, to make a hundred Hiroshimas in China. "Magnanimity in politics," said Edmund Burke, "is not seldom the truest wisdom, and a great empire and little minds go ill together." Imagine an American President saying to the leaders of China and Russia:

"If we should follow the usual course of history we should make war upon you for fear of what you may do a generation hence. Or we should follow the dismal precedent of the Holy Alliance of 1815, and dedicate our wealth and our soundest youth to suppressing any revolt against the existing order anywhere. But we are willing to try a new approach. We respect your peoples and your civilizations as among the most creative in history. We shall try to understand your feelings, and your desire to develop your own institutions without fear of attack. We must not allow our mutual fears to lead us into war, for the unparalleled murderousness of our weapons and yours brings into the situation an element unfamiliar to history. We propose to send representatives to join with yours in a persistent conference for the adjustment of our differences, the cessation of hostilities and subversion, and the reduction of our armaments. Wherever, outside our borders, we may find ourselves competing with you for the allegiance of a people, we are willing to submit to a full and fair election of the population concerned. Let us open our doors to each other, and organize cultural exchanges that will promote mutual appreciation and understanding. We are not afraid that your economic system will displace ours, nor need you fear that ours will displace yours; we believe that each system will learn from the other and be able to live with it in co-operation and peace. Perhaps each of us, while maintaining adequate defenses, can arrange nonaggression and nonsubversion pacts with other states, and from these accords a world order may take form within which each nation will remain sovereign and unique, limited only by agreements freely signed. We ask you to join us in this defiance of history, this resolve to extend courtesy and civilization to the relations among states. We pledge our honor before all mankind to enter into this venture in full sincerity and trust. If we lose in the historic gamble, the results could not be worse than those that we may expect from a continuation of traditional policies. If you and we succeed, we shall merit a place for centuries to come in the grateful memory of mankind."

The general smiles. "You have forgotten all the lessons of history," he says, "and all that nature of man which you described. Some conflicts are too fundamental to be resolved by negotiation; and during the prolonged negotiations (if history may be our guide) subversion would go on. A world order will come not by a gentlemen's agreement, but through so decisive a victory by one of the great powers that it will be able to dictate and enforce international law, as Rome did from Augustus to Aurelius. Such interludes of widespread peace are unnatural and exceptional; they will soon be ended by changes in the distribution of military power. You have told us that man is a competitive animal, that his states must be like himself, and that natural selection now operates on an international plane. States will unite in basic co-operation only when they are in common attacked from without. Perhaps we are now restlessly moving toward that higher plateau of competition; we may make contact with ambitious species on other planets or stars; soon thereafter there will be interplanetary war. Then, and only then, will we of this earth be one."

R E A D I N G 2

Sun Tzu

The Art of War

Laying Plans

Sun Tzu said:

The art of war is of vital importance to the state. It is a matter of life and death, a road either to safety or to ruin. Hence under no circumstances can it be neglected.

The art of war is governed by five constant factors, all of which need to be taken into account. They are: the Moral Law; Heaven; Earth; the Commander; Method and discipline.

The Moral Law causes the people to be in complete accord with their ruler, so that they will follow him regardless of their lives, undismayed by any danger.

Heaven signifies night and day, cold and heat, times and seasons.

Earth comprises distances, great and small; danger and security; open ground and narrow passes; the chances of life and death.

The Commander stands for the virtues of wisdom, sincerity, benevolence, courage, and strictness.

By *Method and discipline* are to be understood the marshaling of the army in its proper subdivisions, the gradations of rank among the officers, the maintenance of roads by which supplies may reach the army, and the control of military expenditure.

These five factors should be familiar to every general. He who knows them will be victorious; he who knows them not will fail.

Therefore, when seeking to determine your military conditions, make your decisions on the basis of a comparison in this wise:

Which of the two sovereigns is imbued with the Moral Law?

Which of the two generals has the most ability?

With whom lie the advantages derived from Heaven and Earth?

On which side is discipline most rigorously enforced? . . .

Which army is the stronger?

On which side are officers and men more highly trained?

In which army is there the most absolute certainty that merit will be properly rewarded and misdeeds summarily punished?

By means of these seven considerations I can forecast victory or defeat. The general who hearkens to my counsel and acts upon it will conquer—let such a one be retained in command! The general who hearkens not to my counsel nor acts upon it will suffer defeat—let such a one be dismissed! But remember: While heeding the profit of my counsel, avail yourself also of any helpful circumstances over and beyond the ordinary rules and modify your plans accordingly.

All warfare is based on deception. Hence, when able to attack, we must seem unable; when using our forces, we must seem inactive; when we are near, we must make the enemy believe we are far away; when far away, we must make him believe we are near. Hold out baits to entice the enemy. Feign disorder, and crush him. If he is secure at all points, be prepared for him. If he is in superior strength, evade him. If your opponent is of choleric temper, seek to irritate him. Pretend to be weak, that he may grow arrogant. If he is taking his ease, give him no rest. If his forces are united, separate them. Attack him where he is unprepared, appear where you are not expected.

The general who wins a battle makes many calculations in his temple before the battle is fought. The general who loses a battle makes but few calculations beforehand. Thus do many calculations lead to victory, and few calculations to defeat; how much more no calculation at all! It is by attention to this point that I can foresee who is likely to win or lose.

On Waging War

In the operations of war, where there are in the field a thousand swift chariots, ten thousand heavy chariots, and a hundred thousand mail-clad soldiers, with provisions enough to carry them a thousand *li,*[1] the expenditure at home and at the front, including entertainment of guests, small items such as glue and paint, and sums spent on chariots and armor, will reach the total of a thousand ounces of silver per day. Such is the cost of raising an army of a hundred thousand men.

When you engage in actual fighting, if victory is long in coming, the men's weapons will grow dull and their ardor will be dampened. If you lay siege to a town, you will exhaust your strength, and if the campaign is protracted, the resources of the state will not be equal to the strain. Never forget: When your weapons are dulled, your ardor dampened, your strength exhausted, and your treasure spent, other chieftains will spring up to take advantage of your extremity. Then no man, however wise, will be able to avert the consequences that must ensue.

Thus, though we have heard of stupid haste in war, cleverness has never been seen associated with long delays. In all history, there is no instance of a country having benefited from prolonged warfare. Only one who knows the disastrous effects of a long war can realize the supreme importance of rapidity in bringing it to a close. It is only one who is thoroughly acquainted with the evils of war who can thoroughly understand the profitable way of carrying it on.

The skillful general does not raise a second levy, neither are his supply wagons loaded more than twice. Once war is declared, he will not waste precious time in waiting for reinforcements, nor will he turn his army back for fresh supplies, but crosses the enemy's frontier without delay. The value of time—that is, being a little ahead of your opponent—has counted for more than either numerical superiority or the nicest calculations with regard to commissariat.

Bring war material with you from home, but forage on the enemy. Thus the army will have food enough for its needs. Poverty of the state exchequer causes an army to be maintained by contributions from a distance. Contributing to maintain an army at a distance causes the people to be impoverished.

On the other hand, the proximity of an army causes prices to go up; and high prices cause people's substance to be drained away. When their substance is drained away, they will be afflicted by heavy exactions. With this loss of substance and exhaustion of strength, the homes of the people will be stripped bare, and their incomes dissipated; at the same time government expenses for broken chariots, worn-out horses, breastplates and helmets, bows and arrows, spears and shields, protective mantlets, draught oxen and heavy wagons, will amount to almost half its total revenue.

A wise general makes a point of foraging on the enemy. One cart-load of the enemy's provisions is equivalent to twenty of one's own, and likewise a single *picul*[2] of his provender is equivalent to twenty from one's own store.

Now, in order to kill the enemy, our men must be roused to anger. For them to perceive the advantage of defeating the enemy, they must also have their rewards. Thus, when you capture spoils from the enemy, they must be used as rewards, so that all your men may have a keen desire to fight, each on his own account.

Therefore in chariot fighting, when ten or more chariots have been taken, those should be rewarded who took the first. Our own flags should be substituted for those of the enemy, and the chariots mingled and used in conjunction with ours. The captured soldiers should be kindly treated and kept. This is called using the conquered foe to augment one's own strength.

In war, then, let your great object be victory, not lengthy campaigns. Thus it may be known that the leader of armies is the arbiter of the people's fate, the man on whom it depends whether the nation shall be in peace or in peril. . . .

The Use of Spies

Raising a host of a hundred thousand men and marching them great distances entails heavy loss on the people and a drain on the resources of the state. The daily expenditure will amount to a thousand ounces of silver. There will be commotion at home and abroad, and men will drop down exhausted on the highways. As many as seven hundred thousand families will be impeded in their labor.

Hostile armies may face each other for years, striving for the victory that is decided in a single day. This being so, *to remain in ignorance of the enemy's condition, simply because one grudges the outlay of a hundred ounces of silver in honors and emoluments, is the height of inhumanity.*

One who acts thus is no leader of men, no present help to his sovereign, no master of victory. What enables the wise sovereign and the good general to strike and conquer, and achieve things beyond the reach of ordinary men, is *foreknowledge.* Now this foreknowledge cannot be elicited from spirits; it cannot be obtained inductively from experience, nor by any deductive calculation.

Knowledge of the enemy's dispositions can only be obtained from other men. Knowledge of the spirit world is to be obtained by divination; information in natural science may be sought by inductive reasoning; the laws of the universe can be verified by mathematical calculation; but the dispositions of the enemy are ascertainable through spies and spies alone.

Hence the use of spies, of whom there are five classes: local spies; internal spies; converted spies; doomed spies; surviving spies.

When these five kinds are all at work, none can discover the secret system. This is called "divine manipulation of the threads." It is the sovereign's most precious faculty.

Having *local spies* means employing the services of the inhabitants of a district. In the enemy's country, win people over by kind treatment, and use them as spies.

Having *inward spies* means making use of officials of the enemy. Worthy men who have been degraded from office, criminals who have undergone punishment; also, favorite concubines who are greedy for gold, men who are aggrieved at being in subordinate positions, or who have been passed over in the distribution of posts, others who are anxious that their side should be defeated in order that they may have a chance of displaying their ability and talents, fickle turncoats who always want to have a foot in each boat. Officials of these several kinds should be secretly approached and bound to one's interests by means of rich presents. In this way you will be able to find out the state of affairs in the enemy's country, ascertain the plans that are being formed against you and, moreover, disturb the harmony and create a breach between the sovereign and his ministers. But there is a necessity for extreme caution in dealing with inward spies . . .

Having *converted spies* means getting hold of the enemy's spies and using them for our own purposes: by means of heavy bribes and liberal promises, detaching them from the enemy's service and inducing them to carry back false information as well as to spy in turn on their own countrymen.

Having *doomed spies* means doing certain things openly for purposes of deception, and allowing our own spies to know of them and, when betrayed, report them to the enemy. We do things calculated to deceive our own spies, who must be led to believe that they have been unwittingly disclosed. Then, when these spies are captured in the enemy's lines, they will make an entirely false report, and the enemy will take measures accordingly, only to find that we do something quite different. The spies will thereupon be put to death.

Surviving spies, finally, are those who bring back news from the enemy's camp. This is the ordinary class of spies, who should form a regular part of the army. *Your surviving spy must be a man of keen intellect, though in outward appearance a fool; of shabby exterior, but with a will of iron. He must be active, robust, endowed with physical strength and courage thoroughly accustomed to all sorts of dirty work, able to endure hunger and cold, and to put up with shame and ignominy . . .*

There must be no more intimate relations in the whole army than those maintained with spies. No other relation should be more liberally rewarded. In no other relation should greater secrecy be preserved.

Spies cannot be usefully employed without a certain intuitive sagacity. Before using spies we must assure ourselves as to their integrity of character and the extent of their experience and skill. A brazen face and a crafty disposition are more dangerous than mountains or rivers; it takes a man of genius to penetrate such.

They cannot be properly managed without benevolence and straightforwardness.

Without subtle ingenuity of mind, one cannot make certain of the truth of their reports.

Be subtle! be subtle! and use your spies for every kind of business.

If a secret piece of news is divulged by a spy before the time is ripe, he must be put to death together with the person to whom the secret was told.

Whether the object be to crush an army, to storm a city, or to assassinate an individual, it is always necessary to begin by finding out the names of the attendants, the aides-de-camp; the doorkeepers, and the sentries of the general in command. Our spies must be commissioned to ascertain these.

The enemy's spies who have come to spy on us must be sought out, tempted with bribes, led away, and comfortably housed. Thus they will become converted spies and available for our service.

It is through the information brought by the converted spy that we are able to acquire and employ local and inward spies. We must tempt the converted spy into our service, because it is he who knows which of the local inhabitants are greedy of gain, and which of the officials are open to corruption.

It is owing to his information, again, that we can cause the doomed spy to carry false tidings to the enemy.

Lastly, it is by his information that the surviving spy can be used on appointed occasions.

The end and aim of spying in all its five varieties is knowledge of the enemy; and this knowledge can only be derived, in the first instance, from the converted spy. He not only brings information himself, but makes it possible to use the other kinds of spies to advantage. Hence it is essential that the converted spy be treated with the utmost liberality . . .

Hence it is only the enlightened ruler and the wise general who will use the highest intelligence of the army for purposes of spying, and thereby they achieve great results.

Spies are a most important element in war, because upon them depends an army's ability to move.

Notes

1. 2.78 modern *li* make a mile. The length may have varied slightly since Sun Tzu's time.

2. A Chinese unit of weight equal to 133.33 pounds.

Martin Van Creveld

The Art of War and Military Thoughts

The origins of military thought are unknown. Since war is among the oldest of human activities, and long antedates the invention of writing, presumably the earliest attempts to think it out have not survived and took the form of poems which were sung or recited on suitable occasions. We do in fact know that many tribal societies have warlike songs. Composed by anonymous bards and often modified to fit subsequent events as they unfold, their purpose is to record glorious deeds that took place in the past, encourage the warriors on one's own side and frighten the enemy. And indeed the Homeric poems, like broadly similar ones in other cultures, appear to have originated in just such a collection of songs.

However revealing and inspiring, poems are no substitute for military theory. . . .

In this connection the vexed question as to whether and how theory influenced action will be largely put aside. At a conference I once attended, one speaker claimed that American "decision-makers" of the Second World War—meaning senior civil servants and generals with research money to spend—treated the social scientists from whom they deigned to commission studies 'as dogs treat lamp-posts'. Upon examination it turned out that one of the social scientists in question happened to be named Ruth Benedict. Her study of Japanese culture, written in 1943–4 and later published under the title *The Chrysanthemum and the Sword,* may or may not have actually influenced any particular decision made during the war—in fact it would be very difficult to tell. More important, though, having sold by the hundreds of thousands, it did more to shape Western, American in particular, notions about Japan than almost any other work before or since, despite the fact that at the time she wrote her study Benedict had never been to Japan, nor did she know Japanese. Certainly it did more than the vast majority of decision-makers whose very names, moderately well known in their own time, have since been forgotten; and many of whom would probably have been unable to put whatever ideas they had about Japan in coherent form even if they had wanted to . . .

Between 1945 and 1991, faced with what was usually understood as unprecedented technological progress, many, perhaps the majority, of writers focused their efforts on the ways in which new weapons would be integrated into future war and influence its shape. Thus, in the 1950s and 1960s, it was often a question of coming to terms with the short- and medium-range missiles then coming into service intercontinental missiles with their nuclear warheads are a different story . . .

The true significance of nuclear weapons was not understood at first. In part this was because there were not too many of them around; nor was it certain that the relatively few and slow bombers capable of carrying them would necessarily reach their targets. Hence it was excusable that many—although not all—senior politicians and military men in the West believed that the next war would be much like the last one, give or take a number of cities turned into radioactive wastes. In 1947, Stalin's previously mentioned picture of total war was reissued specifically with this message in mind. In the face of the American nuclear monopoly of the time, it had to be shown that "adventurist" ideas could not succeed since other factors were even more decisive.

Previously in history, whenever some new and powerful weapon appeared on the scene, it had only been a question of time before it became fully incorporated into military doctrine and, as had happened in the case of the tank and the aircraft-carrier, was turned into the mainstay of that doctrine. From the late 1940s strenuous attempts were made to treat nuclear arms in the same manner, i.e. devise ways for using them in war. First it was the US Air Force which, with its own interests as the sole organization capable of delivering the bomb to target very much in mind, demanded that nuclear bombardment be made the mainstay of American and Western defence, coming up with such aptly named operations as "Bushwhacker," "Dropshot" and "Broiler." Later the idea of "Massive Retaliation" was adopted by the incoming Eisenhower administration. As Secretary of State John Foster Dulles declared in a famous speech, the US would not permit the other side to dictate the site and mode of the next war. Instead, any attempt by the Communists to engage in aggression anywhere in the world *might* be instantly met with means, and at a place, of America's choosing.

By the time it was made, the credibility of this threat was already in some doubt. In September 1949 the Soviet Union had exploded its first atomic bomb and by the early 1950s its arsenal, though still smaller than that of the US, was growing. Given that the US was the first to develop operational H-bombs, possessed far more delivery vehicles and had *deployed* these delivery vehicles across a worldwide chain of bases, it could probably have "won" a nuclear exchange; still this did not address the question as to what would happen if, in the face of an all-out offensive launched by the US air force and navy (which was also acquiring nuclear-capable aircraft), a few Soviet bombs somehow survived in their hideouts and, loaded aboard equally few bombers, found their way to North American targets such as New York and Washington DC. Then, as now, the Dr. Strangeloves of this world tried to exorcize the "bugaboo of radiation" and reassure the public that recovery from a nuclear

war was possible. And then, as now, the question proved unanswerable.

In the late 1950s the situation changed again. Soviet nuclear power was growing, and so were the range and effectiveness of its delivery vehicles in the form of the first intercontinental ballistic missiles. The debate surrounding massive retaliation was replaced, or supplemented, by the question as to how the US itself could be protected against nuclear attack, leading to the emergence of terms such as "city busting" and "counter force," "first strike" and "second strike." A broad consensus was formed that precisely because cities could not be protected against a nuclear offensive it was vital to have forces in place which could survive such an attack and still retaliate with sufficient force to wipe the other side off the map. The outcome was the famous Triad, a vast array of air-borne, sea-borne and land-based nuclear-strike forces linked together by an electronic command system and supposedly capable of "riding out" anything that the Soviet Union could throw at them. Perhaps because the 1962 Missile Crisis had given people a fright, over time the Triad's role in fighting a war tended to be de-emphasized and its deterrent function was given greater prominence. Projected on to the other side, which in spite of its occasional protests to the contrary was supposed to share the same objective, this doctrine became known as "Mutually Assured Destruction" or MAD. . . .

As the millennium comes to an end, two opposing visions of future war seem to be receiving widespread support. One of these still sticks to the framework first created by Clausewitz. Along with the master, it starts from the assumption that war will continue to be used mainly as an instrument of policy at the hand of one state against another. Since reliable defences against nuclear weapons are still not on the horizon, tacitly or explicitly this school finds itself compelled to pretend that they do *not* exist. Thus, at one 1997 conference which dealt with the so-called RMA (revolution in military affairs), a videotape of an imaginary future news broadcast was shown. Cast against the background of Tower Bridge,

London, the announcer pretended to be speaking in the year AD 2020; he started by saying that nuclear weapons had just been abolished.

The danger of nuclear annihilation having been swept away by the stroke of the pen, American analysts in particular talk happily about physical warfare being supplemented by, or even abolished in favour of, "information warfare." Just as the introduction of aircraft during the early years of the twentieth century added a third dimension to warfare, it is argued, so future hostilities will extend into a fourth dimension known as "cyberspace." The electronic circuitry needed for waging information war will be taken straight off the shelves of any electronics store, a proposition which, incidentally, ignores the fact that a single nuclear weapon by virtue of generating an electro-magnetic pulse (EMP) is quite capable of wiping out the communications and data-processing systems of an entire country. The actual conduct of the war will be entrusted to uniformed hackers. Sitting behind screens and hitting buttons, instead of targeting the enemy's men and weapons in the field, they will seek to spoof or jam or saturate the enemy's sensors, disrupt his communications and infiltrate his computers, thus rendering him blind, deaf and mute.

The other school, to which the present author belongs, argues that the proliferation of nuclear weapons has all but brought large-scale interstate warfare to an end. (If nuclear weapons are not used, then large-scale conventional interstate warfare appears to be finished; if they *are* used, then it will already be finished.) Therefore, although isolated attempts to break into the C^3 (or C-cube: command, control, communications) systems of military establishments around the world cannot be excluded and in fact have already been made, large-scale information warfare waged by one state against an equally sophisticated opponent relying on computers, electronic communications and sensors is increasingly unlikely: Designed, financed and maintained by one state for the purpose of fighting another, present-day armed forces are dinosaurs about to disappear; in quantitative terms, and compared with their size at any point since 1945, most of them have already all but disappeared. Furthermore, whereas Clausewitz and his followers looked at war as an instrument in the hands of policy, in fact it is not primarily a rational instrument for the achievement of rational goals. At a deeper level, it would be more correct to say that those goals themselves are but excuses for man's natural desire to fight.

Hence the fact that nuclear weapons are inexorably pushing large-scale inter-state warfare under the carpet, so to speak, should in no way be mistaken for the end of war as such; as Fuller wrote in a footnote to the preface of *Armaments and History* (1946), "one does not eradicate the causes of war by obliterating cities." As Afghanistan and Algeria, Bosnia and Rwanda, and countless other places prove, *Warre* in its elemental Hobbesian sense is not only alive and well but as deadly as ever. Nor should one succumb to the fashionable assumption—which itself is not without its historical predecessors from Edward Gibbon to Norman Angel—that such struggles are necessarily confined to less civilized (read 'developing') countries: Britain for example lost more people to the IRA than during the Suez campaign, the Falklands War and the Gulf War put together. Breaking out now here, now there, limited in geographical scope but often extremely bloody, future war will be waged overwhelmingly by, and against, organizations that are not states. And since they do not own sovereign territory and consequently cannot be threatened with nuclear annihilation, they will be able to fight each other, and the state, to their heart's content. . . .

Questions for Discussion

1. In the reading by Will and Ariel Durant, the philosopher seems to have assumed that all inter-state conflicts are ideological in nature. How would the philosopher address the problem of preventing territorial and economic conflicts?
2. In arguing that war cannot be eliminated from the competitive struggle among nation-states, does the general take into account the scope and lethality of weapons in a nuclear age?
3. Do you agree with the arguments of the general or with the philosopher? What are your reasons?
4. How may the strategies prescribed in Sun Tzu's reading be pursued in a democratic country where transparency is maintained in all government affairs?
5. Why is Sun Tzu's discussion of the use of spies crucial in waging war?
6. How have innovations in weapons technology affected the traditional elements of war such as surprise and speed?
7. Van Creveld formulates two visions of war in the future: the first assumes that war will continue to be used as an instrument of policy by one state against another; the second argues that the proliferation of nuclear weapons has all but brought large-scale interstate warfare to an end. Which vision of the future seems more viable? Why do you think so?

Further Readings

1. Paret, Peter, ed. *Makers of Modern Strategy: from Machiavelli to the Nuclear Age.* Princeton, NJ: Princeton University Press, 1986.
2. Machiavelli, Niccolò. *The Art of War.* Indianapolis: Bobbs-Merrill, 1965.
3. Kagan, Donald. *The Peloponnesian War.* New York: Viking, 2003.
4. Cartledge, Paul. *The Spartans: the World of the Warrior-Heroes of Ancient Greece from Utopia to Crisis and Collapse.* Woodstock, NY: Overlook, 2003.
5. Scavilla, Norma. "Religious Mythology and the Art of War: Comparative Religious Symbolism of Military Violence." *Sociology,* 1982, 9, 4, May–June, 116.
6. Maynard, Kent. "Religious Mythology and the Art of War." *Humanity and Society,* 1982, 6, 2, May, 189–190.
7. Boggs, Carl. "Uncivil Wars: Anti-Politics in a Hobbesian World." *New Political Science,* 35, Spring 1996, 7–19.
8. Berkowitz, Bruce. *The New Face of War: How War will be Fought in the 21st Century.* New York: The Free Press, 2004.
9. Betts, Richard K. "Analysis, War, and Decision: Why Intelligence Failures are Inevitable." *World Politics,* 31, 2, 1978, 61–89.
10. Hughes-Wilson, John. *Military Intelligence Blunders.* London: Constable & Robinson, 1999.

PART II

The War on Terrorism

Warfare, once a well-defined affair, has mutated to take on the shape of the phantom known as "international terrorism." Violence of this unprecedented kind and the absence of any relevant coping strategies, makes it imperative to analyze this phenomenon. This section reviews the various aspects and issues related to international terrorism.

In "America's New War on Terror" Jack Beard traces the history of UN involvement in terrorism-related conflicts, to build the case of self-defense for the United States. International law and precedents from history are used to lend legitimacy to the recent U.S. war in Afghanistan.

The reading "A New Cold War" compares the current phenomenon of international terrorism to its closest precedent in history: the Cold War between the United States and the Soviet Union. It highlights the similarities between the two, such as the clash of rival ideologies and the constant threat of imminent violence. The dissimilarities are also acknowledged, such as the absence of diplomatic options to prevent terrorism.

In "Many Threats of Terror" Richard Garwin discusses the different kinds of threats to which the United States has recently been exposed: chemical, biological, nuclear and cyber terrorism are described in detail.

The change of attitude towards terrorism is analyzed by Bruce Hoffmann in "Rethinking Terrorism and Counter Terrorism since 9/11." He points out the need to recognize its lethality and emphasizes the scope of terrorism, with current examples of its proliferation.

In "Weapons of Mass Salvation" Jeffrey Sacks builds the case against the use of force to counter terrorism. The use of international law is advocated for the peaceful solution of all conflicts including those involving a clash of ideologies. Sacks also highlights the need for the developed world to invest its resources to counter the epidemic of HIV-AIDS and hunger.

Finally, in a penetrating essay entitled "Systemic Analysis of International Terrorism," Fritjof Capra presents a wide range of economic, political, social and psychological determinants of terrorism. He also describes the bizarre phenomenon of suicide bombings.

Jack M. Beard

America's New War on Terror: The Case for Self-Defense under International Law

Introduction

When representatives of fifty countries assembled in San Francisco in 1945 to draw up the United Nations Charter, modern threats of terrorism such as those posed by the Al Qaeda terrorist network were not yet known. The devastation caused by the September 11 terrorist attacks on the United States would not, however, have been an unfamiliar spectacle to the survivors of World War II. The "inherent" right of self-defense in responding to such violent attacks, a right enshrined in Article 51 of the U.N. Charter and understood by the delegates of all states as a long-established principle of customary international law, was a familiar concept in 1945.

It was in accordance with these long-established principles of customary international law and Article 51 that the United States Government reported in a letter to the U.N. Security Council on October 7, 2001, that it had "initiated actions in the exercise of its inherent right of individual and collective self-defence following the armed attacks that were carried out against the United States on 11 September 2001." The letter went on to note that since the September 11 attacks, the U.S. Government had obtained "clear and compelling information that the al-Qaeda organization, which is supported by the Taliban regime in Afghanistan, had a central role in these attacks" and that United States armed forces had initiated actions "designed to prevent and deter further attacks on the United States" including "measures against al-Qaeda terrorist training camps and military installations of the Taliban regime in Afghanistan."

The letter of October 7, 2001 was not the first time the United States has notified the U.N. Security Council of actions involving the use of force against other states and has invoked its inherent right of self-defense in response to terrorist attacks. As discussed below, previous uses of force by the United States against terrorist-supporting states have received varying responses from the international community, given rise to some criticism, and raised a number of international legal questions involving the right of guaranteed self-defense under Article 51 of the U.N. Charter. In contrast, the unprecedented response of the international community to the September 11 terrorist attacks on the United States and important factual and legal distinctions between the circumstances surrounding the September 11 attacks and previous attacks giving rise to the use of force by the United States, demonstrate the propriety of the exercise of self-defense in this case under the U.N. Charter and customary international law.

Previous Uses of Force against Terrorist-Supporting States by the United States

On April 14, 1986, in response to a bombing of a West German discotheque in which an American serviceman and a Turkish woman were killed and more than 230 other persons injured, the United States launched air strikes against five terrorist-related targets in Libya. Based on intercepted and decoded exchanges between Tripoli and the Libyan embassy in East Berlin, the United States claimed that this attack was one of a continuing series of Libyan state-ordered terrorist attacks. The

U.S. Ambassador to the United Nations, Vernon Walters, informed the U.N. Security Council that the United States had acted in self-defense, consistent with Article 51, and that the air strikes were necessary to end Libya's "continued policy of terrorist threats and the use of force, in violation of . . . Article 2(4) of the Charter."

On June 26, 1993, the United States launched a cruise missile attack on Iraq in response to a foiled assassination attempt against former President Bush. Twenty-three Tomahawk missiles were launched at the Iraqi Intelligence Service in Baghdad, causing a number of civilian deaths and destroying much of the complex. On June 27, 1993, U.S. Ambassador to the United Nations Madeleine Albright reported to the U.N. Security Council in this regard: "We responded directly, as we were entitled to do under Article 51 of the United Nations Charter, which provides for the exercise of self-defence in such cases."

In response to the suicide bombings of the U.S. embassies in Tanzania and Kenya, which killed more than two hundred people, including twelve U.S. citizens, and were allegedly perpetrated by the Al Qaeda terrorist network, on August 20, 1998, the United States launched seventy-nine Tomahawk missiles at terrorist training camps in Afghanistan and against a Sudanese pharmaceutical plant that the United States identified as a "chemical weapons facility" associated with Osama bin Laden. The Government of the United States informed the U.N. Security Council that it had repeatedly warned the Government of Sudan and the Taliban regime to shut terrorist organizations down in their respective countries and to "cease their cooperation with the Bin Laden organization." Because the Al Qaeda organization had continued to issue "blatant warnings that 'strikes will continue from everywhere' against American targets" and because further attacks appeared to be in preparation, the United States stated that it "had no choice but to use armed force to prevent these attacks from continuing. In doing so, the United States ha[d] acted pursuant to the right of self-defence confirmed by Article 51. . . ."

International Reaction to Previous Uses of Force by the United States against Terrorist-Supporting States

Previous military actions by the United States against terrorist-supporting states elicited varying responses from the international community and the United Nations. In the case of the 1986 raid on Libya, the United States action was not widely supported. A resolution condemning the U.S. action was introduced in the U.N. Security Council but was vetoed by the United States, France, and the United Kingdom. The U.N. General Assembly adopted a resolution condemning the United States for the attack by a vote of seventy-nine to twenty-eight, with thirty-three abstentions.

In contrast, most states either supported or did not object to the 1993 cruise missile attack on Baghdad in response to the foiled Iraqi assassination attempt on former President Bush, although most of the Arab world expressed regret regarding the attack. In response to the American presentation before the U.N. Security Council, the representatives of other member states either expressed support for the U.S. action or refrained from criticizing it; only China questioned the attack. The General Assembly took no action.

World reaction to the 1998 U.S. cruise missile strikes against terrorist targets in Afghanistan and Sudan in response to the U.S. embassy bombings in East Africa was mixed, with the most intense criticism focused on the Sudan attack. Western European nations supported the U.S. actions to varying degrees, while the Russian President Boris Yeltsin declared that he was "outraged" by the "indecent" behavior of the United States. China issued an ambiguous statement condemning terrorism, and Japan said it "understood America's resolute attitude towards terrorism." In spite of public opinion generally hostile to the United States in the Arab and Muslim world, "most Arab and Muslim Governments remained silent or equivocal about their views on the missile strikes." The U.N. Security Council discussed the matter only briefly, ultimately deferring requests to send an international team of inspectors to the bombed facility in Khartoum to search for evidence of chemical weapons after the United States rebuffed Sudan's requests to produce such evidence. Neither the Security Council nor General Assembly took any formal action in response to the U.S. action against Sudan and Afghanistan.

Previous uses of force by the United States against terrorist-supporting states have thus enjoyed varying levels of support among states and have raised a number of international legal questions. In particular, as noted above, the U.S. raid against Libya in 1986 was not well received. . . .

Assessing a number of factual and legal distinctions between the circumstances surrounding the September 11 attacks and previous terrorist attacks giving rise to the use of force by the United States helps to demonstrate the propriety of the most recent exercise of self-defense under Article 51 and customary international law.

Response of the U.N Security Council

At the outset, the willingness of states and the U.N. Security Council to invoke and affirm the right of self-defense in response to the September 11 terrorist attacks on the United States contrasts sharply with previous terrorist attacks. Before the September 11 terrorist attacks, the U.N. Security Council had never approved a resolution explicitly invoking and reaffirming the inherent right of individual and collective self-defense in response to a particular terrorist attack. It is significant, then, that while the U.N. Security Council stated that it "[u]nequivocally condemn[ed] in the strongest terms the horrifying terrorist attacks which took place on 11 September," it also explicitly and unanimously "[r]ecogniz[ed] the inherent right of individual or collective self-defence in accordance with the Charter." Sixteen days later, the U.N. Security Council again unanimously condemned the terrorist attacks on the United States, explicitly "[r]eaffirming the right of individual or collective

self-defence as recognized by the Charter of the United Nations as reiterated in resolution 1368 (2001). . . ." The Council's unprecedented willingness to invoke and reaffirm self-defense under Article 51 in response to the September 11 terrorist attacks is an important act and, for some states, helped legitimize the U.S. military response as a legal use of force . . .

International Support for the U.S. Military Response under Article 51

A. Decisive Support by Allies and Other States throughout the World in Response to the "Armed Attack"

That the September 11 terrorist attacks can be described as an "armed attack" is implicit in the U.N. Security Council's invocation and reaffirmation of the right of self-defense under Article 51 in Resolutions 1368 and 1373, noted above. Furthermore, the clear and decisive reaction of so many states to the September 11 attacks is significant on this point. In an unprecedented move, the nineteen member countries of the North Atlantic Council of NATO issued a statement on September 12, 2001, agreeing that if it was determined that the September 11 terrorist attacks were directed from abroad against the United States, "it shall be regarded as an action covered by Article 5 of the Washington Treaty, which states that an armed attack against one or more of the Allies in Europe or North America shall be considered an attack against them all." On the basis of subsequent briefings by the United States, NATO determined that the September 11 terrorist attack was indeed directed from abroad and the NATO Secretary General concluded that the attack was an action covered by Article 5 of the Washington Treaty.

In another unprecedented action, this time at a special Washington D.C. meeting of the Organization of American States ("OAS") foreign ministers on September 22, 2001, the twenty-two states of the Western Hemisphere party to the Inter-American Treaty of Reciprocal Assistance

("Rio Treaty") unanimously passed a resolution declaring:

> These terrorist attacks against the United States of America are attacks against all American states, and . . . in accordance with all the relevant provisions of the [Rio Treaty] and the principle of continental solidarity, all States Parties to the Rio Treaty shall provide effective reciprocal assistance to address such attacks and the threat of any similar attacks. . . .

Article 3 of the Rio Treaty, which underlies the September 21 resolution, specifically refers to an "armed attack by any State against an American State."

The unambiguous NATO statements and the OAS delegates' reaffirmation of the Rio Treaty clearly suggest that NATO member states and the states party to the Rio Treaty regarded the September 11 terrorist attacks on the United States as "armed attacks," fully justifying the exercise of the inherent right of self-defense under Article 51 of the U.N. Charter. The European Union ("EU"), along with its member states individually, pledged to support U.S. action against terrorism. Similar views and various offers of support were made by America's Pacific allies, including Australia, New Zealand, Japan, the Philippines, and South Korea. . . .

B. Muslim and Arab States' Reactions

While public opinion in the Arab and Muslim world opposed the U.S. action against Afghanistan, several Arab states such as Bahrain, Egypt, and Jordan expressed support for the U.S. anti-terror campaign. Other Arab states also made significant contributions to U.S. military efforts, including Pakistan by agreeing to support various U.S. military operations in Afghanistan, Saudi Arabia by allowing various operations from Prince Sultan Air Base, and Persian Gulf states such as Oman and Kuwait by allowing use of air bases on their territories. Saudi Arabia and the United Arab Emirates also quickly cut their diplomatic ties with the Taliban, leaving Pakistan as the only state recognizing the Taliban regime. . . . An

emergency meeting of the Organization of the Islamic Conference (OIC), an organization composed of representatives of fifty-six Muslim countries, was nearly unanimous in condemning the September 11 attacks. . . .

Condemnation of the Taliban Regime's Support for Terrorism and Its Link with Al Qaeda

In regard to the link between Al Qaeda and the Taliban Regime, the U.N. Security Council has on numerous occasions made the Taliban's clear and established support of terrorist networks a subject of concern and condemnation. On December 8, 1998, the U.N. Security Council, in noting that it was "deeply disturbed by the continuing use of Afghan territory, especially areas controlled by the Taliban, for sheltering and training terrorists and the planning of terrorist acts," went on to demand that "the Taliban stop providing sanctuary and training for international terrorists and their organizations."

Following the indictment by a U.S. court of Osama bin Laden and his associates for the East Africa U.S. embassy bombings and the Taliban's refusal to turn over Osama bin Laden for trial, the U.N. Security Council again unanimously condemned the continuing use of Afghan territory controlled by the Taliban for sheltering and training terrorists and for planning terrorist acts. Determining that the Taliban's actions constituted a threat to international peace and security, the Council acted under Chapter VII of the U.N. Charter and passed Resolution 1267, which, among other things, "demanded that the Taliban turn over Osama bin Laden without further delay to appropriate authorities in a country where he has been indicted. . . ." After the Taliban rejected all its demands, the Security Council passed Resolution 1333 in which it again condemned the Taliban Regime for its support of international terrorism, deplored its continuing provision of safehaven to Osama bin Laden and his associates, and demanded that the Taliban swiftly close all terrorist training camps on its territory. Citing the Taliban's actions as a threat to international peace and security, the Council imposed a wide variety of economic and diplomatic sanctions on the Taliban, including the freezing of financial assets of Osama bin Laden and the Al Qaeda organization. . . .

Conclusion

While some questions and criticisms have been directed at America's previous uses of force against terrorist supporting states, the case for America's forcible response to the September 11 attacks as being fully consistent with the inherent right of self-defense under customary international law and Article 51 of the U.N. Charter is very strong. The unanimous condemnation of the attacks by the U.N. General Assembly and Se-

curity Council, the affirmation of the right of self-defense by the Security Council, the growing consensus in the international community to hold states accountable for terrorist actions, and the repeated condemnation by the Security Council of the Taliban Regime's support of terrorists in particular, clearly help establish an appropriate framework under international law for the exercise of self-defense by the United States. . . .

If self-defense is to have any meaning in the modern era, international law should not be interpreted to prohibit the United States from exercising its inherent right of self-defense under Article 51 to respond with force against a state that has so directly sheltered, sponsored, and supported the terrorist organizations responsible for the horrific attacks of September 11 on the United States.

J. J. Goldberg

The New Cold War

Not all historic turning points are alike. Some are the obvious kind, moments when great events transpire that change the course of history. Others are simply the points at which we become aware of the changes that have taken place already, while we weren't looking.

September 11, 2001, was the second kind of turning point: not the beginning of America's so-called war against terrorism, but the moment Americans were forcibly awakened to the war that had been declared on them close to a decade earlier.

It took us nearly a decade to realize we were at war, largely because this war did not look like wars we remembered. It was waged episodically, in fits and spurts, albeit with fanatical determination, by shadowy enemies who seemed to have no fixed identity or location. We were not facing some other nation threatening our territory. There were no pitched battles between armies. We had been drawn into a war of ideas, much like the contest between communism and democracy that had just ended. Only now are we coming to understand this. It is a new cold war.

It is time we called it by its name. A cold war is not a quick affair, decided in bold strikes on the battlefield. It allows no sudden, dramatic victory. It is a drawn-out struggle, in which the winning side is the one that offers a better life to more people. It is won by winning over allies and friends. It cannot be fought alone. In a cold war, standing alone means you have lost.

It is time, moreover, to acknowledge the enemy. We were attacked by terrorists on September 11, but we are not at war with terrorism. That is merely a name for the tactic used against us by our foes. The cause for which they fight—the idea that challenges our values—is a militant strain of Islam.

This truth has proven hard to absorb, even a year later. Those who make its case usually do so is terms far too harsh. They present this war as a clash of civilizations, pitting us—meaning, variously, the West, the democracies, the developed nations or Judeo-Christian culture—against the world's 1 billion Muslims. Most of us rightly recoil at that formulation, for that road leads to apocalypse. Instead, rudderless, we grasp at euphemisms and foils: hunting down terrorists, blustering at axes of evil, changing rogue regimes.

What we are up against is something less than a billion Muslims, but more than a few rogues out to make mischief. Our industrial democracies are being challenged by a revolutionary movement that champions a purist Islamic fundamentalism, known as the Salafiyya. Its goal is to restore Muslim society to the supposedly pristine brotherhood of Muhammad and his early disciples. Its enemies are those supposedly decadent Muslim regimes that have strayed from the true path of Muhammad, starting with Egypt and Saudi Arabia, and the supposedly corrupt Western powers that support them. Its allies—starting, so it appears, with Iran—are those revolutionary Islamic regimes that share its commitment to purist Islamic law and its revulsion at the supposed corruption of Western culture.

In some ways this new cold war resembles the last one. Like the communists in their day, the militants of Salafi Islam seek world revolution and promise their adherents a form of heaven. Like communism, Salafi Islam is a mutated strain of a broader value system that is different from ours, but need not be our enemy. Back then, capitalist America was able to make common cause with socialist and labor parties that were as threatened by communism as we were. . . .

As with the last cold war, the terms and scope of this new one are becoming apparent only gradually, amid painful debate. Back then, in the early years of the post-World War II Soviet threat, America responded by launching a witch hunt for suspected communists at home, as though we could depend on society's democratic values by suspending them. It took three turbulent years to fight back the forces of reaction and restore sanity in Washington. Even then, and for years afterward, there was no lack of saber-rattling reactionaries who wanted to end the cold war abruptly and "roll back" communism with a hot, preemptive strike, nuclear if need be. At the other extreme were those liberals who failed to grasp the threat posed by Soviet communism and insisted it could be embraced in friendly coexistence.

Through most of the first cold war, however, America was able to stay the course laid out from the beginning by Harry Truman, Dwight Eisenhower and John F. Kennedy. The madman Stalin and his minions, though they possessed weapons of mass destruction, though they were willing to massacre their own people and invade their neighbors, were kept at bay by a firm mixture of resolve and moderation. Working wisely with our allies in structures of international law and order, following the path of containment, we were able to outlast communism without pushing the world over the edge of nuclear abyss.

In this new cold war, we have not yet reached the stage of wisdom. The days of Truman, Eisenhower and Kennedy are long gone. In their place we have George W. Bush. Under his leadership we strike in every direction at once, seeing our enemy everywhere and nowhere: now in the Salafi extremism of Al Qaeda, now in the cynical Ba'ath secularism of Saddam Hussein's Iraq, now in the very structures of international law that our allies are trying to erect in order to contain these threats in the future. No longer, it seems, do we recoil at the notion of launching preemptive strikes that might unleash apocalyptic responses. We revel in the danger. We dismiss our allies as too hesitant, unwilling to grasp what it means to have enemies. But it is we who have forgotten what it means to have friends.

The first lesson of September 11, that America is at war against a dangerous enemy, has been absorbed. Now it is time for our nation to take a deep, collective breath and begin to absorb the other lessons. We need to talk to one another, to find our missing center. We need to talk to our friends and rebuild our tattered alliances. These things are crucial if we are to find the strength to prevail in a new cold war.

Richard L. Garwin

The Many Threats of Terror

As no commission report could ever do, the terrorist acts of September 11, 2001, have galvanized the United States. More than [three] thousand people died in New York—one of every thousand workers in the city. Taking over a commercial aircraft to use it as a piloted cruise missile evidently exploited a terrible vulnerability of modern society. No commercial pilot could be induced by threats to do this, but the imagination of public officials did not encompass those willing and even wishing to die to kill hundreds or thousands of others.

This instrument of kilo-terrorism is fragile; it can be defeated by not much more than a sturdy locked cockpit. The terrorist planners knew this and went to the trouble, and risked the vulnerability, of planning at least four such hijackings within minutes of one another—too little time to spread the word effectively throughout the aviation system.

My purpose here is to discuss threats and not primarily solutions, although the two are interlinked. If hijacking a passenger aircraft will no longer work, motivated terrorists will doubtless choose something else. I have heard from at least six of my colleagues proposals, for example, to modify the aircraft flight control system so that the pilots can irrevocably switch control to the ground. Or to program the aircraft to automatically land at the nearest suitable airport. Such remedies are unnecessary and distracting. It is enough to lock a strengthened cockpit door and to make all understand that it would not be opened even if hijackers kill the passengers and cabin crew. Clearly, once the aircraft radar transponder is switched to emergency or hijack mode, it should not be possible to switch it back until the aircraft

has landed. There is a case to be made for improved 1990s-era crashproof recorders that will capture video and audio from the cabin as well as the cockpit.

Both smaller and bigger terror weapons exist, and their use may be expected. But even if we have seen the end of hijacked passenger jets as cruise missiles, that is not the end of their equivalent—the use of rented or stolen cargo jets as piloted cruise missiles. Opportunities range from large fleets such as those of UPS or Federal Express to the hundreds of 707s and even 747s available for lease at airports in the United States and elsewhere. More skill but less violence would be involved in stealing such an aircraft. It might be used against buildings or against operating nuclear reactors, which are not designed to withstand the impact of a jumbo jet at high speed. It is relatively simple to have an automatic radar that shuts down a nuclear reactor if a high-speed aircraft is detected within a few seconds of collision; but even in that condition a reactor might suffer a core meltdown because of interference with the emergency core cooling system and other engineered safeguards. . . .

It is doubtful that the terrorists had confidence that the World Trade Center towers would collapse—which they did, not from the impact but from the softening of the steel from the intense fire provided by the aircraft fuel. In fact, the amount of fuel in the form of paper in filing cabinets on a given floor is comparable with that delivered by the plane, but it is more difficult to ignite and easier to put out. It is entirely feasible to build into tall buildings features that would be adequate for fighting such fires and furthermore to equip buildings with means for rapidly bringing firefighters to any floor. This latter might be done on a World Trade Center–like structure by having a number of pulleys of twenty-ton capacity projecting from the roof, with a lead line down near ground level. Firefighters could snag the line and with a ground-based winch pull up a heavy cable which, in turn, could be used to carry platforms, hoses, and pumps to the floors involved. But it would be preferable to have dispersed foam nozzles in a hardened sprinkler system.

Terrorists have other means of turning the strength and assets of American society against itself. These include targeted attacks on chemical plants, but even more important, on shipments of industrial chemicals such as chlorine, which are transported in tank cars or trucks. The terrorist driver might apply for a job with the intent of fitting the tank truck with detonators and exploding it in a community; or such a truck might be ambushed and the material dispersed by a rocket-propelled grenade. While the use of nerve gas or other material would give a far higher number of casualties per ton of material, the vast amounts of dangerous chemicals that move in commerce make this a significant problem.

Some failures to protect particular vulnerable points would cause tremendous damage and inconvenience to modern society—at the major bridges and tunnels, for instance. Not only destruction but radiological contamination of tunnels could be very disturbing, even if it killed few people.

Detonating thousands of tons of ammonium nitrate loaded on a ship in a harbor would have the impact of a small nuclear explosion. Three hundred tons (0.3 kilotons) of ammonium nitrate apparently exploded in France on September 24, killing twenty-nine people and injuring more than 2,500.

Terrorist acts are possible that would be less significant in damage but highly significant in causing terror and weakening perceptions of American strength. Attacks on spectators in a sports stadium seem a particular hazard, especially in the case of events shown on TV. Such an attack could combine explosives and chemical agents; it could even be made by diving a small aircraft loaded with fuel into the stands. The attractiveness of such tactics to terrorists might be reduced by a several-second delay in TV transmission, so that there would be no broadcast, even if thousands of people were killed and several times that number injured.

Concerning nuclear and biological terrorism, the largest amount of damage would be caused either by a nuclear explosion in a city or by a biological warfare attack. It is abundantly clear that the same nineteen terrorists who hijacked the aircraft and destroyed buildings and thousands of lives in what seemed an instant would not have hesitated to detonate a nuclear explosive if they had acquired one. A first-generation (10-kiloton) nuclear explosive would kill at least 100,000 people in a typical urban environment. The theft and detonation of one of the 500-kiloton strategic weapons would probably kill a million people in an instant and flatten 100 square kilometers of buildings. Fifty-five years of development of technology and spread of knowledge make it relatively simple to build a 20-kiloton nuclear weapon if sufficient highly enriched uranium were available, of which there is a thousand-ton surplus in Russia. Much excess plutonium that was developed for making weapons is available as well, although it is somewhat more difficult to use. We must give the security of such materials the attention it deserves.

As for biological warfare, many tons of anthrax may still exist in Russia. Infection can be prevented by prior vaccination; but anthrax is extremely durable as a spore and kills 30 percent or more of the people who have been infected, if there is no adequate prolonged treatment with antibiotics. Even more potentially dangerous are biological warfare agents that are contagious, by contrast with those, such as anthrax, that are simply infectious. High among the contagious agents is smallpox. Although legitimate stocks of smallpox have existed only in two places—in the US and in Russia—it is not precluded that other stocks may have survived the smallpox eradication campaign.

Even though some of these threats are ill defined and it may be hard to prevent their being carried out, some nonspecific solutions are eminently practical. None will give 100 percent protection, but 99 percent protection could be the difference between a million deaths and ten thousand deaths. In a war, that is a great difference. To the 99 percent, it is the difference between life and death. And some of the solutions can be implemented by individual families, corporations, or localities.

The first and most practical defense against biological warfare attack is to maintain "positive" pressure of filtered air within buildings. It takes a very small capital expenditure and a very small expenditure in power to provide a positive pressure so that normal winds will not infiltrate a building, and the anthrax spores or other microbes will be kept out. To do this the air intake to a normal building—whether an office building, an apartment building, or a private house—should be provided with a small blower that delivers air through a High Efficiency Particulate Airfilter (HEPA) at a rate that exceeds the leakage of air in or out of the building. Such "makeup" air will then produce excess pressure in the building so that air flows out through any cracks or apertures, blocking any inflow of unfiltered air. If no form of air intake exists, a window or a portion of a window can be removed to make one. It is interesting to note that any normal building, no matter how tightly closed, will have the same exposure to a biological warfare agent as it would if the windows were wide open—it takes longer for the agent to enter, but it stays there a much longer time. Positive-pressure filtered air largely eliminates this problem.

Other approaches that should be implemented contribute not only to the reduction of threats but to lowering the cost of reducing the threats. Such measures would include sealing at the point of departure trucks, ships, or cargo containers, so that auto parts entering Detroit from Canada, if they were inspected at the factory, would not have to be inspected individually. Electronic manifests and bills of lading could be required in advance, and shipments that comply with these efficiency- and security-based rules would incur less delay and less cost than those shipped the old way.

Similarly, people willing to carry biometric-based identification (a thumbprint plus photo, for instance) could be given "EZ-Pass" treatment. These people would have had a suitable interview and could have provided data to be kept in an electronically accessible file. Those without the EZ-Pass would be delayed longer in driving their trucks into a city or in boarding aircraft.

Thus far, I have discussed a few of the threats that might be expected from terrorists; some of these are greatly increased by the willingness to die for the cause. On the assumption that there are dozens or even hundreds of similar agents already in place, it is unlikely that their motivation can be annulled; hence the critical importance of ensuring that such attempts in the near term will not succeed. Here are some near-term measures:

- To prevent hijacked passenger aircraft being used as a manned cruise missile, strengthen and lock the cockpit door. Assign air marshals to many flights. Ensure that the radar transponder, once switched to emergency mode by a pilot who is being attacked, cannot be switched back.
- To counter the use of rented or stolen large aircraft, ensure that each aircraft landing gear is blocked by heavy concrete barriers or other means that would sound an alarm and disable the gear if moved without authorization.
- Foreign aircraft entering US air space must be subject to the same standards as US aircraft.
- To counter biological warfare, individuals, firms, government, and other organizations should consider installing a unit to provide positive-pressure HEPA-filtered makeup air to their buildings. For most establishments, these units should not be used to guard against biological warfare agents liberated within the building but against those from outside. Because of the far smaller hazard from chemical warfare or industrial chemical attack, HEPA filters should filter only particles from the air. These are typically not individual virus particles, but bacteria or viruses

that are attached to some inert material in the range of diameters from about one to five microns.

■ To facilitate travel and access to sensitive areas, a first-generation biometric identification pass should be made available. Those who have had an adequate interview and have information on file could rapidly be provided with a picture ID augmented by a thumbprint. This would be analogous to the EZ-Pass now widely used at tolls.

■ To facilitate the movement of cargo, more use should be made of sealing at the departure point containers, ships, aircraft, or trucks, so that inspection would occur there with adequate time and space, rather than on the fly at bridges or other choke points. Electronic manifests could be sent ahead and would also accompany the vehicle. Lower customs charges for inspection and accelerated processing would be given to those vehicles and containers packed so as to facilitate high-energy X-ray or neutron scanning. Such vehicles would be processed more rapidly and at a lower cost than those without such helpful features.

There are many more potential terrorists than there are terrorists. In moving against terrorist organizations and states and others supporting ter-

rorism, we need hardly fear that those who are implacable enemies of society will become more deeply implacable. But it would be easy enough to swell the ranks of terrorists with those who up to now have been largely passive. . . .

In taking action against terrorists and their co-conspirators, it would be useful to recall that in the United States conspiracy to commit a crime is in itself an offense. While aiding and abetting the actual crime has the same penalties as the crime itself, conspiracy has a lesser penalty. But one can be imprisoned for conspiracy even if the crime is never committed. Such doctrines could be drawn on to lay the basis for the legitimacy of US action in protecting against and responding to terrorism.

I have neither tried nor succeeded in providing here a complete evaluation of terrorist threats to modern society—let alone a reasoned evaluation of the effectiveness and cost of countermeasures. For instance, cyberterrorism is a serious potential problem, and individual hackers have already caused billions of dollars of damage. It is clear, however, that acting as individuals and as a society as a whole, we will need to make considerable investments in reducing our vulnerability. If we do this wisely and make use of market incentives wherever possible, the cost in efficiency and diversion of resources should be tolerable.

Bruce Hoffman

Rethinking Terrorism and Counterterrorism Since 9/11

The enormity and sheer scale of the simultaneous suicide attacks on September 11 eclipsed anything previously seen in terrorism. Among the most significant characteristics of the operation were its ambitious scope and dimensions; impressive coordination and synchronization; and the unswerving dedication and determination of the 19 aircraft hijackers who willingly and wantonly killed themselves, the passengers, and crews of the four aircraft they commandeered and the approximately 3,000 persons working at or visiting both the World Trade Center and the Pentagon.

Indeed, in lethality terms alone the September 11 attacks are without precedent. For example, since 1968, the year credited with marking the advent of modern, international terrorism, one feature of international terrorism has remained constant despite variations in the number of attacks from year to year. Almost without exception, the United States has annually led the list of countries whose citizens and property were most frequently attacked by terrorists. But, until September 11, over the preceding 33 years a total of no more than perhaps 1,000 Americans had been killed by terrorists either overseas or even within the United States itself. In less than 90 minutes that day, nearly three times that number were killed. To put those uniquely tragic events in context, during the entirety of the twentieth century no more than 14 terrorist operations killed more than 100 persons at any one time. Or, viewed from still another perspective, until the attacks on the World Trade Center and Pentagon, no single terrorist operation had ever killed more than 500 persons at one time. Whatever the met-

ric, therefore, the attacks that day were unparalleled in their severity and lethal ambitions.

Significantly, too, from a purely terrorist operational perspective, *spectacular* simultaneous attacks—using far more prosaic and arguably conventional means of attack (such as car bombs, for example)—are relatively uncommon. For reasons not well understood, terrorists typically have not undertaken coordinated operations. This was doubtless less of a choice than a reflection of the logistical and other organizational hurdles and constraints that all but the most sophisticated terrorist groups are unable to overcome. Indeed, this was one reason why we were so galvanized by the synchronized attacks on the American embassies in Nairobi and Dar-es-Salaam three years ago. The orchestration of that operation, coupled with its unusually high death and casualty tolls, stood out in a way that, until September 11, few other terrorist attacks had. During the 1990s, perhaps only one other terrorist operation evidenced those same characteristics of coordination and high lethality: the series of attacks that occurred in Bombay in March 1993, when 10 coordinated car bombings rocked the city, killing nearly 300 people and wounding more than 700 others. Apart from the attacks on the same morning in October 1983 of the U.S. Marine barracks in Beirut (241 persons were killed) and a nearby French paratroop headquarters (where 60 soldiers perished); the 1981 hijacking of three Venezuelan passenger jets by a mixed commando of Salvadoran leftists and Puerto Rican *independistas;* and the dramatic 1970 hijacking of four commercial aircraft by the PFLP (Popular Front for the Liberation of Palestine), two of which were brought to and then dramatically blown up at Dawson's Field in Jordan, there have been few successfully executed, simultaneous terrorist spectaculars.

Finally, the September 11 attacks not only showed a level of patience and detailed planning rarely seen among terrorist movements today, but the hijackers stunned the world with their determination to kill themselves as well as their victims. Suicide attacks differ from other terrorist operations precisely because the perpetrator's own death is a requirement for the attack's success. . . .

The so-called *Jihad Manual,* discovered by British police in March 2000 on the hard drive of an al Qaeda member's computer is explicit about operational security (OPSEC) in the section that discusses tradecraft. For reasons of operational security, it states, only the leaders of an attack should know all the details of the operation and these should only be revealed to the rest of the unit at the last possible moment. Schooled in this tradecraft, the 19 hijackers doubtless understood that they were on a one-way mission from the time they were dispatched to the United States. Indeed, the video tape of bin Laden and his chief lieutenant, Dr. Ayman Zawahiri, recently broadcast by the Arabic television news station *al Jazeera* contains footage of one of the hijackers acknowledging his impending martyrdom in an allusion to the forthcoming September 11 attacks.

The phenomenon of martyrdom terrorism in Islam has of course long been discussed and examined. The act itself can be traced back to the Assassins, an off-shoot of the Shia Ismaili movement, who some 700 years ago waged a protracted struggle against the European Crusaders' attempted conquest of the Holy Land. The Assassins embraced an ethos of self-sacrifice, where martyrdom was regarded as a sacramental act—a highly desirable aspiration and divine duty commanded by religious text and communicated by clerical authorities—that is evident today. An important additional motivation then as now was the promise that the martyr would feel no pain in

the commission of his sacred act and would then ascend immediately to a glorious heaven, described as a place replete with "rivers of milk and wine . . . lakes of honey, and the services of 72 virgins," where the martyr will see the face of Allah and later be joined by 70 chosen relatives. The last will and testament of Muhammad Atta, the ringleader of the September 11 hijackers, along with a "primer" for martyrs that he wrote, entitled, "The Sky Smiles, My Young Son," clearly evidences such beliefs.

Equally as misunderstood is the attention focused on the hijackers' relatively high levels of education, socioeconomic status, and stable family ties. In point of fact, contrary to popular belief and misconception, suicide terrorists are not exclusively derived from the ranks of the mentally unstable, economically bereft, or abject, isolated loners. In the more sophisticated and competent terrorist groups, such as the LTTE (Liberation Tigers of Tamil Eelam, or Tamil Tigers), it is precisely the most battle-hardened, skilled, and dedicated cadre who enthusiastically volunteer to commit suicide attacks. Observations of the patterns of recent suicide attacks in Israel and on the West Bank and Gaza similarly reveal that the bombers are not exclusively drawn from the maw of poverty, but have included two sons of millionaires. Finally, in the context of the ongoing Palestinian-Israeli conflict, suicide attacks—once one of the more infrequent (though albeit dramatic, and attention-riveting, tactics)—are clearly increasing in frequency, if not severity, assuming new and more lethal forms. . . .

Terrorism's CEO

The cardinal rule of warfare, "know your enemy," was also violated. The United States failed to understand and comprehend Usama bin Laden: his vision, his capabilities, his financial resources and acumen, as well as his organizational skills. The broad outline of bin Laden's curriculum vitae is by now well known: remarkably, it attracted minimal interest and understanding in most quarters prior to September 11. The scion of a porter turned construction magnate whose prowess at making money was perhaps matched only by his countless progeny and devout religious piety, the young Usama pursued studies not in theology (despite his issuance of *fatwas,* or Islamic religious edicts), but in business and management sciences. Bin Laden is a graduate of Saudi Arabia's prestigious King Abdul-Aziz University, where in 1981 he obtained a degree in economics and public administration. . . .

Bin Laden achieved this by cleverly combining the technological munificence of modernity with a rigidly puritanical explication of age-old tradition and religious practice. He is also the quintessential product of the 1990s and globalism. Bin Laden the terrorism CEO could not have existed—and thrived—in any other era. He was able to overcome the relative geographical isolation caused by his expulsion from the Sudan to Afghanistan, engineered by the United States in 1996, by virtue of the invention of the satellite telephone. With this most emblematic technological artifice of 1990s global technology, bin Laden was therefore able to communicate with his minions in real time around the world. Al Qaeda operatives, moreover, routinely made use of the latest technology themselves: encrypting messages on Apple PowerMacs or Toshiba laptop computers, communicating via e-mail or on Internet bulletin boards, using satellite telephones and cell phones themselves and, when travelling by air, often flying first class. . . .

For bin Laden, the weapons of modern terrorism critically are not only the guns and bombs that they have long been, but the mini-cam, videotape, television, and the Internet. The professionally produced and edited two hour al Qaeda recruitment videotape that bin Laden circulated throughout the Middle East during the summer of 2001—which according to Bergen also subtly presaged the September 11 attacks—is exactly such an example of bin Laden's nimble exploitation of "twenty-first-century communications and weapons technology in the service of the most ex-

treme, retrograde reading of holy war."—The tape, with its graphic footage of infidels attacking Muslims in Chechnya, Kashmir, Iraq, Israel, Lebanon, Indonesia, and Egypt; children starving under the yoke of United Nations economic sanctions in Iraq; and most vexatiously, the accursed presence of "Crusader" military forces in the holy land of Arabia, was subsequently converted to CD-ROM and DVD formats for ease in copying onto computers and loading onto the World Wide Web for still wider, global dissemination. An even more stunning illustration of his communications acumen and clever manipulation of media was the pre-recorded, pre-produced, B-roll, or video clip, that bin Laden had queued and ready for broadcast within hours of the commencement of the American air strikes on Afghanistan on Sunday, October 7.

In addition to his adroit marrying of technology to religion and of harnessing the munificence of modernity and the West as a weapon to be wielded against his very enemies, bin Laden has demonstrated uncommon patience, planning, and attention to detail. According to testimony presented at the trial of three of the 1998 East Africa embassy bombers in Federal District Court in New York last year by a former bin Laden lieutenant, Ali Muhammad, planning for the attack on the Nairobi facility commenced nearly five years before the operation was executed. Muhammad also testified that bin Laden himself studied a surveillance photograph of the embassy compound, pointing to the spot in front of the building where he said the truck bomb should be positioned. Attention has already been drawn to al Qaeda's ability to commence planning of another operation before the latest one has been executed, as evidenced in the case of the embassy bombings and the attack 27 months later on the *U.S.S. Cole.* . . .

Indeed, in an age arguably devoid of ideological leadership, when these impersonal forces are thought to have erased the ability of a single man to affect the course of history, bin Laden—despite all efforts—managed to taunt and strike at the United States for years even before September 11. His effective melding of the strands of religious fervor, Muslim piety, and a profound sense of grievance into a powerful ideological force stands—however invidious and repugnant—as a towering accomplishment. In his own inimitable way, bin Laden cast this struggle as precisely the "clash of civilizations" that America and its coalition partners have labored so hard to negate. "This is a matter of religion and creed; it is not what Bush and Blair maintain, that it is a war against terrorism," he declared in a videotaped speech broadcast over *al Jazeera* television on 3 November 2001. "There is no way to forget the hostility between us and the infidels. It is ideological, so Muslims have to ally themselves with Muslims."

Bin Laden, though, is perhaps best viewed as a "terrorist CEO": essentially having applied business administration and modern management techniques to the running of a transnational terrorist organization. Indeed, what bin Laden apparently has done is to implement for al Qaeda the same type of effective organizational framework or management approach adapted by corporate executives throughout much of the industrialized world. Just as large, multinational business conglomerates moved during the 1990s to flatter, more linear, and networked structures, bin Laden did the same with al Qaeda.

Additionally, he defined a flexible strategy for the group that functions at multiple levels, using both top down and bottom up approaches. On the one hand, bin Laden has functioned like the president or CEO of a large multinational corporation: defining specific goals and aims, issuing orders, and ensuring their implementation. This mostly applies to the al Qaeda "spectaculars": those high-visibility, usually high-value and high-casualty operations like September 11, the attack on the *Cole,* and the East Africa embassy bombings. On the other hand, however, he has operated as a venture capitalist: soliciting ideas from below, encouraging creative approaches and "out of the box" thinking, and providing funding

to those proposals he thinks promising. A1 Qaeda, unlike many other terrorist organizations, therefore, deliberately has no one, set modus operandi, making it all the more formidable. Instead, bin Laden encourages his followers to mix and match approaches: employing different tactics and different means of operational styles as needed. At least four different levels of al Qaeda operational styles can be identified:

1. *The professional cadre.* This is the most dedicated, committed, and professional element of al Qaeda: the persons entrusted with only the most important and high-value attacks—in other words, the "spectaculars." These are the terrorist teams that are predetermined and carefully selected, are provided with very specific targeting instructions, and who are generously funded (e.g., to the extent that during the days preceding the September 11 attacks, Atta and his confederates were sending money back to their paymasters in the United Arab Emirates and elsewhere).

2. *The trained amateurs.* At the next level down are the trained amateurs. These are individuals much like, Ahmed Ressam, who was arrested in December 1999 at Port Angeles, Washington State, shortly after he had entered the United States from Canada. Ressam, for example, had some prior background in terrorism, having belonged to Algeria's Armed Islamic Group (GIA). After being recruited into al Qaeda, he was provided with a modicum of basic terrorist training in Afghanistan. In contrast to the professional cadre, however, Ressam was given open-ended targeting instructions before being dispatched to North America. . . . Also, unlike the well-funded professionals, Ressam was given only $12,000 in "seed money" and instructed to raise the rest of his operational funds from petty thievery—for example, swiping cell phones and lap tops around his adopted home of Montreal. He was also told to recruit members for his terrorist cell from among the expatriate Muslim communities in Canada and the United States. In sum, a distinctly more amateurish level of al Qaeda operations than the professional cadre deployed on September 11; Ressam clearly was far less steeled, determined, and dedicated than the hijackers proved themselves to be. . . .

3. *The local walk-ins.* These are local groups of Islamic radicals who come up with a terrorist attack idea on their own and then attempt to obtain funding from al Qaeda for it. This operational level plays to bin Laden's self-conception as a venture capitalist. An example of the local walk-in is the group of Islamic radicals in Jordan who, observing that American and Israeli tourists often stay at the Radisson Hotel in Amman, proposed, and were funded by al Qaeda, to attack the tourists on the eve of the millennium. . . .

4. *Like-minded insurgents, guerrillas, and terrorists.* This level embraces existing insurgent or terrorist groups who over the years have benefited from bin Laden's largesse and/or spiritual guidance; received training in Afghanistan from al Qaeda; or have been provided with arms, material, and other assistance by the organization. These activities reflect bin Laden's "revolutionary philanthropy": that is, the aid he provides to Islamic groups as part of furthering the cause of global jihad. Among the recipients of this assistance have been insurgent forces in Uzbekistan and Indonesia, Chechnya, and the Philippines, Bosnia and Kashmir, and so on. . . .

Underpinning these operational levels is bin Laden's vision, self-perpetuating mythology and skilled acumen at effective communications. His message is simple. According to bin Laden's propaganda, the United States is a hegemonic, status quo power; opposing change and propping up corrupt and reprobate regimes that would not exist but for American backing. Bin Laden also believes that the United States is risk and casualty averse and therefore cannot bear the pain or suffer the losses inflicted by terrorist attack. . . .

Finally, it should never be forgotten that some 20 years ago bin Laden consciously sought to make his own mark in life as a patron of *jihad*—holy war. In the early 1980s, he was drawn to Afghanistan, where he helped to rally—and even more critically, fund—the Muslim guerrilla forces resisting that country's Soviet invaders. Their success in repelling one of the world's two superpowers had a lasting impact on bin Laden. To his mind, Russia's defeat in Afghanistan set in motion the chain of events that resulted in the collapse of the U.S.S.R. and the demise of communism. It is this same self-confidence coupled with an abiding sense of divinely ordained historical inevitability that has convinced bin Laden that he and his fighters cannot but triumph in the struggle against America. Indeed, he has often described the United States as a "paper tiger" on the verge of financial ruin and total collapse—with the force of Islam poised to push America over the precipice. . . .

Today, added to this fundamental enmity is now the even more potent and powerful motivation of revenge for the destruction of the Taliban and America's "war on Islam." To bin Laden and his followers, despite overwhelming evidence to the contrary, the United States is probably still regarded as a "paper tiger," a favorite phrase of bin Laden's, whose collapse can be attained provided al Qaeda survives the current onslaught in Afghanistan in some form or another. Indeed, although weakened, al Qaeda has not been destroyed and at least some of its capability to inflict pain, albeit at a greatly diminished level from September 11, likely still remains intact . . .

Conclusion

Terrorism is perhaps best viewed as the archetypal shark in the water. It must constantly move forward to survive and indeed to succeed. Although survival entails obviating the governmental countermeasures designed to unearth and destroy the terrorists and their organization, success is dependent on overcoming the defenses and physical security barriers designed to thwart attack. In these respects, the necessity for change in order to stay one step ahead of the counterterrorism curve compels terrorists to change—adjusting and adapting their tactics, modus operandi, and sometimes even their weapons systems as needed. The better, more determined, and more sophisticated terrorists will therefore always find a way to carry on their struggle.

The loss of physical sanctuaries—the most long-standing effect that the U.S.-led war on terrorism is likely to achieve—will signal only the death knell of terrorism as it has been known. In a new era of terrorism, "virtual" attacks from "virtual sanctuaries," involving anonymous cyberassaults may become more appealing for a new generation of terrorists unable to absorb the means and methods of conventional assault techniques as they once did in capacious training camps. Indeed, the attraction for such attacks will likely grow as American society itself becomes ever more dependent on electronic means of commerce and communication. One lesson from last October's anthrax cases and the immense disruption it caused the U.S. Postal Service may be to impel more rapidly than might otherwise have been the case the use of electronic banking and other online commercial activities. The attraction therefore for a terrorist group to bring down a system that is likely to become increasingly dependent on electronic means of communication and commerce cannot be dismissed. . . .

Similarly, the attraction to employ more exotic, however crude, weapons like low-level biological and chemical agents may also increase. Although these materials might be far removed from the heinous capabilities of true WMD (weapons of mass destruction) another lesson from last October's anthrax exposure incidents was that terrorists do not have to kill 3,000 people to create panic and foment fear and insecurity: five persons dying in mysterious circumstances is quite effective at unnerving an entire nation. . . .

First, it should be recognized that terrorism is, always has been, and always will be instrumental: planned, purposeful, and premeditated. The challenge that analysts face is in identifying and understanding the rationale and "inner logic" that motivates terrorists and animates terrorism. It is easier to dismiss terrorists as irrational homicidal maniacs than to comprehend

the depth of their frustration, the core of their aims and motivations, and to appreciate how these considerations affect their choice of tactics and targets. To effectively fight terrorism, a better understanding of terrorists and terrorism must be gained than has been the case in the past.

Second, it must be recognized that terrorism is fundamentally a form of psychological warfare. This is not to say that people do not tragically die or that assets and property are not wantonly destroyed. It is, however, important to note that terrorism is designed, as it has always been, to have profound psychological repercussions on a target audience. Fear and intimidation are precisely the terrorists' timeless stock-in-trade. Significantly, terrorism is also designed to undermine confidence in government and leadership and to rent the fabric of trust that bonds society. It is used to create unbridled fear, dark insecurity, and reverberating panic. Terrorists seek to elicit an irrational, emotional response. Countermeasures therefore must be at once designed to blunt that threat but also to utilize the full range of means that can be brought to bear in countering terrorism: psychological as well as physical; diplomatic as well as military; economic as well as persuasion.

Third, the United States and all democratic countries that value personal freedom and fundamental civil liberties will remain vulnerable to terrorism. The fundamental asymmetry of the inability to protect all targets all the time against all possible attacks ensures that terrorism will continue to remain attractive to our enemies. In this respect, both political leaders and the American public must have realistic expectations of what can and cannot be achieved in the war on terrorism and, indeed, the vulnerabilities that exist inherently in any open and democratic society.

Fourth, the enmity felt in many places throughout the world towards the United States will likely not diminish. America is invariably seen as a hegemonic, status quo power and more so as the world's lone superpower. Diplomatic efforts, particularly involving renewed public diplomacy activities are therefore needed at least to effect and influence successor generations of would-be terrorists, even if the current generation has already been missed.

Finally, terrorism is a perennial, ceaseless struggle. Although a war against terrorism may be needed to sustain the political and popular will that has often been missing in the past, war by definition implies finality. The struggle against ter- rorism, however, is never-ending. Terrorism has existed for 2,000 years and owes its survival to an ability to adapt and adjust to challenges and countermeasures and to continue to identify and exploit its opponent's vulnerabilities. For success against terrorism, efforts must be as tireless, innovative, and dynamic as that of the opponent.

Jeffrey Sachs

Weapons of Mass Salvation

If George Bush spent more time and money on mobilising Weapons of Mass Salvation (WMS) in addition to combating Weapons of Mass Destruction (WMD), we might actually get somewhere in making this planet a safer and more hospitable home. WMD can kill millions and their spread to dangerous hands needs to be opposed resolutely. WMS, in contrast, are the arsenal of life-saving vaccines, medicines and health interventions, emergency food aid and farming technologies that could avert literally millions of deaths each year in the wars against epidemic disease, drought and famine. Yet while the Bush administration is prepared to spend $100 billion to rid Iraq of WMD, it has been unwilling to spend more than 0.2% of that sum ($200m) this year on the Global Fund to Fight AIDS, Tuberculosis and Malaria.

The great leaders of the second world war alliance, Franklin Roosevelt and Winston Churchill, understood the twin sides of destruction and salvation. Their war aims were not only to defeat fascism, but to create a world of shared prosperity. Roosevelt talked not only about Freedom from Fear but also Freedom from Want. One of the reasons why the Bush administration is losing the battle for the world's hearts and minds is precisely that it fights only the war on terror, while turning a cold and steely eye away from the millions dying of hunger and disease. When is the last time anybody heard Vice-President Dick Cheney even feign a word of concern for the world's poor?

Last month Mr Bush made a speech to the General Assembly of the United Nations. In calling for action against Iraq, he challenged the international community to live up to its own words.

"We want the United Nations to be effective, and respectful, and successful. We want the resolutions of the world's most important multilateral body to be enforced." He asked whether "the United Nations will serve the purpose of its founding, or will be irrelevant?" The idea that UN commitments should be followed by action is indeed a radical one, especially for the United States, where wilful neglect of its own commitments is the rule.

Just one week before Mr Bush's UN speech, at the Johannesburg World Summit on Sustainable Development, the rich countries promised to put real resources behind the "Millennium Development Goals" of cutting poverty, disease and environmental degradation. They agreed (the United States among them) to "urge the developed countries that have not done so to make concrete efforts towards the target of 0.7% of GNP as ODA (official development assistance) to developing countries." The United States falls $60 billion a year short of that target—a seemingly unbridgeable gap, until one realises that the annual military spending in America has risen by about that amount since Mr Bush entered the White House. The United States spends just 0.1% of GNP on foreign assistance. It is firmly in last place among the 22 donor countries in aid as a share of income, a position it will continue to hold even after the small increases the administration announced earlier this year.

No Conditions, No Excuses

If we were to send teams of "UN development inspectors" into the United States, the results would not be pretty. First, they would discover a nearly total disconnect between global commitments and domestic politics. Mr Bush has not discussed America's commitments at Johannesburg with the American people (and perhaps his aides have not even discussed them with the president).

Second, they would find complete disarray with regard to the organisation, budgeting, and staffing necessary to fulfil the commitments. White House and State Department foreign-policy experts are overwhelmingly directed towards military and diplomatic issues, not development issues. Senior development specialists in the Treasury can be counted on one hand. America's government is not even aware of the gap between its commitments and action, because almost nobody in authority understands the actions that would be needed to meet the commitments.

No serious work whatever is under way within the government to link annual budgetary allocations with the international development goals the United States has endorsed. For example, the Bush administration has failed to produce even one credible document spelling out America's role in a global-scale war against AIDS.

America's planned contribution to the global AIDS fund is around a sixth of what is needed in 2003, according to the fund itself. The evidence shows that $25 billion a year from the donors could avert around 8m deaths each year. The expected $100 billion cost of war against Iraq would therefore be enough to avert around 30m premature deaths from disease, if channelled into a sustained and organised partnership with the poor countries.

There is a way out. It is to empower the United Nations to do what it can truly do: organise a global response to the global challenges of disease control, hunger, lack of schooling and environmental destruction, an effort in which the United States would be a major participant and indeed financier, in exactly the manner that it has repeatedly pledged.

The idea that the UN system could provide real leadership on the great development challenges will strain credulity in some quarters. A steady drumbeat of criticism about the UN agencies during the 1990s, led by right-wing leaders in Congress, has left the impression of nearly moribund institutions, busy securing patronage slots for friends and relatives, and disconnected from the rapid advances in technology, finance and globalisation. Indeed, when I began my own intensive work with the UN agencies three years ago, as chairman of a commission for the World Health Organisation, and then more recently as a special adviser to the secretary-general for the Millennium Development Goals, I was unsure what to expect within the specialised agencies of the United Nations.

Tried and Tested

The truth is almost the opposite of what the UN bashers say. Despite a decade of criticism and budget cuts, the specialised UN agencies have far more expertise and hands-on experience than any other organisations in the world. Even the World Bank, with its knowledge base and ability to disburse and monitor funds in some of the most difficult settings in the world, can address problems of health or environment or other specialised concerns only in partnership with UN agencies that have expertise in these specific areas. No bilateral donor agency can substitute for the scale of UN expertise and engagement, though these agencies can be important partners in a global effort.

This under-appreciated capacity is why the UN system has vastly outperformed expectations in Kosovo, East Timor and other tough assignments in recent years. An agency like the World Health Organisation has a unique mix of technical expertise, legitimacy in all corners of the world, and especially an operational presence on the ground in dozens of the world's poorest and neediest countries. Agencies such as the Food and Agriculture Organisation in Rome became objects of merriment and ridicule among right-wing congressmen in recent years—but of course the constituencies of those senators and congressmen never had to battle the loss of fisheries in Tonle Sap Lake in Cambodia, or drought in AIDS-ravaged southern Africa, as the FAO does each day.

The United Nations, in conjunction with the World Bank, should be asked to take the lead in establishing "Global Frameworks of Action" surrounding each of the major development goals. These frameworks would outline, in broad terms, yet with budgetary guidelines and timetables attached, the specific ways in which rich- and poor-country governments, the private sector, philanthropic foundations and other parts of civil society could get organised to win the fight against poverty and disease. Realistic plans would be based on four Ss: scale, science, specificity, selectivity.

First, the UN plans should address each issue at the appropriate **scale.** Just as there is no point in having weapons inspectors visit only a small fraction of possible weapons sites, there must be no faking it with small-scale AIDS projects that might save one village while leaving whole nations to die. But true scale will cost money, especially from the United States.

Second, the UN should mobilise the best **science** available, as it has done with climate change in the IPCC or with health at the World Health Organisation and UN-AIDS. This means an open, inclusive and consultative process in each area of concern, drawing upon national and international scientific academies, public and private research centres, and academia.

Third, any plan of action must recognise the **specificity** of conditions on the ground. There is no single strategy for fighting AIDS, or preserving forests or combating malaria. Everything depends on physical geography, culture, history and other very local factors. The best way by far to bridge global science and local conditions is to invite national governments and civil society in each country to prepare their own plans of action, with the understanding that meritorious programmes will be funded at the international level. That is the strategy of the Global Environment Facility and the Global Fund to Fight AIDS, Tuberculosis and Malaria. It should be the strategy behind similar efforts for expanding primary education, or providing water and sanitation to impoverished regions.

Fourth, any plan must be **selective,** addressing donor assistance only towards regions that will use it well, and taking a hard-headed approach when corrupt governments are likely to squander the help. On this, the United States is right to demand that aid be linked to good governance and reasonable economic policies. The fallacy in America's approach has been that even well-behaved governments receive only a tiny fraction of the financial help that they really need.

Our interconnectedness on the planet is the dominating truth of the 21st century. One stark result is that the world's poor live, and especially die, with the awareness that the United States is doing little to mobilise the weapons of mass salvation that could offer them survival, dignity and eventually the escape from poverty.

It is time for Mr Bush to take seriously his own statement at the UN that "our commitment to human dignity is challenged by persistent poverty and raging disease." If Mr Bush would only lead his country to that end, not only would he mobilise billions of people in the fight against terrorism, but he would also fulfil his own call for the world to "show that the promise of the United Nations can be fulfilled in our time."

READING 9

Fritjof Capra

A Systemic Analysis of International Terrorism

The horrific terrorist attacks against the United States on September 11 mark the end of an era—the end of over 200 years of invulnerability on our continent. We had heard fundamentalist rhetoric about "striking at the heart of America" for years, but we took it as empty threats. We did not recognize the emergence of a new weapon on the international stage against which we were defenseless—the despair-driven, desperate suicide bomber.[1]

This new form of international terrorism exposes the dangerous fallacy of a national shield against ballistic missiles. Missile defense is of no use whatsoever when terrorists can turn commercial planes into missiles and their fuel tanks into bombs with the help of simple box cutters.

A Systemic Perspective

There is no simple defense against international terrorism, because we live in a complex, globally interconnected world in which linear chains of cause and effect do not exist. To understand this world, we need to think systemically—in terms of relationships, connections, and context.

Understanding international terrorism from a systemic perspective means understanding that its very nature derives from a series of political, economic, and technological problems that are all interconnected. This terrorism is not "mindless," and it is not directed against our "freedom and democracy," as our government wants us to believe.

Terrorism is always a weapon of the politically disempowered and desperate who feel that they are unable to voice their grievances through conventional political processes. In order to combat them effectively, we need to clearly understand the terrorists' frustration.[2]

This does not mean that we should shrink from capturing the terrorists and bringing them to justice. Their crimes are abhorrent beyond words. But we must learn to distinguish between their criminal methods and fundamentalist ideologies on the one hand, and, on the other hand, the often legitimate grievances that drive them into committing such desperate and horrific acts. We cannot fight terrorism effectively without understanding its roots. In the words of Philip Wilcox, who served as US Ambassador at Large for Counterterrorism from 1994 to 1997,

> The most important deficiency in U.S. counterterrorism policy has been the failure to address the root causes of terrorism. Indeed, there is a tendency to treat terrorism as pure evil in a vacuum, to say that changes in foreign policy intended to reduce it will only "reward" terrorists. . . .
>
> But the U.S. should, for its own self-protection, expand efforts to reduce the pathology of hatred before it mutates into even greater danger. Conditions that breed violence and terrorism can at least be moderated through efforts to resolve conflicts and through assistance for economic development, education, and population control.[3]

Understanding the multiple and interdependent roots of terrorism will be the only way to reduce its impact and frequency, and thus to increase our long-term security. Indeed, we owe such a systemic analysis and corresponding action to the victims of the attacks of September 11, as British prime minister Tony Blair has eloquently stated:

> [People] don't want revenge. They want something better in memory of their loved ones. I believe their memorial can and should be greater than simply the punishment of the guilty. It is that out of the shadow of this evil should emerge lasting good: destruction of the machinery of terrorism wherever it is found; hope amongst all nations of a new beginning where we seek to resolve differences in a calm and ordered way; greater understanding between nations and between faiths; and above all justice and prosperity for the poor and dispossessed, so that people everywhere can see the chance of a better future through the hard work and creative power of the free citizen, not the violence and savagery of the fanatic.[4]

A careful exploration of the roots of terrorism shows in particular that much of Islamic fundamentalism is related to the role of the United States in the Middle East and that extremist Islamic movements often arise in direct response to American policies. Of course, the United States is not the only power to blame. There is the insidious legacy of European colonialism; yet American policies since World War II have contributed significantly to the recent rise of fundamentalist Islamic terrorism.[5]

Inappropriateness of Military Strikes

Understandably, the first reaction to the horrendous attacks on the United States is the desire to "strike back." But responding to terrorism with violence, rather than dealing with the context from which it emerged, will continue to create more violence. We must recognize that military actions will not succeed in eliminating the rise of militant Islamic movements. On the contrary, they will result in the deaths of innocent Muslim civilians that will further fuel anti-American hatred.

Retaliatory strikes against suspected terrorist targets trigger further retaliation from terrorists and thus escalate the cycle of violence, as Israel's experience has shown. Surgical strikes make sense only when there are military targets with heavy equipment, which the terrorist networks do not have. Moreover, such strikes are often based on faulty intelligence, which further exacerbates their negative effects. Indeed, whenever the United States has carried out military attacks on terrorist targets in recent years, the attacks have failed or backfired.[6]

Since this terrorism is international, the response has to be international as well. The goals of the coalitions and cooperation within the international community cannot be limited to identifying and capturing the terrorists, as they currently are, but must be extended to addressing the underlying systemic problems. This will be the only way to marginalize the terrorists and strengthen our security in the long run.

America's Image in the World

The terrorism we are concerned with is directed against the United States, and hence the attempt to understand its roots has to begin with the understanding of America's image in the world. This image is multi-faceted. It includes many positive aspects of our society—such as individual liberty, cultural diversity, and economic opportunity—as well as the great enthusiasm for American technology, fashion, sports, and entertainment, especially among the world's youth.

On the other hand, the United States is seen by many as the driving force of a new form of global capitalism that is supported by military force and is often socially unjust and environmentally destructive. Indeed, the buildings attacked by the terrorists on September 11 were proud symbols of American economic power and military might.

The new global capitalism, often referred to as "the new economy," emerged during the last decade of the twentieth century. It is based on sophisticated information and communication technologies and is structured around global networks of financial flows. In spite of great social and cultural diversity, today's world is organized, for the first time in history, according to a common set of economic rules.[7]

These rules are the so-called "free trade" rules that the World Trade Organization (WTO) imposes on its member states. In the mid-1990s this framework for economic globalization was hailed by corporate leaders and politicians as a new order that would benefit all nations, producing worldwide economic expansion whose wealth would "trickle down" to all. However, it soon became apparent to increasing numbers of grassroots activists, both in the United States and around the world, that the new economic rules established by the WTO were manifestly unsustainable and were producing a multitude of interconnected fatal consequences—a breakdown of democracy, more rapid and extensive deterioration of the environment, the spread of new diseases, a disastrous maldistribution of wealth, and increasing poverty and alienation around the world.[8]

It is not difficult to see how these stark global inequities can bring forth desperate, marginalized people who express their hatred and frustration in terrorist suicide attacks. However, there is a nonviolent alternative. During the past years, a powerful worldwide coalition of hundreds of nongovernmental organizations (NGOs) has emerged, which demands greater transparency in the establishment of market rules and independent reviews of the ensuing social and environmental consequences. More recently, this so-called "Seattle Coalition" has begun to propose a whole new set of trade policies that would profoundly change the global economy.[9] After the tragic events of September 11, this work is more important than ever.

U.S. Role in the Middle East

To understand the political context of the recent terrorist attacks, we need to look specifically at the U.S. role in the Middle East. The common view in this country is that we have assumed the role of peacemakers in the region. In other parts of the world, and especially in the Muslim world, the view is quite different. There is widespread anti-American sentiment, based on a number of concerns. They include resentment against

- our uncritical support for the Israeli occupation of Arab land, the dispossession of Palestinians and for state-sponsored assassinations;
- our support of undemocratic and repressive Arab governments, in particular that of Saudi Arabia;
- ten years of sanctions and military attacks against Iraq, which have resulted in the deaths of half a million children;
- our massive military presence in the region (seen by Muslim fundamentalists, especially in Saudi Arabia, as the presence of infidels in the holy land of Islam), as well as our role as the largest supplier of arms in the Middle East.

These grievances have contributed to the rise of several radical Islamic movements, including Hamas and al Qaeda, the terrorist network of Osama bin Laden. Now, why do we support repressive regimes, ignore UN resolutions, and promote violence in the Middle East? The answer, in one word, is "oil." In the view of our government, the access to Persian Gulf oil is essential to the security of the United States. In the Gulf region, like in many other areas in the world, our policies are primarily resource-oriented, designed to support our wasteful economy. Thus, the U.S. role in the Middle East and its contribution to the rise of radical Islamic movements are inextricably linked to our misguided energy policies.

To assure American access to natural resources around the world, the U.S. government continually tries to "stabilize" various regions and, in doing so, has often supported undemocratic and repressive regimes. This has included the training and financing of death squads and other support to governments that have engaged in widespread terrorism against their own populations. Ironically, the U.S. has at times supported hard-line Islamic movements. Indeed, some of the most notorious Islamic terrorists today, including many followers of Osama bin Laden, were originally trained by the CIA.[10]

Our support of repressive governments has helped to encourage underground, often violent, opposition, and the fact that we ourselves have sponsored terrorist attacks undercuts our credibility in the fight against terrorism.

Relationship with Saudi Arabia

To understand the motivation of Osama bin Laden and other Islamic extremists, we need to pay special attention to the U.S. relationship with Saudi Arabia. This relationship is based on an extraordinary bargain, concluded in 1945 between President Roosevelt and King Ibn Saud, according to which Saudi Arabia grants the U.S. unlimited and perpetual access to its oil fields (which contain 25% of the world's known oil reserves!) in exchange for protection of the Saudi royal family against its enemies, both external and internal. This bargain has shaped American foreign and military policy for almost half a century, during which we have protected a totalitarian regime in Saudi Arabia that blatantly disregards basic human rights and tramples democracy.[11]

The main purpose of the Gulf war in 1991, originally code-named "Desert Shield," was not to drive Iraq out of Kuwait, but to protect Saudi Arabia from a possible attack and to guarantee U.S. access to the Saudi oil fields. Since then, the U.S. has maintained and steadily expanded its military presence in the Gulf. In addition we also defend the Saudi regime against its internal enemies. The Saudi Arabian National Guard, which protects the royal family, is almost entirely armed, trained, and managed by the United States.

The goal of Osama bin Laden's terrorist network is to drive the U.S. out of the Gulf region and to replace the corrupt Saudi regime by what they consider an "authentic" Islamic state. Such a state would be modeled after that of the fundamentalist Taliban in Afghanistan, which is many times more repressive than the current Saudi regime, especially in its barbarious treatment of women. Nevertheless, as long as we continue to support the totalitarian system in Saudi Arabia, our support will fuel anti-American hatred.

A Multi-Faceted Anti-Terrorist Strategy

To summarize, at the core of the multiple causes of the recent terrorist attacks against the United States lies the U.S. military presence in the Persian Gulf and our support of the repressive Saudi regime. This presence, in turn, is a consequence of our dependence on Saudi oil, due to many years of misguided energy policies.

Bin Laden's terrorist network has declared an anti-American jihad, a religious war, and finds it easy to recruit volunteers among Muslims who feel frustrated and helpless about other aspects of the U.S. role in the Middle East. These aspects include, in particular, the U.S. support of the Israeli occupation of Arab land and the dispossession of Palestinians; Muslim casualties of U.S.-supported military actions and assassinations, and especially the death of large numbers of civilians in Iraq.

At a deeper level, the extremists often receive sympathy from Islamic fundamentalists who are keenly aware of present global inequities and are struggling to preserve their cultural identity in the face of U.S.-led economic globalization.

The systemic understanding of the background of extremist Islamic terrorism calls for a multi-faceted anti-terrorist strategy. The immediate goal, obviously, is to identify and capture the perpetrators and supporters of the terrorist attacks against the United States, and to bring them to justice before an international court. Since the extension and scope of this terrorism is international, it requires sustained international police work, based on extensive and widespread cooperation among the international community.

This means, in turn, that the United States will have to reverse its recent isolationist stance and become a responsible member of the international community. Instead of weakening or walking away from a series of international treaties and conventions—including the Kyoto protocol on global warming, the Biological Weapons Convention, the World Criminal Court, and the UN Conference on Racism—the Bush Administration needs to realize that cooperation with the United Nations and other multilateral agencies will be vital to increase our own strength and security. Because of our rich cultural diversity, we should be in an ideal position to become active citizens of the world. One fifth of today's Americans, or their parents, were born in other parts of the world; five million of us are Muslims.

In this international collaboration, it will be especially important to enlist the help of Islamic states in portraying the extremists as enemies of Islam, because no true Muslim would take thousands of innocent lives in such reprehensible acts. At the same time, our leaders need to help counteract American religious stereotypes. We need to make it clear that the vast majority of the world's Muslims opposes terrorism and religious intolerance.

Policy Shifts

In the long run, the United States will be able to reduce the terrorist threats only if it adopts a series of policy shifts to deal with the legitimate grievances that often underlie terrorist acts. Systemic thinking means shifting our focus from attempting to crush terrorist movements to pursuing policies that discourage their emergence.

The following two policy shifts would go a long way toward increasing our national security.

1.   A reassessment of U.S. policy in the Persian Gulf, including pressure on the Saudi regime to move toward democratization and the provision of basic human rights.

2.   Promoting a peace agreement that includes the end of Israeli occupation of Palestinian territories and the establishment of a safe and secure

Palestinian state together with the guaranteed existence of an equally safe and secure Israeli state, each with its own territorial integrity. This would bring the United States in line with international law, UN Security Council resolutions, and with the views of virtually the entire international community. In the words of the Israeli novelist and peace activist Amos Oz,

> With or without Islamic fundamentalism, with or without Arab terrorism, there is no justification whatsoever for the lasting occupation and suppression of the Palestinian people by Israel. We have no right to deny Palestinians their natural right to self-determination. [12]

Change of Energy Policy

In order to carry out these shifts of U.S. foreign policy in the Middle East, it will be crucial to sever our dependence on Saudi oil. A shift of energy policy from the current heavy emphasis on fossil fuels to renewable energy sources and conservation is not only imperative for moving toward ecological sustainability, but must also be seen as vital to our security.

More generally, we need to realize that the concept of security needs to be broadened to include considerations such as food security, the security of a healthy environment, social justice, and cultural integrity. In our globally interconnected world, the concept of "national security" is outdated; there can only be global security. A global economic system based on inequity, overconsumption, waste, and exploitation is inherently violent and insecure. An economy based on local self-sufficiency, decentralized renewable energy sources, and the continual cycling of materials will be ecologically and socially sustainable and thus globally secure.

The shift to such a sustainable and secure economy is absolutely feasible with technologies that are available today.[13] In particular, the recent development of efficient hydrogen fuel cells promises to inaugurate a new era in energy production—the "hydrogen economy." A fuel cell is an electrochemical device that combines hydrogen with oxygen to produce electricity and water—and nothing else! This makes hydrogen the ultimate clean fuel. At present, several companies around the world are racing to be the first to produce fuel cell systems to supply electricity for our homes and commercial buildings.

At the same time, car companies are developing hydrogen-powered hybrid-electric cars that will revolutionize the automobile industry. The gradual replacement of the U.S. car fleet with these "hypercars" would eventually save all the oil OPEC now sells and, in addition, would reduce America's CO_2 emissions by about two thirds! Moreover, if a hydrogen tanker struck a reef in Prince William Sound, Alaska, this would have no adverse environmental effects, nor could a hydrogen-fueled airplane be used as a bomb. In both cases, the hydrogen would escape rapidly into the air on impact.

Moral and Political Will

The hydrogen economy will eventually be realized, because it features superior technologies—more economical, safer, and ecologically sustainable. However, this development could be accelerated dramatically with massive investments by the federal government. Such investments would not only bring great environmental and health benefits, but would also significantly increase our security. Moreover, massive federal investments to put a hydrogen infrastructure in place would create tens of thousands of jobs and would give our sagging economy a tremendous boost.

The obstacles that stand in the way of a secure and sustainable future are neither conceptual nor technical. All we need is the moral and political will. To quote Tony Blair once more,

This is a moment to seize. The kaleidoscope has been shaken. The pieces are in flux. Soon they will settle again. Before they do, let us reorder this world around us. . . . Today, humankind has the science and technology to destroy itself or to provide prosperity to all. Yet science can't make that choice for us. Only the moral power of a world acting as a community can. . . . For those people who lost their lives on 11 September and those that mourn them; now is the time for the strength to build that community. Let that be their memorial.[14]

Notes

1. See Robert Fisk, "The Awesome Cruelty of a Doomed People," The Independent, September 12, 2001.

2. See Stephen Zunes, "International Terrorism," Foreign Policy in Focus (www.fpif.org), September 2001.

3. Philip C. Wilcox Jr., "The Terror," New York Review of Books, October 18, 2001.

4. Tony Blair, speech to the Labour Party Conference, Brighton, October 2, 2001.

5. See Stephen Zunes, "U.S. Policy Toward Political Islam," Foreign Policy in Focus (www.fpif.org), June 2001.

6. See refs. 2 and 3.

7. See Manuel Castelis, The Rise of the Network Society, Blackwell, 1996.

8. See Jerry Mander and Edward Goldsmith (eds.), The Case Against the Global Economy, Sierra Club Books, San Francisco, 1996.

9. See International Forum on Globalization, www.ifg.org.

10. See refs. 2 and 5.

11. See Michael Klare, "Asking Why," Foreign Policy in Focus (www.fpif.org), September 2001.

12. Amos Oz, "Struggling Against Fanaticism," New York Times, September 14, 2001.

13. See Paul Hawken, Amory Lovins, and Hunter Lovins, Natural Capitalism, Little Brown, New York, 1999.

14. Tony Blair, ref. 4.

Questions for Discussion

1. The Cold War was a conflict between two countries with recognized governments and defined territories, whereas the "war on terrorism" is not a war against any specific country. Why is it useful to compare the two when such fundamental differences exist between them?

2. Do you think governments should be held accountable for actions of terrorists within their boundaries? What if the terrorists had no affiliation with the state?

3. How feasible is it for the governments of developed countries to address the root causes of global terrorism such as social and political inequality?

4. Do you think Garwin's proposal to counteract threats of terror will ease the fear of the American people?

5. Hoffman, in the last sentence of his article, says "For success against terrorism, efforts must be as tireless, innovative, and dynamic as that of the opponent." Do you think he is suggesting that we retaliate against terrorists with like efforts?

6. What are weapons of mass salvation and how, according to Sachs, should they be used?

7. What does Capra identify as the root causes of anti-American terrorism?

Further Readings

1. Benjamin, Daniel, and Simon Steven, *The Age of Sacred Terror.* New York: Random House, 2002.

2. Ahmed, Eqbal. *Terrorism: Theirs and Ours.* New York: Seven Stories Press, 2001.

3. Skocpol, Theda. "Will 9/11 and the War on Terror Revitalize American Civic Democracy?" *Political Science & Politics,* 2002, 35, 3, Sept., 537–540.

4. Enders, Walter, and Sandler, Todd. "Is Transnational Terrorism Becoming More Threatening? A Time-Series Investigation." *Journal of Conflict Resolution,* 2000, 44, 3, June, 307–332.

5. Jones, Michelle Lim, and Erickson, Victoria Lee. *Surviving Terror: Hope and Justice in a World of Violence.* Grand Rapids, MI: Brazos Press, 2002.

6. Posen, Barry R. "The Struggle Against Terrorism: Grand Strategy, Strategy, and Tactics." *International Security,* 26, 3, Winter 2001–2002, 39–55.

7. Peterson, Peter G. "Public Diplomacy and the War on Terrorism." *Foreign Affairs,* 2002, 81, 5, Sept.–Oct., 74–94.

8. Jenkins, Brian Michael. "Terrorism and Beyond: A 21st Century Perspective." *Studies in Conflict and Terrorism,* 2001, 24, 5, Sept.–Oct., 321–327.

9. Falk, Richard. "Rethinking Counter-Terrorism." *Scandinavian Journal of Development Alternatives,* 1987, 6, 2–3, June–Sept., 19–36.

10. Griffith, Lee. *The War on Terrorism and the Terror of God.* Grand Rapids, MI: Eerdmans, 2002.

11. Tehranian, Majid. "Global Terrorism: Searching for Appropriate Responses." *Pacifica Review,* 2002, 14, 1, Feb., 57–65.

12. Kushner, Harvey W., ed. *The Future Of Terrorism; Violence In The New Millennium.* Thousand Oaks, CA: Sage, 1998, 163–172.

13. Ghosh, Partha S. "International Terrorism: An Unending Malaise." *Indian Journal of Social Science,* 1989, 2, 4, Oct.–Dec., 527–543.

14. Lador-Lederer, J. "A Legal Approach to International Terrorism." *Israel Law Review,* 1974, 9, 2, Apr., 194–220.

15. Lasswell, Harold D. "Terrorism and the Political Process." *Terrorism,* 1978, 1, 3–4, 255–263.

16. Holden, Constance. "Study of Terrorism Emerging as an International Endeavor." *Science,* 1979, 203, 4375, 33–35.

17. Cooper, H. H. A., "Terrorism: The Problem of Definition Revisited." *American Behavioral Scientist,* 2001, 44, 6, Feb., 881–893.

18. Calhoun, Laurie. "The Terrorist's Tacit Message." *Peace Review,* 2002, 14, 1, 85–91.

19. Hoffman, Bruce. "The Logic of Suicide Terrorism." *The Atlantic Monthly,* June 2003, 40–47.

20. Jenkins, Brian Michael. "Terrorism and Beyond: A 21st Century Perspective." *Studies in Conflict and Terrorism,* 2001, 24, 321–327.

PART III

Religious and Secular Theories of Just and Unjust War

It is, indeed, ironic that religion has been a frequent cause of armed conflict, notwithstanding the Sixth Commandment: "Thou shall not kill" or "Thou shall not murder," depending on which theological interpretation of this commandment one accepts. This section presents an overview of different religious perspectives on war based on theology and the social history of religion and its followers. The range of historical narration enables one to assess the extent to which the followers abide by the injunctions of various religions.

In "Ethics and War: A Catholic View," Joseph McKenna discusses the "moral character" of a state. He explores the concept of "self-defense," perhaps the most often employed excuse for recourse to violence. McKenna presents seven conditions or circumstances that justify warfare in the Catholic tradition.

Thomas Paxson, in "The Peace Testimony of the Religious Society of Friends," discusses the philosophy behind the Quakers' legendary opposition to violence. This reading also traces the historical development of the pacifist movement, started by the Religious Society of Friends.

Attached to this reading is the text of a declaration—addressed to King Charles—

made by the leader of the Quakers in the seventeenth century, George Fox, to explain the pacifist beliefs of his community.

The three categories of war in Judaism are described by Michael Walzer in "War and Peace in the Jewish Tradition." He explains how the categories justified in the Judaic tradition include those "Commanded" by God and by Kings. The third category is the "forbidden" wars. It is this third category that is discussed in detail, along with the laws regarding tactics of warfare.

The concept of God-ordained war, which seems to be ingrained in Islamic theology, is elucidated by Sohail Hashmi in "Interpreting the Islamic Ethics of War and Peace." The distinction between the nonviolent pre-Hijra, Makkah period and the post-Hijra, Medinah period is used to trace the development of the concept of Jihad in Islam.

The political philosophy of nonviolence, made famous by Gandhi, is discussed in "Hiṁsā and Ahiṁsā Traditions in Hinduism" by Klaus Klostermaier. The "Mahabharata" is described as the "mother of all battles" and the lessons drawn from this mythical conflict furthered the tradition of "ahiṁsā" or nonviolence in Hindu thought. A contemporary analysis of the current state of militant sectarian violence in India is also explored in light of this concept.

The historical resistance to violence in the Buddhist community is explained in "Peace and Nonviolence in Buddhism" by Roy Amore. He provides a historical context for the develop-ment of this philosophy to enable the reader to comprehend the concept of nonviolence in Buddhism.

In the last reading in this section, Michael Walzer presents a secular view of the ethics of war and its justification in "The Just War." A moral perspective on war is presented devoid of any religious context. Michael Walzer takes a legalist approach towards the problem of justifying violence caused by warfare.

READING 10

Joseph C. McKenna

Ethics and War: A Catholic View

In political terms, war or the threat of war is always an instrument of somebody's policy. It is used to persuade another people to make concessions which are less distasteful to them than the death of their soldiers, the destruction of their wealth, and the occupation of their territory. But the functional description does not convey the stark reality. The tragic finality of instant death, the lingering agony of wounded life, the mental anguish of fear and separation, and the attending train of privation, disease, dishonesty and vice—all these of massive proportions—have been left out. Nuclear war could put the death in tens of millions, deform the bodies and minds of endless generations, and leave the civilized world a charred and blackened wasteland. Normal human sensitivity shudders at this vision. Sensitivity apart, war's coercive purposes repel the humanist as an irrational invasion of man's self-determining dignity. In Christian eyes, to inflict pain on one's fellows clashes with the brotherly ideals which Christ exemplified and preached.

Horrifying though the vision be, inhumane and unchristian though war seem, some segments of mankind still find a promise of gain in the use or threat of force. As long as this is so, the other segments of mankind must deal with a temptation of their own—to cancel out coercion's promise with a menace of counter-coercion. It is this which raises the moral question: Are war and threat of war legitimate, and under what circumstances? How severe may the general be in war, or the statesman in diplomacy? An important restriction of focus in examining such questions must be noted. For all the undoubted impact of environmental interaction on social decisions, the decisions are made by men. It is consequently in the perceptions of solitary minds that the practical permissive or inhibitory influence of moral considerations on community choices must be radicated. The Scholastic moralist wishes to inform the consciences not primarily of nations, but of men.

Divine revelation does not give an unqualified answer to the question of war's legitimacy. Sacred Scripture, read piecemeal with somebody's "inner light" may sound definitive; read in context with the resources of systematic hermeneutics, it remains inconclusive. The "morality of the Sermon on the Mount" is often cited as categorically condemning all resort to force. The Sermon, however, is not all "morality." It includes counsels of perfection as well as minimal commands, ascetical as well as moral guidance. Moreover, in all literalness, it was addressed to individual persons in their individual capacities, not to social collectivities or social leaders as such. Its admonitions to turn the other cheek, to resist not evil, to give your cloak to the man who takes your tunic, and to go two miles with the fellow who makes you go one (*Mt.* 5:39–41) do not necessarily imply, therefore, that the statesman and his nation are morally obliged to sacrifice every other consideration and advantage for the sake of peace. The Sermon's advices must, in fact, be harmonized with the quite different indications which appear elsewhere in Scripture. Among these is the minatory dictum of St. Paul: "But if thou dost what is evil, fear, for not without reason does it [the public power] carry the sword. For it is God's minister, an avenger to execute wrath on him who does evil." (*Rom.* 13:4) While this is directly relevant only to internal social order, it does bestow a positive moral quality

45

upon coercive power in official hands. The interpreter of Scripture must confront with caution, then, even the incisive prohibition in the decalogue: "Thou shalt not kill." (*Ex.* 20:13)

Primitive Christian practices and documents can be, according to Catholic belief, an alternative expression of divine revelation. They reflect the otherwise unrecorded teaching of Christ and the apostles. But these sources are no more decisive than Sacred Scripture as to the moral warrant for war. Despite an apparent reluctance to enter the army, early Christians did serve, and some achieved distinction. The feeling among them that service was incompatible with the new religious spirit hinged not upon the martial purposes of the soldier's profession but upon the idolatrous rites often associated with military life. Origen (d. 254), St. Cyprian (d. 258), and Lactantius (d. 330) can be adduced as denouncing warfare or violence; Tertullian (d. 240) held mutually contradictory positions at different stages of his career. The witness of these men, however, is understandably fragmentary. With the Christian religion persecuted, outlawed, or ignored, formal theorizing on issues of public policy was pointless. When the Edict of Constantine and the emperor's subsequent conversion gave Christians open access to civil office, a new situation was created.

St. Augustine (d. 430) then shaped the broadest early statement on the morality of war. Briefly, this regarded force as, in some situations, justified. The Augustinian statement, despite occasional discordant comments in the Middle Ages, thenceforth remained "in possession" among Catholic thinkers. The chief landmarks in its evolution were the currency given it by Gratian (c. 1150), its distinctive clarification by St. Thomas Aquinas (d. 1274), and its detailed development by the Spanish theologians Francisco Vittoria (d. 1546) and Francisco Suarez (d. 1617). Since the statement is, however, less definitive as early Christian witness than as accepted contemporary doctrine, a complete account of its historical elaboration is not to the point here. It will be enough to set forth the position as it stands today,

incorporating such modifications as have found their way into it during the past three hundred years.

In the opinion of Scholastics, both defensive and offensive war can be morally justified. Supporting argumentation differs for the two types, and the offensive variety is more severely circumscribed. Although Pauline ideas are invoked in the argument, they do not seem strictly necessary; the analysis relies more heavily on reason than on revelation.

At the core of the position is the Scholastic concept of a political society. While this concept admittedly tends to a misleading hypostasization of the state, it does convey reality in terms more meaningful than the positive law fiction of corporate personality. For it relates to the intentions of morality's divine creator rather than to the artifice of human legislators. In the Scholastic view, because a civil society is a natural entity, it is divinely instituted. God, as author of man's natural needs, aptitudes and tendencies, is also author of the social structures which are built upon them. To these social structures, of which the state is one, He has attached certain objective moral characteristics.

One moral characteristic of the state is its obligation to seek the common earthly welfare of its citizens. Linked with this is a second, its right of self-defense. If the evil could with impunity impose their will upon the innocent, social life would be reduced to chaos; for the good of its citizens, then, a state unjustly attacked by force may resist by force.

The right of self-defense is not, however, absolute. It may be exercised only if action is urgently needed and no other remedy is at hand; only so much violence is allowed as will repel the unjust aggressor; a justified attack may not be resisted at all. On these restrictions of the right, Scholastics have long agreed. But two other points have recently attracted closer attention. In an important sense, the right of self-defense is founded on the requirements of a wider, equally natural, but less articulated community—that of mankind. The right aims at preventing international anarchy by restraints placed upon men of ill-will. Conceivably, this purpose would be better served in some circumstances by forbearance than by resistance; where this was the case, the state would be obligated to refrain from action. Secondly, the right of self-defense is founded on the interests of the particular community's own citizens. It aims at protecting their wealth, their lives, and their liberty. Conceivably, this objective, too, could be better achieved by self-abnegation than by self-assertion; and the state would again be obliged to let events take their course.

Another cardinal characteristic of the state is its moral authority. This is its divine authorization to rule, to exercise—with effects in the moral order itself—the functions traditionally identified with governing: to command, judge and execute. While Augustine and his followers here look to the Pauline concept of the public power, the Scholastic can derive this characteristic in sheerly rational terms, as a natural requirement of the community and therefore as a natural endowment bestowed by the community's divine author.

Upon the state's possession of moral authority turns its right of offensive war. The rights of a state or its citizens can be violated in ways other than by invasion: territory or prerogatives owing to the nation can be withheld, or the movement and commerce of its nationals can be seriously impeded. The injustice thus inflicted would call not only for reparation but—in the interests of social order—for punishment. Within a society, the individual is not free to pursue such purposes on his own; he may only appeal to public authority. As between societies, however, there is no one to whom effective appeal can be made. The moral empowerment of the injured state therefore receives a kind of extension: to pass and execute judgment on those who are normally beyond its jurisdiction. Just as the government may right wrongs and punish wrong-doers inside its boundaries, so it may act outside. If need be, it may vindicate its community's rights even by violence. The injured state becomes with respect to another nation "an avenger to execute wrath on him who does evil."

The Scholastic does not, it should be noted, stigmatize legitimate war as the "lesser evil." International crises do not confront him, in this respect at least, with true "dilemmas." Common humanist and Protestant conceptions are quite different. Ernest Lefever, for example, writes unequivocally in a somewhat wider context that "choosing the lesser of two evils . . . is more responsible than an ethic of abstention." Reinhold Niebuhr, adapting classic Lutheran theology, finds man necessitated to sin, not only by the intrinsic corruption of human nature but also by the extrinsic dilemmas of the social milieu. For the Scholastic, by contrast, sin is never inevitable; an act of self-defense or an act of vindicative justice, although imposed by circumstances which are regrettable, is morally good. This conclusion might be censured as leading to an easy identification of selfish national interest with high moral purpose. Yet the doctrine may actually be more humanizing than the other, bleaker, views. It holds conscience to account, first for the reason, then for the measure, of violence—instead of giving over the moral agent to the uninhibited hopelessness which often follows from seeing sin as unavoidable.

The justification of war in general terms does not end the discussion. Conscience must render its account on certain qualifying factors. Unless particular conditions are fulfilled, the general justification has no application to specific cases. These qualifications can be conveniently summarized under seven headings—some of which are more, some less, relevant to the problems of contemporary diplomacy.

First, the war must be declared by legitimate public authority in the country which goes to war. . . . Historically, the condition was invoked in order to limit the military activities of lesser feudal lords. Today, it has a somewhat analogous function even with respect to the major powers. Since, in choosing war or peace, the government of any state acts as surrogate for an unarticulated international authority, its decision must be controlled by international purposes. War must aim at a good which is universal rather than exclusive.

Peace and the sacrifice even of a just claim may therefore be necessary sometimes for the welfare of the wider community.

Second, the injury which the war is intended to prevent or rectify must be real and certain. An imaginary injustice cannot legitimize vindication. Both the right which has been infringed and the alleged infringement of it must have substance. The possibly unjust taking of human life is not within the gambit of the "probabilism" utilized by many Scholastics in appraising most types of moral acts. The right which is at stake in war must therefore be certainly possessed and certainly violated. Some moralists believe, in addition, that a government going to war should know for certain the other party's *moral* culpability, that it should be able to discount with complete assurance any suggestion of inadvertence or ignorance on his part. This belief again is based on the Scholastic notion of civil authority. Because authority is divine in origin and function, only a *moral* fault, as distinguished from a purely juridical, external, offense, can validate its use. As others indicate, however, human knowledge can never be sure of other men's dispositions, on which their moral guilt depends; malicious or not, the external violation of right disturbs social order and justifies its vindication. Typical injuries envisaged by the older moralists, it may be noted, included seizure or retention of territory, breach of the communal or private, the commercial or personal liberties of a country's nationals; and similar impositions on a third state.

Third, the seriousness of the injury must be proportioned to the damages that the war will cause. No criteria are laid down for weighing either factor, except that the assessment must be made in terms of moral rather than material gains and losses. Self-defense, it is agreed, almost always justifies resistance, and the positive vindication of trivial rights is never adequate reason for hostilities. Between these two accepted judgments, however, there is room for widely divergent appraisals. Some commentators contend that no vindication of any right entitles a country to wage war. For them the theory of legitimate

offensive action, although retaining its technical validity, has ceased to be applicable in the modern world. . . .

Fourth—and this is closely linked with the third condition—there must be reasonable hope of success in the waging of the war. If defeat is certain, hostilities will only aggravate the injustice which occasioned them and leave a train of futile sorrow in their path. A nation defending itself against attack, however, may more readily take its chances on fighting, as Finland did in 1939, than a nation on the offensive. In extreme cases the moral value of national martyrdom may compensate for the material destruction of unsuccessful war, as with Belgium in 1914. . . .

Fifth, only as a last resort may hostilities be initiated. A war is clearly pointless if its ends can be attained by less painful means. Negotiation, mediation, arbitration and judicial settlement must be utilized first. Scholastics have in fact demanded, as a necessary prerequisite for military action, an ultimatum or a formal declaration of war, since these are the last measures of persuasion short of force itself. Apart from the possibility that such devices might in fact achieve their appropriate purpose, they can aid in assessing the morality of one's own decision. For they help to establish with certainty any alleged injury as a matter both of law and of fact, by at least hinting at the culpability of a party who shuns them. Moreover, if the rights and wrongs of a situation remain doubtful—in which case war would be immoral—these alternative courses furnish opportunity for compromising the issues.

Sixth, a war may be prosecuted legitimately only insofar as the responsible agents have a right intention. Even good acts are morally perverted if they are done with immoral motives. The significance of this condition should not be discounted simply because the external observer cannot pass judgment on its fulfillment. Governmental authorities are here challenged to confront continually their purposes with the unflinching appraisal of their consciences. A war which is otherwise just becomes immoral if it is waged out of hatred. A war of self-defense becomes immoral if, in its course, it becomes an instrument of expansion. A war to vindicate justice becomes immoral if, as it goes on, it becomes a means of aggrandizement. The facility with which nations rationalize their resort to war is a commonplace of diplomatic historians. The inhibitory influence of conscience is cited less frequently—and even then, with disparaging cynicism; yet it has possibly prevented more wars than this world dreams of. The requirement of right intention can, in addition, debar the rash initiation of war and can bridle the vengeful dispositions which—as Kennan and others have complained—make for the irrational termination of hostilities in "unconditional surrender" when something just as valuable could be achieved faster, more cheaply; and in punitive clauses which fester instead of healing the wounds of the defeated.

Seventh, the particular measures used in conducting the war must themselves be moral. Noble ends do not sanctify ignoble means; evil may not be done that good may come of it. The ramifications of this restriction are wide. It raises questions about the taking of hostages, the handling of prisoners, the employment of deceptive stratagems, and the resort to espionage, and, above all else today, the utilization of nuclear weapons. It might be anticipated that no conceivable use of these armaments can be justified. . . .

With Catholic thought as here presented, it is impossible to reconcile either absolute pacifism or the *Realpolitik* which terminates ethical considerations at the water's edge. The difference between this Catholic view and Protestant or humanist thought of the "realist" tendency is primarily one of emphasis. For the Catholic thinker war is not the lesser of two evils, but the lesser of two goods (one of which appears, at the moment of choice, unattainable). Ethical factors which must be weighed into the political decision for war or peace are more carefully systematized. Even in the conduct of hostilities, moral restraints are regarded as operative. And the moderating factor of "right intention" can contribute to a settlement which is more stable because it is less vindictive. To cite these emphases as "superiorities," however, is less to the purpose than to suggest them as "differences" stimulative of reflection by the many for whom international ethics have, since 1945, acquired new urgency.

Thomas D. Paxson Jr.

The Peace Testimony of the Religious Society of Friends

The Religious Society of Friends (Quakers) has historically opposed war and participation in war, calling on people to live in Christ's peace. Looking to the Spirit acting within the individual and within the community of the faithful, Friends have generally distrusted and avoided systematic theology.[1] The argument that will be developed in this paper rests, significantly, on an appeal to experience.[2]

History

The principal emphasis in early Quakerism was not so much on recovering the early church in an institutional sense as on recovering the life in Christ as lived by the first Christians. Early Friends believed that through experiencing the immediate presence of Christ, human beings could attend directly to the holy Master and harken without intermediary to the Teacher. This message produced in many people a tremendous sense of liberation from both (as they saw it) the dry, empty forms of traditional ritual and ceremony and the social and ecclesiastical hierarchies which in their eyes had been discredited. These "masterless" seekers, whose spiritual needs were not being addressed adequately by the established churches or by radical Puritan groups like the Ranters, were led by George Fox and others to find guidance from Christ's inward teaching. They were eager to live in the Light of Christ and to share the good news that Christ was available to all. . . .

In the 1650s there were many leaders of the movement which became the Religious Society of Friends: Edward Burrough, Edward Byllinge, Margaret Fell, Mary Fisher, Samuel Fisher, George Fox, Elizabeth Hooton, Francis Howgill, John Lilburne, James Nayler, and Isaac Pening-

ton, to mention just a few. Some of these had been active in the Good Old Cause, which brought down the monarchy in the preceding decade. These leaders looked to the New Model Army to bring justice, if not the kingdom of God, to England. Early Friends sought with some success to "convince" soldiers in the army, and newly convinced soldier-Friends often failed to see any problem with remaining soldiers. Indeed, in the mid-1650s Quakers were purged against their will from many military units on the grounds that they undermined military discipline by such actions as refusing to doff their hats to "superiors" and rejecting the use of honorific titles. During this period there is no evidence that either Fox or Nayler, perhaps the most influential of the early "publishers of Truth," tried to talk Quaker soldiers into quitting the military.

From the beginning of the eighteenth century on, Friends tended to assume that Quaker opposition to participation in war was characteristic of the Society from its very inception, but this belief has been challenged by modern historians. One view, that of the British historians Alan Cole, Christopher Hill, and Barry Reay, is that the Peace Testimony[3] did not exist before 1661, though they concede that there were a few pacifists among Friends, such as John Lilburne and the sailor Thomas Lurting . . .

Back in England, on January 6 of 1661, a rebellion was staged against the newly restored monarchy. To indicate that Quakers had no part in this rebellion, a Declaration was written by George Fox and Richard Hubberthorne, "in behalf of the whole body of the Elect People of God who are called Quakers," eschewing violence and any attempt to overthrow the monarchy. It was signed by the authors and ten other prominent Friends and delivered to the king on January 21. This is widely regarded as the initial statement of the Peace Testimony. In the following decades, Friends would be challenged to discern what faithful living required in relation to privateering, obeying calls to watch or to muster, conscription, war taxes, mixed taxes, the manufacture of armaments, and transportation of soldiers and military supplies, among other things.

In 1681, William Penn received a grant to be proprietor of Pennsylvania. He set out to establish a colony that would be governed in a manner consistent with the principles of Friends. It was to have no colonial army or militia; the king was to be responsible for protecting Pennsylvania from privateers and European powers, and Penn adopted a policy of friendly relations with the Delaware, the Native American tribe that lived in southeast Pennsylvania. Nonetheless, in accepting the Charter, Penn accepted the title Captain-General. Until Quakers lost control of the Assembly in 1755, some thirty-seven years after Penn's death, the compromise regarding provincial security was that taxes would be paid for the king's (or queen's) use (which all understood would be used for the royal army), but that there would be no formal provincial army, no conscription, and no taxes explicitly for war. . . .

The Centrality of Peace Witness to the Apostolic Faith

Pilgrim Experience

A familiar and enduring dimension of Friends' unprogrammed meeting for worship is gathering together, in the presence of God, in silent searching. This searching is as multifaceted as prayer. It may include searching for surcease of sorrow, for spiritual sustenance, for guidance; it may include searching in wonder for the face of God; it may include opening oneself attentively to God's searching scrutiny. These common elements of pilgrim experience bring with them an awareness of, among other things, our foolishness, helplessness, and separation from God, and our inability to direct our own spiritual journey. Each of us

knows by experience that we come upon obstacles along the way. When finally, wondrously, "the way opens," as Friends say, permitting us to surmount or pass through an obstacle, we discover that others have gone before us. What may have appeared to us in the experience as a great and glorious revelation, we often see to be commonplace when put into words. We learn that what rose up as mountains for us has been traversed by some without difficulty, and we become aware of things that have not stopped us though they have caused great difficulty for others. We are conscious in all of this that it is none of our doing. We learn the futility of trying to control God; we learn humility—again, and again. . . .

As we travel along the pilgrim path we learn something of what it is to live in the Spirit, however partial and fleeting realization of that life may be. Friends have found that these words—uttered by James Nayler as he lay dying in 1660 after being tortured for blasphemy and later attacked by thieves—resonate with their experience:

> There is a spirit which I feel that delights to do no evil, nor to revenge any wrong, but delights to endure all things, in hope to enjoy its own in the end. Its hope is to outlive all wrath and contention, and to weary out all exaltation and cruelty, or whatever is of a nature contrary to itself. It sees to the end of all temptations. As it bears no evil in itself, so it conceives none in thoughts to any other. If it be betrayed, it bears it, for its ground and spring is the mercies and forgiveness of God. Its crown is meekness, its life is everlasting love unfeigned; it takes its kingdom with entreaty and not with contention, and keeps it by lowliness of mind. In God alone it can rejoice, though none else regard it, or can own its life. . . .[4]

It is the experience of Friends that to the extent to which we live in the awareness of the presence of God, we are called to live under the guidance of that Spirit of which Nayler spoke. . . .

Waging Violent Warfare v. the Lamb's War

The bee lives in a tight and cohesive community, but it gains membership in this community by becoming wholly subordinate to it. The colony is the true organism: it feeds itself; it reproduces; it stores honey to survive the winter. The individual bee is a member, a digit, as it were. As social animals, human beings are susceptible to following the way of the bee, but to do so is dehumanizing. War calls on participants to subordinate themselves to one human community, such as a nation, tribe, or ethnic group. It thus exhibits the triumph of that way of thinking according to which we decide what to do by appeal to the consequences we expect our actions to have, rather than by appeal to absolute moral principles. War also exhibits the triumph of human willfulness over humble attendance to the guidance of the Spirit. From this perspective, "just war" theory rationalizes people's collective assumption of responsibility for justice on earth. But it is not the case that *we* are sovereign. We cannot, acting collectively or individually, make one another just. When I disregard my own limitations (and the limitations of the groups and social institutions I embrace), disregard the teaching and example of Jesus, and assume responsibility for the just behavior of others, attempting to exact justice violently upon them "if necessary," I am supplanting God's judgment with my own. There are elements of willfulness and *hubris* in taking up the sword or gun to impose justice on other human beings, elements quite incompatible with that life in the Spirit to which we are called.

The approach to the centrality of peace witness to the apostolic faith sketched here appeals to an apocalyptic vision that provides support for nonviolence, on the one hand, and for a prophetic calling, on the other. It is suggestive that apocalyptic hopes were high in the first two centuries of the church, among Anabaptists in the sixteenth century, and among radical Puritans and Friends in the seventeenth century. . . .

It is fair to say, I think, that this apocalyptic vision has dimmed among Friends and yet, however they might shrink from (the terminology employed by theologians, there remains among Friends an abiding hope in the coming of God's holy peace and order to this earth and the desire and endeavor to live in that peace and order.

The impulse toward nonresistance found in the words of Nayler quoted earlier is balanced by the prophetic imperative "the Lamb's war," the call

to work against the forces of darkness. Early Friends suffered nonviolently the physical abuse to which their opponents subjected them. While they practiced nonviolent disobedience to those demands of civil authority seen as incompatible with the leadings of the Spirit, they were careful that this disobedience be open, and they accepted the sanctions civil authority levied for that disobedience. In this way the authority of civil government was recognized and respected. The first Friends denounced the evils of their day and engaged actively in lobbying parliament, protector, and then king to change laws and policies seen as unjust. . . .

Toward Reconciliation Regarding Peace Witness

In responding to this familiar criticism, I wish to highlight two developments within the Religious Society of Friends in particular, and the Historic Peace Churches in general, which seem to be facilitating a dialogue that may lead to reconciliation regarding peace witness: (1) the willingness to participate, however critically, in the civil state, and (2) the realization that the third way, between responding to evil with violence and responding to evil with submission to the will of the evildoer, can be much more robust than the unyielding nonresistance of martyrdom. Both of these points warrant some comment. . . .

Although instances of nonviolent *resistance* can be found throughout history, much has been learned about the efficacy of intentionally nonviolent strategies and techniques for combating evil. Whether or not we accept, as Lois Barrett does, Walter Wink's argument in *Engaging the Powers*[5] that Jesus practiced and taught the "third way" of nonviolent action to secure both peace and justice, the Historic Peace Churches have all been influenced by what has been learned about the power of nonviolent direct action for peace and justice. This is a significant shift. In the face of determined evil, nonresistance left the matter of justice almost entirely in God's hands; this was part of the faithful's humble service to God. Nonviolent direct action opened up the possibility of working diligently for justice without violating the proscription against warring with carnal weapons. Indeed, peacemaker teams have been created in the last several years to intervene nonviolently in trouble-spots like Chiapas and Bosnia so as to forestall violence while working for justice.

No one thinks that nonviolent strategies can *guarantee* justice, but neither does anyone think that violent strategies can. The calculations involved in decisions made in the course of nonviolent campaigns include, though they are not limited to, assessments of consequences. This opens up additional areas of common ground between the Historic Peace Churches and others, regardless of whether deontological considerations or those of character also and importantly inform the churches' ethical decisions.

Concluding Remarks

Every person has within, like Saul of Tarsus, that which can respond to divine love, harken to the movement of the Holy Spirit, and hear and respond to God. To say this is not to deny that there are those who refuse to attend and to heed.

It was this faith which led Friends to deal with the Delaware Indians with respect. It is this faith which today underlies the Alternatives to Violence Project (AVP). Just one example of a program that reflects a commitment to peacemaking, AVP was begun in 1974 in response to a request to Quakers from inmates at Greenhaven prison in Stormville, New York; the inmates wanted help persuading teenagers in trouble to abandon violence. The project, as it turned out, focused instead on the adult convicts. It runs workshops to help them discover in themselves irenic alternatives in the sorts of circumstances which otherwise would trigger their acting violently. So successful has the project been in transforming lives that it has spread across the United States and to many other countries throughout the world.

The World Council of Churches has launched a "Programme to Overcome Violence" designed to "challeng[e] and [transform] the global cultural of violence in the direction of a culture of just peace." The even deeper imperative, however, is for the churches to acknowledge the centrality of peace witness to the apostolic faith. In this essay I, as a Friend, have drawn on the experience of Friends, but the intent has been to point to experience which will be familiar in content, if not in context, to Christians generally; it is the experience of the Prince of Peace calling us to rise up and follow, calling us to the Peaceable Kingdom, calling us to live in the Spirit.[6]

Notes

1. Notwithstanding this generalization, several people contributed significantly to the theological framework of Quaker religious thought. These would include George Fox, Robert Barclay, William Penn, Isaac Penington, Margaret Fell, George Keith (who eventually left Quakerism for the Church of England), Samuel Fisher, and Lilias Skene.

2. Those who are interested in seeing a Quaker's justification of the centrality of peace witness to the apostolic faith by appeal to the "New Testament" or "Christian Bible" should read Paul N. Anderson's "Jesus and Peace," in *The Church's Peace Witness,* ed. Marlin E. Miller and Barbara Nelson Gingerich (Grand Rapids: Eerdmans, 1994), pp. 104–30.

3. Wilmer Cooper explains what a Testimony is, as the term is used by Friends, in this way: "From the beginning Friends believed that they could have direct and immediate communication with God which would enable them to discern right ethical choices. But they soon experienced certain common leadings of the Spirit which became formalized into testimonies. These testimonies served as common principles and standards of behavior and action." See *The Testimony of Integrity in the Religious Society of Friends* (Pendle Hill Pamphlet #296, 1991), p. 7. These testimonies are printed in the books of discipline or faith and practice published by yearly meetings. The point the British historians are making is that at least no formal statement representing Friends corporately which condemned participation in war existed before 1661.

4. James Nayler, Works (1716) p. 695, as quoted in Faith and Practice, Philadelphia Yearly Meeting of the Religious Society of Friends (Philadelphia: PYM, 1972), p. 59.

5. Walter Wink, *Engaging the Powers* (Minneapolis: Fortress, 1992). Cf. Barrett, p. 169.

6. I am grateful to the following persons for their reactions to earlier versions of this paper: Martha Grundy, Melissa Meyer, Heather Paxson; my colleagues Sheila Ruth, Clyde Nabe, and Carol Keene; and especially for his detailed, thoughtful, and helpful comments, Dean Freiday.

George Fox and Others

The 1660 Declaration of Friends to Charles II

A Declaration from the Harmless and Innocent People of God, Called Quakers, Against All Sedition, Plotters, and Fighters in the World: For Removing the Ground of Jealousy and Suspicion from Magistrates and People Concerning Wars and Fightings.

Presented to the King upon the 21st day of the 11th Month, 1660.

"Our principle is, and our practices have always been, to seek peace and ensue it; to follow after righteousness and the knowledge of God; seeking the good and welfare, and doing that which tends to the peace of all. We know that wars and fightings proceed from the lusts of men, as James iv. 1–3, out of which the Lord hath redeemed us, and so out of the occasion of war. The occasion of war, and war itself (wherein envious men, who are lovers of themselves more than lovers of God lust, kill, and desire to have men's lives or estates) ariseth from lust. *All bloody principles and practices, as to our own particulars, we utterly deny; with all outward wars and strife, and fightings with—outward weapons, for any end, or under any pretense whatsoever; this is our testimony to the whole world.*

"And whereas it is objected:

"But although you now say 'that you cannot fight, nor take up arms at all, yet if the Spirit move you, then you will change your principle, and you will sell your coat, buy a sword, and fight for the kingdom of Christ.'

"To this we answer, Christ said to Peter, 'Put up thy sword in his place;' though he had said be-

fore, he that had no sword might sell his coat and buy one (to the fulfilling of the law and the Scripture), yet after, when he had bid him put it up, he said, "he that taketh the when the sword, shall perish with the sword. And further, Christ said to Pilate, 'Thinkest thou, that I cannot now pray to my Father, and he shall presently give me more than twelve legions of angels?' And this might satisfy Peter, Luke xxii. 36, after he had put up his sword, when he said to him. 'He that took it, should perish with it;' which satisfieth us, Matt. xxvi. 51–53 And in the Revelation, it is said, 'He that kills with the sword, shall perish with the sword; and here is the faith and the patience of the saints.' And so Christ's kingdom is not of this world, therefore do not his servants fight, as he told Pilate, the magistrate, who crucified him. And did they not look upon Christ as a raiser of sedition? And did he pray, 'Forgive them?' But thus it is that we are numbered amongst transgressors, and fighters, that the Scriptures might be fulfilled.

"That the Spirit of Christ, by which we are guided, is not changeable, so as once to command us from a thing as evil, and again to move unto it; and we certainly know, and testify to the world, that the Spirit of Christ, which leads us into all truth, will never move us to fight and war against any man with outward weapons, neither for the kingdom of Christ, nor for the kingdoms of this world.

"First, Because the kingdom of Christ God will exalt, according to his promise, and cause it to grow and flourish in righteousness; 'not by might, nor by power (of outward sword), but by my Spirit, saith the Lord,' Zech. iv. 6. So those that use any weapon to fight for Christ, or for the establishing of his kingdom or government—their spirit, principle, and practice we deny.

"Secondly, as for the kingdoms of this world, we cannot covet them, much less can we fight for them, but we do earnestly desire and wait, that, by the Word of God's power, and its effectual operation in the hearts of men, the kingdoms of this world may become the kingdoms of the Lord, and of his Christ; that he may rule and reign in men by his Spirit and truth; that thereby all people, out of all different judgements and professions, may be brought into love and unity with God, and one with another; and that they may all come to witness the prophet's words, who said, 'Nation shall not lift up sword against nation, neither shall they learn war any more,' Isa. ii. 4; Mic. iv. 3.

"So we, whom the Lord hath called into the obedience of his truth, have denied wars and fightings, and cannot more learn them. This is a certain testimony unto all the world, of the truth of our hearts in this particular, that as God persuadeth every man's heart to believe, so they may receive it. For we have not, as some others, gone about with cunningly-devised fables, [nor] have we ever denied in practice what we have professed in principle; but in sincerity and truth, and by the word of God, have we laboured to manifest unto all men, that both we and our ways might be witnessed in the hearts of all.

"And whereas all manner of evil hath been falsely spoken of us, we hereby speak the plain truth of our hearts, to take away the occasion of that offense; that so being innocent, we may not suffer for other men's offenses, nor be made a prey of by the wills of men for that of which we were never guilty; but in the uprightness of our hearts *we may, under the power ordained of God for the punishment of evil-doers, and for the praise of them that do well, live* a peaceable and godly life, in all godliness and honesty. For although we have always suffered, and do now more abundantly suffer, yet we know that it is for righteousness' sake; 'for our rejoicing is this, the testimony of our consciences, that in simplicity and godly sincerity, not with fleshly wisdom, but by the grace of God, we have had our conversation in the world,' 2 Cor. i. 12, which for us is a witness for the convincing of our

enemies. For this we can say to all the world, we have wronged no man, we have used no force nor violence against any man: we have been found in no plots, nor guilty of sedition. When we have been wronged, we have not sought to revenge ourselves; we have not made resistance against authority; but wherein we could not obey for conscience' sake we have suffered the most of all people in the nation. We have been counted as sheep for the slaughter, persecuted and despised, beaten, stoned, wounded, stocked, whipped, imprisoned, haled out of synagogues, cast into dungeons and noisome vaults, where many have died in bonds, shut up from our friends, denied needful sustenance for many days together, with other the like cruelties.

"And the cause of all these sufferings is not for any evil, but for things relating to the worship of our God, and in obedience to his requirings. For which cause we shall freely give up our bodies a sacrifice, rather than disobey the Lord: for we know as the Lord hath kept us innocent, so he will plead our cause, when there is none in the earth to plead it. So we, in obedience unto his truth, do not love our lives unto death, that we may do his will, and wrong no man in our generation, but seek the good and peace of all men. He who hath commanded us that we shall not swear at all, Matt. v. 31, hath also commanded us that we shall not kill, Matt. v.; so that we can neither kill men, nor swear for or against them. This is both our principle and practice, and has been from the beginning; so that if we suffer, as suspected to take up arms, or make war against any, it is without any ground from us; for it neither is, nor ever was in our hearts, since we owned the truth of God; neither shall we ever do it, because it is contrary to the Spirit of Christ, his doctrine, and the practices of his apostles; even contrary to him, for whom we suffer all things, and endure all things.

"And whereas men come against us with clubs, staves, drawn swords, pistols cocked, and beat, cut, and abuse us, yet we never resisted them; but to them our hair, backs, and cheeks, have been ready. It is not an honour, to manhood or nobility, to run upon harmless people, who lift not up a hand against them, with arms and weapons.

"Therefore consider these things, ye men of understanding: for plotters, raisers of insurrections, tumultuous ones, and fighters, running with swords, clubs, staves, and pistols, one against another; these, we say, are of the world, and have their foundation from this unrighteous world, from the foundation of which the Lamb hath been slain; which Lamb hath redeemed us from this unrighteous world, and we are not of it, but are heirs of a world of which there is no end, and of a kingdom where no corruptible thing enters. Our weapons are spiritual, and not carnal, yet mighty through God, to the plucking/pulling down of the strongholds of sin and Satan, who is the author of wars, fighting, murder, and plots. Our swords are broken into ploughshares, and spears into pruninghooks, as prophesied of in Micah iv. Therefore we cannot learn war any more, neither rise up against nation or kingdom with outward weapons, though you have numbered us amongst the transgressors and plotters. The Lord knows our innocency herein, and will plead our cause with all people upon earth, at the day of their judgment, when all men shall have a reward according to their works.

"Therefore in love we warn you for your soul's good, not to wrong the innocent, nor the babes of Christ, which he hath in his hand, which he cares for as the apple of his eye; neither seek to destroy the heritage of God, nor turn your swords backward upon such as the law was not made for, i.e., the righteous; but for sinners and transgressors, to keep them down. For those are not peacemakers, nor lovers of enemies, neither can they overcome evil with good, who wrong them that are friends to you and all men, and wish your good, and the good of all people on the earth. If you oppress us, as they did the children of Israel in Egypt, and if you oppress us as they did when Christ was born, and as they did the Christians in the primitive times; we can say, 'The Lord forgive you;' and leave the Lord to deal with you, and not revenge ourselves. If you say, as the council said to Peter and John, 'speak no more in that name;' and if you serve us, as they served the three children spoken of in Daniel,

God is the same that ever he was, that lives for ever and ever, who hath the innocent in his arms.

"O, Friends! offend not the Lord and his little ones, neither afflict his people; but consider and be moderate. Do not run on hastily, but consider mercy, justice, and judgment; that is the way for you to prosper, and obtain favor of the Lord. Our meetings were stopped and broken up in the days of Oliver, under pretense of plotting against him; in the days of the Committee of Safety we were looked upon as plotters to bring in King Charles; and now our peaceable meetings are termed seditious. O! that men should lose their reason, and go contrary to their own conscience; knowing that we have suffered all things, and have been accounted plotters from the beginning, though we have declared against them both by word of mouth and printing, and are clear from any such thing! We have suffered all along, because we would not take up carnal weapons to fight, and are thus made a prey, because we are the innocent lambs of Christ, and cannot avenge ourselves! These things are left on your hearts to consider; but we are out of all those things, in the patience of the saints; and we know, as Christ said, 'He that takes the sword, shall perish with the sword;' Matt. xxvi. 52; Rev. xiii. 10.

"This is given forth from the people called Quakers, to satisfy the king and his council, and all those that have any jealousy concerning us, that all occasion of suspicion may be taken away, and our innocency cleared.

George Fox
Richard Hubberthome
John Stubbs
Francis Howgill
Gerrard Roberts
John Bolton
Leonard Fell
Samuel Fisher
Henry Fell
John Hinde
John Furley Junr.
Thomas Moore
21/11 M/1660

"Postscript. Though we are numbered amongst transgressors, and have been given up to rude, merciless men, by whom our meetings are broken up, in which we edified one another in our holy faith, and prayed together to the Lord that lives for ever, yet he is our pleader in this day. The Lord saith, 'They that feared his name spoke often together' (as in Malachi); which were as his jewels. For this cause, and no evil-doing, are we cast into holes, dungeons, houses of correction, prisons (neither old nor young being spared men nor women), and mad a prey of in the sight of all nations, under the pretense of being seditious, etc., so that all rude people run upon us to take possession. For which we say, 'The Lord forgive them that have thus done to us;' who doth, and will enable us to suffer; and never shall we lift up hand against any that thus use us; but desire the Lord may have mercy upon them, that they may consider what they have done. For how is it possible for them to requite us for the wrong they have done to us? Who to all nations have sounded us abroad as seditious, who were never found plotters against ally, since we knew the life and power of Jesus Christ manifested in us, who hath redeemed us from the world, all works of darkness, and plotters therein, by which we know the election, before the world began. So we say, the Lord have mercy upon our enemies and forgive them, for what they have done unto us!

"O! do as ye would be done by; do unto all men as you would have them do unto you; for this is the law and the prophets.

"All plots, insurrections, and riotous meetings we deny, knowing them to be of the devil, the murderer; which we in Christ, who was before they were, triumph over. And all wars and fightings with carnal weapons we deny, who have the sword of the Spirit; and all that wrong us, we leave to the Lord. This is to clear our innocency from the aspersion cast upon us, that we are seditious or plotters."

Michael Walzer

War and Peace in the Jewish Tradition

The Hebrew word for peace, *shalom,* derives from a root that indicates completion, wholeness, or perfection. As the derivation suggests, peace is not the normal state of the world in this historical age. In its fullest sense, it describes the achievement of the messiah (who must fight wars for the sake of this ultimate peace). It is obviously, then, a desirable and much-desired condition. . . .

Shalom also has a more local and immediate meaning, "not-war," as in the biblical command to "proclaim peace"—that is, to offer one's enemy the opportunity to surrender without fighting. Both surrender and victory bring peace, but this is a temporary condition, also associated with the idea of "rest," as in passages like, "And the land rested from war" (Josh. 11:23). . . .

War, *milkhama,* seems always to have the local and immediate meaning, not-peace; it is a generalized term for "battles." There is no articulated conception of a state of war (like that described, say, by Thomas Hobbes and later political realists). But international society looks in most Jewish writing from the prophets onward very much like a state of war, where violence is the norm and fighting is continuous, or at least endemic. After the destruction of the temple, when Israel no longer figures as a member of international society, the sense of danger, of living always under the threat of violence, colors most Jewish perceptions of the gentile world. The idea that all the nations are hostile to Israel even plays a certain justifying role in arguments (entirely academic) about the legitimacy of preventive attacks. But this experience of generalized and prevailing hostility—conceptualized as *eivah,* enmity, and often given as a reason for prudential behavior—doesn't take on theoretical form, as in the contemporary idea of a "cold war."

The Jewish account of types or categories of war deals only with Jewish wars. So far as the rabbis are concerned, it is a theoretical, and in no sense a practical, typology. It is also an incomplete typology, for it has only two categories where three seem necessary. The first category includes all wars commanded by God; the list is very short, drawn from the biblical accounts of the conquest of the land, though it is subject to some modest rabbinic expansion for the sake of the subsequent defense of the land. The second category includes all "permitted" wars, and seems to be a concession to Israel's kings, since the only examples are the expansionist wars of David. These are the wars that disqualified David from temple-building, but they are permitted to him as king. If he fights, he cannot build, but there is no religious ban on fighting.

The missing third category is the banned or forbidden war. It cannot be the case that all wars not required are permitted, for it is fairly clear that there were wars of which the rabbis disapproved. But the disapproval is usually explained with reference to conditions of various sorts imposed on the permitted wars, not with reference to wars that are never permitted. . . .

In the absence of a developed conception of prohibited wars, there is no limit to the grounds of permissibility. So far as the king's wars are concerned, any ground will serve, including, as we have seen, the glory of the royal name. Some rabbinic commentators were obviously made uncomfortable by such possibilities, and tried to avoid them by a radical reduction of all permitted wars to a single type. Since the nations of the world were assumed to be permanently hostile to Israel and forever plotting acts of aggression, any war against them, whatever its reasons in the

king's mind, served in fact the purposes of prevention: "to diminish the heathen so that they do
not come up against them [the Israelites]."

The clearest statement on preventive and
preemptive attacks, and the only one I have found
that attempts to distinguish between them, comes
from the fourteenth-century sage Menachem
Me'iri, who describes two kinds of permitted
war: when the Israelites fight "against their enemies because they fear lest [their enemies] attack
and when it is known by them that the enemies
are preparing themselves [for an attack]." The
distinction does not seem to make a practical difference, but it follows from this account, as David
Bleich has argued, that "absent clear aggressive
design" (or, at least, a plausible fear that such a
design exists), no military attack is permitted. On
the other hand, Me'iri does not claim here to exhaust the category of permitted war. If the
"enemy" cannot be attacked on the assumption
that he is preparing an attack of his own, he can
be attacked for simpler and grosser reasons, "to
extend the borders . . . ," and so on.

Ruling out these latter wars requires a more
drastic move, giving up not only the assumption
of universal hostility and the idea of "diminishing the heathens" but also the acceptance of
monarchic ambition. The crucial text here comes
from the hand of an eighteenth-century Italian
rabbi, Samuel David Luzzatto, in a commentary
on Deuteronomy 20:10–11. Luzzatto is working
his way out of the commanded/permitted dichotomy, toward something like just/unjust.

> The text does not specify the cause for a per-
> mitted war or [say] whether Israel may wage
> war without cause, merely to despoil and take
> booty, or to expand our domain. [But] it seems
> to me that in the beginning of this section
> [20:1], in saying "When thou goest forth to bat-
> tle against thine enemy," Scripture is determin-
> ing that we may make war only against our
> enemies. The term "enemy" refers only to one
> who wrongs us; hence Scripture is speaking
> only of an invader who enters our domain in
> order to take our land and despoil us. Then we
> are to wage war against him—offering peace
> first.

The repetition of the word "only" (three times)
suggests that Luzzatto knows what he is doing,
even if he seems to commit himself, imprudently,
to fighting only against an invasion-in-progress. I
cannot say, however, that he has had many followers within the *halakhic* community. Secular
Jews commonly assume that the "Jewish tradition" allows only defensive wars, but the evidence
for this is scant.

The more common rabbinic strategy is to retain the broad category of permitted war but to
make the wars that fall within this category very
difficult to fight. Before they can be fought, the
king must meet a set of legal requirements. First,
he must get the approval of the Sanhedrin, and he
must consult the *urim* and *thumim*—two conditions that are literally impossible to meet in these
latter days (and that were already impossible in
talmudic times) since the Sanhedrin can no
longer be convened and the priestly breastplate
through which or on which the urim and thumim
delivered their oracles is long lost. . . .

Then the king's officers must proclaim the
exemptions from military service listed in
Deuteronomy 20:5–8, sending home soldiers
who have recently built a house or planted a vine-
yard or betrothed a wife as well as all those who
are "fearful and faint-hearted." By the time the
early rabbinic commentators finished expanding
on this list, the king could count only on his mercenaries: effectively, there can be no conscription
for permitted wars. Finally, these royal wars can
be fought only after the commanded wars, conquering and securing the land, have been won
(God's battles and our battles come before *his*).
All in all, permitted wars are only barely permitted; they are not, however, positively ruled out—
probably because the Deuteronomic text seems
to countenance territorial expansion—that is,
military campaigns, against "cities which are
very far off from thee" (20:15). . . .

Resistance

It is a commonplace of rabbinic thought that illegal commands of the king should be resisted—or

at least disobeyed. "If the master's orders conflict with the servant's," says Maimonides, answering a rhetorical question in the Talmud, "the master's take precedence. And it goes without saying that if a king ordered [the] violation of God's commandments, he is not to be obeyed." This is the minimalist position; the talmudic texts seem to require active "protest" against the king, though it is not clear exactly what this means, and there is, as usual, no explicit doctrinal elaboration of the duty involved. . . .

Challenging God may be excessive (unwise? imprudent? presumptuous? self-righteous?); challenging kings is not. No doubt, a certain aura of divinity attaches to the person of an anointed king, as David says when he lets pass an opportunity to kill Saul; the king's words, however, are human words, not divine commands. They can be refused. But the king himself, presumably because of his anointment, can only be challenged and overthrown with prophetic support. That seems to be the biblical doctrine, and the doctrine of the rabbis too, though they are not greatly interested in such matters. The gentile kings under whose rule they live must be disobeyed, exactly like Jewish kings, if they command violations of God's law (thus the stories in the book of Daniel), but there is no question of overthrowing them. Indeed, the focus of rabbinic literature, as of popular religious writing throughout the Middle Ages, is on martyrdom, not resistance or rebellion.

Modern Zionist writers have sought to reverse this order of interests, celebrating the Maccabean revolt, for example, as a legitimate and heroic military struggle against a foreign ruler. The rabbis are surprisingly reluctant to offer a similar endorsement, even in their own terms: they would presumably describe the struggle as a commanded war (to defend the land and oppose idolatry within it). But they are more concerned to stress God's miraculous intervention (see, for example, the prayer *al ha'nisim*) than to describe the fight itself, more ready to celebrate Hannah and her seven martyred sons than the military heroes of the revolt.

Had the revolt been a "commanded" war, as Zionists would certainly argue (in their terms: just and necessary), everyone would have been obliged to fight: in commanded wars, the Talmud declares, "all go forth, even a bridegroom from his chamber and a bride from her canopy" (Sotah 44b). But none of the rabbis seems to have questioned the formal announcement of the biblical exemptions reported in 1 Maccabees 3:56 (did they know this text or have access to other historical accounts of the revolt?), even though rabbinic doctrine holds that individuals are to be sent home only in permitted (optional) wars. . . .

Two expansions of the list of individuals not bound to fight in permitted wars are of special interest. First, people, engaged in religiously commanded activities are not required to give up those activities in order to join what will be, after all, a secular struggle. This is the source, or one of the sources, of the exemption of yeshiva students in Israel today (though this exemption can only be claimed by non-Zionists, who do not regard the defense of the present-day state as a "commanded" war). A more radical exemption is suggested by a singular, and until very recently unrepeated, interpretation of the biblical phrase "fearful and faint-hearted." It is a maxim of rabbinic interpretation that doublings of this sort must carry more than one message—since no word in the Bible is superfluous. Hence Rabbi Akiba is quoted as saying that whereas "fearful" refers to the coward, "faint-hearted" must rather mean "soft-hearted" and refer to the compassionate. He goes on to argue that even a soldier who is a "hero among heroes, powerful among the most powerful, but who at the same time is merciful—let him return" (*Tosefta*, Sotah 7:14). This passage has been seized upon by modern commentators (particularly in the United States during the Vietnam War) as a possible foundation for a Jewish form of conscientious objection, though not, obviously, one focused on particular wars. The effort suggests what might be done with the available texts, but it does not connect with anything actually done in the past.

Since commanded/permitted does not translate into just/unjust, there is nothing in the Jewish

tradition that requires, or even that provides a vocabulary for, a moral investigation of particular
Jewish wars. And since for almost two thousand
years there were no wars that demanded investigation, and no political arena within which the investigation would be a relevant activity, questions
of protest, objection, and opposition arise only
marginally and indirectly with reference to the
conduct of war, and not at all with reference to its
overall character. There is no parallel in Jewish
thought to the extensive Catholic discussions
about whether individual soldiers should participate in wars they take to be unjust . . .

Intention

Given the latitudinous ground on which permitted wars may be fought, one would not expect intention to be a central issue in Jewish discussions.
It is certainly central to the tradition as a whole,
playing its expected part in criminal and civil law,
and figuring in what are, from a philosophical
standpoint, very interesting discussions of prayer
and the fulfillment of religious commands. But
no one seems to have taken up the intentions of
kings and warriors—except for Maimonides in
one very strong, but also very odd, statement in
his treatise on the Book of Kings. The statement
is odd because its parallels are more easily found,
as Gerald Blidstein has argued, "in the literature
of crusade and *jihad* than . . . in the Talmud."
Maimonides seems to allow only commanded
wars (though he has an expansive sense of that
category, apparently including within it the war
against idolatry—and the immediately following
section of his treatise contains the more traditional, also rather expansive, account of permitted wars that I have already quoted). Indeed, only
in commanded wars can a singular moral or religious intention be required. The king's "sole aim
and thought," says Maimonides, "should be to
uplift the true religion, to fill the world with righteousness, to break the arm of the wicked and to
fight the battles of the Lord." His warriors are
similarly enjoined: they should know that they
are "fighting for the oneness of God."

Perhaps Maimonides' purpose here is to rule
out wars fought by the king for personal or dynastic reasons (despite his apparent permissiveness
later on) and to admonish warriors who think only
of plunder and booty. The only legitimate reason
for fighting is religious: the elimination of idolatry
from the world. I suppose that this can plausibly be
described as one of the reasons (in the biblical text,
the justifying reason) for the original conquest of
the land: were it not for their "abominations," the
Canaanites would never have been dispossessed.
But the later wars to defend the land—what the elders of Israel called "our battles"—clearly had another reason: they were in no sense religious
crusades, and there would have been no need and,
presumably, no desire to fight them had Midianites
and Philistines remained at home, worshiping
their gods as they pleased. Nor were David's wars
of expansion crusades: his subject peoples in the
north and east were not, so far as we know, denied
their idols. So Maimonides can hardly be describing these latter wars. His most likely purpose is to
describe the intentions of the future king-messiah
and the soldiers who join him. No contemporary
wars would come under his purview. Even if he is
borrowing from Muslim writers here, it would
never have occurred to him that the *jihad* was a
commanded war (but did he secretly admire the
spirit with which it was fought?). In any case, by
stressing the religious motives of the messiah, he is
arguing against any kind of Jewish (national) tri-
umphalism. The messiah will not fight so "that Israel might exercise dominion over the world, or
rule over the heathens." Intentions that may (or
may not) be acceptable in the permitted wars of
premessianic kings are clearly unacceptable in the
days to come. . . .

Conduct

The rabbis did deal fairly extensively with the law
of sieges, in which this issue arises in paradigmatic
form, and they seem to have written, if not with an
explicit recognition of "a halakhic or moral problem," at least with the fate of the besieged civilians
very much in mind. They may have won their

reputation here, for their argument, picked up by Grotius, survived as the radical alternative to the standard version of international siege law.

This is Maimonides' summary (based on a second-century teaching recorded in the *Sifre* to Numbers): "On besieging a city in order to seize it, we must not surround it on all four sides but only on three sides—thus leaving a path of escape for whomever wishes to flee to save his life." Of course, a city surrounded on only three sides is not in fact surrounded. If people can leave, then the food supply inside the city can be stretched out, perhaps indefinitely; or other people can enter, bringing supplies and reinforcements. It is hard to see how the city could ever be taken given this rule, which seems clearly designed for the sake of the inhabitants, not of the army outside, though this is ostensibly a Jewish army. Nachmanides, writing a century after Maimonides, strengthened the rule and added a reason: "We are to learn to deal kindly with our enemy." It is enemy civilians who are treated kindly here, for the ordinary or four-sided siege is a war against civilians. The radicalism of the Jewish law is that it pretty much abolishes siege warfare. But there is no acknowledgment of this, and other legal discussions (see Nachmanides on Deut. 20:19–20) assume the legitimacy of the siege and evince little concern with its impact on the civilian population.

Maimonides also proposes a general rule against the sorts of violence that commonly follow upon a successful siege: anyone "who smashes household goods, tears clothes, demolishes a building, stops up a spring, or destroys articles of food . . . transgresses the command *Thou shalt not destroy.*" This sort of thing the tradition is fairly clear about, and the clarity may help, again, to account for its reputation . . .

Extremity

Jewish discussions about overriding the law or setting it aside in wartime emergencies have focused on religious rather than moral law—sabbath observance above all. The first arguments took place during the Maccabean revolt when Jewish soldiers, attacked on the sabbath and refusing to fight, were massacred by their enemies (1 Macc. 2:32–38). Subsequently, a general decision was made to pursue the military struggle without regard to the sabbath laws. Josephus reports further debates and a similar decision some two centuries later during the Roman war. The rabbis endorsed these decisions, without any specific reference to them, on the grounds of "saving lives." The law was given, they argued, so that we might live by it, not die by it (Sanhedrin 74a). But to this general rule, they made three exceptions: Jews were to accept death rather than violate the laws against idolatry, murder, and incest. If noncombatant immunity rests on the second of these, then it would appear to be safe against emergency. Soldiers cannot deliberately take aim at and kill innocent people to save themselves or even to save the community as a whole. This would at least seem to be the Jewish position, though I do not think it has ever been stated with explicit reference to a military crisis.

All other prohibitions are probably subject to suspension in wartime emergencies: the rules against surrounding a city on four sides, for example, or cutting down fruit trees, or destroying property, can be overridden for the sake of "saving lives" (the Jewish version, perhaps, of military necessity). These prohibitions apply to both commanded and permitted wars, but they apply differently. Commanded wars must be fought even if it is known in advance that the prohibitions will have to be violated in their course, whereas permitted wars are permitted only if it is reasonable to assume that violations will not be necessary. The halakhic principle here is that one should avoid deliberately putting oneself in a position where it will be necessary (and permissible) to break the law. This is the only link that I know of in the Jewish tradition between ius ad bellum and ius in bello: in the case of permitted wars, one must think about how the fighting will be conducted before one can rightly begin it. But once the fighting has actually begun, there is no link at all. . . .

Concluding Note

The clearest need in the tradition that I have been examining is to find some way to a comprehensive and unambiguous account of legitimate and illegitimate, just and unjust, warmaking. Would a category of "prohibited" wars open the way? Such a category would be symmetrical with "commanded" and "permitted," but who, at this late date, could issue the prohibitions? Commanded wars are specifically commanded by God, at least in the original cases, but he is not known to have announced any specific (or general) prohibitions. Nor, however, is he known to have commanded defensive wars; there is no record of such a command in the biblical texts. So, in principle, there could be prohibited wars of aggression in the same style as the commanded wars of defense—derived through interpretation and s'vara (common sense, reasonableness). And commands and prohibitions of this sort might also plausibly be "given" to Jews and Gentiles alike, in contrast to the original command, given to Israel alone. But would these divine commands and prohibitions be, in any sense, authentically *divine*? I cannot answer that question. Perhaps it is better to argue that after the original command, no longer operative, these matters are "not in heaven"—everything else is human work, though still carried on within a religious/legal tradition.

The category of "permitted" wars is well worth preserving, since it answers to certain difficulties in the just/unjust schema. Some just wars seem almost to be "commanded," that is, the goods at stake (the survival of the political community, say) seem urgently in need of defense. *They should be defended,* unless the defense is utterly hopeless, in which case the principle of "saving lives" might justify appeasement or submission. But some just wars are clearly "optional." They can rightly be fought, in response to some small scale aggression, say, but political compromise, even if its terms are unjust, is also a permitted choice. Or, similarly, in the case of preemption: it is obviously permitted, though it may be imprudent, to wait for the enemy attack.

The hardest questions arise in the case of third parties in wars of aggression: they would be justified in coming to the rescue of the victim nation, but are they "commanded" to do that? International law recognizes a right of neutrality, a right that, for obvious reasons, makes many just war theorists uneasy. The issue is not taken up in classical Jewish texts—though individuals in analogous cases in domestic society are not permitted to "stand by the blood of [their] neighbor" (Lev. 19:16). Might states have rights that individuals do not? A theory with three, rather than only two, possibilities at least facilitates the arguments that this question requires. So, once the category of prohibited wars is recognized and elaborated, it would be useful to divide the remaining wars into two kinds: those where the moral assumption is that they *should* be fought, and those where such an assumption is either weak or nonexistent (they *can* be fought). (It also seems plausible to suggest that exemptions from combat make more sense in wars of the second kind than in wars of the first kind.) Permitted wars are the king's wars in the sense that they depend upon a political decision, and so we ought to take an interest, as the rabbis did, in the complexities of the decision-making process.

A similar argument can be made with regard to the conduct of war, where there exists an urgent need to elaborate a full account of noncombatant immunity—a concept frequently intimated in the tradition, but nowhere developed—and to repudiate the moral nihilism of "War is hell." And in both these cases, with reference to the conduct and the classification of war, it is time to work the argument through and refine it out of a much larger number of examples than the Bible offers. After all, the Jewish encounter with war, in one form or another, reaches far across time and space: the Hasmonean wars, the Roman wars, the Crusades, the Christian conquest of Spain, the two world wars, and the Arab–Israeli wars. If the tradition is to serve contemporary uses, it must address itself to the full range of Jewish experience.

Sohail H. Hashmi

Interpreting the Islamic Ethics of War and Peace

Conceptions of War and Peace in the Qur'an

Ibn Khaldun observes in the *Muqadimma,* his celebrated introduction to a history of the world composed at the end of the fourteenth century, that "wars and different kinds of fighting have always occurred in the world since God created it." War is endemic to human existence, he writes, "something natural among human beings. No nation and no race is free from it." Ibn Khaldun's brief comment summarizes rather well the traditional Islamic understanding of war as a universal and inevitable aspect of human existence. It is a feature of human society sanctioned, if not willed, by God Himself. The issues of war and peace thus fall within the purview of divine legislation for humanity. Islam, Muslims like to say, is a complete code of life, and given the centrality of war to human existence, the moral evaluation of war holds a significant place in Muslim ethical/legal discussion. The Islamic ethics of war and peace is therefore derived from the same general sources upon which Islamic law is based.

The first of these sources, of course, is the Qur'an, which is held by Muslims to be God's final and definitive revelation to humanity. The Qur'anic text, like other revealed scriptures, is not a systematic treatise on ethics or law. It is a discursive commentary on the actions and experiences of the Prophet Muhammad, his followers, and his opponents over the course of twenty-three years. But as the Qur'an itself argues in several verses, God's message is not limited to the time and place of its revelation; it is, rather, "a message to all the worlds" (81:27) propounding a

moral code with universal applicability (39:41). "From this commentary emerge broadly defined ethical principles that have been elaborated throughout Islamic history into what may be termed an Islamic conception of divine creation and man's place in it. In other words, although the Qur'an does not present a systematic ethical argument, it is possible to derive a consistent ethical system from it.

Why is humanity prone to war? The Qur'anic answer unfolds in the course of several verses revealed at various times, the essential points of which may be summarized as follows.

First, man's fundamental nature (*fitra*) is one of moral innocence, that is, freedom from sin. In other words, there is no Islamic equivalent to the notion of "original sin." Moreover, each individual is born with a knowledge of God's commandments, that is, with the essential aspects of righteous behavior. But this moral awareness is eroded as each individual encounters the corrupting influences of human society (30:30).

Second, man's nature is to live on the earth in a state of harmony and peace with other living things. This is the ultimate import of the responsibility assigned by God to man as His viceregent (*khalifa*) on this planet (2:30). True peace (*salam*) is therefore not merely an absence of war; it is the elimination of the grounds for strife or conflict, and the resulting waste and corruption (*fasad*) they create. Peace, not war or violence, is God's true purpose for humanity (2:208).

Third, given man's capacity for wrongdoing, there will always be some who *choose* to violate their nature and transgress against God's commandments. Adam becomes fully human only when he chooses to heed Iblis's (Satan's) temptation and disobeys God. As a result of this initial act of disobedience, human beings are expelled from the Garden to dwell on earth as "enemies to each other" (2:36, 7:24). Thus, wars and the evils that stem from them, the Qur'an suggests, are the inevitable consequences of the uniquely human capacity for moral choice. . . .

Fourth, each prophet encounters opposition from those (always a majority) who persist in their rebellion against God, justifying their actions through various self-delusions. One of the principal characteristics of rejection of God (*kufr*) is the inclination toward violence and oppression, encapsulated by the broad concept *zulm*. When individuals choose to reject divine guidance, either by transgressing against specific divine injunctions or by losing faith altogether, they violate (commit zulm against) their own nature (fitra). When Adam and Eve disobey the divine command in the Garden, the Qur'an relates that they cry out in their despair not that they have sinned against God, but that they have transgressed against their own souls (7:23). . . .

Fifth, peace (*salam*) is attainable only when human beings surrender to God's will and live according to God's laws. This is the condition of *islam*, the conscious decision to acknowledge in faith and conduct the presence and power of God. Because human nature is not sufficiently strong to resist the temptation to evil, it is necessary for man to establish a human agency, that is, a state, to mitigate the effects of anarchy and enforce divine law.

Sixth, because it is unlikely that individuals or societies will ever conform fully to the precepts of islam, Muslims must always be prepared to fight to preserve the Muslim faith and Muslim principles (8:60, 73).

The use of force by the Muslim community is, therefore, sanctioned by God as a necessary response to the existence of evil in the world. As the Qur'an elaborates in an early revelation, the believers are those "who, whenever tyranny afflicts them, defend themselves" (42:39). This theme of the just, God-ordained use of force for legitimate purposes is continued in several other verses. In the first verse, which explicitly permits the Muslim community to use armed force against its enemies, the Qur'an makes clear that fighting is a burden imposed upon all believers (not only Muslims) as a result of the enmity harbored by the unbelievers . . . A subsequent verse converts this permission to fight into an injunction. The rationale given for using armed force is quite explicit: "Tumult and oppression (*fitna*) is worse than killing" (2:191).

These two verses clearly undermine the possibility of an Islamic pacifism. One verse in particular offers an implicit challenge to an ethical position based on the renunciation of all violence: "Fighting is prescribed for you, even though it be hateful to you; but it may well be that you hate something that is in fact good for you, and that you love a thing that is in fact bad for you: and God knows, whereas you do not" (2:216). There is, thus, no equivalent in the Islamic tradition of the continuing debate within Christianity of the possibility of just war. There is no analogue in Islamic texts to Aquinas's Question 40: "Are some wars permissible?" The Islamic discourse on war and peace begins from the a priori assumption that some types of war are permissible—indeed, required by God—and that all other forms of violence are, therefore, forbidden.

In short, the Qur'an's attitude toward war and peace may be described as an idealistic realism. Human existence is characterized neither by incessant warfare nor by real peace, but by a continuous tension between the two. Societies exist forever in a precarious balance between them. The unending human challenge is *jihad fi sabil Allah* (struggle in the way of God) . . .

Conceptions of War and Peace in the Sunna

We can construct an outline of the Prophet's approach to the ethics of war and peace not only by referring to the Qur'an, but also by making use of the large body of literature comprising the Prophet's sayings and actions (hadith) and biography (*sira*) compiled between the second and fourth Islamic centuries. It is clear from these records that from an early age, Muhammad was averse to many aspects of the tribal culture in which he was born . . . Throughout the Meccan period of his prophetic mission (610–22 C.E.), he showed no inclination toward the use of force in any form, even for self-defense. On the contrary, his policy can only be described as nonviolent resistance. This policy was maintained in spite of escalating physical attacks directed at his followers and at him personally. . . .

The Prophet's rejection of armed struggle during the Meccan period was more than mere prudence based on the Muslims' military weakness. It was, rather, derived from the Qur'an's still unfolding conception that the use of force should be avoided unless it is, in just war parlance, a "last resort." . . .

Because the Meccan period of the Prophet's mission lasted almost thirteen years, three years longer than the Medinan period, it is absolutely fundamental in the construction of an Islamic ethical system. Clearly, jihad in this extended period of the Prophet's life meant nonviolent resistance. For potential Muslim nonviolent activists, there are many lessons to be learned from the Prophet's decisions during these years. But, regrettably, the Meccan period has received scant attention, either from Muslim activists or from jurists, historians, and moralists.

The period that has been the traditional focus of Muslim and non-Muslim concern in discussing the Islamic approach to war and peace is the decade during which the Prophet lived in Medina (622–32 C.E.). It was in Medina that the Muslims became a coherent community, and it was here that jihad acquired its military component.

According to the early Muslim historians, the Prophet enacted a new policy toward the Quraysh, the ruling tribe of Mecca, within a year of settling in Medina: war aimed at redressing Muslim grievances. He authorized small raids against specific pagan targets, in particular caravans proceeding along the trade route to Syria . . .

Open warfare between the Muslims and the Quraysh was begun with the battle of Badr,

fought in the month of Ramadan in 2 A.H. In the eight years following, the Prophet personally led or authorized over seventy military encounters, ranging in intensity from pitched battles in defense of Medina, to sieges, raids, and skirmishes against enemy targets. Such an astounding number of military engagements could only have had profound implications for the Prophet personally as well as for the nascent Muslim community. The preaching of Islam and the conducting of the community's day-to-day activities had to occur within a milieu characterized by outright warfare against a range of enemies: Quraysh, bedouin tribes, the Jewish tribes of Medina, and the Byzantine empire. The Muslims of this period, according to one report, "did not sleep or wake except with their weapons." Qur'anic verses of the period exhorting the Prophet and his followers to fight suggest the strain that the constant threat of war must have imposed upon the community (8:24, 65).

The battle of Badr was fought when the Prophet was fifty-four years old. And although it is clear that he personally conducted several key campaigns afterward, the combined evidence of the sources indicates that he remained a reluctant warrior. On several occasions he urged the use of nonviolent means or sought an early termination of hostilities, often in the face of stiff opposition from his companions. At the same time, consonant with Qur'anic revelation, he seems to have accepted as unavoidable fighting in defense of what he perceived to be Muslim interests. The essence of his approach to war is crystallized in the following words ascribed to him: "O people! Do not wish to meet the enemy, and ask God for safety, but when you face the enemy, be patient, and remember that Paradise is under the shade of swords." . . .

The medieval theory of an ongoing jihad, and the bifurcation of the world into dar al-Islam and dar al-harb upon which it was predicated, became a fiction soon after it was elaborated by medieval writers. The "house of Islam" disintegrated into a number of rival states, some of whom found themselves allied with states belonging to the "house of war" in fighting their co-religionists. Nevertheless, the idea that "Islam" and the "West" represented monolithic and mutually antagonistic civilizations underlay much Muslim and European writing, particularly during the heyday of European imperialism in the eighteenth and nineteenth centuries. Shades of this viewpoint are very much apparent in our own day. . . .

It is important to recognize that modernists as well as fundamentalists believe that Islamic thought must be revived by returning to the "true sources," that is, the Qur'an and sunna. This approach leads the modernists to challenge many aspects of medieval legal doctrine regarding war and peace, beginning with the division of the world into separate spheres. As they point out, this rigid bifurcation is nowhere to be found in the Qur'an or the traditions of the Prophet. Although the Qur'an's division of mankind into believers and unbelievers lends support for such a view, modernist writers argue that the Qur'anic verses cannot be interpreted to suggest a perpetual state of war between the two, nor any territoriality to the "house of Islam," when these verses are taken in the full context of the Qur'anic message. In one of the leading modernist expositions of Islamic international law, Mohammad Talaat al-Ghunaimi dismisses the dar al-Islam/dar al-harb distinction as an idea introduced by certain medieval legal thinkers in response to their own historical circumstances, but having no basis in Islamic ethics.

Having undermined the medieval dichotomy, the modernists proceed to challenge the medieval conception of "aggressive jihad." Again, their method is to return to the "sources." When the Qur'anic verses and the Prophet's traditions on warfare are studied in their full context, they argue, jihad can only be a war of self-defense. As the influential Egyptian scholar Muhammad Abu Zahra writes, "War is not justified . . . to impose Islam as a religion on unbelievers or to support a particular social regime. The Prophet Muhammad fought only to repulse aggression." . . .

The Conduct of War

Because the goal of jihad is the call to Islam, not territorial conquest or plunder, the right conduct

of Muslim armies has traditionally been an important concern within Islam. The Qur'an provides the basis for *ius in bello* considerations: "And fight in God's cause against those who wage war against you, but do not transgress limits, for God loves not the transgressors" (2:190). The "limits" are enumerated in the practice of the Prophet and the first four caliphs. According to authoritative traditions, whenever the Prophet sent out a military force, he would instruct its commander to adhere to certain restraints. The Prophet's immediate successors continued this practice, as is indicated by the "ten commands" of the first caliph, Abu Bakr:

> Do not act treacherously; do not act disloyally; do not act neglectfully. Do not mutilate; do not kill little children or old men, or women; do not cut off the heads of the palm-trees or burn them; do not cut down the fruit trees; do not slaughter a sheep or a cow or a camel, except for food. You will pass by people who devote their lives in cloisters; leave them and their devotions alone. You will come upon people who bring you platters in which are various sorts of food; if you eat any of it, mention the name of God over it.

Thus, the Qur'an and the actions of the Prophet and his successors established the principles of discrimination and proportionality of means. But as Ibn Rushd's treatise makes clear, the elaboration of these broad principles created serious divisions among medieval jurists. . . .

The legal discussions address three issues: Who is subject to damage in war? What types of damage may be inflicted upon persons? What types of damage may be inflicted upon their property? Underlying the differing opinions on these issues once again are the apparent contradictions between the peace verses and the sword verses. The jurists who contend that the sword verses provide a general rule superseding earlier revelation argue that belief is the decisive factor in establishing immunity from attack. Since verse 9:5, in their view, commands Muslims to fight all polytheists, only women and children (who were specifically designated by the Prophet as immune) are prohibited targets. All able-bodied polytheist males, whether actually fighting or not, may be killed.

Other jurists, who do not consider the peace verses to have been abrogated, maintain that capacity to fight is the only appropriate consideration, and therefore include old men, women, children, peasants, slaves, and hermits among prohibited targets. The prohibition against direct attack, however, does not establish the absolute immunity of noncombatants, because, according to most jurists, all of these persons (except for hermits) are subject to the laws pertaining to prisoners of war. They may be enslaved or ransomed by the Muslim forces. . . .

In current Muslim discourse on war and peace, ius in bello issues receive very little attention. This is true despite the vast changes that have occurred in both the international law and the technology of warfare. The discussion that does occur is usually undertaken by modernists seeking to reinterpret the Qur'an and sunna so that Islamic injunctions correspond to current international practice. Invariably these works concentrate on demonstrating the obsolescence of various aspects of medieval theory, such as the killing or enslavement of prisoners or the distribution of enemy property. More contemporary issues, such as the definition of noncombatant immunity and the use of terrorist methods by some Islamic groups, have yet to be treated systematically.

Far more relevant and interesting discussion of right conduct in war occurs in the context of specific conflicts. During the "war of the cities" toward the end of the Iran–Iraq War, for example, Mehdi Bazargan and the Liberation Movement of Iran (LMI) repeatedly protested that Khomeini was violating Islamic prohibitions against targeting civilians when he authorized missile strikes against Baghdad in retaliation for Iraq's Scud missile attacks against Teheran. . . .

More systematic discussion of just means occurred during the Persian Gulf War. In fact, ius in bello rather than ius ad bellum concerns dominated Muslim debates on the ethics of the conflict. Among the points raised by opponents of the anti-Iraq coalition's policies was that the conflict should be treated as fitna, that is, a dispute among Muslims. The rules concerning fitna developed by medieval jurists do not permit Muslims to ally themselves with non-Muslims, particularly when military decision-making is in non-Muslim hands. The prohibition was based on the belief that unbelievers would not apply the stricter code of conduct incumbent upon Muslims when fighting other Muslims. Critics of the Gulf War have argued that the conduct of the war by the coalition validates the medieval jurists' concerns. The massive air bombardment of Iraq's governmental and industrial facilities, they charge, was disproportionate to the Iraqi provocation and insufficiently discriminated between military and civilian targets. Moreover, the slaughter of Iraqi troops fleeing Kuwait City on the "highway of death" directly contravened one of the central points of Islamic law, namely that the goal of all military campaigns against other Muslims should be to rehabilitate and not to annihilate the transgressing party.

The most glaring area of neglect in contemporary Islamic analyses of ius in bello concerns weapons of mass destruction. So far, no systematic work has been done by Muslim scholars on how nuclear, chemical, and biological weapons relate to the Islamic ethics of war. This is an astonishing fact in light of the development of nuclear technology by several Muslim countries and the repeated use of chemical weapons by Iraq. In discussing the issue with several leading Muslim specialists in international law, I have found a great deal of ambivalence on the subject. Most scholars cite the Qur'anic verse "Hence, make ready against them whatever force and war mounts you are able to muster, so that you might deter thereby the enemies of God" (8:60) as justification for developing nuclear weaponry. Muslims must acquire nuclear weapons, I have been repeatedly told, because their enemies have introduced such weapons into their arsenals. There is unanimous agreement that Muslims should think of nuclear weapons only as a deterrent and that they should be used only as a second-strike weapon. But Islamic discussion of this topic remains at a very superficial level. There is little appreciation of the logistics of nuclear deterrence and of the moral difficulties to which a deterrence strategy gives rise.

Conclusion

Is the Islamic jihad the same as the Western just war? The answer, of course, depends upon who is defining the concepts. But after this brief survey of the debates that have historically surrounded the Islamic approach to war and peace and the controversies that are continuing to this day, I think it is safe to conclude that even though jihad may not be identical to the just war as it has evolved in the West, the similarities between Western and Islamic thinking on war and peace are far more numerous than the differences.

Jihad, like just war, was conceived by its early theorists basically as a means to circumscribe the legitimate reasons for war to so few that peace is inevitably enhanced. Jihad, like just war, is grounded in the belief that intersocietal relations should be peaceful, not marred by constant and destructive warfare. The surest way for human beings to realize this peace is for them to obey the divine law that is imprinted on the human conscience and therefore accessible to everyone, believers and unbelievers. According to the medieval view, Muslims are obliged to propagate this divine law, through peaceful means if possible, through violent means if necessary. No war was jihad unless it was undertaken with right intent and as a last resort, and declared by right authority. Most Muslims today disavow the duty to propagate Islam by force and limit jihad to self-defense. And finally, jihad, like just war, places strict limitations on legitimate targets during war and demands that belligerents use the least amount of force necessary to achieve the swift cessation of hostilities.

Both jihad and just war are dynamic concepts, still evolving and adapting to changing international realities. As Muslims continue to interpret the Islamic ethics of war and peace, their debates on jihad will, I believe, increasingly parallel the Western debates on just war. And as Muslims and non-Muslims continue their recently begun dialogue on the just international order, they may well find a level of agreement on the ethics of war and peace that will ultimately be reflected in a revised and more universal law of war and peace.

Klaus K. Klostermaier

Himsā and Ahimsā Traditions in Hinduism

For many Westerners Mahatma Gandhi (1869–1948) was the true representative of the essence of Hinduism. He embodied the spirit of non-violence (*ahimsā*) and the faith that truth/God (*satya*) will ultimately prevail. His lessons of non-violent resistance were taken up by the leaders of the American civil rights movement and praised, belatedly, by some recent popes. Those who have studied Indian thought under the guidance of the statesman-philosopher Sarvepalli Radhakrishnan (1888–1975) will have learned from his writings that Hinduism is the religion of peace and tolerance, which neither has the need nor the ambition to employ violence in any form. Hinduism is pure spirituality transcending all those conflicts that have drawn other religions into wars of faith with each other or with themselves.

Observers of the Indian contemporary scene must have noticed that fundamentalist political Hindu organizations have been instrumental in provoking a great number of violent confrontations with non-Hindus over such mundane issues as the repossession of the Rāma and Kṛṣṇa janmabhūmīs in Ayodhyā and Mathurā. They openly advocate militant and aggressive Hindu policies *vis-à-vis* non-Hindus. Unsettling and ominous as their speeches and actions might be, threatening the very existence of a free and democratic, pluralistic and secular India, they reflect as genuine and historical a tradition of Hinduism as did Gandhi and Radhakrishnan.

In the following a brief sketch will be provided of six tributaries to the Ganges of Hinduism, some freighted with vessels of war, others carrying messages of peace—some doing both.

Vedic Warriors and Their God

The basic Indian creation myth, fully developed already in the *Rgveda* and forming the preamble to the authoritative *Manusmrti* presents the origin of humankind from a primordial "person" in terms of caste society: *brahmans, ksatriyas, vaisyas,* and *śudras* emerge simultaneously, each with well-defined roles and duties, cooperating for the welfare of society as a whole. Not only are the respective caste duties well marked off against each other, they are exclusive means to attain salvation. Although the pursuit of learning, meditation, and tranquility is the means through which a *brahman* can reach individual perfection, it would be disastrous for anyone else to follow that path. Not only would society suffer for lacking an essential ingredient, that person herself would not find fulfilment and liberation. Birth is destiny. The means to win ultimate felicity for the warrior is fighting a war in defence of *dharma.* Society as a whole cannot exist without the strong arm of the custodians of *dharma,* who, if necessary, will use force to make sure that *adharma* will not win out.

Vedic society, as it is reflected in the *Rgveda* and the *Brāhmaṇas,* did not subscribe to *ahimsā* as its highest ideal, as did later Buddhist and Jain traditions. It not only sanctioned the killing of animals, sometimes in large numbers, for the purpose of the all-important *yajna,* it also gave high standing to its warriors, whose duty it was to kill the enemies of the Vedic religion. The most often invoked deity, Indra, has the attributes of a warrior himself, being praised as 'destroyer of enemies,' 'devastator of cities,' and 'Vrtra-killer.'

For long it was believed that the battles the *Ṛgveda* refers to were reminiscences of the 'Aryan invasion,' the movement of nomadic fair-skinned 'Aryans' from the steppes of southern Russian or inner Asia into the area of today's Punjab . . .

The wars . . . that are reported in the *Ṛgveda*, would have been wars between different clans of the same people, battles between those who considered themselves orthodox and those who had fallen away from Vedic orthodoxy.

Vedic society did not know conscription or total war. Fighting wars was the exclusive business of kṣatriyas. Brahmans were explicitly forbidden to engage in warfare.

The Smṛtis, the law books that codified rather early what must have been traditional practice of the Aryans, encourage kings to wage wars against neighbouring kings: to conquer another kingdom brings as much merit as good administration of one's own realm. And being killed in battle of this nature secures heaven.

Peace Thoughts in the Upaniṣads

The *Upaniṣads,* as can easily be noticed, differ radically in their outlook and orientation from the ritual-and-war dominated *Saṁhitās* and *Brāhmaṇs.* They too are considered *śruti,* revealed sacred word, providing humans with guidance in this life. They are in letter and spirit close to early Buddhist and Jain texts (many of which may be in fact contemporary with the later Upaniṣads) seeking liberation of the spirit from the fetters of rebirth rather than conquest of territory. They were composed by sages who had reached the last of the four brahmanical stages of life: samnyāsa, renunciation, dedicated to finding the Self and the All. Violence and greed had no place in this search. Nor had ritual and sacrifice. *Ahiṁsā,* the refusal to kill animals for the sake of sacrifice

(and for the sake of consumption of meat) became a cornerstone of their practice and teaching: if all life was one, if your own soul once dwelled in the body of an animal, and if the animal was possibly a parent reincarnated, how could you kill it? How would killing animals (or humans!) further your spiritual life? If meditation was the way to reality, if one found the highest fulfillment in one's own heart in an act of spiritual rapture, what purpose would it serve to kill another ensouled being? It only brought bad *karma* and had to be atoned for in later births. Becoming free from the necessity of being reborn, however, was the real aim of life.

The communities of ascetics, who later became known as Buddhists and Jains, apparently originated from the circles of these Upaniṣadic forest-sages and shared many of their practices, even if they developed different ideas of what ultimate liberation consisted in and how it was to be reached. They certainly insisted on *ahiṁsā,* the avoidance of killing of animals for sacrifices, and they emphasized the futility of the ritual-sacrificial complex. As ascetics (though they came from different caste backgrounds) they maintained brahmanic ideals: they were not to engage in wars, not to resist violently, and they had to be prepared to be tortured and killed in the process of promulgating the true *dharma.* Many indeed were. It is from this Upaniṣadic, Buddhist, Jain tradition that modern Hindu notions of *ahiṁsā,* as entertained by Mahatma Gandhi, originated.

"The Mother of All Battles": *The Mahābhārata*

The longest and most famous of all epic poems in the world, the *Mahābhārta,* deals with a war: the most destructive war ever fought, according to Hindu tradition, the war which initiated the Kaliyuga, the age of strife in which we now live. Its description of the eighteen days of battle, which brought to ruin an empire and death to millions of warriors, is the longest and most graphic of its kind. However, the longest of its eighteen *parvans* (books) is called *Śāntiparvan,* Book of Peace. It deals with a great many issues not related to the battle and has been used throughout Indian history as an important source for ethics.

In another section, the *Bhīṣmaparvan,* it reports about a "covenant made between the Kurus, the Pāṇḍavas and the Somakas . . . regarding the different kinds of combat." This probably repeats what was considered traditional conventions of warfare. Battle was to be between equals. One had to give notice and not attack someone in surprise. People not armed should not be fought. Many similar texts can be found in later *smṛti* works which bespeak a tradition of chivalry and of limitation of warfare to the professionals. Under no circumstances were civilians to be brought into the war, and it would have been unthinkable to kill women and children as part of the planned operations. The kind of indiscriminate and total war that is advocated today as "just war" would have been termed "demonic" by the ancient Indians . . .

It was understood that the code of ethics accepted in ordinary life would also apply in times of war. The wholesale destruction of towns and villages, the mass murder of civilians, the raping and looting that are the norm in modern warfare (notwithstanding the idealistic Geneva conventions) would have been unacceptable to traditional Indian society. The kind of warfare introduced by the Muslim conquerors was something totally new to India—it was warfare no longer inspired by the warrior's ambition to win fame and to subdue rival princes, but warfare motivated by religious reasons. It was warfare no longer controlled by a knightly code of war but it was either/or, life and death for all the population of the country, the kind of total war that can only be waged by people who know that God is only with them and not with the enemy, who are unable to see anything but the devil in the faces of their opponents.

War *and* Peace in the *Bhagavadgītā*

Technically, the *Bhagavadgītā* is a part of the *Mahābhārata.* It is however, not considered a mere interpolation in the text, but has been for centuries treated as an independent work: It contains God's revelation imparted as advice to Arjuna at the eve of the great war.

Arjuna is a member of the warrior caste—so are his opponents, members of the same family feuding over succession to the same kingdom. In the beginning Arjuna states his case for nonviolence, for not entering the war, whose terrible outcome has been indicated to him in nightmares and omina. One could call him a "conscientious objector" in today's terms: he is described by Sanjaya, the uninvolved narrator of the story, as "being completely overcome by compassion" (*kṛpayā paramaviṣṭo*). He exhibits signs of physical abhorrence of war, such as paralysis of movement, drying out of his mouth, shaking and aching all over his body. He points to the absurdity of war and the imbalance between the suffering caused by war and the advantages expected. He finds this particular war religiously and morally objectionable too: fighting it will not only rob him of his peace of mind, it also will cause the loss of fulfillment in the beyond, since he is about to kill relations and teachers. War, he maintains, is motivated by greed—an action based on greed cannot be morally right. War is hell and leads to hell. Rather than enjoy kingship won through such a war he would renounce all claims to status and wealth altogether and become a beggar-hermit.

Kṛṣṇa, the voice of God and the protector of *dharma,* states the case for war. He does not deny the truth of what Arjuna has said—but he declares it as relative in the face of an absolute truth that he is going to reveal. On the basis of traditional arguments, Kṛṣṇa declares Arjuna's decision not to fight as militating against the traditions of the race (it is called *anārya,* which would be the Indian equivalent to "Un-American Conduct"), as unprofitable (*ajuṣṭam*), as not designed to gain him heaven (*asvargyam*), "heaven" being the highest aspiration and reward of warriors, and, finally, as dishonourable (*akirtikāraṇam*), "honour" being understood to be the ultimate value for a warrior. On the level of profoundest insight, Arjuna's arguments simply do not apply: since birth and death are necessary corollaries of life, and since souls continuously return after the bodies die (by whatever means), death does not really matter, and the truly wise do not grieve for either past or future. The activity of the war concerns just these mortal bodies—they are not worth more than a garment that one picks up and drops again. At the centre of reality there is no activity: there is, in reality, neither slaying nor being slain. In addition, from a standpoint of ultimate reality, the war has already been fought, the killing has already taken place, the battle anticipated by Arjuna is only a stage demonstration of a play already complete, reflecting an unchanging law of God-created nature and God-maintained world order. . . .

Peace, however, is also taught in the *Bhagavadgītā*: the warrior must reach in his heart the peace that nobody can rob—he must rid himself of greed and anger, which (as Arjuna had said) vitiates any and every activity of war, he must fight as if he did not fight, he must act as if he did not act, he must do everything with a heart free from desire (*niṣkāma karma*). Then, in the midst of the tumult of battle, he will have peace, the only real peace there is. If he retired to a cave in the Himālayas he would not find peace of mind, because he would have abandoned his duty, betraying the cosmic divine plan through which alone he can find personal fulfillment.

The *Bhagavadgītā*, we have to remind ourselves, is not just *a* book among countless others, it is for many Hindus *the* book: God's own word, divine counsel to follow in times of inner and outer turmoil. The choice between peace and war, violence and non-violence is not ours: our *dharma* places us in specific positions, God's inscrutable plans make wars happen and cease.

Non-Violence as Unconditional Prerequisite for Seekers

. . . The Indian fondness for classification is at work also in the schematic demonstration of the varieties of *hiṁsā /ahiṁsā*. *Hiṁsā* (violence) as a vice can be either perpetrated by the violent person herself, caused by her, or permitted by her. In all these cases it arises out of anger, greed, or delusion. Each of these forms of violence can occur in a mild, medium, or strong form. Altogether, then, we have twenty-seven different forms of *hiṁsā* to be eradicated and counteracted by twenty-seven different forms of *ahiṁsā*.

The *Yoga Sūtras* insist that the vow of *ahiṁsā* (as of all other *yamas*) is "universal, and not limited by life-state, space, time and circumstances," that is, it insists that it is not sufficient to observe *ahiṁsā* in just certain areas or with regard to certain places or times. *Hiṁsā* is defined as any violation of living beings—by contrast *ahiṁsā* would be the habit of not inflicting any pain on any living being whatsoever. The *Yoga Sūtras* describe as the result of *ahiṁsā* that "hostilities are being given up in the presence (of the practitioner)." This statement provided inspiration for Gandhi: he firmly believed that the mere presence of a genuinely non-violent person would be sufficient to stop a violent person from proceeding with violence.

Ahiṁsā is one of five "universal habits" that have to be practised together to make a person fit to enter the path of liberation. If a person practised *ahiṁsā* alone and would not be truthful or honest in her dealings with other people, she could not claim to qualify for Yoga. For Gandhi too, *ahiṁsā* and *satya* were the two pillars of moral life upon which all activity, public and private, had to rest.

The Extension of Ahiṁsā to Premā: The Vaiṣṇava Contribution

From the fifth century onwards Hinduism, properly speaking, developed largely in reaction against Buddhism and Jainism, which at that time were the majority religions of India. Hinduism nominally maintained its Vedic base and insisted on the performance of rituals, but it appropriated many (probably indigenous) elements like temples, images, and a large number of new, revealed scriptures, the *Purāṇas, Āgamas,* and *Tantras.* It also became sectarian in the sense that groups of devotees rallied around a particular deity, such as Śiva, Viṣṇu, Śakti, Surya, and

Gaṇeśa, who for their followers became the Supreme, identified with the Upaniṣadic *brahman*. Large numbers of professional priests and theologians catered to the needs of the people in this sectarian context, developing impressive and extensive systems of religious theory and practice. Śaivism and Śāktism continued the practice of animal (and even human!) sacrifices (possibly they not only preserved the ancient Vedic practice but took over such atavistic customs from indigenous populations) and of frenzied orgies in honour of their deities. Vaiṣṇavism, on the other side, seemed to have absorbed not only many former Buddhists but also much of the ethos of Buddhism, with its emphasis on non-violence. There are no animal (or human) sacrifices in Vaiṣṇavism, and Vaiṣṇavas are vegetarians as a matter of religious principle. Their abhorrence of violence also shows in their more gentle forms of asceticism: there is no self-mutilation of the type often found among Śaivas and no self-decapitation as practised by some Śāktas as the supreme act of devotion. Vaiṣṇavas honour Viṣṇu with flowers, fruit, incense, and hymns. They practice fasting and meditation and aim not only at not violating other living beings but at embracing all of them with love. Viṣṇu, as the "friend of all living beings," is immanent in all that lives. It was especially the movement around Caitanya in sixteenth-century Bengal, later called Gauḍīa-Vaiṣṇavism, which saw in Kṛṣṇa the 'archetype of love' and in religion the way to reach that state of being where everything appears as an expression of this divine love. It is quite evident that each and every action—in deed, word, or thought—that would violate love would be prohibited.

It was probably as much under the influence of Vaiṣṇavism as under that of the Christian gospels, that Mahātmā Gandhi began translating the word *ahiṁsā* as love: a positive engagement on behalf of living beings rather than a mere refraining from injury, as the word originally meant. . . .

Conclusion

Hinduism in our time—like other mass religions—is polarized in its attitudes to peace and war. For a time it seemed that Gandhi's interpretation of Hinduism (as of all religion worth its name) as an expression of *satya* and *ahiṁsā*, truth and love would prevail, and that Hinduism would become a major pacifist force in the world. Christians joined the Gandhian movement and Westerners became Hindus in the belief that here was a religion that took seriously not only Jahwe's commandment "thou shalt not kill" but also Jesus' injunction of brotherly love extended to all humankind. Not all those who were attracted by Gandhianism stayed with it. Some resented what they saw as a certain disregard for the human individual, who was to become an instrument for the realization of an abstract ideal. Gandhi obviously did not mind the suffering and death of millions, as long as it was in pursuit of the ideal of non-violence. Martyrdom for the sake of a distant *Rāmarājya* was something to be sought for; ordinary life with its ordinary human satisfactions did not count much in the scheme. Gandhi's interpretation of Hinduism as a religion of non-violence and truth brought forth the Hindu opposition. Today we see the reawakening of a form of traditional Hinduism that perceives in militancy for the sake of Bhārat Mātā the genuine expression of the Hindu spirit.

Modern militant Hinduism began with Dayananda Saraswati and his Ārya Samāj: it was first directed against Christian missions and Muslims in India. It broadened its base with the emergence of the Hindu Mahāsabhā a generation later, in protest against what some Hindus perceived to be the surrender of the Indian Congress to Muslim pressure. It was intended to be a militant Hindu political party that uncompromisingly strove for a Hindu-dominated independent India. The Hindu Mahāsabhā had found in Vir Savarkar its greatest and most strident ideologue. A contemporary of Gandhi and Nehru, he relentlessly attacked both the Gandhian principle of *ahiṁsā* and Nehru's idea of a pluralistic secular state. He maintained that "the belief in absolute non-violence . . . evinces no mahatmaic saintliness but a monomaniacal senselessness" and that "the militarization and industrialization of the Hindus must constitute our immediate objective."

The Rastria Swayamsevak Sangh, a Hindu Mahā-sabhā front organization, built up from the 1930s onward a kind of private army in the service of militant Hinduism. It has grown and been amplified by private Hindu armies under other names, most of them under the umbrella of the Hindu Viśva Pariṣad, which was formed in 1964 in Bombay to counteract what was perceived as a Christian missionary threat in connection with the World Eucharistic Congress in Bombay.

Nobody who has followed events in India since independence can be unaware of the many brutal and large-scale communal riots. While certainly not the only culprits, Hindu militants have openly advocated violence and incited their followers to aggression against non-Hindus in the name of Hinduism. The advocates of non-violence are not entirely missing, but they seem to be in a minority nowadays. It does no longer seem possible idealistically to argue with Gandhi that *ahiṁsā*, understood as universal love, is the central truth of Hinduism. Today's militant Hindus have all the arguments of the late twentieth-century real world on their side: large numbers of followers, the power to coerce events in their direction, the will to use any means in pursuit of their interests, and the disregard for minorities who are too weak to resist with force.

I do not wish to end on such a pessimistic note. Could we then, by way of a somewhat more positive conclusion, suggest a concept made popular by Kaka Kalelkar, a devoted Gandhian, but also reflecting much of the spirit of traditional India as well, namely, the notion of *samanvaya*. *Samanvaya* means harmonization, it designates the method of resolving contradictions and conflicts. The term was used by Śankara as the title to the first section of his commentary on the *Brahmasūtras,* where he shows that the various apparently contradictory Upaniṣadic statements about *brahman* can be reconciled with an in-depth understanding of *brahman.* The surface meaning of various scriptural statements may appear to differ and disagree, but there is a common intentionality of all scripture that is found through a depth hermeneutics. Kaka Kalelkar, following Gandhi, applied the principle of *samanvaya* to the plurality of religions that, in the course of history, has not only led to intellectual exclusivism and spiritual absolutism, but also to violent conflict and to mutual destruction. *Samanvaya* does not dissolve the differences that characterize the different traditions of humankind, but it allows us to recognize their family resemblance and to come together in a "familyhood of religions." That might be the best we can do at present in order to activate the potential for inner and outer peace, which Hinduism no doubt possesses.

Roy C. Amore

Peace and Non-Violence in Buddhism

Non-Violence Values along the Ancient Ganges

An ethic of non-violence was central to Buddhism from its inception. Buddhism, as we know it, arose in the Ganges region of northern India approximately twenty-five hundred years ago. To the people of the day this area was known as the Middle Region, lying between the oceans of the Jambu Continent (Jambudvipa)—jambu are a fruit still to be found in the markets of India. During the seventh and sixth centuries BCE this Middle Region had undergone political transformation in the form of a consolidation from a region with numerous small kingdoms and republics to a region consisting of four large kingdoms. The rapid changes had been set in motion by a population explosion based upon the introduction of iron technology, especially the iron ploughshare, into the area. Each kingdom had as its capital a major city in which the various sciences of the day thrived. These included both economic staples such as metal working, textile manufacturing, medicine, nutrition, and writing, as well as the sciences characteristic of ancient cities such as mathematics, logic, astronomy/astrology, and political science.

The economy of the Middle Region thrived because of the interplay of three sectors: (1) a rich, expanding agricultural base with large estates owned by a ruling-class of landlords and worked by commoners and slaves, (2) a newly formed trade business conducted along a caravan route that crossed the region from east to west, and (3) an emerging banking industry complete with money lending and coinage.

The emergence of the large kingdoms created great wealth as well as power among the rul-ing kshatriya class, and the thriving trade business created wealth among the merchant class. Furthermore, some members of the brahman class held wealth in the form of land and especially cattle, the traditional form of wealth. Upper-class males had a strong grip on power and prestige, but some upper-class women were well educated and enjoyed wealth and prestige.

The Buddhist texts normally only mention the kshatriyas when speaking about the republics, as opposed to the kingdoms. The republics were ruled by an aristocracy of kshatriya clans, it seems. Another matter that emerges in the Buddhist texts in a way curiously different than what we would expect from reading brahmanical literature is that the vaishya, merchant class, is seldom mentioned. Instead, the picture of social life in ancient India that one gets from the Buddhist texts is that of a brahman class of landowners/priests; a ruling house in the kingdoms or a ruling, kshatriya class in the republics; a householder class; and various service occupations.

Hidden beneath the peace and prosperity were serious social and ideological divisions, however. There were tensions between the upper classes and the commoners, as we would expect, but the new money economy had created a large urban merchant class whose wealth and financial power outstripped its social status. The brahman class, being more conservative, was critical of money lending, and the ruling class looked down upon the merchants as landless. Furthermore, brahmans and kshatriyas took pride from the Purusha creation hymn in the Rig Veda, which gave them high status as, respectively, the mouth and arm of the sacrificed primordial "person" (*purusha*). The ruling-class writers of the law books sometimes went so far as to group the merchant, vaishya class together with the commoner, shudra class.

In addition to the tension between the new urban rich and the traditional landed rich, the region had undergone an infusion of Aryan culture in recent centuries. The kshatriya and brahman classes were the elite of an Aryan culture that had entered the region from farther west. It introduced new languages, marriage customs, political norms, and social conventions to the Middle Region. Important everyday things such as new forms of pottery and metal working were introduced as well.

For our analysis of non-violence, the most important cultural tension was between the brahman priests and the traditional spirituality of the region. It is very difficult to prove that a distinct regional religious tradition did exist, because the written sources we now have are the products of the brahman elite. However, there are linguistic and archaeological data that lend support to the claim that the religion of the brahmans had been superimposed upon the traditional spirituality of the region. It seems worthwhile to reconstruct this traditional religion, for it forms the basis of two for the world's living religions that have non-violence at the heart of their teachings, Buddhism and Jainism.

Along the Ganges were camps that served as the centres for various religious teachers. Many of the teachers were brahmans, but these open-air seminaries admitted non-brahman students (*shramana*) as well. Normally, only males were admitted, it seems, but the Jain leader Parshva founded an order for females as early as the tenth century BCE according to Jain tradition. And Shakyamuni Buddha, somewhat reluctantly we are told, instituted a monastic order for women as well as men. Each camp had its spiritual master, who laid down a discipline (*vinaya*) and a set of teachings (*dharma*). There was a fierce rivalry among the masters as they competed for students and respect. Like university students today, the students of ancient India checked out the various teachers, looking for one whose combination of teachings and discipline suited the student.

There were areas of general agreement among the masters. With regard to discipline, all the teachers required the students to take a vow of celibacy. There were always dietary restrictions, the most common one being the avoidance of meat eating on the grounds that killing animals caused them suffering. Most masters required their disciples to rise quite early and to spend many hours working to sustain the camp as well as at meditating and learning. These religious training camps were the forerunners of the later monastic movement of India, and perhaps beyond.

Students were expected to engage in ascetic practices, denying themselves bodily pleasures for the sake of spiritual development. Some of the ascetic practices were relatively mild, by *their* standards, such as standing or sitting in a fixed posture for several hours at a time, or fasting during full moon days, or sleeping on the ground. Other practices were quite severe; such as exposing oneself to rain for long periods in the cool season, or standing nude in the sun for hours during the hot season, or piercing one's skin with metal objects, or going without food or water for very long periods.

The ethical values of the masters were rooted in the concept of *ahiṁsā*, which literally means non-harming. It was this issue that most seriously divided the brahmans from the non-brahman teachers who represented the traditional values of the Middle Region. The differing value systems came into sharpest focus over the issue of performing the animal sacrifices required in the brahmanical tradition. The brahmanical definition of the unethical person was one who was not a sacrificer, whereas the Ganges masters defined the unethical person as one who harmed living beings. One value system required animal sacrifices, while the other condemned them.

The tension between the brahman sacrificers and the Ganges masters is apparent in one of the animal stories included in the Buddhist Jataka collection. The story tells about a brahman who ordered his servants to bathe and garland a goat in preparation for a sacrifice. While being washed in the river, it suddenly laughs, then cries. When asked to explain the laughter, the goat tells the brahman that it laughed with delight when it realized that this was its last rebirth as a goat, and that its next birth would be as a human. As for the crying, the goat explains that in further reflecting about its past rebirths, it recalled that the reason it had been condemned to hundreds of rebirths as a goat was because in its last human rebirth it had been a brahman who committed the bad karma action of killing a goat as part of a sacrifice. It cried when it thought about the suffering its current brahman owner would have to endure in his own future rebirths! Needless to say, the brahman decided not to sacrifice that goat, and to adopt the value of *ahiṁsā.*

Another Buddhist scripture satirizes the brahman sacrifice, and in the typical style of the Buddha, gives an alternate explanation of the elements of a "true sacrifice." According to the story a brahman named "Sharptooth," which is not meant to be taken as a real name, came to the Buddha to ask about the proper use of the sacred implements of the sacrifices—which is about as likely, historically, as a Jewish temple priest asking Jesus about how to use the fire tongs at the Jerusalem temple! The Buddha responded by telling the story of a past king named Wide-Realm who abandoned his plan to sponsor a Vedic sacrifice of hundreds of animals in favour of a more modest, egalitarian offering dedicated not to the gods, but to the welfare to all living creatures. Unlike the brahmanical sacrifices, no commoners were forced to provide labour for the sacrifice. As a follow-up to his sacrifice, King Wide-Realm set up food and medicine distribution places throughout his kingdom in order to provide the basic welfare of all and to eliminate the poverty that breeds crime. The brahman Sharptooth got the message and went forth to do likewise.

The Buddhist disciples, or "renouncers," had to set themselves apart from the world of the householder, but those who were of brahman background had to renounce that as well. They gave up their cooking pots, the tuft of hair at the back of their heads, and the utensils used in carrying out the Vedic sacrifices.

The most zealous proponents of *ahiṁsā* wore masks over their faces and strained their drinking water to avoid unintentionally killing insects. The Jain leader Mahavira advocated these extreme forms of *ahiṁsā.* Sakyamuni Buddha did not advocate these practices, but did encourage his disciples to avoid stepping on earthworms, and so forth.

The attempts to live one's everyday life according to the principle of *ahiṁsā* was not limited to those who had taken religious vows. Some lay-people, or "householders," gave up hunting or fishing as occupations. Others even shied away from farming because ploughing involved killing insects. Most householders seemed to have continued to eat meat, even if they did not kill the animal, but one group took *ahiṁsā* to an interesting level. They lived as vegetarians most of the year, but once a year a group of the males killed one elephant for a communal feast. The idea was that they got nutrition from the animal while limiting their bad karma to that generated by a single act of harming, and that bad karma was shared by a group!

Buddhist Social Ethic

What effect did this strong personal *ahiṁsā* ethic have on the Buddhist social ethic? Before addressing that question, however, we should respond to the criticism that Buddhism may not actually have a social ethic. It is true that the emphasis of Buddha's teaching was on one's personal behaviour and the goal of purifying one's mind (*citta*). Most Buddhists are familiar with the following Dharmapada verse, which is cited as a summation of Buddhist thought:

> The avoidance of all evil,
> The cultivation of wholesome
>   consciousness,
> The purification of the mind
> This is the teaching of the buddhas.

This is an individual ethic. Indeed, it has been argued that the modern understanding of the individual first appeared in Buddhist texts.

The Buddhist project was to improve society at large by purifying the motives of individuals. Basing their approach on what appeared to work in the real world, as we might say, they held that a cadre of tranquil, generous, non-violent persons could be the catalyst for social transformation.

Although the pacifist impulse in early Buddhism was focused on individuals, there was a drive towards social reform as well. The reforms centered upon the abuses of the brahmans and the responsibilities of the kshatriyas. In contrast to our era, the business class does not come under serious criticism.

Shakyamuni Buddha was critical of the privileges assumed by the brahmans as a social class and as an hereditary priesthood. With techniques such as the following, he challenged the idea that social status could or should be derived from birth status rather than personal achievement: "Ask not about a person's birth status (*jati*, caste), ask about a person's character." A whole chapter of the Dharmapada, one of the most popular of the Buddhist scriptures, is dedicated to the claim that the "true brahman" is one who has purified the mind, as opposed to one who is merely born into the priestly class. In this way, the Buddha argued that the real brahmans were those who had made progress on the spiritual path. To put the matter in terms of our topic, the true "holy ones" are those who live by the principle of *ahiṁsā* and not those who officiate at the animal sacrifices. The *ahiṁsā* ethic thereby led to a challenge to the theoretical underpinnings of the Indian social order. The implication was that the Rig Veda's Purusha hymn, which has its counterparts in other ancient Indo-European cultures, was wrong to lay down sacrifice as the model spiritual activity and wrong to legitimize a hereditary class system.

As for the kshatriyas, the ethic of non-violence led Shakyamuni Buddha to criticize their practice of undertaking wars to expand one's territory. The main object of the wars of aggression during the Buddha's time was to gain control over strategic points on the banks of the Ganges. Such territorial wars were as old and well established in Indo-European culture as animal sacrifices. The cattle raid carried out by the third of the three legendary heros in Indo-European mythology legitimized, even idealized, wars of aggression by the ruling kshatriya class. One time, according to the Buddhist texts, Shakyamuni Buddha was staying in the vicinity of a battlefield on which the armies of the kingdoms of Magadha and Savatthi were fighting. The king of Magadha had started the war to expand his territory, and he had decisively won the battle and forced the other king into retreat. When Buddha's disciples reported the battle to him, he explained that the Magadhan king was evil, and the Savatthi king was good. The good king had been defeated, but only temporarily, Buddha predicted. His point was not so much a prediction of the future but rather an expression of the basic *ahiṁsā* teaching that "conquest leads only to more fighting." In the words of the Dhammapada,

> Hatreds are never ended or calmed by hate,
> Hatreds are only calmed by non-hate.
> This is an everlasting principle.

Buddhist thought speaks against poverty on the grounds that it directly causes suffering to the poor and indirectly causes crime, which brings suffering to others. This means that the Buddhist condemnation of poverty is linked only indirectly to the ethic of *ahiṁsā*.

Early Buddhism had two very different approaches to poverty. In the first it called upon the king to set up food stations to provide rice and curries for the poor. The obligation of the government to provide such rice kitchens is found throughout the early Buddhist literature, but I cannot find in the Buddhist texts any standards given for who qualifies to receive the free food. There *seems* to be no concern that the welfare rolls would grow too big. Was there so little concern because the food was second rate? Perhaps, but certain kings who are especially virtuous made a point of eating at their own rice stations, and the texts stress that the food should be of a good variety. It would seem that in ancient India, as in modern southern Asia, it is considered an insult not to serve a variety of curries with the rice.

In the second approach to poverty, Buddhism put the onus upon government to alleviate poverty. A king who fails to rule by righteousness (*dharma*) allows poverty and, therefore, crime to increase. Another cause of poverty is a government that over-taxes the people to build up the royal treasury. Whether the taxes take the form of goods or of services—a common form of taxation in traditional India—the result is that the people have less time and money to use for their own basic needs. One Buddhist sutra makes the very modern-sounding point that the hoarding of wealth by the wealthy few causes poverty among the disadvantaged.

Most references to giving in the Buddhist texts refer to donations to the Sangha, and in Buddhist karma theory such gifts to worthy persons are the most meritorious. However, as Lily De Silva rightly notes, Buddhist thought also strongly endorses charity to the poor. Besides recommending gifts to the monks, Buddhist texts "also speak of Kapanas 'destitutes,' *addhikas,* 'wayfarers,' *vanibbakas,* 'vagabonds,' and *yacakas,* 'beggars,' to whom also should be given."

The *ahiṃsā* ethic also led to a critique of abuse against women and female infants. The Buddha even dared, according to the text, to chastise a king for his improper attitude of disappointment at the birth of a daughter. Shakyamuni's admonition to him tried to put a positive twist to the birth of a daughter, by pointing out that a daughter might be better than a son. She might, he suggests, be very wise and virtuous. Unfortunately, from our perspective, the reasons given for preferring a baby girl are definitely of a pre-feminist nature—such as, she may be outstanding at virtues such as being a good wife and honouring her mother-in-law, and she may make the king a proud grandfather by bearing sons who do great things. But whatever the cultural standards may be for taking pride in one's children, the point remains that the non-violence impulse in Buddhism made some progress in correcting the age-old social preference for male offspring. The Buddhist teaching is in sharp contrast with brahmanical prayers, offered on behalf of the sponsor of the Vedic sacrifice, "for sons and long life" as a reward for undertaking the ritual.

Unlike early Christianity, Buddhism enjoyed royal patronage from the start, for the Buddha himself converted several regional kings. As in other matters, Buddhists took a middle position on the matter of law and order. They sanctioned the use of punishment, even capital punishment, for the control of crime, but at the same time they condemned the use of unjust or unnecessarily cruel punishments. Their ethic of non-violence was considered applicable to the king's personal and judicial behaviour and to the nature of the laws he proclaimed. In short, the king was not considered an absolute authority in Buddhism, but was required to operate within the confines of *dharma* as understood by the Buddhist tradition.

The famous king known in the West as Ashoka is known to Buddhists as Dharma Ashoka. This title has several connotations. Besides distinguishing him from another Indian king named Ashoka, the name implies both the sense of "Ashoka, who was concerned with Dharma" and "Ashoka, the Righteous."

The story of Dharma Ashoka is so well known that for our purposes it is necessary only to call attention briefly to the role he plays in the institutionalization of the Buddhist ethic of nonviolence. Having inherited the throne from his father and grandfather, who had driven the Macedonians out of central India, Ashoka had annexed even more territory to the south and west, such that he ruled an empire that included most of modern India. The Buddhist histories claim that as a result of Ashoka's reflection on a particularly bloody war with the east coast kingdom of Kalinga, he underwent a conversion to Buddhism and began promoting the ethic of nonviolence. Probably his family had previously been supporters of *ahiṃsā* traditions, such as Jainism, and so his conversion to Buddhism was not a major shift.

Ashoka called, according to his famous rock edits, for a *dharma* conquest, as opposed to further military conquests. In the message posted in the Kalinga area, he expresses remorse at having been responsible for the death and suffering of so many people. His government's ideals include security, self-control, impartiality, and cheerfulness for all living creatures in his empire. Ashoka spells out his "conquest by *dharma*" and claims that it is spreading within the Indian continent and among the Alexandrian kingdoms, whose kings he names. Ashoka states that real satisfaction in ruling over people comes only from inducing them to follow *dharma*.

Ashoka juxtaposes his own pledge to be just and moderate in punishment with a warning to his Kalinga subjects and the nearby tribal people that he will not hesitate to deal firmly with rebels and criminals, despite his commitment to non-violence. Ashoka's promotion of *dharma* becomes a model for later Buddhist rulers. Wars of aggression and cruel or unjust punishments were considered to be against *dharma,* but the govern-ment was thought to have the duty to punish criminals and rebels. By the end of Ashoka's reign, the new Buddhist sociopolitical order had spread to governments beyond India. . . .

Conclusion

The pacifist impulse in Buddhism is rooted in the ethic of non-violence that was the characteristic spiritual value along the ancient Ganges. This *ahiṁsā* ethic gave rise to a personal ethical system that encouraged non-harming occupations, vegetarianism, and kindness to all living creatures. On the political level, the *ahiṁsā* ethic gave shape to ethical guidelines for rulers which discouraged wars of aggression, hunting, and cruelty towards enemies and criminals. It recognized a need for the punishment of crimes and wars of defence.

Michael Walzer

The Just War

The Legalist Paradigm

If states actually do possess rights more or less as individuals do, then it is possible to imagine a society among them more or less like the society of individuals. The comparison of international to civil order is crucial to the theory of aggression. I have already been making it regularly. Every reference to aggression as the international equivalent of armed robbery or murder, and every comparison of home and country or of personal liberty and political independence, relies upon what is called the *domestic analogy.* Our primary perceptions and judgments of aggression are the products of analogical reasoning. When the analogy is made explicit, as it often is among the lawyers, the world of states takes on the shape of a political society the character of which is entirely accessible through such notions as crime and punishment, self-defense, law enforcement, and so on.

These notions, I should stress, are not incompatible with the fact that international society as it exists today is a radically imperfect structure. As we experience it, that society might be likened to a defective building, founded on rights; its superstructure raised, like that of the state itself, through political conflict, cooperative activity, and commercial exchange; the whole thing shaky and unstable because it lacks the rivets of authority. It is like domestic society in that men and women live at peace within it (sometimes), determining the conditions of their own existence, negotiating and bargaining with their neighbors. It is unlike domestic society in that every conflict threatens the structure as a whole with collapse. Aggression challenges in directly and is much more dangerous than domestic crime, because there are no policemen. But that only means that

the "citizens" of international society must rely on themselves and on one another. Police powers are distributed among all the members. And these members have not done enough in the exercise of their powers if they merely contain the aggression or bring it to a speedy end—as if the police should stop a murderer after he has killed only one or two people and send him on his way. The rights of the member states must be vindicated, for it is only by virtue of those rights that there is a society at all. If they cannot be upheld (at least sometimes), international society collapses into a state of war or is transformed into a universal tyranny.

From this picture, two presumptions follow. The first, which I have already pointed out, is the presumption in favor of military resistance once aggression has begun. Resistance is important so that rights can be maintained and future aggressors deterred. The theory of aggression restates the old doctrine of the just war: it explains when fighting is a crime and when it is permissible, perhaps even morally desirable. The victim of aggression fights in self-defense, but he isn't only defending himself, for aggression is a crime against society as a whole. He fights in its name and not only in his own. Other states can rightfully join the victim's resistance; their war has the same character as his own, which is to say, they are entitled not only to repel the attack but also to punish it. All resistance is also law enforcement. Hence the second presumption: when fighting breaks out, there must always be some state against which the law can and should be enforced. Someone must be responsible, for someone decided to break the peace of the society of states. No war, as medieval theologians explained, can be just on both sides.

There are, however, wars that are just on neither side, because the idea of justice doesn't pertain to them or because the antagonists are both aggressors, fighting for territory or power where they have no right. The first case I have already alluded to in discussing the voluntary combat of aristocratic warriors. It is sufficiently rare in human history that nothing more need be said about it here. The second case is illustrated by those wars that Marxists call "imperialist," which are not fought between conquerors and victims but between conquerors and conquerors, each side seeking dominion over the other or the two of them competing to dominate some third party. Thus Lenin's description of the struggles between "have" and "have-not" nations in early twentieth-century Europe: ". . . picture to yourselves a slave-owner who owned 100 slaves warring against a slave-owner who owned 200 slaves for a more 'just' distribution of slaves. Clearly, the application of the term 'defensive' war in such a case . . . would be sheer deception . . ." But it is important to stress that we can penetrate the deception only insofar as we can ourselves distinguish justice and injustice: the theory of imperialist war presupposes the theory of aggression. If one insists that all wars on all sides are acts of conquest or attempted conquest, or that all states at all times would conquer if they could, then the argument for justice is defeated before it begins and the moral judgments we actually make are derided as fantasies. Consider the following passage from Edmund Wilson's book on the American Civil War:

> I think that it is a serious deficiency on the part of historians . . . that they so rarely interest themselves in biological and zoological phenomena. In a recent . . . film showing life at the bottom of the sea, a primitive organism called a sea slug is seen gobbling up small organisms through a large orifice at one end of its body; confronted with another sea slug of an only slightly lesser size, it ingurgitates that, too. Now the wars fought by human beings are stimulated as a rule . . . by the same instincts as the voracity of the sea slug.

There are no doubt wars to which that image might be fit, though it is not a terribly useful image with which to approach the Civil War. Nor does it account for our ordinary experience of international society. Not all states are sea-slug states, gobbling up their neighbors. There are always groups of men and women who would live if they could in peaceful enjoyment of their rights and who have chosen political leaders who represent that desire. The deepest purpose of the state is not ingestion but defense, and the least that can be said is that many actual states serve that purpose. When their territory is attacked or their sovereignty challenged, it makes sense to look for an aggressor and not merely for a natural predator. Hence we need a theory of aggression rather than a zoological account.

The theory of aggression first takes shape under the aegis of the domestic analogy. I am going to call that primary form of the theory the *legalist paradigm,* since it consistently reflects the conventions of law and order. It does not necessarily reflect the arguments of the lawyers, though legal as well as moral debate has its starting point here. Later on, I will suggest that our judgments about the justice and injustice of particular wars are not entirely determined by the paradigm. The complex realities of international society drive us toward a revisionist perspective, and the revisions will be significant ones. But the paradigm must first be viewed in its unrevised form; it is our baseline, our model, the fundamental structure for the moral comprehension of war. We begin with the familiar world of individuals and rights, of crimes and punishments. The theory of aggression can then be summed up in six propositions.

1. *There exists an international society of independent states.* States are the members of this society, not private men and women. In the absence of a universal state, men and women are protected and their interests represented only by their own governments. Though states are founded for the sake of life and liberty, they cannot be challenged in the name of life and liberty by any other states. Hence the principle of non-intervention, which I will analyze later on. The rights of private persons can be recognized in international society, as in the UN

Charter of Human Rights, but they cannot be enforced without calling into question the dominant values of that society: the survival and independence of the separate political communities.

2. *This international society has a law that establishes the rights of its members—above all, the rights of territorial integrity and political sovereignty.* Once again, these two rest ultimately on the right of men and women to build a common life and to risk their individual lives only when they freely choose to do so. But the relevant law refers only to states, and its details are fixed by the intercourse of states, through complex processes of conflict and consent. Since these processes are continuous, international society has no natural shape; nor are rights within it ever finally or exactly determined. At any given moment, however, one can distinguish the territory of one people from that of another and say something about the scope and limits of sovereignty.

3. *Any use of force or imminent threat of force by one state against the political sovereignty or territorial integrity of another constitutes aggression and is a criminal act.* As with domestic crime, the argument here focuses narrowly on actual or imminent boundary crossings: invasions and physical assaults. Otherwise, it is feared, the notion of resistance to aggression would have no determinate meaning. A state cannot be said to be forced to fight unless the necessity is both obvious and urgent.

4. *Aggression justifies two kinds of violent response: a war of self-defense by the victim and a war of law enforcement by the victim and any other member of international society.* Anyone can come to the aid of a victim, use necessary force against an aggressor, and even make whatever is the international equivalent of a "citizen's arrest." As in domestic society, the obligations of bystanders are not easy to make out, but it is the tendency of the theory to undermine the right of neutrality and to require widespread participation in the business of law enforcement. In the Korean War, this partic-

ipation was authorized by the United Nations, but even in such cases the actual decision to join the fighting remains a unilateral one, best understood by analogy to the decision of a private citizen who rushes to help a man or woman attacked on the street.

5. *Nothing but aggression can justify war.* The central purpose of the theory is to limit the occasions for war. "There is a single and only just cause for commencing a war," wrote Vitoria, "namely, a wrong received." There must actually have been a wrong, and it must actually have been received (or its receipt must be, as it were, only minutes away). Nothing else warrants the use of force in international society—above all, not any difference of religion or politics. Domestic heresy and injustice are never actionable in the world of states: hence, again, the principle of nonintervention.

6. *Once the aggressor state has been militarily repulsed, it can also be punished.* The conception of just war as an act of punishment is very old, though neither the procedures nor the forms of punishment have ever been firmly established in customary or positive international law. Nor are its purposes entirely clear: to exact retribution, to deter other states, to restrain or reform this one? All three figure largely in the literature, though it is probably fair to say that deterrence and restraint are most commonly accepted. When people talk of fighting a war against war, this is usually what they have in mind. The domestic maxim is, punish crime to prevent violence; its international analogue is, punish aggression to prevent war. Whether the state as a whole or only particular persons are the proper objects of punishment is a harder question. . . . But the implication of the paradigm is clear: if states are members of international society, the subjects of rights, they must also be (somehow) the objects of punishment.

Questions for Discussion

1. How do McKenna's principles of a just war apply to wars based on religious ideologies in which people declare war on each other in order to expand the influence of their religions?
2. What distinguishes the Catholic or Scholastic view of war from other theories presented in this section on theories of just and unjust war?
3. Is there any situation in which Quakers would justify the use of violence?
4. How would you analyze the wars fought between Arabs and Israelis in light of the theory presented by Walzer in his reading?
5. How does the Islamic concept of Jihad apply to the conflict among Islamic countries?
6. How does the Islamic concept of war differ from or resemble other religious theories about war?
7. What does the Gandhian philosophy have to say about the acquisition and development of nuclear weapons as a deterrent?
8. How does the Buddhist peace tradition deal with the principle of self-defense?
9. After reviewing Walzer's last reading in this section, what are his parameters of a just war?
10. When, if ever, do you suppose Walzer would justify a preemptive war and a preventive war?

Further Readings

1. Christiano, Kevin J. "Conflict and Order in Roman Catholic Thought." *Research in Human Social Conflict,* 2000, 2, Mar., 229–246.
2. Hauerwas, Stanley. "Christian Non-Violence" in Jon L. Berquist, ed., *Strike Terror No More: Theology, Ethics, and the New War.* St. Louis: Chalice Press, 2002.
3. Bartoli, Andrea. "Christianity and Peacebuilding" in Harold Coward and Gordon S. Smith, eds., *Religion and Peacebuilding.* New York: State University of New York Press, 2004, 147–166.
4. Martin-Baro, Ignacio. "Religion as an Instrument of Psychological Warfare." *Journal of Social Issues,* 1990, 46, 3, Fall, 93–107.
5. Thompson, Henry O. *World Religions in War and Peace.* Jefferson, NC: McFarland & Company, 1988.
6. Roberts, Helen. "Witness against War: Researching the History of the Quaker Peace Testimony." *Quaker Studies,* 2002, 7, 1, Sept., 79–100.
7. Brutz, Judith L., and Allen, Craig M. "Religious Commitment, Peace Activism, and Marital Violence in Quaker Families." *Journal of Marriage and the Family,* 1986, 48, 3, Aug., 491–502.
8. Safi, Louay M. "Peace and Limits of War: Transcending Classical Conception of Jihad." *International Institute of Islamic Thought,* 2001.
9. Benhabib, Seyla. "Unholy Wars." *Constellations,* 2002, 9, 1, Mar., 34–45.
10. Mohammad, Fida. "Jihad as Terrorism: The Western Media and the Defamation of the Qu'ran" in Jeff Ferrell and Neil Websdale, eds., *Making Trouble: Cultural Constructions of Crime, Deviance, and Control.* Hawthorne, NY: Aldine De Gruyter, 1999, 303–317.
11. Ulmen, Gary. "Just Wars or Just Enemies?" *Telos,* 1996, 109, Fall, 99–112.
12. Hass, Peter J. "The Just War Doctrine and Post Modern Warfare. Strike Terror No More" in Jon L. Berquist, ed., *Strike Terror No More: Theology, Ethics, and the New War.* St. Louis: Chalice Press, 2002.
13. Smock, David R. *Religious Perspectives on War: Christian, Muslim, and Jewish Attitudes toward Force,* Revised Edition. Washington, DC: United States Institute of Peace Press, 2002.

14. Gopin, Mark. "Judaism and Peacebuilding" in Harold Coward and Gordon S. Smith, eds., *Religion and Peacebuilding.* New York: State University of New York Press, 2004, 111–127.

15. Denny, Frederick M. "Islam and Peacebuilding: Continuities and Transitions" in Harold Coward and Gordon S. Smith, eds., *Religion and Peacebuilding.* New York: State University of New York Press, 2004, 129–146.

16. Gandhi, Rajmohan. "Hinduism and Peacebuilding" in Harold Coward and Gordon S. Smith, eds., *Religion and Peacebuilding.* New York: State University of New York Press, 2004, 45–68.

17. Berling, Judith A. "Confucianism and Peacebuilding" in Harold Coward and Gordon S. Smith, eds., *Religion and Peacebuilding.* New York: State University of New York Press, 2004, 93–110.

18. Weigel, George, "Religion and Peace: An Argument Complexified." *The Washington Quarterly,* Spring 1991, 27–39.

19. Johnson, James Turner. "Can a Pacifist Have a Conversation with Augustine? 'A response to Alain Epp Weaver.'" *Journal of Religious Ethics,* 29, Spring 2001, 87.

20. Starr, Jerold M. "Religious Preference, Religiosity, and Opposition to War." *Sociological Analysis,* 1975, 36, 4, 323–334.

IV
PART

Theories of the Causes of War

Biological Theories

The contribution of human genes to the phenotype has been exhaustively debated by biologists and genetic scientists alike. However, this topic is now also being discussed by social scientists in the context of genetic contributions to the human capacity for aggression. Various theories have been developed to assess the extent to which the human propensity for violence has its roots in the genetic evolution of mankind. Many theorists believe that aggression is an instinct for self-preservation that has evolved and developed through the process of natural selection. Those who do not believe in the genetic origins of aggression, criticize such theories for justifying violence. Those who agree, however, insist that it is only an objective analysis of the relationship between human psychology and genetics and that it would lead to a better understanding of the issue. This section deals with this ongoing debate.

Irenaus Eibl-Eibesfeldt, in "Biology of Peace and War," differentiates between two kinds of aggression found in humans: intragroup aggression and intergroup aggression. She establishes the phylogenetic nature of intragroup aggression in humans and how intergroup aggression is a product of biological natural selection and cultural evolution. Warfare is defined by the author as an elaborate and developed form of intergroup warfare and thus finds its origins in the genetic make-up of humans. The concept of "pseudospeciation" is advanced as a mechanism which enhances the evaluation of one's in-group and demonizes an out-group, thus promoting violence.

The second reading in this section is a reproduction of the "Seville Statement on Violence." The statement is a joint declaration by a committee of 20 international scholars and the representatives of UNESCO to oppose the idea of aggression being a genetically ingrained characteristic of human beings. This reading denies the "scientific" validity of the theory that humans are naturally predisposed towards violence.

The original Seville statement was widely criticized by various members of the scientific community. The credentials of the committee members were questioned and there was some speculation about their motives for drafting and signing the statement. The third reading of this section, "The Seville Statement on Violence Revisited," was written by two of the 20 signatories of the original statement in response to the criticisms.

Irenaus Eibl-Eibesfeldt

The Biology of Peace and War

Is Aggression Inevitable?

In recent years, aggression and war have been the subject of much discussion, sparked off by Konrad Lorenz, who in *On Aggression* (first published in 1963) advanced the idea that aggressive behavior performs functions in the service of the preservation of the species and has been programmed into animals as the result of phylogenetic adaptations, with the result that an innate aggressive drive causes them to fight members of their own species—their conspecifics. Lorenz based this theory on innumerable observations of animals, and pointed to some striking parallels that suggest that the same applies to man.

These conclusions were vigorously disputed. Lorenz's opponents accused him of rashly and unjustifiably extrapolating findings from the animal kingdom to man; in particular, they attacked his concept of drives. They maintained that human aggression is reactive and is acquired rather than innate, since anthropological findings show that by no means all peoples are aggressive; especially, they claimed that hunters and food gatherers, who represent the earliest stage of cultural evolution still observable today, are characterized by a high degree of peacefulness, which makes it legitimate to conclude that prehistoric man also lived in peace.

Some critics further denied that the aggressive behavior observed in individual animals and men had anything to do with the phenomenon of war; they insisted that its causes do not lie in animals' or men's nature, but can be explained adequately by cultural and historical factors. Hollitscher says, for instance: "War as an institutionalized political means of applying extraeconomic pressure came into existence only after the development of the private ownership of the means of production with which antagonistic societies began"; and he also accuses ethologists of making the mistake of dealing with man as if he were an animal.

Lorenz has also been criticized for explaining away aggressive behavior as "natural," thus allegedly encouraging a fatalism that puts ammunition into the hands of those who believe in the basic immutability of human society. Underlying this view is the fallacious idea that what is inborn cannot be affected by education.

Critics of the ethological approach frequently write as if ethologists were blind to the tremendous importance of cultural and environmental factors. The discussion of aggression in particular is burdened with this misconception. In a discussion on research into aggression published in 1974, Erich Fromm writes: "What could be more welcome to people . . . who are afraid and feel themselves incapable of changing the course of things leading to destruction than Konrad Lorenz's theory that violence springs from our animal nature and derives from an "untamable drive to aggression." But Lorenz never talked of an "untamable drive to aggression"; on the contrary, he insists that human aggression is the greatest of all dangers at the present time and that it will not be overcome if it is accepted as inevitable, as a metaphysical truth, but only if its causes are scientifically investigated. As he said in 1963:

> With humanity in its present cultural and technological situation, we have good reason to consider intra-specific aggression the greatest of all dangers. We shall not improve our chances of counteracting it if we accept it as something metaphysical and inevitable, but on the other hand, we shall perhaps succeed in finding reme-

dies if we investigate the chain of its natural causation. Wherever man has achieved the power of voluntarily guiding a natural phenomenon in a certain direction, he has owed it to his understanding of the chain of causes which formed it. Physiology, the science concerned with the normal life processes and how they fulfill their species-preserving function, forms the essential foundation for pathology, the science investigating their disturbances.

Also, Lorenz has repeatedly repudiated the foolish "biologism" that sees in man "nothing but" an animal.

In considering here the various arguments advanced in the light of recently established facts, my primary concern will be whether aggressive behavior is programmed into animals and men by hereditary factors and, if so, how. I shall draw on findings in the fields of animal ethology, physiology, developmental psychology, and anthropology, and I shall examine manifestations in different cultures of aggressive behavior, its development in the young, the situations that act as releasing stimuli, as well as the various patterns of aggression control. I hope in this way to uncover both the motives that lead to aggressive conflict and those that underlie the resolution of conflict.

A comparison of the processes of phylogenetic adaptation with those of cultural adaptation reveals striking resemblances between the two that in many cases can be regarded as the result of selective pressures working in the same direction. This is especially evident if biological and cultural patterns of aggression control are compared. There are many parallels, resulting from their function, between the dueling of vertebrates and culturally ritualized competitive combat among men. I shall suggest that biological development and cultural development obey the same functional laws, and that, to a certain extent, cultural evolution thus repeats biological evolution at a higher level of the developmental spiral. If this hypothesis is correct, as I hope to show, our knowledge of biological evolution should enable us both to determine our position in cultural development and to make predictions about its further course. . . .

Intergroup Aggression and War

Animals and birds fight for the possession of females or the defense of hunting grounds or for leadership of the herd, but it is said that they do not fight each other to the death as men do in war. . . . These facts indicate that the human institution of war is more than the human form of the aggressive drive that is inherent in every animal. War must be a human aberration or aggravation of the aggressive drive. It must also be a product of tradition and not of instinct.

Arnold Toynbee

The Cultural Evolution to War

In discussing the functional laws of phylogenetic cultural evolution, I mentioned that, under the formative influence of similar selective pressures, cultural evolution copies biological evolution at a higher level of the development spiral. The formation of species, therefore, has its counterpart in cultural pseudospeciation. Cultures mark themselves off from each other as if they were different species, and so adapt themselves to different niches. To emphasize their difference from others, representatives of different groups describe themselves as human, while all others are dismissed as nonhuman or not fully equipped with all the human values. This cultural development is based on biological preadaptations, above all, on our innate rejection of strangers, which leads to the demarcation of the group.

Group identity is brought about by aggression; with it, the group assures itself of territory, which it collectively defends against strangers. Up to this point, there is no basic difference between human conditions and those we encountered among the chimpanzees. But the possession of weapons enables men to kill one another.

Weapons were certainly a vital factor in the development of destructive aggression. Weapons . . . have to a certain extent circumvented our innate inhibitions. A rapid blow with a weapon can eliminate a fellow human before he has a chance of appealing to our sympathy by an appropriate gesture of submission. This is even more likely to be the case if the killing is done from a distance, for instance, with an arrow. Nevertheless, we must bear in mind that, in spite of the possession of weapons, intragroup aggression seldom becomes destructive. But intergroup aggression—war—is essentially destructive, and must therefore have some other basis. The vital role is played here by cultural pseudospeciation. The fact that the other party is often denied a share in our common humanity shifts the conflict to the interspecific level, and interspecific aggression is generally destructive in the animal kingdom too. . . .

Clearly, I make a sharp distinction between war as a product of cultural evolution and the essentially biologically determined forms of individualized intragroup aggression. The destructive character of war developed culturally hand in hand with man's pseudospeciation. That does not mean it has no biological roots. We are preadapted to it both by our inborn rejection of strangers and our inborn readiness for aggressive action. The fear of strangers is still an important factor in releasing group aggression, and it is utilized to the collective aggression of war. War developed as a cultural mechanism for spacing out strangers, and in this territorial function, it is comparable with biologically determined forms of territorial aggression. It is wrong to equate it with a pathological degeneration such as murder, as is done by, among others, Fromm, who sees the root of the evil in sadism and necrophilia.

Conradt takes the view that uninhibited intergroup aggression—war—is a species-specific characteristic of man. If he had said universal instead of species-specific, I should have agreed. But he holds that uninhibited intergroup aggression is a congenital human characteristic. He argues that the acceleration of human evolution is explicable only on the basis of intergroup selection, that increasing stress does not cause murder rates to escalate into warlike clashes ("as the environmental theory would lead one to expect"), that war is completely different in kind from escalated criminality, and that wars take place in the absence of any kind of stress situation—all of

which is true. He also points out the double morality that exists in relation to killing, which results in the fact that killing in war is not punished even when the victims are defenseless women and children. . . .

Conradt rightly sees the necessity of differentiating between intergroup and intragroup aggression, but his conclusion that war is a new phylogenetic acquisition of man is not convincing. The mechanisms of pseudospeciation that result in groups marking themselves off from and dehumanizing other groups and the invention of weapons—all of which are preliminary conditions for the destructive aggression of war—are clearly the result of cultural evolution.

Causes and Functions of War

I am in accord with Quincy Wright's definition of war as armed conflict between groups. As I have said, war is the result of cultural evolution, and its origins reach far back into the early history of mankind.

"At no period in human history was there a golden age of peace," declares Quincy Wright, one of the leading experts in this field. Only if one takes a narrower view of war, regarding it, as Clausewitz does, as a rational instrument of foreign policy aimed at forcing one's will on another party, can war be regarded as a discovery of civilization. Then, as Clausewitz says, it is "the continuation of politics by other means."[1] Such civilized warfare assumes the existence of laws that define the states of war and peace and lay down rules of behavior for each. The difference between this kind of war and war among primitives is only one of degree, however, for among primitives too, conventions frequently exist governing the course of conflict, particularly between related tribes. At all events, war at this level is a socially recognized form of intergroup conflict that includes violence. Both the legal and the social definitions distinguish between the state of war and the state of peace. . . .

War among primitives is often limited to raids to which they stalk or creep up to the enemy, using tactics reminiscent of hunting. Wilhelm, for instance, describes a raid by one group of !Kung Bushmen on another. There had been a quarrel over some game, and a man had been killed. The band that had suffered this loss sought revenge . . .

If we desire to eliminate war, we must first establish whether it performs functions in inter-human relations, and if so, what functions. I have already stated my view that war is the result of cultural evolution whose direction is determined by selection. In accordance with this, war should demonstrably contribute to the preservation of a culture. This conflicts with the view that war appears only as a phenomenon concomitant to other functional systems or as a morbid degeneration of them. Walsh puts forward the highly speculative view that fathers send their sons to war to punish them for their oedipal wishes. According to this theory, war would be the result of paternal hatred without having any other function. Fromm distinguishes between beneficial and malignant aggression. The former is described as a phylogenetically programmed impulse to attack whenever vital interests of the individual or the species are threatened. This defensive aggression contributes to the preservation of the individual or the species, and it ceases with the disappearance of the threat. Malignant aggression is characterized by destructiveness and cruelty and is based on sadism and necrophilia—character traits that occasionally appear as morbid developments in man.

Certainly, sadism exists as a pathological phenomenon, and it is often responsible for the atrocities ordered by many rulers. Apart from these, it offers no explanation whatsoever of the phenomenon of war, in which atrocities do sometimes occur, though they do not play an essential role. In many wars, chivalrous rules are actually observed.

Discussion of the phenomenon of war suffers from a certain confusion in the use of the terms "cause" and "function." In speaking of the cause of war, we sometimes mean the immediate occasion for it, or the reasons for it advanced by some people. The term is also used in an evolu-

tionary sense, referring to the selective pressure that "caused" a development. It is this that I mean when I look for the "function" of a development, and I shall be guided in my search by the observable consequences of warlike conflicts. . . .

The history of mankind down to the present day is the history of the successful conqueror. Whether or not territorial gain plays a part in the subjective motivation of war is a completely secondary question in that respect. What counts is the result.

I emphasize this because Chagnon, in his otherwise admirable studies, repeatedly insists that the warlike Yanomami Indians do not aim at territorial gain: "Territorial gains are neither intended nor achieved in the carrying out of these conflicts. This has certain consequences for the theories of aggression based on territorial behavior, particularly in the form developed in the recent books of Ardrey and Lorenz."

Although the declared objectives of their wars are to capture women and to show other groups that they are ready to defend their sovereignty by force, nevertheless, the demonstrable result, apart from the capture of women and the gain in prestige, is that the winners often exterminate the losers or force them to abandon territory. It is this result that counts, even though the motivations put forward by those involved are different. In other cultures, men go to war to distinguish themselves, but the result is the same. The selective advantage for the group is independent of the individuals frame of mind. A young man courting a girl does not by any means invariably connect this with the intention of becoming a father of a healthy baby as quickly as possible. Wright states this clearly: "The function of an activity may be broader than its intention."

The territorial function of war has been plainly seen by many anthropologists. According to Morey and Marwitt the centralized tribes of the South American lowlands engaged in wars that served to acquire land and raise tribute and provided an answer before the days of European influence to the problem of population pressure on a limited area of cultivable land. The aggressivity of the groups had an obviously ecological basis. . . .

Wars are fought for hunting grounds, pasture land, and arable land, and if in earlier times, climatic alterations made a group's living area inhospitable, it was actually compelled to find new territory by force of arms. The drying up of the Central Asian steppes set the Mongol peoples in motion, and their warlike expeditions took them all the way to Europe. Their clash with the Teutonic peoples in turn forced the latter to migrate. Overpopulation, too—as the consequence of technical or medical discoveries, for instance—can force human groups to migrate.

The fact that wars are about territory has often been clearly recognized by those involved: "But of the cities of these people, which the Lord thy God doth give thee for an inheritance, thou shalt save alive nothing that breatheth: But thou shalt utterly destroy them; namely, the Hittites, and the Amorites, the Canaanites, and the Perizzites, the Hivites, and the Jebusites; as the Lord thy God hath commanded thee" (Deut. 20: 16–17).

"And they utterly destroyed all that was in the city, both man and woman, young and old, and ox, and sheep, and ass, with the edge of the sword" (Josh. 6: 21).

It was perfectly clear to the lawgiver who proclaimed these things that his people needed their neighbors' land as a settlement area. Since men normally have strong inhibitions against aggression directed at women and children, this massacre dictated by cold utilitarian considerations had to be represented as a divine command. Such commands, however, have not always been obeyed. With the further development of civilization, humanitarian considerations came increasingly to prevail. Victors satisfied themselves with reducing their enemies to subjection, extracting tribute from them, and imposing their own culture on them. Also, their labor power, for which there had been no use at lower cultural levels, came to be appreciated. The conquered were then wiped out not biologically but culturally. In this way, cultures gradually developed their own

dynamism independently of their agents. And cultural formulas were able to demonstrate their usefulness and impose themselves independently of their biological agents.

War is a means that aids groups to compete for the wealth essential to life (land, mineral resources, etc.). It has also been said that it serves the purpose of keeping population growth in check, but that is certainly a secondary effect. It has been claimed that it serves to regulate psychological variables (the abreaction of psychological tensions): here individual motivations are confused with selective advantage.

If one asks whether modern war still performs functions I have described, the answer is yes, up to the present day, insofar as it has been conducted with the methods in use up to the Second World War. Modern warfare also leads to the acquisition of land and access to raw materials and labor. There are divergent views about the outcome of a nuclear war—whether it would be worth the victor's while—but the most vivid imagination is hardly sufficient to visualize the resulting devastation.

War is to be attributed neither to degenerate, misdirected animal instincts nor to necrophilia nor to any other pathological degeneration of basic human impulses. It is not a functionless deviation, but a specifically human form of intergroup aggression that helps human groups to acquire land and natural resources. We gladly ignore these unpleasant facts. We want to live in peace, and in accordance with the principle of "What ought not be, cannot be," we delude ourselves and shut our eyes to the problem. That only makes the inevitable awakening more unpleasant. It is surely better to see plainly that war performs definite functions and face up to that truth. The fact that it performs these functions does not mean that they can be performed in no other way. Better solutions can be devised, but they presuppose that the functions of war are apprehended in nonwarlike fashion. No one can expect that nations reduced to poverty because they are refused access to vital raw materials will tolerate that situation passively. No one can expect that people living in a country growing more and more inhospitable because of a change of climate will wait for death by starvation without doing anything about it. In such situations, a group will sooner or later take positive action; its only alternative is to reconcile itself to its fate and go under. . . .

Conclusion

Man's intergroup aggression, however, generally aims at destruction. This is the result of cultural pseudospeciation, in the course of which human groups mark themselves off from others by speech and usages, and describe themselves as human and others as not fully human. Underlying this is the innate disposition that manifests itself in the infant's fear and rejection of strangers as well as in primate territoriality, but it is only through man's suppression of his similarly innate inclination to band formation that a sharp demarcation of groups takes place. Thus war developed as a cultural mechanism in the competition of groups (pseudospecies) for space and raw materials. The theory that war first developed in the Neolithic age with the development of horticulture and agriculture does not stand up to critical examination; there is evidence of armed clashes as early as the Paleolithic period. Moreover, present-day hunters and gatherers have been shown to be mostly territorial; they fight for the possession of hunting and gathering grounds.

War is primarily destructive, but as in the development from destructive to ritualized fighting, we see the beginnings of cultural ritualizations of war in the form of conventions that prevent excessive bloodshed. This is obviously of selectionistic advantage. But development in this direction assumes that the functions of war, in the competition for land, for instance, can be performed in some other way, even including war without bloodshed. Among other things, the defeated must be able to retreat, which is a condition for their being spared in the dueling of animals. This is no longer possible for man because there is a shortage of empty spaces, and thus a limit is set to an automatic further humanization of war. But there are other preadaptations that could bring about a cultural development to peace. In the course of cultural pseudospeciation, man has superimposed a cultural norm filter that commands him to kill upon his biological norm filter, which forbids him to kill.

This leads to a conflict of norms, of which man is aware through the conscience that pricks him as soon as he apprehends the enemy that confronts him as a fellow human being. Finally, he shows the same signals that normally have a conciliatory effect in intragroup relations and release sympathy. There is an abundance of observations that reinforce this assumption; victorious warriors, for example, often have to perform penitential rituals before being fully reintegrated into their community.

The root of the universal desire for peace lies in this conflict between cultural and biological norms, which makes men want to bring their biological and cultural norm filters into accord. Our conscience remains our hope, and based on this, a rationally guided evolution could lead to peace. This presupposes recognition of the fact that war performs functions that will have to be performed in some other way, without bloodshed. Those who do not see this and dismiss war as a pathological phenomenon are guilty of a dangerous simplification, since it naturally will not occur to them that those who want peace will have to find a different way of carrying out the functions of war. Man's motivational structure makes him perfectly capable of peaceful coexistence in modern mass society, and education for peace must be primarily education in tolerance in the sense of willingness to understand.

Note

1. "An act of violence to force the other party to carry out our will . . . continuation of political relations, carrying them out by other means."

The Seville Statement on Violence

The Seville Statement on Violence was drafted by an international committee of 20 scholars at the 6th International Colloquium on Brain and Aggression held at the University of Seville, Spain, in May 1986, with support from the Spanish Commission for UNESCO. The Statement's purpose is to dispel the widespread belief that human beings are inevitably disposed to war as a result of innate, biologically determined aggressive traits.

UNESCO adopted the Seville Statement at its 25th General Conference Session in Paris, October 17–November 16, 1989. The Statement has been formally endorsed by scientific organizations and published in journals around the world. UNESCO is preparing a brochure to be used in teaching young people about the Statement.

In August 1987 the Council of Representatives of the American Psychological Association voted to endorse the Seville Statement. The Board of Scientific Affairs emphasized that this is not a scientific statement on the issue of specific inherited behavioral traits. It is, rather, a social statement designed to eliminate unfounded stereotypic thinking on the inevitability of war. . . .

Believing that it is our responsibility to address from our particular disciplines the most dangerous and destructive activities of our species, violence and war; recognizing that science is a human cultural product which cannot be definitive or all-encompassing; and gratefully acknowledging the support of the authorities of Seville and representatives of Spanish UNESCO; we, the undersigned scholars from around the world and from relevant sciences, have met and arrived at the following Statement on Violence. In it, we challenge a number of alleged biological findings that have been used, even by some in our disciplines, to justify violence and war. Because the alleged findings have contributed to an atmosphere of pessimism in our time, we submit that the open, considered rejection of these misstatements can contribute significantly to the International Year of Peace.

Misuse of scientific theories and data to justify violence and war is not new but has been made since the advent of modern science. For example, the theory of evolution has been used to justify not only war, but also genocide, colonialism, and suppression of the weak.

We state our position in the form of five propositions. We are aware that there are many other issues about violence and war that could be fruitfully addressed from the standpoint of our disciplines, but we restrict ourselves here to what we consider a most important first step.

It is scientifically incorrect to say that we have inherited a tendency to make war from our animal ancestors. Although fighting occurs widely throughout animal species, only a few cases of destructive intra-species fighting between organized groups have ever been reported among naturally living species, and none of these involve the use of tools designed to be weapons. Normal predatory feeding upon other species cannot be equated with intra-species violence. Warfare is a peculiarly human phenomenon and does not occur in other animals.

The fact that warfare has changed so radically over time indicates that it is a product of culture. Its biological connection is primarily through language which makes possible the coordination of groups, the transmission of technology, and the use of tools. War is biologically possible, but it is not inevitable, as evidenced by its variation in occurrence and nature over time and space. There are cultures which have not engaged in war for centuries, and there are cultures which have engaged in war frequently at some times and not at others.

It is scientifically incorrect to say that war or any other violent behavior is genetically programmed into our human nature. While genes are involved at all levels of nervous system function, they provide a developmental potential that can be actualized only in conjunction with the ecological and social environment. While individuals vary in their predispositions to be affected by their experience, it is the interaction between their genetic endowment and conditions of nurturance that determines their personalities. Except for rare pathologies, the genes do not produce individuals necessarily predisposed to violence. Neither do they determine the opposite. While genes are co-involved in establishing our behavioral capacities, they do not by themselves specify the outcome.

It is scientifically incorrect to say that in the course of human evolution there has been a selection for aggressive behavior more than for other kinds of behavior. In all well-studied species, status within the group is achieved by the ability to cooperate and to fulfill social functions relevant to the structure of that group. "Dominance" involves social bondings and affiliations; it is not simply a matter of the possession and use of superior physical power, although it does involve aggressive behaviors. Where genetic selection for aggressive behavior has been artificially instituted in animals, it has rapidly succeeded in producing hyper-aggressive individuals; this indicates that aggression was not maximally selected under natural conditions. When such experimentally-created hyper-aggressive animals are present in a social group, they either disrupt its social structure or are driven out. Violence is neither in our evolutionary legacy nor in our genes.

It is scientifically incorrect to say that humans have a "violent brain." While we do have the neural apparatus to act violently, it is not automatically activated by internal or external stimuli. Like higher primates and unlike other animals, our higher neural processes filter such stimuli before they can be acted upon. How we act is shaped by how we have been conditioned and socialized. There is nothing in our neurophysiology that compels us to react violently.

It is scientifically incorrect to say that war is caused by "instinct" or any single motivation. The emergence of modern warfare as been a journey from the primacy of emotional and motivational factors, sometimes called "instincts," to the primacy of cognitive factors. Modern war involves institutional use of personal characteristics such as obedience, suggestibility, and idealism; social skills such as language; and rational considerations such as cost-calculation, planning, and information processing. The technology of modern war has exaggerated traits associated with violence both in the training of actual combatants and in the preparation of support for war in the general population. As a result of this exaggeration, such traits are often mistaken to be the causes rather than the consequences of the process.

We conclude that biology does not condemn humanity to war, and that humanity can be freed from the bondage of biological pessimism and empowered with confidence to undertake the transformative tasks needed in this International Year of Peace and in the years to come. Although these tasks are mainly institutional and collective, they also rest upon the consciousness of individual participants for whom pessimism and optimism are crucial factors. Just as "wars begin in the minds of men," peace also begins in our minds. The same species who invented war is capable of inventing peace. The responsibility lies with each of us.

Seville, May 16, 1986

Signatories

David Adams, Psychology, Wesleyan University, Middletown, Connecticut, U.S.A.

S. A. Barnett, Ethology, The Australian National University, Canberra, Australia

N. P. Bechtereva, Neurophysiology, Institute for Experimental Medicine of Academy of Medical Sciences of U.S.S.R., Leningrad, U.S.S.R.

Bonnie Frank Carter, Psychology, Albert Einstein Medical Center, Philadelphia, Pennsylvania, U.S.A.

Jose M. Rodriguez Delgado, Neurophysiology, Centro de Estudios Neurobiologicos, Madrid, Spain

Jose Luis Diaz, Ethology, Instituto Mexicano de Psiquiatria, Mexico D.F., Mexico

Andrzej Eliasz, Individual Differences Psychology, Polish Academy of Sciences, Warsaw, Poland

Santiago Genoves, Biological Anthropology, Instituto de Estudios Antropologicos, Mexico D.F., Mexico

Benson E. Ginsburg, Behavior Genetics, University of Connecticut, Storrs, Connecticut, U.S.A.

Jo Groebel, Social Psychology, Erziehungswissenschaftliche Hochschule, Landau, Federal Republic of Germany

Samir-Kumar Ghosh, Sociology, Indian Institute of Human Sciences, Calcutta, India

Robert Hinde, Animal Behavior, Cambridge University, United Kingdom

Richard E. Leakey, Physical Anthropology, National Museums of Kenya, Nairobi, Kenya

Taha M. Malasi, Psychiatry, Kuwait University, Kuwait

J. Martin Ramirez, Psychobiology, Universidad de Sevilla, Spain

Federico Mayor Zaragoza, Biochemistry, Universidad Autonoma, Madrid, Spain

Diana L. Mendoza, Ethology, Universidad de Sevilla, Spain

Ashis Nandy, Political Psychology, Center for the Study of Developing Societies, Delhi, India

John Paul Scott, Animal Behavior, Bowling Green State University, Bowling Green, Ohio, U.S.A.

Riitta Wahlstrom, Psychology, University of Jyvaskyla, Finland

John Paul Scott
Benson E. Ginsburg

The Seville Statement on Violence Revisited

It is now the eighth anniversary of the Seville Statement on Violence (issued May 16, 1986; published in the *American Psychologist* October 1990), and we welcome the opportunity provided by Beroldi (1994) to call it to the attention of psychologists once again. The Statement was arrived at in conjunction with the United Nations International Year of Peace (1986) and the Sixth International Colloquium on the Brain and Aggression held at Seville, Spain, in May of that year with the joint sponsorship of the Department of Psychobiology of Seville University and the Spanish Commission for UNESCO. Some 50 scholars from 16 countries participated in the colloquium by invitation, and a number of the key papers were published in full (Ramirez, Hinde, & Groebel, 1987). A multidisciplinary subgroup of 20 invited participants from 12 countries, all well recognized in their respective fields (which included psychology, ethology, neurophysiology, biological anthropology, behavior genetics, social psychology, sociology, animal behavior, and political psychology), met for a three-day retreat to address the problem of whether violence and war are biologically inevitable. There were no political litmus tests applied to any of us, and regardless of our academic disciplines or political orientations, we could not conclude, on the basis of the evidence we had researched, that the most critical answers were to be found solely in biology. It therefore became important to submit the Statement to organizations representing other disciplines, particularly psychology, to focus attention on and to stimulate additional research in this vitally important area.

The endorsement of the Statement by the American Psychological Association (APA) constitutes, in our view, a socially and scientifically responsible action. Had Beroldi (1994) chosen to address this area as a scientist, by providing evidence expanding or refuting or questioning the validity of any of the conclusions embodied in the Statement and thereby contributing to our knowledge in the field, he would have helped fulfill the objectives that the signatories and the APA sought to attain by calling the Statement to the attention of the scientific community. Instead, he has taken a political ad hominem position, questioning the motivations and competences of the signatories. As a separate issue, he raises objections to the introductory rhetoric preceding the Statement and the phrase "It is scientifically incorrect" that precedes each of the Statement's conclusions. Beroldi's attribution of a political position for which the Statement is essentially a front is based on comments by David Adams, whom Beroldi cites and with whom he disagrees. These are not part of the Statement.

To consider Beroldi's (1994) contentions objectively, it is necessary to relate them to the Statement itself. . . .

In his opening statement, Beroldi (1994) asserts that he is viewing the Statement from an evolutionary perspective, thereby implying that the signatories either were not doing so or, as he maintains later, lacked the competence to do so ("most of the signatories lack citations in the germinal literature in this field," p. 848). Robert Hinde, Santiago Genovese, and Richard Leakey are internationally known and respected. We ourselves received our doctorates under the direction of Sewall Wright, one of the preeminent evolutionary biologists of our time, and have received national and international awards in the area of evolution and behavior. Scott's (1989) most recent book is an application of systems theory to evolution. This is in addition to several other books and several hundred papers. Where has Beroldi been looking, and, as he has raised the issue, what are his credentials?

In moving from appeals to authority (Beroldi, 1994, cites his own) to the Statement itself, the Statement's five propositions constitute the basis for the endorsement by the APA and other scientific societies. These propositions are self-explanatory, terse summaries based on reviews and discussion of the pertinent literature. There is nothing political in them. It would therefore be "scientifically incorrect," in terms of the available literature in 1986 as known to the participants, to defend the obverse of any of the five propositions.

With respect to the introductory and concluding paragraphs surrounding the five propositions, one can write one's own rhetoric, but the misuse of scientific theories in a societal context has fed the "we–they" dichotomy that not only served Hitler's objectives but is still espoused by various groups and is fueling inter- and intra-societal conflicts today. One might find more felicitous language, but insofar as the Seville Statement calls attention to the most pressing behavioral problems of our society—violence and war—and addresses these in terms of the nature of human nature, it shifts the emphasis from biology to psychology. The APA has endorsed it, should have endorsed it, and will, we hope, improve on it in ways that will stimulate more effective research on the basis of which policy decisions can be made. We hope that Beroldi will be among those who will make constructive contributions in this area.

References

Beroldi, G. (1994). Critique of the Seville Statement on Violence. *American Psychologist, 49,* 847–848.

Scott, J. P. (1989). *The evolution of social systems* (Monographs in Psychobiology: An Integrated Approach, Vol. 3). New York: Gordon & Breach.

Ramirez, J. M., Hinde, R. A., & Groebel, J. (Eds). (1987). *Essays on violence* (Series on psychobiology). Seville, Spain: University of Seville Publications.

Questions for Discussion

1. What do you think of Eibl-Eibesfeldt's theory of aggression? Is aggression instinctual or is it culturally acquired?
2. Do you agree with Eibl-Eibesfeldt that "education in tolerance" is the only way to bring about peace? Is this realistic or plausible?
3. What scientific evidence is there for the absence of a biological basis for human beings' use of warfare?
4. Appraise the persuasiveness of the "Seville Statement on Violence."
5. Eibl-Eibesfeldt advances the critical concept of "cultural pseudospeciation" to explain intergroup aggression. Explore the implications of this concept for intergroup violence and war.

Further Readings

1. Crook, D. P. *Darwinism, War and History: The Debate over the Biology of War from the "Origin of Species" to the First World War.* Cambridge: Cambridge University Press, 2003.
2. Harrison, Mark. "Darwinism War and History: The Debate over the Biology of War from the 'Origin of Species' to the First World War." *Social History of Medicine,* 1996, 9, 2, Aug., 267–276.
3. Blanchard, D. Caroline, and Blanchard, Robert J. "Emotions as Mediators and Modulators of Violence: Some Reflections on the 'Seville Statement on Violence.' " *Social Research,* 2000, 67, 3, Fall, 683–708.
4. Kaye, Howard L. "The Biology of Peace and War: Men, Animals, and Aggression." *Sociology,* 1980, 7, 5, July–Aug., 141–142.
5. Tinbergen, N. "On War and Peace in Animals and Man: An Ethologist's Approach to the Biology of Aggression." *Science,* 1968, 160, 3835, June, 28, 1411–1418.

Economic Theories

This section explores the economic aspects of organized warfare. The economic motives for war, the economic factors that contribute to war, and the lucrative economic institutions such as arms manufacturers (both state and nonstate), that sustain war are analyzed in the following readings.

In the first reading in this section, "Economics of War and Peace," Christopher Mark Davis explores the theories developed by Paul Kennedy and others, and explains the different mechanisms through which capitalist and Marxist economies pursue their war systems. He explains how imperialist wars were driven by economic factors which led to the military development of imperialist powers.

"The Rise and Fall of the Great Powers," by Paul Kennedy, explains the cyclic mechanism by which states acquire hegemonic status and then lose it. The main agent in this cycle is warfare and the preparation for war. Kennedy invokes historical examples to illustrate the pattern. It entails acquisition of a vast territory, control of material resources leading to economic development, followed by military aggrandizement, increasing involvement in world affairs and an eventual implosion of centralized authority. Military ambition is characterized by the author as the key factor in bringing about the downfall of

any political establishment, however grand and powerful. Military development may be the mechanism through which states acquire imperial power, but an eventual imbalance in the military and economic assets is responsible for the downfall of an imperial power.

In "The Arms Bonanza," James Adams discusses the economics of the weapons industry. This reading cites the Iran-Iraq war as an example of how the profit motive of the firms in this industry perpetuated the war, and how some countries sold arms to both sides simultaneously, thus enabling them to sustain the war. This reading also gives an account of how weapons firms circumvent international law to sell arms to various rebel groups in different regions of the world, thus fueling violence. Some governments evade their own state policies to sell weapons to combatants. This reading contributes to one's understanding of the power wielded by the weapons industry over governments.

The last reading in this section, "The Global Arms Trade" by William M. Evan, presents an analysis of current trends in global arms trade. It presents data on the world's major suppliers and recipients of conventional weapons. Besides the India-Pakistan war, the Iran-Iraq war and Gulf War I, this reading also includes a profile of the weapons industry during the most recent conflict in Iraq: Gulf War II. A list of firms that provided Iraq with its conventional weapons is also included along with the nationalities of these firms. Some surprising data emerge through this analysis of the arms industry. The operations of the "Military Industrial Complex" are explained and the arms policies of the world's largest weapons supplier, the United States, are analyzed.

Christopher Mark Davis

The Economics of War and Peace

Many of the major studies of the international system attach importance to economic factors as causes of wars and determinants of their outcomes. For example, Paul Kennedy argues that:

> . . . there exists a dynamic for change, driven chiefly by economic and technological developments, which then impact on social structures, political systems, military power, and the position of individual states and empires . . . all the major shifts in the world's military power balances have followed alterations in the productive balances . . . the rising and falling of the various empires and states in the international system has been confirmed by the outcomes of the major Great Power wars, where victory has always gone to the side with the greatest material resources.

Quincy Wright examines the economics of war in ten sections of his book, amounting to about 100 pages. He briefly surveys the main schools of economics and asserts that little work has been done on this subject because most economists consider it to be on the periphery of, or outside, their field: "Economists have not discussed war very much. . . . Most of the writing on economic causes of war has been by historians or publicists not by economists. . . . In the standard texts on economics, however, war figures almost not at all." This is an inaccurate portrayal of the contributions of economists, who have produced many important studies of the economics of war over the centuries. He recognizes that Marxists have a theory of war that claims:

> . . . that war as well as other evils grew from the struggle of economic classes manifested in modern times by the phenomena of capitalism and imperialism. . . . Among the economic "forces" often said by these writers to cause

war are "capitalism," "imperialism," "the international arms trade" and "international finance."

These causes are examined in a superficial manner and all are summarily dismissed: "Most economists have found that economic theory and historical evidence give little support for these assertions." In contrast, he argues that growing economic interdependence acts to reduce the threat of war and that there are strong economic motivations for disarmament.

Evolution of Civilizations and War

The dynamics and features of civilizations were of first-order importance in Quincy Wright's analysis of war. He accepts Arnold Toynbee's idea that history is characterized by the rise and fall of civilizations that is caused by a variety of factors, economics being only a minor and indirect one. He divides the history of civilizations into four stages, but gives them different names; they are birth, rise, decline, and fall . . . they are heroic age, time of troubles, universal state, and disintegration. He identifies 26 civilizations in the ancient world and dates the stages of their histories. Although ancient history had a cyclical pattern, with some progress observable over time, the Renaissance in Europe was identified by him as a turning point in human history. Modern civilization subsequently developed in Europe in accordance with "humanist" values and spread over the world. Wright considered that the European-based civilization of his time constituted the pinnacle of human spiritual and intellectual achievement. However, history would not end until all people and states accepted "modernism" and reformed international institutions

101

and relations so that they conformed to the values of world civilization.

Quincy Wright argues that there are several relationships between civilizations and war. Periods of transition from one stage of civilization to another are associated with a higher probability of conflict. He claims that certain civilizations were more warlike and effective in the military sphere than others, but this had little to do with economics. He analyzes progress in military technique (which includes military technology, organization and operations) over time in the different civilizations. But he does not clearly connect technological progress with economic features of a civilization. He thinks that modern civilization is especially effective in developing military technologies, but that the result has been to make warfare too destructive to initiate. . . .

Economic Systems and War

Although Quincy Wright did not believe in economic determinants of either history or wars, the book expresses clear views about the relationship between economic systems and warfare. As mentioned above, he claims that modern capitalism, with its market economy and democratic political system, is the most peaceful economic system in history. In contrast, collectivist economies (he calls them "state socialist") are highly correlated with aggression and war: "Socialist economies have produced the most warlike states in history. . . . Socialist states have ended to be more militarized, regimented, dictatorial, self-sufficient and bellicose than liberal states." The causality of his argument, though, is that warlike civilizations or states adopt "socialism" in order to wage war more effectively, rather than that a "socialist" economy causes them to become warlike. It should be noted that his conception of state socialism is idiosyncratic, since the countries that are alleged to possess such a system include ancient Assyria, Inca Peru, Sparta and contemporary (1930s) Italy, Germany, Russia and Japan. This indicates that he has a limited understanding of the Soviet command economy and conceptually cannot distinguish it from the quite different

capitalist economies in the fascist states of Italy and Germany.

In Soviet Marxist thinking there is a clear connection between economic systems and war. All pre-socialist types (slave, feudal, capitalist) engage in aggressive warfare due to economic dynamics. The most warlike and dangerous economic systems in history are those characterized by bourgeois governments, finance capital, and imperialist external policies (modern capitalism). The most peaceful one yet to emerge is that of state socialism in the USSR. After capitalism is overthrown, it will be possible to move beyond socialism to communism, which will be associated with the elimination of contradictions and conflict and the emergence of a peaceful world.

Economic Foundations of Military Power

In the quotation at the start of this section, Kennedy makes a clear connection between economic power (an aggregate measure of human resources, capital stock and raw materials) and military capabilities. The importance of the economic base in sustaining modern warfare and in prevailing in a war of attrition, such as World War I, was discussed in numerous books published in the interwar period. The treatment of this issue by Quincy Wright is uneven. There is ample material on military technology (weapons) in many sections of the book. But technological innovation is treated as though it is autonomous from the economic system, rather than endogenous to it. He recognizes that since the eighteenth century industrial power has had a growing impact on warfare, and even gives the title of 'industrialization and nationalistic wars' to the brief history of military technique in the period 1789–1914. Despite this, he devotes scant attention to the production potential of nations, defense industry, or military research and development processes. When he does mention the impact of industry on war, it usually is in combination with other factors:

> The skills involved in modern military techniques tend to be less the capacity to command armed forces in the field and more the capacity to

manage the national economy, to sustain the national morale, to destroy the enemy's morale and economy, and to handle neutrals diplomatically—in other words, the role of strictly military operations in wars between states of equal technological development has tended to decline . . .

The studies of Quincy Wright led him to . . . conclude that war was caused by disequilibrium in at least one of the following dimensions: technological, psychic, social and intellectual. He did not believe that economic factors were important in causing wars and criticized those who alleged that they were, primarily the Marxists, citing the works of Angell, Viner and Robbins for support. With respect to World War II, he quotes with approval from a 1940 study that concluded: "The role of economic factors in the peace failure of 1919–39 was not of first importance." This assertion is contrary to the findings of Milward, who explicitly cites economic factors as causes of the war:

> Far from having economic reservations about warfare as policy, both the German and Japanese governments were influenced in their decisions for war by the conviction that war might be an instrument of economic gain. Although economic considerations were in neither case prime reasons in the decision to fight, both governments held a firmly optimistic conviction that war could be used to solve some of their more long-term economic difficulties.

Marx and Engels somewhat neglected the topic of economic causes of war. Lenin initially blamed the wars of capitalist nations on militarism, profit-driven arms races and struggles over and in colonies. Hilferding and Luxembourg argued that modern states with a finance capital system need to expand externally to obtain supplies and markets. The military is used to support imperialist policies and wars are a probable, but not certain, outcome of the conflicts between the expansionist powers. In his 1915 book on *Imperialism and World Economy* Bukharin not only strengthened the link between economic causes and war, but made the latter the inevitable outcome of the former:

> . . . the prime cause and the moving force in wars is not the existence of arms (although wars

are obviously impossible without arms) but, on the contrary, the inevitableness of economic conflicts conditions the existence of arms. This is why in our times, when economic conflicts have reached an unusual degree of intensity, we are witnessing a mad orgy of armaments.

Theoretical arguments that the dynamics of the imperialist economies inevitably generated instability, rivalry, arms races and wars were further elaborated over subsequent decades by Soviet analysts. Their findings are fundamentally different from those of Quincy Wright.

Economic Interdependence and War

In the interwar period numerous economists supported the view that the modern market economies of Europe and North America were becoming increasingly interdependent and that this had reduced the likelihood of war. Quincy Wright clearly was influenced by their findings and incorporated them into his arguments:

> While the necessity of state defense was not denied, the initiation of war was considered both politically and economically irrational, and it was anticipated that war would disappear as civilization advanced . . . the cost of modern war is always beyond any possible economic gain.

He believed that armed conflict was contrary to modernizing trends and that in his period war had no useful function. In an economically interdependent world with sophisticated weapons technologies, states would be reluctant to resort to war because of its enormous costs.

The Marxists had a less optimistic interpretation of the world economic system. They considered the leading imperialist powers to be predators with respect to the countries of Asia, Africa and Latin America. The integration of the colonies with the metropolitan nation was exploitive in nature and maintained by military force. The theory of imperialism portrayed the leading capitalist states as competitors striving to create their own trading blocs rather than as co-operative trading partners in an integrated world economy.

Paul Kennedy

The Rise and Fall of the Great Powers

The relative strengths of the leading nations in world affairs never remain constant, principally because of the uneven rate of growth among different societies and of the technological and organizational breakthroughs which bring a greater advantage to one society than to another. For example, the coming of the long-range gunned sailing ship and the rise of the Atlantic trades after 1500 was not *uniformly* beneficial to all the states of Europe—it boosted some much more than others. In the same way, the later development of steam power and of the coal and metal resources upon which it relied massively increased the relative power of certain nations, and thereby decreased the relative power of others. Once their productive capacity was enhanced, countries would normally find it easier to sustain the burdens of paying for large-scale armaments in peacetime and of maintaining and supplying large armies and fleets in wartime. It sounds crudely mercantilistic to express it this way, but wealth is usually needed to underpin military power, and military power is usually needed to acquire and protect wealth. If, however, too large a proportion of the state's resources is diverted from wealth creation and allocated instead to military purposes, then that is likely to lead to a weakening of national power over the longer term. In the same way, if a state overextends itself strategically—by, say, the conquest of extensive territories or the waging of costly wars—it runs the risk that the potential benefits from external expansion may be outweighed by the great expense of it all—a dilemma which becomes acute if the nation concerned has entered a period of relative economic decline. The history of the rise and later fall of the leading countries in the Great Power system since the advance of western Europe in the sixteenth century—that is, of nations such as Spain, the Netherlands, France, the British Empire, and currently the United States—shows a very significant correlation *over the longer term* between productive and revenue-raising capacities on the one hand and military strength on the other. . . .

. . . At the beginning of the sixteenth century it was by no means apparent that the last-named region [Europe] was destined to rise above all the rest. But however imposing and organized some of those oriental empires appeared by comparison with Europe, they all suffered from the consequences of having a centralized authority which insisted upon a uniformity of belief and practice, not only in official state religion but also in such areas as commercial activities and weapons development. The lack of any such supreme authority in Europe and the warlike rivalries among its various kingdoms and city-states stimulated a constant search for military improvements, which interacted fruitfully with the newer technological and commercial advances that were also being thrown up in this competitive, entrepreneurial environment. Possessing fewer obstacles to change, European societies entered into a constantly upward spiral of economic growth and enhanced military effectiveness which, over time, was to carry them ahead of all other regions of the globe.

While this dynamic of technological change and military competitiveness drove Europe forward in its usual jostling, pluralistic way, there still remained the possibility that one of the contending states might acquire sufficient resources to surpass the others, and then to dominate the continent. For about 150 years after 1500, a dynastic-religious bloc under the Spanish and Austrian Habsburgs seemed to threaten to do just that, and the efforts of the other major European states to check this "Habsburg bid for mastery.". . . The chief theme of this [reading] is that despite the great resources possessed by the Habsburg monarchs, they steadily overextended themselves in the course of repeated conflicts and became militarily top-heavy for their weakening economic base. If the other European Great Powers also suffered immensely in these prolonged wars, they managed—though narrowly—to maintain the balance between their material resources and their military power better than their Habsburg enemies.

The Great Power struggles which took place between 1660 and 1815 cannot be so easily summarized as a contest between one large bloc and its many rivals. It was in this complicated period that while certain former Great Powers like Spain and the Netherlands were falling into the second rank, there steadily emerged five major states (France, Britain, Russia, Austria, and Prussia) which came to dominate the diplomacy and warfare of eighteenth-century Europe, and to engage in a series of lengthy coalition wars punctuated by swiftly changing alliances. This was an age in which France, first under Louis XIV and then later under Napoleon, came closer to controlling Europe than at any time before or since; but its endeavors were always held in check, in the last resort at least, by a combination of the other Great Powers. Since the cost of standing armies and national fleets had become horrendously great by the early eighteenth century, a country which could create an advanced system of banking and credit (as Britain did) enjoyed many advantages over financially backward rivals. But the factor of geographical position was also of great importance in deciding the fate of the Powers in their many, and frequently changing, contests—which helps to explain why the two "flank" nations of Russia and Britain had become much more important by 1815. Both retained the capacity to intervene in the struggles of west-central

Europe while being geographically sheltered from them; and both expanded into the *extra-*European world as the eighteenth century unfolded, even as they were ensuring that the continental balance of power was upheld. Finally, by the later decades of the century, the Industrial Revolution was under way in Britain, which was to give that state an enhanced capacity both to colonize overseas and to frustrate the Napoleonic bid for European mastery.

For an entire century after 1815, by contrast, there was a remarkable absence of lengthy coalition wars. A strategic equilibrium existed, supported by all of the leading Powers in the Concert of Europe, so that no single nation was either able or willing to make a bid for dominance. The prime concerns of government in these post-1815 decades were with domestic instability and (in the case of Russia and the United States) with further expansion across their continental landmasses. This relatively stable international scene allowed the British Empire to rise to its zenith as a global power, in naval and colonial and commercial terms, and also interacted favorably with its virtual monopoly of steam-driven industrial production. By the second half of the nineteenth century, however, industrialization was spreading to certain other regions, and was beginning to tilt the international power balances away from the older leading nations and toward those countries with both the resources and organization to exploit the newer means of production and technology. Already, the few major conflicts of this era—the Crimean War to some degree but more especially the American Civil War and the Franco-Prussian War—were bringing defeat upon those societies which failed to modernize their military systems, and which lacked the broad-based industrial infrastructure to support the vast armies and much more expensive and complicated weaponry now transforming the nature of war.

As the twentieth century approached, therefore, the pace of technological change and uneven growth rates made the international system much more unstable and complex than it had been fifty years earlier. This was manifested in the frantic post-1880 jostling by the Great Powers for additional colonial territories in Africa, Asia, and the Pacific, partly for gain, partly out of a fear of being eclipsed. It also manifested itself in the increasing number of arms races, both on land and at sea, and in the creation of fixed military alliances, even in peacetime, as the various governments sought out partners for a possible future war. Behind the frequent colonial quarrels and international crises of the pre-1914 period, however, the decade-by-decade indices of economic power were pointing to even more fundamental shifts in the global balances—indeed, to the eclipse of what had been, for over three centuries, essentially a *Eurocentric* world system. Despite their best efforts, traditional European Great Powers like France and Austria-Hungary, and a recently united one like Italy, were falling out of the race. By contrast, the enormous, continent-wide states of the United States and Russia were moving to the forefront, and this despite the inefficiencies of the czarist state. Among the western European nations only Germany, possibly, had the muscle to force its way into the select league of the future world Powers. Japan, on the other hand, was intent upon being dominant in East Asia, but not farther afield. Inevitably, then, all these changes posed considerable, and ultimately insuperable, problems for a British Empire which now found it much more difficult to defend its global interests than it had a half-century earlier.

Although the major development of the fifty years after 1900 can thus be seen as the coming of a bipolar world, with its consequent crisis for the "middle" Powers . . . this metamorphosis of the entire system was by no means a smooth one. On the contrary, the grinding, bloody mass battles of the First World War, by placing a premium upon industrial organization and national efficiency, gave imperial Germany certain advantages over the swiftly modernizing but still backward czarist Russia. Within a few months of Germany's victory on the eastern front, however, it found itself facing defeat in the west, while its allies were similarly collapsing in the Italian, Balkan, and Near Eastern

theaters of the war. Because of the late addition of American military and especially economic aid, the western alliance finally had the resources to prevail over its rival coalition. But it had been an exhausting struggle for all the original belligerents. Austria-Hungary was gone, Russia in revolution, Germany defeated; yet France, Italy, and even Britain itself had also suffered heavily in their victory. The only exceptions were Japan, which further augmented its position in the Pacific; and, of course, the United States, which by 1918 was indisputably the strongest Power in the world.

The swift post-1919 American withdrawal from foreign engagements, and the parallel Russian isolationism under the Bolshevik regime, left an international system which was more out of joint with the fundamental economic realities than perhaps at any time in the five centuries covered in this [*The Rise and Fall of Great Powers*]. Britain and France, although weakened, were still at the center of the diplomatic stage, but by the 1930s their position was being challenged by the militarized, revisionist states of Italy, Japan, and Germany—the last intent upon a much more deliberate bid for European hegemony than even in 1914. In the background, however, the United States remained by far the mightiest manufacturing nation in the world, and Stalin's Russia was quickly transforming itself into an industrial superpower. Consequently, the dilemma for the *revisionist* "middle" Powers was that they had to expand soon if they were not to be overshadowed by two continental giants. The dilemma for the status quo middle Powers was that in fighting off the German and Japanese challenges, they would most likely weaken themselves as well. The Second World War, for all its ups and downs, essentially confirmed those apprehensions of decline. Despite spectacular early victories, the Axis nations could not in the end succeed against an imbalance of productive resources which was far greater than that of the 1914–1918 war. What they did achieve was the eclipse of France and the irretrievable weakening of Britain—before they themselves were overwhelmed by superior force. By 1943, the bipolar world forecast decades earlier had finally arrived, and the military balance had once again caught up with the global distribution of economic resources.

The last two chapters of [*The Rise and Fall of Great Powers*] examine the years in which a bipolar world did indeed seem to exist, economically, militarily, and ideologically—and was reflected at the political level by the many crises of the Cold War. The position of the United States and the USSR as Powers in a class of their own also appeared to be reinforced by the arrival of nuclear weapons and long-distance delivery systems, which suggested that the strategic as well as the diplomatic landscape was now entirely different from that of 1900, let alone 1800.

And yet the process of rise and fall among the Great Powers—of differentials in growth rates and technological change, leading to shifts in the global economic balances, which in turn gradually impinge upon the political and military balances—had not ceased. Militarily, the United States and the USSR stayed in the forefront as the 1960s gave way to the 1970s and 1980s. Indeed, because they both interpreted international problems in bipolar, and often Manichean, terms, their rivalry has driven them into an ever-escalating arms race which no other Powers feel capable of matching. Over the same few decades, however, the global productive balances have been altering faster than ever before. The Third World's share of total manufacturing output and GNP, depressed to an all-time low in the decade after 1945, has steadily expanded since that time. Europe has recovered from its wartime batterings and, in the form of the European Economic Community, has become the world's largest trading unit. The People's Republic of China is leaping forward at an impressive rate. Japan's postwar economic growth has been so phenomenal that, according to some measures, it recently overtook Russia in total GNP. By contrast, both the American and Russian growth rates have become more sluggish, and their shares of global production and wealth have shrunk dramatically since the 1960s. Leaving aside all the smaller nations, therefore, it is plain that there already exists a *multi*polar world once

more, if one measures the economic indices alone. Given this book's [*The Rise and Fall of Great Powers*] concern with the interaction between strategy and economics, it seemed appropriate to offer a final (if necessarily speculative) chapter to explore the present disjuncture between the military balances and the productive balances among the Great Powers; and to point to the problems and opportunities facing today's five large politico-economic "power centers"—China, Japan, the EEC, the Soviet Union, and the United States itself—as they grapple with the age-old task of relating national means to national ends. This history of the rise and fall of the Great Powers has in no way come to a full stop. . . .

. . . [T]he problem which historians—as opposed to political scientists—have in grappling with general theories is that the evidence of the past is almost always too varied to allow for "hard" scientific conclusions. Thus, while it is true that some wars (e.g., 1939) can be linked to decision-makers' fears about shifts taking place in the overall power balances, that would not be so useful in explaining the struggles which began in 1776 (American Revolutionary War) or 1792 (French Revolutionary) or 1854 (Crimean War). In the same way, while one could point to Austria-Hungary in 1914 as a good example of a "falling" Great Power helping to trigger off a major war, that still leaves the theorist to deal with the equally critical roles played then by those "rising" Great Powers, Germany and Russia. Similarly, any general theory about whether empires pay, or whether imperial control is affected by a measurable "power-distance" ratio, is likely—from the conflicting evidence available—to produce the banal answer sometimes yes, sometimes no.

Nevertheless, if one sets aside *a priori* theories and simply looks at the historical record of "the rise and fall of the Great Powers" over the past five hundred years, it is clear that some generally valid conclusions can be drawn—while admitting all the time that there may be individual exceptions. For example, there is detectable a causal relationship between the shifts which have occurred over time in the general economic and productive balances and the position occupied by individual Powers in the international system. The move in trade flows from the Mediterranean to the Atlantic and northwestern Europe from the sixteenth century onward, or the redistribution in the shares of world manufacturing output away from western Europe in the decades after 1890, are good examples here. In both cases, the economic shifts heralded the rise of new Great Powers which would one day have a decisive impact upon the military/territorial order. This is why the move in the global productive balances toward the "Pacific rim" which has taken place over the past few decades cannot be of interest merely to economists alone.

Similarly, the historical record suggests that there is a very clear connection *in the long run* between an individual Great Power's economic rise and fall and its growth and decline as an important military power (or world empire). This, too, is hardly surprising, since it flows from two related facts. The first is that economic resources are necessary to support a large-scale military establishment. The second is that, so far as the international system is concerned, both wealth and power are always *relative* and should be seen as such. Three hundred years ago, the German mercantilist writer von Hornigk observed that

> whether a nation be today mighty and rich or not depends not on the abundance or security of its power and riches, but principally on whether its neighbors possess more or less of it.

. . . The Netherlands in the mid-eighteenth century was richer in *absolute* terms than a hundred years earlier, but by that stage was much less of a Great Power because neighbors like France and Britain had "more . . . of it" (that is, more power and riches). The France of 1914 was, absolutely, more powerful than that of 1850—but this was little consolation when France was being eclipsed by a much stronger Germany. Britain today has far greater wealth, and its armed forces possess far more powerful weapons, than in its mid-Victorian prime; that avails it little when its share

of world product has shrunk from about 25 percent to about 3 percent. If a nation has "more . . . of it," things are fine; if "less of it," there are problems.

This does not mean, however, that a nation's relative economic and military power will rise and fall *in parallel.* Most of the historical examples covered here suggest that there is a noticeable "lag time" between the trajectory of a state's relative economic strength and the trajectory of its military/territorial influence. Once again, the reason for this is not difficult to grasp. An economically expanding Power—Britain in the 1860s, the United States in the 1890s, Japan today—may well prefer to become rich rather than to spend heavily on armaments. A half-century later, priorities may well have altered. The earlier economic expansion has brought with it overseas obligations (dependence upon foreign markets and raw materials, military alliances, perhaps bases and colonies). Other, rival Powers are now economically expanding at a faster rate, and wish in their turn to extend their influence abroad. The world has become a more competitive place, and market shares are being eroded. Pessimistic observers talk of decline; patriotic statesmen call for "renewal."

In these more troubled circumstances, the Great Power is likely to find itself spending much *more* on defense than it did two generations earlier, and yet still discover that the world is a less secure environment—simply because other Powers have grown faster, and are becoming stronger. Imperial Spain spent much more on its army in the troubled 1630s and 1640s than it did in the 1580s, when the Castilian economy was healthier. Edwardian Britain's defense expenditures were far greater in 1910 than they were at, say, the time of Palmerston's death in 1865, when the British economy was relatively at its peak; but which Britons by the later date felt more secure? The same problem, it will be argued below, appears to be facing both the United States and the USSR today. Great Powers in relative decline instinctively respond by spending more on "security," and thereby divert potential resources from "investment" and compound their long-term dilemma.

Another general conclusion which can be drawn from the five-hundred-year record presented here is that there is a very strong correlation between the eventual outcome of the *major coalition wars* for European or global mastery, and the amount of productive resources mobilized by each side. This was true of the struggles waged against the Spanish-Austrian Habsburgs; of the great eighteenth-century contests like the War of Spanish Succession, the Seven Years War, and the Napoleonic War; and of the two world wars of this century. A lengthy, grinding war eventually turns into a test of the relative capacities of each coalition. Whether one side has "more . . . of it" or "less of it" becomes increasingly significant as the struggle lengthens.

One can make these generalizations, however, without falling into the trap of crude economic determinism. Despite this book's [*The Rise and Fall of the Great Powers*] abiding interest in tracing the "larger tendencies" in world affairs over the past five centuries, it is *not* arguing that economics determines every event, or is the sole reason for the success and failure of each nation. There simply is too much evidence pointing to other things: geography, military organization, national morale, the alliance system, and many other factors can all affect the relative power of the members of the states system. In the eighteenth century, for example, the United Provinces were the richest parts of Europe, and Russia the poorest—yet the Dutch fell, and the Russians rose. Individual folly (like Hitler's) and extremely high battlefield competence (whether of the Spanish regiments in the sixteenth century or of the German infantry in this century) also go a long way to explain individual victories and defeats. What does seem incontestable, however, is that in a long-drawn-out Great Power (and usually coalition) war, victory has repeatedly gone to the side with the more flourishing productive base—or, as the Spanish captains used to say, to him who has the last escudo. Much of what follows will confirm that cynical but essentially correct judgment. And it is precisely because the power position of the leading nations has closely paralleled their relative economic position over the past five centuries that it seems worthwhile asking what the implications of today's economic and technological trends might be for the current balance of power. This does not deny that men make their own history, but they do make it within a historical circumstance which can restrict (as well as open up) possibilities. . . .

James Adams

The Arms Bonanza

Like many of the great conflicts, the start of the Iran–Iraq war on September 22, 1980 was low key, an unlikely beginning to what was to become the biggest conventional war since World War II. President Saddam Hussein of Iraq had told his neighbours that he planned to teach the ambitious Ayatollah Khomeini a lesson by giving Iran a bloody nose. His troops advanced with the blessing of the moderate Arab states, all of whom feared the threat posed by the Khomeini brand of Islamic fundamentalism.

It is an old axiom of warfare never to attack a revolution, and Saddam Hussein found that the Iranians were a much tougher opposition than he had expected. Although the Iraqi forces seized large tracts of Iranian territory within the first two weeks, Hussein's offer then of a negotiated peace was turned down. Indeed, the Iranians drew on a seemingly inexhaustible supply of troops filled with revolutionary fervour, who rushed to the front and held off later Iraqi attacks.

Over the next eight years, the fortunes of the war changed between the sides, with both countries regularly proclaiming the start of another "final offensive" which never quite materialised.

The tactics used in the war were reminiscent of those employed on the Somme in the First World War: trench warfare and soldiers in wave attacks which took no real advantage of the new weaponry available to both sides.

Inevitably, such a traditional approach to modern war was enormously expensive both in arms and men. The exact number of casualties on both sides is difficult to obtain with any accuracy but western intelligence sources generally seem to agree on a total figure of around 500,000. To kill that many people, both sides spent around

$500 billion, a substantial proportion of this on weapons, in what was the single largest bonanza for freelance arms dealers seen anywhere in the world at any time.

The war came at a time of declining export markets for arms and provided a useful outlet for companies and countries desperate to keep their flagging industries working. Although most countries in both west and east remained officially neutral in the war, a new underground network of dummy companies, shady dealers and willing shippers sprang up, often with the approval of governments.

In fact, there was an extraordinary feeding frenzy by the sharks of the arms business. Fifty countries sold arms to the protagonists in the war. Of those fifty, four countries sold only to Iraq, eighteen to Iran and twenty-eight, including France, China, Italy, South Africa, Britain, the United States and West Germany sold weapons to both sides.

From the start of the war, most of Iran's purchases of arms were arranged through the Iranian Military Procurement Offices, also known as the Logistics Support Centre in the headquarters of the National Iranian Oil Company, based at 4 Victoria Street, London. The sixth-floor offices, next door to the British government's Department of Trade and Industry, housed between twenty and forty Iranians and a further 200 locally hired staff whose sole job was to find and buy arms.

On the face of it, this was a peculiar state of affairs, since the British government, along with most other western nations, had a ban on arms sales to Iran. In fact, the British made a clear decision to allow the offices to operate precisely because they were so centrally located. The British Security Service, commonly known as MI5, mounted a major intelligence operation against the centre and its employees. With the help of the intelligence monitoring centre at GCHQ in Cheltenham, the Security Service was able to routinely listen to all telephone calls, intercept all telexes and facsimile messages and, using other systems, observe and listen to conversations between arms dealers and the Iranians.

Despite such surveillance, the Iranians were occasionally able to circumvent the British watchers. In 1986, the then government-owned Royal Ordnance Factory in Bridgwater, Somerset, signed a contract with a Greek company to sell 2,362 kilograms of Tetryl, a detonating explosive. The contract was given an export license but the cargo, packed in twenty containers, was eventually diverted via Yugoslavia to Iran.

The British government responded with justifiable anger. But, as with any other western countries, there was a strong element of hypocrisy in the British policy in the war. Officially neutral and with a ban of arms sales to either side, there was clearly a willingness to exploit the war if political criticism could be contained.

Two landing craft built by Yarrow shipyard were delivered to Iran in May 1985. The ships had originally been ordered by the Shah and were supposed to be used for disaster relief. The British maintained they had to fulfil the contract and had received reassurances from the Iranians that the vessels would not be used in the war. Of course, as the British might reasonably have guessed, once delivered, the ships were immediately taken over by the Iranian navy and used in the war.

In 1986, the British authorised the sale of six radar systems made by Plessey and worth $370m to Iran. Once again, the Iranians promised to use the equipment only for civilian purposes.

The procurement office in London was closed in September 1987, following an Iranian attack on the British tanker *Gentle Breeze* in the Persian Gulf.

Until the closure of the offices, the British were able to build up a detailed picture of Iran's war effort by the nature of its arms purchases.

This information was routinely shared with the United States and other western allies and enabled western countries to intercept a number of illegal arms deals.

The first deal attempted by the London buyers was illustrative of the problems they would face in the years to come. An Iranian expatriate, Behnam Nodjoumi, agreed to sell the Iranians 8,000 US TOW anti-tank missiles. The missiles did not exist and Iranian military officers sent to Belgium to inspect the cargo were kidnapped and made to send false messages back to London authorising the deal. Police arrested Nodjoumi just before the cash was due to be handed over. He was later sentenced to ten years in prison.

The war did not simply encourage confidence men to sell weapons that did not exist. It was also an opportunity for governments to make huge legitimate profits. At the start of the war, Iran was almost entirely dependent on the west for arms. The United States had been the main supplier of arms to the Shah, with the result that the Iranian air force flew American aircraft and the army drove American tanks. Such a commitment to one source can bring advantages in purchasing discounts and ease of training but it also makes the country concerned dependent on a single source of spares. After the revolution Iran had to search the world for US-made equipment and steadily diversify its arms buying. All that meant paying a premium above the market price for every missile and shell.

Those premiums attracted every type of arms dealer to the Iranian honeypot: the underground dealers from the illegal arms market, governments who made no secret of their deals with the protagonists, and companies and governments which operated entirely in secret.

Even such nominally neutral countries as Sweden and Switzerland profited from the war. Iran bought two hundred Scandia trucks and large numbers of Boghammer fast patrol boats from Sweden. It also bought around four hundred RBS–70 laser-guided anti-aircraft missiles from the Bofors division of the Swedish arms company Nobel.

Switzerland sold Iran six Pontius PC–7 training aircraft in August 1984 for $4m and helpfully included detailed plans for converting the aircraft from civilian to military use.

The eagerness to feed at the trough made for some unlikely eating companions. Both China and North Vietnam, which had fought against each other, supplied weapons to Iran. In fact, for the first two years of the war, China supplied Iraq with around $3 billion of arms. Then, realising that Iran was prepared to pay higher prices for a wider range of goods, the Beijing government switched sides and began supplying fighters, small arms and missiles at the rate of around $1 billion a year to Iran.

For North Vietnam, which had captured billions of dollars worth of American arms in the fall of South Vietnam in 1975, the war opened up a new and highly profitable market. In the course of the war they supplied US M–48 tanks, M–113 armoured personnel carriers and millions of rounds of ammunition worth more than $1 billion. . . .

The arms business used to be considered a disreputable and amoral one. It was argued that killing machines should not be sold and that they should be manufactured only for defensive purposes. It was also argued that most developing nations could not afford the weapons they were being offered and arms dealers were therefore encouraging such countries to increase their debt. These arguments are still heard occasionally but now most governments that have weapons to sell, do so. Driven by the need to produce exports, foreign exchange and a healthy domestic industry in Britain, for example, Prime Minister Margaret Thatcher has personally intervened in two of the country's largest arms deals—with Saudi Arabia and Malaysia—to ensure that Britain won the contract.

Of course, there will always be back-street dealers, techno-mercenaries who are uninterested in the consequences of what they do and only care about the profit. What is different about today is that governments and reputable companies are willing to join in and sell anything to almost anyone. Given the worldwide condemnation of Colonel Gadaffi in Libya and his proven sponsorship of terrorism, it is depressing that western companies, led by West Germany, helped him establish a plant to build chemical weapons. It is also depressing that America, knowing of Pakistan's attempts to develop a nuclear weapon, did nothing effective to stop them.

But if the developed nations show insufficient restraint, the newcomers to the business show none at all. Brazil, with one of the highest debts in the world, needs to sell arms to survive. South Africa needs to sell arms to support its ailing economy and is already isolated from the world community. Today, both these nations make some of the finest missiles, guns and support equipment in the world and will happily sell any of it anywhere, to anyone.

Not only is the arms business more diverse and the weapons it produces more powerful, but new weapons of mass destruction are on the horizon that will make even the most insignificant dictator a real power in the world.

Chemical and biological weapons are now cheap to make and available to most developing countries. But this is only the beginning. The full potential of genetically engineered weapons is not yet understood. So far only the Soviets are thought to have made the designer weapons available by this method. If western intelligence reports are accurate, then the world will see for the first time a weapon of enormous destructive power that can be applied with absolute precision to have very specific effects—the ultimate weapon. The technology for this is becoming widely available also. It is only a matter of time before Libya, Iraq or South Africa decide that, for them too, this is the weapon of choice.

In the past, developing nations have argued that if the major powers are allowed to possess nuclear weapons then they should be allowed their own, affordable weapons of equal destructive power. This has always been a specious argument. The transfer of war technology of whatever kind should be strictly controlled. Some controls, such as the Non-Proliferation Treaty and various export restrictions on arms and technology imposed by individual countries, already exist. But even in countries like the United States, which has pioneered many of the arms control measures, there appears to be a lack of serious political will to enforce such measures. Even when illegal activities are discovered, if action against them is politically inconvenient, then nothing is done. Thus Pakistan and Israel have continued to develop a nuclear capability while receiving substantial US aid, and Egypt has organised the smuggling of restricted technology from the US and has been rewarded for its efforts with new and better weaponry.

The United States and Europe, which together possess much of the technology wanted by the developing world, will continue to be a marketplace for the covert buying of arms, and for the smuggling of arms and technology. It is here that a control regime has to start and it is here that such a regime has to be effectively enforced.

Unless new and effective enforcement regimes are introduced, armies in west and east will be faced with large Third World forces of almost equal firepower. Recent wars in Afghanistan, Angola and Lebanon have already demonstrated this growth in military capability where small forces can defeat much larger armies. This matters because since the end of World War II, it is the unmatched strength of the few major military powers that has kept the ambitions of smaller nations in check. Wholesale proliferation of new weapons of frightening power will reduce that influence, with serious consequences for the world.

William M. Evan

The Global Arms Trade

To give arms to all men who offer an honest price for them without respect of persons or principles: to aristocrats and republicans, to Nihilist and Catholic, to burglar and policeman, to black man, white man and yellow man, to all sorts and conditions, all nationalities, all faiths, all follies, all causes, and all crimes.[1]

The proliferation of civil wars and international wars—whether in Europe, Africa, South Asia, Latin America or the Middle East—depends upon the unrestrained arms trade. The principal exporters of arms are: the U.S., Russia, France, the U.K. and Germany; and the principal importers of arms are Taiwan, China, Saudi Arabia, Turkey and India. In Table 24.1, I present data on the top 12 suppliers and recipients of major conventional weapons for the period 1997–2001. During this five-year period, the total arms sales for the top 12 arms suppliers was approximately $100 billion. The U.S. accounted for 45% of the total arms sales and Russia accounted for 17%.

The global arms trade is driven by "economic factors on the supply side and political factors on the demand side."[2] In addition, the arms trade undergirds the military-industrial complex in the exporting countries and strengthens the influence of the military in the recipient countries.[3]

I am especially indebted to my friend Lana Yang who invited me to present a paper at the World Congress of the International Associated of Educators for World Peace in Lake Maggiore, Italy. Her contributions to the mission of IAEWP inspired me to write this paper. Moreover, since I was unable to personally attend the World Congress, she generously offered to read my paper for me. For many helpful editorial and substantive suggestions, I am also deeply indebted to Professors Nelson N. Foote, Andrew Lamas, Mark Manion, Morris Mendelson, Edward B. Shils, Dr. John Burroughs, Dr. Bruce Nevin and Samuel M. Hughes.

In a penetrating analysis of the global arms trade, Keller identifies four trends that

> . . . do not bode well for international peace and security. The first of these is the apparent support among governments for the transfer of potent weapons—advanced attack aircraft, submarines, tanks, missiles, munitions, radars, and the like—to the less developed world. A second trend is the formation of business alliances among arms manufacturers of different nations. Third, advanced civil technology is increasingly being adapted to military purposes. And finally, technologies that support weapons of mass destruction are being acquired by more countries in the developing world.[4]

Another well-known fact about the global arms trade is that it is highly lucrative;[5] hence weapons manufacturers have cultivated customers for their weapons needs irrespective of political, economic or ideological considerations, as we shall see when I discuss several case studies of wars.

Some Case Studies

I shall now consider several case studies of how the arms trade perpetuates international conflicts.

The Iran–Iraq War

On the 22nd of September 1980, Iraq attacked Iran in an effort to conquer Khuzestan and thus cut off

■ **TABLE 24.1**

The Top 12 Suppliers and Recipients
of Major Conventional Weapons,
1997–2001 (Figures are expressed in
US $m. at constant [1990] prices)

Suppliers		Recipients	
U.S.A.	44 821	Taiwan	11 397
Russia	17 354	China	7 117
France	9 808	Saudi Arabia	6 717
U.K.	6 699	Turkey	5 028
Germany (FRG)	4 821	India	4 710
Ukraine	2 627	Greece	4 436
Netherlands	1 862	South Korea	3 931
Italy	1 671	Egypt	3 250
China	1 555	Japan	3 203
Belarus	1 518	Pakistan	2 931
Sweden	1 123	Israel	2 835
Israel	975	U.K.	2 680

Source: Table 8A.1 and 8A.2: Bjorn Hagelin, Pieter D.
Wezeman, Siemon T. Wezeman and Nicholas
Chipperfield, "The Volume of Transfers of Major
Conventional Weapons: By Recipients and Suppliers,
1997–2001," *SIPRI Yearbook 2000* Oxford: Oxford
University Press, 2002, pp. 403–408. Copyright ©
Stockholm International Peace Research Institute. Used
with permission.

Tehran from its main refineries and ports. Iran and Iraq fought the longest and most destructive war ever waged between Third World countries. The loss in human lives was enormous: Iran sustained over 300,000 fatalities and Iraq between 100,000 and 150,000 fatalities.[6] The war unleashed a frenzy of arms sales, with the USSR, France and Germany selling arms to *both* protagonists; and the U.S., because of the collapse of its relationship with Iran—following the victory of Khomeini's regime—found itself selling arms to Iraq.

If the U.N. had intervened and imposed an embargo on the export of arms to Iran and Iraq, the war would have ended long before 8 years elapsed. Sadly, this did not occur, not because of

an oversight but because several of the permanent members of the Security Council were busy profiting from the sale of arms to *both* countries.

The Indo-Pakistan Wars

For almost 50 years India and Pakistan have waged three wars, two over Kashmir—1947–49 and 1964–65—and one over Bengal (1971–72). Although total military casualties were very slight in all three wars, there were *one million civilian casualties* during the Bengali War.[7]

In the 1970s, both India and Pakistan embarked on a program to develop nuclear weapons; and in 1998 both countries detonated nuclear weapons to develop their nuclear arsenals. Since they have achieved an approximate degree of nuclear parity, they are able to deter each other from launching a nuclear attack—as happened during the Cold War between the U.S. and the Soviet Union. Hence, MAD, or mutual assured destruction, will, hopefully, prevent the outbreak of a nuclear war between these countries. It will not, however, deter them from waging a conventional war. And a conventional war between India and Pakistan would be extremely dangerous because it could potentially turn nuclear by the vanquished country.[8] Thus, each of these South Asian antagonists has an incentive to import vast quantities of high-tech conventional weapons.

In Table 24.2, I present data on the arms-trade partners of India and Pakistan during 1993–2002. Although Russia and China are the principal suppliers for India and Pakistan, respectively, it is also noteworthy that five countries—The Netherlands, Ukraine, France, U.K. and Italy—supply arms to *both* antagonists without regard to political or ideological considerations.

The Persian Gulf Wars

At the end of the Iran–Iraq war in 1988, Iraq embarked on a campaign to replenish its arsenals of conventional and non-conventional weapons. It reached out to many countries far beyond the Middle East and regardless of religious, political or ideological divides.

■   **TABLE 24.2**
Arms-Trade Partners of India and Pakistan, 1993–2002

Imported Weapons to India (IND) in 1993–2002

	1993	1994	1995	1996	1997	1998	1999	2000	2001	2002	Total 93–02	% of *total*
Russia	311	251	574	628	1127	362	913	420	693	1529	6808	75
Netherlands	75	75	77	75	87	80	54	18	39		580	6
German (FRG)	22	182	11	15	15	11	11	44	11	11	333	4
Slovakia			67	74	74				40	40	295	3
U.K.	14	14	86	22	51	15	12			9	223	3
France	31	31	30	26	20	1	19	19	19	15	211	2
Israel					27	39	8	27	68	19	188	2
Ukraine			9		55	17	26	26	17	17	167	2
Poland						1	9	17	67	27	121	1
Singapore	2				38	19					59	1
Kyrgyzstan		57									57	1
Italy								10	10	2	22	0
South Korea	4			4	4	4					16	0
South Africa							6		5		11	0
Year total	459	553	911	844	1498	549	1058	581	969	1669	9091	100

Imported Weapons to Pakistan (PAK) in 1993–2002

	1993	1994	1995	1996	1997	1998	1999	2000	2001	2002	Total 93–02	% of *total*
China	537	207	174	70	25	23	5	55	16	718	1830	31
Ukraine					420	440	420				1280	22
France	5	5	3	59	5	62	326	92	85	315	957	16
U.K.	169	340									509	9
U.S.A.	18	18	18	198	128	18	5			5	408	7
Italy	68	68	50	45				1	38	128	398	7
Russia			34	81						99	214	4
Netherlands		44	1		19	19					83	1
Belarus					26	26	26				78	1
Sweden	19	3	3	3	3	3	4	4	4	4	50	1
Lebanon									45		45	1
North Korea			10	10							20	0
Indonesia										10	10	0
New Zealand		3									3	0
Slovakia	0										0	0
Year total	816	688	283	466	636	591	786	152	188	1279	5885	100

Source: SIPRI Arms Transfers Database, http://projects.sipri.se/armstrade/Tnd_Ind_IND_PAKMpts93_02.pdf
Figures are trend-indicator values expressed in US $m. at constant (1990) prices. Copyright © Stockholm International Peace Research Institute. Used with permission.

Although Gulf War I in 1991 was relatively brief, the level of destruction to Iraq's military matériel was enormous. Iraq's response was to increase its weapons shopping spree right through the 1990s and even right up to the start of Gulf War II on March 20, 2003. The extent of this arms build-up became clear when Iraq submitted, on December 7, 2002, its 12,000 page weapons dossier to the U.N. Security Council. Only the five permanent Security Council members—in contrast to the ten non-permanent members—received the unexpurgated version of Iraq's weapons-program declaration. Even before this dossier was released, there were reports that it would name the corporations that supplied Iraq with the wherewithal to develop biological, chemical and nuclear weapons. This suspicion was confirmed when the report was leaked to a leftist German daily newspaper *Die Tageszeitung,* which received the original, uncensored dossier.

In Table 24.3, I present the names of the corporations that supplied Iraq's weapons program. In aggregate terms, there are:

24 American firms

3 Chinese firms

8 French firms

17 British firms

6 USSR/Russian firms

5 Japanese firms

3 Dutch firms

7 Belgium firms

3 Spanish firms, and

2 Swedish firms

A note accompanying this surprising document, prepared by *Die Tageszeitung,* states without explanation that "the 80 German companies named in the dossier were not included in the list." To illustrate the extent of involvement of German companies, however, I shall list 16 firms—identified by the Iraq Watch[9]—that supplied Iraq with equipment for its missile and nuclear program:

1. Siemens
2. H&H Metalform
3. Mauserwerke Obendorf
4. Karo
5. Gerber
6. Inwako
7. Dietrich Hinze
8. Karl-Heinz Schwaz
9. Daimler-Benz
10. Leybold
11. Leifeld and Company
12. Rhan-Bayern Fahrzengeban
13. Saarstahl
14. Strabag
15. Werner Beaujean
16. Tramac

A week before Gulf War II began, William Safire, columnist for *The New York Times,* asserted that:

> France, China and Syria all have a common reason for keeping American and British troops out of Iraq: the three nations may not want the world to discover that their nationals have been illicitly supplying Saddam Hussein with materials used in building long-range surface-to-surface missiles.[10]

And several days after the start of Gulf War II, the U.S. government lodged a complaint with Moscow "over the sales by Russian companies of anti-tank missiles and jamming equipment to the Iraqi military."[11] A State Department official charged that "such equipment in the hands of Iraq may pose a direct threat to U.S. and coalition armed forces."[12,12a]

Once again we see that the pursuit of profits from the arms trade takes precedence over political and even military considerations.

The Military-Industrial Complex: A Driving Force of the Global Arms Trade

Few social scientists, let alone presidents of the U.S., have coined a concept that has become the object of scholarly inquiry as well as part of the layman's vocabulary. The concept in question, the "military-industrial complex," was first

The Corporations That Supplied Iraq's Weapons Program

KEY

B = biological weapon program

R = rocket program

A = nuclear weapon program

C = chemical weapon program

K = conventional weapons, military logistics, supplies at the Iraqi Ministry of Defense, and building of military plants

U.S.A.

1. Honeywell (R, K)
2. Spectra Physics (K)
3. Semetex (R)
4. TI Coating (A, K)
5. Unisys (A, K)
6. Sperry Corp. (R, K)
7. Tektronix (R, A)
8. Rockwell (K)
9. Leybold Vacuum Systems (A)
10. Finnigan-MAT-US (A)
11. Hewlett-Packard (A, R, K)
12. Dupont (A)
13. Eastman Kodak (R)
14. American Type Culture Collection (B)
15. Alcolac International (C)
16. Consarc (A)
17. Carl Zeiss–U.S. (K)
18. Cerberus (LTD) (A)
19. Electronic Associates (R)
20. International Computer Systems (A, R, K)
21. Bechtel (K)
22. EZ Logic Data Systems, Inc. (R)
23. Canberra Industries Inc. (A)
24. Axel Electronics Inc. (A)

In addition to these 24 companies home-based in the U.S.A. are 50 subsidiaries of foreign enterprises which conducted their arms business with Iraq from within the U.S. Also designated as suppliers for Iraq's arms programs (A, B, C & R) are the U.S. Ministries of Defense, Energy, Trade and Agriculture as well as the Lawrence Livermore, Los Alamos and Sandia National Laboratories.

China

1. China Wanbao Engineering Company (A, C, K)
2. Huawei Technologies Co. Ltd (K)
3. China State Missile Company (R)

France

1. Commissariat a l'Energie Atomique (A)
2. Sciaky (A)
3. Thomson CSF (A, K)
4. Aerospatiale and Matra Espace (R)
5. Cerbag (A)
6. Protec SA (C)
7. Thales Group (A)
8. Societé Général pour les Techniques Nouvelles (A)

Great Britain

1. Euromac Ltd–U.K. (A)
2. C. Plath-Nuclear (A)
3. Endshire Export Marketing (A)
4. International Computer Systems (A, R, K)
5. MEED International (A, C)
6. Walter Somers Ltd. (R)
7. International Computer Limited (A, K)
8. Matrix Churchill Corp. (A)
9. Ali Ashour Daghir (A)
10. International Military Services (R) (part of the U.K. Ministry of Defence)
11. Sheffield Forgemasters (R)
12. Technology Development Group (R)
13. International Signal and Control (R)
14. Terex Corporation (R)
15. Inwako (A)
16. TMG Engineering (K)
17. XYY Options, Inc. (A)

USSR/Russia

1. Soviet State Missile Co. (R)
2. Niikhism (R)
3. Mars Rotor (R)
4. Livinvest (R)
5. Russia Aviatin Trading House (K)
6. Amsar Trading (K)

Japan

1. Fanuc (A)
2. Hammamatsu Photonics KK (A)
3. NEC (A)
4. Osaka (A)
5. Waida (A)

(continued)

■ **TABLE 24.3** (continued)

The Netherlands

1.   Melchemie B.V. (C)
2.   KBS Holland B.V. (C)
3.   Delft Instruments N.V. (K)

Belgium

1.   Boehler Edelstahl (A)
2.   NU Kraft Mercantile Corporation (C)
3.   OIP Instrubel (K)
4.   Phillips Petroleum (C)
5.   Poudries Réunies Belge SA (R)
6.   Sebatra (A)
7.   Space Research Corp. (R)

Spain

1.   Donabat (R)
2.   Treblam (C)
3.   Zayer (A)

Sweden

1.   ABB (A)
2.   Saab-Scania (R)

Source: From the article "Blühende Geschäfte" by Andreas Zumach, first published in *taz - die tageszeitung,* No. 6934, 19 Dec. 2002, page 3. Copyright © *taz - die tageszeitung.* Used with permission.

Note: The 80 German companies named in the dossier were not included in this list.

articulated by President Eisenhower in his farewell address on January 17, 1961, in the following terms:

> This conjunction of an immense Military Establishment and a large arms industry is new in the American experience. The total influence—economic, political, even spiritual—is felt in every city, every statehouse, every office of the Federal Government . . .
>
> In the councils of government, we must guard against the acquisition of unwarranted influence whether sought or unsought, by the military-industrial complex. The potential for the disastrous rise of misplaced power exists and will persist.

> We must never let the weight of this combination endanger our liberties or democratic processes.[13]

The term "military-industrial complex" caught the imagination of social scientists and laymen alike. Social scientists from different disciplines—political scientists, sociologists and economists—hastened to explore the concept and its implicit propositions:

> The prolonged state of international tension that has existed since 1945, has been characterized by high levels of military expenditure by the major powers, especially the United States and the Soviet Union. These high levels of expenditure have given rise to powerful domestic

groups within the major states who have vested interests in the continuance of military spending and international conflict.

The military-industrial complex rationalizes high levels of military spending with an ideology of international conflict, mainly the ideology of the Cold War.[14]

Social scientists embedded this concept in different theoretical frameworks. Marxists interpreted this concept as evidence of the effort of the American ruling class to cope with the internal contradictions of capitalism by pursuing its imperialist and hegemonic objectives. Macrosociologists and political scientists related this concept to the controversy between the theories of elitism and pluralism in American society. Those subscribing to the political pluralist view of American society questioned the empirical validity of the implicit theory of the military-industrial complex (MIC).

An Interorganizational Network Perspective

In contrast with the perspectives previously mentioned, I shall consider the military-industrial complex from an interorganizational network perspective. In the past few decades, organizational researchers have focused their attention on "interorganizational networks" as a unit of analysis.[15] Instead of studying interactions within single organizations or within dyadic interorganizational relations, researchers have increasingly taken as the object of inquiry recurrent interactions among three or more organizations or networks of organizations.

Although the MIC suggests a relationship between the military and the industry, clearly other types of organizational actors are involved, such as political organizations, research and development laboratories and trade unions. For reasons of parsimony, I will consider a triadic network of military, industrial and political entities. As it happens, my decision coincides with C. Wright Mills'[16] contention, which antedates the coining of the term military-industrial complex, that linkages between the military elite, the economic elite and the political elite have profound consequences for the functioning of American society.

The American Military-Industrial Complex

Each of the major global exporters of weapons—namely, the U.S., Russia, Britain, France and Germany—has a thriving military-industrial complex. Because of the absence of comparative information on this international phenomenon, I shall examine the recurrent interactions among the following participants in the American MIC: The Department of Defense, the principle component of the Executive Branch apart from the Presidency; the Congress, especially the Armed Services Committees and the Defense Appropriations Subcommittees; and the defense contractors. Each of the three organizational participants in the network are linked together by a number of resource flows, namely money, personnel and influence, as shown in Figure 24.1. In other words, there is a multiplicity of ties linking the three categories of organizational actors.

Military budgets are formulated by the DoD in consultation with the Presidency. Informally, defense contractors exert influence on the budget process by advocating the funding of projects initiated by DoD, with or without the participation of defense contractors. A campaign of lobbying is then mounted by DoD personnel in support of the defense budget bill, in the course of which various *quid pro quos* are worked out, such as that the DoD will agree to establish military bases in congressional districts requested by influential Congressmen, who in turn promise to approve the appointment of new officers and the granting of new commissions.

After Congress passes the military budget, the DoD contracts with defense firms for weapons systems, munitions, material, etc.: retired military officers are offered senior executive appointments by defense contractors; and in turn, some corporate executives are offered civilian appointments in the Pentagon for brief "tours of duty," one function of which is to perfect their

■ **FIGURE 24.1**
American Military-Industrial Complex

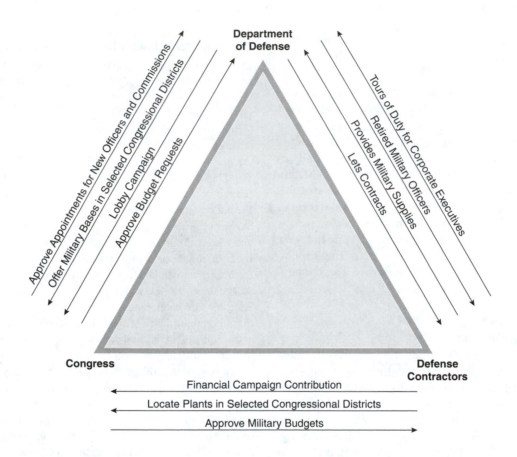

knowledge of the culture of the system with which they plan to have a long-term relationship.

Defense contractors reward Congressmen for supporting DoD budget requests by making financial contributions, via Political Action Committees, to the re-election campaigns of congressmen. They also express their gratitude for favors granted by promising to locate plants, often via subcontractors, to create jobs for constituents who vote in favor of DoD budgetary requests.

To illustrate the functioning of the MIC, a brief sketch of the history of the B-1 program is instructive.[17] The B-1 program was initiated by the Air Force during the Cold War as a bomber with the capability of penetrating Soviet defenses and dropping nuclear bombs. Originally, the

specifications called for bombers capable of speeds in excess of 2,000 miles per hour, which would cost $29 million dollars each. Over time, the speed dropped to 738 miles per hour, but the price as reported by the Air Force rose to $200 million and eventually to $400 million dollars, according to the Congressional Budget Office. Since 1960, three U.S. presidents have rejected the B-1 program on the grounds that on-going improvements in Soviet air defenses would defeat the mission of the B-1 program. Nevertheless, Rockwell International, the prime contractor, persisted in its lobbying campaign with DoD personnel who were not persuaded by the Air Force, and with congressmen who preferred the Stealth program instead.

To overcome opposition in Congress, Rockwell International developed a "national production strategy" according to which it would disperse B-1's production among thousands of subcontractors.

> Thus nearly everyone in Congress has a company back home with a stake in the B-1. In fact, 48 of 50 states have a piece of the bomber's production (the exceptions are Alaska and Hawaii). The average state stake in B-1 contracts is $780 million, using the Congressional Budget Office's estimated cost of $39.8 billion for 100 planes.[18]

In January 1982, after 20 years of opposition to a bomber of doubtful utility, Congress approved the B-1 program for the production of 100 bombers at a cost of $20.5 billion dollars. Rockwell International, the prime beneficiary, stands to gain $13.5 billion in contracts and about $400 million in profits for its role in building the 100 planes. The author of this case study concludes:

> And if there is a moral to the story, it is this: the close alliance among the Pentagon brass, the defense contractors and members of Congress has bred a weapons buying system that produces profits and promotions in peace time, even if it provides questionable tools for War.[19]

The interorganizational linkages identified in the American MIC involve continuous communication among the three actors, so much so that it leads to the emergence of a community of interests among them. A network of recurrent resource flows has predictable consequences for Congressional decisions with respect to weapons procurement, defense spending and defense policies. Regardless of domestic or foreign economic and political developments, budgetary allocations continue to be made for research, development and production of a variety of weapons systems. This phenomenon has led political scientists to describe the network of organizational linkages existing in the MIC as an "iron triangle":

> Once molded, the triangle sets with the rigidity of iron. The Three participants exert strenuous effort to keep it isolated and protected from outside points of view. In time they become unwitting victims of their own isolation, convinced that they are acting not only in their own but in the public interest.[20]

Policy Dilemmas

Can the American iron triangle be penetrated and eventually resolved? In the course of time, endogenous countervailing forces may emerge that will weaken the MIC, e.g. because of whistle-blowing by retired military officers, retired or defeated congressmen, and corporate executives whose firms have lost out in competitive bids for defense contracts.

As for exogenous countervailing forces to combat the MIC, I can envision possible development, though admittedly of very low probability, namely, the growth of peace-oriented non-governmental organizations (NGOs), owing to the initiatives of professional elites of such diverse institutions as medicine, law, science, engineering, business, education, etc., who are beginning to voice opposition to the threat of nuclear war and weapons of mass destruction. If such peace NGOs reach a "critical mass," they can conceivably have a significant impact on penetrating the iron triangle.

Urgent Need for Effective Regulation of the Global Arms Trade

To promote world peace, national, regional and global restrictions are urgently needed to limit the transfer of arms from one country to another. To restrict the sale of arms that are used in civil and international wars, a first crucial step is for all countries—claiming to advocate peaceful international relations—to impose *effective* export control laws on weapons systems

Export Control Laws

In a comprehensive and brilliant socio-legal[21] analysis of U.S. export control statutes, Sievert concludes that although U.S. statutes were somewhat effective during the 50 years of the Cold War, their post–Cold War performance in ensuring national security has been dismal.[22] For example, in the six years before Gulf War I, "U.S. exporters shipped $1.5 billion in equipment to Iraq—including $100 million in high speed computers—and that a significant portion of these exports were directly utilized in Saddam Hussein's nuclear weapons program. Congressional hearings subsequently confirmed that Iraq's nuclear, missile, artillery, and fire control programs were all dramatically enhanced by the purchase of U.S. technology."[23]

Sievert identified six major problems with the U.S. export control system:

1. *Complexity.* There is a multiplicity of statutes, each of which has its own set of numerous implementing directives, for example, The Trading With the Enemy Act (TWEA), The International Traffic in Arms Regulations (ITAR) and the Export Administration Regulations (EAR).

2. *Multilayered Bureaucracy.* The export control system is administered by no less than six federal agencies: the departments of State, Commerce, Customs, Defense, Energy and the Treasury.

3. *No Statutory Duty to Inquire as to the End Use.* If a company receives an order from an overseas buyer for a product that does not need a license, the exporter is not required to investigate how the product will eventually be used.

4. *Problem of Enforcement.* Any individual or corporation who violates export regulations can face suspension of export privileges or a fine of up to $104,000. Suspension, however, requires evidence of repeated violations, and fines of $100,000 fail to act as a deterrent because exports yield enormous profits.

5. *Weak International Controls.* There is a lack of effective international controls on militarily sensitive technology.

6. *Policy Decisions on Arms Sales.* Although the export control statutes express the intent of Congress to "reduce the international trade in implements of war" and to protect U.S.

national security, policy decisions by the executive branch of the government change over time and have resulted in the United States "becoming the arms merchant to the world."[24]

In short, "because of the failure of our export control system . . . we are increasingly in danger of being attacked by weapons which we, in effect, have helped to make."[25]

House of Representatives 772[26]

In 1995, two congressmen (Senator Mark Hatfield, R-Oregon and Representative Cynthia McKinney, D-Georgia) introduced a courageous bill that would have established a set of significant policy guidelines for exporting arms. Known as H.R. 772, this bill would have prohibited military assistance and arms transfers to foreign governments that are a) undemocratic, b) do not adequately protect human rights, c) are engaged in acts of armed aggression or d) are not fully participating in the United Nations Register of Conventional Arms. Unfortunately, this bill was never passed by Congress.

The International Code of Conduct on Arms Transfers

At the international level, a bold and imaginative effort was initiated in 1995 by Dr. Oscar Arias, former president of Costa Rica and a Nobel Peace Laureate. He invited 19 fellow Nobel Peace Laureates, to join him in developing an International Code of Conduct on Arm Transfers.[27] This remarkable code requires arms suppliers to certify that all arms recipients meet the following criteria:

1. compliance with international human rights,
2. compliance with international humanitarian laws [laws of warfare: 1907 Hague Convention, Geneva Conventions, 1949, and Protocol 1, 1977],
3. respect for democratic rights,
4. respect for international arms embargoes and military sanctions,
5. participate in the U.N. Register of Conventional Arms,

6. commitment to promote regional peace, security and stability,

7. opposition to terrorism, and

8. promotion of human development.

This code has since been submitted to the European Union and to the U.N. General Assembly. However, the probability of adoption and implementation of this code by both of these organizational entities is, alas, very slim indeed. Although 189 member states comprise the U.N. General Assembly, the majority of these countries are *importers* of vast quantities of arms either for domestic security purposes or for deterrence of their hostile neighbors. As for the European Union, many of the original 15 members are large *exporters* of arms and hence have a disincentive to regulate the arms trade. If the International Code of Conduct on Arms Transfers were ever submitted to the U.N. Security Council, it would undoubtedly meet a similar fate because the five permanent council members are among the largest *suppliers* of arms in the world. Thus, it is evident that the prospects for regulating the global arms trade with the help of the organs of the United Nations appear dim indeed.

Conclusion

The only possible *current* remedy for the chaos characterizing the global arms trade is to activate thousands of non-governmental organizations (NGOs). The growth of civil society in various countries augurs well for the mobilization of such international organizations to condemn the unrestrained flow of deadly weapons. "Merchants of Death," in democratic as well as in nondemocratic countries, need to be exposed.

Our analysis points to the following four conclusions, all of which are based on a common assumption, namely, that NGOs, not nation-states, can make the initiative to remedy the deplorable state of governance of the global arms trade:

First, NGOs might consider a strategy of vigorously lobbying members of the House of Representatives and the Senate to revive the H.R. 772 bill to regulate the arms trade. A major hurdle of such an effort is the anticipated opposition from recipients of campaign financing and from the benefactors, many of whom, no doubt, are arms manufacturers.

Second, NGOs might also consider petitioning the member states of the U.N. General Assembly to pass a resolution supporting the International Code of Conduct on Arms Transfers so it can become part of international law.

Third, NGOs should seek to persuade the ten non-permanent members of the Security Council to introduce a resolution supporting the International Code of Conduct on Arms Transfers, even if it means confronting the anticipated self-serving opposition from the five permanent members.

Fourth, a legal case could conceivably be made by, for example, Amnesty International, that major weapons exporters are responsible for the death of countless civilians, especially in the developing world. In Sudan, for instance, where a fratricidal war between the North and the South has been waged for two decades, Amnesty International lawyers could construct a case against, say, a British manufacturer of cluster bombs—an indiscriminate weapon—that it sold to the combatants and thus endangered the lives of Sudanese civilians. Since Britain has ratified the Rome Treaty establishing the International Criminal Court (ICC), Amnesty International might well decide to submit such a case for prosecution by the ICC. Amnesty International lawyers might claim that individuals involved in the supply of weapons could be prosecuted under provision 2(b) (IV) of Article 8 on War Crimes and provision 3(d) of Article 25 on individual criminal responsibility. Pursuing such a legal strategy in order to create a remedy against the depredations of "merchants of death"—if it were successful—would result in a landmark decision.[28]

Notes

1. This is the creed of the arms maker in Bernard Shaw's "Major Barbara," quoted in H. E. Engelbrecht and F. C. Hanighan, *Merchants of Death,* New York:

The Garden City Publishing Co. Inc., 1937. Shaw's portrait of Undershaft, as the archetype of the capitalist, is that of an immoral munitions monger.

2. Edward B. Atkeson, "The World's Biggest Growth Engine," *The International Economy,* January/February 1993, p. 33.

3. Cf. Marek Thee, "Militarism and Militarization," *World Encyclopedia of Peace,* Vol. III (second edition), Dobbs Ferry, N.Y. Oceana Publications, Inc., pp. 260–264.

4. William W. Keller, *Arm in Arm: The Political Economy of the Global Arms Trade,* New York Basic Books, 1995, p. x.

5. Cf. James Adams, *Engines of War: Merchants of Death and the News Arms Race,* New York: The Atlantic Monthly Press, 1990.

6. Herbert K. Tillema, *International Armed Conflict since 1945: A Bibliographic Handbook of Wars and Military Intervention,* Boulder: Westview Press, 1991, p. 152.

7. Tillema, *op.cit.,* p. 235.

8. Cf. William M. Evan and Francis A. Boyle, "Kashmir: Invoking International Law to Avoid Nuclear War," *Counterpunch,* June 4, 2002; Gabriel Kolko, *Another Century of War?* N.Y.: W. W. Norton & Co., 2002, p. 64.

9. Iraq Watch Org is published by the Wisconsin Project on Nuclear Arms Control, a Washington-based research group.

10. William Safire, "The French Connection," *The New York Times,* March 12, 2003.

11. James Harding, "U.S. Anger at Russian Sales of Missiles," *The Financial Times,* March 24, 2003, p. 6.

12. *Ibid.*

12a. It is indeed noteworthy that James Risen of *The New York Times.* (March 5, 2004, p. 1) reports:

A group of Russian engineers secretly aided Saddam Hussein's long-range ballistic missile program, providing technical assistance for prohibited Iraqi weapons projects even in the years just before the war that ousted him from power, American government officials say.

13. Dwight D. Eisenhower, "President Eisenhower's Farewell to the Nation," U.S. Department of State, *Bulletin,* vol. 4, February 4, 1961.

14. Steven Rosen, "Testing the Theory of the Military-Industrial Complex," in Steven Rosen, ed.,

Testing the Theory of the Military-Industrial Complex. Lexington, Mass.: Lexington Books, 1973, pp. 2–4.

15. William M. Evan, *Interorganizational Relations,* London: Penguin Books, 1976. Howard E. Aldrich, *Organizations and Environments,* Englewood Cliffs, New Jersey: Prentice-Hall, 1979. Robert N. Stern, "The Development of an Interorganizational Control Network: The Case of Intercollegiate Athletics," *Administrative Science Quarterly,* vol. 24, June 1979, pp. 252–266.

16. C. Wright Mills, *The Power Elite,* New York: Oxford University Press, 1956.

17. If adequate data were already available about the Bush administration's national missile defense program, that would have been selected instead as a case study of the operations of the MIC.

18. Frank Greve, "Is the B-1 a Plane Whose Time Has Come?" *The Philadelphia Inquirer Magazine,* March 17, 1984, pp. 20–25, 29–31. Quote is on p. 30.

19. *Ibid.*, p. 22.

20. Gordon Adams, *The Politics of Defense Contracting: The Iron Triangle,* New Brunswick: Transaction Books, 1982.

21. Cf. William M. Evan, *Social Structure and Law,* Newbury Park: Sage Publications, 1990.

22. Ronald J. Sievert, "Urgent Message to Congress—Nuclear Triggers to Libya, Missile Guidance to China, Air Defense to Iraq, Arms Supplier to the World: Has the Time Finally Arrived to Overhaul the U.S. Export Control Regime? The Case for Immediate Reform of Our Outdated, Ineffective, and Self-Defeating Export Control System," 37 *Texas International Law Journal,* 89, Winter 2002.

23. *Ibid.,* p. 91.

24. *Ibid.,* p. 104.

25. *Ibid.,* p. 89.

26. Full Text of bill as introduced in the 104 Congress, 1995, H.R. 772.

27. http://www.arias.or.cr/fundarias/cpr/codel.shtml

28. I am deeply indebted to Dr. John Burroughs of the Lawyers' Committee on Nuclear Policy for making me aware of this possible legal strategy against arms manufacturers.

Questions for Discussion

1. Do you think capitalism promotes war?
2. How does competition in the marketplace get projected onto foreign policy?
3. If market economies are becoming increasingly interdependent, do you think this will reduce the likelihood of war?
4. What are the implications of Paul Kennedy's analysis in "The Rise and Fall of the Great Powers" for the economic and military dilemmas facing the United States?
5. What can the UN do about arms suppliers who operate legally and illegally to supply arms to warring countries, thereby prolonging conflicts?
6. What is the relationship between international conflicts and the global arms trade?
7. What is the relationship between the military-industrial complex in the United States and elsewhere in terms of the growth of global arms trade.

Further Readings

1. Robin, Ron. *The Making of the Cold War Enemy: Culture and Politics in the Military-Industrial Complex.* Princeton, NJ: Princeton University Press, 2003.
2. Lumpe, Lora, ed. *Running Guns: The Global Black Market in Small Arms.* New York: Zen Books, 2000.
3. Blanton, Shannon Lindsey. "The Role of Arms Transfers in the Quest for Human Security." *Journal of Political and Military Sociology,* 2001, 29, 2, Winter, 240–258.
4. Mayer, Jane. "Contract Sport: What Did the Vice President Do for Halliburton?" *The New Yorker,* 2004, 16, February, 23.
5. Neuman, Stephanie G. "The Arms Trade, Military Assistance, and Recent Wars: Change and Continuity." *Annals of the American Academy of Political and Social Science,* 1995, 541, Sept., 47–74.
6. Barnaby, Frank. "The Dynamics of World Armaments: An Overview." *International Social Science Journal,* 1976, 28, 2, 245–265.
7. Kende, Istvan. "Dynamics of Wars, of Arms Trade and of Military Expenditure in the 'Third World,' 1945–1976." *Instant Research on Peace and Violence,* 1977, 7, 2, 59–67.
8. Neuman, Stephane G. "The Arms Trade, Military Assistance, and Recent Wars: Change and Continuity." *Annals of the American Academy of Political and Social Science,* 1995, 541, Sept., 47–74.
9. Harkavy, Robert E. "The Changing International System and the Arms Trade." *Annals of the American Academy of Political and Social Science,* 1994, 535.

Technological Theories

Innovations in weapons technology used to be considered a major consequence of warfare, a prime example being the development of the atomic bomb during World War II. The demand for new and more effective weapons was a result of armed confrontation between the warring states—Allied and Axis powers. This section revises this concept. In the last few decades, the focus has shifted and the discussion is centered around the likelihood of war being caused by a proliferation of conventional and nonconventional weapons.

The first reading, "War in the Atomic Age" by Bernard Brodie, was written in the immediate aftermath of the bombing of Hiroshima and Nagasaki. Brodie has summarized the issues that arose about the development of nuclear technology in its nascent stage. The power of the A-bomb and the futility of conventional forms of defense such as a superior air force capacity are discussed. He concludes that because the advancement of nuclear weaponry will diminish the importance of the number of conventional bombs owned by a state, there is an incentive to further develop the delivery sys-

tems for nuclear weapons. Brodie also speculates about the future potential for sabotage of these weapons, the availability of raw missile material and the possibilities of nuclear proliferation.

In "Technology and War," Van Creveld discusses the growing importance of computerization and information technology in modern warfare. The emergence of nuclear weapons has revolutionized the military and modern warfare as well. "The possibility that nuclear war . . . would literally mean the end of the war" prompted the superpowers to undertake various programs of arms control.

In "World War III? Now?," Geoffrey Forden explains how the USSR's deteriorated nuclear arsenal and outdated satellite detection systems might cause an accidental nuclear war. The author stresses the need for information sharing even if the United States has to financially assist Russia in upgrading its detection system.

Anthony Cordesman, in "Chemical Weapons as Means of Attack," explains the threat posed by biological and chemical weapons in the hands of terrorist organizations. This reading discusses the specific chemical and biological agents that may be employed as well as the mechanisms that may be adopted to permit their use. The simplicity and ease of their use is highlighted to explain why chemical and biological weapons are an immediate threat.

The last reading in this section specifically discusses biological weapons and the possibility of their use against civilian populations by terrorist organizations. The possible means of defense against such weapons is also discussed.

Bernard Brodie

War in the Atomic Age

It is already known to us all that a war with atomic bombs would be immeasurably more destructive and horrible than any the world has yet known. That fact is indeed portentous, and to many it is overwhelming. But as a datum for the formulation of policy it is in itself of strictly limited utility. It underlines the urgency of our reaching correct decisions, but it does not help us to discover which decisions are in fact correct.

Men have in fact been converted to religion at the point of the sword, but the process generally required actual use of the sword against recalcitrant individuals. The atomic bomb does not lend itself to that kind of discriminate use. The wholesale conversion of mankind away from those parochial attitudes bound up in nationalism is a consummation devoutly to be wished and, where possible, to be actively promoted. But the mere existence of the bomb does not promise to accomplish it at an early enough time to be of any use. The careful handling required to assure long and fruitful life to the Age of Atomic Energy will in the first instance be a function of distinct national governments, not all of which, incidentally, reflect in their behavior the will of the popular majority.

Governments are of course ruled by considerations not wholly different from those which affect even enlightened individuals. That the atomic bomb is a weapon of incalculable horror will no doubt impress most of them deeply. But they have never yet responded to the horrific implications of war in a uniform way. Even those governments which feel impelled to the most drastic self-denying proposals will have to grapple not merely with the suspicions of other governments but with the indisputable fact that great nations have very

recently been ruled by men who were supremely indifferent to horror, especially horror inflicted by them on people other than their own.

Statesmen have hitherto felt themselves obliged to base their policies on the assumption that the situation might again arise where to one or more great powers war looked less dangerous or less undesirable than the prevailing conditions of peace. They will want to know how the atomic bomb affects that assumption. They must realize at the outset that a weapon so terrible cannot but influence the degree of probability of war for any given period in the future. But the degree of that influence or the direction in which it operates is by no means obvious. . . .

Thus, a series of questions present themselves. Is war more or less likely in a world which contains atomic bombs? If the latter, is it *sufficiently* unlikely—sufficiently, that is, to give society the opportunity it desperately needs to adjust its politics to its physics? What are the procedures for effecting that adjustment within the limits of our opportunities? And how can we enlarge our opportunities? Can we transmute what appears to be an immediate crisis into a long-term problem, which presumably would permit the application of more varied and better considered correctives than the pitifully few and inadequate measures which seem available at the moment?

It is precisely in order to answer such questions that we turn our attention to the effect of the bomb on the character of war. We know in advance that war, if it occurs, will be very different from what it was in the past, but what we want to know is: How different, and in what ways? A study of those questions should help us to discover the conditions which will govern the pursuit of security in the future and the feasibility of proposed measures for furthering that pursuit. At any rate, we know that it is not the mere existence of the weapon but rather its effects on the traditional pattern of war which will govern the adjustments which states will make in their relations with each other. . . .

Presented below are a number of conclusions concerning the character of the bomb which seem to this writer to be inescapable. Some of the eight points listed already enjoy fairly universal acceptance; most do not. After offering with each one an explanation of why he believes it to be true, the writer will attempt to deduce from these several conclusions or postulates the effect of the bomb on the character of war.

I. The power of the present bomb is such that any city in the world can be effectively destroyed by one to ten bombs.

While this proposition is not likely to evoke much dissent, its immediate implications have been resisted or ignored by important public officials. These implications are twofold. First, it is now physically possible for air forces no greater than those existing in the recent war to wipe out all the cities of a great nation in a single day—and it will be shown subsequently that what is physically possible must be regarded as tactically feasible. Secondly, with our present industrial organization the elimination of our cities would mean the elimination for military purposes of practically the whole of our industrial structure. But before testing these extraordinary implications, let us examine and verify the original proposition.

The bomb dropped on Hiroshima completely pulverized an area of which the radius from the point of detonation was about one and one-quarter miles. However, everything to a radius of two miles was blasted with some burning and between two and three miles the buildings were about half destroyed. Thus the area of total destruction covered about four square miles, and the area of destruction and substantial damage extended over some twenty-seven square miles.

The bomb dropped on Nagasaki, while causing less damage than the Hiroshima bomb because of the physical characteristics of the city, was nevertheless considerably more powerful. . . .

The city of New York is listed in the *World Almanac* as having an area of 365 square miles. But it obviously would not require the pulverization of every block of it to make the whole area one of complete chaos and horror. Ten well-placed bombs of the Nagasaki type would eliminate that city as a contributor to the national economy, whether for peace or war, and convert it instead into a catastrophe area in dire need of relief from outside. If the figure of ten bombs be challenged, it need only be said that it would make very little difference militarily if twice that number of bombs were required. Similarly, it would be a matter of relative indifference if the power of the bomb were so increased as to require only five to do the job. Increase of power in the individual bomb is of especially little moment to cities of small or medium size, which would be wiped out by one bomb each whether that bomb were of the Nagasaki type or of fifty times as much power. No conceivable variation in the power of the atomic bomb could compare in importance with the disparity in power between atomic and previous types of explosives.

The condition at this writing of numerous cities in Europe and Japan sufficiently underlines the fact that it does not require atomic bombs to enable man to destroy great cities. TNT and incendiary bombs when dropped in sufficient quantities are able to do a quite thorough job of it. For that matter, it should be pointed out that a single bomb which contains in itself the concentrated energy of 20,000 tons of TNT is by no means equal in destructive effect to that number of tons of TNT distributed among bombs of one or two tons each. The destructive radius of individual bombs of any one type increases only with the cube root of the explosive energy released, and thus the very concentration of power in the atomic bomb prevents the full utilization of its tremendous energy. The bomb must be detonated from an altitude of at least 1,000 feet if the full spread of its destructive radius is to be realized, and much of the blast energy is absorbed by the air above the target. But the sum of initial energy is quite enough to afford such losses.

It should be obvious that there is much more than a logistic difference involved between a situation where a single plane sortie can cause the destruction of a city like Hiroshima and one in which at least 500 bomber sorties are required to do the same job. Nevertheless, certain officers of the United States Army Air Forces, in an effort to "deflate" the atomic bomb, have observed publicly enough to have their comments reported in the press that the destruction wrought at Hiroshima could have been effected by two days of routine bombing with ordinary bombs. Undoubtedly so, but the 500 or more bombers needed to do the job under those circumstances would if they were loaded with atomic bombs be physically capable of destroying 500 or more Hiroshimas in the same interval of time. That observation discounts certain tactical considerations. . . .

II. No adequate defense against the bomb exists, and the possibilities of its existence in the future are exceedingly remote.

This proposition requires little supporting argument in so far as it is a statement of existing fact. But that part of it which involves a prediction for the future conflicts with the views of most of the high-ranking military officers who have ventured opinions on the implications of the atomic bomb. No layman can with equanimity differ from the military in their own field, and the present writer has never entertained the once-fashionable view that the military do not know their business. But, apart from the question of objectivity concerning professional interests—in which respect the record of the military profession is neither worse nor better than that of other profession—the fact is that the military experts have based their arguments mainly on presumptions gleaned from a field in which they are generally not expert, namely, military *history*. History is at best an im-

perfect guide to the future, but when imperfectly understood and interpreted it is a menace to sound judgment.

The defense against hostile missiles in all forms of warfare, whether on land, sea, or in the air, has thus far depended basically on a combination of, first, measures to reduce the number of missiles thrown or to interfere with their aim (i.e., defense by offensive measures) and, secondly, ability to absorb those which strike. . . . London was defended against the German V-1, or "buzz-bomb," first by concerted bombing attacks upon the German experimental stations, industrial plants, and launching sites, all of which delayed the V-1 attack and undoubtedly greatly reduced the number of missiles ultimately launched. Those which were nevertheless launched were met by a combination of fighter planes, anti-aircraft guns, and barrage balloons. Towards the end of the eighty-day period which covered the main brunt of the attack, some 75 per cent of the bombs launched were being brought down, and, since many of the remainder were inaccurate in their flight, only 9 per cent were reaching London.[1] These London was able to "absorb"; that is, there were casualties and damage but no serious impairment of the vital services on which depended the city's life and its ability to serve the war effort.

It is precisely this ability to absorb punishment, whether one is speaking of a warship or a city, which seems to vanish in the face of atomic attack. For almost any kind of target selected, the so-called "static defenses" are defenses no longer. For the same reason too, mere reduction in the number of missiles which strike home is not sufficient to save the target, though it may have some effect on the enemy's selection of targets. The defense of London against V-1 was considered effective, and yet in eighty days some 2,300 of those missiles hit the city. The record bag was that of August 28, 1944, when out of 101 bombs which approached England 97 were shot down and only four reached London. But if those four had been atomic bombs, London survivors would not have considered the record good. . . .

III. The atomic bomb not only places an extraordinary military premium upon the development of new types of carriers but also greatly extends the destructive range of existing carriers.

World War II saw the development and use by the Germans of rockets capable of 220 miles' range and carrying approximately one ton each of TNT. Used against London, these rockets completely baffled the defense. But for single-blow weapons which were generally inaccurate at long distances even with radio control,[2] they were extremely expensive. It is doubtful whether the sum of economic damage done by these missiles equaled the expenditure which the Germans put into their development, production, and use. At any rate, the side enjoying command of the air had in the airplane a much more economical and longer-range instrument for inflicting damage on enemy industry than was available in the rocket. The capacity of the rocket-type projectile to strike without warning in all kinds of weather with complete immunity from all known types of defenses guaranteed to it a supplementary though subordinate role to bomber-type aircraft. But its inherent limitations, so long as it carried only chemical explosives, were sufficient to warrant considerable reserve in predictions of its future development.

However, the power of the new bomb completely alters the considerations which previously governed the choice of vehicles and the manner of using them. A rocket far more elaborate and expensive than the V-2 used by the Germans is still an exceptionally cheap means of bombarding a country if it can carry in its nose an atomic bomb. The relative inaccuracy of aim—which continued research will no doubt reduce—is of much diminished consequence when the radius of destruction is measured in miles rather than yards. And even with existing fuels such as were used in the German V-2, it is theoretically feasible to produce rockets capable of several thousands of miles of range, though the problem of controlling the flight of rockets over such distances is greater than is generally assumed. . . .

With atomic bombs, however, the considerations . . . which so severely limit bombing range tend to vanish. There is no question of increasing the number of bombs in order to make the sortie profitable. One per plane is quite enough. The gross weight of the atomic bomb is secret, but even if it weighed four to six tons it would still be a light load for a B-29. It would certainly be a sufficient pay load to warrant any conceivable military expenditure on a single sortie. The next step then becomes apparent. Under the callously utilitarian standards of military bookkeeping, a plane and its crew can very well be sacrificed in order to deliver an atomic bomb to an extreme distance. We have, after all, the recent and unforgettable experience of the Japanese *Kamikaze*.[3] Thus, the plane can make its entire flight in one direction, and, depending on the weight of the bomb and the ultimate carrying capacity of the plane, its range might be almost as great with a single atomic bomb as it would be with no bomb load whatever. The non-stop flight during November, 1945, of a B-29 from Guam to Washington, D.C., almost 8,200 statute miles, was in this respect more than a stunt.[4]

If it be true, as has been hinted,[5] that the B-29 is the only existing bomber which can carry the atomic bomb, the fact might argue an even greater gross weight for the bomb than that surmised above. It might of course be that a bomb having a lighter container would still be highly effective though less efficient, but in any case we know that there is no need for the bomb to be *heavier* than either the Hiroshima or the Nagasaki bomb. The plane which carried the Hiroshima bomb apparently flew a distance of 3,000 miles, and bombers of considerably greater carrying capacity are definitely beyond the blueprint stage. With the bomb weight remaining fixed, the greater capacity can be given over entirely to fuel load and thus to added range. The great-circle-route distance between New York and Moscow is only 4,800 miles. With planes following the great-circle routes even across the Arctic wastes, as will undoubtedly prove feasible, it appears that no major city in either the Soviet Union or the

United States is much beyond 6,000 miles from the territories of the other. And if American forces are able to utilize bases in northern Canada, the cities of the Soviet Union are brought considerably closer.

Under the conditions just described, any world power is able from bases within its own territories to destroy most of the cities of any other power. It is not *necessary,* despite the assertions to the contrary of various naval and political leaders including President Truman, to seize advanced bases close to enemy territory as a prerequisite to effective use of the bomb. [6] . . .

The facts just presented do not mean that distance loses all its importance as a barrier to conflict between the major power centers of the world. It would still loom large in any plans to consolidate an atomic bomb attack by rapid invasion and occupation. It would no doubt also influence the success of the bomb attack itself. Rockets are likely to remain of lesser range than aircraft and less accurate near the limits of their range, and the weather hazards which still affect aircraft multiply with distance. Advanced bases will certainly not be valueless. But it is nevertheless a fact that under existing technology the distance separating, for example, the Soviet Union from the United States offers no direct immunity to either with respect to atomic bomb attack, though it does so for all practical purposes with respect to ordinary bombs.[7]

IV. Superiority in air forces, though a more effective safeguard in itself than superiority in naval or land forces, nevertheless fails to guarantee security.

This proposition is obviously true in the case of very long range rockets, but let us continue to limit our discussion to existing carriers. In his *Third Report to the Secretary of War,* dated November 12, 1945, General H. H. Arnold, commanding the Army Air Forces, made the following statement: "Meanwhile [i.e., until very long range rockets are developed], the only known effective means of delivering atomic bombs in their present stage of development is the very heavy bomber, and that is certain of success only when the user has air superiority."[8]

This writer feels no inclination to question General Arnold's authority on matters pertaining to air combat tactics. However, it is pertinent to ask just what the phrase "certain of success" means in the sentence just quoted, or rather, how much certainty of success is necessary for each individual bomb before an atomic bomb attack is considered feasible. In this respect one gains some insight into what is in General Arnold's mind from a sentence which occurs somewhat earlier on the same page in the *Report:* "Further, the great unit cost of the atomic bomb means that as nearly as possible every one must be delivered to its intended target." Here is obviously the major premise upon which the conclusion above quoted is based, and one is not disputing General Arnold's judgment in the field of his specialization by examining a premise which lies wholly outside of it.

When the bombs were dropped on Hiroshima and Nagasaki in August, 1945, there were undoubtedly very few such bombs in existence—which would be reason enough for considering each one precious regardless of cost. But the cost of their development and production then amounted to some two billions of dollars, and that figure would have to be divided by the number made to give the cost of each. If, for example, there were twenty in existence, the unit cost would have to be reckoned at $100,000,000. That, indeed, is a staggering sum for one missile, being approximately equivalent to the cost of one *Iowa* class battleship. It is quite possible that there were fewer than twenty at that time, and that the unit cost was proportionately higher. . . .

V. Superiority in numbers of bombs is not in itself a guarantee of strategic superiority in atomic bomb warfare.

Under the technical conditions apparently prevailing today, and presumably likely to continue for some time to come, the primary targets for the atomic bomb will be cities. One does not shoot rabbits with elephant guns, especially if there are elephants available. The critical mass conditions to which the bomb is inherently subject place the minimum of destructive energy of the individual unit at far too high a level to warrant its use against any target where enemy strength is not already densely concentrated. Indeed, there is little inducement to the attacker to seek any other kind of target. If one side can eliminate the cities of the other, it enjoys an advantage which is practically tantamount to final victory, provided always its own cities are not similarly eliminated.

The fact that the bomb is inevitably a weapon of indiscriminate destruction may carry no weight in any war in which it is used. Even in World War II, in which the bombs used could to a large extent isolate industrial targets from residential districts within an urban area, the distinctions imposed by international law between "military" and "non-military" targets disintegrated entirely.[9]

How large a city has to be to provide a suitable target for the atomic bomb will depend on a number of variables—the ratio of the number of bombs available to the number of cities which might be hit, the wastage of bombs in respect to each target, the number of bombs which the larger cities can absorb before ceasing to be profitable targets, and, of course, the precise characteristics and relative accessibility of the individual city. Most important of all is the place of the particular city in the nation's economy. We can see at once that it does not require the obliteration of all its towns to make a nation wholly incapable of defending itself in the traditional fashion. Thus, the number of *critical* targets is quite limited, and the number of hits necessary to win a strategic decision—always excepting the matter of retaliation—is correspondingly limited. That does not mean that additional hits would be useless but simply that diminishing returns would set in early; and after the cities of, say, 100,000 population were eliminated the returns from additional bombs expended would decline drastically. . . .

We cannot, of course, assume that if a race in atomic bombs develops each nation will be content to limit its production after it reaches

what it assumes to be the critical level. That would in fact be poor strategy, because the actual critical level could never be precisely determined in advance and all sorts of contingencies would have to be provided for. Moreover, nations will be eager to make whatever political capital (in the narrowest sense of the term) can be made out of superiority in numbers. But it nevertheless remains true that superiority in numbers of bombs does not endow its possessor with the kind of military security which formerly resulted from superiority in armies, navies, and air forces.

VI. The new potentialities which the atomic bomb gives to sabotage must not be overrated.

With ordinary explosives it was hitherto physically impossible for agents to smuggle into another country, either prior to or during hostilities, a sufficient quantity of materials to blow up more than a very few specially chosen objectives. The possibility of really serious damage to a great power resulting from such enterprises was practically nil. A wholly new situation arises, however, where such materials as U-235 or Pu-239 are employed, for only a few pounds of either substance are sufficient, when used in appropriate engines, to blow up the major part of a large city. Should those possibilities be developed, an extraordinarily high premium will be attached to national competence in sabotage on the one hand and in countersabotage on the other. The F.B.I. or its counterpart would become the first line of national defense, and the encroachment on civil liberties which would necessarily follow would far exceed in magnitude and pervasiveness anything which democracies have thus far tolerated in peacetime.

However, it would be easy to exaggerate the threat inherent in that situation, at least for the present. From various hints contained in the *Smyth Report*[10] and elsewhere,[11] it is clear that the engine necessary for utilizing the explosive, that is, the bomb itself, is a highly intricate and fairly massive mechanism. The massiveness is not something which we can expect future research to diminish. It is inherent in the bomb. The mechanism and casing surrounding the explosive element must be heavy enough to act as a "tamper," that is, as a means of holding the explosive substance together until the reaction has made substantial progress. Otherwise the materials would fly apart before the reaction was fairly begun. And since the *Smyth Report* makes it clear that it is not the tensile strength of the tamper but the inertia due to mass which is important, we need expect no particular assistance from metallurgical advances.[12]

The designing of the bomb apparently involved some of the major problems of the whole "Manhattan District" project. The laboratory at Los Alamos was devoted almost exclusively to solving those problems, some of which for a time looked insuperable. The former director of that laboratory has stated that the results of the research undertaken there required for its recording a work of some fifteen volumes.[13] The detonation problem is not even remotely like that of any other explosive. It requires the bringing together instantaneously in perfect union of two or more subcritical masses of the explosive material (which up to that moment must be insulated from each other) and the holding together of the combined mass until a reasonable proportion of the uranium or plutonium atoms have undergone fission. A little reflection will indicate that the mechanism which can accomplish this must be ingenious and elaborate in the extreme, and certainly not one which can be slipped into a suit case.

It is of course possible that a nation intent upon perfecting the atomic bomb as a sabotage instrument could work out a much simpler device. Perhaps the essential mechanism could be broken down into small component parts such as are easily smuggled across national frontiers, the essential mass being provided by crude materials available locally in the target area. Those familiar with the present mechanism do not consider such an eventuation likely. And if it required the smuggling of whole bombs, that too is perhaps possible. But the chances are that if two or three were successfully introduced into a country by stealth,

the fourth or fifth would be discovered. Our federal police agencies have made an impressive demonstration in the past, with far less motivation, of their ability to deal with smugglers and saboteurs. . . .

VII. In relation to the destructive powers of the bomb, world resources in raw materials for its production must be considered abundant.

Everything about the atomic bomb is overshadowed by the twin facts that it exists and that its destructive power is fantastically great. Yet within this framework there are a large number of technical questions which must be answered if our policy decisions are to proceed in anything other than complete darkness. Of first importance are those relating to its availability.

The manner in which the bomb was first tested and used and various indications contained in the *Smyth Report* suggest that the atomic bomb cannot be "mass produced" in the usual sense of the term. It is certainly a scarce commodity in the sense in which the economist uses the term "scarcity," and it is bound to remain extremely scarce in relation to the number of TNT or torpex bombs of comparable size which can be produced. To be sure, the bomb is so destructive that even a relatively small number (as compared with other bombs) may prove sufficient to decide a war, especially since there will be no such thing as a "near miss"—anything near will have all the consequences of a direct hit. However, the scarcity is likely to be sufficiently important to dictate the selection of targets and the circumstances under which the missile is hurled.

A rare explosive will not normally be used against targets which are naturally dispersed or easily capable of dispersion, such as ships at sea or isolated industrial plants of no great magnitude. Nor will it be used in types of attack which show an unduly high rate of loss among the attacking instruments—unless, as we have seen, the target is so important as to warrant high ratios of loss provided one or a few missiles penetrate to it. In these respects the effects of scarcity in the explosive materials are intensified by the fact that it requires certain minimum amounts to produce an explosive reaction and that the minimum quantity is not likely to be reduced materially, if at all, by further research.[14]

The ultimate physical limitation on world atomic bomb production is of course the amount of ores available for the derivation of materials capable of spontaneous atomic fission. The only basic material thus far used to produce bombs is uranium, and for the moment only uranium need be considered.

VIII. Regardless of American decisions concerning retention of its present secrets, other powers besides Britain and Canada will possess the ability to produce the bombs in quantity within a period of five to ten years hence.

This proposition by-passes the possibility of effective international regulation of bomb production being adopted within that period. . . . One may anticipate, however, to the extent of pointing out that it is difficult to induce nations like the Soviet Union to accept such regulation until they can start out in a position of parity with the United States in ability to produce the bomb. The State Department Board of Consultants' report of March 16, 1946, acknowledges as much when it states that "acceleration" of the disappearance of our monopoly must be "inherent in the adoption of any plan of international control.". . .

Notes

1. Duncan Sandys, *Report on the Flying Bomb*, pamphlet issued by the British Information Services, September, 1944, p. 9.

2. Accuracy is of course a matter of definition. Lieut. Col. John A. O'Mara of the United States Army considers the V-2 an accurate missile because at 200 miles' range some 1,230 out of the 4,300 launched against England were able to hit the target, "which was the London area." New York *Times,* March 8, 1946, p. 7. In the text [on page 132] the writer is merely using a different base of comparison from the

one Lieut. Col. O'Mara has in mind, namely, the capabilities of the bombing aircraft at any distance within its flying radius.

3. On several occasions the United States Army Air Forces also demonstrated a willingness to sacrifice availability of planes and crews—though not the lives of the latter—in order to carry out specific missions. Thus in the Doolittle raid against Japan of April, 1942, in which sixteen Mitchell bombers took off from the carrier *Hornet,* it was known beforehand that none of the planes would be recovered even if they succeeded in reaching China (which several failed to do for lack of fuel) and that the members of the crews were exposing themselves to uncommon hazard. And the cost of the entire expedition was accepted mainly for the sake of dropping sixteen tons of ordinary bombs! Similarly, several of the Liberators which bombed the Ploesti oil fields in August, 1943, had insufficient fuel to return to their bases in North Africa and, as was foreseen, had to land in neutral Turkey where planes and crews were interned.

4. See New York *Times,* November 21, 1945, p. 1. It should be noticed that the plane had left about 300 gallons, or more than one ton, of gasoline upon landing in Washington. It was of course stripped of all combat equipment (e.g., armor, guns, ammunition, gun-directors, and bomb-sights) in order to allow for a greater gasoline load. Planes bent on a bombing mission would probably have to carry some of this equipment, even if their own survival were not an issue, in order to give greater assurance of their reaching the target.

5. See [p. 132]

6. See President Truman's speech before Congress on the subject of universal military training, reported in the New York *Times,* October 24, 1945, p. 3.

7. Colonel Clarence S. Irvine, who commanded the plane which flew non-stop from Guam to Washington, was reported by the press as declaring that one of the objects of the flight was "to show the vulnerability of our country to enemy air attack from vast distances." New York *Times,* November 21, 1945, p. 1.

8. See printed edition of the *Report,* p. 68. In the sentence following the one quoted, General Arnold adds that this statement is "perhaps true only temporarily," but it is apparent from the context that the factor he has in mind which might terminate its "truthfulness"

is the development of rockets comparable to the V-2 but of much longer range. The present discussion is not concerned with rockets at all.

9. This was due in part to deliberate intention, possibly legal on the Allied side under the principle of retaliation, and in part to a desire of the respective belligerents to maximize the effectiveness of the air forces available to them. "Precision bombing" was always a misnomer, though some selectivity of targets was possible in good weather. However, such weather occurred in Europe considerably less than half the time, and if the strategic air forces were not to be entirely grounded during the remaining time they were obliged to resort to "area bombing." Radar, when used, was far from being an approximate substitute for the human eye.

10. Henry D. Smyth, *Atomic Energy for Military Purposes, The Official Report on the Development of the Atomic Bomb under the Auspices of the United States Government, 1940–1945,* Princeton, Princeton University Press, 1945, paragraphs 12.9–12.22.

11. General Arnold, for example, in his *Third Report to the Secretary of War,* asserted that at present the only effective means of delivering the atomic bomb is the "very heavy bomber." See printed edition, p. 68.

12. One might venture to speculate whether the increase in power which the atomic bomb is reported to have undergone since it was first used is not due to the use of a more massive tamper to produce a more complete reaction. If so, the bomb has been increasing in weight rather than the reverse.

13. J. Robert Oppenheimer, *op. cit.,* p. 9.

14. The figure for critical minimum mass is secret. According to the *Smyth Report,* it was predicted in May, 1941, that the critical mass would be found to lie between 2 kg. and 100 kg. (paragraph 4.49), and it was later found to be much nearer the minimum predicted than the maximum. It is worth noting, too, that not only does the critical mass present a lower limit in bomb size, but also that it is not feasible to use very much more than the critical mass. One reason is the detonating problem. Masses above the critical level cannot be kept from exploding, and detonation is therefore produced by the instantaneous assembly of subcritical masses. The necessity for *instant and simultaneous* assembly of the masses used must obviously limit their number. The scientific explanation of the critical mass condition is presented in the *Smyth Report* in paragraphs 2.3, 2.6, and 2.7. One must always distinguish, however, between the chain reaction which occurs in the plutonium-producing pile and that which occurs in the bomb. Although the general principles determining critical mass are similar for the two reactions, the actual mass needed and the character of the reaction are very different in the two cases. See also *ibid.,* paragraphs 2.35, 4.15–17, and 12.13–15.

Martin Van Creveld

Technology and War

Computerized War

One very important result of the invention of invention . . . is the extraordinary complexity of "modern" warfare as compared to all its predecessors. In part, this complexity simply reflects the growing sophistication of the hardware itself. After all, there is no comparing a modern self-propelled gun with its tens of thousands of precision-made components, to the artillery of 50, or even 15, years ago. However, the complexity of individual pieces of hardware only forms a relatively small part of the problem. Other factors are the momentous variety of equipment used in modern war; the need to back up that equipment with hundreds of thousands, even millions, of different spare parts that often require different kinds of storage facilities and have different expected life spans; the need to train, organize, and cater to the needs of the many classes of specialized personnel who alone are capable of maintaining, repairing, and operating the equipment; and the task of merging both hardware and personnel into integrated teams, capable of surviving on the battlefield and of fulfilling their missions under the tremendous pressures it brings to bear. Since there is a sense in which war has always been war, none of these problems is essentially new. Nor do I claim that they are, except to note that the degree of complexity has increased the difficulties by many orders of magnitude.

To look at the matter from a "cybernetic" point of view, the cardinal result of the invention of invention, and the accelerated pace of technological innovation, was a vast increase in the amount of information needed to "run" any military unit, make any decision, carry out any mission, conduct any operation, campaign, or war. As might be expected, this fact strongly influenced the organization of military headquarters. While Napoleon had still been able to emulate Alexander and concentrate most command functions in his own hands, the middle decades of the nineteenth century saw the emergence of a new institution, the modern general staff. The rise of the general staff is best understood as a direct outcome of the need for more and better data-processing. At the same time, it was itself the cause for further growth.

In 1870, the German General Staff consisted of some 70 officers, few of whom were so specialized that they could not, in a pinch, take over each other's jobs. Less than three decades later the number of officers entitled to wear the coveted crimson stripes had passed the 200 mark, not counting several hundred more who had been detailed to the headquarters of every army, corps, and division. Specialization and professionalization proceeded apace, the simple and flexible structure of 1870 gradually turning into a bureaucratic monster. Since similar developments were taking place in the armies of other countries, it is not surprising that the diaries and memoirs coming out of World War I are riddled with complaints concerning the way in which modern technology was helping turn war into an exercise in management. By 1918, it sometimes seemed that as many forms had to be filled out as shells and bullets were fired at the enemy. . . .

Because the drive towards more and more complex technology continued after 1945, and because the world's most advanced armed forces tended to be at peace during that period, free rein was given to the pressure towards overorganization that is inherent in any bureaucratic structure. As the number of fighting troops generally declined, there was a great increase in the number of services, arms, branches, departments, and military occupation specialities (MOS) into which they were divided. Sheer complexity made it impossible for officers to command as many men as they did previously, with the result that arm for arm, and level for level, the size of military formations generally declined. Everything else being equal, this in turn made for a taller command structure, and so the merry-go-round continued. The most advanced armed forces piled staff upon staff and folder upon folder. The German Bundeswehr—by no means the worst of the lot—offers a perfect example. As compared to the old Wehrmacht, it saw the percentage of *Führungstruppen* (literally "command-troops") increase fivefold between 1945 and 1975.

Thus technology gave birth to complexity, complexity to an extraordinary requirement for information, and the requirement for information to paperwork. The avalanche of paperwork that is threatening the most advanced modern armies would have overwhelmed them long ago had it not been for the introduction of mechanical data-processing equipment. This, again, was hardly an original military development. Instead, its beginnings are usually associated with the name of an American statistician, Herman Hollerith, whose ticker-tape-operated machines were developed from those used in the weaving industry (the Jackard Loom), and intended for use in processing the 1890 national census data. In 1910 one of Hollerith's associates invented the punched card as a means for storing data. Thereupon they incorporated manufacturing and selling, computing, tabulating, and recording equipment. During the period between the wars the use of mechanical calculators, data-processing equipment, and printers gradually spread in the administration of business organizations of every kind, though some organizations proved more resistant than others. By World War II, in the U.S. Army at any rate, their use had become a self-evident necessity. Their ubiquitous presence was captured in Joseph Heller's novel, *Catch-22,* where a character named

Major Major was promoted to Major by an IBM machine with a sense of humor.

Another use to which early calculating and tabulating equipment was put was data processing for the purpose of aeronautical research, pioneered by a German engineer, Konrad Zuse, with his *Z 3* machine built in Berlin in 1941. More exciting was the deciphering of German military radio traffic, a task that was begun by Polish Intelligence and later taken over and developed by the British, who gave it the name of Ultra. At the heart of Ultra was the Bomba, or Bomb, which was an electromechanical calculator capable of operating at speeds much higher than those of any other data-processing device available at the time. It thus permitted the millions of different combinations formed by different settings of the wheels on the German Enigma encoding machine to be run through within a reasonable period of time, usually six to seventy-two hours from the moment the broadcasts were intercepted. Similar machines were employed by U.S. Intelligence. Known under the code name of Magic, they helped crack various Japanese diplomatic and naval codes and thereby contributed greatly to victory in the Pacific war.

Yet another military use of data-processing equipment was in antiaircraft defense work. In this field everything depended on the coordination of radar sets, searchlights, guns, and fighter aircraft, a job that had to be performed rapidly and with great accuracy. Mechanical and electromechanical calculators capable of meeting those requirements were already available, so that it was only natural to harness them for this work. For both sides, but particularly for the Germans, the goal was to construct defenses capable of covering entire countries and even continents. These defenses, comprising many different devices, had to be capable of identifying attacking aircraft, tracking their movements, ascertaining their exact altitude, speed, and bearing, and finally laying the guns in such a way that a shell leaving the muzzle at something close to 1 kilometer a second would accurately hit an enemy aircraft flying at 400 kilometers per hour at several kilometers altitude.

Since the Luftwaffe did not possess much strategic bombing capability after 1941, Allied land-based antiaircraft defenses never grew as sophisticated as their German counterparts. However, much effort went into attempts to defeat the Japanese dive-bombers and torpedo aircraft, a related and, in some ways even more difficult problem since it involved shooting at planes that not only engaged in violent maneuvering but often came in too low for radar to give advance warning. In any event, the conflict came to an end before either side was able to achieve complete integration of all systems or to develop automation very far. However, the steps already taken clearly pointed the way to the future.

The calculating machines built and employed during World War II had two principal disadvantages. First, they included numerous moving mechanical components. This meant complexity, a large size-to-power ratio, and relatively low computing speeds. Second, in so far as they were not able to choose between alternative operations—a capability known as "branching," and already envisaged by Charles Babbage for his analytical Engine of the 1830s—they represented high-power calculators rather than true computers. The first of these problems was solved in 1946 when J. Presper Eckert built ENIAC (Electronic Numerical Integrator and Calculator), thereby doing away with cogwheels and replacing them by electronic circuits, albeit large and clumsy ones. The second problem was solved in 1947 when John von Neumann invented stored programming.

Though the development of the digital computer was now essentially complete, there followed a tremendous number of improvements in detail. In the 1950s, transistor-based machines began replacing their vacuum-tube predecessors. During the sixties, these were in turn replaced by models based on integrated circuits, which kept getting smaller and smaller in size. Progress in software and peripheral equipment has been equally tumultuous, so that the cost of per-byte data processing has been falling by a factor of 10 per decade during each of the last four decades.

Since computers were originally considered rather esoteric, one would expect the field to owe everything to civilians and nothing to the military. Nevertheless, the military, particularly in America, had been involved with computers almost from the beginning, not only as users but also as active consumers who, beginning in World War II, frequently laid down specifications and provided funds for development. Undoubtedly, one important reason behind the love story between brasshats and their computers is the sheer size of armed forces as compared to virtually all other social organizations. If the military was to be administered with anything like the efficiency of other organizations, automation represented the only way. Second and perhaps more important, computers with their binary on-off logic seem to appeal to the military mind. This is because the military, in order to counter the inherent confusion and danger of war, is forever seeking ways to make communications as terse and unambiguous as humanly possible. Computers by their very nature do just that. Had they only been able to stand at attention and salute, in many ways they would have made ideal soldiers.

The affinity between computers and the kind of mind that is cultivated by the armed forces has also been responsible for another phenomenon. Though recent issues of the *Military Review,* and the issues of 40 years ago, are both written in English, the differences between them are striking. Older articles contained a much higher proportion of verbs and adjectives. Recent ones, by contrast seem to consist almost exclusively of nouns. These are often strung together into acronyms, most of which are used to designate machines. . . .

As the military of many countries strove to automate their operations during the 1950s, the first fields to be affected were personnel administration, record keeping, and many aspects of logistics such as requisitioning, and keeping track of spare parts—in brief, the "business of war" which takes place at one remove from the enemy's hostile action. The point of the exercise was to increase cost efficiency, a term which seems to have originated in the big business firms and which now stood for all that was desirable in life. It called for the use of computers to establish constant centralized control, either directly from the Pentagon War Room, or from similar installations around the world, over the exact whereabouts, status, and condition of the last nut and bolt intended for the last tank of the last battalion.

From the administrative aspects of war, the impact of computers spread to communications, where they allowed the replacement of manual and mechanical switchboards by fully automated electronic switchboards for telephones, teleprinters, and other electronic means of data transmission. By 1964, those switchboards had become sufficiently small and reliable for the U.S. Army to pioneer the construction of a fully automatic military communications system in Vietnam, a first-ever innovation. Once integrated, all-electronic, communications networks had become available, the next logical step was to use them to link the computers employed by various parts of the organization, thus permitting human operators to be taken out of the loop to an ever-growing extent. Beginning with the Strategic Air Command, whose World Wide Military Command and Control System (WWMCCS) became operational in 1962, each individual command—navy, marines, ground forces, personnel, matériel, the lot—invested in its own worldwide, integrated, real-time communications system. . . .

Since computers were now capable of receiving data from sources that were hundreds or even thousands of kilometers away, predicting their next success was easy. Beginning in the late sixties, computers were provided with direct links, either through wire or wireless, to a variety of electronic, optical and acoustic sensors such as cameras, television, radar, infrared, and sonar. The purpose of these sensors was to provide up-to-date intelligence by picking up the "signature" left by the opponent's operations, which in practice meant anything from the patrols of his missile-launching submarines to the state of his crops. Sensors in an endless variety of types and sizes could be located on the ground, at sea, in the air or, from 1965 on,

aboard spy satellites that were put on the top of rockets and shot into outer space. By linking them with computers, it was possible for incoming data to be continuously gathered, automatically stored, and held in constant readiness for instant monitor display and printout.

Computers, however, could do more than this. Provided they were fed with the necessary software, there was no reason why they could not classify incoming signals according to predetermined criteria, thus taking over some of the functions previously allotted to intelligence analysts. Furthermore, if a computer was capable of identifying a threat—if, that is, the difference between an American and a Soviet soldier could be formalized—there was no reason why it could not sound the alarm. It would even cause the appropriate weapons to be directed and activated automatically without any need for human interference. Throughout the sixties and the seventies, the automatic battlefield has been the subject of much speculation. Things have not yet proceeded that far, in large part because many potential war environments turned out to be much too complicated to be "understood" even by the best available computer programs.

There were two important exceptions. Complete automation, or something very near it, appeared both practicable and necessary in air warfare where the environment is very simple and speeds very great. The radar-linked, computer-guided missile systems that became operational from the mid-sixties occasionally proved themselves very effective. However, they could also be too effective. The problems associated with automated warfare received an interesting demonstration in the 1973 Arab-Israeli War, when the most advanced air defense system built until that time was activated on the Golan Heights. It defeated, or at any rate helped neutralize, the redoubtable Israeli Air Force, but only at the cost of bringing down dozens of Syrian aircraft as well. The Egyptians, who were operating a similar system over the Suez Canal, fared even worse. Since they rightly feared hitting their own planes, the latter for the most part remained on the ground.

Complete automation could also have been applied to the kind of strategic nuclear warfare associated with land-based missiles. In the late fifties, the construction of a "doomsday machine" had been regarded as technically feasible. Such a machine would identify an enemy attack, and respond by firing warheads at stationary, predetermined targets. However, the risk of a breakdown was considered too great, rightly so if one thinks of the numerous false alarms that have been caused by malfunctioning computer chips and by radar mistaking flocks of geese for enemy missiles. Acting on the assumption that humans possess better judgment than any machine yet built, the United States (and, as far as we know, the USSR as well) have accordingly decided to desist from taking the final step towards automation. The pressing of the firing button has been left to men of flesh and blood who, in order to be on the safe side, always operate in pairs so as to prevent unauthorized action by an individual. As an additional safeguard, they also carry pistols with which to shoot each other in case either one of them should go berserk.

The shining goal which computers, purchased at enormous expense, were supposed to attain was cost effectiveness in administration, communications, intelligence, and ultimately in operations. However, these results were not always achieved in practice. As many horror stories from Vietnam in particular attest, the administrative overcentralization that is always a possible outcome of good communications often led to gross waste and inefficiency, impossibly long reaction times, and a loss of initiative at the lower levels of the military hierarchy. Part of the blame for the frequent failure of automation to achieve many of the claims made on its behalf can be laid on human error, administrative inefficiency, and the incompleteness of the systems themselves (one of the cardinal consequences of the invention of invention is precisely that all systems are necessarily incomplete all of the time). However, the most important causes for failure must be sought on a deeper level. . . .

If present-day computers are to be used at all, it is first of all necessary to model and quan-

tify the fields with which they deal. This explains why the first military domains penetrated by computers have been those which are easiest to quantify, namely personnel administration, logistics, intelligence, and finally the operation of certain weapons in certain environments. However, the process did not stop at this point. As the role of computers grew, this fact itself compelled people to quantify and model war. By so doing, automation helped modify their thinking about it. . . .

Nuclear War

If computers represented one new technology to emerge out of World War II, forever changing the course of history, nuclear energy was another, and militarily it was even more important. Like the majority of man's more esoteric discoveries, the origins of nuclear energy owed little either to war or to men in uniform. The work that started with the discovery of radioactivity by Becquerel in 1896 was carried on by Planck (quantum mechanics) and Einstein (relativity theory) early in the twentieth century. Centering around the University of Goettingen, research into the nature of the atom proceeded during the 1920s. It resulted in many fresh insights, such as the Schroedinger equations and Heisenberg's Uncertainty Law. The first cyclotron, or atom-smashing machine, was built during the thirties. Finally, uranium was artificially split for the first time in a Berlin laboratory in 1938. Though the meaning of this achievement was not immediately grasped even by those who brought it about, it later turned out to be a critical turning point.

Possibly because few people were capable of seeing the atom's practical uses, least of all its military uses, nuclear research before 1939 had been completely open and international. In 1940, this situation came to an abrupt end. As people already noted at the time, this was itself a sure sign that the military was waking up to its significance. The story of what happened next is, again, fairly familiar. If Germany held the lead initially, this was rapidly lost owing to a number of critical scientific errors, combined with a failure of vision on the part of the German military, industry, and government. The American government and military, too, had to be prodded by Leo Szilard and Albert Einstein before they agreed to go into atomic energy research. Once the decision to do so had been made in 1941, however, there was mounted a scientific and industrial effort that was far beyond the resources of any other country at the time. If only because it alone could afford the tremendous duplication and waste associated with any crash program, the United States was able to build the first bombs. These were dropped on Hiroshima and Nagasaki in August 1945.

Early reactions to the appearance of the bomb were, as might be expected, marked by considerable confusion aggravated by the fact that, right from the beginning, every kind of institutional interest was mixed up in the debate. On one extreme were those who insisted that nuclear weapons, though undoubtedly very powerful, were basically no different from any others; hence, that the fundamentals of war and of warmaking potential would not be affected by them to any considerable extent. On the other hand, as early as 1945 there emerged a school of thought that tended to regard nuclear weapons not only as unprecedentedly powerful, but as qualitatively different from any of their predecessors. It was argued then, and still is often argued today, that there can be no effective defense against these weapons. Consequently, their only rational use— if that indeed is the right word—would be for the purpose of deterrence and preventing war.

Looking back at the debate with the benefit of hindsight, a strong case can be made that both sides were right. So long as they were relatively scarce, but assuming both sides had them, nuclear weapons would greatly increase the destructiveness of military conflict without, however, altering its fundamental nature. Indeed, the failure of the United States to derive any critical benefits from its four-year monopoly over these weapons suggests that, provided the gap in other resources was not completely unbridgeable, war would not even change its nature if the bomb were possessed by one side only. Had the United States heeded the advice of extremists and used its relatively small stockpile of atomic weapons to bomb the Soviet Union in 1945–49, no doubt the latter country would have suffered horrendously. However, assuming she would not have been brought to her knees, the war would have been derided by the balance of both countries' overall resources, and here the advantages were by no means all on one side.

On the other extreme, assume a situation in which one side (or each side) possesses enough bombs to completely and instantaneously destroy the other, regardless of any defensive measures that the latter might take. In that case victory would go to the side that was the first to strike, though in the absence of a defense there could hardly be a question of war properly speaking. Next, assume that each side is unable to prevent his own destruction by an enemy first strike, but is fully capable of destroying him even after absorbing such a strike. In that case, the use of nuclear weapons to achieve "complete" victory will have the effect not only of revolutionizing war but of turning it into an unprecedentedly effective form of suicide.

Thus, the bomb could be used in war only if its power to destroy were not absolute but either limited or capable of being resisted. If its power were absolute, then there would be no war, though a one-sided act of destruction might still take place. Almost incidentally, the old truth that any weapon can be countered is thereby stood on its head. In a situation where two opponents have enough nuclear weapons to destroy each other, these weapons will be useful *only* if they are capable of being countered in one way or another. . . .

To look at the question from another angle, it is clear that the weapons, their delivery vehicles, and the defenses that may be built against them—in brief, technology—only comprise a fairly small part of the nuclear equation. Compared to the remaining parts of the equation, however, the technological considerations involved are relatively simple, a fact which turns it into a suitable starting point for thought. To proceed in chronological order, the construction and dropping of the first atomic bombs was followed first by their proliferation in the hands of the United States and then in the hands of other countries as well. Many of these bombs had much greater yields than the original ones, but a real breakthrough in this field was only achieved in 1952 when the first hydrogen device was exploded. Unlike their atomic predecessors, hydrogen bombs are based on fusion rather than fission processes. This means that, provided one is prepared to pay the price in size and weight, their yield is essentially unlimited. Theoretically, and probably in practice as well, it was possible to build a weapon sufficiently powerful to annihilate a small country in a single blow, although the construction of a bomb large enough to do the same to a medium-sized nation seems unfeasible (or undesirable) at present.

In any case, it was only during the early years that designers and engineers concentrated on maximizing yield. Since at least the explosion of the first hydrogen device, greater efforts have gone into three directions. First, successful attempts were made to produce low-yield weapons which could be used selectively (in the vicinity of one's own troops, for example) and without necessarily unleashing the full fury of the enemy's reaction. Second, development focused on maximizing some of the effects of nuclear weapons, such as blast, while minimizing others such as radiation. These attempts have also been successful to the point where bombs, like ice cream, can be had in a variety of sizes and flavored to the user's tastes. Third and technologically most difficult, bombs have been progressively miniaturized. Understandably, the data on this subject are among the most classified of all. Nevertheless it is known that, if the original bomb dropped on Hiroshima weighed some 10 tons and had a yield of under 20 kilotons, devices can now be made weighing under 500 kilograms and yielding perhaps 200 kilotons.

At the time of their first appearance, the size and bulk of nuclear weapons made them capable of being carried only by heavy bombers. Their miniaturization since then has made them deliverable by many different vehicles, including fighter-bombers, missiles, cruise missiles, artillery shells and—one shudders to think—even by an ordinary car or van. Over time, the various delivery vehicles in use by armed forces around the world have tended to become not only smaller but much more accurate. This in turn made possible further reductions in yield, until the smallest weapons now deployed probably have an explosive force equivalent to perhaps one or two kilotons or even less. Even so, a weapon of this size is an awesome thing. By comparison, the so called blockbusters of World War II fame only contained 10 tons of TNT.

Traditionally, the most important way in which countries defended themselves against bombing attacks was by whittling down the other side's bomber force. However, since many an individual nuclear weapon is quite capable of reducing an entire city to ashes, it was clear that attrition rates much higher than any attained in World War II would be required if the defense was not to be altogether hopeless. During the decade and a half after 1945, early-warning and antiaircraft defense systems improved very greatly and were extended to the point that they covered entire hemispheres. Nevertheless, no side felt so confident of its ability to escape destruction as to risk an all-or-nothing confrontation. During this period, too, the difficulties of the defense were multiplied by the introduction of numerous new vehicles, each possessing different characteristics, and capable of delivering warheads to their targets. Particularly when intercontinental ballistic missiles, or ICBMs, reached operational status in the early sixties, the problem of defending a country against total destruction began to look insoluble.

Depending on one's understanding of nuclear devices either as more powerful versions of ordinary weapons or as completely different and revolutionary ones, this perceived vulnerability to nuclear destruction would lead to either of two different conclusions. The first, especially prevalent in the Soviet Union where military policy tends to be made by the military, was that war if it came would have to open with a crippling first strike against the other side's nuclear weapons and delivery vehicles. The second, more congenial to the United States (which allows civilians a greater role in formulating military policy), was that the most powerful "strategic" nuclear warheads at any rate should never be used except for the purpose of deterrence which, to be on the safe side, had to be reinforced by all possible means. Thus, a given way of thought when combined with an institutional interest led one side to concentrate on constructing a first-strike war-fighting capability which would be activated if war came. Following a different logic, and reflecting a rather different institutional setup, the other side concentrated on establishing a second-strike force which, by threatening instant and overwhelming retaliation, would hopefully prevent war from taking place at all. The distinction between the two views is subtle, but important when it comes to force-structure and consequently to technological choices and the allocation of resources.

If a country's purpose is to be capable of fighting a war, the means for doing so have to be safeguarded against the worst the enemy can do. If the aim is to prevent war by deterrence, then too a force is required that is capable of surviving the worst that the enemy might do, and still inflicting "unacceptable" damage. Either way, it is necessary to set up on the ground, or launch into space, an immensely complicated array of electronic systems, whose task is to offer round-the-clock surveillance, real-time early warning (at the speed ballistic missiles travel, even real-time warning cannot offer more than half an hour's breathing space), and hardened command and control facilities capable of sending one's own delivery vehicles on their way. The vehicles themselves have to be physically protected against a possible disarming first strike by the enemy, a protection that might take any of a number of forms. At its simplest, all that is necessary is to multiply their number and keep them well dispersed. Next, the vehicles in question can be made more difficult to hit by shifting them from one place to

another, putting them on permanent airborne patrol, mounting them in superhardened underground silos, hiding them under the surface of the sea, or using any number of even more esoteric techniques. Given a will and sufficient resources, and disparate military services each clamoring for possession of its own nuclear delivery vehicles, there is nothing to prevent all these methods from being applied at once. If no individual method is capable of offering an acceptable degree of security, several of them together probably can. If it is not possible to protect all one's delivery vehicles, it is certainly possible to protect enough of them to kill the enemy not once but many times over.

Thus security, interpreted in somewhat different ways on each side of the Iron Curtain, was the slogan in the name of which the decision-makers of the 1960s went to work. It was a task in which they were remarkably successful, producing as they did a system which, in its main outline, has lasted to the present day. However, seen from a different perspective the outcome has been that both superpowers enjoy less, rather than more, security than ever before. This is because peace was bought at the expense of instituting a modern sword of Damocles. Taking the form of many tens of thousands of megatons, the sword was hung above the rivals (and much of the remaining world as well) and could come crashing down at any moment. Furthermore, as nuclear weapons became more numerous and were put into the hands of different states and organizations, the risk of an accidental or unauthorised release was probably increased. The United States, and presumably the Soviet Union as well, has taken numerous and infinitely complex precautions to prevent this from happening. Some precautions, in the form of "hot" or "red" lines linking the national command centers, have also been taken to minimize the damage if it does happen. Nevertheless, at the moment of writing, a nuclear war triggered off by an accident or misunderstanding remains a possibility which, however remote, need happen just once for civilization as we know it to come to an end.

Given the law of averages, which modern science tells us governs all seemingly random events, one might argue that such a possibility is bound to arise sooner or later.

The possibility that nuclear war, whatever its origin, would literally mean the end of the world led to yet another outcome. If only because neither side was completely immune to the pressure of domestic and international opinion, and because both sought to impose some limits on the other's forces, the years since 1958 have been characterized by almost continuous talks aimed at various sorts of arms limitations. These efforts have brought some results, as may be seen from the Nuclear Test Ban Treaty, the Nonproliferation Treaty, SALT (Strategic Arms Limitation Treaties) I and II (the latter unsigned, but more or less observed by both sides), and the recent agreement limiting medium-range missiles in Europe. The most important treaties have put limits on the size of the superpowers' nuclear arsenals and also on the kinds of weapons and delivery vehicles that could be deployed. In the United States, critics of the treaties have argued that they tend to freeze some of the advantages in the number and power of delivery vehicles that the Soviets are believed to have enjoyed since the early seventies. Supporters, on the other hand, emphasize that the treaties only refer to existing weapons and therefore tend to work in favor of the technologically innovative side. Both arguments are probably correct.

Complicated as it is, the SALT I Treaty reflects the technology of the sixties. At that time it was widely felt, that each side's force of missiles, whether ground- or submarine-launched, was invulnerable to a first strike, hence that mutual deterrence—sometimes referred to as MAD, or Mutual Assured Destruction—was securely established. The ink on the treaty had scarcely dried, however, when further technological advances began to undermine this belief. The most important single development took the form of ballistic missiles carrying multiple independent reentry vehicles, or MIRV. Entering operational service in the early seventies, MIRV contradicted SALT I

and the assumptions on which it was based in two ways. First, the new warheads were sufficiently accurate to knock out not only cities and industries but missiles in their silos. Second, the sheer number of reentry vehicles mounted on top of each missile now made it possible to knock out several enemy missiles by using just one, thus eliminating the enemy's missiles and still retain a large number of one's own ready for use. The combination of great accuracy and an exchange ratio unfavorable to the defense was perceived to endanger the survivability of second strike forces, or at least those parts of them that were land-based. This was known as the window of vulnerability.

The second technological development that threatened each side's force of ICBMs was the introduction of the cruise missile. First developed by the Germans during World War II, cruise missiles were subsequently experimented with by the armed forces of various nations, but for a long time were not perceived to offer any special advantages as compared to manned bombers and ICBMs. During the seventies, however, the simultaneous maturing of several new technologies made it possible to build small, pilotless craft powered by miniature jet engines and capable of carrying a payload over ranges of up to 2,000 km. Unlike many present-day manned bombers, modern cruise missiles are capable of flying so low over the ground as to be detectable only by immensely complex, immensely expensive airborne detection systems. Unlike ICBMs, they do not rely on inertial guidance but are guided to their targets by a system known as TERCOM (Terrain Contour Matching) which consists essentially of a radar scanning the area overflown and comparing it to a digital map stored in an onboard computer memory. Like the MIRVed ICBM, cruise missiles are exceedingly accurate. Like the MIRVed ICBM, too, this accuracy should permit them to destroy missiles in their silos.

As is almost always the case when a new technology arises, reactions to it were mixed. In the eyes of some, the capability for knocking out missiles in their silos and thus of eliminating one side's deterrent forces (even if it were only the land-based deterrent forces that were being threatened) appeared so awesome that they wished to turn the clock back and revert to the "one missile, one warhead" technology of the sixties. Others, perhaps more realistically, emphasized that cruise missiles in particular may actually strengthen deterrence. This is because these weapons, being small and provided with their own guidance system, are capable of being launched not just from stationary silos but also from ground vehicles, aircraft, ships, and even the torpedo tubes of submerged submarines. This makes them difficult to find, and hence invulnerable to a disarming first strike. Furthermore, cruise missiles sufficiently accurate to hit missile-silos should also be capable of scoring a bull's eye on individual command centers. This prospect, it is argued, presents decision makers at all levels with the strongest possible incentive to refrain from going to war because, in that case, they themselves will be the first to be vaporized.

The basic assumption on which MAD rests—namely, that in an age of nuclear abundance no means in the world can save a country's population and industry from being wiped out by a determined adversary, and that this is a good thing because stability will result—this assumption itself has its critics. Attempts to build anti-ballistic missile defenses were undertaken by both superpowers during the late sixties but, particularly in the face of the rise of MIRV, appeared sufficiently unpromising for a ceiling to be put on them by SALT I. A decade later, however, the prospect arose of one day defeating ICBMs with the aid of much more sophisticated technology that has been appropriately dubbed "Star Wars." If it is ever built, a ballistic missile defense system (BMD) will be based either on earth or in space aboard satellites. It will consist of an immensely complex array of sensors and computers, whose task will be to identify missiles after launch, distinguish them from decoys, and track them. This accomplished, the missiles will be destroyed by firing lasers, beams of charged particles, or so-called rail-guns which are devices for firing minuscule pellets of metal at velocities far in excess

of anything attainable by ordinary guns. Any missiles that get through, or else the warheads which they release, will be engaged by earth-based guided missiles now under development.

The merits of building a ballistic missile defense system are very such in dispute. Advocates claim that, in a crisis, even a partial ballistic missile defense will be better than none and that the side possessing such a defense will accordingly be in a better position to raise the stakes ("achieve escalation dominance," is the technical term for this) in a game of nuclear blackmail. Opponents reply that such a defense probably cannot be made to work. Even if it can, its effectiveness against a well-coordinated first strike will be marginal. At most, so the argument goes, the defense may be effective against a "ragged" second strike; however, it is precisely here that the danger lies, for a defense that puts the Soviet Union's retaliatory capability in doubt might compel that country to adopt the first strike strategy that the United States fears most. The debate, consisting of an endless series of arguments and counterarguments none of which can really be "proved," goes on. . . .

Since agreement is lacking on the conceptual level—it is not even clear whether the Strategic Defense Initiative (SDI) is intended to protect America's cities or her missile sites alone—BMD at present appears to share the fate of many past military technological innovations. These, precisely because they were so new, were driven less by any clear idea as to their usefulness or even desirability than by the foibles of the powers that be. To give the matter an additional twist, those powers are said to be engaged in a deliberate attempt to create institutional support for the program by sinking tremendous resources into research and development. However, neither the size of the enterprise nor the excellence of the scientific research which it involves are in themselves sufficient to guarantee its ultimate usefulness. Even if a BMD system is built and is successful, or indeed particularly if this should happen, the other superpower will not be far behind. Ways of defeating SDI are, as a matter of fact, not difficult to think of: among numerous other possibilities, many more missiles might be built to swamp the system, or the boost phase in which missiles are particularly vulnerable might be reduced by introducing new fuels, or else that phase can be eliminated altogether by placing warheads permanently in orbit. As these examples show, there is no reason to think that the Soviet reaction will necessarily be symmetrical to, or as expensive as, the American challenge.

Almost from the day of their inception, nuclear weapons were regarded in two distinct ways. On one side were those who regarded them as qualitatively different and, therefore, as too terrible to use for any purpose except deterrence pure and simple. On the other, there were those who conceived them as fundamentally similar to, if much more powerful than, all previous weapons. Over the last 40 years, and in spite of repeated warnings that some novel technology just around the corner was about to change everything, by and large the former view seems to have prevailed. The result has been that no nuclear weapons have been used since Nagasaki and that the world has greatly benefited from what appears to be a fairly stable balance of terror. Though not excluding crises, some of them nerve-wracking to participants and spectators whose fate depended on issues about which they knew little and cared even less, this balance has at any rate kept the nuclear powers from going at each other's vitals.

The threatening presence of nuclear weapons thus seems to have contributed to the rise of a form of strategic stability which, though certainly capable of being disrupted at any moment, looks real enough to most people. Precisely because it does, however, decision-makers have been wondering how far they—and, of course, the other side—can go without upsetting it; and, specifically, whether the balance of terror necessarily precluded the use of *any* nuclear weapons under *any* kind of circumstances. The question was largely academic so long as bombs were huge and strategic delivery systems scarcely capable of hitting anything smaller than cities. Since the mid-sixties, however, the growing accuracy of delivery vehicles has permitted much smaller warheads to be fielded, with the result that the problem has been put at the very center of strategic thought. In the United States, and to a lesser extent in the USSR as well, it has led to much talk of "flexible options" and "surgical strikes," neither of which are anything but euphemisms for nuclear attacks against "limited" targets. The underlying idea is that, by destroying no more than a few million people out of a superpower's population, such attacks will hopefully not provoke the injured party to retaliate with all his might. Of all the debates that have been called forth by the prevailing nuclear equilibrium, this one is in some ways the furthest removed from reality, which is not to say that it is also the least dangerous.

Geoffrey E. Forden

World War III? Now?

Cambridge, Mass. Now that decisions on deploying a missile defense system will be put off until at least early next year, it's time to deal with a less sweeping but more immediate life-and-death issue: the crumbling of satellites that can prevent accidental launches of Russia's nuclear weapons.

For a picture of what these satellites are intended to do, consider a famous near-disaster on the American side in 1979. A training tape simulating a massive Soviet nuclear attack was accidentally run on the computers of the North American Aerospace Defense Command. Everyone thought it was real, and crews prepared to launch American missiles in retaliation. What stopped them were our early-warning satellites, which showed there were no Soviet missiles in the air.

On at least two other occasions, once each in the United States and Russia, space-based sensors played the same lifesaving role after other systems sent mistaken warnings.

Russia and the United States still have thousands of missiles ready to launch at each other on a few minutes' notice. American leaders still have satellite warning systems to prevent accidental launches when other systems give false warnings. But most of Russia's early-warning satellites have stopped functioning or wandered out of their assigned orbits.

In 1995, when the Russian system was still in good repair, some Russian military people misinterpreted a NASA research rocket as an attack designed to blind their radars to incoming American missiles. Fortunately, their satellite warning system, still providing 24-hour space-based surveillance of American missile fields, showed them they were wrong.

Satellites and sensing devices are expensive and technically complex, and they need regular maintenance and replacement. Russian factories that produced the parts have closed, and scientists who know how to work with the systems have been forced to seek other jobs. Clearly, it's in the American interest to step in.

The United States should immediately spend about $160 million to get five Russian early-warning satellites—ready to go but languishing on the ground—into space. Next, we should make a firm commitment to financing joint research with Russia into new, less costly satellite missile sensors that Russia could more easily afford. The Clinton administration has tied its backing to demands for Russian concessions on missile defense.

Getting Russian satellites functioning would be far more effective than a joint early-warning center in Moscow that was also proposed by the Clinton administration. At this center, American and Russian military personnel would sit side by side, looking at computer screens displaying the data from their own early-warning systems but free to look over each other's shoulders. If Russia suspected the United States was launching a missile attack, would its leaders really believe American computer screens that did not show it?

Regardless of whether a missile defense is eventually approved, the relatively inexpensive safety systems needed to prevent a mistaken attack from Russia's still powerful missile force cannot be allowed to fail.

Anthony Cordesman

Chemical Weapons as Means of Attack

Chemical weapons have not been used effectively in attacks on the American homeland. Reports that the bombers of the World Trade Center [February 26, 1996] considered trying to add a chemical weapon like sodium cyanide to their explosives seem to be untrue, and led to an unsubstantiated assertion by the trial judge. There have, however, been a number of attempts to use chemical weapons by domestic extremists and individuals. For example, in 1997, members of the KKK plotted to place an improvised explosive device on a hydrogen sulfide tank at a refinery near Dallas, Texas. There is a well-established, low-level risk that such weapons will be used in the future, although there is no way to predict the frequency of such attacks, their scale, potential success, or lethality.

There are a wide range of countries involved in the development of chemical weapons. Table 28.1 provides a recent unclassified US intelligence summary [of] chemical weapons activities by nation. It is only a partial list. The US intelligence community is tracking a total of approximately 25 nations which are believed to be carrying out some form of state-sponsored chemical and/or biological weapons development. As has been discussed earlier, at least two foreign terrorist groups are also believed to have active chemical and biological weapons efforts.

The Impact and Variety of Possible Chemical Weapons

Experts like the Center for Disease Control have found that the US may face a wide range of threats from different types of chemical weapons and toxic agents, many of which are not normally considered to be weapons. A CDC study notes that the chemical agents that might be used by terrorists range from sophisticated military agents to toxic chemicals commonly used in industry. The criteria the CDC suggested for determining priority chemical agents include:

- chemical agents already known to be used as weaponry;
- availability of chemical agents to potential terrorists;
- chemical agents likely to cause major morbidity or mortality;
- potential of agents for causing public panic and social disruption; and
- agents that require special action for public health preparedness.

The CDC lists several categories of chemical agents as presenting enough of a threat to require active public health planning. These include nerve agents, such as tabun (ethyl N, N-dimethylphosphoramidocyanidate), Sarin (isopropyl methylphosphanofluoridate), soman (pinacolyl methyl phosphonofluoridate), GF (cyclohexylmethylphosphonofluoridate), and VX (o-ethyl-[S]-[2-diisopropylaminoethyl]-methylphosphonothiolate). They include blood agents such as hydrogen cyanide and cyanogen chloride; and blister agents such as lewisite (an aliphatic arsenic compound, 2-chlorovinyldichloroarsine), nitrogen and sulfur mustards, and phosgene oxime. And, they include pulmonary agents like phosgene, chlorine, and vinyl chloride; and incapacitating agents like BZ (3-quinuclidinyl benzilate).

Other agents on the CDC's list are more commercial in character. They include heavy metals like arsenic, lead, and mercury; and

■ **TABLE 28.1**
US Department of Defense Estimate of Potential National
Threats Intentions Involving Chemical Weapons

China

Beijing is believed to have an advanced chemical warfare program including research and development, production, and weaponization capabilities. China's chemical industry has the capability to produce many chemicals, some of which have been sought by states trying to develop a chemical warfare capability. Foreign sales of such chemicals have been a source of foreign exchange for China. The Chinese government has imposed restrictions on the sale of some chemical precursors and its enforcement activities generally have yielded mixed results. While China claims it possesses no chemical agent inventory, it is believed to possess a moderate inventory of traditional agents. It has a wide variety of potential delivery systems for chemical agents, including cannon artillery, multiple rocket launchers, mortars, land mines, aerial bombs, SRBMs, and MRBMs.

Chinese military forces most likely have a good understanding of chemical warfare doctrine, and its forces routinely conduct defensive chemical warfare training. Even though China has ratified the CWC, made its declaration, and subjected its declared chemical weapons facilities to inspections, we believe that Beijing has not acknowledged the full extent of its chemical weapons program.

India

India is an original signatory to the CWC. In June 1997, it acknowledged that it had a dedicated chemical warfare production program. This was the first time India had publicly admitted that it had a chemical warfare effort. India also stated that all related facilities would be open for inspection, as called for in the CWC, and subsequently, it has hosted all required CWC inspections. While India has made a commitment to destroy its chemical weapons, its extensive and well-developed chemical industry will continue to be capable of producing a wide variety of chemical agent pre-cursors should the government change its policy. In the past, Indian firms have exported a wide array of chemical products, including Australia Group-controlled items, to several countries of proliferation concern in the Middle East. (Australia Group-controlled items include specific chemical agent precursors, microorganisms with biological warfare applications, and dual-use equipment that can be used in chemical or biological warfare programs.) Indian companies could continue to be a source of dual-use chemicals to countries of proliferation concern.

Iran

Iran has acceded to the Chemical Weapons Convention (CWC) and in a May 1998 session of the CWC Conference of the States Parties, Tehran, for the first time, acknowledged the existence of a past chemical weapons program. Iran admitted developing a chemical warfare program during the latter stages of the Iran-Iraq War as a "deterrent" against Iraq's use of chemical agents against Iran. Moreover, Tehran claimed that after the 1988 cease-fire, it "terminated" its program. However, Iran has yet to acknowledge that it, too, used chemical weapons during the Iran-Iraq War.

Nevertheless, Iran has continued its efforts to seek production technology, expertise and precursor chemicals from entities in Russia and China that could be used to create a more advanced and self-sufficient chemical warfare infrastructure. As Iran's program moves closer to self-sufficiency, the

(continued)

potential will increase for Iran to export dual-use chemicals and related equipment and technologies to other countries of proliferation concern. In the past, Tehran has manufactured and stockpiled blister, blood and choking chemical agents, and weaponized some of these agents into artillery shells, mortars, rockets, and aerial bombs. It also is believed to be conducting research on nerve agents. Iran could employ these agents during a future conflict in the region. Lastly, Iran's training, especially for its naval and ground forces, indicates that it is planning to operate in a contaminated environment.

Iraq

Since the Gulf War, Baghdad has rebuilt key portions of its industrial and chemical production infrastructure; it has not become a state party to the CWC. Some of Iraq's facilities could be converted fairly quickly to production of chemical warfare agents. Following Operation Desert Fox, Baghdad again instituted a rapid reconstruction effort on those facilities to include former dual-use chemical warfare-associated production facilities, destroyed by U.S. bombing. In 1999, Iraq may have begun installing or repairing dual-use equipment at these and other chemical warfare-related facilities. Previously, Iraq was known to have produced and stockpiled mustard, tabun, sarin, and VX, some of which likely remain hidden. It is likely that an additional quantity of various precursor chemicals also remains hidden.

In late 1998, UNSCOM reported to the UN Security Council that Iraq continued to withhold information related to its chemical program. UNSCOM cited an example where Baghdad seized from inspectors a document discovered by UNSCOM inspectors, which indicated that Iraq had not consumed as many chemical munitions during the Iran-Iraq War as had been declared previously by Baghdad. This document suggests that Iraq may have an additional 6,000 chemical munitions hidden. Similarly, UNSCOM discovery in 1998 of evidence of VX in Iraqi missile warheads showed that Iraq had lied to the international community for seven years when it repeatedly said that it had never weaponized VX.

Iraq retains the expertise, once a decision is made, to resume chemical agent production within a few weeks or months, depending on the type of agent. However, foreign assistance, whether commercial procurement of dual-use technology, key infrastructure, or other aid, will be necessary to completely restore Iraq's chemical agent production capabilities to pre-Desert Storm levels. Iraqi doctrine for the use of chemical weapons evolved during the Iran-Iraq War, and was fully incorporated into Iraqi offensive operations by the end of the war in 1988. During different stages of that war, Iraq used aerial bombs, artillery, rocket launchers, tactical rockets, and sprayers mounted in helicopters to deliver agents against Iranian forces. It also used chemical agents against Kurdish elements of its own civilian population in 1988.

Libya

Libya has made progress with its chemical warfare effort. However, it remains heavily dependent on foreign suppliers for precursor chemicals, mechanical and technical expertise, and chemical warfare-related equipment. From 1992 to 1999, UN sanctions continued to limit the type and amount of support Tripoli receives from abroad. However, following the suspension of UN sanctions in April 1999, Libya wasted no time in reestablishing contacts with foreign sources of expertise, parts, and precursor chemicals for its program. Clearly, Tripoli has not given up its goal of reestablishing its offensive chemical warfare ability and continues to pursue an indigenous chemical warfare production capability.

Prior to 1990, Libya produced about 100 tons of chemical agents—mustard and some nerve agent—at a chemical facility at Rabta. However, it ceased production there in 1990 due to intense international media attention and the possibility of military intervention, and fabricated a fire to make the Rabta facility appear to have been seriously damaged. Libya maintains that the facility is a pharmaceutical production plant and announced in September 1995 that it was reopening the Rabta pharmaceutical facility. Although production of chemical agents has been halted, the Rabta facility remains part of the Libyan chemical weapons program, and future agent production cannot be ruled out. After 1990, the Libyans shifted their efforts to trying to build a large underground chemical production facility at Tarhunah. However, the pace of activity there has slowed, probably due to increased international attention. The Libyans claim that the Tarhunah tunnel site is a part of the Great Man-made River Project, a nationwide irrigation effort. Libya has not become a state party to the CWC.

North Korea

Like its biological warfare effort, we believe North Korea has had a long-standing chemical warfare program. North Korea's chemical warfare capabilities include the ability to produce bulk quantities of nerve, blister, choking, and blood agents, using its sizeable, although aging, chemical industry. We believe it possesses a sizeable stockpile of these agents and weapons, which it could employ should there be renewed fighting on the Korean peninsula.

North Korea is believed to be capable of weaponizing such stocks for a variety of delivery means. These would include not only ballistic missiles, but also artillery and aircraft, and possibly unconventional means. In fact, the United States believes that North Korea has some long-range artillery deployed along the demilitarized zone (DMZ) and ballistic missiles, some of which could deliver chemical warfare agents against forward-based U.S. and allied forces, as well as against rear-area targets. North Korean forces are prepared to operate in a contaminated environment; they train regularly in chemical defense operations and are taught that South Korean and U.S. forces will employ chemical munitions. North Korea has not signed CWC, nor it is expected to do so in the near future.

Pakistan

Pakistan ratified the CWC in October 1997 and did not declare any chemical agent production or development. Pakistan has imported a number of dual-use chemicals that can be used to make chemical agents. These chemicals also have commercial uses and Pakistan is working towards establishing a viable commercial chemical industry capable of producing a variety of chemicals, some of which could be used to make chemical agents. Chemical agent delivery methods available to Pakistan include missiles, artillery, and aerial bombs.

Russia

Moscow has acknowledged the world's largest stock pile of chemical agents of 40,000 metric tons of agent. The Russian chemical warfare agent inventory consists of a comprehensive array of blister, choking, and nerve agents in weapons and stored in bulk. These agents can be employed by tube and rocket artillery, bombs, spray tanks, and SRBM warheads. In addition, since 1992, Russian scientists familiar with Moscow's chemical warfare development program have been

(continued)

■ **T A B L E   2 8 . 1**   (continued)

publicizing information on a new generation of agents, sometimes referred to as "Novichoks." These scientists report that these compounds, some of which are binaries, were designed to circumvent the CWC and to defeat Western detection and protection measures. Furthermore, it is claimed that their production can be hidden within commercial chemical plants. There is concern that the technology to produce these compounds might be acquired by other countries.

As a state party to the CWC, Russia is obligated to declare and destroy its chemical weapons stockpile and to forego the development, production, and possession of chemical weapons. However, we believe that the Russians probably have not divulged the full extent of their chemical agent and weapon inventory. Destruction facilities are being planned at Shchuch'ye and Gornyy, two of the seven declared storage locations for the Russian chemical warfare stockpile; these efforts are being funded in large part by foreign assistance programs.

Nevertheless, Russia admitted it could not meet its first obligation to destroy one percent of its stockpile by April 2000. Subsequently, the Organization for the Prohibition of Chemical Weapons (OPCW) granted Russia an extension until April 2002, but with the stipulation that it must also meet 20 percent destruction deadline by the same date, as called for under the CWC. However, international experts agree that it will be extremely difficult for Russia to destroy its huge chemical arsenal by 2007 as mandated by the CWC. Even if Russia were to be granted a five-year extension by the OPCW, it is unlikely that Russia's declared stockpile will be completely destroyed because of serious technical, ecological, financial, and political problems.

Syria

Syria is not a state party to the CWC and has had a chemical warfare program for many years, although it has never used chemical agents in a conflict. Damascus already has a stockpile of the nerve agent sarin that can be delivered by aircraft or ballistic missiles. Additionally, Syria is trying to develop the more toxic and persistent nerve agent VX. In the future, Syria can be expected to continue to improve its chemical agent production and storage infrastructure. Damascus remains dependent on foreign sources for key elements of its chemical warfare program, including precursor chemicals and key production equipment. For example, during 1999, Syria sought chemical warfare-related precursors and expertise from foreign sources.

Sudan

Sudan has been interested in acquiring a chemical warfare capability since the 1980s and has sought assistance from a number of countries with chemical warfare programs. We believe that Iraq, in particular, has provided technical expertise to Khartoum. In addition, the finding of a known VX precursor chemical near a pharmaceutical facility in Khartoum suggests that Sudan may be pursuing a more advanced chemical warfare capability. Sudan acceded to the CWC in 1999, although allegations of Sudanese chemical warfare use against rebels in southern Sudan have persisted. These, and prior allegations of chemical warfare use, have not been confirmed. Further, Khartoum's desire to present a more moderate image and alleviate its international isolation will cause Sudan to proceed with its chemical warfare program with caution.

Source: Adapted by Anthony H. Cordesman from Department of Defense, *Proliferation and Response,* January 2001

volatile toxins like benzene, chloroform, and tri-halomethanes. Other agents include explosive nitro compounds and oxidizers, such as ammonium nitrate combined with fuel oil. They include pulmonary agents like phosgene, chlorine, and vinyl chloride; persistent and nonpersistent pesticides; and dioxins, furans, and polychlorinated biphenyls (PCBs). They include flammable industrial gases and liquids like gasoline, propane; and poison industrial gases, liquids, and solids, like the cyanides, and nitriles. Finally, they include corrosive industrial acids and bases like nitric and sulfuric acid.

Many of the items the CDC list are widely available on the US market and include commercial organo-phospates and parathion, and the military lists of possible agents is much longer and includes additional toxic smokes, herbicides, flame materials, and toxic industrial compounds. As a result, it is hardly surprising that CDC studies also note that there as no way to predict precisely what chemicals might be used, particularly in low level attacks. . . .

The Probable Lethality and Effectiveness of Chemical Attacks

Just as it is easy to underestimate the importance of conventional explosives, it is easy to exaggerate the lethality of most chemical weapons. Many forms of lower level attacks using chemical weapons might do no more or less damage than attacks using conventional weapons. For example, the World Trade Center bombing (in 1993) killed six and injured over 1,000, and could easily have killed hundreds if the bomb had been better placed. Large high explosive weapons can easily be equal to both chemical and radiological weapons as "weapons of mass destruction."

It is also an illusion that the effects of chemical weapons are always radically worse or more repellant than the damage done by conventional weapons. No one who has actually visited a battlefield and seen anyone with a fragmentation wound in the stomach and then seen a prisoner affected by a moderate dose of mustard gas is going to accept for a second that one casualty is somehow worse than another. . . .

Military estimates of lethality also generally assume prompt medical action and some assume rapid decontamination or evacuation of the area. Response can fail or be ineffective if it is not properly organized. Chemical weapons can have lingering effects as poisons, and act as contact or food poisons for days after they cease to be effective as mass agents. BVX, HD, HN, L, and HL are all persistent agents that can remain lethal for weeks. Effective and timely decontamination could well be impossible. Casualty recognition can be difficult with some weapons, where there is either a psychomimetic agent or a quiescent period in terms of symptoms. In some cases, the use of antidotes like Atropine could create medical problems of their own. In others, severe exposure can require up to a week of intensive treatment for nerve gas, and months to years for inhaled blistering agents. . . .

The Aum Shinrikyo Case Study

Aum Shinrikyo makes an interesting case study of what a terrorist organization can do. It is somewhat misleading for GAO to state that Aum Shinrikyo did not cause more deaths "despite substantial financial assets, well-equipped laboratories, and educated scientists working in the laboratories . . . because of the poor quality of the chemical agent and the dissemination technique used." Aum experimented with a wide range of chemical weapons, including nerve agents like Sarin, tabun, soman, and VX, and considered hydrogen cyanide, and possibly phosgene and mustard. Aum selected Sarin precisely because it was relatively easy to manufacture, and any problems with the result are more a reflection on Aum's peculiar internal structure and lack of effective organization than the technical problems in manufacturing chemical weapons per se.

Aum does seem to have been successful in buying the formula for Sarin from a Russian and in getting all of the necessary equipment to make it successfully. It is also important to note that Iraq produced its first mustard gas in small lots at a university affiliated facility in less than six months, and initially rejected rushing forward with the manufacture of Sarin because it was not persistent and was unstable under heat and daylight conditions, and not because of the difficulty in making small amounts.

Aum attempted several different chemical attacks. It evidently staged its first attack on a rival religious leader in 1993, but its first successful attack was on the judges in a civil suit against Aum in Matsumoto in June 1994, where a heating element, fan, and sprayer on a refrigeration truck were used to kill seven people and injure 144. The Tokyo subway attack that took place in March 1995 killed only 12 people but injured more than 1,000. The delivery mechanism consisted of plastic bags of Sarin punctured in subway cars, where puddles of diluted Sarin were allowed to evaporate. This was an extremely crude delivery method, and even so the Japanese authorities reported some effects for as many as 5,000 people, and the prosecutors claimed 3,398 were injured.

Better tactics in using the same dissemination technique could easily have produced far more lethal results, and there are a number of simple and more effective dissemination techniques. For example, Aum Shinrikyo would have achieved high lethality efforts introducing the same agent into the closed air systems in many high rise office buildings, or simply by releasing pools of Sarin over wide areas in the floor of the Kasumigaseki subway station, rather than leaving it in bags in subway cars. Aum planned similar attacks for May 5, 1995 and July 4, 1995, and it is still unclear why they failed. . . .

Anthony Cordesman

Biological Weapons as Means of Attack

One way to describe the risks posed by biological weapons is to describe the world that existed when natural outbreaks of disease were a recurrent fact of life, and the impact of disease on the Americas. A recent WHO study provides a good overview of the impact of disease on history,

It is arguable whether war or the devastation wrought by infectious disease has had a greater historic influence on political boundaries. Up until the Second World War, it was pestilence—and not warfare—that claimed the lives of Europe's soldiers. Napoleon Bonaparte can lay blame for his ignominious retreat from Moscow—not on the Russians, nor even the Russian winter. By far, his deadliest opponent was typhus; a louse-borne infection that reduced a healthy Grande Armee of 655,000 to a pitiful and demoralized 93,000—who wound up straggling home and surviving just long enough to pass the rickettsia on to neighbours and loved ones. The subsequent epidemic killed another two million, carrying off 250,000 civilians in Germany alone.

In the New World, it was not superior Spanish firepower, nor their reliance on horses that resulted in the conquest and enslavement of the Amerindians. By far the greatest allies of the self-proclaimed, "liberators of the heathens" were smallpox, influenza and measles. Formerly unknown in the Americas, the first recorded smallpox epidemic hit the fledgling colony of Santo Domingo in 1495, destroying 80% of the local indigenous population. That same outbreak was also responsible for the deaths of hundreds of Spanish soldiers after the battle of Vega Real in 1495. . . .

Biological weapons have never been used successfully in large-scale combat, or in effective covert and terrorist attacks. Japan was the only nation in World War II that made confirmed use of biological weapons, and it used relatively crude means. While Japan used biological weapons against some 12 Chinese cites, the total number of deaths does not seem to have exceeded 10,000, and many such deaths were caused by experiments conducted under controlled conditions that used human beings as live subjects. Other nations confined their efforts to experimentation or to developing such weapons for retaliatory purposes. For example, Britain produced over five million seed cakes of animal Anthrax to be dropped by bombers during World War II. . . . Table 29.1 shows that unclassified US intelligence lists a number of countries where biological weapons efforts are continuing, and US intelligence experts indicate that a classified list would be over twice as long.

The technology necessary to produce biological weapons is proliferating as part of the broad transfer of biotechnology throughout the world. Many, if not most of the key technologies involved are now commercialized for food processing and pharmaceutical purposes. Modern biological weapons have become far more lethal and easy to deliver since World War II and have been stockpiled. For example US had stockpiles of seven weapons in 1969, at the time it renounced the use of biological weapons, and then was testing advanced biological warheads for the Polaris and Snark cruise missile. Russia, France, Britain, China, North Korea, also had extensive stocks of such weapons in 1972, when the Biological Weapons Convention (BWC) was opened for signature. In spite of the fact that some 140 nations have now signed or ratified the BWC, US intelligence exports estimate that at least 15 countries still stockpile such weapons.

China

China continues to maintain some elements of an offensive biological warfare program it is believed to have started in the 1950s. China possesses a sufficiently advanced biotechnology infrastructure to allow it to develop and produce biological agents. Its munitions industry is sufficient to allow it to weaponize any such agents, and it has a variety of delivery means that could be used for biological agent delivery. China is believed to possess an offensive biological warfare capability based on technology developed prior to its accession to the BWC in 1984. China actively participates in international efforts to negotiate a BWC compliance protocol.

Since 1984, China consistently has claimed that it never researched, produced, or possessed any biological weapons and never would do so. Nevertheless, China's declarations under the voluntary BWC declarations for confidence building purposes are believed to be inaccurate and incomplete, and there are some reports that China may retain elements of its biological warfare program.

India

India has many well-qualified scientists, numerous biological and pharmaceutical production facilities, and biocontainment facilities suitable for research and development of dangerous pathogens. At least some of these facilities are being used to support research and development for biological warfare defense work. India has ratified the BWC.

Iran

Iran has a growing biotechnology industry, significant pharmaceutical experience and the overall infrastructure to support its biological warfare program. Tehran has expanded its efforts to seek considerable dual-use biotechnical materials and expertise from entities in Russia and elsewhere, ostensibly for civilian reasons. Outside assistance is important for Iran, and it is also difficult to prevent because of the dual-use nature of the materials and equipment being sought by Iran and the many legitimate end uses for these items.

Iran's biological warfare program began during the Iran-Iraq war. Iran is believed to be pursuing offensive biological warfare capabilities and its effort may have evolved beyond agent research and development to the capability to produce small quantities of agent. Iran has ratified the BWC.

Iraq

Iraq's continued refusal to disclose fully the extent of its biological program suggests that Baghdad retains a biological warfare capability, despite its membership in the BWC. After four and one-half years of claiming that it had conducted only "defensive research" on biological weapons Iraq declared reluctantly, in 1995, that it had produced approximately 30,000 liters of bulk biological agents and/or filled munitions. Iraq admitted that it produced anthrax, botulinum toxins and aflatoxins and that it prepared biological agent-filled munitions, including missile warheads and aerial bombs. However, UNSCOM believed that Iraq had produced substantially greater amounts than it has admitted—three to four times greater.

Iraq also admitted that, during the Persian Gulf War, it had deployed biological agent-filled munitions to air-fields and that these weapons were intended for use against Israel and coalition forces in Saudi Arabia. Iraq stated that it destroyed all of these agents and munitions in 1991, but it has provided insufficient credible evidence to support this claim.

The UN believes that Baghdad has the ability to reconstitute its biological warfare capabilities within a few weeks or months, and, in the absence of UNSCOM inspections and monitoring during 1999 and 2000, we are concerned that Baghdad again may have produced some biological warfare agents.

Libya

Libya has ratified the BWC, but has continued a biological warfare program. This program has not advanced beyond the research and development stage, although it may be capable of producing small quantities of biological agent. Libya's program has been hindered by the country's poor scientific and technological base, equipment shortages, and a lack of skilled personnel, as well as by UN sanctions in place from 1992 to 1999. Without foreign assistance and technical expertise to help Libya use available dual-use materials, the Libyan biological warfare program is not likely to make significant progress beyond its current stage. On the other hand, with the suspension of UN sanctions, Libya's ability to acquire biological-related equipment and expertise will increase.

North Korea

North Korea has acceded to the Biological and Toxin Weapons Convention (BWC), but nonetheless has pursued biological warfare capabilities since the 1960s. Pyongyang's resources include a rudimentary (by Western standards) biotechnical infrastructure that could support the production of infectious biological warfare agents and toxins such as anthrax, cholera, and plague. North Korea is believed to possess a munitions-production infrastructure that would allow it to weaponize biological warfare agents and may have biological weapons available for use.

Pakistan

Pakistan is believed to have the resources and capabilities to support a limited biological warfare research and development effort. Pakistan may continue to seek foreign equipment and technology to expand its bio-technical infrastructure. Pakistan has ratified the BWC and actively participates in compliance protocol negotiations for the treaty.

Russia

The FSU offensive biological program was the world's largest and consisted of both military facilities and civilian research and development institutes. According to Ken Alibek, the former Deputy Director of BIO-PREPARAT, the principal Soviet government agency for biological weapons research and development, by the early 1970s, the Soviet Union had developed a biological warfare employment doctrine, where biological weapons were categorized as strategic or operational. Alibek stated that they were not to be employed as tactical weapons. Strategic biological agents, those to be used on "deep targets," such as the continental United States, were the lethal variety and included smallpox, anthrax, and plague. Operational agents, those intended

(continued)

■ **TABLE 29.1** **(continued)**

for use on medium-range targets, but well behind the battlefront, were the incapacitating variety and included tularemia, glanders, and Venezuelan equine encephalitis.

For both strategic and operational employment, the Soviet goal was to create large numbers of casualties and extensive disruption of vital civilian and military activities. The Former Soviet Biological Warfare Program was a massive program involving tens of thousands of personnel. Thousands of tons of agent reportedly produced annually, including anthrax, smallpox, plague, tularemia, glanders, and Venezuelan equine encephalitis. Perceived for strategic use against targets in the United States. Dual-use nature of virtually all materials involved in production process makes it difficult to determine conclusively the exact size and scope of the former Soviet program, or any remaining effort

The former Deputy Director further stated that although the Soviet Union became a signatory to the 1972 BWC, it continued a massive program to develop and manufacture biological weapons, Alibek claims that in the late-1980s and early-1990s, over 60,000 people were involved in the research, development, and production of biological weapons in the Soviet Union. The annual production capacity of all of the facilities involved was several thousand tons of various agents.

The Russian government has publicly committed to ending the former Soviet biological weapons program and claims to have ended the program in 1992. Nevertheless, serious concerns remain about Russia's offensive biological warfare capabilities and the status of some elements of the offensive biological warfare capability inherited from the FSU. Since the breakup of the Soviet Union, more extensive downsizing and restructuring of the program have taken place. Many of the key research and production facilities have taken severe cuts in funding and personnel. However, some key components of the former Soviet program may remain largely intact and may support a possible future mobilization capability for the production of biological agents and delivery systems. Despite Russian ratification of the BWC, work outside the scope of legitimate biological defense activity may be occurring now at selected facilities within Russia, and the United States continues to receive unconfirmed reports of some ongoing offensive biological warfare activities.

Syria

Syria has signed but not r   the BWC but nonetheless is pursuing the development of biological weapons. Syria   echnical infrastructure is capable of supporting limited agent development. However, th   ians are not believed to have begun any major effort to put biological agents into weap   . Without significant foreign assistance, it is unlikely that Syria could manufacture signific   amounts of biological weapons for several years.

Source: Adapted by Anthony H. C   esman from Department of Defense, *Proliferation and Response,* January 2001

Categorizing the Biological Threat

Modern biological weapons take many different forms and offer many potential advantages. They employ living agents or toxins produced by natural or synthetic agents to kill or injure humans, domestic animals, and crops. . . .

Such weapons fall into five main medical categories: Bacterial agents (Anthrax, plague, brucellosis, typhoid fever); rickettsial agents (typhus, Rocky Mountain spotted fever, Q-fever); viral agents (smallpox, influenza, yellow fever, encephalitis, dengue fever, chikungunga, Rift Valley Fever, and hemorrhagic fevers like Ebola,

Marburg and Lassa); toxins (botulinum, staphylococcus enterotoxin, shigella toxin, aflatoxin); and fungal (coccidiodomyocosis). There are other anti-plant and anti-animal weapons that are not used against humans.

The US Center for Disease Control (CDC) has concluded that the U.S. public health system and primary health-care providers must be prepared to address a wide variety of biological agents, including pathogens that are rarely seen in the United States. It has stated that,

> "High-priority agents include organisms that pose a risk to national security because they"
>
> - can be easily disseminated or transmitted person-to-person;
> - cause high mortality, with potential for major public health impact;
> - might cause public panic and social disruption; and
> - require special action for public health preparedness

There are many different ways to categorize biological weapons according to lethality. The CDC divides such weapons into three main categories: Category A, Category B, and Category C. The Category A weapons are high-priority agents that include organisms that pose a risk to national security because they can be easily disseminated or transmitted person-to-person; cause high mortality, with potential for major public health impact; might cause public panic and social disruption; and require special action for public health preparedness. These category A weapons include:

- variola major (smallpox);
- *Bacillus anthracis* (Anthrax);
- *Yersinia pestis* (plague);
- *Clostridium botulinum* toxin (botulism);
- *Francisella tularensis* (tularaemia);
- filoviruses,
  - Ebola hemorrhagic fever,
  - Marburg hemorrhagic fever; and
- arenaviruses,
  - Lassa (Lassa fever),

- Junin (Argentine hemorrhagic fever) and related viruses.

Category B agents include biological weapons that are moderately easy to disseminate; cause moderate morbidity and low mortality; and require specific enhancements of CDC's diagnostic capacity and enhanced disease surveillance. They include

- *Coxiella burnetti* (Q Fever);
- *Brucella* species (brucellosis);
- *Burkholderia mallei* (glanders);
- alphaviruses,
  - Venezuelan encephalomyelitis,
  - eastern and western equine encephalomyelitis;
- ricin toxin from *Ricinus communis* (castor beans);
- epsilon toxin of *Clostridium perfringens;* and
- *Staphylococcus* enterotoxin B.

There is a subset of Category B agents that include pathogens that are food- or waterborne. These pathogens include but are not limited to

- *Salmonella* species,
- *Shigella dysenteriae,*
- *Escherichia coli* O157:H7,
- *Vibrio cholerae,* and
- *Cryptosporidium parvum.*

Category C agents have third priority, and include emerging pathogens that could be engineered for mass dissemination in the future because of their availability; ease of production and dissemination; and potential for high morbidity and mortality and major health impact. Preparedness for Category C agents requires ongoing research to improve disease detection, diagnosis, treatment, and prevention, and these weapons include:

- Nipah virus,
- hantaviruses,
- tickborne hemorrhagic fever viruses,
- tickborne encephalitis viruses,
- yellow fever, and
- multidrug-resistant tuberculosis.

Many of these weapons offer a means of attack that is potentially cheap, lethal, and hard to detect. At the same time, much depends on how well they are weaponized, both in terms of the agent chose and the way in which it is prepared, stored, and delivered. For example, the same disease is generally far more lethal in the form of a dry micropowder that can be disseminated and inhaled over a wide area than in the form of a wet agent. Explosive warheads may waste much of the agent while spraying it upwind in a line source delivery may be highly effective. Wind patterns, temperature, and the presence of ultraviolet light can affect both the lethality and active life of the agent. As a result, the same amount of the same agent can be several orders of magnitude more lethal under optimal weaponization and delivery conditions and potentially highly lethal agents can have minimal effectiveness under the wrong weaponization and delivery conditions.

The CDC also warns that there is no way to know in advance which newly emergent pathogens might be employed by terrorists and that it is imperative to link "bioterrorism preparedness efforts with ongoing disease surveillance and outbreak response activities as defined in CDC's emerging infectious disease strategy." . . .

The Lethality and Effectiveness of Current Biological Weapons

Table 29.2 shows that biological weapons can be far more lethal than chemical weapons. According to this chart, the lethal dose for botulinum toxin, for example, is 0.001 micrograms per kilogram of body weight, while the lethal dose for VX—the most lethal form of nerve gas—is 15 micrograms per kilogram of body weight. In theory, one milligram of Anthrax spores contains one million infective doses. . . .

■ **TABLE 29.2**
The Comparative Effects of Biological, Chemical, and Nuclear Weapons Delivered against a Typical Urban Target

Using missile warheads: Assumes one Scud-sized warhead with a maximum payload of 1,000 kilograms. The study assumes that the biological agent would not make maximum use of this payload capability because this is inefficient. It is unclear [if] this is realistic.

	Area Covered in Square Kilometers	Deaths Assuming 3,000–10,000 People Per Square Kilometer
Chemical: 300 kilograms of Sarin nerve gas with a density of 70 milligrams per cubic meter	0.22	60–200
Biological: 30 kilograms of Anthrax spores with a density of 0.1 milligram per cubic meter	10	30,000–100,000
Nuclear: One 12.5 kiloton nuclear device achieving 5 pounds per cubic inch of over-pressure	7.8	23,000–80,000
One 1 megaton hydrogen bomb	190	570,000–1,900,000

■ **TABLE 29.2** (continued)

Using one aircraft delivering 1,000 kilograms of Sarin nerve gas or 100 kilograms of Anthrax spores: Assumes the aircraft flies in a straight line over the target at optimal altitude and dispensing the agent as an aerosol. The study assumes that the biological agent would not make maximum use of this payload capability because this is inefficient. It is unclear [if] this is realistic.

	Area Covered in Square Kilometers	Deaths Assuming 3,000–10,000 People Per Square Kilometer
Clear sunny day, light breeze:		
Sarin Nerve Gas	0.74	300–700
Anthrax Spores	46	130,000–460,000
Overcast day or night, moderate wind:		
Sarin Nerve Gas	0.8	400–800
Anthrax Spores	140	420,000–1,400,000
Clear calm night:		
Sarin Nerve Gas	7.8	3,000–8,000
Anthrax Spores	300	1,000,000–3,000,000

Source: Adapted by Anthony H. Cordesman from Office of Technology Assessment, *Proliferation of Weapons of Mass Destruction: Assessing the Risks,* US Congress OTA-ISC-559, Washington, August, 1993, pp. 53–54.

Rocco Casagrande

Technology against Terror

Are We Under Attack?

Biological warfare is insidious. Airborne clouds of bacterial or viral agents are nearly invisible and odorless; people who inhale the agents would not know they had been attacked until they fell ill days later. By that time, it might be too late to treat those victims or to protect others from infection. Although most biological agents are not very contagious, in many instances the unknowingly infected could pass on the disease.

Fortunately, the incubation period of biological agents provides a window of time in which public health officials could quarantine and treat victims and vaccinate others. Prior to the onset of symptoms, many diseases caused by biological agents are treatable with antibiotics; after symptoms appear, some victims will be beyond treatment.

Early detection is particularly important because many of the diseases caused by biological warfare agents trigger initial symptoms, such as fever and nausea, that could easily be mistaken for the flu. Medical students are generally taught the phrase "When you hear hoofbeats, think horses—not zebras," as a way to remind them to rule out common disorders before considering more exotic diagnoses. Although this dictum saves time and effort in everyday situations, it could lead doctors to initially overlook a biological attack. For this reason, some biological detectors are colloquially referred to as zebra chips, or Z chips, because they can tip off physicians that a metaphorical zebra is on the loose.

Biological warfare can be waged by contaminating food or water supplies or via disease-carrying insects such as mosquitoes, but these methods are unlikely to affect thousands of victims during a single attack. Biological weapons reach the level of weapons of mass destruction—with a potential for human casualties rivaling that of nuclear weapons—only when they are disseminated through the air as a breathable aerosol of particles about one millionth of a meter in size. These tiny droplets can float through the air for long distances and become lodged deep within the lungs to cause dangerous systemic infections.

Airborne biological agents are tough to detect, however, because of their variety: they can come in the form of bacteria, viruses or nonliving toxins produced by microbes. Biological agents can be deadly, even when extremely dilute. A healthy person breathes in roughly six liters of air a minute, and certain pathogens can cause disease when as few as 10 organisms are inhaled. To protect people who are present for short periods in a contaminated area, a device would have to pick up two individual pathogens per liter of air—an extremely daunting task.

Deploying the Defense

A biological attack could occur anytime, anywhere. Madmen bent on killing as many people as possible could just as easily release a cloud of pathogens at a rural state fair as they could unleash a biological agent in an urban subway train during rush hour. (In the former case, however, they would have to pick an overcast day: bright sunlight kills most microbes.)

Since September 11, 2001, the fear of a terrorist attack has pervaded the thinking of events planners from New York City to Punxsutawney, Pa., which beefed up security this past Groundhog Day to foil possible attacks. Although the diversity and abundance of potential targets will make it impossible or impractical to protect all of them completely, properly deploying biological detectors could reduce the likelihood that the worst attacks would succeed.

Currently, biological agent detectors are too expensive and require too much maintenance to be placed on every street corner. Common sense dictates, however, that certain events or locations deserve tighter security because of their importance or the large number of potential victims there. The Capitol building and the Pentagon are at the heart of U.S. democracy and power and therefore deserve around-the-clock biological surveillance. Eventually technology may progress to the point where biological agent detectors will be reliable, cheap and self-sufficient enough to guard the municipal buildings of every major city.

Unfortunately, no biological agent detector available now can both distinguish harmful organisms from benign ones and monitor its surroundings constantly for pathogens. Some devices cannot collect samples automatically and require a human operator. Others can take samples mechanically, by sampling air or water, but are able to do so only when directed by an operator, who must acquire the samples at intervals to allow adequate time for analysis. Operators could take samples at set times—such as every hour or as soon as the previous sample was analyzed—but a cloud of biological agents could pass over an area or be dispersed in a matter of minutes. Taking samples at the wrong time could miss an attack.

Some detectors are linked to lidar systems or particle counters and collect samples only when a cloud of particles of the right size is present. Similar systems could be used to test the water that flows in the water mains that supply sensitive buildings: if the particle count in a water main spiked, the device would divert a sample of water for further analysis.

A system that could monitor its environment continuously, analyze samples rapidly and operate at low cost would be ideal, but such a system has yet to be perfected. In the meantime, epidemiologists and computer scientists have collaborated to create a database for monitoring the symptoms of patients who visit emergency rooms to detect the earliest signs of a biological attack. The protocol relies on handheld devices that physicians use to upload symptom information to a database that can pick up patterns of illness— such as an unusual number of flu-like illnesses outside flu season that are consistent with the leading edge of a biological attack.

One such system—known as the Lightweight Epidemiology Advanced Detection and Emergency Response System (LEADERS)—has been used since to mine hospital databases in areas near major events such as political party conventions, the Super Bowl and the World Series. Mindful of the fact that most people do not go to the hospital when they think they have the flu, programmers are adding metrics into the LEADERS database such as sales of over-the-counter medications, sick-day tallies and tollbooth receipts (sick people are less likely to drive). Ideally, these databases would log patient information from all over the nation constantly so that attacks in the country could be detected early, no matter where, when or how they occur.

Questions for Discussion

1. Bearing in mind that Brodie's reading was written before the beginning of the nuclear arms race between the former USSR and the United States, are the theories explored in this reading still valid?
2. To what extent may innovations in weapons technology account for the incidence of war in the recent past?
3. Do you think nuclear weapons are qualitatively different from, or fundamentally similar to, conventional weapons?
4. If two new nuclear powers, India and Pakistan, for example, were to exchange information regarding their nuclear capabilities, would this not defeat the purpose of developing nuclear weapons in the first place?
5. What is your opinion of Forden's satellite proposal?
6. Should the U.S. government allocate funds to find antidotes to the various chemical and biological weapons, now that the threat of their usage has been renewed by an increase in terrorist activities?
7. What do you think will be a bigger modern-day threat: nuclear, chemical, or biological weapons? Why?
8. Are adequate steps being taken to safeguard nuclear weapons technology against the threat of terrorism?

Further Readings

1. Rabinowitch, Eugene. *The Dawn of a New Age: Reflections on Science and Human Affairs.* Chicago: University of Chicago, 1963, 327.
2. Hacker, Barton C. "Military Institutions, Weapons, and Social Change: Toward a New History of Military Technology." *Technology and Culture,* 1994, 35, 4, Oct., 768–834.
3. McMahon, Peter. "Technology and Globalisation: An Overview." *Prometheus,* 2001, 19, 3, Sept., 211–222.
4. Richter, Maurice N., Jr. "Technology and Society: Historical Perspective." *Society for the Study of Social Problems,* 1977.
5. Wright, Robert. "The Threat of Chemical and Biological Weapons." *Philosophy and Social Action,* 1996, 22, 1, Jan.–Mar., 43–52.
6. Zilinskas, Raymond A. "Biological Warfare and the Third World." *Politics and the Life Sciences,* 1990, 9, 1, Aug., 59–76.
7. Stanton, John J. "Terror in Cyberspace: Terrorists Will Exploit and Widen the Gap between Governing Structures and the Public." *American Behavioral Scientist,* 2002, 45, 6, Feb., 1017–1032.
8. Ballard, James David, and Hornick, Joseph G. 'Technological Facilitation of Terrorism: Definitional, Legal, and Policy Issues." *American Behavioral Scientist,* 2002, 45, 6, Feb., 989–1017.
9. Bowers, Stephen R., and Keys, Kimberly R. "Technology and Terrorism: The New Threat for the Millennium." *Conflict Studies,* 1998, 309, May, 1–24.
10. Cohen, Eliot A. "World War IV." *The New York Times,* November 20, 2001.

Political Theories

The international political system consists of a population of states with vastly different resources and with asymmetric power relations. On the one hand, this system encourages competition for resources among larger states and, on the other, it encourages hegemonic domination of smaller states. The dynamics of the hegemonic system determine stability or instability of the international political system. The two readings in this section deal with issues pertaining to interstate relations and their impact on the possibility of warfare.

In "Multipolar Systems and International Stability," Karl Deutsch and David Singer explain how different international power-sharing systems can account for the likelihood of interstate conflict. The authors explain how the multipolar configuration reduces the likelihood of war by minimizing the chances of unilateral action by any one state. It also accelerates the interaction op-

portunities for states, compelling them to refrain from military action against one another. According to the authors, however, multipolar systems are unstable in the long term.

In the second reading, "The Spread of Nuclear Weapons: A Debate," Kenneth Waltz and Scott Sagan debate whether horizontal proliferation of nuclear weapons increases or decreases the possibility of warfare.

Waltz sets forth his theory that the possession of nuclear weapons by many states would *decrease* the chances of nuclear war. He discusses criticisms of his theory and explains how heads of state are rational players and would never use nuclear weapons to prevent the annihilation of their countries. Waltz emphatically supports the principle of rational deterrence.

In a reply to Waltz, Sagan discusses how nuclear proliferation *increases* the chances of accidental nuclear war. He stresses the possibility of deterrence failure due to miscommunication or sabotage by nonstate actors. Sagan also observes that military leaders are, in fact, prone to risk the use of nuclear weapons. He also highlights the fact that some countries lack the mechanisms for stable civilian control, making them more "inward-looking" in terms of foreign policy. Finally, Sagan contests that heads of state are rational actors.

Karl W. Deutsch
J. David Singer

Multipolar Systems and International Stability

In the classical literature of diplomatic history, the balance-of-power concept occupies a central position. Regardless of one's interpretation of the term or one's preference for or antipathy to it, the international relations scholar cannot escape dealing with it. The model is, of course, a multifaceted one, and it produces a fascinating array of corollaries; among these, the relationship between the number of actors and the stability of the system is one of the most widely accepted and persuasive. That is, as the system moves away from bipolarity toward multipolarity, the frequency and intensity of war should be expected to diminish.

To date, however, that direct correlation has not been subjected to rigorous scrutiny by either abstract or empirical test. For the most part, it has seemed so intuitively reasonable that a few historical illustrations have been accepted as sufficient. This is, on balance, not enough to support a lawful generalization; it must eventually be put to the historical test. This will be done eventually, but in the interim this hypothesis should at least be examined on formal, abstract grounds. The purpose of this article, therefore, is to present two distinct—but related—lines of formal, semi-quantitative, argument as to why the diffusion-stability relationship should turn out as the theoretician has generally assumed and as the historian has often found to be the case.

A Probabilistic Concept of International Political Stability

Stability may, of course, be considered from the vantage point of both the total system and the individual states comprising it. From the broader, or systemic, point of view, we shall define stability as the probability that the system retains all of its essential characteristics; that no single nation becomes dominant; that most of its members continue to survive; and that large-scale war does not occur. And from the more limited perspective of the individual nations, stability would refer to the probability of their continued political independence and territorial integrity without any significant probability of becoming engaged in a "war for survival." The acceptable level of this probability—such as 90, or 95, or 99 per cent—seems to be intuitively felt by political decision-makers, without necessarily being made explicit, but it could be inferred by investigators in the analysis of particular cases. A more stringent definition of stability would require also a low probability of the actors' becoming engaged even in limited wars . . .

The Accelerated Rise of Interaction Opportunities

The most obvious effect of an increase in the number of independent actors is an increase in the number of possible pairs or dyads in the total system. This assumes, of course, that the number of independent actors is responsive to the general impact of coalition membership, and that as a nation enters into the standard coalition it is much less of a free agent than it was while non-aligned. That is, its alliance partners now exercise an inhibiting effect—or perhaps even a veto—upon its freedom to interact with non-alliance nations.

This reduction in the number of possible dyadic relations produces, both for any individual nation and for the totality of those in the system, a corresponding diminution in the number of opportunities for interaction with other actors. Although it must be recognized at the outset that, in the international system of the nineteenth and twentieth centuries, such opportunities are as likely to be competitive as they are to be cooperative, the overall effect is nevertheless destabilizing. The argument is nothing more than a special case of the widely employed pluralism model.

In that model, our focus is on the degree to which the system exhibits negative feedback as well as cross-pressuring. By negative—as distinguished from positive or amplifying—feedback, we refer to the phenomenon of self-correction: as stimuli in one particular direction increase, the system exhibits a decreasing response to those stimuli, and increasingly exhibits tendencies that counteract them. This is the self-restraining system, manifested in the automatic pilot, the steam-engine governor, and most integrated social systems, and it stands in contrast to the self-aggravating system as seen in forest fires, compound interest, nuclear fission, runaway inflation or deflation, and drug addiction.[1]

The pluralistic model asserts that the amplifying feedback tendency is strengthened, and the negative feedback tendency is weakened, to the extent that conflict positions are superimposed or reinforcing. Thus, if all clashes and incompatibilities in the system produce the same divisions and coalitions—if all members in class Blue line up *with* one another and *against* all or most of those in class Red—the line of cleavage will be wide and deep, with positive feedback operating both within and between the two classes or clusters. But if some members of class Blue have some incompatible interests with others in their class, and an overlap of interests with some of those in Red, there will be some degree of negative or self-correcting feedback both within and between the two classes.

This notion is analogous to that of cross-cutting pressure familiar to the student of politics.

Here we observe that every individual plays a fairly large number of politically relevant roles and that most of these pull him in somewhat different attitudinal, behavioral, and organizational directions. For example, if an individual is (1) a loving parent, (2) a member of a militant veterans' organization, (3) owner of a factory, and (4) a Catholic, the first and third factors will tend to deflect him toward a "coexistence" foreign policy, the second will pull him toward a "holy war" orientation, and his religious affiliation will probably (in the 1960's) produce a deep ambivalence. Likewise, following Ralf Dahrendorf's formulation, if status difference is a major determinant of conflict exacerbation, and an individual is head of a family, a bank teller, and president of the lodge, he will coalesce with and against different people on different issues.[2] In each of these cases, his relatively large number of interaction opportunities produces a set of cross-pressures such as largely to inhibit any superimposition or reinforcement. The consequence would seem to favor social stability and to inhibit social cleavage; increasing differentiation and role specialization in industrial society has, in a sense, counteracted the Marxian expectation of class warfare.

Thus, in any given bilateral relationship, a rather limited range of possible interactions obtains, even if the relationship is highly symbiotic. But as additional actors are brought into the system, the range of possible interactions open to each—and hence to the total system—increases. In economics, this accretion produces the transformation from barter to market, and in any social setting it produces a comparable increase in the range and flexibility of possible interactions. Traditionally, social scientists have believed—and observed—that as the number of possible exchanges increases, so does the probability that the "invisible hand" of pluralistic interests will be effective. One might say that one of the greatest threats to the stability of any impersonal social system is the shortage of alternative partners.

If we assume, then, that any increase in the number of independent actors *is* conducive to stability, the question remains as to the quantitative nature of this correlation. Is there any particular level at which the system cannot be made more stable by the addition of new actors, or less stable by the loss of existing actors? Is there, furthermore, some critical level at which small changes become crucial? Our response must be based, of course, on the degree to which each single increment or decrement affects the number of possible dyads, or bilateral interaction opportunities, in the system. That effect is found by applying the standard formula for possible pairs: $\frac{N(N-1)}{2}$; thus, in a purely bipolar system, only one dyad or pair is possible, while a tripolar situation produces three pairs, four actors produce six pairs, five produce ten possible pairings, and so on, as shown in Figure 31.1.

This figure indicates rather dramatically the degree to which the number of independent ac-tors affects the possible number of dyads, and thus interaction opportunities. Even as we move from bipolarity to a tripolar system, the interaction opportunities within the system triple, and when another single actor is added the possible dyadic relations increase by three, and so on, with each addition in the actor column producing an increment of $N-1$ in the interaction opportunity column. Intuitively, the student of international politics would note that until N reaches five, there is an insufficient number of possible dyads, and that beyond that level the stability-enhancing in-crement begins to grow very sharply.

So far, we have operated from the conserva-tive assumption that all nations have identical in-terests, concerns, and goals, and though we would not want to exaggerate in the opposite di-rection, one cannot overlook the diversity that does exist. A landlocked nation can hardly offer fishing rights in its coastal waters, an agricultural

■ **FIGURE 31.1**
Interaction Opportunity

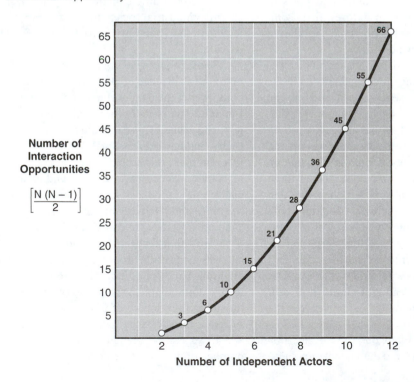

surplus nation will seldom purchase those same foodstuffs, two underdeveloped nations are most unlikely to exchange machine tools, and a permanent member of the Security Council cannot be expected to give much for assurance of a seat in that organ. Every nation's needs and supplies differ, and the more nations there are, the greater will be the number and diversity of trade-offs available to the total system. As possible trade-offs increase, the greater the possibility for compensatory and stabilizing interactions to occur. That is, in a system characterized by conflict-generating scarcities, each and every increase in opportunities or cooperation (i.e., to engage in a mutually advantageous trade-off) will diminish the tendency to pursue a conflict up to, and over, the threshold of war.

Finally, membership in an alliance not only exercises a negative quantitative impact on a nation's interaction opportunities, but affects the quality of those that do continue to exist. On the one hand, the pattern-maintenance needs of the alliance will be such as to *minimize* (a) the range of issues over which it will conflict with an alliance partner, and (b) the intensity of such intra-alliance conflicts as are permitted. On the other hand, the establishment of such clear-cut ingroup–outgroup division can only lead to an *increase* in the range and intensity of any conflicts with non-alliance actors.

To summarize, one logical explanation for the correlation between number of independent actors and the probability of armed conflict lies in the realm of enhanced interaction opportunities, observed in terms of their quanity, diversity, and qualities. . . .

Some Implications for the Diffusion of Nuclear Weapons

If an increase in the number and diplomatic mobility of actors may slow down the process of arms escalation, it would by the same reasoning also slow down any process of de-escalation. Here, too, a one-sided arms reduction in a two-power world may elicit an equal response by the other power, while in a multipolar world the effect of any such unilateral initiative would be much weaker.

If we are chiefly interested in rapid de-escalation—that is, in partial or complete disarmament—a multipolar world may prove more intractable than a bipolar one; and we may view the emergence of French, German, Japanese, or Communist Chinese national power with justified alarm. If we are mainly concerned, on the contrary, with preventing any rapid escalation of the two-power arms competition between the United States and the Soviet Union, a shift toward a multipolar world may appear preferable.

At this point, of course, the bare and abstract arguments pursued thus far become quite insufficient. In our analysis of alternative international power systems we have abstracted from all other qualities of the states, governments, and national political systems within them. At the point of policy choice, however, these hitherto neglected aspects may be the decisive ones. A bipolar system in which each of the two rival powers is likely to be moderate and cautious in its policy initiatives and responses might be a great deal safer than a multipolar world containing one or several well-armed powers whose governments or politically relevant strata were inclined to incompetence or recklessness. As elsewhere, so also in international politics a stable general system could be wrecked by the introduction of unstable components.

At the present time, the importance of this latter point may well be decisive. Each of the present major nuclear powers—the United States, Britain, and the Soviet Union—has been politically stable, in the sense that each has retained its particular type of government for over forty years. None of these three countries has been notable for initiating large and reckless military enterprises. Among the middle-level and smaller powers most likely to press for nuclear weapons during the next decade—which include France, Germany, Japan, Mainland China, Nationalist China, and perhaps Egypt and others—there are several whose recent history lacks any comparable evidence of stability in domestic institutions and caution in international affairs. If this stage should be followed by the dissemination of nuclear weapons among a still larger number of countries, including inevitably at least some with still less stable domestic regimes and less cautious military policies, the instability of the international system would be still more dangerous. For these reasons, any successful efforts by the United States and other powers to slow down the dissemination of nuclear weapons would tend to increase the stability of the entire international system . . .

One other problem, however, should be discussed here: the time horizon under which the stability of international systems is evaluated. A multipolar world, though often more stable in the short run than a bipolar one, has its own problem of long-run political stability, and it is to this that we must now turn our attention.

The Long-Run Instability of Multipolar Systems

On the basis of these considerations, it might seem that a multipolar system could last forever, or for a very long time, by always opposing the ambitions of its currently top-ranking member; and this is indeed what some writers have claimed as a virtue of the balance-of-power system. In each of the sections above, however, we have dealt with considerations of an essentially short or middle-run nature, with a rather incomplete view as the natural consequence.

There are at least two analytic reasons why this relatively benign long-run outcome cannot be expected. For one thing, if we accept the usual zero-sum assumption of Machiavelli and the classic theory of games—according to which any gain by one contender can occur only through an equal loss by one or more of his rivals—then we must assume that each contending power ordinarily will try to acquire all the territory and population it can at the expense of its rivals, and that it will do nothing to create new rivals for itself. The model thus provides for the possibility of the destruction of states whose rulers misjudged the

precise balance of strength at the moment, or whose economies and populations no longer yielded the increasing increments in arms spending and military effort required by the competition, but this model does not provide for the creation of new states. If the probability of states' perishing is small, but larger than zero, and the probability of substantial new powers' arising is zero in terms of this model, then the model will predict a diminishing number of effective contenders, leading eventually to a two-power world or to the survival of a single power, as in the case of the reduction of the many governments of classic antiquity to the two-power clash of Rome and Carthage, and of Rome's final long monopoly of power in the Mediterranean world until new forces entered from outside the region.

The second line of reasoning is based on considerations of statistics. Thus far we have taken probabilities only in terms of their central tendencies, rather than in terms of the variance of possible outcomes and their distribution. If we assume these outcomes to be normally distributed around some mean, then the usual outcome of an increment in threat by power A against power B in a multipolar system will consist in both A's and B's finding enough allies, respectively, to match the power of their respective coalitions and to produce the relatively moderate outcomes predicted by the classic balance-of-power model. In rare cases, however, corresponding to one tail of the distribution, state A will find a great preponderance of allies and become able to destroy its current enemy, B, completely; and in other rare cases—corresponding to the other tail of the distribution—A must expect to find itself facing an overwhelming coalition of adversaries that will destroy it. In the short run, only the moderate central tendencies of the distribution of outcomes of the coalition-forming process will be frequent enough to be taken into account, but in the long run the balance-of-power world must be expected to produce eventually dramatic and catastrophic changes, both locally and at last at the system level. The number of years after which long-run rather than short-run phenomena are likely to prevail will depend on the frequency of international crises, and on the shape of the distribution of balanced and unbalanced coalitions, respectively, as outcomes of the coalition-forming process.

This expectation seems in good agreement with the historical data. No balance-of-power system has lasted longer than a few centuries, and most of the original powers contending in such systems have survived as independent powers only for much shorter periods.

The classic descriptive and analytical views of two-power confrontations and of the balance of power among several contenders have been formalized by several writers. The most prominent models, of the tight bipolar and multipolar world, respectively, can be interpreted in terms of the dynamic model of conflict by Lewis F. Richardson. The results suggest that the Richardson model, with very simple assumptions, can be made to include the bipolar and multipolar models as special cases. This combined model then suggests some general inferences in predictions about trends that appear to accord well with historical data. In the long run, according to this model, even multipolar systems operating under the rules of balance-of-power policies are shown to be self-destroying, but both in the short and the long run the instability of tight bipolar systems appears to be substantially greater. It seems plausible that, *if the spread of nuclear weapons could be slowed down or controlled,* a transition from the bipolar international system of the early 1950's to an increasingly multipolar system in the 1960's might buy mankind some valuable time to seek some more dependable bases for world order.

Notes

1. For an application of these and related concepts to a range of political questions, see Karl W. Deutsch, *The Nerves of Government* (New York 1963).

2. Ralf Dahrendorf, "Toward a Theory of Social Conflict," *Journal of Conflict Resolution,* 11 (June 1958), 176–77.

Kenneth N. Waltz
Scott D. Sagan

The Spread of Nuclear Weapons: A Debate

More May Be Better

Kenneth N. Waltz

What will the spread of nuclear weapons do to the world? I say "spread" rather than "proliferation" because so far nuclear weapons have proliferated only vertically as the major nuclear powers have added to their arsenals. Horizontally, they have spread slowly across countries, and the pace is not likely to change much. Short-term candidates for the nuclear club are not numerous, and they are not likely to rush into the nuclear business. One reason is that the United States works with some effect to keep countries from doing that.

Nuclear weapons will nevertheless spread, with a new member occasionally joining the club. Membership grew to twelve in the first fifty years of the nuclear age, and that number includes three countries who suddenly found themselves in the nuclear military business as successor states to the Soviet Union. A 50 percent growth of membership in the next decade would be surprising. Since rapid changes in international conditions can be unsettling, the slowness of the spread of nuclear weapons is fortunate. Someday the world will be populated by fifteen or eighteen nuclear-weapon states (hereafter referred to as nuclear states). What the further spread of nuclear weapons will do to the world is therefore a compelling question. . . .

What Will the Spread of Nuclear Weapons Do to the World?

Contemplating the nuclear past gives ground for hoping that the world will survive if further nuclear powers join today's (club). This hope is called into question by those who believe that the infirmities of some new nuclear states and the delicacy of their nuclear forces will work against the preservation of peace and for the fighting of nuclear wars. The likelihood of avoiding destruction as more states become members of the nuclear club is often coupled with the question of *who* those states will be. What are the likely differences in situation and behavior of new as compared to old nuclear powers? . . .

Examining the supposedly unfortunate characteristics of new nuclear states removes some of one's worries. One wonders why their civil and military leaders should be less interested in avoiding their own destruction than leaders of other states have been. Nuclear weapons have never been used in a world in which two or more states had them. Still, one's feeling that something awful will emerge as new nuclear powers are added to the present group is not easily quieted. The fear remains that one state or another will fire its new nuclear weapons in a coolly calculated preemptive strike, or fire them in a moment of panic, or use them to launch a preventive war. These possibilities are examined in the next section. Nuclear weapons, so it is feared, may also be set off anonymously, or used to back a policy of blackmail, or be used in a combined conventional-nuclear attack. . . .

States are deterred by the prospect of suffering severe damage and by their inability to do much to limit it. Deterrence works because nuclear weapons enable one state to punish another state severely without first defeating it. "Victory," in Thomas Schelling's words, "is no longer a prerequisite for hurting the enemy." Countries armed only with conventional weapons can hope that their military forces will be able to limit the damage an attacker can do. Among countries armed with strategic nuclear forces, the hope of avoiding heavy damage depends mainly on the attacker's restraint and little on one's own efforts. . . .

Conclusion

The conclusion is in two parts. The first part applies the above analysis to the present. The second part uses it to peer into the future.

What Follows from My Analysis?

Many more countries can make nuclear weapons than do. One can believe that American opposition to nuclear arming stays the deluge only by overlooking the complications of international life. Any state has to examine many conditions before deciding whether or not to develop nuclear weapons. Our opposition is only one factor and is not likely to be the decisive one. Many states feel fairly secure living with their neighbors. Why should they want nuclear weapons? Some countries, feeling threatened, have found security through their own strenuous efforts and through arrangements made with others. South Korea is an outstanding example. Many officials believe that South Korea would lose more in terms of American support if it acquired nuclear weapons than it would gain by having them. Further, on occasion we might slow the spread of nuclear weapons by *not* opposing the nuclear weapons programs of some countries. When we oppose Pakistan's nuclear program, we are saying that we disapprove of countries developing nuclear weapons no matter what their neighbors do.

The gradual spread of nuclear weapons has not opened the nuclear floodgates. Nations attend to their security in ways they think best. The fact that so many more countries can make nuclear weapons than do says more about the hesitation of countries to enter the nuclear military business than about the effectiveness of American nonproliferation policy. We should suit our policy to individual cases, sometimes bringing pressure against a country moving toward nuclear-weapons capability and sometimes quietly acquiescing. No one policy is right in all cases. We should ask what the interests of other countries require before putting pressure on them. Some countries are likely to suffer more in cost and pain if they remain conventional states than if they become nuclear ones. The measured spread of nuclear weapons does not run against our interests and can increase the security of some states at a price they can afford to pay.

What Does the Nuclear Future Hold?

What will a world populated by a larger number of nuclear states look like? I have drawn a picture of such a world that accords with experience throughout the nuclear age. Those who dread a world with more nuclear states do little more than assert that more is worse and claim without substantiation that new nuclear states will be less responsible and less capable of self control than the old ones have been. They feel fears that many felt when they imagined how a nuclear China would behave. Such fears have proved unfounded as nuclear weapons have slowly spread. I have found many reasons for believing that with more nuclear states the world will have a promising future. I have reached this unusual conclusion for four main reasons.

First, international politics is a self-help system, and in such systems the principal parties determine their own fate, the fate of other parties, and the fate of the system. This will continue to be so.

176 PART FOUR Theories of the Causes of War

Second, given the massive numbers of American and Russian warheads, and given the impossibility of one side destroying enough of the other side's missiles to make a retaliatory strike bearable, the balance of terror is indestructible. What can lesser states do to disrupt the nuclear equilibrium if even the mighty efforts of the United States and the Soviet Union did not shake it?

Third, nuclear weaponry makes miscalculation difficult because it is hard not to be aware of how much damage a small number of warheads can do. Early in [the twentieth] century Norman Angell argued that war could not occur because it would not pay. But conventional wars have brought political gains to some countries at the expense of others. Among nuclear countries, possible losses in war overwhelm possible gains. In the nuclear age Angell's dictum becomes persuasive. When the active use of force threatens to bring great losses, war becomes less likely. This proposition is widely accepted but insufficiently emphasized. Nuclear weapons reduced the chances of war between the United States and the Soviet Union and between the Soviet Union and China. One must expect them to have similar effects elsewhere. Where nuclear weapons threaten to make the cost of wars immense, who will dare to start them?

Fourth, new nuclear states will feel the constraints that present nuclear states have experienced. New nuclear states will be more concerned for their safety and more mindful of dangers than some of the old ones have been. Until recently, only the great and some of the major powers have had nuclear weapons. While nuclear weapons have spread, conventional weapons have proliferated. Under these circumstances, wars have been fought not at the center but at the periphery of international politics. The likelihood of war decreases as deterrent and defensive capabilities increase. Nuclear weapons make wars hard to start. These statements hold for small as for big nuclear powers. Because they do, the gradual spread of nuclear weapons is more to be welcomed than feared.

More Will Be Worse

Scott D. Sagan

Why should we worry about the spread of nuclear weapons? The answer is by no means obvious. After all, we have lived with nuclear deterrence for half a century now. The two superpowers maintained a long peace throughout the Cold War, despite deep political hostilities, numerous crises, and a prolonged arms race. Why should we expect that the experience of future nuclear powers will be any different? . . .

Such optimistic views of the effects of nuclear proliferation have not escaped criticism, of course, and a number of scholars have argued that nuclear deterrence may not be stable in specific regional settings. What is missing in the debate so far, however, is an alternative *theory* of the consequences of nuclear proliferation; an alternative that is a broader conception of the effects of nuclear weapons proliferation on the likelihood of war. In this [reading] I present such an alternative, rooted in organization theory, which leads to a far more pessimistic assessment of the future prospects for peace.

There are two central arguments. First, I argue that professional military organizations—because of common biases, inflexible routines, and parochial interests—display organizational behaviors that are likely to lead to deterrence failures and deliberate or accidental war. Unlike the widespread psychological critique of rational deterrence theory—which maintains that some political leaders may lack the intelligence . . . or emotional stability to make deterrence work—this organizational critique argues that military organizations, unless professionally managed through a checks-and-balances system of strong civilian control, are unlikely to fulfill the operational requirements for stable nuclear deterrence.

Second, I argue that there are strong reasons to believe that future nuclear-armed states will lack the positive mechanisms of civilian control. Many current and emerging proliferators have either military-run governments or weak civilian-led governments in which the professional military has a strong and direct influence on policymaking. In such states, the biases, routines, and parochial interests of powerful military organizations, not the "objective" interests of the state, can determine state behavior. In addition, military organizations in many proliferators are "inward-looking," focusing primarily on issues of domestic stability and internal politics, rather than on external threats to national security. When such militaries are in power, senior officers' energies and interests necessarily shift away from professional concerns for the protection of national security; when civilians are in power, but are extremely fearful of military coups, defense policy is designed to protect their regime, not the nation's security, and officers are promoted according to their personal loyalty to current leaders, not their professional competence. In either case, such extensive military involvement in domestic politics, whether active or latent, means that the military's professional competence as a fighting force, and also as a manager of a deterrent force, will suffer.

What are the likely effects of the spread of nuclear weapons? My argument proceeds in three steps. First, I contrast the assumptions and logic of proliferation optimists to the assumptions and logic of a more pessimistic organizational-level approach to nuclear proliferation. Next, I compare the two theories' predictions about three major operational requirements of deterrence and, in each case, I present the existing empirical evidence concerning each requirement. Finally, at the end of the [reading], I present some lessons for international relations theory and United States nonproliferation policy.

Rational Deterrence Theory and Organization Theory Compared

Rational Deterrence Theory

. . . Anyone—political leader or man in the street—can see that catastrophe lurks if events spiral out of control and nuclear warheads begin to fly." Given that the costs of nuclear war are so high, even a small risk of war can produce strong deterrence. Because "a nation will be deterred from attacking even if it believes that there is only a possibility that its adversary will retaliate," Waltz maintains that "the probability of major war among states having nuclear weapons approaches zero." If this is true, then the spread of nuclear weapons should have very positive consequences: "The likelihood of war decreases as deterrent and defensive capabilities increase. Nuclear weapons make wars hard to start. These statements hold for small as for big nuclear powers. Because they do, the gradual spread of nuclear weapons is more to be welcomed than feared" . . .

Within the rational deterrence framework, three major operational requirements for stable nuclear deterrence exist: 1) there must not be a preventive war during the transition period when one state has nuclear weapons and the other state is building, but has not yet achieved, a nuclear capability; 2) both states must develop, not just the ability to inflict some level of unacceptable damage to the other side, but also a sufficient degree of "second-strike" survivability so that its forces could retaliate if attacked first; and 3) the nuclear arsenals must not be prone to accidental or unauthorized use. Nuclear optimists believe that new nuclear powers will meet these requirements because it is in these states' obvious interests to do so. This is, as I will show, [a] very problematic belief.

An Organizational Perspective

The assumption that states behave in a basically rational manner is of course an assumption, not an empirically tested insight. International relations scholars often assume high degrees of rationality, not because it is accurate, but because it is helpful: it provides a relatively simple way of making predictions, by linking perceived interests with expected behavior. The rational-actor view is clearly not the only one possible, however, and it is not the only set of assumptions that lead to useful predictions about nuclear proliferation.

An alternative set of assumptions views government leaders as intending to behave rationally, yet sees their beliefs, the options available to them, and the final implementation of their decisions as being influenced by powerful forces within the country. If this is the case, organization theory should be useful for the study of the consequences of proliferation. This is important, since such an organizational perspective challenges the central assumption that states behave in a self-interested, rational manner.

Two themes in organization theory focus attention on major impediments to pure rationality in organizational behavior. First, large organizations function within a severely "bounded," or limited, form of rationality: they have inherent limits on calculation and coordination and use simplifying mechanisms to understand and respond to uncertainty in the outside world. Organizations, by necessity, develop routines to coordinate action among different units: standard operating procedures and organizational rules, not individually reasoned decisions, therefore govern behavior. Organizations commonly "satisfice": rather than searching for the policy that maximizes their utility, they often accept the first option that is minimally satisfying. Organizations are often myopic: instead of surveying the entire environment for information, organizational members have biased searches, focusing only on specific areas stemming from their past experience, recent training, and current responsibility. Organizations suffer from "goal displacement": they often become fixated on narrow operational measurements of goals and lose focus on their overall objectives. Organizational filters continually shape the beliefs and actions of individuals. As James March and Herbert Simon put it, "the world tends to be perceived by the organization members in terms of the particular concepts that are reflected in the organization's vocabulary. The particular categories it employs are reified, and become, for members of the organization, attributes of the world rather than mere conventions."

Second, complex organizations commonly have multiple, conflicting goals, and the process by which objectives are chosen and pursued is intensely political. From such a political perspective,

actions that cut against the interests of the organization's leadership are often found to serve the narrow interests of some units within the organization. Organizations are not simply tools in the hands of higher-level authorities but are groups of self-interested and competitive subunits and actors. . . . And even when a professional military service or command acts in relatively rational ways to maximize *its* interests—protecting its power, size, autonomy or organizational essence—such actions do not necessarily reflect the organizational interests of the military as a whole, much less the national interests of the state. To the degree that such narrow organizational interests determine state behavior, a theory of "rational" state action is seriously weakened. . . .

Bringing Organizations into Counter-Proliferation Policy

What are the policy implications of my organizational-level approach to nuclear proliferation? First, and most obviously, this approach suggests that the United States is quite correct to maintain an active nuclear nonproliferation policy. A world with more nuclear-armed states may be our fate; it should not be our goal. It is highly unfortunate, in this regard, that a growing number of defense analysts in new nuclear nations read the arguments of the U.S. nuclear optimists, most prominently the writings of Kenneth Waltz, and now cite that literature to legitimize the development of nuclear arsenals in their nations. It is fortunate, however, that U.S. government officials have not been convinced of the merits of the optimists' views, and there is little evidence that U.S. policy is going to move away from its strong opposition to the further spread of nuclear weapons.

Second, a more effective approach to nuclear proliferation would add a larger dose of intellectual persuasion to our current policy efforts, which are aimed primarily at restricting the supply of materials and providing security guarantees to potential nuclear states. There are ongoing debates—often in secret, sometimes in the open—about the wisdom of developing nuclear weapons in many of these countries. To influence such debates, non-proliferation advocates need to develop better understandings of the perceptions and interests of the domestic organizational actors involved. Decisionmakers in potential nuclear powers do not need to be told that proliferation is not in the *United States's* interests. They need to be convinced that it is not in *their* interest. Civilian leaders, military leaders, and wider publics alike in these states need to be reminded that the development of nuclear weapons will make their states targets for preventive attacks by their potential adversaries, will not easily lead to survivable arsenals, and will raise the specter of accidental or unauthorized uses of nuclear weapons. Just as importantly, they also need to be persuaded that nuclear proliferation may not be in their narrow self-interest as civilian leaders seeking for political power, as militaries seeking autonomy, and as citizens seeking safety.

Finally, an organizational approach offers a valuable, but pessimistic, perspective on efforts to manage proliferation if it occurs despite U.S. attempts to prevent it. At one level, an implication of an organizational perspective is that the United States should cooperate with new nuclear states—sharing knowledge of organizational structures, technology, and experience—to reduce the dangerous consequences of the spread of nuclear weapons. At a deeper level, however, the most disturbing lesson of this analysis is that, for organizational reasons, such cooperative efforts are not likely to succeed.

This is true with respect to all three of the requirements of deterrence. First, the most important step the United States could take to reduce the likelihood of military biases leading to preventive war in the new nuclear nations would be to encourage sustained civilian control of the military, with appropriate checks and balances, in those states. Such efforts are unlikely, however, to be completely effective. In some new nuclear states, strong military organizations are unlikely to give up their current positions of significant decisionmaking power and influence. In some other nuclear states, unpopular civilian

regimes will not create competent, professional military organizations, since they might serve as a threat to the regime's power. In either case, appropriate civil-military relations are problematic. Efforts to improve civil-military relations are therefore likely to be most effective precisely where they are least needed.

Second, to enhance survivability of new nuclear forces, the United States could also consider cooperating with new nuclear states—sharing information on delivery-system technology, operational practices, and advanced warning systems—to help them create invulnerable forces. This policy, however, is also unlikely to be widely implemented. Not only will U.S. policymakers fear that such cooperative efforts would signal that the United States is not really opposed to the further spread of nuclear weapons, but the leaders of new nuclear states, and especially the leaders of their military organizations, will also not want to discuss such sensitive issues in detail, fearing that it will expose their own nuclear vulnerabilities and organizational weaknesses to the United States.

Third, the large risk of nuclear accidents in these countries suggests that the United States may want to share information on such subjects as electronic locking devices, weapons-safety design improvements, and personnel reliability programs. To the degree that the United States can share technology that only improves weapons safety and security, but does not enhance readiness to use the forces, such efforts would be helpful. A broad policy to make the weapons of new nuclear nations safer could be highly counterproductive, however, if it led them to believe that they could safely operate large nuclear arsenals on high states of alert.

Indeed, an organizational perspective on nuclear safety suggests that we need a paradigm shift in the way we think about managing proliferation. The United States should not try to make new nuclear nations become like the superpowers during the cold war, with large arsenals ready to launch at a moment's notice for the sake of deterrence; instead, for the sake of safety, the

United States and Russia should try to become more like some of the nascent nuclear states, maintaining very small nuclear capabilities, with weapons components separated and located apart from the delivery systems, and with civilian organizations controlling the warheads.

Finally, if my theories are right, the U.S. defense department should be telling new nuclear states, loudly and often, that there are inherent limits to nuclear weapons safety. If my theories are right, however, the U.S. defense department will not do this, because this would require it to acknowledge to others, and itself, how dangerous our own nuclear history has been. The important and difficult task of persuasion will therefore fall largely upon individuals outside the organizations that have managed U.S. nuclear weapons.

Questions for Discussion

1. During the bipolar decades of the Cold War, international security issues were centered mainly around the United States and the Soviet Union. In the present multipolar system, security issues are similar; however, they have become more globalized in the form of terrorism. In the light of these facts, how do the two types of international political systems (bipolar and multipolar) differ in terms of stability?

2. Do you agree with Deutsch and Singer's theory that a multipolar system is more stable than a bipolar system?

3. Given the phenomenon of nuclear proliferation, how would you address the increase in the possibility of an accidental nuclear war?

4. How would you explain the fact that Pakistan and India have not been engaged in a full-scale war ever since the two countries developed their nuclear weapons programs?

5. Sagan and Waltz engage in a thorough debate on the spread of nuclear weapons. In what respects do these two authors differ in their assessment of whether the spread of nuclear weapons will increase or decrease the chances of nuclear war? Who do you agree with and why?

Further Readings

1. Kegley, Charles W., Jr., and Raymond, Gregory A. "Must we Fear a Post-Cold War Multipolar System?" *Journal of Conflict Resolution,* 1992, 36, 3, Sept., 573–585.

2. Rosecrance, Richard N. "Bipolarity, Multipolarity, and the Future" in James N. Rosenau, ed., *International Politics and Foreign Policy.* New York: The Free Press, 1969, 325–335.

3. Huntington, Samuel P. "The Lonely Superpower." *Foreign Affairs,* 1999, 78, 2, March–April, 35–49.

4. El Baradei, Mohamed. "Saving Ourselves from Self-Destruction." *The New York Times,* February 12, 2004.

5. Broad, William J. "How the World Can Be Saved, Redux." *The New York Times,* February 15, 2004.

6. Gowa, Joanne, and Mansfield, Edward D. "Power Politics and International Trade." *American Political Science Review,* 1993, 87, 2, June, 408–420.

7. Friedberg, Aaron L. "Ripe for Rivalry: Prospects or Peace in a Multipolar Asia." *International Security,* 1993–1994, 18, 3, Winter, 5–33.

8. Elman, Colin. "Horses for Courses: Why Not Neorealist Theories of Foreign Policy?" *Security Studies,* 1996, 6, 1, Autumn, 7–53.

9. Hopf, Ted. "Polarity, the Offence-Defense Balance, and War." *American Political Science Review,* 1991, 85, 2, June, 475–493.

10. Smoke, Richard. *War: Controlling Escalation.* Cambridge: Harvard University Press, 1977.

11. Brodie, Bernard. *War and Politics.* New York: Macmillan, 1973.

12. Topper, Keith. "The Theory of International Politics? An Analysis of Neorealist Theory." *Human Studies,* 1998, 21, 2, Apr., 57–186.

13. Coffey, Joseph I. *Nuclear Proliferation: Prospects, Problems and Solutions.* Philadelphia: American Academy of Political and Social Science, 1977.

14. Dunn, Lewis A. *Controlling the Bomb: Nuclear Proliferation in the 1980s.* New Haven, CT: Yale University Press, 1982.

Psychological Theories

The psychological factors that contribute to traits such as aggression and anger have long been linked with the tendency to engage in armed conflict. These feelings, which are generated on an individual level and may be transformed on an aggregate level, result in a tendency for leaders to have recourse to warfare. This section explores various aspects of the relationship between psychology and conflict.

In "Frustration Aggression Hypothesis," Neal Miller and his co-authors explain the relationship between aggressive behavior and frustration and vice versa. The ambiguity regarding "instigation" of aggression and the actual occurrence of an aggressive act due to frustration is clarified by the authors in this reading. They further explain that it may be difficult to observe "instigation" to aggression, and a manifestation of such thoughts may or may not occur as these acts are socially punishable. The implications of this seminal hypothesis for armed conflicts are also formulated by the authors of this reading.

In "Why Men Fight: Psychological Determinants," Jerome Frank relates the tendency to kill to psychological aspects of violence. Frank discusses different ways in which aggression is instigated in children, as this characteristic is more observable in children due to a lack of social inhibitions. He argues that this happens mainly through individual punishment, group punishment, imitation of angry adults, conflict with an external or an internal source, boredom and violation of expectations. Exposure to a hostile or angry environment and a demand for unfailing obedience by their elders may develop an aggressive streak within children. This reading also outlines the circumstances which promote the expression of frustration and anger in group and individual settings.

In "Nobody Wanted War," Ralph White presents six psychological "misperceptions" usually associated with warring states. World War I is used as an example to explain the nature of these misperceptions and their effects on the psychology of a group. After articulating how a group's image of itself and of its enemy facilitates the outbreak of violence against another group, White proceeds to differentiate between the immediate "precipitating" causes of a conflict and the long-term, underlying causes. He also poses questions pertaining to the specific causes of World War I and the psychology of the Austrians, Germans and Russians.

In "Know Your Enemy: a Psychological Profile of Terrorism," Colin Ross advocates the adoption of a psychological approach to the problem of terrorism. He wonders why $40 billion were allocated to clean up the debris of the World Trade Center while only one million dollars were allocated to the problems of posttraumatic stress disorders. The author acknowledges the fact that many terrorists are beyond psychological therapy but that the future recruitment of people into the suicide-bombing terrorist organizations may be prevented by making an effort to understand the psychological profiles of these individuals.

The "Einstein–Freud Correspondence on War" is a remarkable exchange of ideas between the world's two most famous scientists. This correspondence resulted from Einstein's query about the possibility of a psychological solution to warfare. After setting forth his own brilliant political and social theory of war, Einstein asked Freud if the propensity towards violence is psychologically ingrained in the human mind. Freud's reply to this letter is a classic summary of his theoretical perspective on the issue.

Neal E. Miller
Robert R. Sears
O. H. Mowrer
Leonard W. Doob
John Dollard

The Frustration-Aggression Hypothesis

The frustration-aggression hypothesis is an attempt to state a relationship believed to be important in many different fields of research. It is intended to suggest to the student of human nature that when he sees aggression he should turn a suspicious eye on possibilities that the organism or group is confronted with frustration; and that when he views interference with individual or group habits, he should be on the look-out for, among other things, aggression. This hypothesis is induced from commonsense observation, from clinical case histories, from few experimental investigations, from sociological studies and from the results of anthropological field work. The systematic formulation of this hypothesis enables one to call sharp attention to certain common characteristics in a number of observations from all of these historically distinct fields of knowledge and thus to take one modest first step toward the unification of these fields.

A number of tentative statements about the frustration-aggression hypothesis have recently been made by us in a book.[1] Unfortunately one of these statements, which was conspicuous because it appeared on the first page, was unclear and misleading as has been objectively demonstrated by the behavior of reviewers and other readers. In order to avoid any further confusion it seems advisable to rephrase this statement, changing it to one which conveys a truer impression of the authors' ideas. The objectionable phrase is the last half of the

proposition: "that the occurrence of aggression always presupposes the existence of frustration, and contrariwise, that the existence of frustration always leads to some form of aggression."

The first half of this statement, the assertion that the occurrence of aggression always presupposes frustration, is in our opinion defensible and useful as a first approximation, or working hypothesis. The second half of the statement, namely, the assertion "that the existence of frustration always leads to some form of aggression" is unfortunate from two points of view. In the first place it suggests, though it by no means logically demands, that frustration has no consequences other than aggression. This suggestion seems to have been strong enough to override statements appearing later in the text which specifically rule out any such implication.[2] A second objection to the assertion in question is that it fails to distinguish between instigation to aggression and the actual occurrence of aggression. Thus it omits the possibility that other responses may be dominant and inhibit the occurrence of acts of aggression. In this respect it is *inconsistent* with later portions of the exposition which make a distinction between the instigation to a response and the actual presence of that response and state that punishment can inhibit the occurrence of acts of aggression.[3]

Both of these unfortunate aspects of the former statement may be avoided by the following rephrasing: Frustration produces instigations to a number of different types of response, one of which is an instigation to some form of aggression.

This rephrasing of the hypothesis states the assumption that was actually used throughout the main body of the text. Instigation to aggression may occupy any one of a number of positions in the hierarchy of instigations aroused by a specific situation which is frustrating. If the instigations to other responses incompatible with aggression are stronger than the instigation to aggression, then these other responses will occur at first and prevent, at least temporarily, the occurrence of acts of aggression. This opens up two further possibilities. If these other responses lead to a reduction in the instigation to the originally frustrated response, then the strength of the instigation to aggression is also reduced so that acts of aggression may not occur at all in the situation in question. If, on the other hand, the first responses do not lead to a reduction in the original instigation, then the instigations to them will tend to become weakened through extinction so that the next most dominant responses, which may or may not be aggression, will tend to occur. From this analysis it follows that the more successive responses of non-aggression are extinguished by continued frustration, the greater is the probability that the instigation to aggression eventually will become dominant so that some response of aggression actually will occur. Whether or not the successive extinction of responses of non-aggression must inevitably lead to the dominance of the instigation to aggression depends, as was clearly stated in later pages of the book, upon quantitative assumptions beyond the scope of our present knowledge.[4,5]

Frustration produces instigation to aggression but this is not the only type of instigation that it may produce. Responses incompatible with aggression may, if sufficiently instigated, prevent the actual occurrence of acts of aggression. In our society punishment of acts of aggression is a frequent source of instigation to acts incompatible with aggression.

When the occurrence of acts of aggression is prevented by more strongly instigated incompatible responses, how is the existence of instigation to aggression to be determined? If only the more direct and overt acts of aggression have been inhibited, as is apt to be the case because such acts are the most likely to be punished, then the instigation to aggression may be detected by observing either direct or less overt acts of aggression. If even such acts of aggression are inhibited, then a different procedure must be employed. Two such procedures are at least theoretically possible. One is to reduce the competing instigations, such as fear of punishment, and observe whether or not acts of aggression then occur. The other is to confront the subject with an additional frustration which previous experiments have demonstrated would by itself be too weak to arouse an instigation strong enough to override the competing responses inhibiting the aggression in question. If the instigation from this additional frustration now results in an act of aggression, then it must have gained its strength to do so by summating with an already present but inhibited instigation to aggression. The presence of the originally inhibited instigation to aggression would be demonstrated by the effects of such summation. Thus the fact that an instigation may be inhibited does not eliminate all possibility of experimentally demonstrating its presence.

At this point two important related qualifications of the hypothesis may be repeated for emphasis though they have already been stated in the book. It is not certain how early in the infancy of the individual the frustration-aggression hypothesis is applicable, and no assumptions are made as to whether the frustration-aggression relationship is of innate or of learned origin.

Now that an attempt has been made to clarify and to qualify the hypothesis, four of the chief lines of investigation which it suggests may be briefly considered.[6]

1. An attempt may be made to apply the hypothesis to the integration and elucidation of clinical and social data. Here the fact that certain forms of aggression are spectacularly dangerous to society and to the individual is relevant. This means that acute personality conflicts are apt to arise from the problem of handling aggression and that the problem of aggression is apt to play an important role in shaping certain great social institutions such as the in-group as an organization against the out-group.

2. An attempt may be made to formulate more exactly the laws determining the different ways in which instigation to aggression will be expressed under specified circumstances. Some of the problems in this field are suggested by the phenomena of displacement of the object of aggression, change in the form of aggression, and catharsis of aggression.

3. An attempt may be made to secure more information concerning the other consequences which frustration may produce in addition to the instigation to aggression. Such an attempt would lead into studies of rational thought and problem solution as suggested in the classical work of John Dewey, and into studies of experimental extinction, trial-and-error learning, substitute response and regression.[7] Work along this line of investigation may deal either with the clinical and social significance of these other consequences of frustration or with the discovery of the laws governing them.

4. An attempt may be made to improve or to reformulate the basic frustration-aggression hypothesis itself. The determination of the laws which allow one to predict exactly under which circumstances instigation to aggression may be expected to occupy the dominant, the second, the third, or some other position in the hierarchy of instigations aroused by a frustrating situation is a most important problem of this type. Another problem is the reduction of the frustration-aggression hypothesis to more fundamental principles and the more accurate restatement of the hypothesis in terms of the more basic principles. One of the steps in this direction would be to scrutinize any exceptions to the hypothesis as now formulated. Another step would involve a careful study of the early stages of the socialization of the individual in an attempt to analyze the interlocking roles of three factors: first, innate physiological reaction patterns; second, learning mechanisms; and third, the structure of the social maze which poses the learning dilemmas and contains the rewards and punishments. An empirical and theoretical analysis along these lines might lead to a fundamental reformulation giving a closer approximation of the socially and scientifically useful truths imperfectly expressed in the present frustration-aggression hypothesis.

Notes

1. J. Dollard, L. W. Doob, N. E. Miller, O. H. Mowrer, and R. R. Sears. *Frustration and aggression.* New Haven: Yale University Press, 1939.

2. *Op. cit.,* pp. 8–9, 19, 58, 101–102.

3. *Ibid.,* pp. 32–38; also 27, 39–50, 75–87, 111, 166. In this later exposition a distinction is made not only between instigation to aggression and acts of aggression but also between conspicuous acts of overt aggression and inconspicuous acts of non-overt aggression. It is assumed that the former are more apt to be culturally inhibited by strong punishments than the latter.

4. *Op. cit.,* p. 40.

5. The notions used here are similar to those employed by Professor Hull in describing trial-and-error learning. See Hull, C. L. Simple trial-and-error learning—an empirical investigation, *J. Comp. Psychol.,* 1939, 27, 233–258.

6. Both of the first two of these chief lines of investigation have been developed at length in *Frustration and Aggression.* No attempt was made there to elaborate upon either the third or the fourth. Thus that first effort does not purport to be a complete systematization of all principles within a single field, but rather, an exploratory attempt to apply a strictly limited number of principles to several different fields. *Op. cit.,* pp. 18, 26.

7. These problems are discussed in more detail by Dr. Sears in the next paper of this series, "Non-aggressive responses to frustration." [*Psychological Review,* 1941, 48, 343–346.]

Jerome D. Frank

Why Men Fight: Psychosocial Determinants

The ultimate act of war is killing: no matter how indirect the method, how complex the chain of command, how intricate the team cooperation necessary to launch a weapon, or how many of the enemy killed at once, the final act is that of a single person. The inquiry into the psychosocial causes of war should thus begin by reviewing the causes of aggressive behavior in individuals. . . .

Humans respond not to events but to their meanings and can read into any event an endless variety of meanings. In humans as in other animals a physical attack will incite aggression, but so too will a dare, an insult to one's wife, spitting on the flag, or a military command.

Aggression's forms are as varied as their instigators—verbal abuse, physical assault, a lawsuit, complaining to the police, releasing a nuclear bomb. Since this chapter deals mainly with psychological experiments, the behaviors used as indicators of aggression are rather mild—killing, needless to say, is not among them—but since they do involve the infliction of psychological or physical pain, it may not be too far-fetched to assume that if additional conditions were also fulfilled, some of their determinants could contribute to the impulse to kill.

Although aggression can be generated by such varied motives as hate, revenge, protection of self-esteem, obedience to orders, or altruism, fight patterns in themselves are morally neutral: to murder a man for pay is regarded as wicked but to kill someone who attacks your child or your country is considered virtuous, as is supporting your family by prizefighting. The purpose of aggressive acts, as defined here, is to make the victim suffer: the sight of his victim's humiliation, fear, or pain may be actively pleasurable to an angry person and incite him to further violence, while other of his opponent's acts will inhibit it—again the variety is immense. A human aggressor may be satisfied by any behavior that indicates submission, as long as it is the behavior he set out to elicit.

There is the story of a nursery school child who became angry with a playmate and started to hit him. The teacher, attempting to divert him, handed him a doll and suggested that he hit it instead. He hit it a couple of times, then disgustedly threw it across the room, saying, "I want it to say 'Ouch!' "

The Instigator and Target of Aggression

Illustrated here is the failure of an aggression-discharging mechanism: if for any reason a person cannot attack the source of his anger, he may "displace" the attack to a substitute object, just like a fighting fish or a monkey. Displacement may be illustrated by another story, hopefully apocryphal: a blacksmith in a little Swiss village was convicted of murder and sentenced to be hanged. But since he was the only blacksmith and could not be spared, they hanged one of the village's seven tailors instead.

Humans have the capacity to displace their aggression to a remarkable degree, but a bit of experimental evidence suggests that they may obtain more relief by attacking the source of their anger rather than a substitute. The experimenter, who was also their teacher, angered some undergraduates by heckling them while they counted backwards from a hundred by twos as fast as they could, making sure that they could not finish in the allotted time. He then told them to ask a "victim"—

either himself or a fellow undergraduate—to guess the number they were thinking of, between one and ten, and to shock him every time he missed, over a series of ten trials. The measurement of anger was a rise in blood pressure—readings were taken before and after the heckling, and then after shocking the victim—and the central finding was that blood pressure rose significantly after the heckling and stayed up after shocking the undergraduate, but fell significantly after shocking the teacher, who had caused all the trouble.[1]

An analogous finding was that experimental subjects directed more aggression to a person who had insulted them, the greater his resemblance to a person in a film who was the object of justified aggression.

How Children Learn Aggression

It seems reasonable to suppose that a person's childhood experiences may affect his propensity to resort to violence in later life. The possibility that knowledge about early determinants of aggression may prove to have at least some remote relevance to the prevention of war thus justifies some consideration of the relationship to childhood aggression of individual and group methods of punishment, and of imitation.

Individual Punishment

. . . Because of its many possible meanings, however, the effect of childhood punishment on stimulating or inhibiting later aggressiveness is complex. In general, punishments range between two poles: infliction of bodily pain and withdrawal of affection. The latter is always involved, at least implicitly, and used alone, it seems more effective in causing the child to internalize the parents' standards and feel guilty when he does the disapproved act, even in their absence. Corporal punishment elicits compliance from the child when the punishing agent is present—actually or in his mind—but he is less apt to feel guilty and more inclined to feel anger and resentment at the frustrating parent, which may strengthen his tendency to be aggressive.

A comparative study of delinquent and nondelinquent middle-class adolescent boys has shown that children whose families freely use corporal punishment are more aggressive than those whose families do not. In humans, as in animals, the infliction of pain is a powerful stimulus to fighting. Two caged rats or monkeys, for example, will promptly attack each other if simultaneously given a painful shock, exhibiting an inborn response which takes precedence over more appropriate responses like pressing a lever to turn off the shock. If the same kind of reflex reaction can be seen as causing a spanked child to attack a toy or a playmate, this would partially explain why physical punishment may make children prone to fight. Since they are not allowed to attack their parents, children must seek outside targets—an activity reinforced by the characteristic approval of physically aggressive parents.

One subtle experiment illustrates a principle—termed the "strain toward consistency"—which is applicable, as we shall see, at the level of national as well as personal behavior. The study involved dissuading children from choosing to play with an attractive toy which they were shown along with others. Some were threatened with severe and some with mild punishment if they played with it, and all the children obeyed the prohibition. Asked to rate the toy's attractiveness three weeks to two months later, the children threatened with severe punishment still found it attractive, while those threatened with mild punishment derogated it. The assumption on which the experiment was based, and which it therefore may be said to support (although the findings could be explained in many other ways), is that the child must be able to explain to himself why he behaves inconsistently by avoiding the attractive toy. The threat of severe punishment for playing with it is sufficient reason, so he can still regard it as attractive; but if the threatened punishment is too mild to justify his avoidance, the most readily available reason is that the toy wasn't attractive after all. In other words, the most effective way to change a person's attitude toward an act to be deterred is apparently a threat "severe enough to induce momentary compliance yet mild enough to provide inadequate justification for that compliance." An ingenious statesman will perhaps find a way to apply this principle to deter his nation's enemies.

Group Punishment and Aggression

In keeping with the individualistic competitive orientation of American culture, educational methods, like those of childrearing, apply rewards and punishments to the child as an individual. Each child is expected to be concerned only with his own advancement and with the success or failure of his performance, not with that of the rest of the class or group. . . .

Imitation

Imitation is a very rapid and effective method of learning, and this may be another reason why children of parents who use corporal punishment may be more aggressive than children of those who do not.

Imitation of aggressive parents can be enhanced by what psychoanalytic theory terms "identification with the aggressor": "By impersonating the aggressor, assuming his attributes or imitating his aggression, the child transforms himself from the person threatened to the person making the threat," thereby presumably counteracting the anxiety the aggressor has aroused.

Children who do not have a parental model for aggression may develop the habit of not fighting—which in itself can be an aggression inhibitor. This principle has been used to explain why, if brought together before fighting patterns have developed, such "natural enemies" as dogs and cats grow up in perfect harmony, their innate patterns of fighting apparently either inhibited by other habits of not fighting or simply atrophied through disuse.

The power of imitation to instigate aggression in children has been elegantly demonstrated by a series of experiments with nursery school children about four years old. In the initial experiment they watched an adult playing with some toys: half saw him attack a large inflated doll while the other half saw him play quietly with some Tinker Toys. The experimenter then mildly frustrated the children by permitting them to play briefly with some very attractive toys, then interrupting them and taking them into a room containing the doll and other toys. If they did what the model had done to the doll and used his words, their aggressive behavior was classified as imitative; if they did different things, attacked different toys, or used different aggressive expressions, it was nonimitative. Boys and girls alike who had witnessed the aggressive model showed more of both types of aggression than did those who had seen the non-aggressive one—showing that an aggressive model stimulates both imitative and non-imitative aggressive behavior in young children. . . .

Immediate Instigators of Aggression

Having reviewed some possible predisposers to aggressive behavior, we now turn to aspects of the immediate situation that can elicit it. The dominant theory holds that all instigators to aggression can be regarded as forms of frustration—that is, as events that block ongoing goal-directed behavior. The subjective response to frustration is anger; the objective response, verbal or physical attack on the frustrating agent.

Rather than attempting to force all inciters to aggression into the procrustean bed labeled "frustration," we shall consider them under five headings—conflict, violation of expectations, boredom, contagion, and obedience—of which only the first three are clearly forms of frustration. Contagion and obedience could be subsumed under this concept only by considerable mental gymnastics; their major effect is to determine the form aggressive behavior takes, but they can also instigate it directly.

Conflict

Conflict is a ubiquitous and powerful form of frustration, one which frequently instigates violent behavior. Hostile feelings are especially likely to be aroused by some features of conflict between individuals. Actual or threatened bodily attack not only blocks one's progress toward a goal, including the universal goal of preserving life and limb, but can drive him further from it. Such a threat or attack arouses fear, which instigates flight or submission, but if these are perceived to be impossible, it becomes a stimulus to counterattack. The victim may perceive counterattack to be the best defense; or he may feel cornered although he is not physically trapped: the feeling that submission or flight would disgrace him in his own opinion or in that of persons who matter to him has the same psychological effect. Under these circumstances fear becomes a powerful motive for aggression, and with the change in behavior it becomes mingled with anger. . . .

Violation of Expectations

The most aggravating aspect of frustration may be that it violates expectations, in fact, even with chimpanzees: "When a chimpanzee in heat is introduced into the next cage, the male . . . comes as close as he can until he is stopped by the intervening cage wire. . . . At this time he shows no anger. . . . But the anger becomes highly predictable if the male is first led to expect, by the caretaker's actions, that he will be admitted to the female cage and then is not." Analogously, the bridge player who loses through his partner's error gets angry not at his opponents but at the partner, whom he expects not to let him down; the motorist rushing to work is more annoyed by the man ahead of him who stalls at a green light than at the driver who stops at a red one. . . .

The power of disappointed expectations to arouse aggression is perhaps pointed up most significantly by the fact that members of a deprived nation or segment of society become violent only when, expecting to better their lot, they find themselves unable to do so. Calcutta slum dwellers are incomparably worse off than the Negro citizens of Detroit; yet the latter exploded with rage and frustration, while the Indians, who until recently lived out their miserable existences in apathetic resignation, are only now becoming restive.

What has happened is that the mass media have made the poor much more aware than ever before that they are not getting their share of the world's increasing affluence—their once absolute deprivation has become relative deprivation.[1] And their sense of frustration is heightened because both democratic and communist ideologies hold out universal affluence as a legitimate expectation—nay, a right—and their hopes of achieving it are raised by the loosening of traditional social and political structures.

Boredom

The absence of certain stimuli can be as frustrating as the presence of others. Men, like rats, dogs, and monkeys, hunger for stimulation and excitement, and when life does not offer enough, they are prone to make some. It has been suggested that boredom, which stimulates the human propensity for mischief-making, is a major source of delinquency: "The delinquent is stuck with his boredom, stuck inside it, stuck to it, until for two or three minutes he 'lives'; he goes on a raid around the corner and feels the thrill of risking his skin or his life as he smashes a bottle filled with gasoline on some other kid's head. In a sense, it is his trip to Miami. It makes his day. It is his shopping tour. It gives him something to talk about for a week. It is *life*. Standing around with nothing coming up is as close to dying as you can get. Unless one grasps the power of boredom, the threat of it to one's existence, it is impossible to 'place' the delinquent as a member of the human race."

Because modern industrial societies have not found ways of keeping everybody busy, the ranks of the idle contain large numbers of young men—some unemployed, but others, their energies and abilities meeting insufficient challenge, for whom life is too easy. The reading about or viewing of violence, which enables such people to identify with the aggressor as well as with criminal acts, might be analogous to the appetitive behavior of animals whose environment contains no suitable target for aroused aggression. Bored young men thus constitute a reservoir of latent violence that national leaders can direct toward other nations.

Implicit in all of this is that it is far too optimistic to think that aggression would vanish if everyone were affluent and well fed, for it is not even theoretically possible to eliminate human aggression by removing all frustration. Frustration cannot be eliminated from life because humans, never satisfied, keep pushing until they come to a barrier—erected by the natural environment or by others who are also in process of aggrandizing themselves or their groups—at which point they become frustrated.

This analysis of frustration and aggression, however, does suggest two hopeful possibilities: it is possible to decrease frustration in a society by increasing the general level of well-being, providing channels for advancement, and the like; it is also possible to teach people to adjust their expectations to reality. And just as humans can always find targets for their rage, they can also find substitute ways of expressing it, including many which are socially useful—the social reformer who expresses his anger by fighting injustice probably obtains as much relief and satisfaction as the hoodlum who beats up an old man.

Contagion

Conflict, boredom, and other forms of frustration arouse aggressive impulses, but the aroused person's actions depend in part on the behavior of others in his environment. That the presence of others behaving violently seems to be powerfully stimulating is indicated by the fact that most senseless violence is perpetrated by gangs: the individuals, needing the support of their fellows, egg each other on and commit excesses as mob members that they would not dream of alone. . . .

Obedience

So far it has been assumed that most aggressive behavior is an expression of anger or hatred. This may be true in civilian life and these feelings sometimes contribute to the soldier's aggressiveness in hand-to-hand fighting. But the combat soldier's main motive for killing—especially as methods of killing become increasingly impersonal—is obedience: soldiers go into battle, fire cannon, and drop bombs simply because they have been ordered to do so, and not primarily because they hate the enemy.

Obedience to legitimate authority is one of the strongest motivating forces in the life of all normal members of organized societies, a fact that American students of psychology seem to have systematically minimized, perhaps because it does not fit the image of the self-reliant, ruggedly individualistic American. Yet the most cursory glance at history reveals the virtually unlimited power of a duly constituted authority to control his subjects' behavior, and this holds for aggression, both toward self and toward others. Subordinates have been known to commit suicide on order from their chief; and Henri Christophe, an early dictator of Haiti, is said to have shown his power by ordering his soldiers to march over the edge of the citadel cliff.

The power of obedience as a motivating force was brought into sharp focus by the Eichmann trial: was this man who was instrumental in the extermination of millions of Jews a sadistic monster or simply an efficient bureaucrat carrying out orders? Rather than entering into this unresolved controversy, let us turn to an experiment designed to test the limits of the power of obedience to cause someone to inflict pain on an innocent victim.

The subjects—normal American college students and adults—believed that the purpose of the experiment was to study the effect of punishment on learning. Each subject was to present a fellow subject (actually an experimenter's accomplice) with a simple learning task and shock him each time he made a mistake. Every detail of the setting was arranged so that the subject was completely convinced that he was administering shocks. The shocks were administered by a machine on which the voltage level was plainly marked, starting with 15 volts and increasing by 15-volt steps to 450 volts; the levels were also labeled: 300 volts was "intense shock" and 420 "danger, severe shock," with the two highest levels marked only "XXX." Before the experiment began the subject saw electrodes placed on the accomplice, who was then strapped to a chair in a neighboring room.

The actual experiment involved signaling a series of problems to the accomplice, who signaled his answer back. The accomplice made frequent errors in accordance with a prearranged schedule, and since the subject had been told to increase the shock by 15 volts after each error, he had to keep increasing the severity of the shock. At 300 volts the accomplice pounded the wall and thereafter stopped signaling answers; at this point the subject was told to regard failure to respond as an error and to continue to administer shocks. The accomplice pounded the wall once more at 315 volts, and then was not heard from again. Whenever the subject demurred, the experimenter told him to continue, with increasing urgency, the most forceful command being: "You have no other choice, you *must* go on."

The findings are disturbing: all subjects administered shocks up to 300 volts ("painful shock"), and 62 per cent went to the maximum—450 volts (two levels beyond "danger, severe shock").

Subsequent studies showed that the closer the victim was to the subject psychologically, the less likely the subject was to be obedient. But even when they had to hold the struggling, screaming victim's hand on the shock plate, 30 per cent of the subjects went on to give the maximum shock.[2]

Over 90 per cent of the subjects would participate in giving the maximum shock if they were required to perform only one step in a chain, such as throwing a master switch that permitted someone else to give the shock.

The degree of psychological closeness of the experimenter influenced the subjects' obedience in the opposite direction. The number of subjects who gave the full shock was about three times as great when the experimenter was in the room as it was when, after giving the original instructions, he left and gave his orders by telephone.

Although sadism may have facilitated an occasional subject's obedience (one or two were

horrified to discover that they felt pleasure when administering the shocks), the main determinant seems to be that the experimenter mobilized habits of obedience ingrained in all members of organized societies and also absolved the subject of guilt, since responsibility rested with the experimenter. A person submitting to a legitimate authority hands his conscience over, in effect, for since the authority decides what is right and wrong, the subordinate's own conscience is suspended.

Considering the intensity of indoctrination and training and the power of military authority, the proportion of soldiers attacking an enemy under orders would be expected to be considerably greater than the proportion of subjects in the experiments who obediently gave the full shock. Actually it was less—only 15 to 25 per cent of American soldiers in World War II fired their guns in combat, perhaps because the victims were psychologically closer and the authority more remote. Nuclear weapons are fired by a team against distant victims. The experiments suggest that these conditions should elicit ready obedience, so it is not surprising that when the commander of a Polaris submarine was asked how it felt to be the man whose act could unleash the submarine's destructive power, he replied: "I've never given it any thought. But, if we ever have to hit, we'll hit. And there won't be a second's hesitation." Fortunately obedience is as powerful an inhibitor of aggression as an instigator of it. Military authority forbids soldiers from killing except under very special circumstances and . . . obedience can restrain normally aggressive men from resorting to violence, even under extreme provocation.

Group Organization and Individual Aggression

In the process of becoming a member of any organized society each person must repeatedly block old habits and attitudes in order to learn new ones, and members of the same society are bound to collide as they struggle to find their niches in the social structure. Thus, in humans, as in animals, social living arouses a certain amount of aggression, necessary for the group's formation and maintenance. In all societies internal conflicts are inhibited by each member's belonging to several groups whose interests coincide in some respects and differ in others, and strong pressure is exerted not to carry any given conflict too far, for an enemy when one set of interests is salient may be required as an ally when another set comes to the fore. Interlocking group memberships may suffice to keep the peace even in societies which lack officials with power to judge quarrels and enforce their decisions: "These societies are so organized into a series of groups and relationships, that people who are friends on one basis are enemies on another. Herein lies social cohesion, rooted in conflict between men's different allegiances."

In stabilized societies that have developed adequate machinery for the peaceful resolution of disputes, the mere threat of physical violence is enough to secure redress of grievances. To gain concessions from their opponents, leaders of dissident groups, even those committed to nonviolence, threaten that they will not be able to restrain their followers from violence. It has been suggested that since elections can be viewed as ways in which elites measure their relative strengths—analogous to choosing up sides in a game—their effectiveness in such societies depends on their implicit threat of violence. The outcome predicts the winner in case of a violent showdown, which then becomes superfluous.

Group Disorganization and Violence

There seems to be an optimal degree of social control from the standpoint of minimizing frustrations. The frustrations of life under a rigidly organized, repressive system are too obvious to require elaboration. Since members of such a society cannot express their aggression toward their government, they displace it to external targets . . .

But that too little social control can be equally frustrating is possibly a plausible explanation of why, in both human and animal societies,

overt violence is most likely to occur before a firm social organization has been achieved or when it has broken down. In animal societies violence is at its peak while the social structure is forming—when territories are being staked out and dominance hierarchies established. The state of rapidly developing societies like the emerging nations may be analogous: individual citizens have not yet found their places or determined the limits of their powers, and the rules of the game have not been established. Under these circumstances there is bound to be much jockeying for power and wealth—sometimes by means which the adversary regards as illegitimate—and citizens constantly regarding each other as committing fouls. Furthermore, since individuals are prone to overestimate their capacities in comparison with their rivals', discrepancies between hopes and achievements are pronounced. Rapidly innovating societies, such as practically all industrialized nations today, could be expected to show similar characteristics, because their dominance hierarchies are constantly shifting and the rules changing to fit new circumstances.

The breakdown of social organization in an already established society has similar effects. In animal societies one source of this breakdown is overcrowding, such as characterized monkey colonies in zoos before its disastrous effects were recognized. Perhaps a similar phenomenon contributes to the high crime rates of densely populated city slums, although it is difficult to determine the relative contributions of overcrowding, poverty, poor education, and other factors. Part of the finding is attributable to attitudes of law enforcement agencies: since slum dwellers are booked for minor crimes more frequently than their better situated fellow citizens, there is a greater discrepancy between reported crime rates than between actual ones in the two areas. . . .

Socially Sanctioned Violence

All societies provide safety-valves for release of aggression in the form of permissible behavior, sharply limited in time and space and hedged by rules and customs that permit the discharge of aggression in ways that do not destroy the group.

Some of these safety valves permit actual killing. Some societies have sporadically allowed an individual to kill quite a few people before the fit passed or he himself was killed—the Vikings' *Berserkgang,* for example, possibly precipitated by eating certain mushrooms, and the Malays' *Amok.* That even these behaviors are not entirely attributable to the psychopathology of the killers is indicated by the fact that both abruptly disappeared. Going berserk vanished in the twelfth century after having plagued the Vikings for about three centuries, and *Amok* disappeared when the Dutch, sensing that it was basically a dramatic way of committing suicide, prevented the *Amok* runner from being killed but instead sentenced him to life imprisonment at hard labor.

Other societies have permitted or even encouraged the discharge of pent-up aggression by violence against minority groups. As in such examples as the Jews in Czarist Russia or the Chinese in Indonesia in 1965, since the groups chosen as scapegoats usually cannot adequately defend themselves, are suitable targets for projection and displacement, and are not fully integrated into the society, attacking them does not seriously disrupt the social structure.

Notes

1. "A generation or two ago the Colombian peasant was considerably more content with his lot in life. But the cheap transistor radio has changed that. Today the native of even the most remote Andean village is aware that a different way of life is available to some, if not yet to him. The result has been a new feeling of frustration and resentment."

2. In view of the ethical questions raised by this experiment, unusual care was taken at its conclusion to explain the procedure to the subjects and to give them ample opportunity to work through their feelings.

Ralph K. White

Nobody Wanted War

The Sequence of Events, 1914

Since the sequence of events is important in understanding how the First World War began, and since even the bare essentials may be hazy in many readers' minds, a brief summary is presented herewith:

June 28, 1914. The Austrian Archduke Francis Ferdinand was assassinated in Sarajevo by a militant Serbian nationalist protesting against the Austro-Hungarian rule over Serbians and other Yugoslavs.

At that time the Austro-Hungarian empire in Central Europe included not only what is now Austria and Hungary but also what is now Czechoslovakia, most of what is now Yugoslavia, and much of what is now Poland and Rumania. All of these nationalities were restless, even though the Austro-Hungarian rule over them was relatively mild and progressive. A very dangerous element in the situation, from the Austrian point of view, was the small independent nation of Serbia, just south of Austria-Hungary, which was obviously hoping to expand by uniting with its Yugoslav brothers then under Austro-Hungarian rule. From the Austrians' point of view, therefore, the murder of the Archduke was extremely dangerous as a symptom of the disintegration their empire was faced with, since they regarded the murder as instigated by "criminal" Serbian nationalists aided and abetted by the Serbian government in Belgrade.

July 5. The German Kaiser and his Chancellor, Bethmann-Hollweg, assured their ally, Austria-Hungary, of German support if Austria decided to react "firmly" to the Serbian danger.

July 23. Austria-Hungary sent Serbia an ultimatum making a number of demands.

July 25. Serbia replied to the ultimatum accepting all of the demands but one—the one that provided for Austro-Hungarian participation in police activity within Serbia. Austria-Hungary, regarding this last demand as crucial, rejected the Serbian reply, broke off diplomatic relations, and began to prepare for war.

Feverish diplomatic activity ensued. Russia, enormously larger than Austria, regarded Serbia as her protégé and protested Austria's action. Germany however, also much stronger than Austria and with a much more modern and efficient army than Russia's, stood firmly by Austria and seemed clearly ready to fight at Austria's side if Austria were attacked by Russia. France was similarly allied with Russia. England, loosely allied with France and Russia in the Triple Entente, did her best to get the issue resolved by negotiation, but failed.

July 29. Germany tried unsuccessfully to keep Austria from attacking Serbia.

By this time, however, a new and decisive element was entering the situation: the mobilization of Russia's enormous but cumbersome military machine. The Germans, thoroughly alarmed by the prospect of a war on two fronts, with Russia on one side and France on the other, demanded that Russia stop her mobilization. Russia refused and the war began with a German strike at France through Belgium, which consolidated British feeling and ensured that Britain would enter the war on the anti-German side.

Austrian Perceptions

On the day when Austria-Hungary broke relations with Serbia, setting in motion the escalation that transformed a local dispute into a world war, the perception of the situation in Austrian minds was radically different from the perception of it in the minds of Austria's enemies—a perception that sustained those enemies (ultimately including the United States) through more than four years of one of the bloodiest wars in history. Austria's enemies saw her declaration of war on Serbia as cold-blooded, calculating aggression. In their minds, the militarists who ruled Imperial Germany and controlled Austria had decided to use the minor Serbian dispute as a pretext to launch a war that they believed would give them mastery, first of Europe and then of the world.

Historical scholarship in the 1920s established a view of these events that includes a more understandable conception of what was in Austrian minds at the time. Historians are now in fair agreement that Austria, not Germany, was the prime mover. Germany clearly tried to prevent a major European war. From the Austrian point of view Serbia was carrying on an intolerable agitation against Austria-Hungary, not even stopping at assassination, that had to be punished. Unless Serbia was punished, nationalist agitation throughout the Austro-Hungarian Empire would get worse, threatening its very existence.

To be sure, there were other thoughts in the minds of Austrians. One was the terrifying possibility of a larger war. Russia, with her enormous army, might come in. But surely (the Austrians thought) the Czar of Russia, who lived in fear of assassination himself, must realize that the Hapsburg emperor could not tolerate the sort of agitation that had prompted the assassination of the Archduke. He must see that Austria-Hungary's very existence as a bastion of civilization and order in Central Europe depended on her standing firm in this new crisis and teaching the conspirators in Belgrade an unforgettable lesson. Since the German Kaiser had seen the justice of Austria's position and was standing firmly by her, the Czar would hardly be so rash as to intervene; he must know that the consequences of a world war would be incalculable. In any case, the risk must be run; if the Serbian nationalist agitation

among the Serbs and Croats still under Austrian rule were allowed to continue, it could quickly spread to the other nationalities within the Austro-Hungarian family of nations, and Austria-Hungary herself would disappear as a Great Power—which was, of course, unthinkable.

If this is a fair picture of what was happening in Austrian minds, it suggests that their reality world was distorted by six forms of misperception:

1. A diabolical enemy-image
2. A virile self-image
3. A moral self-image
4. Selective inattention
5. Absence of empathy
6. Military overconfidence

1. *The Diabolical Enemy-Image:* In the central focus of Austrian minds was the "criminal" character of the "assassins" who had violated all standards of human decency and were endangering the very survival of the beneficent Austro-Hungarian empire. In this black-and-white picture the black was more fully in focus than the white. To Austrians it seemed that such men, and the conspiracy in Belgrade that was responsible for their actions (though this point remained controversial to detached observers) were so flagrantly evil that all right-minded people, even Russians, must see the need to "punish" them.

The Germans too saw devils. Although before July 30 they only gave "loyal" support to Austria (and, on July 29, tried unsuccessfully to restrain her), on July 30 the news of Russian mobilization threw the Germans into panic. To the Kaiser it appeared that the Russians, French, and British were seizing upon the Serbian dispute as a pretext to attack both Germany and Austria. In an extraordinary instance of displacement of hostility, at precisely the moment when the British were trying desperately to stave off major war, the Kaiser saw them as the head and center of a plot against him. On the margin of a diplomatic note he wrote: "The net has been suddenly thrown over our head, and England sneeringly reaps the most brilliant success of her persistently prosecuted, purely *anti-German world policy,* against which we have proved ourselves helpless, while she twists the noose of our political and economic destruction out of our fidelity to Austria, as we squirm isolated in the net (italics in the original)." Though the Kaiser could scarcely be called psychotic, this passage has the ring of pure paranoia. To him, the British plot was real. With Germany's very existence at stake, he felt that Russia should be given no more time to get its enormous but cumbersome military machine under way. He decided on a strike-first policy, and once that decision was made, the Great War had begun.

2. *The Virile Self-Image:* In 1914, the Austrians were not alone in their preoccupation with prestige and their feeling that humiliation would be intolerable. Each of the Great Powers feared "losing our position as a Great Power" and sinking to the status of a second-class power. In each case, after a firm stand had been taken, governments were acutely conscious of the danger of backing down, or seeming to back down. They were less vividly aware of the pain and death of tens of millions of human beings that might result if there were no compromise. This was true until the general Russian mobilization, when fear took over as the ruling emotion in Germany, if not in Austria-Hungary, and led directly to a strike-first policy. Before that time, the ruling emotion had been not fear of attack but fear of humiliation. The chief dimension in which national decision-makers judge themselves, and expected to be judged by others, was not good vs. bad, or right vs. wrong, but strong vs. weak. The essential goal apparently was to be, and to seem, strong and courageous. The essential thing was to take a firm stand, a strong stand, and to do it with such firmness and such obvious lack of fear, on one's own part and on the part of one's allies, that the potential enemy would surely back down.

3. *The Moral Self-Image:* In the crisis of 1914 the Austrians had a black-and-white picture in which only evil was attributed to the Serbian enemy and only good [to] the Austro-Hungarian self. While their own moral nobility was perhaps

less salient in the Austrians' minds than the diabolical character of the enemy or their own need to take a firm stand in the interest of self-preservation, the Austrian self that they thought worth preserving was also noble: peace-loving (they never for a moment sought a bigger war, and always feared it), civilized (they were a bastion of civilization in a Central Europe threatened by the barbarian tide of pan-Slavism), economically rational (their empire was prospering in unity and would suffer economically if broken up), orderly (the Serbian assassins were violating elementary standards of law and order), and democratic (theirs was a limited monarchy, and the subject peoples were advancing toward full autonomy as rapidly as possible).

It is not necessary to deny some truth in each of these propositions; it is necessary only to notice that the Austrians' picture was expurgated at one crucial point. It did not include even a candid consideration of the possibility that this noble nation might now be committing aggression. The Austrian ultimatum to Serbia included what the Serbs regarded as a virtual demand for submission to Austrian authority, and when this was not clearly accepted by Serbia, Austria broke relations and began to mobilize for war. In the eyes of most of the world, this was aggression. It was aggression also by almost any clear definition of the term; for example, if aggression is defined as the use of force or threat of force on another nation's territory and against the wishes of the majority of the politically conscious people of that nation, Austria's action was aggression, however much it may have been provoked. But the Austrians did not call it that, or seriously think about what to call it. To them it was not aggression at all, but a firm stand, or bringing the criminals to justice. Here again there was selective inattention. The charge of aggression was not answered in their minds; it was ignored.

There was also in their minds a curious sort of automatism—a feeling that they could not do otherwise. The initial steps on the road to war were taken with a feeling of necessity; to do otherwise would be suicide. Once the initial steps were taken, Austrian minds were gripped by what Anatol Rapoport has called "the blindness of involvement." As the Emperor Francis Joseph put it, "We cannot go back now." All moral guilt was thus shifted from the Austrians themselves to an impersonal Fate or Necessity. This was shown most strikingly at two key points: Austria's refusal to reconsider her course of action on July 25, when the conciliatory Serbian reply to the Austrian ultimatum was seen even by the German Kaiser as "doing away with every reason for war," and her refusal to draw back even when Germany, on July 29, exerted very strong pressure on her to do so. On that day the German Chancellor, Bethmann-Hollweg, wired the Austrians: "we cannot allow Vienna to draw us lightly, and without regard to our advice, into a worldwide conflagration." Berchtold, the Austrian Foreign Minister, had the bit in his teeth, and had put on blinders; with a "courageous" unwillingness to consider any alternative course of action, he stepped over the brink of the precipice.

The strong German pressure on Austria to draw back also points up how mistaken our own diabolical image of Germany was, throughout the First World War. Americans generally assumed that Austria, much weaker than Germany, must have been playing a subordinate role in the Kaiser's plans for war and world conquest. Actually Austria, encouraged by the "blank check" which Germany had heedlessly given her on July 5, went a good deal further than Germany wanted her to. The "puppet" got out of hand. Like much of history, this series of events was largely a matter of sheer thoughtlessness and failure to communicate. Germany can be blamed not so much for malice or for dreams of world conquest as for ordinary carelessness. She should have tried sooner and harder to stop Austria. But one thing is now fairly well agreed upon by scholars: Germany did not try to precipitate a European war. She tried to prevent it.

4. *Selective Inattention:* Of all the psychological mechanisms involved in the misperceptions we have been considering, perhaps most pervasive is one that in some contexts may be called "resis-

tance" or "repression" (though the Freudians give a more restricted meaning to each of these terms). Harry Stack Sullivan has referred to it more broadly as "selective inattention." It is involved on both sides of a black-and-white picture, when white or gray elements on the enemy side are glossed over and attention focuses only on the black, and vice versa.

In nations stumbling toward war there are usually at least three other definable types or aspects of selective inattention: narrow time-perspective, narrow space-perspective, and absence of empathy. The Austrians in 1914 were vividly aware of only one aspect of the future as they perceived it: the catastrophic disintegration that they thought likely (with much reason) if they could not cope firmly with Serbian nationalism. But the parts of this anxiety-filled image were not cognitively well defined. It did not distinguish clearly, for example, between what would happen if they merely dealt firmly with Serbian and other agitators within their own borders and what would happen if, in the process of punishing Serbia, they sent troops across their borders into a neighboring state. To the rest of the world this distinction seemed the distinction between legitimate maintenance of internal stability and illegitimate aggression that could precipitate world war. But in anxious Austrian minds it was all of a piece: a need to punish Serbia, as vigorously as possible, in order to prevent destruction and vindicate the image of Austria-Hungary as a virile nation.

In addition, the Austrians failed to pay attention to other future possibilities, including Russian intervention, and the kind of breakup of the Austrian empire that later occurred as a result of the war that Austria herself precipitated.

A restriction in the Austrians' space-perspective was represented by their failure to pay much attention to countries other than the two that were the main focus of their attention (themselves and Serbia), and the two that were somewhat in the periphery (Russia, whose intervention they feared, and Germany, whose strong stand by Austria was counted on to deter Russian intervention). Two countries that were soon to become involved, France and England, were present in Austrian minds but apparently not seriously considered. America, which was to join the Allies nearly three years later—partly because of the American impression at the outset that Germany and Austria had committed aggression—was apparently not considered at all.

5. *Absence of Empathy:* Even in the case of Serbia, the enemy that was in the bright central focus of Austrian attention, the Austrians seemed to fail almost completely to realize how the situation looked from another point of view. They did not see that to a Serbian patriot the Austrian demands appeared to be naked aggression, calling for a struggle to the last drop of patriotic Serbian blood. They did not see how Russian pride, smarting after a number of setbacks including the high-handed Austrian annexation of Bosnia six years earlier, would respond to a new arbitrary extension of German–Austrian power in an area where the Russians felt that their honor and their interest were involved. They failed to see that, while the Russian Czar himself was peacefully inclined and would try to avoid a major war, his close advisers were not necessarily so pacific, and that Russia might become entangled in a situation in which its pride and prestige were so deeply involved that war might seem the only alternative to intolerable humiliation. Like the Germans, the Austrians resisted negotiations, which would have compelled them to see clearly and to cope with other viewpoints. They failed to anticipate the swing of the pendulum of the Kaiser's mood from careless overconfidence to panic once the Russian general mobilization had started and the British entry into the war seemed likely.

The Austrians failed to see how the British and French would fear a collapse of the balance of power if they left Russia to fight alone against a smaller but far more efficient German army, or how British public opinion would react if the panicky Germans, anxious to capitalize on their one great asset, the superior efficiency and speed of their forces, were to invade France through Belgium. They did not realize that America would regard their attack on Serbia as a big country bul-

lying a small one, and would similarly regard Germany's march through Belgium—that America's sympathies would be immediately engaged on the side of the Allies, and the way would thus be prepared for America ultimately to enter the war. In short, the Austrians were so wrapped up in their own anxiety and their own righteous indignation that they had little attention left for considering what was real to anyone else.

6. *Military Overconfidence:* It is paradoxical but true that exaggerated fear can be combined with exaggerated military confidence. The Austrians, for example, had what now seems an exaggerated fear of the spreading disaffection of nationalities within their empire that would result if they failed to take a stand against Serbia. At the same time, until the Russian mobilization, they were excessively confident that they could teach Serbia a lesson and, with strong German support, keep Russia from intervening. Like the Germans, they pinned their hopes on the possibility of localizing the issue, enjoying mastery and venting righteous indignation within a small sphere while remaining safe from the mastery impulse and the righteous indignation of others in a larger sphere. They were wrong. They misperceived. Reality differed from their perception of it chiefly in that they were inattentive to the possibility that strong allies of Serbia (Russia, France, Britain, America) might scorn to be intimidated by the Kaiser's appearance at Austria's side "in shining armor." They did not see that their potential enemies, like themselves, might be living up to an indomitable self-image, fearful of showing fear, and therefore irrationally ready to fight.

Underlying Causes

The causes of any war are usually discussed under two heads: immediate, "precipitating" causes—assumed to be relatively superficial—and long-term, underlying causes. Up to this point our analysis of World War I has been only in terms of its immediate or precipitating causes. Is this superficial? Were there deeper causes that have not been touched?

Certainly there were other forces at work. Four factors often cited as underlying causes are nationalism, militarism, economic imperialism, and the system of competitive alliances into which Europe was divided in 1914. Each of these had deep historical roots, and the mere mention of them is enough to suggest how much has been omitted in the above historical sketch. But even in this brief discussion it is appropriate to ask two questions:

Were the immediate, precipitating causes perhaps less superficial than is commonly supposed?

After all, these are the causes that were most directly, demonstrably related to the fateful decision that directly produced the war. Austria's breaking of relations with Serbia and her mobilization for war, Russia's general mobilization, the panicky German response to Russian mobilization—these actions, and the motives, assumptions, and misperceptions that produced them, were direct and unequivocal causes of the war's outbreak. Abstractions such as militarism and economic imperialism are both more indirectly and more equivocally related to what occurred.

Take, for instance, militarism. This high-level abstraction, insofar as it means anything beyond our dislike of war and of the arms associated with it, has two concrete meanings: an arms race, with its concomitant of heightened fear and suspicion, and a disproportionate influence of military men in the decisions that lead to war.

An arms race certainly existed in the years before 1914, especially in the competition between the German and the French armies and between the German and the British navies. But it would be hard to show that either race contributed even indirectly to the decisions of the Austrians, the Russians, and the Germans that directly precipitated war.

As for undue influence of military men upon diplomatic decisions, it probably existed in Russia but not, to any high degree, in either Austria or Germany. In Austria the decisions were apparently made primarily by the civilian Foreign Minister, Berchtold, backed by the Emperor, Francis Joseph, and in Germany by the civilian Chancellor, Bethmann-Hollweg, backed by the Kaiser. In neither case is it clear that militarism had any essential part in what occurred.

Economic imperialism as a cause of war has been the favored explanation of Marxists and others who have pictured the First World War as the inevitable outcome of capitalist rivalry for markets, raw materials, and investment opportunities. Innumerable writers have discovered in economic imperialism a profound and "scientific" explanation for the mystery of the occurrence of war in a world in which the common people, at least, hate war. But this explanation is hard to reconcile with the stubborn, inconvenient fact that the prime movers in starting the First World War were not the advanced capitalist nations, Great Britain, France, and Germany. The prime movers were Serbia, Austria-Hungary, and Russia, which were engaged not in a scramble for overseas markets and raw materials but in an old-fashioned struggle for territory, power, prestige, national independence, and (at least in Austrian minds) rational survival.

Competitive alliances also call for consideration as one of the forces behind the war. It is true that the alliance of Germany with Austria-Hungary, the alliance of France with Russia and the looser entente that included Great Britain as well as France and Russia were crucial factors in the immediate, dramatic spread of the war. Once Austria and Russia were embroiled, the war spread and became a conflagration that included Germany, France, and Great Britain. A local conflict was transformed, senselessly, into a general one. A distinction should be made, however, between factors that caused the war and factors that caused it to spread. The initial conflict was essentially between Austria and Serbia, with Russia's support of Serbia serving to bring two major countries, Austria and Russia, into collision. That presumably would have occurred whether either country had allies or not. Germany at first gave Austria a blank check, but later tried to restrain her. If that attempt had succeeded, the war probably would not have occurred, and the alliance system would have had to be credited with stopping a war instead of producing one.

Nationalism, however, was clearly a basic cause. The crisis of 1914 was shot through with nationalism from beginning to end. To take just one country: Austria's diabolical image of Serbia was an image of a national enemy, endangering Austria's national survival. Her virile and moral self-image was an image of a national self. Her selective inattention shielded her from disturbances of a national black-and-white picture and from reconsidering a course of action that she regarded, however mistakenly, as essential to national survival. (Sinking to the status of second-class power seemed to the Austrians almost equivalent to national extinction.) The empathy that Austria's decision-makers did not have was empathy with national enemies, and Berchtold's jaunty, feckless overconfidence was overconfidence in a national self, backed by a national ally.

Every step in our analysis could be described also as a study of one or another aspect of nationalism, defined provisionally as identification of individuals and governments alike) with a national self-image and a consequent mobilization of powerful motives—such as the desire for power and prestige—on behalf of that image. Negatively, nationalism can be described as an absence of any concept of a self larger than the nation. With the possible exception of the Catholic church, and of course their alliance with Germany, the Austrians in 1914 had virtually no supranational self-images (such as Europe, or the United Nations, or the human race), with which they could identify. The same can be said of all other actors in the drama.

Earlier national history and underlying causes—including psychological ones—may be important, then, in helping to account for the growth and shaping of the nationalism that now seems to have been of decisive importance during the war crisis itself. And that leads to a second question:

Were psychological factors, including misperception, important also in the growth of nationalism, and should they therefore be recognized among the underlying as well as the precipitating causes of the war?

For full understanding of the nationalism that pervaded Europe in 1914, the history of the preceding two or three centuries must be studied. For example, Austria's glorious victories over the Turks and Metternich's special dynastic version of nationalism help one to understand the atmosphere and rhetoric of Vienna in 1914.

The historical record alone, however, is hardly enough to explain it. It is also important to ask whether Austrian and other nationalists derived unconscious satisfactions, throughout these centuries, from picturing their own nations as virile and moral, whether (more mysteriously) they also drew unconscious satisfaction from picturing their enemies as diabolical, and if so, why. One must ask whether there is a deep psychological need to identify with symbols of *something* larger and better than the individual self, and try to analyze the social factors that link this need to some symbols (religious, ideological, or rational) rather than others. . . .

Colin A. Ross

Know Your Enemy: A Psychological Profile of Terrorism

In the five months since the World Trade Center and Pentagon attacks, I have not heard the words posttraumatic stress disorder (PTSD) pronounced once on television. I have on my desk a report stating that $40 billion was allocated to cleanup of the World Trade Center site, of which $1 million was allocated to mental health. We are spending 40,000 times as much on the physical pile of rubble as we are on our minds, souls and psyches.

Don't get me wrong. The physical cleanup is absolutely necessary and I support it fully, for several reasons: as a symbolic healing of the wound; to show the terrorists that we can recover; to find the bodies and body parts for the relatives; for security, investigational and intelligence reasons; and so the area can start being used again, whether for a building or a park.

But does a 40,000:1 ratio make sense? Not to me. I think we are being too macho about the psychological impact of the attack. We seem to regard it as weak or unpatriotic to have PTSD. I saw this when I was at a conference on trauma and dissociation in Barcelona a few years ago. A psychiatrist stated that there are no cases of PTSD in the Basque region of Spain, which has experienced a lot of terrorism. This is preposterous clinically, and I regard it as a macho political statement, posing as a medical analysis. We seem to be doing the same thing here. In that regard, we are behaving like the terrorists, who also deny that they are affected by the trauma they have experienced.

If I was going to work therapeutically with the suicide bomber, I would try to get inside his mind and his world-view. This is called empathy. I would begin by explaining to him that I view suicide bombings as moral and legal crimes which can never be justified. I would explain that I am fully in support of the U.S. military, diplomatic, intelligence and economic war against terrorism. But, I would say, I am there to work with him as a human being, setting aside his violent and dangerous behavior.

The terrorist's participation in the therapy would be voluntary and he would stop it at any time without consequences. If he ever called me as an expert witness in a legal proceeding, I would tell the jury what I understood, but I would not apologize for, excuse, or sugar-coat his terrorist activities. I am not soft on crime. The purpose of the therapy would be to treat his mental health problems, conflicts and addictions, just as it would be for anyone.

Since this hypothetical young man is a Muslim and a member of al-Queda, I would explain to him . . . I would explain to him how I see the criminal justice system operating in America, under the heading of "tough on crime." I would point out to him that I live in Texas, a death penalty state of which President Bush was formerly Governor.

In America, you are not allowed to have empathy for a murderer. You are not allowed to take his childhood trauma into account in legal proceedings. If you do, you are dismissed as a bleeding-heart liberal who is pushing the "abuse excuse." In America, murderers are not allowed to be victims of trauma. There are two rigid categories: tough on crime-no empathy; and soft on crime-empathy.

In order to avoid being soft on crime, American courts ban empathy. This results in absurd claims by psychiatrists and prosecutors that serial killers, or mothers who murder their babies, are not insane. The system blocks acknowledging the insanity in order to block a soft sentence. . . .

All terrorists see themselves as victims, and see their terrorist activities as a legitimate counter-response to the crimes of their perpetrators. I would show the suicide bomber that I believe in and practice another option: tough on crime-empathy. I will not excuse him, but neither will I demonize him.

I would then give him my analysis of demonization. Osama bin Laden has defined America as Satan. He allows no empathy and no negotiation, and he is locked in a fight to the death with the Evil America. He is the victim and America is the perpetrator, in his mind.

America is simply the mirror image. For America, bin Laden is Satan, there is no negotiation, and the goal is the capture and death of bin Laden, either in a military action or through execution at an American jail.

Both sides have adopted an absolute, black-and-white position of good-versus-evil. There is really no difference between the psychology of the two sides. From the perspective of the citizens of America, we are perfectly justified in taking bin Laden dead or alive. Bin Laden's perspective is the flip opposite. He feels fully justified in killing innocent children at the World Trade Center. What is the difference between al-Queda and America, then?

The suicide bomber thinks I am working on excusing or justifying bin Laden's murder of American civilians. I am not. I am explaining to the suicide bomber my assumptions and point of view, in order to form a treatment relationship with him. The psychology of al-Queda and America today are mirror opposites of each other in many ways. But not the behavior.

America is not perfect by any means, but the two opponents are very different. The United States has never killed thousands of Muslim civilians on purpose in a military operation. The September 11 attacks did nothing but increase the total Muslim casualties in the war between Mus-

lim terrorists and America, if we count the Muslims who will die from the American response.

In the therapy, I would emphasize the similarities in order to point out the differences. It is a combination of empathy and toughness.

The psychology of demonization is alive and well in America. . . . After some discussion of the psychology of demonization with the hypothetical suicide bomber, I would next launch into a character analysis of bin Laden, first his positive traits. Osama bin Laden is:

- Highly intelligent
- Well educated
- Charismatic
- Dedicated to his cause
- Well organized
- The most newsworthy person on the planet
- The successful architect of a huge impact on America and the world
- Resourceful
- Tenacious
- Devout
- Proud

This is an accurate and factual list. Its purpose would be to un-demonize bin Laden, and thereby, by association, un-demonize the suicide bomber.

I would then ask about bin Laden's children, of whom there are fifteen by four wives. Where are they? In the five months since the World Trade Center, I have not heard or read one mention of them. Are they in the caves with their father? At another target site? Even in Afghanistan? Are they alive or dead? So far, no one in the American media, at least while I have been reading newspapers and watching TV, has bothered to ask these questions.

What if bin Laden's children are inside caves or buildings we plan to target with smart bombs or Special Forces troops? Collateral damage? Bin Laden is Satan for killing innocent women and children at the World Trade Center, but we seem unconcerned about his children. What? We don't even have intelligence on the location of bin Laden's children? Or we do, but it's classified?

Why does no journalist ask these tough questions? Is it un-American to be concerned about the welfare of Osama bin Laden's children? It better not be.

In my hypothetical psychotherapy, the suicide bomber is now reinforced in his view of America as Satan and bin Laden and his family as victims.

At this point I would turn the tables. Where did Osama bin Laden start out? In Saudi Arabia with a net worth of hundreds of millions of dollars. He received the best education, flew in private jets, rubbed shoulders with royalty and billionaire capitalists, and has four wives. He could provide his children the best the world has to offer, whether that be a medical education at Harvard or fully subsidized beachcombing in Hawaii.

But where are his children? Living in rags in caves? Waiting to be killed by the U.S. military as "collateral damage?" The U.S. never talks about his children, but neither does he. And what about bin Laden's wives? Does he beat them? Where are they and what are their futures, compared to the wealth and opportunity he could have provided?

If bin Laden lived in America and removed his children from the life of a multi-millionaire to hide them in caves, keep them from school, and expose them to military attack, they would be apprehended by Child Protective Services. We would define him as a perpetrator of child abuse and neglect.

Why would Osama bin Laden abuse and neglect his own children? He is one of fifty-two siblings by thirteen wives of his father. Did he ever get what he needed from his own father, emotionally and spiritually? No way. Osama bin Laden must have been an extremely emotionally neglected child. The one-on-one time he got with his father as a child was probably zero. He never learned how to love and be loved by his father, to honor or be honored by his father. This is my theory, not something I know for a fact.

Osama bin Laden would have to feel hurt, lonely, unloved, rejected and abandoned by his parents, simply because of the structure of his family, not even counting his father's religious, social, and business commitments. He would have to resent the empty material substitutes for love he got from them, no matter how numerous and opulent they were.

Then what happened? The thoughtful, devout Osama became the black sheep of his family. This was not all his family's fault, but it wasn't all his fault either. I don't know exactly why, out of all those siblings, only Osama became the greatest terrorist on the planet, but he did.

Start out with the hurt, rejection and anger he already felt by age ten. Then add on being disowned by your family and country, having your passport revoked, being exiled to the Sudan then Afghanistan, and you have an extremely hurt, rejected and vengeful man.

What happens next? It is unbearably painful to feel the full brunt of the hurt and rejection by mom and dad, which is the core of the pain. So what do you do? Displace it. It is not a complicated equation.

The empty, materialist, capitalist father has betrayed his son. Not only his son, but his country, race and religion, in Osama bin Laden's mind. How? The Evil Father has aligned himself with a puppet regime in Saudia Arabia, which is in turn pandering to the Great America. America is aligned with the Satanic Jews in the Jewish oppression of Muslims in Palestine. The America Satan placed his troops in Saudia Arabia on a long-term basis after the Gulf War. Bingo.

All the hatred is directed at America. This is much less painful than directing the anger at your father, because if you feel that anger, soon you will fall into the underlying feelings, which are those of a sad, lost, scared, lonely boy who longs for his father's love, his father's touch, and his father's approving words, but who will never get them.

It is easier to kill Americans than to acknowledge and feel that underlying grief about your mother and father. This is the basic psychology of trauma.

It is more powerful, stronger and safer to be the perpetrator, because then you do not have to feel the pain of victimhood. In clinical work I see this all the time—people jump into the perpetrator role in order not to feel the powerless, helpless terror of the victim. You can escape your own terror by terrorizing others. Osama bin Laden calls this behavior a jihad. In east LA it is called a drive-by shooting. Bin Laden is a drive-by shooter on a world geopolitical stage; the world is his gang neighborhood.

Next I would talk about the reward offered to the suicide bomber, which is seventy-two virgins in heaven. I would point out the contradiction. Bin Laden attacks America as an infidel land of alcohol and prostitution, low morals, and spiritual emptiness. But what is the heavenly reward he offers the suicide bomber? Eternal residence at a personal Playboy Mansion.

Ramzi Yousef, who is in jail for the 1993 World Trade Center bombing, lived a life of sex, drugs and rock and roll in the west for years, as did other Muslim terrorists, including bin Laden. Bin Laden drank, got in bar fights, womanized and lived the life of the rich Saudi playboy in Beirut, from 1973 to 1975. He became increasingly devout and fundamentalist after the fall of Beirut, which interrupted his trips here.

Terrorists are basically attacking the enemy within. They lust after and long for the sexual company of voluptuous women, but they suppress that in themselves with religious fundamentalism, and try to exterminate it outside themselves as well. The terrorists are attacking their own image in a mirror.

The problem is, this isn't just psychology. A lot of people died on September 11. Does the suicide bomber really want to be a pawn in the trauma-driven psychodrama of his terrorist leaders? What if the seventy-two virgins will never show up in the after-world? What if that was a con job, not a spiritual fact? How does he know for sure? These are questions I would ask the suicide bomber—I would basically be using the same procedures described in the cult deprogramming literature.

Then I would get into the personal history of the suicide bomber himself. Did he also miss out

on his father's love? Was his teenage sexuality honored and fulfilled by his culture, or stifled? Did he get to make love in the back seat of a car, or watch a sexy movie? No. He had no opportunity and his needs were suppressed and condemned by his cultural leaders. They forgot to tell him about their own sexual escapades in the west. And they offered him as an eternal reward, the very thing they condemned.

The seventy-two virgins in heaven have no more rights than women did under the Taliban regime. They are just objects. Under the Taliban women were executed in public for adultery, while the greatest martyrs to the faith got seventy-two virgins in heaven. Sometimes the number is seventy virgins and seventy wives, which would way out-perform Osama bin Laden's father. Now we are getting into the suicide bomber's anger and grief about his mother. If mother and all women with her are controlled objects, sometimes virgin sex slaves in heaven, sometimes adulterous whores on earth, then the terrorist feels no pain about the love he missed out on. The objectification of women is a psychological defense. The terrorist doesn't feel any pain about the fact that cardboard silhouettes of women, including his mother, did not love him, because they are just objects for use, abuse and disposal, in this world and the next. He need not care about them, or about their feelings for him. The terrorist's personal psychological defense is reinforced by his culture, his government, his religious leaders, and his terrorist programmers.

Next, in the therapy, I might describe the suicide bomber I read about in a book. This young man was captured before he could blow himself up. When asked how he justified the killing of innocent women and children, he replied that all citizens of Israel are responsible for the crimes of their state. There are no innocents in Demon-Israel. The rights of the individual are erased by the crimes of the state. This is the standard propaganda response, and the young man had been well programmed with it.

The young man was asked what he missed due to his life as a terrorist. His answer? Soccer.

It turned out that the young man was an avid soccer fan, knew a lot about the Israeli soccer team, and admired the top Israeli players.

The person questioning him then asked if he would be willing to commit suicide in a packed soccer stadium, if assigned that mission. He said that he could not do that.

Hello. This is not an evil maniac, a monster, or a fanatic. This is a teenager, a soccer fan, a sexually frustrated, poor and oppressed human being with no future. The cure to terrorism is to reach the traumatized human being underneath the disguise of terrorist. The young man could not kill at a soccer stadium because soccer put him in touch with his own humanity, and the humanity of his targets.

The suicide bomber has been brainwashed by his culture, his religion and his terrorist leaders. He has been sold a lie about getting a permanent pass to the Playboy Mansion. He wants the same thing that red-blooded American boys want: to be a sports star and have a hot girlfriend, plus money and a good car. For that we call him Satan?

If the young man in therapy with me could learn to accept, tolerate and honor his own loss and grief, he would not need to be a perpetrator. Then he could be a person.

Am I proposing that the war against terrorism should be psychotherapy? No. That would be absurd. Many terrorists are too far-gone for any psychological strategy to have any effect. The solutions for them are military.

I am talking about the long-term cure for terrorism. If we continue to demonize the children in Muslim cultures, we are creating the next generation of terrorists. The more we nuke the committed terrorist, the more we confirm his worldview and stoke the fires of his terrorism. This problem cannot be bombed into oblivion.

Two things are simultaneously true. We need to disarm and neutralize the leaders of terrorism—at military, financial, logistical and operational levels. But we also need a viable long-term solution to terrorism. Long-term, the solution is psychological warfare. We have to win the war in the mind. Smart bombs and Special Forces

are useless in that theater, just as psychotherapy is useless in the sphere of operation of the military. You can't neutralize Osama bin Laden with psychotherapy, and you can't solve terrorism solely by force. We have to get out of either-or, black and white, all-or-nothing thinking. The solution requires military, intelligence, political, diplomatic and economic strategies. But it also requires psychology.

The way to win the psychological war against terrorism is not to define it as a war. Psychologically, terrorism is all about trauma. The trauma causes a splitting of the psyche into good and evil, then the evil is projected out onto a foreign target. The way to destroy the evil within is to cast it out and fight it as an external enemy. It is a hopeless war because the real enemy is within. The oppression of women in the Taliban regime was an external mirror image of oppression within the minds of Taliban leaders. They were trying to control and punish women because if they didn't, free women would remind them of the power of their mothers to deny them love, strength and freedom.

Do I know this to be a scientific fact? Hardly. Have I ever been to Afghanistan or interviewed a member of the Taliban? No. But I understand trauma.

The way to disarm the terrorists, long-term, has got to be understanding then intervening in their psychology. We could hire all the angry fifteen-year old Muslims in Africa, Asia and the Middle East as consultants to us on the problems of the Middle East. Pay for their education. Feed their brothers and sisters. Treat them as human beings. Honor their religion. Build soccer stadiums. And be tough on the adults in their culture who preach hate, violence and terror.

But first we need to get our own house in order. I was at a restaurant a few months ago and went to the men's restroom. There was a picture of Osama bin Laden in the men's urinal. I can see the humor in that, but Osama bin Laden is a human being. He was not born a terrorist. He did not ask to be ignored by his father. He did not ask to be supported by the CIA during the

Afghan war against Russia, then abandoned by that arm of the American state when Russia was expelled.

The point at which the CIA dropped Osama bin Laden as an asset was a crucial point in recent history. A different intervention at that point of time might have prevented the September 11 World Trade Center attack. Of course, hindsight is always perfect, and there is nothing worse than an armchair quarterback who has all the answers but never actually played the game. But if we forget this lesson we will be doomed to repeat it. If we had understood both bin Laden's psychology and his tremendous skills, gifts and dedication, we could have continued to support him, and he might have been less likely to turn on America.

I want to be absolutely clear on this. I am looking back in time as a civilian at the decision to drop bin Laden as an asset. I am sure I am ignorant of numerous binds, conflicts and competing priorities that had to be factored into the decision. All I am suggesting is that we might run some different scenarios on this decision, then use them to assess similar situations that will crop up in the future, for instance in Somalia.

It is Osama bin Laden's gifts and dedication which make him such a dangerous enemy. Those, combined with the equation we helped solidify in his mind by dumping him as an asset: America = Great Satan = Israel = Saudi Royal family = dad. Our foreign policy needs to take the psychology of terrorism into account. Terrorists are driven by psychological motives, and we have to understand their minds in order to devise strategies which can turn them into assets instead of enemies.

I am not talking about pandering to terrorists. Before Osama bin Laden was America's Satan, he was America's employee. In a way, he is like the disgruntled American employee who comes back to work with an assault rifle the day after he is fired. The purpose of the analysis is not to be soft on terrorists, it is to formulate a meaningful psychological warfare strategy to prevent future drive-by shootings on the world stage.

Osama bin Laden is absolutely responsible for the choices and decisions he has made as an adult. These include thousands of counts of murder stemming from September 11, 2001, for which he will die, or has already died. He knew the rules going in and he will pay the price. . . .

Hatred, anger and demonization will never solve the problem of terrorism. If we piss on the face of Osama bin Laden, we are defiling Allah and guaranteeing a jihad against ourselves. We do not have to hate bin Laden in order to be tough on him.

Every time I read that Osama bin Laden is the most hated man in America, I know that our culture is part of the problem, not part of the solution. Our own hatred is recoiling back on us. Call it karma, call it what you like. It is un-American to hate another human being, I believe. Or at least it should be. We have everything turned upside down. If we think it is patriotic and American to hate Osama bin Laden, then we have lost and evil has won. We have accepted the demon inside ourselves and projected it back on him. He will accept it from us and send it back again.

It takes two to tango, and it is a dance of death. We need to step out of the dance, out of the cycle of demonization and warfare. We might do that, as a culture, within the foreseeable future, though the odds are slim.

Albert Einstein
Sigmund Freud

Exchange of Correspondence on War

Dear Mr. Freud:

The proposal of the League of Nations and its International Institute of Intellectual Co-operation at Paris that I should invite a person, to be chosen by myself, to a frank exchange of views on any problem that I might select affords me a very welcome opportunity of conferring with you upon a question which, as things now are, seems the most insistent of all the problems civilization has to face. This is the problem: Is there any way of delivering mankind from the menace of war? It is common knowledge that, with the advance of modern science, this issue has come to mean a matter of life and death for civilization as we know it; nevertheless, for all the zeal displayed, every attempt at its solution has ended in a lamentable breakdown.

I believe, moreover, that those whose duty it is to tackle the problem professionally and practically are growing only too aware of their impotence to deal with it, and have now a very lively desire to learn the views of men who, absorbed in the pursuit of science, can see world problems in the perspective distance lends. As for me, the normal objective of my thought affords no insight into the dark places of human will and feeling. Thus, in the inquiry now proposed, I can do little more than to seek to clarify the question at issue and, clearing the ground of the more obvious solutions, enable you to bring the light of your far-reaching knowledge of man's instinctive life to bear upon the problem. There are certain psychological obstacles whose existence a layman in the mental sciences may dimly surmise, but whose interrelations and vagaries he is incompetent to fathom; you, I am convinced, will be able to suggest educative methods, lying more or less outside the scope of politics, which will eliminate these obstacles.

As one immune from nationalist bias, I personally see a simple way of dealing with the superficial (i.e., administrative) aspect of the problem: the setting up, by international consent, of a legislative and judicial body to settle every conflict arising between nations. Each nation would undertake to abide by the orders issued by this legislative body, to invoke its decision in every dispute, to accept its judgments unreservedly and to carry out every measure the tribunal deems necessary for the execution of its decrees. But here, at the outset, I come up against a difficulty; a tribunal is a human institution which, in proportion as the power at its disposal is inadequate to enforce its verdicts, is all the more prone to suffer these to be deflected by extrajudicial pressure. This is a fact with which we have to reckon; law and might inevitably go hand in hand, and juridical decisions approach more nearly the ideal justice demanded by the community (in whose name and interests these verdicts are pronounced) insofar as the community has effective power to compel respect of its juridical ideal. But at present we are far from possessing any supranational organization competent to render verdicts of incontestable authority and enforce absolute submission to the execution of its verdicts. Thus I am led to my first axiom: The quest of international security involves the unconditional surrender by every nation, in a certain measure, of its liberty of action—its sovereignty that is to say—and it is clear beyond all doubt that no other road can lead to such security.

The ill success, despite their obvious sincerity, of all the efforts made during the last decade to reach this goal leaves us no room to doubt that strong psychological factors are at work which paralyze these efforts. Some of these factors are not far to seek. The craving for power which characterizes the governing class in every nation is hostile to any limitation of the national sovereignty. This political power hunger is often supported by the activities of another group, whose aspirations are on purely mercenary, economic lines. I have especially in mind that small but determined group, active in every nation, composed of individuals who, indifferent to social considerations and restraints, regard warfare, the manufacture and sale of arms, simply as an occasion to advance their personal interests and enlarge their personal authority.

But recognition of this obvious fact is merely the first step toward an appreciation of the actual state of affairs. Another question follows hard upon it: How is it possible for this small clique to bend the will of the majority, who stand to lose and suffer by a state of war, to the service of their ambitions? (In speaking of the majority I do not exclude soldiers of every rank who have chosen war as their profession, in the belief that they are serving to defend the highest interests of their race, and that attack is often the best method of defense.) An obvious answer to this question would seem to be that the minority, the ruling class at present, has the schools and press, usually the Church as well, under its thumb. This enables it to organize and sway the emotions of the masses, and makes its tool of them.

Yet even this answer does not provide a complete solution. Another question arises from it: How is it that these devices succeed so well in rousing men to such wild enthusiasm, even to sacrifice their lives? Only one answer is possible. Because man has within him a lust for hatred and destruction. In normal times this passion exists in a latent state, it merges only in unusual circumstances; but it is a comparatively easy task to call it into play and raise it to the power of a collective psychosis. Here lies, perhaps, the crux of all the complex factors we are considering, an enigma that only the expert in the lore of human instincts can resolve.

And so we come to our last question. Is it possible to control man's mental evolution so as to make him proof against the psychosis of hate and destructiveness? Here I am thinking by no means only of the so-called uncultured masses. Experience proves that it is rather the so-called "intelligentsia" that is most apt to yield to these disastrous collective suggestions, since the intellectual has no direct contact with life in the raw but encounters it in its easiest, synthetic form—upon the printed page.

To conclude: I have so far been speaking only of wars between nations; what are known as international conflicts. But I am well aware that the aggressive instinct operates under other forms and in other circumstances. (I am thinking of civil wars, for instance, due in earlier days to religious zeal, but nowadays to social factors; or, again, the persecution of racial minorities.) But my insistence on what is the most typical, most cruel and extravagant form of conflict between man and man was deliberate, for here we have the best occasion of discovering ways and means to render all armed conflicts impossible.

I know that in your writings we may find answers, explicit or implied, to all the issues of this urgent and absorbing problem. But it would be of the greatest service to us all were you to present the problem of world peace in the light of your most recent discoveries, for such a presentation well might blaze the trail for new and fruitful modes of action.

Yours very sincerely,
A. Einstein

Freud's reply, dated Vienna, September 1932:

Dear Mr. Einstein:

When I learned of your intention to invite me to a mutual exchange of views upon a subject which not only interested you personally but seemed deserving, too, of public interest, I cordially assented. I expected you to choose a problem lying on the borderland of the knowable, as it stands today, a theme which each of us, physicist and psychologist, might approach from his own angle, to meet at last on common ground, though setting out from different premises. Thus the question which you put me—what is to be done to rid mankind of the war menace?—took me by surprise. And, next, I was dumfounded by the thought of my (of *our,* I almost wrote) incompetence; for this struck me as being a matter of practical politics, the statesman's proper study. But then I realized that you did not raise the question in your capacity of scientist or physicist, but as a lover of his fellow men, who responded to the call of the League of Nations much as Fridtjof Nansen, the polar explorer, took on himself the task of succoring homeless and starving victims of the World War. And, next, I reminded myself that I was not being called on to formulate practical proposals but, rather, to explain how this question of preventing wars strikes a psychologist.

But here, too, you have stated the gist of the matter in your letter—and taken the wind out of my sails! Still, I will gladly follow in your wake and content myself with endorsing your conclusions, which, however, I propose to amplify to the best of my knowledge or surmise.

You begin with the relations between might and right, and this is assuredly the proper starting point for our inquiry. But, for the term *might,* I would substitute a tougher and more telling word: *violence.* In right and violence we have today an obvious antinomy. It is easy to prove that one has evolved from the other and, when we go back to origins and examine primitive conditions, the solution of the problem follows easily enough. I must crave your indulgence if in what follows I speak of well-known, admitted facts as though they were new data; the context necessitates this method.

Conflicts of interest between man and man are resolved, in principle, by the recourse to violence. It is the same in the animal kingdom, from which man cannot claim exclusion; nevertheless, men are also prone to conflicts of opinion, touching, on occasion, the loftiest peaks of abstract thought, which seem to call for settlement by quite another method. This refinement is, however, a late development. To start with, group force was the factor which, in small communities, decided points of ownership and the question which man's will was to prevail. Very soon physical force was implemented, then replaced, by the use of various adjuncts; he proved the victor whose weapon was the better, or handled the more skillfully. Now, for the first time, with the coming of weapons, superior brains began to oust brute force, but the object of the conflict remained the same: one party was to be constrained, by the injury done him or impairment of his strength, to retract a claim or a refusal. This end is most effectively gained when the opponent is definitely put out of action—in other words, is killed. This procedure has two advantages: the enemy cannot renew hostilities, and, secondly, his fate deters others from following his example. Moreover, the slaughter of a foe gratifies an instinctive craving—a point to which we shall revert hereafter. However, another consideration may be set off against this will to kill: the possibility of using an enemy for servile tasks if his spirit be broken and his life spared. Here violence finds an outlet not in slaughter but in subjugation. Hence springs the practice of giving quarter; but the victor, having from now on to reckon with the craving for revenge that rankles in his victim, forfeits to some extent his personal security.

Thus, under primitive conditions, it is superior force—brute violence, or violence backed by arms—that lords it everywhere. We know that in the course of evolution this state of things was modified, a path was traced that led away from violence to law. But what was this path? Surely it issued from a single verity: that the superiority of one strong man can be overborne by an alliance of many weaklings, that *l'union fait la force.* Brute force is overcome by union; the allied might of scattered units makes good its right against the isolated giant. Thus we may define "right" (i.e., law) as the might of a community. Yet it, too, is nothing else than violence, quick to attack whatever individual stands in its path, and it employs the selfsame methods, follows like ends, with but one difference: it is the communal, not individual, violence that has its way. But, for the transition from crude violence to the reign of law, a certain psychological condition must first obtain.

The union of the majority must be stable and enduring. If its sole *raison d'être* be the discomfiture of some overweening individual and, after his downfall, it be dissolved, it leads to nothing. Some other man, trusting to his superior power, will seek to reinstate the rule of violence, and the cycle will repeat itself unendingly. Thus the union of the people must be permanent and well organized; it must enact rules to meet the risk of possible revolts; must set up machinery insuring that its rules—the laws—are observed and that such acts of violence as the laws demand are duly carried out. This recognition of a community of interests engenders among the members of the group a sentiment of unity and fraternal solidarity which constitutes its real strength.

So far I have set out what seems to me the kernel of the matter: the suppression of brute force by the transfer of power to a larger combination, founded on the community of sentiments linking up its members. All the rest is mere tautology and glosses. Now the position is simple enough so long as the community consists of a number of equipollent individuals. The laws of such a group can determine to what extent the individual must forfeit his personal freedom, the right of using personal force as an instrument of violence, to insure the safety of the group. But such a combination is only theoretically possible; in practice the situation is always complicated by the fact that, from the outset, the group includes elements of unequal power, men and women, elders and children, and, very soon, as a result of war and conquest, victors and the vanquished—i.e., masters and slaves—as well. From this time on the common law takes notice of these inequalities of power, laws are made by and for the rulers, giving the servile classes fewer rights. Thenceforward there exist within the state two factors making for legal instability, but legislative evolution, too: first, the attempts by members of the ruling class to set themselves above the law's restrictions and, secondly, the constant struggle of the ruled to extend their rights and see each gain embodied in the code, replacing legal disabilities by equal laws for all. The second of these tendencies will be particularly marked when

there takes place a positive mutation of the balance of power within the community, the frequent outcome of certain historical conditions. In such cases the laws may gradually be adjusted to the changed conditions or (as more usually ensues) the ruling class is loath to rush in with the new developments, the result being insurrections and civil wars, a period when law is in abeyance and force once more the arbiter, followed by a new regime of law. There is another factor of constitutional change, which operates in a wholly pacific manner, viz.: the cultural evolution of the mass of the community; this factor, however, is of a different order and can only be dealt with later.

Thus we see that, even within the group itself, the exercise of violence cannot be avoided when conflicting interests are at stake. But the common needs and habits of men who live in fellowship under the same sky favor a speedy issue of such conflicts and, this being so, the possibilities of peaceful solutions make steady progress. Yet the most casual glance at world history will show an unending series of conflicts between one community and another or a group of others, between large and smaller units, between cities, countries, races, tribes and kingdoms, almost all of which were settled by the ordeal of war. Such war ends either in pillage or in conquest and its fruits, the downfall of the loser. No single all-embracing judgment can be passed on these wars of aggrandizement. Some, like the war between the Mongols and the Turks, have led to unmitigated misery; others, however, have furthered the transition from violence to law, since they brought larger units into being, within whose limits a recourse to violence was banned and a new regime determined all disputes. Thus the Roman conquest brought that boon, the *pax Romana,* to the Mediterranean lands. The French kings' lust for aggrandizement created a new France, flourishing in peace and unity. Paradoxical as its sounds, we must admit that warfare well might serve to pave the way to that unbroken peace we so desire, for it is war that brings vast empires into being, within whose frontiers all warfare is proscribed by a strong central power. In practice, however, this end is not attained, for as a rule the fruits of victory are but short-lived, the new-created unit falls asunder once again, generally because there can be no true cohesion between the parts that violence has welded. Hitherto, moreover, such conquests have only led to aggregations which, for all their magnitude, had limits, and disputes between these units could be resolved only by recourse to arms. For humanity at large the sole result of all these military enterprises was that, instead of frequent, not to say incessant, little wars, they had now to face great wars which, for all they came less often, were so much the more destructive.

Regarding the world of today the same conclusion holds good, and you, too, have reached it, though by a shorter path. There is but one sure way of ending war and that is the establishment, by common consent, of a central control which shall have the last word in every conflict of interests. For this, two things are needed: first, the creation of such a supreme court of judicature; secondly, its investment with adequate executive force. Unless this second requirement be fulfilled, the first is unavailing. Obviously the League of Nations, acting as a Supreme Court, fulfills the first condition; it does not fulfill the second. It has no force at its disposal and can only get it if the members of the new body, its constituent nations, furnish it. And, as things are, this is a forlorn hope. Still we should be taking a very shortsighted view of the League of Nations were we to ignore the fact that there is an experiment the like of which has rarely—never before, perhaps, on such scale—been attempted in the course of history. It is an attempt to acquire the authority (in other words, coercive influence), which hitherto reposed exclusively in the possession of power, by calling into play certain idealistic attitudes of mind. We have seen that there are two factors of cohesion in a community: violent compulsion and ties of sentiment ("identifications," in technical parlance) between the members of the group. If one of these factors becomes inoperative, the other may still suffice to hold the group together. Obviously such notions as these can only be significant when they are the expression of deeply rooted sense of unity, shared by all. It is necessary, therefore, to gauge the efficacy of such sentiments. History tells us that,

on occasion, they have been effective. For example, the Panhellenic conception, the Greeks' awareness of superiority over their barbarian neighbors, which found expression in the Amphictyonies, the Oracles and Games, was strong enough to humanize the methods of warfare as between Greeks, though inevitably it failed to prevent conflicts between different elements of the Hellenic race or even to deter a city or group of cities from joining forces with their racial foe, the Persians, for the discomfiture of a rival. The solidarity of Christendom in the Renaissance age was no more effective, despite its vast authority, in hindering Christian nations, large and small alike, from calling in the Sultan to their aid. And, in our times, we look in vain for some such unifying notion whose authority would be unquestioned. It is all too clear that the nationalistic ideas, paramount today in every country, operate in quite a contrary direction. Some there are who hold that the Bolshevist conceptions may make an end of war, but, as things are, that goal lies very far away and, perhaps, could only be attained after a spell of brutal internecine warfare. Thus it would seem that any effort to replace brute force by the might of an ideal is, under present conditions, doomed to fail. Our logic is at fault if we ignore the fact that right is founded on brute force and even today needs violence to maintain it.

I now can comment on another of your statements. You are amazed that it is so easy to infect men with the war fever, and you surmise that man has in him an active instinct for hatred and destruction, amenable to such stimulations. I entirely agree with you. I believe in the existence of this instinct and have been recently at pains to study its manifestations. In this connection may I set out a fragment of that knowledge of the instincts, which we psychoanalysts, after so many tentative essays and gropings in the dark, have compassed? We assume that human instincts are of two kinds: those that conserve and unify, which we call "erotic" (in the meaning Plato gives to Eros in his Symposium), or else "sexual" (explicitly extending the popular connotation of "sex"); and, secondly, the instincts to destroy and kill, which we assimilate as the aggressive or destructive instincts. These are, as you perceive, the well-known opposites, Love and Hate, transformed into theoretical entities; they are, perhaps, another aspect of those eternal polarities, attraction and repulsion, which fall within your province. But we must be chary of passing overhastily to the notions of good and evil. Each of these instincts is every whit as indispensable as its opposite, and all the phenomena of life derive from their activity, whether they work in concert or in opposition. It seems that an instinct of either category can operate but rarely in isolation; it is always blended ("alloyed," as we say) with a certain dosage of its opposite, which modifies its aim or even, in certain circumstances, is a prime condition of its attainment. Thus the instinct of self-preservation is certainly of an erotic nature, but to gain its end this very instinct necessitates aggressive action. In the same way the love instinct, when directed to a specific object, calls for an admixture of the acquisitive instinct if it is to enter into effective possession of that object. It is the difficulty of isolating the two kinds of instinct in their manifestations that has so long prevented us from recognizing them.

If you will travel with me a little further on this road, you will find that human affairs are complicated in yet another way. Only exceptionally does an action follow on the stimulus of a single instinct, which is *per se* a blend of Eros and destructiveness. As a rule several motives of similar composition concur to bring about the act. This fact was duly noted by a colleague of yours, Professor G. C. Lichtenberg, sometime Professor of Physics at Göttingen; he was perhaps even more eminent as a psychologist than as a physical scientist. He evolved the notion of a "Compass-card of Motives" and wrote: "The efficient motives impelling man to act can be classified like the thirty-two winds and described in the same manner; *e.g., Food-Food-Fame* or *Fame-Fame-Food."* Thus, when a nation is summoned to engage in war, a whole gamut of human motives may respond to this appeal—high and low motives, some openly avowed, others slurred over. The lust for aggression and destruction is certainly included; the innumerable cruelties of history and man's daily life confirm its prevalence

and strength. The stimulation of these destructive impulses by appeals to idealism and the erotic instinct naturally facilitate their release. Musing on the atrocities recorded on history's page, we feel that the ideal motive has often served as a camouflage for the lust of destruction; sometimes, as with the cruelties of the Inquisition, it seems that, while the ideal motives occupied the foreground of consciousness, they drew their strength from the destructive instincts submerged in the unconscious. Both interpretations are feasible.

You are interested, I know, in the prevention of war, not in our theories, and I keep this fact in mind. Yet I would like to dwell a little longer on this destructive instinct which is seldom given the attention that its importance warrants. With the least of speculative efforts we are led to conclude that this instinct functions in every living being, striving to work its ruin and reduce life to its primal state of inert matter. Indeed, it might well be called the "death instinct"; whereas the erotic instincts vouch for the struggle to live on. The death instinct becomes an impulse to destruction when, with the aid of certain organs, it directs its action outward, against external objects. The living being, that is to say, defends its own existence by destroying foreign bodies. But, in one of its activities, the death instinct is operative *within* the living being and we have sought to trace back a number of normal and pathological phenomena to this *introversion* of the destructive instinct. We have even committed the heresy of explaining the origin of human conscience by some such "turning inward" of the aggressive impulse. Obviously when this internal tendency operates on too large a scale, it is no trivial matter; rather, a positively morbid state of things; whereas the diversion of the destructive impulse toward the external world must have beneficial effects. Here is then the biological justification for all those vile, pernicious propensities which we are now combating. We can but own that they are really more akin to nature than this our stand against them, which, in fact, remains to be accounted for.

All this may give you the impression that our theories amount to a species of mythology and a gloomy one at that! But does not every natural science lead ultimately to this—a sort of mythology? Is it otherwise today with your physical sciences?

The upshot of these observations, as bearing on the subject in hand, is that there is no likelihood of our being able to suppress humanity's aggressive tendencies. In some happy corners of the earth, they say, where nature brings forth abundantly whatever man desires, there flourish races whose lives go gently by, unknowing of aggression or constraint. This I can hardly credit; I would like further details about these happy folk. The Bolshevists, too, aspire to do away with human aggressiveness by insuring the satisfaction of material needs and enforcing equality between man and man. To me this hope seems vain. Meanwhile they busily perfect their armaments, and their hatred of outsiders is not the least of the factors of cohesion among themselves. In any case, as you too have observed, complete suppression of man's aggressive tendencies is not in issue; what we may try is to divert it into a channel other than that of warfare.

From our "mythology" of the instincts we may easily deduce a formula or an indirect method of eliminating war. If the propensity for war be due to the destructive instinct, we have always its counteragent, Eros, to our hand. All that produces ties of sentiment between man and man must serve us as war's antidote. These ties are of two kinds. First, such relations as those toward a beloved object, void though they be of sexual intent. The psychoanalyst need feel no compunction in mentioning "love" in this connection; religion uses the same language: Love thy neighbor as thyself. A pious injunction, easy to enounce, but hard to carry out! The other bond of sentiment is by way of identification. All that brings out the significant resemblances between men calls into play his feeling of community, identification, whereon is founded, in large measure, the whole edifice of human society.

In your strictures on the abuse of authority I find another suggestion or an indirect attack on the war impulse. That men are divided into the leaders and the led is but another manifestation of their inborn and irremediable inequality. The second class constitutes the vast majority; they need a high command to make decisions for them, to which decisions they usually bow without demur. In this context we would point out that men should be at greater pains than heretofore to form a superior class of independent thinkers, unamenable to intimidation and fervent in the quest of truth, whose function it would be to guide the masses dependent on their lead. There is no need to point out how little the rule of politicians and the Church's ban on liberty of thought encourage such a new creation. The ideal conditions would obviously be found in a community where every man subordinated his instinctive life to the dictates of reason. Nothing less than this could bring about so thorough and so durable a union between men, even if this involved the severance of mutual ties of sentiment. But surely such a hope is utterly utopian, as things are. The other indirect methods of preventing war are certainly more feasible, but entail no quick results. They conjure up an ugly picture of mills that grind so slowly that, before the flour is ready, men are dead of hunger.

As you see, little good comes of consulting a theoretician, aloof from worldly contact, on practical and urgent problems! Better it were to tackle each successive crisis with means that we have ready to our hands. However, I would like to deal with a question which, though it is not mooted in your letter, interests me greatly. Why do we, you and I and many another, protest so vehemently against war, instead of just accepting it as another of life's odious importunities? For it seems a natural thing enough, biologically sound and practically unavoidable. I trust you will not be shocked by my raising such a question. For the better conduct of an inquiry it may be well to don a mask of feigned aloofness. The answer to my query may run as follows: Because every man has a right over his own life and war destroys lives that were full of promise; it forces the individual into situations that shame his manhood, obliging him to murder fellow men, against his will; it ravages material amenities, the fruits of human toil, and much besides. Moreover, wars, as now conducted, afford no scope for acts of heroism according to the old ideals and, given the high perfection of modern arms, war today would mean the sheer extermination of one of the combatants, if not of both. This is so true, so obvious, that we can but wonder why the conduct of war is not banned by general consent. Doubtless either of the points I have just made is open to debate. It may be asked if the community, in its turn, cannot claim a right over the individual lives of its members. Moreover, all forms of war cannot be indiscriminately condemned; so long as there are nations and empires, each prepared callously to exterminate its rival, all alike must be equipped for war. But we will not dwell on any of these problems; they lie outside the debate to which you have invited me. I pass on to another point, the basis, as it strikes me, of our common hatred of war. It is this: We cannot do otherwise than hate it. Pacifists we are, since our organic nature wills us thus to be. Hence it comes easy to us to find arguments that justify our standpoint.

This point, however, calls for elucidation. Here is the way in which I see it. The cultural development of mankind (some, I know, prefer to call it civilization) has been in progress since immemorial antiquity. To this *processus* we owe all that is best in our composition, but also much that makes for human suffering. Its origins and causes are obscure, its issue is uncertain, but some of its characteristics are easy to perceive. It well may lead to the extinction of mankind, for it impairs the sexual function in more than one respect, and even today the uncivilized races and the backward classes of all nations are multiplying more rapidly than the cultured elements. This process may, perhaps, be likened to the effects of domestication on certain animals—it clearly involves physical changes of structure—but the view that cultural development is an organic process of this order has not yet become generally familiar. The psychic changes which accompany this process of cultural change are striking, and not to be gainsaid. They consist in the progressive rejection of instinctive ends and a scaling down of instinctive reactions. Sensations which delighted our forefathers have become neutral or unbearable to us; and, if our ethical and aesthetic ideals have undergone a change, the causes of this are ultimately organic. On the psychological side two of the most important phenomena of culture are, firstly, a strengthening of the intellect, which tends to master our

instinctive life, and, secondly, an introversion of the aggressive impulse, with all its consequent benefits and perils. Now war runs most emphatically counter to the psychic disposition imposed on us by the growth of culture; we are therefore bound to resent war, to find it utterly intolerable. With pacifists like us it is not merely an intellectual and affective repulsion, but a constitutional intolerance, an idiosyncrasy in its most drastic form. And it would seem that the aesthetic ignominies of warfare play almost as large a part in this repugnance as war's atrocities.

How long have we to wait before the rest of men turn pacifist? Impossible to say, and yet perhaps our hope that these two actors—man's cultural disposition and a well-founded dread of the form that future wars will take—may serve to put an end to war in the near future, is not chimerical. But by what ways or byways this will come about, we cannot guess. Meanwhile we may rest on the assurance that whatever makes for cultural development is working also against war.

With kindest regards and, should this exposé prove a disappointment to you, my sincere regrets,

Yours,

Sigmund Freud

Einstein addressed the following letter to Freud on December 3, 1932:

You have made a most gratifying gift to the League of Nations and myself with your truly classic reply. When I wrote you I was thoroughly convinced of the insignificance of my role, which was only meant to document my good will, with me as the bait on the hook to tempt the marvelous fish into nibbling. You have given in return something altogether magnificent. We cannot know what may grow from such seed, as the effect upon man of any action or event is always incalculable. This is not within our power and we do not need to worry about it.

You have earned my gratitude and the gratitude of all men for having devoted all your strength to the search for truth and for having shown the rarest courage in professing your convictions all your life. . . .

Questions for Discussion

1. What bearing does the relationship between frustration and aggression have on the causes of war?
2. What are the implications of the relationship between frustration and aggression for preventing war?
3. What is the difference between the frustration felt by an individual and by a group of people, and how does that affect the tendency toward aggression?
4. To what extent do you think "psychosocial determinants," as described by Frank, can be used to identify a group of people who pose a threat to peace?
5. Ross wonders why the United States has allocated hardly any resources to analyze posttraumatic stress disorders following September 11. Why do you think this is the case?
6. How important is it to evaluate the motives behind the acts of terrorists?
7. If, according to Freud, human beings are inherently predisposed toward warfare, then wouldn't it be better if that possibility were explored and corrected through biological, namely genetic, means?
8. In the remarkable exchange of correspondence between Einstein and Freud, both pin their hopes for world peace on an international body, such as the League of Nations or the United Nations. Do you think their optimism is justified?

Further Readings

1. Glad, Betty, ed. *Psychological Dimensions of War.* Newbury Park, CA: Sage Publications, 1990.
2. Anderson, Anne, and Christie, Daniel J. "Some Contributions of Psychology to Policies Promoting Cultures of Peace." *Peace and Conflict: Journal of Peace Psychology,* 2001, 7, 2, 173–185.
3. Baistow, Karen. "Problems of Powerlessness: Psychological Explanations of Social Inequality and Civil Unrest in Post-War America." *History of the Human Sciences,* 2000, 13, 3, Aug., 95–116.
4. Volkan, Vamik D. "Ethnicity and Nationalism: A Psychoanalytic Perspective." *Applied Psychology,* 1998, 47, 1, Jan., 45–57.
5. Altemeyer, Bob. "Marching in Step: A Psychological Explanation of State Terror." *The Sciences,* 1988, 28, 2, Mar.–Apr., 30–38.
6. Newman, Graeme R, and Lynch, Michael J. "From Feuding to Terrorism: The Ideology of Vengeance." *Contemporary Crises,* 1987, 11, 3, 223–242.
7. Dutter, Lee E. "Ethno-Political Activity and the Psychology of Terrorism." *Terrorism,* 1987, 10, 3, 145–163.
8. Senghaas-Knobloch, Eva, and Volmnerg, Birgit. 'Towards a Social Psychology of Peace." *Journal of Peace Research,* 1988, 25, 3, Sept., 245–256.
9. Akhtar, Salman. "The Psychodynamic Dimension of Terrorism." *Psychiatric Annals,* 1999, 29, 6, June, 350–355.
10. Demause, Lloyd. "The Childhood Origins of Terrorism." *The Journal of Psychohistory,* 2002, 29, 4 Spring, 340-348.
11. Fields, Rona M. "Child Terror Victims and Adult Terrorists." *Journal of Psychohistory,* 1979, 7, 71–75.
12. Olsson, Peter A. "The Terrorist and the Terrorized: Some Psychoanalytic Consideration." *The Journal of Psychohistory,* 1988, 16, 1, Summer, 47–60.

Sociological and Anthropological Theories

It has been argued that war is a byproduct of social structure and cultural evolution. This section presents an overview of the issue from the perspectives of sociology and anthropology.

In "Warfare is only an Invention—Not a Biological Necessity," Margaret Mead refutes the argument that warfare is a sociological inevitability. She dissents from the view that warfare is a sociological phenomenon that has evolved due to human beings' primitive instincts to survive in a harsh environment. She cites the Eskimo community as an example; in spite of their inclement surroundings, there is a complete absence of organized violence in their community. A similar argument is made by referring to Australian aborigines and other native populations. Throughout this reading, Mead reiterates her belief that despite facing the most difficult environmental conditions, these native tribes have not engaged in warfare. She concludes that warfare is an invention of the so called "civilized" world and is not inherent in the social evolution of mankind.

Bronislow Malinowski provides an anthropological perspective on the causes of war in his essay "An Anthropological Analysis of War." He acknowledges confusion that exists in anthropology regarding warfare. The confusion is caused by various concepts such as nationalism, race and ethnicity. Malinowski argues that although aggressive instincts may be harbored and promoted by a given cultural group, this is not tantamount to promoting warfare. He states that anger is fostered through cultural evolution and is directed toward out-groups. Aggression toward out-groups is not a consequence of anthropological characteristics of a group. It is, therefore, not valid to say that warfare is an ingrained part of cultural development. Malinowski distinguishes six modes of aggression and use of violence, only two of which he considers manifestations of war: military expeditions of organized pillage, slave-raiding and collective robbery; and wars between two culturally differentiated groups as an instrument of national policy.

In "Why Nations Go to War," John Stoessinger identifies the chief reasons for international conflict as being leaders' over-confidence regarding the outcome of war, a firm belief in the brief duration of war, a misperception of enemy's power and character, and insecurity regarding the enemy's intentions. The author also explains the sources of these principal beliefs and how leaders may rally their people's support. He cites various recent examples from the Middle East, where leaders' ideas and beliefs have thrust their entire nations into armed conflict.

Margaret Mead

Warfare Is Only an Invention— Not a Biological Necessity

Is war a biological necessity, a sociological inevitability or just a bad invention? Those who argue for the first view endow man with such pugnacious instincts that some outlet in aggressive behavior is necessary if man is to reach full human stature. It was this point of view which lay back of William James's famous essay, "The Moral Equivalent of War," in which he tried to retain the warlike virtues and channel them in new directions. A similar point of view has lain back of the Soviet Union's attempt to make competition between groups rather than between individuals. A basic, competitive, aggressive, warring human nature is assumed, and those who wish to outlaw war or outlaw competitiveness merely try to find new and less socially destructive ways in which these biologically given aspects of man's nature can find expression. Then there are those who take the second view: warfare is the inevitable concomitant of the development of the state, the struggle for land and natural resources of class societies springing, not from the nature of man, but from the nature of history. War is nevertheless inevitable unless we change our social system and outlaw classes, the struggle for power, and possessions; and in the event of our success warfare would disappear, as a symptom vanishes when the disease is cured.

One may hold a sort of compromise position between these two extremes; one may claim that all aggression springs from the frustration of man's biologically determined drives and that, since all forms of culture are frustrating, it is certain each new generation will be aggressive and the aggression will find its natural and inevitable

expression in race war, class war, nationalistic war and so on. All three of these positions are very popular today among those who think seriously about the problems of war and its possible prevention, but I wish to urge another point of view, less defeatist perhaps than the first and third, and more accurate than the second: that is, that warfare, by which I mean recognized conflict between two groups *as groups,* in which each group puts an army (even if the army is only fifteen pygmies) into the field to fight and kill, if possible, some of the members of the army of the other group—that warfare of this sort is an invention like any other of the inventions in terms of which we order our lives, such as writing, marriage, cooking our food instead of eating it raw, trial by jury or burial of the dead, and so on. Some of this list any one will grant are inventions: trial by jury is confined to very limited portions of the globe; we know that there are tribes that do not bury their dead but instead expose or cremate them; and we know that only part of the human race has had the knowledge of writing as its cultural inheritance. But, whenever a way of doing things is found universally, such as the use of fire or the practice of some form of marriage, we tend to think at once that it is not an invention at all but an attribute of humanity itself. And yet even such universals as marriage and the use of fire are inventions like the rest, very basic ones, inventions which were perhaps necessary if human history was to take the turn that it has taken, but nevertheless inventions. At some point in his social development man was undoubtedly without the institution of marriage or the knowledge of the use of fire.

The case for warfare is much clearer because there are peoples even today who have no warfare. Of these the Eskimo are perhaps the most conspicuous examples, but the Lepchas of Sikkim described by Geoffrey Gorer in *Himalayan Village* are as good. Neither of these peoples understands war, not even defensive warfare. The idea of warfare is lacking, and this idea is as essential to really carrying on war as an alphabet or a syllabary is to writing. But whereas the Lepchas are a gentle, unquarrelsome people, and the advocates of other points of view might argue that they are not full human beings or that they had never been frustrated and so had no aggression to expand in warfare, the Eskimo case gives no such possibility of interpretation. The Eskimo are not a mild and meek people; many of them are turbulent and troublesome. Fights, theft of wives, murder, cannibalism, occur among them—all outbursts of passionate men goaded by desire or intolerable circumstance. Here are men faced with hunger, men faced with loss of their wives, men faced with the threat of extermination by other men, and here are orphan children, growing up miserably with no one to care for them, mocked and neglected by those about them. The personality necessary for war, the circumstances necessary to goad men to desperation are present, but there is no war. When a traveling Eskimo entered a settlement he might have to fight the strongest man in the settlement to establish his position among them, but this was a test of strength and bravery, not war. The idea of warfare, of one *group* organizing against another *group* to maim and wound and kill them was absent. And without that idea passions might rage but there was no war.

But, it may be argued, isn't this because the Eskimo have such a low and undeveloped form of social organization? They own no land, they move from place to place, camping, it is true, season after season on the same site, but this is not something to fight for as the modern nations of the world fight for land and raw materials. They have no permanent possessions that can be looted, no towns that can be burned. They have

no social classes to produce stress and strains within the society which might force it to go to war outside. Doesn't the absence of war among the Eskimo, while disproving the biological necessity of war, just go to confirm the point that it is the state of development of the society which accounts for war, and nothing else?

We find the answer among the pygmy peoples of the Andaman Islands in the Bay of Bengal. The Andamans also represent an exceedingly low level of society; they are a hunting and food-gathering people; they live in tiny hordes without any class stratification; their houses are simpler than the snow houses of the Eskimo. But they knew about warfare. The army might contain only fifteen determined pygmies marching in a straight line, but it was the real thing none the less. Tiny army met tiny army in open battle, blows were exchanged, casualties suffered, and the state of warfare could only be concluded by a peace-making ceremony.

Similarly, among the Australian aborigines, who built no permanent dwellings but wandered from water hole to water hole over their almost desert country, warfare—and rules of "international law"—were highly developed. The student of social evolution will seek in vain for his obvious causes of war, struggle for lands, struggle for power of one group over another, expansion of population, need to divert the minds of a populace restive under tyranny, or even the ambition of a successful leader to enhance his own prestige. All are absent, but warfare as a practice remained, and men engaged in it and killed one another in the course of a war because killing is what is done in wars.

From instances like these it becomes apparent that an inquiry into the causes of war misses the fundamental point as completely as does an insistence upon the biological necessity of war. If a people have an idea of going to war and the idea that war is the way in which certain situations, defined within their society, are to be handled, they will sometimes go to war. If they are a mild and unaggressive people, like the Pueblo Indians, they may limit themselves to defensive warfare; but they will be forced to think in terms of war because there are peoples near them who have warfare as a pattern, and offensive, raiding, pillaging warfare at that. When the pattern of warfare is known, people like the Pueblo Indians will defend themselves, taking advantage of their natural defenses, the *mesa* village site, and people like the Lepchas, having no natural defenses and no idea of warfare, will merely submit to the invader. But the essential point remains the same. There is a way of behaving which is known to a given people and labeled as an appropriate form of behavior; a bold and warlike people like the Sioux or the Maori may label warfare as desirable as well as possible; a mild people like the Pueblo Indians may label warfare as undesirable; but to the minds of both peoples the possibility of warfare is present. Their thoughts, their hopes, their plans are oriented about this idea, that warfare may be selected as the way to meet some situation.

So simple peoples and civilized peoples, mild peoples and violent, assertive peoples, will all go to war if they have the invention, just as those peoples who have the custom of dueling will have duels and peoples who have the pattern of vendetta will indulge in vendetta. And, conversely, peoples who do not know of dueling will not fight duels, even though their wives are seduced and their daughters ravished; they may on occasion commit murder but they will not fight duels. Cultures which lack the idea of the vendetta will not meet every quarrel in this way. A people can use only the forms it has. So the Balinese have their special way of dealing with a quarrel between two individuals: if the two feel that the causes of quarrel are heavy they may go and register their quarrel in the temple before the gods, and, making offerings, they may swear never to have anything to do with each other again. Today they register such mutual "not-speaking" with the Dutch government officials. But in other societies, although individuals might feel as full of animosity and as unwilling to have any further contact as do the Balinese, they cannot register their quarrel with the gods and go on quietly about their business because registering

quarrels with the gods is not an invention of which they know.

Yet, if it be granted that warfare is after all an invention, it may nevertheless be an invention that lends itself to certain types of personality, to the exigent needs of autocrats, to the expansionist desires of crowded peoples, to the desire for plunder and rape and loot which is engendered by a dull and frustrating life. What, then, can we say of this congruence between warfare and its uses? If it is a form which fits so well, is not this congruence the essential point? But even here the primitive material causes us to wonder, because there are tribes who go to war merely for glory, having no quarrel with the enemy, suffering from no tyrant within their boundaries, anxious neither for land nor loot nor women, but merely anxious to win prestige which within that tribe has been declared obtainable only by war and without which no young man can hope to win his sweetheart's smile of approval. But if, as was the case with the Bush Negroes of Dutch Guiana, it is artistic ability which is necessary to win a girl's approval, the same young man would have to be carving rather than going out on a war party.

In many parts of the world, war is a game in which the individual can win counters—counters which bring him prestige in the eyes of his own sex or of the opposite sex; he plays for these counters as he might, in our society, strive for a tennis championship. Warfare is a frame for much prestige-seeking merely because it calls for the display of certain skills and certain virtues; all of these skills—riding straight, shooting straight, dodging the missiles of the enemy and sending one's own straight to the mark—can be equally well exercised in some other framework and, equally, the virtues—endurance, bravery, loyalty, steadfastness—can be displayed in other contexts. The tie-up between proving oneself a man and proving this by a success in organized killing is due to a definition which many societies have made of manliness. And often, even in those societies which counted success in warfare a proof of human worth, strange turns were given to the idea, as when the plains Indians gave their highest awards to the man who touched a live enemy rather than to the man who brought in a scalp—from a dead enemy—because the latter was less risky. Warfare is just an invention known to the majority of human societies by which they permit their young men either to accumulate prestige or avenge their honor or acquire loot or wives or slaves or sago lands or cattle or appease the blood lust of their gods or the restless souls of the recently dead. It is just an invention, older and more widespread than the jury system, but none the less an invention.

But, once we have said this, have we said anything at all? Despite a few instances, dear to the hearts of controversialists, of the loss of the useful arts, once an invention is made which proves congruent with human needs or social forms, it tends to persist. Grant that war is an invention, that it is not a biological necessity nor the outcome of certain special types of social forms, still, once the invention is made, what are we to do about it? The Indian who had been subsisting on the buffalo for generations because with his primitive weapons he could slaughter only a limited number of buffalo did not return to his primitive weapons when he saw that the white man's more efficient weapons were exterminating the buffalo. A desire for the white man's cloth may mortgage the South Sea Islander to the white man's plantation, but he does not return to making bark cloth, which would have left him free. Once an invention is known and accepted, men do not easily relinquish it. The skilled workers may smash the first steam looms which they feel are to be their undoing, but they accept them in the end, and no movement which has insisted upon the mere abandonment of usable inventions has ever had much success. Warfare is here, as part of our thought; the deeds of warriors are immortalized in the words of our poets; the toys of our children are modeled upon the weapons of the soldier; the frame of reference within which our statesmen and our diplomats work always contains war. If we know that it is not inevitable, that it is due to historical accident that warfare is one of the ways in which we think of behaving, are we given any hope by that? What hope is

there of persuading nations to abandon war, nations so thoroughly imbued with the idea that resort to war is, if not actually desirable and noble, at least inevitable whenever certain defined circumstances arise?

In answer to this question I think we might turn to the history of other social inventions, and inventions which must once have seemed as firmly entrenched as warfare. Take the methods of trial which preceded the jury system: ordeal and trial by combat. Unfair, capricious, alien as they are to our feeling today, they were once the only methods open to individuals accused of some offense. The invention of trial by jury gradually replaced these methods until only witches, and finally not even witches, had to resort to the ordeal. And for a long time the jury system seemed the one best and finest method of settling legal disputes, but today new inventions, trial before judges only or before commissions, are replacing the jury system. In each case the old method was replaced by a new social invention; the ordeal did not go out because people thought it unjust or wrong, it went out because a method more congruent with the institutions and feelings of the period was invented. And, if we despair over the way in which war seems such an ingrained habit of most of the human race, we can take comfort from the fact that a poor invention will usually give place to a better invention.

For this, two conditions at least are necessary. The people must recognize the defects of the old invention, and some one must make a new one. Propaganda against warfare, documentation of its terrible cost in human suffering and social waste, these prepare the ground by teaching people to feel that warfare is a defective social institution. There is further needed a belief that social invention is possible and the invention of new methods which will render warfare as out-of-date as the tractor is making the plow, or the motor car the horse and buggy. A form of behavior becomes out-of-date only when something else takes its place, and in order to invent forms of behavior which will make war obsolete, it is a first requirement to believe that an invention is possible.

Bronislaw Malinowski

An Anthropological Analysis of War

Anthropology has done more harm than good in confusing the issue by optimistic messages from the primeval past, depicting human ancestry as living in the golden age of perpetual peace. Even more confusing is the teaching of those who maintain or imply that war is an essential heritage of man, a psychological or biological destiny from which man never will be able to free himself.

There is, however, a legitimate role for the anthropologist. Studying human societies on the widest basis in time perspective and spatial distribution, he should be able to tell us what war really is. Whether war is a cultural phenomenon to be found at the beginnings of evolution; what are its determining causes and its effects; what does it create and what does it destroy—these are questions which belong to the science of man. The forms, the factors, and the forces which define and determine human warfare should, therefore, be analyzed in a correct anthropoligical theory of war. . . .

Dictated by common sense, indispensable to sound statesmanship, running through abstract and philosophic reflection, persistent in and above the battle cries of intrenched armies and scheming diplomacies, the main problem of today is simple and vital: shall we abolish war or must we submit to it by choice or necessity? Is it desirable to have permanent peace and is this peace possible? If it is possible, how can we implement it successfully? There is obviously a price and a great price to be paid for any fundamental change in the constitution of mankind. Here, clearly, the price to be paid is the surrender of state sovereignty and the subordination of all political units to world-wide control. Whether this is a smaller or greater sacrifice

in terms of progress, culture, and personality than the disasters created by war is another problem, the solution of which may be foreshadowed in anthropological arguments.

I think that the task of evaluating war in terms of cultural analysis is today the main duty of the theory of civilization. In democratic countries public opinion must be freed from prejudice and enlightened as regards sound knowledge. The totalitarian states are spending as much energy, foresight, and constructive engineering on the task of indoctrinating the minds of their subjects as in the task of building armaments. . . .

The problem of what war is as a cultural phenomenon naturally falls into the constituent issues of the biological determinants of war, its political effects, and its cultural constructiveness. In the following discussion of pugnacity and aggression we shall see that even preorganized fighting is not a simple reaction of violence determined by the impulse of anger. The first distinction to emerge from this analysis will be between organized and collective fighting as against individual, sporadic, and spontaneous acts of violence—which are the antecedents of homicide, murder, and civic disorder, but not of war. We shall then show that organized fighting has to be fully discussed with reference to its political background. Fights within a community fulfil an entirely different function from intertribal feuds or battles. Even in these latter, however, we will have to distinguish between culturally effective warfare and military operations which do not leave any permanent mark either in terms of diffusion, of evolution, or of any lasting historical aftereffect. From all this will emerge the concept of "war as an armed contest between two independent political units, by means of organized military force, in the pursuit of a tribal or national policy." With this as a minimum definition of war, we shall be able to see how futile and confusing it is to regard primitive brawls, scrimmages, and feuds as genuine antecedents of our present world-catastrophe.

War and Human Nature

We have, then, first to face the issue of "aggressiveness as instinctual behavior"; in other words, of the determination of war by intrinsically biological motives. Such expressions as "war is older than man," "war is inherent in human nature," "war is biologically determined" have either no meaning or they signify that humanity has to conduct wars, even as all men have to breathe, sleep, breed, eat, walk, and evacuate, wherever they live and whatever their civilization. Every schoolboy knows this and most anthropologists have ignored the facts just mentioned. The study of man has certainly evaded the issue concerning the relation between culture and the biological foundations of human nature.

Put plainly and simply, biological determinism means that in no civilization can the individual organism survive and the community continue without the integral incorporation into culture of such bodily functions as breathing, sleep, rest, excretion, and reproduction. This seems so obvious that it has been constantly overlooked or avowedly omitted from the cultural analyses of human behavior. Since, however, the biological activities are in one way determinants of culture, and since, in turn, every culture redefines, overdetermines and transmutes many of these biological activities, the actual interrelation and interdependence cannot be left outside anthropological theory. We shall have briefly to define in what sense certain phases of human behavior are biological invariants and then apply our analysis to aggression and pugnacity. . . .

Can we regard pugnacity and aggressiveness and all the other reactions of hostility, hate, and violence as comparable to any vital sequence so far discussed? The answer must be an emphatic negative. Not that the impulse of aggression, violence, or destruction be ever absent from any human group or from the life of any human being. If the activity of breathing be interrupted by accident or a deliberate act of another individual, the immediate reaction to it is a violent struggle to remove the obstacle or to overcome the human act of aggression. Kicking, biting, pushing, immediately start; a fight ensues, which has to end with the destruction of the suffocated organism or the removal of the obstacle. Take away the food from the hungry child or dog or monkey and you will provoke immediately strong hostile reactions. Any interference with the progressive course of sexual preliminaries—still more, any interruption of the physiological act—leads in man and animal to a violent fit of anger.

This last point, however, brings us directly to the recognition that the impulse of anger, the hostilities of jealousy, the violence of wounded honor and sexual and emotional possessiveness are as productive of hostility and of fighting, direct or relayed, as is the thwarting in the immediate satisfaction of a biological impulse.

We could sum up these results by saying that the impulse which controls aggression is not primary but derived. It is contingent upon circumstances in which a primary biologically defined impulse is being thwarted. It is also produced in a great variety of nonorganic ways, determined by such purely cultural factors as economic ownership, ambition, religious values, privileges of rank, and personal sentiments of attachment, dependence, and authority. Thus, to speak even of the *impulse* of pugnacity as biologically determined is incorrect. This becomes even clearer when we recognize, by looking at the above diagram, that the essence of an impulse is to produce a clear and definite bodily reaction, which again produces the satisfaction of the impulse. In human societies, on the contrary, we find that the impulse of anger is in almost every case transformed into chronic states of the human mind or organism—into hate, vindictiveness, permanent attitudes of hostility. That such culturally defined sentiments can lead, and do lead, to acts of violence, simply means that acts of violence are culturally, not biologically, determined. Indeed, when we look at the actual cases of violent action, individual, or collective and organized, we find that most of them are the result of purely conventional, traditional, and ideological imperatives, which have nothing whatsoever to do with any organically determined state of mind.

It is interesting to find that when the argument for a biological or psychological determinism of aggressiveness as something inherent in man's animal nature is put forward, examples from prehuman behavior are easy to find. It is easy to show that dogs, apes, baboons, and even birds fight over females, food, spatial or territorial rights. The study of immature children in primitive tribes, or in our own nurseries, discloses that the argument by violence is very often used and has to be constantly watched over and regulated by adults. This, indeed, might have suggested to any competent observer that the elimination of violence and of aggression, and not its fostering, is the essence of any educational process.

When we are faced with the question where, how, and under what circumstances, acts of purely physiological aggression occur among human adults, we come again to an interesting result. Cases of sound, normal people attacking, hurting, or killing one another under the stress of genuine anger do occur, but they are extremely, indeed, negligibly, rare. Think of our own society. You can adduce an indefinite number of cases from a mental hospital. You can also show that within very specialized situations, such as in prisons or concentration camps, in groups cooped up by shipwreck or some other accident, aggression is fairly frequent. Such a catastrophe as a theater on fire or a sinking boat has sometimes, but not always, the effect of producing a fight for life, in which people are trampled to death and bones broken through acts of violence, determined by panic and fear. There are also cases in every criminal record, primitive or civilized, of homicidal injuries or bruises which

occur under outbursts of anger and hatred, or a fit of jealousy. We see that "aggressiveness" within the framework of an adult cultural group is found under the headings of "panic," "insanity," "artificial propinquity," or else that it becomes the type of antisocial and anticultural behavior called "crime." It is always part and product of a breakdown of personality or of culture. It is not a case of a vital sequence which has to be incorporated into every culture. Even more, since it is a type of impulsive sequence which constantly threatens the normal course of cultural behavior, it has to be and is eliminated.

The Harnessing of Aggression by Culture

Another interesting point in the study of aggression is that, like charity, it begins at home. Think of the samples given above. They all imply direct contact and then the flaring-up of anger over immediate issues, where divergent interests occur, or, among the insane, are imagined to occur. Indeed, the smaller the group engaged in co-operation, united by some common interests, and living day by day with one another, the easier it is for them to be mutually irritated and to flare up in anger. Freud and his followers have demonstrated beyond doubt and cavil that within the smallest group of human co-operation, the family, there frequently arise anger, hatred, and destructive, murderous impulses. Sexual jealousies within the home, grievances over food, service, or other economic interests occur in every primitive or civilized household. I have seen myself Australian aborigines, Papuans, Melanesians, African Bantus, and Mexican Indians turning angry or even flaring into a passion on occasions when they were working together, or celebrating feasts, or discussing some plans or some issues of their daily life. The actual occurrence, however, of bodily violence is so rare that it becomes statistically negligible. . . .

Those who maintain that "natural aggressiveness" is a permanent cause of warfare would have to prove that this aggressiveness operates more as between strangers than between members of the same group. The facts taken from ethnographic evidence give an entirely different answer. Tribal strangers are above all eliminated from any contact with one another. Thus, the Veddas of Ceylon have arrangements by which they can transact exchange of goods and give symbolic messages to their neighbors—the Tamils and Singhalese—without ever coming face to face with them. The Australian Aborigines have an elaborate system of intertribal avoidances. The same applies to such primitive groups as the Punans of Borneo, the Firelanders, and the Pygmies of Africa and Malaysia. . . .

The Contribution of Anthropology to the Problem of War

As regards the theoretical gains, we have shown that war cannot be regarded as a fiat of human destiny, in that it could be related to biological needs or immutable psychological drives. All types of fighting are complex cultural responses due not to any direct dictates of an impulse but to collective forms of sentiment and value. As a mechanism of organized force for the pursuit of national policies war is slow in evolving. Its incidence depends on the gradual development of military equipment and organization, of the scope for lucrative exploits, of the formation of independent political units.

Taking into account all such factors, we had to establish, within the genus of aggression and use of violence, the following distinctions: (1) Fighting, private and angry, within a group belongs to the type of breach of custom and law and is the prototype of criminal behavior. It is countered and curbed by the customary law within institutions and between institutions. (2) Fighting, collective and organized, is a juridical mechanism for the adjustment of differences between constituent groups of the same larger cultural unit. Among the lowest savages these two types are the only forms of armed contest to be found. (3) Armed raids, as a type of man-hunting sport, for purposes of head-hunting, cannibalism, human sacrifices, and the collection of other tro-

phies. (4) Warfare as the political expression of early nationalism, that is, the tendency to make the tribe-nation and tribe-state coincide, and thus to form a primitive nation-state. (5) Military expeditions of organized pillage, slave-raiding, and collective robbery. (6) Wars between two culturally differentiated groups as an instrument of national policy. This type of fighting, with which war in the fullest sense of the word began, leads to conquest, and, through this, to the creation of full-fledged military and political states, armed for internal control, for defense and aggression. This type of state presents, as a rule, and for the first time in evolution, clear forms of administrative, political, and legal organization. Conquest is also of first-rate importance in the processes of diffusion and evolution.

The types of armed contest, listed as (4) and (6) and these two only, are, in form, sociological foundations, and in the occurrence of constructive policy are comparable with historically defined wars. Every one of the six types here summed up presents an entirely different cultural phase in the development of organized fighting. The neglect to establish the differentiation here introduced has led to grave errors in the application of anthropological principles to general problems concerning the nature of war. The crude short-circuiting—by which our modern imperialisms, national hatreds, and world-wide lust of power have been connected with aggression and pugnacity—is largely the result of not establishing the above distinctions, of disregarding the cultural function of conflict, and of confusing war, as a highly specialized and mechanized phenomenon, with any form of aggression.

We can determine even more precisely the manner in which anthropological evidence, as the background of correct understanding and informed knowledge, can be made to bear on some of our current problems. In general, of course, it is clear that since our main concern is whether war will destroy our Western civilisation or not, the anthropological approach, which insists on considering the cultural context of war, might be helpful.

Especially important in a theoretical discussion of whether war can be controlled and ultimately abolished, is the recognition that war is not biologically founded. The fact that its occurrence cannot be traced to the earliest beginnings of human culture is significant. Obviously, if war were necessary to human evolution; if it were something without which human groups have to decay and by which they advance; then war could not be absent from the earliest stages, in which the actual birth of cultural realities took place under the greatest strains and against the heaviest odds. A really vital ingredient could not, therefore, be lacking in the composition of primitive humanity, struggling to lay down the foundations of further progress.

War, looked at in evolutionary perspective, is always a highly destructive event. Its purpose and *raison d'être* depend on whether it creates greater values than it destroys. Violence is constructive, or at least profitable, only when it can lead to large-scale transfers of wealth and privilege, of ideological outfit, and of moral experience. Thus, humanity had to accumulate a considerable stock of transferable goods, ideas, and principles before the diffusion of those through conquest, and even more, the pooling and the reorganization of economic, political, and spiritual resources could lead to things greater than those which had been destroyed through the agency of fighting. . . .

Thus, the general formula which anthropological analysis imposes on sound and enlightened statesmanship is the complete autonomy of each cultural group, and the use of force only as a function of law within, and in foreign relations, a policing of the world as a whole.

John G. Stoessinger

Why Nations Go to War

I decided to embark on six case studies of the major international wars fought in this century: the two world wars, Korea, Vietnam, India and Pakistan, and the Arab states and Israel. What interested me most in each case was the "moment of truth" when leaders crossed the threshold into war. I decided to "blow up" that fateful moment, to capture it in flight, as it were, in all its awesome tragic meaning. In the process, I sought answers to the questions that have always haunted me: At what moment did the decision to go to war become irreversible? Who bore the responsibility and why? Could the disaster have been averted? Did the six cases, different though they were, reveal some common truths about war in our time?

As a final case study in this revision, I have chosen to examine the Iran-Iraq War. In many ways, this conflict resembles World War I, complete with an arsenal of horrors including trench warfare, poison gas, and the extinction of an entire generation of young men on both sides. When shall we ever learn?

It has been fashionable to assert that war is not an illness, but, like aggression, an ineradicable part of human nature. I challenge this assumption. Whereas aggression may be inherent, war is learned behavior, and as such can be unlearned and ultimately selected out entirely. Humans have dispensed with other habits that previously seemed impossible to shed. For example, during the Ice Age, when people lived in caves, incest was perfectly acceptable, whereas today incest is almost universally taboo. Cannibalism provides an even more dramatic case. Thousands of years ago, human beings ate one another and drank one another's blood. That, too, was part of "human nature." Even a brief

century ago, millions of Americans believed that God had ordained white people to be free and black people to be slaves. Why else would He have created them in different colors? Yet slavery, once considered part of "human nature," was abolished because human beings showed a capacity for growth. Growth came slowly, after immense suffering, but it *did* come. "Human nature" had been changed. Like slavery and cannibalism, war too can be eliminated from humankind's arsenal of horrors.

It seems, however, that people abandon their bad habits only when catastrophe is close at hand. The intellect alone is not enough. We must be shaken, almost shattered, before we change. A grave illness must pass its crisis before it is known whether the patient will live or die. Most appropriately, the ancient Chinese had two characters for crisis, one connoting danger and the other opportunity. The danger of extinction is upon us, but so is the opportunity for a better life for all people on this planet.

We must therefore make an effort to look Medusa in the face and to diagnose the sickness. Diagnosis is no cure, of course, but it is the first and the most necessary step. I shall attempt this diagnosis by suggesting certain common themes from the seven case studies.

When I first began work on the cases, I did not know what conclusions I would draw. I was afraid, in fact, that I might reach no general conclusions whatsoever. The landscape of war differed so much from case to case that I despaired of finding a reliable road map. As my work progressed, however, certain common themes emerged. Gradually, they took shape and meaning, and as I reached the end of my journey, they thrust themselves before me with clarity and force. Rather than state these themes as definitive conclusions, I prefer to set them forth in the hope that they might engage the reader in a dialogue. . . .

The first general theme that compels attention is that no nation that began a major war in this century emerged a winner. Austria-Hungary and Germany, which precipitated World War I, went down to ignominious defeat; Hitler's Germany was crushed into unconditional surrender; the North Korean attack was thwarted by collective action and ended in a draw; although the Vietnam war ended in a Communist victory, it would be far too simple to blame the Communists exclusively for its beginning; the Arabs who invaded the new Jewish state in 1948 lost territory to the Israelis in four successive wars; Pakistan, which sought to punish India through preemptive war, was dismembered in the process. And Iraq, which invaded Iran in 1980 hoping for a quick victory, had to settle for a costly stalemate eight years and half a million casualties later.

In all cases, those who began a war took a beating. Neither the nature nor the ideology of the government that started a war made any difference. Aggressors were defeated whether they were capitalists or Communists, white or non-white, Western or non-Western, rich or poor. . . .

In the atomic age, war between nuclear powers is suicidal; wars between small countries with big friends are likely to be inconclusive and interminable; hence decisive war in our time has become the privilege of the impotent. It has become almost banal to say that the atomic age has fundamentally altered the nature of war. No nuclear power can tell another: "Do as I say or I shall kill you," but is reduced to saying: "Do as I say or I shall kill us both," which is an entirely different matter. Thus, when everybody is somebody, nobody is anybody. But it is not only nuclear countries that cannot win wars against each other. A small country with a close tie to a big ally also can no longer be defeated. The wars in Korea, Vietnam, and the Middle East all illustrate this point. The North Koreans

were unable to defeat South Korea so long as the United States was willing to support the South and neutralize the North's successes. And the South Koreans could not defeat the North so long as China and the Soviet Union were willing to render assistance. Thus the Korean War ended with the frontiers virtually unchanged. The main difference was the large number of dead Koreans on *both* sides. In Vietnam, the Soviet Union and China sent enough supplies to offset the results of American bombings; and the deserts of the Middle East became veritable proving grounds for the testing of new superpower weapons. Thus wars between small nations with big friends will be interminable so long as the ally of the weaker side is willing to continue his support. Neither side can win; only the casualties mount. In our time, decisive victories seem possible only for nations without big friends or for the impotent. Bangladesh was able to break away from Pakistan because none of the great powers considered the issue important enough to restore the status quo by force of arms. Nor did the genocidal violence perpetrated by the Tutsi tribe against the Hutu people in Central Africa stir the great powers into action. Thus the paradox of war in the atomic age may be summarized as follows: the power of big states vis-à-vis each other has been reduced, if not altogether canceled out, while the power of small and friendless states vis-à-vis each other has been proportionately enhanced.

In our time, unless the vanquished is destroyed completely, a victor's peace is seldom lasting. Those peace settlements that are negotiated on a basis of equality are much more permanent and durable. In 1918 Germany was defeated but not crushed, Versailles became the crucible for Hitler's Germany, which was then brought down only through unconditional surrender. The Korean settlement was negotiated between undefeated equals. Both sides were unhappy, but neither side was so unhappy that it wished to overturn the settlement and initiate yet another war. An uneasy armistice or truce was gradually recognized as a possible basis for a peace settlement. The relative insecurity of each side thus became the guarantor of the relative security of both. Israel learned this lesson in October 1973. The victor's peace of 1967 had left the Arabs in a state of such frustration that they were compelled to try their hand at war once more. With their dignity restored in 1973, they found it psychologically possible, a decade and a half later, to confront the Israelis with a new and most effective challenge: the Palestinian uprising.

With regard to the problem of the outbreak of war, the case studies indicate the crucial importance of the personalities of leaders. I am less impressed by the role of abstract forces, such as nationalism, militarism, or alliance systems, which traditionally have been regarded as the causes of war. Nor does a single one of the seven cases indicate that economic factors played a vital part in precipitating war. The personalities of leaders, on the other hand, have often been decisive. The outbreak of World War I illustrates this point quite clearly. Conventional wisdom has blamed the alliance system for the spread of the war. Specifically, the argument runs, Kaiser Wilhelm's alliance with Austria dragged Germany into the war against the Allied Powers. This analysis, however, totally ignores the role of the Kaiser's personality during the gathering crisis. Suppose Wilhelm had had the fortitude to continue his role as mediator and restrain Austria instead of engaging in paranoid delusions and accusing England of conspiring against Germany. The disaster might have been averted; the conventional wisdom would then have praised the alliance system for saving the peace instead of blaming it for causing the war. In truth the emotional balance or lack of balance of the German Kaiser turned out to be absolutely crucial. Similarly, the relentless mediocrity of the leading personalities on all sides no doubt contributed to the disaster. If one looks at the outbreak of World War II, there is no doubt that the victor's peace of Versailles and the galloping inflation of the 1920s brought about the rise of Nazi Germany. But once again, it was the personality of Hitler that was decisive. A more ra-

tional leader would have consolidated his gains and certainly would not have attacked the Soviet Union. And if Russia had to be attacked, then a rational man would have made contingency plans to meet the Russian winter instead of counting blindly on an early victory. In the Korean War the hubris of General MacArthur probably prolonged the conflict by two years, and in Vietnam the fragile egos of at least two American presidents who could not face the facts first escalated the war quite disproportionately and then postponed its ending quite unreasonably. In the Middle East the volatile personality of Gamal Abdel Nasser was primarily responsible for the closing of the Gulf of Aqaba, the event which precipitated the Six-Day War of 1967. In 1971 Yahya Khan, the leader of West Pakistan, took his country to war with India because he would not be cowed by a woman. And in the 1980s, Saddam Hussein of Iraq and the Ayatollah Khomeini of Iran—both zealots and fanatics—fought a holy war against each other. In all these cases, a fatal flaw or ego weakness in a leader's personality was of crucial importance. It may, in fact, have spelled the difference between the outbreak of war and the maintenance of peace.

The case material reveals that perhaps the most important single precipitating factor in the outbreak of war is misperception. Such distortion may manifest itself in four different ways: in a leader's image of himself; a leader's view of his adversary's character; a leader's view of his adversary's intentions toward himself and finally, a leader's view of his adversary's capabilities and power. Each of these is of such importance that it merits separate and careful treatment.

There is a remarkable consistency in the self-images of most national leaders on the brink of war. Each confidently expects victory after a brief and triumphant campaign. Doubt about the outcome is the voice of the enemy and therefore inconceivable. This recurring optimism is not to be dismissed lightly by the historian as an ironic example of human folly. It assumes a powerful emotional momentum of its own and thus itself becomes one of the causes of war. Anything that fuels such optimism about a quick and decisive victory makes war more likely, and anything that dampens it becomes a cause of peace.

This common belief in a short, decisive war is usually the overflow from a reservoir of self-delusions held by the leadership about both itself and the nation. The Kaiser's appearance in shining armor in August 1914 and his promise to the German nation that its sons would be back home "before the leaves had fallen from the trees" was matched by similar expressions of overconfidence and military splendor in Austria, Russia, and the other nations on the brink of war. Hitler's confidence in an early German victory in Russia was so unshakable that no winter uniforms were issued to the soldiers and no preparations whatsoever made for the onset of the Russian winter. In November 1941, when the mud of autumn turned to ice and snow, the cold became the German soldier's bitterest enemy. Tormented by the Arctic temperatures, men died, machines broke down, and the quest for warmth all but eclipsed the quest for victory. Hitler's hopes and delusions about the German "master race" were shattered in the frozen wastes of Russia. The fact that Hitler had fought in World War I and seen that optimism crumble in defeat did not prevent its reappearance. When North Korea invaded South Korea, her leadership expected victory within two months. The Anglo-French campaign at Suez in 1956 was spurred by the hope of a swift victory. In Pakistan Yahya Khan hoped to teach Indira Gandhi a lesson modeled on the Six-Day War in Israel. In Vietnam every American escalation in the air or on the ground was an expression of the hope that a few more bombs, a few more troops, would bring decisive victory. And in the Middle East, Saddam Hussein of Iraq expected a quick victory over Iran. What he got instead was a bloody stalemate.

Thus leaders on all sides typically harbor self-delusions on the eve of war. Only the war itself then provides the stinging ice of reality and ultimately helps to restore a measure of perspec-

tive in the leadership. The price for this recapture of reality is high indeed. It is unlikely that there ever was a war that fulfilled the initial hopes and expectations of *both* sides.

Distorted views of the adversary's character also help to precipitate a conflict. As the pressure mounted in July 1914, the German Kaiser explosively admitted that he "hated the Slavs, even though one should not hate anyone." This hatred no doubt influenced his decision to vacate his role as mediator and to prepare for war. Similarly, his naive trust in the honesty of the Austrian leaders prompted him to extend to them the blank-check guarantee that dragged him into war. In reality the Austrians were more deceitful than he thought and the Russians more honest. Worst of all, the British leadership, which worked so desperately to avert a general war, was seen by Wilhelm as the center of a monstrous plot to encircle and destroy the German nation. Hitler too had no conception of what Russia really was like. He knew nothing of the history and depth of the Russian land and believed that it was populated by subhuman barbarians who could be crushed with one decisive stroke and then made to serve as slaves for German supermen. This relentless hatred and contempt for Russia became a crucial factor in Hitler's ill-fated assault of 1941. Perhaps the most important reason for the American military intervention in Vietnam was the misperception of the American leadership about the nature of Communism in Asia. President Lyndon Johnson committed more than half a million combat troops to an Asian land war because he believed that Communism was still a monolithic octopus with North Vietnam its tentacle. He did this more than a decade after the death of Stalin, at a time when Communism had splintered into numerous ideological and political fragments. His total ignorance of Asia in general and of Vietnam in particular made him perceive the Vietnam war in terms of purely Western categories: a colossal shoot-out between the forces of Communism and those of anti-Communism. The fact that Ho Chi Minh saw the Americans as the successors of

French imperialism whom he was determined to drive out was completely lost on the president. Virtue, righteousness, and justice were fully on his side, so Johnson thought. America, the child of light, had to defeat the child of darkness in a twentieth-century crusade. . . .

When a leader on the brink of war believes that his adversary will attack him, the chances of war are fairly high. When both leaders share this perception about each other's intent, war becomes a virtual certainty. The mechanism of the self-fulfilling prophecy is then set in motion. When leaders attribute evil designs to their adversaries, and they nurture these beliefs for long enough, they will eventually be proved right. The mobilization measures that preceded the outbreak of World War I were essentially defensive measures triggered by the fear of the other side's intent. The Russian czar mobilized because he feared an Austrian attack; the German Kaiser mobilized because he feared the Russian "steamroller." The nightmare of each then became a terrible reality. Stalin was so imprisoned by the Marxist dogma that capitalists would always lie that he disbelieved Churchill's truthful warnings about Hitler's murderous intent to the extent that Russia almost lost the war. . . .

Arabs and Israelis and Indians and Pakistanis generally expected nothing but the worst from one another, and these expectations often led to war. The conviction held by Syria and Egypt after 1967 that Israel intended to hold onto the occupied territories forever was the immediate precipitating cause of the October War of 1973, in which the Arabs made a desperate attempt to reconquer their lost lands. And Yahya Khan's perception of India's intention to fight on the side of the secessionist movement in Bengal led directly to his abortive and suicidal air attack.

A leader's misperception of his adversary's power is perhaps the quintessential cause of war. It is vital to remember, however, that it is not the actual distribution of power that precipitates a war; it is the way in which a leader thinks that power is distributed. A war will start when nations disagree over their perceived strength. The war itself then becomes a dispute over measurement. Reality is gradually restored as war itself cures war. And the war will end when the fighting nations perceive each other's strength more realistically. . . .

One of the clearest examples of . . . misperception of this kind took place in the Korean War. MacArthur, during his advance through North Korea toward the Chinese border, stubbornly believed that the Chinese Communists did not have the capability to intervene. When the Chinese did cross the Yalu River into North Korea, MacArthur clung to the belief that he was facing 40,000 men, while in truth the figure was closer to 200,000. And when the Chinese forces temporarily withdrew to assess their impact on MacArthur's army, the American general assumed that the Chinese were badly in need of rest after their encounter with superior Western military might. And when the Chinese attacked again and drove MacArthur all the way back to South Korea, the leader of the UN forces perceived this action as a "piece of treachery worse even than Pearl Harbor." The most amazing aspect of this story is that the real facts were quite available to MacArthur from his own intelligence sources, if only the general had cared to look at them. But he knew better and thus prolonged the war by two more years. Only at war's end did the Americans gain respect for China's power and take care not to provoke her again beyond the point of no return. Yet in the Vietnam war, the American leadership committed precisely the same error vis-à-vis North Vietnam. Five successive presidents believed that Ho Chi Minh would collapse if only a little more military pressure were brought to bear on him either from the air or on the ground. The North Vietnamese leader proved them all mistaken, and only when America admitted that North Vietnam could not be beaten did the war come to an end. In both Korea and Vietnam the price of reality came high indeed. As these wars resolved less and less, they tended to cost more and more in blood and treasure. The number of dead on all sides bore mute testimony to the fact that America had to fight two of the most terrible and divisive wars in her entire history before she gained respect for the realities of power on the other side. In 1948 the Arabs believed that an invasion by five Arab armies would quickly put an end to Israel. They were mistaken. But in 1973 Israel, encouraged to the point of hubris after three successful wars, viewed Arab power only with contempt and its own as unassailable. That too was wrong, as Israel had to learn in the bitter war of October 1973. In Pakistan Yahya Khan had to find out to his detriment that a woman for whom he had nothing but disdain was better schooled in the arts of war than he, did not permit her wishes to dominate her thoughts, and finally managed to dismember Pakistan. And in the Persian Gulf, the invading Iraqis were amazed at the "fanatical zeal" of the Iranians, whom they had underestimated.

Thus, on the eve of each war, at least one nation misperceives another's power. In that sense the beginning of each war is a misperception or an accident. The war itself then slowly, and in agony, teaches the lesson of reality. And peace is made when reality has won. The outbreak of war and the coming of peace are separated by a road that leads from misperception to reality. The most tragic aspect of this truth is that war has continued to remain the best teacher of reality and thus has been the most effective cure for war.

As we move toward the close of the twentieth century, we face an awesome paradox: never before in history have we prepared so feverishly for a war that no one wants. No analysis of war in our time would be complete without at least a glance at our simultaneous efforts to build—and then destroy, or at least control—weapons that could incinerate the earth.

The following is an eyewitness description of Hiroshima shortly after the city was destroyed by an atomic bomb in August 1945:

> People are still dying, mysteriously and horribly--people who were uninjured in the cataclysm—from an unknown something which I can only describe as the atomic plague.

Hiroshima does not look like a bombed city. . . . I write these facts as dispassionately as I can, in the hope that they will act as a warning to the world. In this first testing ground of the atomic bomb . . . it gives you an empty feeling in the stomach to see such man-made devastation. . . . I could see about three miles of reddish rubble. That is all the atomic bomb left. . . . The Police Chief of Hiroshima . . . took me to hospitals where the victims of the bombs are still being treated. In these hospitals I found people who, when the bomb fell, suffered absolutely no injuries, but now are dying from the uncanny aftereffects. For no apparent reason their health began to fail. They lost appetite. Their hair fell out. Bluish spots appeared on their bodies. And then bleeding began from the ears, nose and mouth.

At first, the doctors told me, they thought these were the symptoms of general debility. They gave their patients Vitamin A injections. The results were horrible. The flesh started rotting away from the hole caused by the injection of the needle. And in every case the victim died.

A peculiar odour . . . given off by the poisonous gas still issues from the earth soaked with radioactivity; against this the inhabitants all wear gauze masks over their mouths and noses; many thousands of people have simply vanished—the atomic heat was so great that they burned instantly to ashes—except that there were no ashes—they were vaporised.

. . . Yet despite all the progress made, war is still a very real danger. In the past the anarchic nature of the nation-state system was chiefly responsible for wars. Now the future may bring new challenges to our survival that emanate from nonstate entities. Self-styled patriots, liberation groups, criminal elements, and even individual terrorists may soon have access to nuclear technology and subject national leaders to atomic blackmail. When one considers the fact that in 1976 an undergraduate physics student at Princeton University was able to write, with the use of publicly available materials, a paper describing how to build an atom bomb, that possibility does not seem at all farfetched. If the world's poor and hungry remain unable to persuade the world's rich to share their wealth more equitably, then violence becomes an increasingly probable scenario. Hence, as the twentieth century draws to a close, wars may erupt in the cracks of the state system as easily as among sovereign states themselves. . . .

Despite the persistence of so much human tragedy and folly, it is nevertheless possible to conclude this study on a note of hope. Neither the American people nor the Russian people want a nuclear war. In both nations the level of consciousness against war has been raised. In the United States, if the nation's leaders get too close to the brink, the people tend to act as a corrective.

In the Soviet Union, the memory of war and devastation acts as a similar corrective. This popular sentiment against nuclear death finally led to some meaningful disarmament. And there is hope now for more. Certainly all men and women of goodwill must continue to work in that direction. *There has been a slow dawning of compassion and global consciousness over humanity's bleak skies in our generation.* This has manifested itself both in a new awareness of and even resistance to the havoc that war wreaks on the human spirit. Our sense of logic no longer finds it acceptable to consider throwing a human being into a fire an atrocity, while condoning the military operation of throwing fire on many human beings.

Questions for Discussion

1. Which of the following propositions most accurately describes war: a biological necessity, a sociological inevitability, or an invention? Why?

2. How do anthropologists, such as Mead and Malinowski, analyze the causes of war?

3. Stoessinger says "No nation that began a major war in this century emerged as a winner," but he says that the opposite was true in the nineteenth century. What do you think accounts for this change? Do you think it will change again in the twenty-first century? Why do you think so?

Further Readings

1. Schmidt, Bettina E., and Schroder, Ingo W., eds. *Anthropology of Violence and Conflict.* London: Routledge, 2001.

2. Otterbein, Keith F. A. "History of Research on Warfare in Anthropology." *American Anthropologist,* 1999, 101, 4, Dec., 794–805.

3. Dawson, Doyne. "Evolutionary Theory and Group Selection: The Question of Warfare." *History and Theory,* 1999, 38, 4, Dec., 79–100.

4. Beiburg, Federico, and Goldman, Marcio. "Anthropology and Politics in Studies of National Character." *Cultural Anthropology,* 1998, 13, 1, Feb., 56–81.

5. Wilson, Robin. "The Politics of Contemporary Ethno-Nationalist Conflicts." *Nations and Nationalism,* 2001, 7, 3, July, 365–384.

6. Dawson, Doyne. "Evolutionary Theory and Group Selection: The Question of Warfare." *History and Theory,* 1999, 38, 4, Dec., 79–100.

7. Crook, D. P. *Darwinism War and History: The Debate over the Biology of War from the "Origin of Species" to the First World War.* Cambridge: Cambridge University Press, 2003.

8. Cooter, Roger. "Discourses on War." *Studies in History and Philosophy of Science,* 1995, 26, 4, Dec., 637–647.

PART V

Theories and Strategies for the Prevention of War

Negotiation Strategies

Negotiation strategies are considered one of the foremost conflict-resolution options to prevent war. Nation-states pay increasing attention to diplomatic options before engaging in armed conflict. In this section Roger Fisher and William Ury explain the viability of this option and ways to increase its efficacy in crisis solving.

In "Getting to Yes: Negotiating Agreement without Giving Up" Fisher and Ury provide a systematic analysis of the problems encountered by negotiators, along with a set of guidelines to overcome such problems. They present the following five negotiation strategies.

The first strategy, "position bargaining," is identified by Fisher and Ury as being extremely detrimental to any negotiation process. The gap between the parties is widened if they argue over the validity of their positions instead of debating options

to bridge that gap. Position bargaining increases the likelihood of a breakdown of negotiations between the parties. The authors state that two kinds of bargaining positions, usually identified by negotiators as soft and hard positions, are both inefficient. The former makes one vulnerable to coercion, and the latter runs the risk of causing a breakdown.

The authors then explore another strategic option they designate as "principled bargaining," which focuses on the *interests* of the respective parties. This alternative mode of bargaining, according to Fisher and Ury, creates an environment for a successful outcome of negotiations.

The second strategy is to differentiate between a dispute itself and the individuals involved. This reading explains how important it is to realize that negotiators on both sides are humans and that their perceptions and personal feelings may differ. By taking into account these differences, negotiators may pave the way for successful negotiations. It is imperative to maintain communications on both sides to ensure meaningful dialogue.

The third strategy is to turn negotiations into a mutual problem-solving process rather than a bargaining game. To recognize that both parties will benefit equally by finding a viable and mutually-acceptable solution to the problem, both sides should strive to find such a solution. This can be done by exploring and identifying common interests.

The fourth strategy is to increase the options for both sides to make it easier for them to accept one, by creating solutions in which one party does not have to lose if the other wins. In other words, the challenge is to create a *win–win* situation for both parties. Fisher and Ury emphasize the importance of helping the other side solve their problems and thus argue that all problems in a negotiation process should be mutually oriented.

The fifth strategy identified by the authors is the creation of an objective framework for conducting negotiations. Fair rules and standards applicable to all involved parties are essential if negotiations are to lead to a successful outcome.

Roger Fisher
William Ury

Getting to Yes: Negotiating Agreement without Giving Up

Don't Bargain over Positions

Whether a negotiation concerns a contract, a family quarrel, or a peace settlement among nations, people routinely engage in positional bargaining. Each side takes a position, argues for it, and makes concessions to reach a compromise. . . .

Arguing over Positions Produces Unwise Agreements

When negotiators bargain over positions, they tend to lock themselves into those positions. The more you clarify your position and defend it against attack, the more committed you become to it. The more you try to convince the other side of the impossibility of changing your opening position, the more difficult it becomes to do so. Your ego becomes identified with your position. You now have a new interest in "saving face"—in reconciling future action with past positions—making it less and less likely that any agreement will wisely reconcile the parties' original interests.

The danger that positional bargaining will impede a negotiation was well illustrated by the breakdown of the talks under President Kennedy for a comprehensive ban on nuclear testing. A critical question arose: How many on-site inspections per year should the Soviet Union and the United States be permitted to make within the other's territory to investigate suspicious seismic events? The Soviet Union finally agreed to three inspections. The United States insisted on no less than ten. And there the talks broke down—over positions—despite the fact that no one understood whether an "inspection" would involve one person looking around for one day, or a hundred people prying indiscriminately for a month. The parties had made little attempt to design an inspection procedure that would reconcile the United States's interest in verification with the desire of both countries for minimal intrusion.

As more attention is paid to positions, less attention is devoted to meeting the underlying concerns of the parties. Agreement becomes less likely. Any agreement reached may reflect a mechanical splitting of the difference between final positions rather than a solution carefully crafted to meet the legitimate interests of the parties. The result is frequently an agreement less satisfactory to each side than it could have been.

Arguing over Positions Is Inefficient

Bargaining over positions creates incentives that stall settlement. In positional bargaining you try to improve the chance that any settlement reached is favorable to you by starting with an extreme position, by stubbornly holding to it, by deceiving the other party as to your true views, and by making small concessions only as necessary to keep the negotiation going. The same is true for the other side. Each of those factors tends to interfere with reaching a settlement promptly. The more extreme the opening positions and the smaller the concessions, the more time and effort it will take to discover whether or not agreement is possible.

The standard minuet also requires a large number of individual decisions as each negotiator decides what to offer, what to reject, and how much of a concession to make. Decision-making is difficult and time-consuming at best. Where each decision not only involves yielding to the other side but will likely produce pressure to yield further, a negotiator has little incentive to move quickly. Dragging one's feet, threatening to walk out, stonewalling, and other such tactics become commonplace. They all increase the time and costs of reaching agreement as well as the risk that no agreement will be reached at all.

Arguing over Positions Endangers an Ongoing Relationship

Positional bargaining becomes a contest of will. Each negotiator asserts what he will and won't do. The task of jointly devising an acceptable solution tends to become a battle. Each side tries through sheer will power to force the other to change its position. "I'm not going to give in. If you want to go to the movies with me, it's *The Maltese Falcon* or nothing." Anger and resentment often result as one side sees itself bending to the rigid will of the other while its own legitimate concerns go unaddressed. Positional bargaining thus strains and sometimes shatters the relationship between the parties.

When There Are Many Parties, Positional Bargaining Is Even Worse

Although it is convenient to discuss negotiation in terms of two persons, you and "the other side," in fact, almost every negotiation involves more than two persons. Several different parties may sit at the table, or each side may have constituents, higher-ups, boards of directors, or committees with whom they must deal. The more people involved in a negotiation, the more serious the drawbacks to positional bargaining.

If some 150 countries are negotiating, as in various United Nations conferences, positional bargaining is next to impossible. It may take all to say yes, but only one to say no. Reciprocal concessions are difficult: to whom do you make a concession? Yet even thousands of bilateral deals would still fall short of a multilateral agreement. In such situations, positional bargaining leads to the formation of coalitions among parties whose shared interests are often more symbolic than substantive. At the United Nations, such coalitions produce negotiations between "the" North and "the" South, or between "the" East and "the" West. Because there are many members in a group, it becomes more difficult to develop a common position. What is worse, once they have painfully developed and agreed upon a position, it becomes much harder to change it. Altering a position proves equally difficult when additional participants are higher authorities who, while absent from the table, must nevertheless give their approval.

Many people recognize the high costs of hard positional bargaining, particularly on the parties and their relationship. They hope to avoid them by following a more gentle style of negotiation. Instead of seeing the other side as adversaries, they prefer to see them as friends. Rather than emphasizing a goal of victory, they emphasize the necessity of reaching agreement. In a soft negotiating game the standard moves are to make offers and concessions, to trust the other side, to be friendly, and to yield as necessary to avoid confrontation.

[Table 41.1] illustrates two styles of positional bargaining, soft and hard. Most people see their choice of negotiating strategies as between these two styles. Looking at the table as presenting a choice, should you be a soft or a hard positional bargainer? Or should you perhaps follow a strategy somewhere in between?

The soft negotiating game emphasizes the importance of building and maintaining a relationship. Within families and among friends much negotiation takes place in this way. The process tends to be efficient, at least to the extent of producing results quickly. As each party competes with the other in being more generous and more forthcoming, an agreement becomes highly likely. But it may not be a wise one. The results may not be as tragic as in the O. Henry story about an impoverished couple in which the loving wife sells her hair in order to buy a handsome chain for her husband's watch, and the unknowing husband sells his watch in order to buy beautiful combs for his wife's hair. However, any negotiation primarily concerned with the relationship runs the risk of producing a sloppy agreement.

■ **TABLE 41.1**

PROBLEM
Positional Bargaining: Which Game Should You Play?

Soft	Hard
Participants are friends.	Participants are adversaries.
The goal is agreement.	The goal is victory.
Make concessions to cultivate the relationship.	Demand concessions as a condition of the relationship.
Be soft on the people and the problem.	Be hard on the problem and the people.
Trust others.	Distrust others.
Change your position easily.	Dig in to your position.
Make offers.	Make threats.
Disclose your bottom line.	Mislead as to your bottom line.
Accept one-sided losses to reach agreement.	Demand one-sided gains as the price of agreement.
Search for the single answer: the one *they* will accept.	Search for the single answer: the one *you* will accept.
Insist on agreement.	Insist on your position.
Try to avoid a contest of will.	Try to win a contest of will.
Yield to pressure.	Apply pressure.

More seriously, pursuing a soft and friendly form of positional bargaining makes you vulnerable to someone who plays a hard game of positional bargaining. In positional bargaining, a hard game dominates a soft one. If the hard bargainer insists on concessions and makes threats while the soft bargainer yields in order to avoid confrontation and insists on agreement, the negotiating game is biased in favor of the hard player. The process will produce an agreement, although it may not be a wise one. It will certainly be more favorable to the hard positional bargainer than to the soft one. If your response to sustained, hard positional bargaining is soft positional bargaining, you will probably lose your shirt.

There Is an Alternative

If you do not like the choice between hard and soft positional bargaining, you can change the game.

The game of negotiation takes place at two levels. At one level, negotiation addresses the sub-

stance; at another, it focuses—usually implicitly—on the procedure for dealing with the substance. The first negotiation may concern your salary, the terms of a lease, or a price to be paid. The second negotiation concerns how you will negotiate the substantive question: by soft positional bargaining, by hard positional bargaining, or by some other method. This second negotiation is a game about a game—a "meta-game." Each move you make within a negotiation is not only a move that deals with rent, salary, or other substantive questions; it also helps structure the rules of the game you are playing. Your move may serve to keep the negotiations within an ongoing mode, or it may constitute a game-changing move.

This second negotiation by and large escapes notice because it seems to occur without conscious decision. Only when dealing with someone from another country, particularly someone with a markedly different cultural background, are you likely to see the necessity of establishing some accepted process for the substantive negotiations. But whether consciously or not, you are negotiating procedural rules with every move you make, even if those moves appear exclusively concerned with substance.

The answer to the question of whether to use soft positional bargaining or hard is "neither." Change the game. At the Harvard Negotiation Project we have been developing an alternative to positional bargaining: a method of negotiation explicitly designed to produce wise outcomes efficiently and amicably. This method, called *principled negotiation* or *negotiation on the merits,* can be boiled down to four basic points.

These four points define a straightforward method of negotiation that can be used under almost any circumstance. Each point deals with a basic element of negotiation, and suggests what you should do about it.

People: Separate the people from the problem.

Interests: Focus on interests, not positions.

Options: Generate a variety of possibilities before deciding what to do.

Criteria: Insist that the result be based on some objective standard.

The first point responds to the fact that human beings are not computers. We are creatures of strong emotions who often have radically different perceptions and have difficulty communicating clearly. Emotions typically become entangled with the objective merits of the problem. Taking positions just makes this worse because people's egos become identified with their positions. Hence, before working on the substantive problem, the "people problem" should be disentangled from it and dealt with separately. Figuratively if not literally, the participants should come to see themselves as working side by side, attacking the problem, not each other. Hence the first proposition: *Separate the people from the problem.*

The second point is designed to overcome the drawback of focusing on people's stated positions when the object of a negotiation is to satisfy their underlying interests. A negotiating position often obscures what you really want. Compro-

mising between positions is not likely to produce an agreement which will effectively take care of the human needs that led people to adopt those positions. The second basic element of the method is: *Focus on interests, not positions.*

The third point responds to the difficulty of designing optimal solutions while under pressure. Trying to decide in the presence of an adversary narrows your vision. Having a lot at stake inhibits creativity. So does searching for the one right solution. You can offset these constraints by setting aside a designated time within which to think up a wide range of possible solutions that advance shared interests and creatively reconcile differing interests. Hence the third basic point: Before trying to reach agreement, *invent options for mutual gain.*

Where interests are directly opposed, a negotiator may be able to obtain a favorable result simply by being stubborn. That method tends to reward intransigence and produce arbitrary results. However, you can counter such a negotiator by insisting that his single say-so is not enough and that the agreement must reflect some fair standard independent of the naked will of either side. This does not mean insisting that the terms be based on the standard you select, but only that some fair standard such as market value, expert opinion, custom, or law determine the outcome. By discussing such criteria rather than what the parties are willing or unwilling to do, neither party need give in to the other; both can defer to a fair solution. Hence the fourth basic point: *Insist on objective criteria.*

The method of principled negotiation is contrasted with hard and soft positional bargaining in [Table 41.2], which shows the four basic points of the method in boldface type.

The four basic propositions of principled negotiation are relevant from the time you begin to think about negotiating until the time either an agreement is reached or you decide to break off the effort. That period can be divided into three stages: analysis, planning, and discussion.

During the *analysis* stage you are simply trying to diagnose the situation—to gather information, organize it, and think about it. You will want to consider the people problems of partisan perceptions, hostile emotions, and unclear com-

■ **TABLE 41.2**

PROBLEM		SOLUTION
Positional Bargaining: Which Game Should You Play?		Change the Game— Negotiate on the Merits
Soft	**Hard**	**Principled**
Participants are friends.	Participants are adversaries.	Participants are problem-solvers.
The goal is agreement.	The goal is victory.	The goal is a wise outcome reached efficiently and amicably.
Make concessions to cultivate the relationship.	Demand concessions as a condition of the relationship.	**Separate the people from the problem.**
Be soft on the people and the problem.	Be hard on the problem and the people.	Be soft on the people, hard on the problem.
Trust others.	Distrust others.	Proceed independent of trust.
Change your position easily.	Dig in to your position.	**Focus on interests, not positions.**
Make offers.	Make threats.	Explore interests.
Disclose your bottom line.	Mislead as to your bottom line.	Avoid having a bottom line.
Accept one-sided losses to reach agreement.	Demand one-sided gains as the price of agreement.	**Invent options for mutual gain.**
Search for the single answer: the one *they* will accept.	Search for the single answer: the one *you* will accept.	Develop multiple options to choose from; decide later.
Insist on agreement.	Insist on your position.	**Insist on objective criteria.**
Try to avoid a contest of will.	Try to win a contest of will.	Try to reach a result based on standards independent of will.
Yield to pressure.	Apply pressure.	Reason and be open to reason; yield to principle, not pressure.

munication, as well as to identify your interests and those of the other side. You will want to note options already on the table and identify any criteria already suggested as a basis for agreement.

During the *planning* stage you deal with the same four elements a second time, both generating ideas and deciding what to do. How do you propose to handle the people problem? Of your interests, which are most important? And what are some realistic objectives? You will want to generate additional options and additional criteria for deciding among them.

Again during the *discussion* stage, when the parties communicate back and forth, looking toward agreement, the same four elements are the best subjects to discuss. Differences in perception, feelings of frustration and anger, and difficulties in communication can be acknowledged and addressed. Each side should come to understand the interests of the other. Both can then jointly generate options that are mutually advantageous and seek agreement on objective standards for resolving opposed interests.

To sum up, in contrast to positional bargaining, the principled negotiation method of focusing on basic interests, mutually satisfying options, and fair standards typically results in a *wise* agreement. The method permits you to reach a gradual consensus on a joint decision *efficiently* without all the transactional costs of digging in to positions only to have to dig yourself out of them. And separating the people from the problem allows you to deal directly and empathetically with the other negotiator as a human being, thus making possible an *amicable* agreement. . . .

Separate the People from the Problem

Everyone knows how hard it is to deal with a problem without people misunderstanding each other, getting angry or upset, and taking things personally. . . .

Negotiators Are People First

A basic fact about negotiation, easy to forget in corporate and international transactions, is that you are dealing not with abstract representatives of the "other side," but with human beings. They have emotions, deeply held values, and different backgrounds and viewpoints; and they are unpredictable. So are you. . . .

Failing to deal with others sensitively as human beings prone to human reactions can be

disastrous for a negotiation. Whatever else you are doing at any point during a negotiation, from preparation to follow-up, it is worth asking yourself, "Am I paying enough attention to the people problem?"

Separate the Relationship from the Substance; Deal Directly with the People Problem

Dealing with a substantive problem and maintaining a good working relationship need not be conflicting goals if the parties are committed and psychologically prepared to treat each separately on its own legitimate merits. Base the relationship on accurate perceptions, clear communication, appropriate emotions, and a forward-looking, purposive outlook. Deal with people problems directly; don't try to solve them with substantive concessions.

Perception

Understanding the other side's thinking is not simply a useful activity that will help you solve your problem. Their thinking *is* the problem. Whether you are making a deal or settling a dispute, differences are defined by the difference between your thinking and theirs. . . .

Put Yourself in Their Shoes. How you see the world depends on where you sit. People tend to see what they want to see. Out of a mass of detailed information, they tend to pick out and focus on those facts that confirm their prior perceptions and to disregard or misinterpret those that call their perceptions into question. Each side in a negotiation may see only the merits of its case, and only the faults of the other side's.

The ability to see the situation as the other side sees it, as difficult as it may be, is one of the most important skills a negotiator can possess. It is not enough to know that they see things differently. If you want to influence them, you also need to understand empathetically the power of their point of view and to feel the emotional force with which they believe in it. . . .

Understanding their point of view is not the same as agreeing with it. It is true that a better understanding of their thinking may lead you to revise your own views about the merits of a situation. But that is not a *cost* of understanding their point of view, it is a *benefit*. It allows you to reduce the area of conflict, and it also helps you advance your newly enlightened self-interest. . . .

Discuss Each Other's Perceptions.   One way to deal with differing perceptions is to make them explicit and discuss them with the other side. As long as you do this in a frank, honest manner without either side blaming the other for the problem as each sees it, such a discussion may provide the understanding they need to take what you say seriously, and vice versa.

It is common in a negotiation to treat as "unimportant" those concerns of the other side perceived as not standing in the way of an agreement. To the contrary, communicating loudly and convincingly things you are willing to say that they would like to hear can be one of the best investments you as a negotiator can make. . . .

Face-Saving: Make Your Proposals Consistent with Their Values.   In the English language, "face-saving" carries a derogatory flavor. People say, "We are doing that just to let them save face," implying that a little pretense has been created to allow someone to go along without feeling badly. The tone implies ridicule.

This is a grave misunderstanding of the role and importance of face-saving. Face-saving reflects a person's need to reconcile the stand he takes in a negotiation or an agreement with his principles and with his past words and deeds. . . .

Face-saving involves reconciling an agreement with principle and with the self-image of the negotiators. Its importance should not be underestimated. . . .

Emotion

In a negotiation, particularly in a bitter dispute, feelings may be more important than talk. The parties may be more ready for battle than for co-operatively working out a solution to a common problem. People often come to a negotiation realizing that the stakes are high and feeling threatened. Emotions on one side will generate emotions on the other. Fear may breed anger, and anger, fear. Emotions may quickly bring a negotiation to an impasse or an end.

First Recognize and Understand Emotions, Theirs and Yours.   Look at yourself during the negotiation. Are you feeling nervous? Is your stomach upset? Are you angry at the other side? Listen to them and get a sense of what their emotions are. You may find it useful to write down what you feel—perhaps fearful, worried, angry—and then how you might like to feel—confident, relaxed. Do the same for them.

In dealing with negotiators who represent their organizations, it is easy to treat them as mere mouthpieces without emotions. It is important to remember that they too, like you, have personal feelings, fears, hopes, and dreams. Their careers may be at stake. There may be issues on which they are particularly sensitive and others on which they are particularly proud. Nor are the problems of emotion limited to the negotiators. Constituents have emotions too. A constituent may have an even more simplistic and adversarial view of the situation. . . .

Make Emotions Explicit and Acknowledge Them as Legitimate.   Talk with the people on the other side about their emotions. Talk about your own. It does not hurt to say, "You know, the people on our side feel we have been mistreated and are very upset. We're afraid an agreement will not be kept even if one is reached. Rational or not, that is our concern. Personally, I think we may be wrong in fearing this, but that's a feeling others have. Do the people on your side feel the same way?" Making your feelings or theirs an explicit focus of discussion will not only underscore the seriousness of the problem, it will also make the negotiations less reactive and more "pro-active." Freed from the burden of unexpressed emotions, people will become more likely to work on the problem.

Communication

Without communication there is no negotiation. Negotiation is a process of communicating back and forth for the purpose of reaching a joint decision. Communication is never an easy thing, even between people who have an enormous background of shared values and experience. Couples who have lived with each other for thirty years still have misunderstandings every day. It is not surprising, then, to find poor communication between people who do not know each other well and who may feel hostile and suspicious of one another. Whatever you say, you should expect that the other side will almost always hear something different.

There are three big problems in communication. First, negotiators may not be talking to each other, or at least not in such a way as to be understood. Frequently each side has given up on the other and is no longer attempting any serious communication with it. Instead they talk merely to impress third parties or their own constituency.

Even if you are talking directly and clearly to them, they may not be hearing you. This constitutes the second problem in communication. Note how often people don't seem to pay enough attention to what you say. Probably equally often, you would be unable to repeat what they had said. In a negotiation, you may be so busy thinking about what you are going to say next, how you are going to respond to that last point or how you are going to frame your next argument, that you forget to listen to what the other side is saying now. Or you may be listening more attentively to your constituency than to the other side. Your constituents, after all, are the ones to whom you will have to account for the results of the negotiation. They are the ones you are trying to satisfy. It is not surprising that you should want to pay close attention to them. But if you are not hearing what the other side is saying, there is no communication.

The third communication problem is misunderstanding. What one says, the other may misinterpret. Even when negotiators are in the same room, communication from one to the other can seem like sending smoke signals in a high wind. . . .

What can be done about these three problems of communication?

Listen Actively and Acknowledge What Is Being Said.   The need for listening is obvious, yet it is difficult to listen well, especially under the stress of an ongoing negotiation. Listening enables you to understand their perceptions, feel their emotions, and hear what they are trying to say. Active listening improves not only what you hear, but also what they say. If you pay attention and interrupt occasionally to say, "Did I understand correctly that you are saying that . . . ?" the other side will realize that they are not just killing time, not just going through a routine. They will also feel the satisfaction of being heard and understood. It has been said that the cheapest concession you can make to the other side is to let them know they have been heard.

Standard techniques of good listening are to pay close attention to what is said, to ask the other party to spell out carefully and clearly exactly what they mean, and to request that ideas be repeated if there is any ambiguity or uncertainty. Make it your task while listening not to phrase a response, but to understand them as they see themselves. Take in their perceptions, their needs, and their constraints. . . .

Prevention Works Best

The techniques just described for dealing with problems of perception, emotion, and communication usually work well. However, the best time for handling people problems is before they become people problems. This means building a personal and organizational relationship with the other side that can cushion the people on each side against the knocks of negotiation. It also means structuring the negotiating game in ways that separate the substantive problem from the relationship and protect people's egos from getting involved in substantive discussions. . . .

Separating the people from the problem is not something you can do once and forget about; you have to keep working at it. The basic approach is to deal with the people as human beings and with the problem on its merits. . . .

Focus on Interests, Not Positions

Consider the story of two men quarrelling in a library. One wants the window open and the other wants it closed. They bicker back and forth about how much to leave it open: a crack, halfway, three quarters of the way. No solution satisfies them both.

Enter the librarian. She asks one why he wants the window open: "To get some fresh air." She asks the other why he wants it closed: "To avoid the draft." After thinking a minute, she opens wide a window in the next room, bringing in fresh air without a draft.

For a Wise Solution Reconcile Interests, Not Positions

This story is typical of many negotiations. Since the parties' problem appears to be a conflict of positions, and since their goal is to agree on a position, they naturally tend to think and talk about positions—and in the process often reach an impasse.

The librarian could not have invented the solution she did if she had focused only on the two men's stated positions of wanting the window open or closed. Instead she looked to their underlying interests of fresh air and no draft. This difference between positions and interests is crucial.

Interests Define the Problem. The basic problem in a negotiation lies not in conflicting positions, but in the conflict between each side's needs, desires, concerns, and fears. The parties may say:

"I am trying to get him to stop that real estate development next door."

Or "We disagree. He wants $50,000 for the house. I won't pay a penny more than $47,500."

But on a more basic level the problem is:

"He needs the cash; I want peace and quiet."

Or "He needs at least $50,000 to settle with his ex-wife. I told my family that I wouldn't pay more than $47,500 for a house."

Such desires and concerns are *interests*. Interests motivate people; they are the silent movers behind the hubbub of positions. Your position is something you have decided upon. Your interests are what caused you to so decide.

Reconciling interests rather than positions works for two reasons. First, for every interest there usually exist several possible positions that could satisfy it.

When you do look behind opposed positions for the motivating interests, you can often find an alternative position which meets not only your interests but theirs as well. In the Sinai, demilitarization was one such alternative.

Reconciling interests rather than compromising between positions also works because behind opposed positions lie many more interests than conflicting ones.

Behind Opposed Positions Lie Shared and Compatible Interests, as well as Conflicting Ones. We tend to assume that because the other side's positions are opposed to ours, their interests must also be opposed. If we have an interest in defending ourselves, then they must want to attack us. If we have an interest in minimizing the rent, then their interest must be to maximize it. In many negotiations, however, a close examination of the underlying interests will reveal the existence of many more interests that are shared or compatible than ones that are opposed. . . .

How Do You Identity Interests?

The benefit of looking behind positions for interests is clear. How to go about it is less clear. A position is likely to be concrete and explicit; the interests underlying it may well be unexpressed, intangible, and perhaps inconsistent. How do you go about understanding the interests involved in a negotiation, remembering that figuring out *their* interests will be at least as important as figuring out *yours*?

Ask "Why not?" Think about Their Choice. One of the most useful ways to uncover interests is first to identify the basic decision that those on the other side probably see you asking them for, and then to ask yourself why they have not made that decision. What interests of theirs stand in the way? If you are trying to change their minds, the starting point is to figure out where their minds are now. . . .

Now analyze the consequences, as the other side would probably see them, of agreeing or refusing to make the decision you are asking for. You may find a checklist of consequences such as the following helpful in this task:

Impact on my interests

- Will I lose or gain political support?
- Will colleagues criticize or praise me?

Impact on the group's interests

- What will be the short-term consequences? The long-term consequences?
- What will be the economic consequences (political, legal, psychological, military, etc.)?
- What will be the effect on outside supporters and public opinion?
- Will the precedent be good or bad?
- Will making this decision prevent doing something better?
- Is the action consistent with our principles? Is it "right"?
- Can I do it later if I want?

In this entire process it would be a mistake to try for great precision. Only rarely will you deal with a decision-maker who writes down and weighs the pros and cons. You are trying to understand a very human choice, not making a mathematical calculation.

Realize That Each Side Has Multiple Interests.

In almost every negotiation each side will have many interests, not just one. As a tenant negotiating a lease, for example, you may want to obtain a favorable rental agreement, to reach it quickly with little effort, and to maintain a good working relationship with your landlord. You will have not only a strong interest in *affecting* any agreement you reach, but also one in *effecting* an agreement. You will be simultaneously pursuing both your independent and your shared interests.

A common error in diagnosing a negotiating situation is to assume that each person on the other side has the same interests. This is almost never the case. . . .

To understand [a] negotiator's interests means to understand the variety of somewhat differing interests that he needs to take into account.

The Most Powerful Interests Are Basic Human Needs. In searching for the basic interests behind a declared position, look particularly for those bedrock concerns which motivate all people. If you can take care of such basic needs, you increase the chance both of reaching agreement and, if an agreement is reached, of the other side's keeping to it. Basic human needs include:

- security
- economic well-being
- a sense of belonging
- recognition
- control over one's life

As fundamental as they are, basic human needs are easy to overlook. In many negotiations, we tend to think that the only interest involved is money. Yet even in a negotiation over a monetary figure, such as the amount of alimony to be specified in a separation agreement, much more can be involved. What does a wife really want in asking for $500 a week in alimony? Certainly she is interested in her economic well-being, but what else? Possibly she wants the money in order to feel psychologically secure. She may also want it for recognition: to feel that she is treated fairly and as an equal. Perhaps the husband can ill afford to pay $500 a week, and perhaps his wife does not need that much, yet she will likely accept less only if her needs for security and recognition are met in other ways.

Talking about Interests

The purpose of negotiating is to serve your interests. The chance of that happening increases when you communicate them. The other side may not know what your interests are, and you may not know theirs. One or both of you may be focusing on past grievances instead of on future concerns. Or you may not even be listening to each other. How do you discuss interests constructively without getting locked into rigid positions? . . .

Acknowledge Their Interests as Part of the Problem.   Each of us tends to be so concerned with his or her own interests that we pay too little heed to the interests of others.

People listen better if they feel that you have understood them. They tend to think that those who understand them are intelligent and sympathetic people whose own opinions may be worth listening to. So if you want the other side to appreciate *your* interests, begin by demonstrating that you appreciate *theirs*. . . .

You will satisfy your interests better if you talk about where you would like to go rather than about where you have come from. Instead of arguing with the other side about the past—about last quarter's costs (which were too high), last week's action (taken without adequate authority), or yesterday's performance (which was less than expected)—talk about what you want to have happen in the future. Instead of asking them to justify what they did yesterday, ask, "Who should do what tomorrow?"

Be Concrete But Flexible.   In a negotiation you want to know where you are going and yet be open to fresh ideas. To avoid having to make a difficult decision on what to settle for, people will often go into a negotiation with no other plan than to sit down with the other side and see what they offer or demand.

How can you move from identifying interests to developing specific options and still remain flexible with regard to those options? To convert your interests into concrete options, ask yourself, "If tomorrow the other side agrees to go along with me, what do I now think I would like them to go along with?" To keep your flexibility, treat each option you formulate as simply illustrative. Think in terms of more than one option that meets your interests. "Illustrative specificity" is the key concept.

Much of what positional bargainers hope to achieve with an opening position can be accomplished equally well with an illustrative suggestion that generously takes care of your interest. For example, in a baseball contract negotiation,

an agent might say that "$250,000 a year would be the kind of figure that should satisfy Cortez's interest in receiving the salary he feels he is worth. Something on the order of a five-year contract should meet his need for job security."

Having thought about your interests, you should go into a meeting not only with one or more specific options that would meet your legitimate interests but also with an open mind. An open mind is not an empty one.

Be Hard on the Problem, Soft on the People.   You can be just as hard in talking about your interests as any negotiator can be in talking about his position. In fact, it is usually advisable to be hard. It may not be wise to commit yourself to your position, but it is wise to commit yourself to your interests. . . .

Negotiating hard for your interests does not mean being closed to the other side's point of view. Quite the contrary. You can hardly expect the other side to listen to your interests and discuss the options you suggest if you don't take their interests into account and show yourself to be open to their suggestions. Successful negotiation requires being both firm *and* open. . . .

Invent Options for Mutual Gain

Diagnosis

As valuable as it is to have many options, people involved in a negotiation rarely sense a need for them. In a dispute, people usually believe that they know the right answer—their view should prevail. In a contract negotiation they are equally likely to believe that their offer is reasonable and should be adopted, perhaps with some adjustment in the price. All available answers appear to lie along a straight line between their position and yours. Often the only creative thinking shown is to suggest splitting the difference.

In most negotiations there are four major obstacles that inhibit the inventing of an abundance of options: (1) premature judgment; (2) searching for the single answer; (3) the assumption of a fixed pie; and (4) thinking that "solving their problem is their problem." In order to overcome these constraints, you need to understand them.

Premature Judgment.   Inventing options does not come naturally. *Not* inventing is the normal state of affairs, even when you are outside a stressful negotiation. If you were asked to name the one person in the world most deserving of the Nobel Peace Prize, any answer you might start to propose would immediately encounter your reservations and doubts. How could you be sure that that person was the *most* deserving? Your mind might well go blank, or you might throw out a few answers that would reflect conventional thinking: "Well, maybe the Pope, or the President."

Nothing is so harmful to inventing as a critical sense waiting to pounce on the drawbacks of any new idea. Judgment hinders imagination. . . .

Searching for the Single Answer.   In most people's minds, inventing simply is not part of the negotiating process. People see their job as narrowing the gap between positions, not broadening the options available. They tend to think, "We're having a hard enough time agreeing as it is. The last thing we need is a bunch of different ideas." Since the end product of negotiation is a single decision, they fear that free-floating discussion will only delay and confuse the process.

If the first impediment to creative thinking is premature criticism, the second is premature closure. By looking from the outset for the single best answer, you are likely to short-circuit a wiser decision-making process in which you select from a large number of possible answers.

The Assumption of a Fixed Pie.   A third explanation for why there may be so few good options on the table is that each side sees the situation as essentially either/or—either I get what is in dispute or you do. A negotiation often appears to be a "fixed-sum" game; $100 more for you on the price of a car means $100 less for me. Why bother to invent if all the options are obvious and I can satisfy you only at my own expense?

Thinking That "Solving Their Problem Is Their Problem."   A final obstacle to inventing realistic options lies in each side's concern with only its own immediate interests. For a negotiator to reach an agreement that meets his own self-interest he needs to develop a solution which also appeals to the self-interest of the other. Yet emotional involvement on one side of an issue makes it difficult to achieve the detachment necessary to think up wise ways of meeting the interests of both sides: "We've got enough problems of our own; they can look after theirs." There also frequently exists a psychological reluctance to accord any legitimacy to the views of the other side; it seems disloyal to think up ways to satisfy them. Shortsighted self-concern thus leads a negotiator to develop only partisan positions, partisan arguments, and one-sided solutions.

Prescription

To invent creative options, then, you will need (1) to separate the act of inventing options from the act of judging them; (2) to broaden the options on the table rather than look for a single answer; (3) to search for mutual gains; and (4) to invent ways of making their decisions easy. Each of these steps is discussed below.

Separate Inventing from Deciding.   Since judgment hinders imagination, separate the creative act from the critical one; separate the process of thinking up possible decisions from the process of selecting among than. Invent first, decide later.

As a negotiator, you will of necessity do much inventing by yourself. It is not easy. By definition, inventing new ideas requires you to think about things that are not already in your mind. You should therefore consider the desirability of arranging an inventing or brainstorming session with a few colleagues or friends. Such a session can effectively separate inventing from deciding.

A brainstorming session is designed to produce as many ideas as possible to solve the problem at hand. The key ground rule is to postpone all criticism and evaluation of ideas. The group simply invents ideas without pausing to consider whether they are good or bad, realistic or unrealistic. With those inhibitions removed, one idea should stimulate another, like firecrackers setting off one another.

In a brainstorming session, people need not fear looking foolish since wild ideas are explicitly encouraged. And in the absence of the other side, negotiators need not worry about disclosing confidential information or having an idea taken as a serious commitment.

There is no one right way to run a brainstorming session. Rather, you should tailor it to your needs and resources. In doing so, you may find it useful to consider the following guidelines.

Before brainstorming:

1. *Define your purpose.* Think of what you would like to walk out of the meeting with.

2. *Choose a few participants.* The group should normally be large enough to provide a stimulating interchange, yet small enough to encourage both individual participation and free-wheeling inventing—usually between five and eight people.

3. *Change the environment.* Select a time and place distinguishing the session as much as possible from regular discussion. The more different a brainstorming session seems from a normal meeting, the easier it is for participants to suspend judgment.

4. *Design an informal atmosphere.* What does it take for you and others to relax? It may be talking over a drink, or meeting at a vacation lodge in some picturesque spot, a simply taking off your tie and jacket during the meeting and calling each other by your first names.

5. *Choose a facilitator.* Someone at the meeting needs to facilitate—to keep the meeting on track, to make sure everyone gets a chance to speak, to enforce any ground rules, and to stimulate discussion by asking questions.

During brainstorming:

1. *Seat the participants side by side facing the problem.* The physical reinforces the psychological. Physically sitting side by side can reinforce the mental attitude of tackling a common problem together. People facing each other tend to respond personally and engage in dialogue or argument; people sitting side by side in a semicircle of chairs facing a blackboard tend to respond to the problem depicted there.

2. *Clarify the ground rules, including the no-criticism rule.* If the participants do not all know each other, the meeting begins with introductions all around, followed by clarification of the ground rules. Outlaw negative criticism of any kind.

Joint inventing produces new ideas because each of us invents only within the limits set by our working assumptions. If ideas are shot down unless they appeal to all participants, the implicit goal becomes to advance an idea that no one will shoot down. If, on the other hand, wild ideas are encouraged, even those that in fact lie well outside the realm of the possible, the group may generate from these ideas other options that *are* possible and that no one would previously have considered.

Other ground rules you may want to adopt are to make the entire session off the record and to refrain from attributing ideas to any participant.

3. *Brainstorm.* Once the purpose of the meeting is clear, let your imaginations go. Try to come up with a long list of ideas, approaching the question from every conceivable angle.

4. *Record the ideas in full view.* Recording ideas either on a blackboard or, better, on large sheets of newsprint gives the group a tangible sense of collective achievement; it reinforces the no-criticism rule; it reduces the tendency to repeat; and it helps stimulate other ideas.

After brainstorming:

1. *Star the most promising ideas.* After brainstorming, relax the no-criticism rule in order to winnow out the most promising ideas. You are still not at the stage of deciding; you are merely nominating ideas worth developing further. Mark those ideas that members of the group think are best.

2. *Invent improvements for promising ideas.* Take one promising idea and invent ways to make it better and more realistic, as well as ways to carry it out. The task at this stage is to make the idea as attractive as you can. Preface constructive criticism with: "What I like best about that idea is . . . Might it be better if . . . ?"

3. *Set up a time to evaluate ideas and decide.* Before you break up, draw up a selective and improved list of ideas from the session and set up a time for deciding which of these ideas to advance in your negotiation and how.

Consider brainstorming with the other side. Although more difficult than brainstorming with your own side, brainstorming with people from the other side can also prove extremely valuable. It is more difficult because of the increased risk that you will say something that prejudices your interests despite the rules established for a brainstorming session. You may disclose confidential information inadvertently or lead the other side to mistake an option you devise for an offer. Nevertheless, joint brainstorming sessions have the great advantages of producing ideas which take into account the interests of all those involved, of creating a climate of joint problem-solving, and of educating each side about the concerns of the other.

To protect yourself when brainstorming with the other side, distinguish the brainstorming session explicitly from a negotiating session where people state official views and speak on the record. People are so accustomed to meeting for the purpose of reaching agreement that any other purpose needs to be clearly stated.

To reduce the risk of appearing committed to any given idea, you can make a habit of advancing at least two alternatives at the same time. You can also put on the table options with which you obviously disagree. "I could give you the house for nothing, or you could pay me a million dollars in cash for it, or. . . ." Since you are plainly not proposing either of these ideas, the ones which follow are labeled as mere possibilities, not proposals. . . .

But whether you brainstorm together or not, separating the act of developing options from the act of deciding on them is extremely useful in any negotiation. Discussing options differs radically from taking positions. Whereas one side's position will conflict with another's, options invite other options. The very language you use differs. It consists of questions, not assertions; it is open, not closed: "One option is . . . What other options have you thought of?" "What if we agreed to this?" "How about doing it this way?" "How would this work?" "What would be wrong with that?" Invent before you decide.

Broaden Your Options. Even with the best of intentions, participants in a brainstorming session are likely to operate on the assumption that they are really looking for the *one* best answer, trying to find a needle in a haystack by picking up every blade of hay.

At this stage in a negotiation, however, you should not be looking for the right path. You are developing room within which to negotiate. Room can be made only by having a substantial number of markedly different ideas—ideas on which you and the other side can build later in the negotiation, and among which you can then jointly choose . . .

Multiply options by shuttling between the specific and the general: The Circle Chart. The task of inventing options involves four types of thinking. One is thinking about a particular problem—the factual situation you dislike, for example, a smelly, polluted river that runs by your land. The second type of thinking is descriptive analysis—you diagnose an existing situation in general terms. You sort problems into categories and tentatively suggest causes. The river water may have a high content of various chemicals, or too little oxygen. You may suspect various upstream industrial plants. The third type of thinking, again in general terms, is to consider what ought, perhaps, to be done. Given the diagnoses you have made, you look for prescriptions that theory may suggest, such as reducing chemical effluent, reducing diversions of water, or bringing fresh water from some other river. The fourth and final type of thinking is to come up with some specific and feasible suggestions for action. Who might do what tomorrow to put one of these general approaches into practice? For instance, the state environmental agency might order an upstream industry to limit the quantity of chemical discharge.

The Circle Chart [in Figure 41.1] illustrates these four types of thinking and suggests them as steps to be taken in sequence. If all goes well, the specific action invented in this way will, if adopted, deal with your original problem.

The Circle Chart provides an easy way of using one good idea to generate others. With one useful action idea before you, you (or a group of you who are brainstorming) can go back and try to identify the general approach of which the action idea is merely one application. You can then think up other action ideas that would apply the same general approach to the real world. Similarly, you can go back one step further and ask, "If this theoretical approach appears useful, what is the diagnosis behind it?" Having articulated a

■ **FIGURE 41.1**
Circle Chart
The Four Basic Steps in Inventing Options

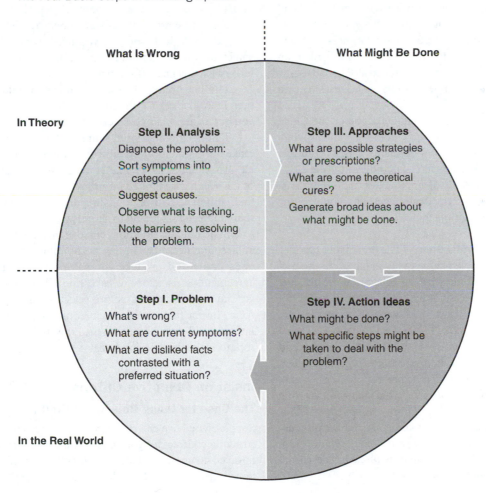

diagnosis, you can generate other approaches for dealing with a problem analyzed in that way, and then look for actions putting these new approaches into practice. One good option on the table thus opens the door to asking about the theory that makes this option good and then using that theory to invent more options. . . .

Look through the eyes of different experts. Another way to generate multiple options is to examine your problem from the perspective of different professions and disciplines.

In thinking up possible solutions to a dispute over custody of a child, for example, look at the problem as it might be seen by an educator, a banker, a psychiatrist, a civil rights lawyer, a minister, a nutritionist, a doctor, a feminist, a football coach, or one with some other special point of view. If you are negotiating a business contract, invent options that might occur to a banker, an inventor, a labor leader, a speculator in real estate, a stockbroker, an economist, a tax expert, or a socialist.

You can also combine the use of the Circle Chart with this idea of looking at a problem through the eyes of different experts. Consider in turn how each expert would diagnose the situation, what kinds of approaches each might suggest, and what practical suggestions would follow from those approaches. . . .

Look for Mutual Gain.   The third major block to creative problem-solving lies in the assumption of a fixed pie: the less for you, the more for me. Rarely if ever is this assumption true. First of all, both sides can always be worse off than they are now. Chess looks like a zero-sum game; if one loses, the other wins—until a dog trots by and knocks over the table, spills the beer, and leaves you both worse off than before.

Even apart from a shared interest in averting joint loss, there almost always exists the possibility of joint gain. This may take the form of developing a mutually advantageous relationship, or of satisfying the interests of each side with a creative solution.

Identify shared interests.   In theory it is obvious that shared interests help produce agreement. By definition, inventing an idea which meets shared interests is good for you and good for them. In practice, however, the picture seems less clear. In the middle of a negotiation over price, shared interests may not appear obvious or relevant. How then can looking for shared interests help? . . .

Three points about shared interests are worth remembering. First, shared interests lie latent in every negotiation. They may not be immediately obvious. Ask yourself: Do we have a shared interest in preserving our relationship? What opportunities lie ahead for cooperation and mutual benefit? What costs would we bear if negotiations broke off? Are there common principles, like a fair price, that we both can respect?

Second, shared interests are opportunities, not godsends. To be of use, you need to make something out of them. It helps to make a shared interest explicit and to formulate it as a shared *goal.*

The tax holiday for new industries would then represent not a concession by the mayor to you but an action in pursuit of your shared goal.

Third, stressing your shared interests can make the negotiation smoother and more amicable. Passengers in a lifeboat afloat in the middle of the ocean with limited rations will subordinate their differences over food in pursuit of their shared interest in getting to shore. . . .

In a complex situation, creative inventing is an absolute necessity. In any negotiation it may open doors and produce a range of potential agreements satisfactory to each side. Therefore, generate many options before selecting among them. Invent first; decide later. Look for shared interests and differing interests to dovetail. And seek to make their decision easy.

Insist on Objective Criteria
The Case for Using Objective Criteria

Suppose you have entered into a fixed-price construction contract for your house that calls for reinforced concrete foundations but fails to specify how deep they should be. The contractor suggests two feet. You think five feet is closer to the usual depth for your type of house.

Now suppose the contractor says: "I went along with you on steel girders for the roof. It's your turn to go along with me on shallower foundations." No owner in his right mind would yield. Rather than horse-trade, you would insist on deciding the issue in terms of objective safety standards. "Look, maybe I'm wrong. Maybe two feet is enough. What I want are foundations strong and deep enough to hold up the building safely. Does the government have standard specifications for these soil conditions? How deep are the foundations of other buildings in this area? What is the earthquake risk here? Where do you suggest we look for standards to resolve this question?"

It is no easier to build a good contract than it is to build strong foundations. If relying on objective standards applies so clearly to a negotiation between the house owner and a contractor, why not to business deals, collective bargaining, legal settlements, and international negotiations? Why not insist that a negotiated price, for example, be based on some standard such as market value, replacement cost, depreciated book value, or competitive prices, instead of whatever the seller demands?

In short, the approach is to commit yourself to reaching a solution based on principle, not pressure. Concentrate on the merits of the problem, not the mettle of the parties. Be open to reason, but closed to threats.

Principled Negotiation Produces Wise Agreements Amicably and Efficiently.   The more you bring standards of fairness, efficiency, or scientific merit to bear on your particular problem, the more likely you are to produce a final package that is wise and fair. The more you and the other side refer to precedent and community practice, the greater your chance of benefiting from past experience. And an agreement consistent with precedent is less vulnerable to attack. If a lease contains standard terms or if a sales contract conforms to practice in the industry, there is less risk that either negotiator will feel that he was harshly treated or will later try to repudiate the agreement.

A constant battle for dominance threatens a relationship; principled negotiation protects it. It is far easier to deal with people when both of you are discussing objective standards for settling a problem instead of trying to force each other to back down.

Approaching agreement through discussion of objective criteria also reduces the number of commitments that each side must make and then unmake as they move toward agreement. In positional bargaining, negotiators spend much of the time defending their position and attacking the other side's. People using objective criteria tend to use time more efficiently talking about possible standards and solutions.

Independent standards are even more important to efficiency when more parties are involved. In such cases positional bargaining is difficult at best. It requires coalitions among parties; and the more parties who have agreed on a position, the more difficult it becomes to change that position. Similarly, if each negotiator has a constituency or has to clear a position with a higher authority, the task of adopting positions and then changing them becomes time-consuming and difficult. . . .

Developing Objective Criteria

Carrying on a principled negotiation involves two questions: How do you develop objective criteria, and how do you use them in negotiating?

Whatever method of negotiation you use, you will do better if you prepare in advance. This certainly holds true of principled negotiation. So develop some alternative standards beforehand and think through their application to your case.

Fair Standards.   You will usually find more than one objective criterion available as a basis for agreement. Suppose, for example, your car is demolished and you file a claim with an insurance company. In your discussion with the adjuster, you might take into account such measures of the car's value as (1) the original cost of the car less depreciation; (2) what the car could have been sold for; (3) the standard "blue book" value for a car of that year and model; (4) what it would cost to replace that car with a comparable one; and (5) what a court might award as the value of the car.

In other cases, depending on the issue, you may wish to propose that an agreement be based upon:

market value	what a court would
precedent	decide
scientific judgment	moral standards
professional	equal treatment
standards	tradition
efficiency	reciprocity
costs	etc.

At a minimum, objective criteria need to be independent of each side's will. Ideally, to assure a wise agreement, objective criteria should be not only independent of will but also both legitimate and practical. In a boundary dispute, for example, you may find it easier to agree on a physically salient feature such as a river than on a line three yards to the east of the riverbank.

Objective criteria should apply, at least in theory, to both sides. You can thus use the test of reciprocal application to tell you whether a proposed criterion is fair and independent of either party's will. If a real estate agency selling you a house offers a standard form contract, you would be wise to ask if that is the same standard form they use when *they* buy a house. In the international arena, the principle of self-determination is notorious for the number of peoples who insist on it as a fundamental right but deny its applicability to those on the other side. Consider the Middle East, Northern Ireland, or Cyprus as just three examples.

Fair Procedures.   To produce an outcome independent of will, you can use either fair standards for the substantive question or fair procedures for resolving the conflicting interests. Consider, for example, the age-old way to divide a piece of cake between two children: one cuts and the other chooses. Neither can complain about an unfair division.

This simple procedure was used in the Law of the Sea negotiations, one of the most complex negotiations ever undertaken. At one point, the issue of how to allocate mining sites in the deep seabed deadlocked the negotiation. Under the terms of the draft agreement, half the sites were to be mined by private companies, the other half by the Enterprise, a mining organization to be owned by the United Nations. Since the private mining companies from the rich nations had the technology and the expertise to choose the best sites, the poorer nations feared the less knowledgeable Enterprise would receive a bad bargain.

The solution devised was to agree that a private company seeking to mine the seabed would present the Enterprise with *two* proposed mining sites. The Enterprise would pick one site for itself and grant the company a license to mine the other. Since the company would not know which site it would get, it would have an incentive to make both sites as promising as possible. This simple procedure thus harnessed the company's superior expertise for mutual gain.

A variation on the procedure of "one cuts, the other chooses" is for the parties to negotiate what they think is a fair arrangement before they go on to decide their respective roles in it. In a divorce negotiation, for example, before deciding which parent will get custody of the children, the parents might agree on the visiting rights of the other parent. This gives both an incentive to agree on visitation rights each will think fair.

As you consider procedural solutions, look at other basic means of settling differences: taking turns, drawing lots, letting someone else decide, and so on.

Frequently, taking turns presents the best way for heirs to divide a large number of heirlooms left to them collectively. Afterwards, they can do some trading if they want. Or they can make the selection tentative so they see how it comes out before committing themselves to accept it. Drawing lots, flipping a coin, and other forms of chance have an inherent fairness. The results may be unequal, but each side had an equal opportunity.

Letting someone else play a key role in a joint decision is a well-established procedure with almost infinite variations. The parties can agree to submit a particular question to an expert for advice or decision. They can ask a mediator to help them reach a decision. Or they can submit the matter to an arbitrator for an authoritative and binding decision.

Professional baseball, for example, uses "last-best-offer arbitration" to settle player salary disputes. The arbitrator must choose between the last offer made by one side and the last offer made by the other. The theory is that this procedure puts pressure on the parties to make their proposals more reasonable. In baseball, and in states where this form of arbitration is compulsory for certain public employee disputes, it does seem to produce more settlements than in comparable circumstances where there is a commitment to conventional arbitration; those parties who don't settle, however, sometimes give the arbitrator an unpleasant choice between two extreme offers.

Negotiating with Objective Criteria

Having identified some objective criteria and procedures, how do you go about discussing them with the other side?

Negotiating on the merits has three basic elements:

1. Frame each issue as a joint search for objective criteria.
2. Reason and be open to reason as to which standards are most appropriate and how they should be applied.
3. Never yield to pressure, only to principle.

In short, focus on objective criteria firmly but flexibly.

Frame Each Issue as a Joint Search for Objective Criteria.   If you are negotiating to buy a house, you might start off by saying: "Look, you want a high price and I want a low one. Let's figure out what a *fair* price would be. What objective standards might be most relevant?" You and the other side may have conflicting interests, but the two of you now have a shared goal: to determine a fair price. You might begin by suggesting one or

more criteria yourself—the cost of the house adjusted for depreciation and inflation, recent sale prices of similar houses in the neighborhood, or an independent appraisal—and then invite the seller's suggestions. . . .

Reason and Be Open to Reason.   What makes the negotiation a *joint* search is that, however much you may have prepared various objective criteria, you come to the table with an open mind. In most negotiations, people use precedent and other objective standards simply as arguments in support of a position. A policemen's union might, for example, insist upon a raise of a certain amount and then justify their position with arguments about what police in other cities make. This use of standards usually only digs people even deeper into their position.

Going one step further, some people begin by announcing that their position is an issue of principle and refuse even to consider the other sides case. "It's a matter of principle" becomes a battle cry in a holy war over ideology. Practical differences escalate into principled ones, further locking in the negotiators rather than freeing them.

This is emphatically *not* what is meant by principled negotiation. Insisting that an agreement be based on objective criteria does not mean insisting that it be based solely on the criterion *you* advance. One standard of legitimacy does not preclude the existence of others. What the other side believes to be fair may not be what you believe to be fair. You should behave like a judge; although you may be predisposed to one side (in this case, your own) you should be willing to respond to reasons for applying another standard or for applying a standard differently. When each party is advancing a different standard, look for an objective basis for deciding between them, such as which standard has been used by the parties in the past or which standard is more widely applied. Just as the substantive issue itself should not be settled on the basis of will, neither should the question of which standard applies.

In a given case there may be two standards (such as market value and depreciated cost) which produce different results, but which both parties agree seem equally legitimate. In that case, splitting the difference or otherwise compromising between the results suggested by the two objective standards is perfectly legitimate. The outcome is still independent of the will of the parties.

If, however, after a thorough discussion of the merits of an issue you still cannot accept their proposed criteria as the most appropriate, you might suggest putting them to a test. Agree on someone you both regard as fair and give him or her a list of the proposed criteria. Ask the person to decide which are the fairest or most appropriate for your situation. Since objective criteria are supposed to be legitimate and because legitimacy implies acceptance by a great many people, this is a fair thing to ask. You are not asking the third party to settle your substantive dispute—just to give you advice on what standard to use in settling it.

The difference between seeking agreement on the appropriate principles for deciding a matter and using principles simply as arguments to support positions is sometimes subtle, but always significant. A principled negotiator is open to reasoned persuasion on the merits; a positional bargainer is not. It is the combination of openness to reason with insistence on a solution based on objective criteria that makes principled negotiation

so persuasive and so effective at getting the other side to play.

Never Yield to Pressure. Consider once again the example of negotiating with the contractor. What if he offers to hire your brother-in-law on the condition that you give in on the depth of the foundations? You would probably answer, "A job for my brother-in-law has nothing to do with whether the house will be safely supported on a foundation of that depth." What if the contractor then threatens to charge you a higher price? You would answer the same way: "We'll settle that question on the merits too. Let's see what other contractors charge for this kind of work," or "Bring me your cost figures and we'll work out a fair profit margin." If the contractor replies, "Come on, you trust me, don't you?" you would respond: "Trust is an entirely separate matter. The issue is how deep the foundations have to be to make the house safe."

Pressure can take many forms: a bribe, a threat, a manipulative appeal to trust, or a simple refusal to budge. In all these cases, the principled response is the same: invite them to state their reasoning, suggest objective criteria you think apply, and refuse to budge except on this basis. Never yield to pressure, only to principle.

Questions for Discussion

1. With respect to the negotiation process, as analyzed by Fisher and Ury, which do you think is the most important factor to consider: interests, options, people, or objective criteria? Why?
2. When one of the two negotiating parties has a marked political and financial advantage, would the negotiation strategies of Fisher and Ury still be valid for the less powerful party?
3. Fischer and Ury's *Getting to Yes: Negotiating Agreement without Giving Up* has been a phenomenal bestseller. What, in your judgment, are the strengths and weaknesses of their theory?

Further Readings

1. Small, Richard G. *Bargaining for Advantage: Negotiation Strategies for Reasonable People.* Viking Press/Penguin Books: New York, 1999.
2. Olekalns, Mara, and Smith, Philip L. "Social Value Orientations and Strategy Choices in Competitive Negotiations." *Personality and Social Psychology Bulletin*, 1999, 25, 6, June, 657–668.
3. Lawler, Edward J, Ford, Rebecca, and Large, Michael D. "Unilateral Initiatives as a Conflict Resolution Strategy." *Social Psychology Quarterly*, 1999, 62, 3, Sept., 240–256.
4. Alberstein, Michal. "Negotiating through Paradoxes: Rationality, Practicality, and Naïve Realism (Or: Enjoy your Biases)." *Studies in Law, Politics, and Society*, 2001, 22, 1, 197–232.
5. Hisschemoller, Matthijs, and Hoppe, Rob. "Coping with Intractable Controversies: The Case for Problem Structuring in Policy Design and Analysis." *Knowledge and Policy*, 1995–1996, 8, 4, Winter, 40–60.
6. Carment, David, and James, Patrick. "Two-Level Games and Third-Party Intervention: Evidence from Ethnic Conflict in the Balkans and South Asia." *Canadian Journal of Political Science*, 1996, 29, 3, Sept., 521–554.
7. Burr, Anne M. "Ethics in Negotiation: Does Getting to Yes Require Candor?" *Dispute Resolution Journal,* 56, 2001, May–July, 8.
8. Zartman, I. William, ed. *Elusive Peace: Negotiating an End to Civil Wars.* Washington D.C.: The Brookings Institution, 1995.
9. Evan, William M., and MacDougall, John A. "Inter-Organizational Conflict: A Labor-Management Bargaining Experiment." *Journal of Conflict Resolution*, 1968, XI, 113–125.

Nonviolent Strategies

Strategies of nonviolence are presented in this section, not merely as a way to prevent war, but also as a mechanism to oppose and end existing armed conflicts. Here, the rationale for such strategies is discussed along with their logic and effectiveness.

"Politics of Nonviolent Action" by Gene Sharp presents a summary of three methods by which an armed conflict may be avoided. Sharp introduces "conversion" as the capacity to convince one's opponent of the validity of one's claim in a dispute. This prevents the opponent from resorting to violence. The second method, namely "accommodation," involves achieving a better understanding of the opponent's legitimate concerns and therefore increases the likelihood of reaching a compromise. The third

option, "nonviolent coercion," entails using normative force against an opponent to get him to yield to demands. The author identifies this option as being the most difficult to implement.

In "The Nonviolent Moment as Peak Experience" Michael Nagler emphasizes the development of a nonviolent attitude on a personal level and describes how that attitude translates into the dynamics of a large group. He explains the importance of numbers in nonviolence movements and how individuals can make a difference by realizing the spiritual aspect of nonviolence. The author refutes the notion that nonviolence is tantamount to apathy or inaction. He explains how peace must be actively and arduously pursued by peace activists.

In "Toward a Confederation of Israel, Palestine, and Jordan," William M. Evan traces the struggle for peace in the Middle East for over five decades. To resolve the Palestinian–Israeli conflict, a Palestine state is long overdue. Progress toward this resolution could be facilitated if Palestinian and Israeli leaders were to explore the implementation of a proposal for a confederation of Israel, Palestine, and Jordan. Some benefits of a confederation are outlined. The author also underscores the need for an International Commission to explore the problems of establishing a confederation.

Gene Sharp

The Politics of Nonviolent Action

Three Ways Success May Be Achieved

Nonviolent struggle can only be successful when the necessary conditions exist or have been created. Despite the improvised character of most nonviolent action in the past, successes from which we can learn have occurred. Even failures can provide important insights. As understanding of the requirements for effectiveness grows, the proportion of successes is likely to increase. The question then increasingly becomes *how* success can be achieved.

The influences, causes and processes involved in producing success in nonviolent convict are diverse, complicated and intermeshed. The determining combination of influences, pressures and forces will never be precisely the same, the possible combinations being infinite. It would be a distortion to impose on them an unnatural uniformity or an artificial simplicity.

It is, however, possible to distinguish three broad processes, or mechanisms, by which the complicated forces utilized and produced by nonviolent action influence the opponent and his capacity for action and thereby perhaps bring success to the cause of the grievance group. These are *conversion, accommodation* and *nonviolent coercion*. . . .

In *conversion* the opponent has been inwardly changed so that he wants to make the changes desired by the nonviolent actionists. In *accommodation,* the opponent does not agree with the changes (he has not been converted), and he could continue the struggle (he has not been nonviolently coerced), but nevertheless he has concluded that it is best to grant some or all of the

demands. He may see the issues as not so important after all, the actionists as not as bad as he had thought, or he may expect to lose more by continuing the struggle than by conceding gracefully. In *nonviolent coercion* the opponent has not changed his mind on the issues and wants to *continue* the struggle, but is *unable* to do so; the sources of his power and means of control have been taken away from him without the use of violence. This may have been done by the nonviolent group or by opposition and noncooperation among his own group (as, mutiny of his troops), or some combination of these.

Advocates and practitioners of nonviolent action have differed in their attitudes to these mechanisms. All too often their attitudes have been oversimplified, focusing primarily on the extremes of complete conversion or full nonviolent coercion. Thus, exponents of a nonviolence derived from religious conviction who emphasize conversion frequently see nonviolent coercion as closer to violence than to their own beliefs. Exponents of nonviolent coercion (say, use of the general strike to achieve social revolution) often deny even the possibility of conversion, and see that approach as alien to their own efforts. There are also middle positions. The choice of a preferred mechanism will influence the conduct of the struggle, including the strategy, tactics and methods used, the public statements made, the "tone" of the movement, and the responses to the opponent's repression. A choice or preference by actionists of one of these mechanisms is possible and even necessary, whether on ethical or strategic grounds. In practice, however, matters are rarely clear and simple between pure conversion and strict coercion, as exponents of these extreme mechanisms would have us believe. Not only may the mechanisms be variously combined and play different roles in the various stages of the struggle; different persons and subgroups within the opponent group may be diversely affected or even unaffected by the nonviolent action. We shall return to the ethical significance of these complexities later. First we must examine the three broad mechanisms of change themselves.

Conversion

"By conversion we mean that the opponent, as the result of the actions of the nonviolent person or group, comes around to a new point of view which embraces the ends of the nonviolent actor." This change may be influenced by reason, argumentation and other intellectual efforts. It is doubtful, however, that conversion will be produced solely by intellectual effort. Conversion is more likely to involve the opponent's emotions, beliefs, attitudes and moral system.

Seeking Conversion. While Gandhi did not in certain circumstances rule out actions which produced change by accommodation or even nonviolent coercion, he sought to achieve the change as far as possible by means which did not "humiliate" the opponent "but . . . uplift him." Gandhi's statements provide good illustrations of this objective of conversion. He wrote to the Viceroy in 1930: "For my ambition is no less than to convert the British people through nonviolence, and thus make them see the wrong they have done to India." On another occasion he wrote that a *satyagrahi* never seeks to influence the "wrong-doer" by inducing fear; instead the appeal must always be "to his heart. The Satyagrahi's object is to convert, not coerce, the wrong-doer." The aim of nonviolent action with this motivation is thus not simply to free the subordinate group, but also to free the opponent, who is thought to be imprisoned by his own system and policies.

In line with this attitude, while maintaining their internal solidarity and pursuing the struggle, the nonviolent actionists will emphasize that they intend no personal hostility toward the members of the opponent group. Instead, the actionists may regard the conflict as a temporary, but necessary, disruption which will make possible deeper unity and cooperation between the two groups in the future. Gandhi said: "My non-cooperation is non-cooperation with evil, not with the evil-doer." He added that he wished by noncooperation to induce the opponent to cease inflicting the evil or harm so that cooperation would be possible on a different basis. "My non-cooperation is with methods and systems, never with men." This aim of conversion has in certain situations had significant effects on the opponent group. Replacement of hostile personal attitudes by positive attitudes will reduce the pressure on the opponent group to be defensively aggressive. "Thus the opponents may be influenced to engage in fewer acts of provocative hostility, and, in the long-run, some of their leaders and part of the membership may even become motivated to live up to the other group's view of them as potential allies."

The extreme Gandhian emphasis on conversion is translated into action only rarely. However, efforts to convert sometimes occur in the absence of such a doctrine, and conversion sometimes occurs without conscious efforts. Also, conversion of *some* members of the opponent group (say, soldiers) may contribute to change by accommodation or nonviolent coercion.

Conversion efforts may sometimes take place side by side with the application or other nonviolent pressures, such as economic or political noncooperation. For example, even as Philadelphia merchants were in late 1765 cancelling orders already placed with British merchants and launching a campaign of economic noncooperation in an effort to obtain repeal of the Stamp Act, they sent a memorial to British merchants in which they urged those same merchants to help the Americans achieve repeal of the Act and the removal of certain commercial restrictions. Almost exactly three years later under comparable conditions a similar memorial was sent from Philadelphia, seeking support for repeal of the Townshend duties.

The opponent group of course consists of many members and a variety of subgroups, and the nonviolent group will be unable to apply equal influences for conversion to all of these. Furthermore, the nonviolent group may deliberately choose to concentrate its efforts to achieve conversion on certain persons or subgroups in the opponent camp. When the most direct personal contact in the course of the struggle occurs between the nonviolent actionists and the opponent's agents of repression—his police and troops—the actionists may attempt to convert these agents, instead of the general public or the policy makers. . . .

At one extreme, if members of the nonviolent group are not even regarded as fellow human beings, the chances of achieving conversion by nonviolent suffering are likely to be nil. This barrier needs to be examined.

The closeness or distance between the contending groups will help to determine the effect of the suffering of the nonviolent group on members of the opponent group. If the opponent group sees the grievance group as members of "a common moral order," this perception is likely to encourage better treatment and a more sympathetic response to their challenge. Conversely, if the subordinates are regarded as outside such a common moral order, or as traitors to it, or as inferiors or nonhumans, the opponent group is more likely to be both cruel and indifferent to their sufferings. . . .

Although believers in principled nonviolence derived from religious sources most often are the exponents of conversion, this mechanism occurs in the absence of such beliefs and even when conversion is not deliberately sought. For example, most of the attitudes thought to be needed to achieve conversion were apparently absent in the Irish peasants' boycott of the now famous Captain Boycott. . . . Although economically ruined by the peasants' action in 1879, he returned in 1883 from New York to Ireland, but this time as a *supporter* of the Irish cause. This does not show that the peasants' boycott alone had changed his opinions, but that his personal experience was

bound to have played a role in his thinking about conditions in Ireland.

Theory and opinions from Gandhi and others on how conversion operates may best be understood if an example of change by conversion is described first: the Quakers' struggle in Puritan Massachusetts Bay Colony, 1656–75. When the Quakers attempted to proselitize in Puritan Massachusetts they became involved in a nonviolent action campaign for religious liberty. The Puritans regarded Quakerism as a "sink of blasphemies" and Quakers themselves as "ravening wolves." They were accused of defiance of the ministry and the courts, naked dancing, and a plot to burn Boston and kill the inhabitants. Perhaps most important, a grant of religious toleration would have ended the Puritan theocracy and political ideal. The Puritans believed they had a religious duty to persecute those who spread religious "error."

Two women Quakers were the first to arrive; they were sent back to England on the next boat. Two days later eight more Quakers arrived; despite harsh penalties the numbers constantly increased as they waged "a direct frontal attack." They met in private homes, tried to speak after sermons in churches, spoke during their own trials and from their jail cell windows, issued pamphlets and tracts, returned to the colony in defiance of the law, held illegal meetings, refused to pay fines, and when imprisoned refused to work at the cost of food being denied them. Despite expulsions, whippings through towns and executions, the Quakers repeatedly returned. One already banished on pain of death walked calmly into the court where another was on trial for his life.

Initially the general public and the theocratic leaders were united in favor of the persecution. Gradually, however, a split developed as the public began to see the Quakers in a new light. Sympathizers began to pay the jailers' fees and at night passed food to the Quakers through jail windows. The bearing of the Quakers as they were whipped and executed convinced people that they had "the support of the Lord" and were "the Lord's people." The Governor expressed his determination to continue executions so long as the Quakers persisted. . . .

If the opponent recognizes the sincerity of the nonviolent group, this may be a very important step toward respect for them and toward a reconsideration of the issues. Gandhi saw respect of the opponent for the nonviolent actionists as an achievement which heralded approaching success. He argued that at the approach of this stage, the nonviolent actionists must conduct themselves with special care. . . .

Nonviolent actionists may, of course, not even attempt to convert the opponent. Or they may be willing to try to do so, while being ready after a certain point to use full nonviolent coercion. Nonviolent action can achieve social and political objectives by means other than conversion.

Difficulties in producing conversion have led many exponents and practitioners of nonviolent action, among them James Farmer, to reject the attempt to achieve it, and to concentrate on change by accommodation or nonviolent coercion: "In the arena of political and social events, what men feel and believe matters much less than what, under various kinds of external pressures, they can be made to *do*." Attention now turns to the mechanisms of change by *accommodation* and *nonviolent coercion*.

Accommodation

Accommodation as a mechanism of nonviolent action falls in an intermediary position between conversion and nonviolent coercion. In accommodation the opponent is neither converted nor nonviolently coerced; yet there are elements of both involved in his decision to grant concessions to the nonviolent actionists. This may be, as has been suggested, the most common mechanism of the three in successful nonviolent campaigns. In the mechanism of accommodation the opponent resolves to grant the demands of the nonviolent actionists without having changed his mind fundamentally about the issues involved. Some other factor has come to be considered more important than the issue at stake in the conflict, and the opponent is therefore willing to yield on the issue

rather than to risk or to experience some other condition or result regarded as still more unsatisfactory. The main reason for this new willingness to yield is the changed social situation produced by the nonviolent action. Accommodation has this in common with nonviolent coercion. In both mechanisms, action is "directed toward . . . a change in those aspects of the situation which are regarded as productive of existing attitudes and behavior." This means that the actionists

> . . . operate on the situation within which people must act, or upon their perception of the situation, without attempting directly to alter their attitudes, sentiments or values. The pressure for a given type of behavior then comes either from (a) revealing information which affects the way in which individuals visualize the situation, or from (b) actual or potential alteration of the situation itself.

In nonviolent coercion the changes are made when the opponent no longer has an effective choice between conceding or refusing to accept the demands. In accommodation, however, although the change is made in response to the altered situation, it is made while the opponent still has an effective choice before him, and before significant nonviolent coercion takes place. The degree to which the opponent accepts this change as a result of influences which would potentially have led to his conversion, or as the result of influences which might have produced nonviolent coercion, will vary. Both may be present in the same case. Sometimes other factors not capable of leading to either extreme may contribute to achieving accommodation. . . .

The factors influencing accommodation may be summarized as the degree of conflict of interest, all factors influencing the conversion mechanism, actual and potential support for the nonviolent actionists and their cause in the opponent's group and among third parties, the degree of effectiveness of the opponent's repression and other countermeasures, economic losses produced by the conflict, the estimated present and future strength of the nonviolent actionists, and the estimated chances of victory and defeat and their consequences.

But not even accommodation may be achieved, for there are clearly some types of opponents who may be unwilling to grant any demands of the nonviolent group. Even if they know that they may be finally defeated, such opponents may prefer to remain firm to the end. For these cases, too, the question arises as to whether nonviolent action can win except by a change of will in the opponent? Is there such a thing as *nonviolent coercion?*

Nonviolent Coercion

In some cases of nonviolent action, the opponent is neither converted nor does he decide to accommodate to the actionists' demands. Instead he may be determined to win full victory against them. Under some circumstances he may do so, or he may at least achieve temporary success in crushing the actionists. Failure of both conversion and accommodation does not, however, always mean victory for the opponent. The demands of the nonviolent group may also be achieved *against* the will of the opponent, that is, he may be *nonviolently coerced.* This type of nonviolent change has often been neglected in favor of the other two mechanisms.

As James Farmer has pointed out, when change by conversion and accommodation is believed to be unrealistic, neglect of the mechanism of nonviolent coercion has left the field clear for advocates of violence:

> Perhaps we at CORE have failed to show how effective and virile nonviolence can be. . . . We must show that nonviolence is something more than turning the other cheek, that it can be aggressive within the limits a civilized order will permit. Where we cannot influence the heart of the evil-doer, we can force an end to the evil practice.

Roughly speaking, nonviolent coercion may take place in any of three ways: 1) the defiance may become too widespread and massive to be controlled by the opponent's repression; 2) the

noncooperation and defiance may make it impossible for the social, economic and political system to operate unless the actionists' demands are achieved; 3) even the opponent's ability to apply repression may be undermined and may at times dissolve. In any of these cases, or any combination of them, despite his resolution not to give in, the opponent may discover that it is impossible for him to defend or impose his objectionable policies or system. In such an instance, the change will have been achieved by nonviolent coercion.

The Concept of Nonviolent Coercion.   The concept of coercion is not limited to the effects of threat or use of physical violence. Neither the *Oxford Dictionary* nor the *Webster Dictionary* suggests that its definition is restricted to the impact of that pressure or force which comes from physical violence. On the contrary, it is often made clear that coercion can be effected by nonphysical pressures including moral force. Instead of violence, the key factors in coercion are: 1) whether the opponent's will is blocked despite his continued efforts to impose it, and 2) whether the opponent is *able* to act in an effort to implement his will. These two aspects are emphasized by Paullin and Lakey. "Coercion is the use of either physical or intangible force to compel action contrary to the will or reasoned judgement of the individual or group subjected to such force." "Coercion . . . is taking away from the opponent either his ability to maintain the status quo or his ability to effect social change." The concept of "coercion" is thus a very broad one, which clearly includes the imposition of certain conditions by means of nonviolent action without the opponent's agreement.

There is, however, a vast difference between nonviolent coercion and what might be called violent coercion. As Bondurant points out: "The difference between violent coercion in which deliberate injury is inflicted upon the opponent and nonviolent coercion in which injury indirectly results is a difference of such great degree that it is almost a difference of kind." Involved in the former is the deliberate intention of *inflicting* physical injury or death; in the latter, the coercion largely arises from noncooperation, a refusal of the non-violent group to submit despite repression, and at times removal of the opponent's ability to inflict violence: "nonviolent coercion forces the opponent to accept the [nonviolent actionists'] demands even though he disagrees with them, has an unfavorable image of [the nonviolent group], and would continue resisting if he could." In such cases the nonviolent actionists have so grown in numbers and strength, or the opponent's sources of repressive sanctions have been so weakened, or both, that the opponent is unable to continue to impose his will on the subordinates. The opponent can no longer wield power contrary to the wishes of the nonviolent group.

Nonviolent coercion is not simply a creation of theoretical speculation. Nor is it even a forecast of future potentialities of the technique based on extensions of previous experience. Despite the improvised nature of most past cases of nonviolent action, nonviolent coercion has sometimes occurred. In other cases it has nearly taken place. Noncooperation has sometimes been so effective that temporary paralysis of the opponent's power has been achieved, but total collapse of his regime did nevertheless not result. The regime may have regained ground because of the actionists' failure to capitalise strategically on the situation, the introduction of resistance violence or other disruptive influences, or some other factor. For example, as described earlier, effective British power in several of the American colonies was for a time paralysed and it even collapsed in the face of noncooperation. . . .

Some Factors Influencing Nonviolent Coercion.
There is no single pattern for producing nonviolent coercion. The factors which produce it occur in different combinations and proportions; there appear to be at least eight such factors. The role and combination of these will not be the same when the nonviolent coercion has been largely produced by mutiny, for example, as when the coercion has been achieved by economic and political paralysis. The contribution of each factor will depend upon the degree to which it regulates one

or more of the opponent's necessary sources of power.

Generally speaking, nonviolent coercion is more likely where the *numbers* of nonviolent actionists are very large, both in absolute numerical terms and in proportion to the general population. It is then possible for the defiance to be too massive for the opponent to control; paralysis by noncooperation is more likely. There, too, may be a greater chance of interfering with the sources of power which depend upon manpower, skilled or unskilled.

The *degree of the opponent's dependence* on the nonviolent actionists for the sources of his power is also important. The greater the dependence, the greater the chances of nonviolent coercion. It therefore becomes important to consider exactly *who* is refusing assistance to the opponent. "The extent of nonparticipation required to produce measurable political effects varies with the strategic position of the strikers," argued Hiller. Under certain circumstances the opponent may be relatively indifferent to large numbers of noncooperating subjects and in other circumstances he may be nonviolently coerced by the action of a relatively few.

The *ability* of the nonviolent group *to apply the technique* of nonviolent action will be very important. The role of fighting skill here is comparable to its importance in any other type of combat. Skill here includes the capacity to choose strategy, tactics and methods, the times and places for action, etc., and ability to act in accordance with the dynamics and requirements of this nonviolent technique. Ability to apply nonviolent action skillfully will help to overcome the weaknesses of the nonviolent group, to capitalize on the opponent's weaknesses, and to struggle against the opponent's countermeasures.

Whether or not nonviolent coercion is achieved will also depend on *how long* the defiance and noncooperation can be maintained. A massive act of noncooperation which collapses after a few hours cannot nonviolently coerce anyone. Willingness and ability to maintain nonviolent action for a sufficient duration despite repression are necessary to reduce or sever sources of the opponent's power.

The sympathy and support of *third parties* for the nonviolent group may be important in producing nonviolent coercion if the opponent depends on them for such things as economic resources, transportation facilities, military supplies and the like. Such supplies may then be cut off and his power position thereby undermined.

The *means of control and repression* which the opponent can use, and for how long, in an attempt to force a resumption of cooperation and obedience are also important. Even more important is the actionists' response to them.

The final factor contributing to nonviolent coercion is *opposition within the opponent group* either to the policies at issue or to the repression, or to both. The number of dissidents, the intensity of their disagreement, the types of action they use, and their positions in the social, economic and political structure will all be important here. On occasion splits in the ruling group itself may occur. Should this happen, or should a general strike or major mutiny of troops or police take place in opposition to repression of the nonviolent actionists, it would be a major factor in producing nonviolent coercion.

Michael N. Nagler

The Nonviolent Moment as Peak Experience

Either I don't give in to my rage, which means going crazy . . . or I give in to it, which means I go to jail.

—Franklin Smith, American teenager

When my spiritual teacher was still living in India, on the Nilgiri Hills, he had a friend who was very much like himself: a compassionate, sensitive nature with strong feelings about justice and fairness. One morning the two of them were walking through the bazaar and came upon a villager with a caged bear. The cage was so small that the poor beast could hardly turn around; it seemed to Sri Easwaran and his friend to be crying out for help with its eyes. They walked off without speaking. Later that day, Easwaran went to call on his friend and found him trembling with anger. "I'm going to take my gun to the bazaar," he burst out. "I'm going to set that bear free, and shoot anyone who tries to stop me."

"Wait a minute," Easwaran put in hastily. "Hold on just a bit. Let me see what I can do."

First he went around to the owner to try to reason with him. It turned out the man, a simple villager, was from his own state of Kerala, so it wasn't hard to broach the subject after chatting a while in their native language. "Look here, don't you think that creature is suffering in such a small cage?"

"Do you think I like to keep him penned up like that?" he explained. "But what can I do? A new cage would cost me more than a month's earnings."

"Would you be willing to use a decent cage if I could get one built for you?"

"Of course."

Next stop: the local carpenter. By luck, he turned out to be a Kerala man also. Easwaran explained the situation and then came to the point. "You give me your rock-bottom price for a new cage."

"Brother, I have a family to feed; but for you . . . "

Then back to his angry friend. "Suppose we could get a better cage built for so-and-so many rupees and the owner agreed to use it, would you put up the money?"

"Gladly. . . . But that owner will never agree."

"He's already agreed."

Sri Easwaran was as angry as his friend at the sight of the dumb animal's suffering. That's important to realize; but equally important is the key difference in approach. The one saw a path to a solution, and quickly took it, while the other was hung up between the choices with which we're all too familiar, the dilemma that teenager Franklin Smith calls "living a crazy man or dying a sane one." And so he fumed, while Sri Easwaran set about writing a happy ending for the bear, for his friend, the carpenter, the owner— and doubtless himself.

Only a minor event, if you want to look at it that way, but you could also look at it as a parable. How many crises does our government face every year to which it reacts with either violence or capitulation, either imposing sanctions, as with Iraq, or fuming helplessly, as with Bosnia, East Timor or Tibet?

It is all rather reminiscent of the two kinds of student—or rather two kinds of training given to students—in the Davitz experiment. The nonviolent are not people who don't feel anger. On the contrary, they can often prize anger (at least, the kind of anger Sri Easwaran and his friend felt) because first of all that capacity to feel for others, which sometimes means getting angry over what is happening to them, is one of the things that makes us fully human. Second, and more important, that kind of anger is potentially the emotive power to correct the situation. For, in the light of the Davitz experiment, we would not say that Sri Easwaran did what he did in spite of his anger; he did it *with* his anger. By not giving in to his angry impulse to do something to that bear owner but instead looking for a constructive way to help the bear *and* its owner, he unconsciously converted the energy he was feeling as anger into constructive effort. Emotions are power. By themselves, however, they are not necessarily wisdom. Wisdom was for him to choose, which he did. In that choice, blocking one path, he opened the other.

This impromptu "shuttle diplomacy" was actually a fairly obvious solution, when you think about it. The trouble is that when we get angry, most of us can't think about it. Just when we're motivated to do something, we lose sight of the obvious thing to do. As an old proverb has it, "Anger is a wind that blows out the lamp of the mind"—unless our mind is alert enough to set its sails for a better course.

If one still thinks this was a small event, we can think back to one which had exactly the same dynamic, but changed the course of history. I am thinking of the anger Gandhi experienced that fateful night of May 31, 1893, when he was thrown off the train at Pietermaritzburg a week after his arrival in South Africa. This was no minor irritation; according to his own testimony, Gandhiji was furious. That, along with the fact that Gandhi is more than usually articulate about his inner experiences, is what makes this event (among millions of similar insults we human be-

ings endure at one another's hands) such an important window into the dynamics of nonviolent conversion. The first clue as to how he finally succeeded, after a night of bitter reflection, to see the creative way out is that he didn't take the insult personally. He saw in it the whole tragedy of man's inhumanity to man, the whole outrage of racism. Not, "They can't do this to me," but, "How can we do this to one another?" The second clue is the state of his faith in human nature. Already at that period he believed that people could not stay blind to the truth forever. He did not yet know how to wake them up; he just knew they could not want to stay forever asleep. That is how he was able to find the third way between running home to India and suing the railroad company.

Imagine the old-fashioned locomotive carrying this "coolie barrister" from Durban up the mountains to Pretoria, standing at the station in Pietermaritzburg with a good head of steam. You could shovel in more coal and bottle up all that power and pretend it wasn't there until finally it exploded, or you could open the valves and scald everyone on the platform—but surely you would want to use it to drive the train. This is what Gandhiji was going through with all the emotional power built up in him by the accumulated insults he had met since his arrival at the Durban pier. He chose neither to "pocket the insult," as he says, nor to lash out at the immediate source of the pain. He launched what was to become the greatest experiment in social change in the modern world.

Within a few years of this event, Gandhi was working fifteen hours a day, seven days a week at a pace that would frighten even an advanced workaholic. Two secretaries could not keep up with his correspondence, any more than they could keep up with his breathtaking "walks" when he scampered off down the road each evening like a sandpiper. On a lecture tour to Gujarat taking him to two, sometimes three villages a day, he had to remind those arranging his punishing itinerary that he was only mortal. He kept this pace up for over fifty years, taking breaks only when conveniently detained in "his Majesty's prison." What untold damage that energy would have wrought if it had been stifled inside him, as it was in millions of other Indians groaning silently under the heel of an increasingly destructive colonization, or vented as raw violence, as was dangerously close to happening with many of them.

Peak Experience

The escape from violence is often experienced as a kind of strange joy. You pay a price, often a heavy one, but the sudden discovery of the creative path out of the dilemma between fear and anger, capitulation and attack, comes with a great feeling of release. It has been called, as in Buddhism, the "middle way," but the best expression for it comes from someone who experienced it under extreme duress, Andrew Young, who uses the words of an old spiritual, "The Way Out of No Way."

An episode that beautifully illustrates this way occurred during a march for voter's rights in Birmingham in 1964. The marchers, mostly black, were converging on City Hall when they suddenly found their way blocked by a phalanx of police and firemen. They hadn't prepared for this eventuality, and not knowing what else to do, they knelt down to pray. One of those marchers reports what happened next:

> [After a while, we] became "spiritually intoxicated," as another leader described it. . . . This was sensed by the police and firemen and it began to have an effect on them. . . . I don't know what happened to me. I got up from my knees and said to the cops: 'We're not turning back. We haven't done anything wrong. All we want is our freedom. How do you feel doing these things?' The Negroes started advancing and Bull Connor [the notorious segregationist police commissioner] shouted: "Turn on the water!" But the firemen did not respond. Again he gave the order and nothing happened. Some observers claim they saw the firemen crying. Whatever happened, the Negroes went through the lines.

Political power, we hear, grows out of the barrel of a gun; but in this case the police had all the guns, while the marchers, it would seem, had all the power.

Whether we call it "integrative power" or say this was an "act of love," the experiences of Joan Black [found in original publication] in her ER and the marchers confronted with cold authority in Birmingham, different as those experiences are, give a sense of how potent a force is involved here and how many ways it can manifest itself. What happened in Birmingham would seem to be as strong as mob violence, only somehow its reverse. What is the source of this power?

In both cases, the source is an intense fear reaction, *which was not acted on.* It was acted *out,* you could say, the way Sri Easwaran did not act on his angry thoughts but channeled them into creative action. The marchers could have given up and gone home, or they could have attacked the police and firemen. But they didn't want to just react, like automata. They were on a higher plane just then. Shortly before, one of their leaders had said, "We're going to win our freedom, and as we do it we're going to set our white brothers free." They breathed the heady air of freedom, and walked on.

And the firemen whose hands were frozen on the nozzles of their hoses? In them, as Gandhi would put it, their dormant reason was "compelled to be free." A confrontation like this, where feelings are intense on both sides and one of them precipitates an unexpected, successful outcome by a clear and clarifying act of courage, is what one scholar calls the "nonviolent moment." From the point of view of the nonviolent actor, we can call it a peak experience. A peak experience is one in which we are thrown back onto deeper resources by an emotional challenge.

One of the participants in the 1960 sit-ins at cafeterias in the South who was beaten by a racist mob can add for us some very clear insight into the psychology of such an experience. "You feel the pain," he said, "but you don't become bitter, you don't become hostile. . . . You sort of lose yourself. . . . You become involved in the circumstances of others." There is nothing super-natural about being able to carry out this kind of struggle, and there certainly is no guarantee that suffering will not come our way. But like a moun-tain climber pushing forward into the thin, bitter air of an icy peak, or a ballet dancer pushing her or his body beyond limits, there is such a thing as rising above pain. In the 1996 Olympics Kerri Strug gave her coach "one more jump," landing on a badly sprained ankle, and the whole world winced watching her face twitch at her otherwise perfect landing. There is this difference: the non-violent actor is deliberately seeking to manifest the pain that others are trying not to see. So in his or her case, the pain is not just something to put up with along the way; it's part of the point.

The fact is, even if you don't stick your neck out in today's world, pain happens. It's very im-portant to remember that when people say non-violence is risky, that people get attacked when minding their own business and not even dream-ing of changing the world, and there is a nonvio-lent way to respond to that kind of pain as well, as the following story illustrates.

One day in 1992 an eighty-year-old woman was mugged and badly hurt in New York City. Eileen Egan, however, was not your typical mug-ging victim. She was a lifetime peace activist, a coworker of Dorothy Day and Mother Teresa, who naturally saw things a little differently than most people. A good writer, she was also able to articulate her vision, for example, in a pithy in-terview in *Parade* magazine two years after the at-tack, called "I Refuse To Live In Fear." Egan is another insightful spokesperson for the kind of experience we're talking about, and its long-term results. Without using the word "nonviolence," she managed to describe precisely what makes this principle work, and in everyday language we can all follow. She started from the assumption, she tells us, that the worst result of the attack was not her broken hip and ribs but the potential "bro-kenness" of her fellow-feeling toward the man who attacked her. Like the effect of television vi-olence, the effect of real violence will, if we let it, spread into our feelings toward all our relation-

ships. Egan was extremely concerned not to let that happen. Instead of letting herself get vindic-tive, then, she tried to make friends with her at-tacker, staying in touch with him as he wended his way through the prison system, and she de-scribes how it helped her avoid the "posttrau-matic stress" that might have followed such a brutal attack. Note that so far *he* doesn't seem much affected by her generosity; but that doesn't prevent her from benefiting from it. She explains,

I've forgotten about the attack completely. I used to get nervous when somebody came up behind me, but that's gone now. There are so many more important things to worry about in the world.

But wasn't she angry? Of course, but she had something to do with her anger, so it left no scars. Remember nurse Black?: "I saw a sick person and had to take care of her." We saw this early on [in the original publication] in the case of Karen Ridd, and we'll continue to see it behind every example of real nonviolence we meet. One of the things, then, that accompanies the peak experience, maybe that makes it possible, is a higher vision. In the nonviolent person's outlook even an attacker is a person. He or she will not dehumanize another human, even one who has dehumanized himself.

And that vision has another aspect. Practi-cally all the rescuers who risked their lives to help Jews and other refugees during the Holocaust felt "that what an individual did, or failed to do, mat-tered;" that "they could influence events . . . [and so] what they did, or failed to do, mattered a great deal." Along with the vision that we are all human together, each of us equally real, there is a sense that human action and your own emo-tional struggle to act well is very meaningful; you're deeply aware that your efforts have an im-pact on the world. As Egan says, "If somebody has chosen a life of violence and doesn't get the result he expected from his victim [i.e., fear and anger], it may help him to see life differently." Kindness begets kindness, visions communicate, mood affects mood. Advertisers exploit our im-pressionability all the time—why can't we? As of

1992, Egan had not seen much of an answering mood from her former assailant. Not a problem. Perhaps he was touched, but not ready to let on. In any case *she* certainly reaped benefits from her attitude, benefits that a professional counselor would be thrilled to impart.

Berta Passweg was a Jewish refugee who had escaped to Egypt. One day, a friend in Alexandria said, "Berta, you should pray for Hitler." Seeing Berta's shock she explained, "Not that he succeeds with his evil intentions, but that God changes his mind." When Berta was finally able to do this, she found that "I don't think it had any effect on Hitler, but it had an effect on me. . . . All hate and bitterness against the Germans had just vanished and I could meet and talk with them without resentment."

For Berta Passweg and Eileen Egan, unlike Joan Black or Karen Ridd, the violence had already happened. In the former cases we are talking about healing, not preventing, violence—healing and not letting it spread. We are also talking about an individual rather than a group, compared to the Freedom Riders or the Birmingham marchers. These would seem to be incidentals that don't affect the basic principle or the way the peak experience feels and works: either way, purpose overrides pain.

I mentioned that we can see the same dynamic in groups and in individuals. Yet it is important to start with the individual, rather than the big march or the strike, even though most people associate nonviolence with group actions. Actors can, of course, get swept up in a wave of group enthusiasm, but the real source of nonviolent power is still coming from within them, and neither they nor we should lose sight of that. Groups don't have emotions, only individuals do.

The founding moment of Satyagraha, in my view, is the famous oath taken in the Empire Jewish Theater of Johannesburg on September 11, 1906, when a packed audience of Indians swore not to obey laws that were about to be passed depriving them of their basic human dignity. Gandhiji's explanation of the oath's meaning for each one in that vast crowd sheds light on the roots of its power in the individual.

> It is quite unlikely, but even if everyone else flinched leaving me alone to face the music, I am confident that I would never violate my pledge.

He asked each one of them to "search their hearts" and take the pledge only if it were really a matter between himself and God, notwithstanding what anyone else or the group as a whole would do. In other words, though the oath-taking was to be done *en masse* it was not a mass action; it was a summation of individual actions. That was to remain its sustaining power.

Eighty years later, Cardinal Jaime Sin would say this about the huge "people power" uprising in the Philippines that dislodged Ferdinand Marcos.

> It was amazing. It was two million independent decisions. Each one said, in his heart, "I will do this," and they went out.

Since violence and nonviolence come about subtly, long before they are seen in outward action, it should not be too surprising if certain traits of character or norms of a whole culture are causing violence without our being aware of it. Our modern culture has quite a few of these, and one of them is the way "we've started to understand every human encounter as a symbolic clash of group interests," as writer Louis Menand points out. "Violence can be talked about to the abstract, but violence, like sex, never occurs in the abstract. . . . Groups are essentially imaginary. Souls are real, and they can be saved, or lost, only one at a time."

There is a certain dehumanization inherent in the temptation to see people as a group—be it a corporation, a state, a race, even a gender—instead of seeing them as individuals. In nonviolence, at any rate, you never do this. How could you? For "soul-force" you need souls. In a group act of soul-force numbers can be handy, but they're never essential. "In Satyagraha it is never the numbers that count," Gandhiji said. "Strength of numbers is the delight of the timid. The valiant of spirit glory in fighting alone."

Developing Nonviolence: Making the Moment Last

A few years before Karen Ridd's team got to Guatemala, Sue Severin, a Marin County, California health educator, found herself so frustrated and angry over the terror imposed on Nicaraguan villagers by the Reagan era policy of "low-intensity conflict" that she set aside her career and volunteered for a highly dangerous project: to join a faith-based citizens group going down to document terrorist activity along the Honduran border. It was an effective way of converting her anger to useful action and, like many nonviolent projects, it led further than she anticipated. It was on this mission that Sue and the other North American team members stumbled onto the power of *nonviolent interposition,* or more specifically the technique that is now called *protective accompaniment.* Wherever they went, particularly during their longish stay in the formerly besieged village of Jalapa, there were no Contra attacks. So on their return to the States, Sue and others decided they had no choice but to go back and offer the protection of their presence to the people among whom they had lived, and to do it in as many areas as possible. Naturally, this was a frightening prospect, and she was as frightened as anyone while sitting in her comfortable, safe home in Marin County reading about what "the Contra" was doing in those remote jungle villages. But, as Dutch child rescuer Cornelia Knottnerus also found, "The best antidote to fear is action." Strangely enough, while Sue and the others were actually in Nicaragua, fear was never a problem.

> While I was there I never felt fear. I think the main reason was, I was there out of choice. . . . I found—much to my surprise—that I became very calm in danger. I'm a Quaker and don't go very much with "God" language, but the only way I can explain it is, I felt I was in the hands

of God: not safe—that I wouldn't be hurt—but that I was where I was supposed to be, doing what I was supposed to be doing. And this can be addictive. Maybe that's why we kept going back.

We began this chapter with a story that illustrates the conversion of anger. By this time we've seen that fear, too, can become fuel for the fire of unsentimental, active love when one chooses the nonviolence response.

Severin's reminiscence offers a number of other insights. She clarifies something about the feeling of empowerment, almost of invincibility, that sometimes comes over nonviolent actors and enables them to face and often overcome danger with preternatural courage—the Birmingham marchers' "spiritual intoxication." As she points out, it is not a naive feeling of invulnerability as though they were temporarily teenagers again. It is something both subtler and more realistic: what empowers you is the conviction that what you are going through is meaningful. In Severin's words, this is what you are "supposed to be doing," and these words are echoed by Marge Argelyan from Chicago, who did very similar work in Hebron in 1996. "This experience had the most integrity of any work I've done." They were echoed by Solange Muller, daughter of the Assistant Secretary General of the UN, at a meeting in New York. "When you find work like that, you never go back."

In times like ours, when life has become meaningless for so many, it's not hard to understand how the taste of nonviolent struggle can be "addictive." Just listen to testimonies from the women and men who risked their lives to save Jewish and other victims of the Holocaust.

Professor and Mrs. Ege played a prominent role in the highly successful Danish rescue operation. Mrs. Ege: "We helped the Jews because it meant that for once in your life you were doing something worthwhile. . . . I think that the Danes should be equally grateful to the Jews for giving them an opportunity to do something decent and meaningful." A trapeze artist, Speedy

Larking, said it with less restraint: "I feel—hang it—I feel like throwing myself down on the road and saying, 'Thank you!' " But it is a physician, Dr. Strandbygaard, who really takes our breath away. "Isn't this strange? . . . It's almost like experiencing again the overwhelming love of one's youth."

Heady stuff. These intense, fulfilling moments, we have said so far, come from the inner struggle to control our "biological" response of fight or flight. Such a struggle can lead to a peak experience that often has its effect on our opponents. It *always* has effects, like those we've just been hearing about, on the doer—on ourselves. Next chapter [not included here] we'll focus on the obvious question: how and with what degree of reliability can we expect our opponent to "get it"? But it's not quite time yet to leave the world of the actor's own inner experience.

In the grip of nonviolence, people experience more intensely. Life feels more "real." It is like the strange feeling of Yeats' Irish airman, who has no earthly reason to be risking his life fighting for the British.

Nor law, nor duty bade me fight,
Nor public men, nor cheering crowds,
A lonely impulse of delight
Drove to this tumult in the clouds;
I balanced all, brought all to mind,
The years to come seemed waste of breath,
A waste of breath the years behind
In balance with this life, this death.

It is like that experience, of course, but rather different. In war you are risking your life to kill others; in nonviolence you're risking your life (if necessary) so that no one else will be killed—ultimately so that no one will ever have to face death again at the hands of their fellow humans. Nonviolence is what William James was looking for: the moral equivalent of war.

In one's own nonviolent moment a flash of spiritual light momentarily rends the darkness of the prevailing image of ourselves as a separate, competitive, neo-Darwinian animal who knows nothing but threat force. . . .

One time or another, I think we've all had glimpses of a peak experience. Though it happened over thirty years ago, I vividly remember one afternoon in Berkeley when I was playing basketball with five other guys in Live Oak Park. All of a sudden—maybe one of us had just sunk a really pretty shot—the three of us, my teammates and myself, were in a rally. We were invincible. It was magic; every pass connected, every shot sank. It was more like a ballet than three guys playing ball. Then it ended. The spell—or whatever it was—broke. We went back to being our bumbling selves, and I don't even think we won the game. An actor, an athlete, a dancer, even a professor has peak moments when suddenly they "get it," or "it clicks." The difference is that a professional actor or athlete or whatever learns how to reenter that state on demand, so that with enough training he or she can make it happen whenever it's needed. There is nothing particularly mysterious about this, even though the "learning" that's involved has to be more than just at the conscious level. The training of a "career satyagrahi," who will need to keep certain "natural" reactions under control when he or she is at that lunch counter—or of someone who wants to stay alive some day in a dark alley—is very similar. You learn to be calmly alert under any stress.

The fact is that neither Joan Black nor the Birmingham marchers nor Karen Ridd nor Sue Severin nor Eileen Egan were totally unprepared for their nonviolent moment. Joan Black was on duty in an emergency room. Her medical training and her setting predisposed her to see a distraught person as a person—someone who needed help. Karen Ridd and Sue Severin were carrying out a nonviolent mission for which they had had a modest amount of training. The Birmingham marchers were in the midst of a long drawn-out nonviolent struggle, in which they had perhaps some training and certainly the rare benefit of inspired leadership.

This was also the case with Jawaharlal Nehru. Like thousands of his countrymen, the future Prime Minister of free India was drawn to the Mahatma's nonviolence, but there was more to it than just getting the idea, as he discovered when he was caught in a *lathi* charge by mounted police during a peaceful demonstration in Lucknow in 1928. (A *lathi,* or *lathee*, is a metal-tipped bamboo staff that Indian and British police used liberally in those days.)

> And then began a beating of us, and battering with lathees and long batons both by the mounted and the foot police. It was a tremendous hammering, and the clearness of vision that I had had the evening before left me. All I knew was that I had to stay where I was and must not yield or go back. I felt half blinded with the blows, and sometimes a dull anger seized me and a desire to hit out. I thought how easy it would be to pull down the police officer in front of me from his horse and to mount up myself, but long training and discipline held, and I did not raise a hand, except to protect my face from a blow.

William M. Evan

Toward a Confederation of Israel, Palestine and Jordan

The struggle for peace in the Middle East has been long and tortuous. After [over] five decades of Arab-Israeli conflict and five wars, the 1993 Oslo Accords were a hopeful breakthrough. That one of the architects of this agreement, Yitzhak Rabin, was soon the victim of an Israeli assassin's bullet dramatizes the perplexing nature of the Arab-Israeli conflict.

With few notable exceptions, leaders of the Middle East countries have not approached the Palestinian-Israeli conflict with a determined problem-solving orientation, let alone with a vision.[1] . . .

Regardless of the [long] gestation period, Palestinian statehood is a foregone conclusion. Some rudimentary building blocks of statehood are already in existence: a legislature (the Palestinian Legislative Council); an executive branch (a revered leader, Arafat, who still commands the grudging respect of most, if not all, of his fellow Palestinians, and a Palestinian cabinet); a law enforcement system of thousands of police officers; an airport; national symbols (flag and anthem); and, last but not least, an expanding territory.

To be sure, there are many seemingly intractable problems requiring negotiations between Israelis and Palestinians, including an equitable distribution of water resources, control of borders, the refugee problem, the percentage of West Bank land to be ceded to Palestinians, the status of East Jerusalem, and so on. These and other problems would lend themselves to mutually acceptable solutions if [Israeli and Palestinian leaders] were to explore a confederation proposal, advanced in 1991 by the Jerusalem Center for Public Affairs.[2]

The purpose of this essay is to provide a rationale for a confederation of Israel, Palestine and Jordan.

Concept of a Confederation

In a confederation, "constituent states retain . . . their political independence but band together in perpetual union under a common constitution to form a joint government for quite specific and limited purposes. . . . The appeal of a confederation is in its provision of greater autonomy for the constituent units. . . ."[3]

In his 1991 book, Daniel Elazar, a well-known scholar on federalism, set forth 11 possible federal proposals for the Arab-Israeli conflict.[4] However, writing as he did, before the Oslo Accords and before the signing of a peace treaty between Israel and Jordan, Elazar did not entertain the option of a confederation of Israel, Palestine and Jordan. Another reason is that Elazar did not believe that a Palestine state on the West Bank and Gaza would be a prudent risk, either politically or militarily. Like some other Israelis, Elazar evidently subscribed to the idea that Jordan is, in effect, a Palestine state, since the majority of its inhabitants are ethnically Palestinians.

Shimon Peres is now a strong advocate of a Palestinian state, but when he wrote about it in 1993,[5] he advocated a confederation quite different from the tri-state proposal advanced in this essay: "The political structure best suited to the limitations and possibilities of the area is a Jordanian-Palestinian confederation for political matters, and a Jordanian-Palestinian-Israeli 'Benelux' arrangement for economic affairs . . ."[6] by which Peres means a customs union.

There are a number of confederations in existence, of which Canada and Switzerland are two noteworthy examples. Canada's confederation consists of 10 provinces, one of which is Quebec. For many years, a secessionist movement has been active in Quebec, a French-speaking province that seeks to free itself from the domination of the English-speaking provinces. In a recent referendum in Quebec, a secessionist proposal was narrowly defeated. The Canadian government has sought to counter the Quebecois secessionist movement by revising its constitution to further protect the economic and cultural interests of the population of Quebec.

In 1991, Switzerland celebrated the 700th anniversary of the founding of its confederation. Surmounting political, religious, linguistic and other divisions—not to mention recurrent military incursions—26 cantons were established, providing for cantonal autonomy and democracy. Under the 1874 constitution, the cantons hold all power not specifically delegated to the federal authorities. The durability and success of the Swiss confederation are remarkable considering that it integrates diverse cultural populations: Italian, French and German.

Unlike some of the confederations that have foundered, Canada and Switzerland have succeeded in meeting the expectations of its citizens of diverse cultural and linguistic backgrounds by safeguarding two fundamental institutions: democratic governance and constitutionalism. These appear to be two prerequisites for a successful confederation. As Elazar put it, ". . . No federation or confederation could work unless all its constituent units were governed democratically. . . ."[7] The fact that only one of the three states, namely Israel, presently claims to fulfill these two prerequisites, is a problem that would have to be addressed in the process of developing a confederation.

Jordan, a constitutional monarchy, is introducing some limited democratic forms by virtue of the fact that the royal family has granted the people the right to organize parties and hold democratic elections "even if their platforms do not match the King's ideas."[8]

The political situation in Palestine has not yet progressed in the direction of full democratization, for though Arafat was elected in legitimate elections, there is much to criticize, especially as regards human rights. The transition of Jordan and Palestine to full-fledged democratic polities is essential not only for the success of the confederation, but also for peace and security in the Middle East. For, as Russett and other political scientists have observed, democracies do not, as a rule, wage war against one another.[9]

While creating a new political authority, the proposed confederation would preserve the integrity of the three constituent states. Whatever joint confederal functions are consensually agreed upon would be incorporated in a constitution to govern the confederation.

Each of the three constituent states would benefit from joining such a confederation. By identifying areas of commonality, significant economic and political developments could be achieved. Several examples of joint efforts will be outlined to make the point.

Some Benefits of Confederation

A Common Labor Pool

Eliminating barriers to the free movement of labor would activate market forces to the mutual benefit of the three states. Large reserves of unemployed Palestinians would seek jobs in Israel; similarly, substantial numbers of unemployed Jordanians would freely move across the Jordan River in search of jobs. The flow of labor, however, would not be in one direction only. Israel has a surfeit of Soviet-trained engineers and scientists who are presently underemployed. If they could cross the borders of Palestine and Jordan, they could perform an entrepreneurial function in developing small and medium-size enterprises.

Israeli Entrepreneurship and Capital

New economic opportunities in Palestine and Jordan would beckon Israeli entrepreneurs who have innovative ideas as well as access to capital markets. This would introduce a new element of dynamism in the economies of Jordan and Palestine. Jordanian and Palestinian entrepreneurs would be able to tap into Israeli experience in accessing global financial sources of capital. Joint ventures by Israeli, Jordanian and Palestinian entrepreneurs would flourish in the course of time.

Developing Ports of Commerce

Each of the three states has ports that are presently underdeveloped. Expanding and modernizing them would have a catalytic effect on exports and imports from around the world. Large infrastructure projects, such as ports, have to enjoy a certain minimum level of usage for economies of scale to kick in. If each country insists on building and operating individual ports, none of these facilities would achieve the threshold of usage necessary for cost savings to materialize. Such large infrastructure projects as ports are ideally suited for joint ventures to avoid duplication of facilities. For example, the port project in Aqaba, Jordan, if it were undertaken jointly with Israel, would greatly expand commerce for both countries.

Developing Water Resources

The Middle East has one of the most acute water shortages in the world. Syria and Iraq are at the mercy of Turkey for the waters of the Tigris and the Euphrates. Jordan is hostage to Syria upstream—for water of the Yarmuk—and to Israel downstream—for water of the Jordan River. Israel's water comes from three main sources: the Sea of Galilee, which is fed by the Jordan River; and two aquifers, one of which is in the occupied territories of the West Bank. This problem is on the agenda of the ongoing negotiations. The present inequitable allocation of water resources is evident when one compares the annual consumption in cubic meters for all purposes (domestic, industrial and agricultural) of Israel, Jordan and Palestine (West Bank and Gaza).

■ **TABLE 44.1.**
Annual Per-Capita
Consumption of Water in
Cubic Meters for All Purposes

Average Consumption	
Israel	400–450
Jordan	173–185
West Bank	110–170
Gaza	75–110

Sources: Peter Glick, *Water in Crisis,* Oxford University Press, 1993; U.S. National Academy of Sciences, *Water for the Future,* 1999; Thomas Naff, *Amer Middle East Water Data Base.*

A confederation would highlight the need for exploring joint efforts to develop new sources of water, instituting a program of conservation and achieving a more equitable allocation of water among the three states. Admittedly, because of its much higher level of economic development than either Palestine or Jordan, Israel requires more water resources. For this reason, Israel is presently negotiating with Turkey to deliver several million cubic meters of water per year to Israel by pipe or tanker or "medusa" bag. While this strategy might solve some of Israel's water problems, it would leave the serious water conflicts with Palestine and Jordan unresolved. On the other hand, a confederation would, in principle, enable the three states to cooperate in planning for the development of new water supplies, e.g., by investing in a program of desalination—a project that would very likely elicit financial support from the World Bank. It is noteworthy that Israel is now considering helping fund the development of three multimillion-dollar desalination plants in Egypt to meet the needs of both countries.[10]

Development of Infrastructure

Palestine and Jordan are both in need of extensive development of their infrastructure—such as roads, bridges, sewage plants, utilities, etc.—if their economic development is to be accelerated. A confederation would facilitate this and increase the chances that the World Bank would support such development projects, since multilateral agencies may balk at providing funds for facilities that are cost-efficient only if they are used close to capacity. The laws of economics, instead of parochial national considerations, should guide such decisions. Infrastructure developed from the perspective of a confederation, rather than within the framework of individual countries, is likely to be much more cost-effective.

Development of Tourism

Tourism, one of the fastest-growing industries in the world, would be substantially stimulated by the establishment of a confederation of Israel, Palestine and Jordan. According to the *Yearbook of Tourism Statistics,*[11] Israeli tourism revenues increased close to threefold from 1990 to 1997 (from $1.4 billion per year to $3.4 billion), whereas Jordan's tourism revenues remained almost static ($336 million to $376 million). With the elimination of the present relatively impenetrable borders between the three states, tourists, especially religious pilgrims eager to visit biblical sites, would very likely flock to all three states.

Progress Toward a Middle East Common Market

The proposed tri-state confederation would enable the parties to take the first critical steps toward implementing an idea considered for many years, namely, the establishment of a Middle East Common Market. When Israel finally enters into peace treaties with Syria and Lebanon, these countries, along with Egypt, could also become members of the Middle East Common Market. The European Common Market experience is an inspiring model to emulate: France and Germany, bitter enemies in the Second World War, established the Coal and Steel Community in 1952, thus developing a program of economic cooperation which led, decades later, to the formation of the European Union. A similar process could well develop in the Middle East.

Health Care Systems

The foregoing examples of joint confederal efforts need not be confined to economic activities; they could also extend to the social realm. As a highly industrialized country, Israel has a well-developed health-care system. And yet, like other Western countries, it suffers from a maldistribution of physicians, clinics and hospitals. Advances in telecommunications technology, namely, developments in telemedicine, are seeking to overcome this problem. Israelis living in the north and south of the country, at considerable distances from medical centers in Jerusalem, Haifa and Tel Aviv, are the beneficiaries of advanced medical care by experts with the help of telecommunication satellites. Telecardiology and teleradiology are prime examples of the application of telemedicine. This technology could readily be applied to the extensive health-care problems of Palestine and Jordan, where the health-care facilities are relatively underdeveloped.

Political Multiplier Effects

The defense budgets of Israel and Jordan could be substantially reduced as a result of joining a confederation. Progress in turning swords into plowshares would encourage the signing of peace treaties with Syria and Lebanon. Thus, a *regional* peace dividend could be achieved, which in turn could contribute to a *global* peace dividend.

Problem of Refugees

Another highly contentious problem is the plight of the millions of Palestinian refugees dispersed in Lebanon, Syria, Jordan, the West Bank and Gaza since the war in 1948. Palestinians argue that they, like the Jews, are entitled to a "right of return" to their homeland. The establishment of a Palestinian state would enable the new state to absorb a portion of the estimated 3.5 million refugees. A confederation would seek to address the problem of the Palestinian Diaspora by exploring the feasibility of resettlement as well as a program of compensation and reparations.

Status of Jerusalem

Such a confederal arrangement could provide the framework for solving the much-contested and highly emotional problem of Jerusalem. Jewish fundamentalists, dedicated to the building of the Third Temple, are as fervently devoted to the eventual coming of the Messiah as are Christian fundamentalists to the Second Coming of Jesus, and Muslim fundamentalists to the coming of the Mahdi, the Muslim Messiah.[12] Instead of dividing this historic city, a "Solomonic" solution would be to preserve it as a united city for all three monotheistic religions, but not necessarily under the exclusive control of Israel. It could become simultaneously the capital of Israel, the capital of the new Palestine state, as well as the capital of the confederation. Finally, the principal holy places—the Temple Mount, the Western Wall, the Dome of the Rock, Al-Aqsa Mosque, the Holy Sepulcher, etc.—could come under the joint rule of the three states forming the confederation.

Need for an International Commission to Develop Plans for the Confederation

The foregoing examples of joint efforts through a confederation are intended to underscore opportunities for mutual benefits from cooperative ventures. A commission comprised of the ministers of economics, finance and trade of Israel, Jordan and Palestine, could develop detailed confederation plans that could be implemented early in the new millennium.

One of the tasks of such a compromise would be to elicit the political and economic support for the confederation of the U.S. and the European Union. It would also be important for the commission to seek to overcome any opposition from Arab states, especially from the neighboring states of Syria and Lebanon. It is very likely that Egypt would be supportive of the confederation, and that Saudi Arabia would, at least, not oppose it. Last, but not least, the commission would have to secure the cooperation of multilateral agencies, such as the International Monetary Fund and the World Bank, to provide funding to implement the establishment of a confederation.

Conclusion

From a geopolitical standpoint, a confederation of Israel, Palestine and Jordan is an idea whose time has come. Developing a detailed blueprint for a confederation is obviously not feasible or necessary at this juncture. The crucial question is whether Israeli and Palestinian leaders have the courage and vision to explore a confederal form of government as a strategic political mechanism for achieving durable peace and cooperation in the Middle East.

Notes

1. Shimon Peres, one of the architects of the Oslo Accords, deserves recognition for his sustained and imaginative commitment to the Mideast peace process. See Shimon Peres with Aryeh Naor, *The New Middle East,* New York: Henry Holt, 1993.

2. Cf. Daniel J. Elazar, *Two Peoples, One Land,* New York: University Press of America, 1991, p. viii. For a recent discussion of a confederation proposal, see Shosh Shor, "From Sword into Plowshare: Regional Arrangements for Israel and Palestinians?" *Jerusalem Letter / Viewpoints,* Jerusalem Center for Public Affairs, No. 411, 1 August, 1999, p. 2.

3. Ibid., pp. 43, 106.

4. Ibid., p. 101.

5. Peres with Naor, op. cit, p. 175.

6. Ibid., p. 173.

7. Elazar, op. cit. p. 106.

8. Peres with Naor, op. cit, p. 177.

9. Cf. Bruce M. Russett, *Grasping the Democratic Peace: Principles of a Post Cold-War World,* Princeton, N.J.: Princeton University Press, 1993.

10. Stephen J. Glain, "Arab Investment Stirs: With Peace or Without," *Wall Street Journal,* September 20, 1999, p. 1.

11. Madrid: World Tourism Organization, 1999, Vol. 48, pp. 106, 117; Vol. 51, pp. 117, 124.

12. Jeffrey Goldberg, "Israel's Y2K Problem," *The New York Times Magazine,* October 3, 1999, pp. 38–43, 52, 65, 76–77.

Questions for Discussion

1. Are there any conflicts in the history of the world that have been avoided by means of nonviolent protests or demonstrations?
2. Can accommodation, as analyzed by Sharp, be interpreted as a form of appeasement?
3. What are the essential elements of making a nonviolence movement successful?
4. Do you think that mass protests are enough to change the policies of government officials?
5. What objective may be achieved through civil disobedience?
6. Discuss some of the hurdles that need to be overcome if a confederation of Palestine, Israel and Jordan was to be established.
7. What problems do you foresee of Israel and Jordan joining such a confederation?

Further Readings

1. Gier, Nicholas F. *The Virtue of Nonviolence.* Albany: State of New York Press, 2004.
2. Jett, Dennis. *Why Peacekeeping Fails.* New York: Palgrave Macmillan, 2001.
3. Kriesberg, Louis. "The Growth of the Conflict Resolution Field," in Chester A. Crocker, Fen Osler Hampson, and Pamela Aall, eds., *The Challenges of Managing International Conflict.* Washington, D.C.: United States Institute of Peace Press, 2001, 407–426.
4. Otunnu, Olara. *Peacemaking and Peacekeeping for the New Century.* Boston: Rowman and Littlefield Publishers, 1998.
5. Bharadwaj, L. K. "Principled versus Pragmatic Nonviolence." *Peace Review*, 1998, 10, 1, March, 79–81.
6. Devi, Sharmila, "Peace Advocated Thinks Businnes is the Key." *The Financial Times,* Sept. 22, 2003, 10.
7. Lijphart, Arend. "Consociation and Federation: Conceptual and Empirical Links." *Canadian Journal of Political Science,* 1979, XII, 3, Sept., 499–515.
8. Galtung, Johan, *Peace by Peaceful Means: Peace and Conflict, Development and Civilization.* London: Sage, 1996.
9. Chekki, Dan A. "Some Traditions of Nonviolence and Peace." *International Journal on World Peace*, 1993, 10, 3, Sept. 47–54.
10. Fisher, George. "The 'New Politics' of Gandhi." *Social Policy*, 1983, 13, 4, Spring, 61–64.
11. Boulding, Elise. "Building a Culture of Peace: Some Priorities." *NWSA Journal*, 2001, 13, 2, Summer, 55–59.
12. King, Blair B. "Gandhi, Nonviolence, and the Holocaust." *Peace and Change*, 1991, 16, 2, Apr., 176–196.
13. Spodek, Howard. "From Gandhi to Violence: Ahmedabad's 1985 Riots in Historical Perspective." *Modern Asian Studies*, 1989, 23, 4, Oct., 765–795.
14. Bharadwaj, L. K. "The Contribution of Gandhian Thinking to the Understanding of the World Crisis." *International Review of Sociology*, 1984, 20, 1–3, Apr.–Dec., 65–99.
15. Horovitz, David. "A Glimmer of Peace." *The New York Times*, March 10, 2004, A27.

International Law

International law has become an increasingly significant institutional mechanism in restraining states from using force against other states. Besides preventing the occurrence of war, it provides a mechanism for a possible peaceful settlement of disputes.

In "The Rights of War and Peace," Hugo Grotius articulated the notion of a regulated conflict for the first time. As the "father of international law" Grotius wrote his treatise in 1625 to outline the parameters of a just war and the means that may be adopted during such a war. The first part of this reading explains the rights of groups and the second part examines the rights of individuals during the course of a violent conflicts. Status and rights of a neutral party, and of civilians, are explicated by Grotius. The ideas presented in this reading form the basis of present day international law as they bear on the conduct of war and crimes committed during an armed conflict.

In "War Crimes," William M. Evan explains how the military personnel of any warring state dehumanize the enemy, and thereby overcome any inhibitions they might have against fighting other human beings.

The author asserts that military indoctrination tends to provide the conditions for the perpetration of war crimes. History of international and domestic legislation regarding the prevention of war crimes has been traced from the ancient Chinese war customs to the fourth Geneva Convention. To further elucidate the issue, specific war crime issues from recent wars are documented.

"Legality of the Threat or Use of Nuclear Weapons" is an advisory opinion issued by the International Court of Justice (ICJ) at the request of the General Assembly. This advisory opinion clarifies the position of the ICJ on this issue. It also suggests the need for specific conventions prohibiting the use of, as well as the threat of the use of, nuclear weapons.

"Constitution of Japan, Article 9" is a unique document in the world's history. Following World War II, Japan, in its constitution, renounced war and refused to maintain a land and air force.

In "Kashmir: Invoking International Law to Avoid Nuclear War," William M. Evan and Francis A. Boyle urge the application of international law to resolve the Kashmir dispute. The authors assert that since both India and Pakistan are members of the 1899 Hague convention for the Pacific Settlement of International Disputes, they are undermining international law by threatening to use military force. Article 8 of the Hague convention establishes a procedure for mediation. The U.S. government, joined by others, should invoke this provision to peacefully resolve this dispute. The application of international law to the Kashmir conflict is especially crucial because both countries have nuclear weapons, which they may be tempted to deploy in the event of a war.

Hugo Grotius

The Rights of War and Peace

What is Lawful in War

I. Having . . . considered by what persons, and for what causes, war may be justly, declared and undertaken, the subject necessarily leads to an inquiry into the circumstances, under which war may be undertaken, into the extent, to which it may be carried, and into the manner, in which its rights may be enforced. Now all these matters may be viewed in the light of privileges resulting simply from the law of nature and of nations, or as the effects at some prior treaty or promise. But the actions, which are authorized by the law of nature, are those that are first entitled to attention.

II. In the first place, as it has occasionally been observed, the means employed in the pursuit of any object must, in a great degree, derive the complexion of their moral character from the nature of the end to which they lead. It is evident therefore that we may justly avail ourselves of those means, provided they be lawful, which are necessary to the attainment of any right. *Right* in this place means what is strictly so called, signifying the moral power of action, which any one as a member of society possesses. On which account, a person, if he has no other means of saving his life, is justified in using any forcible means of repelling an attack, though he who makes it, as for instance, a soldier in battle, in doing so, is guilty of no crime. For this is a right resulting not properly from the crime of another, but from the privilege of self-defence, which nature grants to every one. Besides, if any one has sure and undoubted grounds to apprehend imminent danger from any thing belonging to another, he may seize it without any regard to the guilt or innocence of that owner. Yet he does not by that seizure become the proprietor of it. For that is not necessary to the end he has in view. He may detain it as a precautionary measure, till he can obtain satisfactory assurance of security.

Upon the same principle any one has a natural right to seize what belongs to him, and is unlawfully detained by another: or, if that is impracticable, he may seize something of equal value, which is nearly the same as recovering a debt. Recoveries of this kind establish a property in the things so reclaimed; which is the only method of restoring the equality and repairing the breaches of violated justice. So too when punishment is lawful and just, all the means absolutely necessary to enforce its execution are also lawful and just, and every act that forms a part of the punishment, such as destroying an enemy's property and country by fire or any other way, falls within the limits of justice proportionable to the offence.

III. In the second place, it is generally known that it is not the origin only of a just war which is to be viewed as the principal source of many of our rights, but there may be causes growing out of that war which may give birth to additional rights. As in proceedings at law, the sentence of the court may give to the successful litigant other rights besides those belonging to the original matter of dispute. So those who join our enemies, either as allies or subjects, give us a right of defending ourselves against them also. So too a nation engaging in an unjust war, the injustice of which she knows and ought to know, becomes liable to make good all the expenses and losses incurred, because she has been guilty of occasioning them. In the same manner those powers, who become auxiliaries in wars undertaken without any reasonable grounds, contract a degree of guilt and render themselves liable to punishment in proportion to the injustice of their measures. Plato approves of war conducted so far, as to compel the aggressor to indemnify the injured and the innocent.

IV. In the third place, an individual or belligerent power may, in the prosecution of a lawful object, do many things, which were not in the contemplation of the original design, and which in themselves it would not be lawful to do. Thus in order to obtain what belongs to us, when it is impossible to recover the specific thing, we may take more than our due, under condition of repaying whatever is above the real value. For the same reason it is lawful to attack a ship manned by pirates, or a house occupied by robbers, although in that ship, or that house there may be many innocent persons, whose lives are endangered by such attack.

But we have had frequent occasion to remark, that what is conformable to right taken in its strictest sense is not always lawful in a moral point of view. For there are many instances, in which the law of charity will not allow us to insist upon our right with the utmost rigour. A reason for which it will be necessary to guard against things, which fall not within the original purpose of an action, and the happening of which might be foreseen: unless indeed the action has a tendency to produce advantages, that will far outweigh the consequences of any accidental calamity, and the apprehensions of evil are by no means to be put in competition with the sure hopes of a successful issue. But to determine in such cases requires no ordinary penetration and discretion. But wherever there is any doubt, it is always the safer way to decide in favour of another's interest, than to follow the bent of our own inclination. "Suffer the tares to grow, *says our divine teacher,* least in rooting up the tares you root up the wheat also.". . .

V. It frequently occurs as a matter of inquiry, how far we are authorized to act against those, who are neither enemies, nor wish to be thought so, but who supply our enemies with certain articles. For we know that it is a point, which on former and recent occasions has been contested with the greatest animosity; some wishing to enforce with all imaginary rigour the rights of war, and others standing up for the freedom of commerce.

In the first place, a distinction must be made between the commodities themselves. For there are some, such as arms for instance, which are only of use in war; there are others again, which are of no use in war, but only administer to luxury; but there are some articles, such as money, provisions, ships and naval stores, which are of use at all times both in peace and war.

As to conveying articles of the first kind, it is evident that any one must be ranked as an enemy, who supplies an enemy with the means of prosecuting hostilities. Against the conveyance of commodities of the second kind, no just complaint can be made.—And as to articles of the third class, from their being of a doubtful kind, a distinction must be made between the times of war and peace. For if a power can not defend itself, but by intercepting the supplies sent to an enemy, necessity will justify such a step, but upon condition of making restoration, unless there be some additional reasons to the contrary. But if the conveyance of goods to an enemy tends to obstruct any belligerent power in the prosecution of a lawful right, and the person so conveying them possesses the means of knowing it; if that power, for instance, is besieging a town, or blockading a port, in expectation of a speedy surrender and a peace, the person, who furnishes the enemy with supplies, and the means of prolonged resistance, will be guilty of an aggression and injury towards that power. He will incur the same guilt, as a person would do by assisting a debtor to escape from prison, and thereby to defraud his creditor. His goods may be taken by way of indemnity, and in discharge of the debt. If the person has not yet committed the injury, but only intended to do so, the aggrieved power will have a right to detain his goods, in order to compel him to give future security, either by putting into his hands hostages, or pledges; or indeed in any other way. But if there are evident proofs of injustice in an enemy's conduct the person who supports him in such a case, by furnishing him with succours, will be guilty not barely of a civil injury, but his giving assistance will amount to a crime as enormous, as it would be to rescue a criminal in the very face of the judge. And on that account the injured power may proceed against him as a criminal, and punish him by a confiscation of his goods.

These are the reasons, which induce belligerent powers to issue manifestoes, as an appeal to other states, upon the justice of their cause, and their probable hopes of ultimate success. This question has been introduced under the article, which refers to the law of nature, as history supplies us with no precedent to deduce its establishment from the voluntary law of nations. . . .

VI. Wars, for the attainment of their objects, it cannot be denied, must employ force and terror as their most proper agents. But a doubt is sometimes entertained, whether stratagem may be lawfully used in war. The general sense of mankind seems to have approved of such a mode of warfare. For Homer commends his hero, Ulysses, no less for his ability in military stratagem, than for his wisdom. Xenophon, who was a philosopher as well as a soldier and historian, has said, that nothing can be more useful in war than a well-timed stratagem, with whom Brasidas, in Thucydides agrees, declaring it to be the method from which many great generals have derived the most brilliant reputation. And in Plutarch, Agesilaus maintains, that deceiving an enemy is both just and lawful. The authority of Polybius may be added to those already named; for he thinks, that it shows great talent in a general to avail himself of some favourable opportunity to employ a stratagem, than to gain an open battle. This opinion of poets, historians, and philosophers is supported by that of Theologians. For Augustin has said that, in the prosecution of a just war, the justice of the cause is no way affected by the attainment of the end, whether the object be accomplished by stratagem or open force, and Chrysostom, in his beautiful little treatise on the priestly office, observes, that the highest praises

are bestowed on those generals, who have practised successful stratagems. Yet there is one circumstance, upon which the decision of this question turns more than upon any opinion even of the highest authority, and that is, whether stratagem ought to be ranked as one of those evils, which are prohibited under the maxim of not doing evil, that good may ensue, or to be reckoned as one of those actions, which, though evil in themselves, may be so modified by particular occasions, as to lose their criminality in consideration of the good, to which they lead.

VII. There is one kind of stratagem, it is proper to remark, of a negative, and another of a positive kind. The word stratagem, upon the authority of Labeo, taken in a negative sense, includes such actions, as have nothing criminal in them, though calculated to deceive, where any one, for instance, uses a degree of dissimulation or concealment, in order to defend his own property or that of others. So that undoubtedly there is something of harshness in the opinion of Cicero, who says there is no scene of life, that will allow either simulation, or dissimulation to be practised. For as you are not bound to disclose to others all that you either know or intend; it follows that, on certain occasions, some acts of dissimulation, that is, of concealment may be lawful. This is a talent, which Cicero in many parts of his writings, acknowledges that it is absolutely necessary for statesmen to possess. The history of Jeremiah, in the xxxviiith chapter of his prophecy, furnishes a remarkable instance of this kind.

The Right of Killing Enemies, in Just War, to be Tempered with Moderation and Humanity

I. and II. Cicero, in the first book of his offices, has finely observed, that "some duties are to be observed even towards those, from whom you have received an injury. For even vengeance and punishment have their due bounds." And at the same time he extols those ancient periods in the Roman government, when the events of war were mild, and marked with no unnecessary cruelty.

The explanations given in the first chapter of this book [*The Rights of War and Peace*] will point out the cases, where the destruction of an enemy is one of the rights of lawful war, according to the principles of strict and internal justice, and where it is not so. For the death of an enemy may proceed either from an accidental calamity, or from the fixed purpose of his destruction.

No one can be justly killed by design, except by way of legal punishment, or to defend our lives, and preserve our property, when it cannot be effected without his destruction. For although in sacrificing the life of man to the preservation of perishable possessions, there may be nothing repugnant to strict justice, it is by no means consonant to the law of charity.

But to justify a punishment of that kind, the person put to death must have committed a crime, and such a crime too, as every equitable judge would deem worthy of death. Points, which it is unnecessary to discuss any further, as they have been so fully explained in the chapter on punishments [not included here].

III. In speaking of the calamities of war, as a punishment, it is proper to make a distinction between misfortune and injury. For a people may sometimes be engaged in war against their will, where they cannot be justly charged with entertaining hostile intentions. . . .

IV. and V. Between complete injuries and pure misfortunes there may be sometimes a middle kind of actions, partaking of the nature of both, which can neither be said to be done with known and willful intention, nor yet excused under colour of ignorance and want of inclination. Acts of pure misfortune neither merit punishment, nor oblige the party to make reparation for the loss occasioned. Hence many parts of history supply us with distinctions that are made between those who are the authors of a war, and principals in it, and those who are obliged to follow others, as accessories in the same.

VI. But respecting the authors of war, a distinction is to be made also, as to the motives and causes of war: some of which though not actually just, wear an appearance of justice, that may impose upon the well meaning. The writer to Herennius lays it down as the most equitable vindication of injury, where the party committing it, has neither been actuated by revenge, nor cruelty; but by the dictates of duty and an upright zeal.

Cicero, in the first book of his offices, advises the sparing of those, who have committed no acts of atrocity and cruelty in war, and that wars, undertaken to maintain national honour, should be conducted upon principles of moderation. And, in one of his letters, adverting to the war between Pompey and Caesar, he describes the struggle between those two illustrious men, as involved in so much obscurity of motives and causes, that many were perplexed in deciding which side to embrace. In his speech too for Marcellus, he remarks that such uncertainty might be attended with error, but could never be charged with guilt.

VII. Such forbearance in war is not only a tribute to justice, it is a tribute to humanity, it is a tribute to moderation, it is a tribute to greatness of soul. It was in this moderation, says Sallust, the foundation of Roman greatness was laid. Tacitus describes his country-men as a people no less remarkable for their courage in the field, than for their humanity to the vanquished and suppliant.

On this subject, there is a brilliant passage in the fourth book to Herennius, where it is said, "It was an admirable resolution of our ancestors, never to deprive a captive prince of his life. For it would be truly a violation of common justice to abuse, by wanton cruelty and rigour, the power over those, whom fortune has put into our hands, by reducing them from the high condition, in which she had placed them before; their former enmity is forgotten. Because it is the characteristic of bravery to esteem opponents as enemies, while contending for victory, and to treat them as men, when conquered, in order to soften the calamities of war, and improve the terms and relations of peace. But it may be asked, if the enemy now treated with this indulgence would have shown the same lenity himself. To which a reply may be made, that he is not an object of imitation in what he would have done, so much as in what he ought to have done."

VIII. Though there may be circumstances, in which absolute justice will not condemn the sacrifice of lives in war, yet humanity will require that the greatest precaution should be used against involving the innocent in danger, except in cases of extreme urgency and utility.

IX. After establishing these general principles, it will not be difficult to decide upon particular cases. Seneca says, that "in the calamities of war children are exempted and spared, on the score of their age, and women from respect to their sex." In the wars of the Hebrews, even after the offers of peace have been rejected, God commands the women and children to be spared.

Thus when the Ninevites were threatened with utter destruction, on account of their grievous crimes, a mitigation of the sentence was allowed, in compassion to the many thousands, who were of an age incapable of making a distinction between right and wrong.

If God, from whose supreme gift the life of man proceeds, and on whose supreme disposal it depends, prescribes to himself a rule like this, it is surely incumbent upon men, who have no commission, but for the welfare and preservation of the lives of men, to act by the same rule. Thus age and sex are equally spared, except where the latter have departed from this privilege by taking arms, or performing the part of men.

X. The same rule may be laid down too with respect to males, whose modes of life are entirely remote from the use of arms. And in the first class of this description may be placed the ministers of religion, who, among all nations, from times of the most remote antiquity have been exempted from bearing arms.—Thus, as may be seen in sacred history, the Philistines, being enemies of the Jews, forbore doing harm to the company of prophets, that was at Gaba: and David fled with Samuel to another place, which the presence of a prophetic company protected from all molestation and injury.

Plutarch relates of the Cretans, that when all order among them was entirely broken by their civil broils, they abstained from offering violence to any member of the priesthood, or to those employed in the sacred rites belonging to the dead. From hence the Greeks came to denote a general massacre by the proverbial expression of no one being left to carry fire to the altar.

Equally privileged with the holy priesthood are those, who devote their lives to the pursuit of letters, and other studies beneficial to mankind.

XI. Diodorus bestows an encomium upon the Indians, who, in all their wars with each other, forbore destroying or even hurting those employed in husbandry, as being the common benefactors of all. Plutarch relates the same of the ancient Corinthians and Megarensians, and Cyrus sent a message to the king of Assyria to inform him that he was willing to avoid molesting all who were employed in tilling the ground.

XII. To the above catalogue of those exempted from sharing in the calamities war, may be added merchants, not only those residing for a time in the enemy's country, but even his natural-born, and regular subjects: artisans too, and all others are included; whose subsistence depends upon cultivating the arts of peace.

XIII. and XIV. More civilized manners having abolished the barbarous practice of putting prisoners to death for the same reason, the surrender of those, who stipulate for the preservation of their lives either in battle, or in a siege, is not to be rejected.

The Romans, when investing towns, always accepted offers of capitulation, if made before the battering ram had touched the walls. Caesar gave notice to the Atuatici, that he would save their city, if they surrendered, before the battering ram was brought up. And in modern times it is the usual practice, before shells are thrown, or mines sprung, to summon places to surrender, which are thought unable to hold out—and where places are stronger, such summons is generally sent, before the storming is made.

XV. and XVI. Against these principles of natural law and equity an objection is sometimes derived from the necessity of retaliation, or striking terror, in cases of obstinate resistance. But such an objection is by no means just. For after a place has surrendered, and there is no danger to be apprehended from the prisoners, there is nothing to justify the further effusion of blood.—Such rigour was sometimes practised, where there were any enormous acts of injustice, or any violation of faith; it was practised also upon deserters, if taken.

Sometimes, where very important advantages may attend striking a terror, by preventing the same crimes in future from being committed, it may be proper to exercise the right of rigour in its full extent. But an obstinate resistance, which can be considered as nothing but the faithful discharge of a trust, can never come within the description of such delinquencies, as justify extreme rigour.

XVII. Where delinquencies indeed are such as deserve death, but the number of offenders is very great, it is usual, from motives of mercy, to depart in some degree from the right of enforcing the whole power of the law: the authority for so doing is founded on the example of God himself, who commanded such offers of peace to be made to the Canaanites, and their neighbors, the most wicked of any people upon the face of the earth, as might spare their lives upon the condition of their becoming tributaries.

XVIII. From the opinions advanced and maintained above, it will not be difficult to gather the principles of the law of nature respecting hostages.

At the time, when it was a general opinion that every one had the same right over his life, as over his property, and that right, either by express or implied consent was transferred from individuals to the state, it is not surprising that we should read of hostages, though harmless and innocent as individuals, being punished for the offences of the state: and, in this case, the consent of the state to such a regulation implies that of individuals, who have originally resigned their own will to that of the public; in whom, after such resignation, it indubitably vested.

But when the day-spring rose upon the world, men, obtaining clearer views of the extent of their power, found that God, in giving man dominion over the whole earth, reserved to himself the supreme disposal of his life, so that man cannot resign to anyone the right over his own life or that of another.

XIX. By way of conclusion to this subject it may be that all actions no way conducive to obtain a contested right, or to bring the war to a termination, but calculated merely to display the strength of either side are totally repugnant to the duties of a Christian and to the principles of humanity. So that it behoves Christian princes to prohibit all unnecessary effusion of blood, as they must render an account of their sovereign commission to him, by whose authority, and in whose stead, they bear the sword.

William M. Evan

War Crimes

When government leaders decide to go to war, their military establishments devote considerable effort to training and indoctrinating their troops (Janowitz, 1971, 1972; Barber 1972). Training either conscripts or volunteers in the arts of warfare, in the use of weapons—especially state-of-the-art weapons—is not enough. They also need indoctrination in why they are fighting their enemy and in hating their enemy, so they will be psychologically prepared to kill and risk being killed (Hovland *et al.,* 1949:21–50). The net effect of the deliberate and systematic socialization process, developed by the armed forces of all countries, is to dehumanize the enemy.

Another general feature of all wars is that, regardless of the level of planning and preparedness, warfare involves a measure of uncertainty and unpredictability—otherwise referred to as the "fog of war." Regardless of how tight the chain of command is in a given army, navy or airforce, military commanders are incapable of always maintaining complete control at all times of their troops in combat. Victory on the battlefield—and possibly even defeat—creates opportunities for exploiting the vanquished and subjugated population, thereby paving the way for the commission of a variety of war crimes. Thus, in virtually all wars the phenomenon of war crimes occurs.

Laws and Customs of War

The very concept of war crimes presupposes that a set of rules governing warfare has been violated. This is indeed paradoxical: notwithstanding the readiness to engage in a manifestly inhuman activity of killing one's enemies, there is a perceived need to limit the nature and scope of the havoc inflicted on one's enemy. This need arises not out of altruism but because of the awareness of the potential destructive consequences of war for all warring parties. As a consequence, "laws and customs of war" have emerged over the centuries in various countries. Unwritten rules, or customs, governing warfare were developed as a means of maintaining strict control and discipline over troops and to keep up morale. Such customs were also especially necessary when an army was "deep in enemy territory in order to avoid antagonizing . . . the local population" (Röing, 1975:140).

In ancient China, there were various customs governing war, for example, the prohibition against waging war during planting and harvesting seasons. Writing in the fourth century B.C., Sun Tzu, author of the classic *The Art of War,* states that it is forbidden to injure a previously wounded enemy or to strike elderly men:

> Treat the captives well, and care for them. All the soldiers taken must be cared for with magnanimity and sincerity so that they may be used by us (Quoted in Friedman, 1972:3).

In ancient Rome, customs of war were articulated by government officials. Thus Cicero declared that "some duties are to be observed even toward those from whom you have received an injury. For even vengeance and punishment have their due bounds" (Grotius, 1901:359). And Tacitus "describes his countrymen as a people no less remarkable for their courage in the field, than for their humanity to the vanquished and suppliant" (Grotius, 1901:361).

During the middle ages, there were elaborate rituals and rules governing combat between knights. But as soon as other categories of combatants appeared—e.g., burghers and farmers who did not feel bound by the rules of the age of chivalry—they proceeded to violate the laws and customs of war. A dramatic example of this occurred in the "battle of the golden spurs" on July 11, 1302:

> Local farmers defeated the knights by taking the easy measure of killing or wounding their horses. This way of fighting although extremely effective was, in fact, a violation of the laws of war at that time. (Röling, 1975:140).

Other laws of war during the medieval period were influenced by Christianity. For example, at the Lateran Council in 1215, the use of the crossbow was prohibited between Christian knights engaged in battle; it was, however, permissible against Turks. The penalty for using the crossbow against Christians was excommunication.

In 1474, 27 judges of the Holy Roman Empire tried and convicted Peter von Hagenbach in Breisach, Germany for violating the "laws of God and man" by allowing his troops to rape and kill innocent civilians and pillage their property (Bassiouni, 1991:1).

By far the most significant turning point in the development of laws and customs of war was the pioneering work of Hugo Grotius *The Rights of War and Peace.* First published in 1625, it deals systematically with the rules of warfare from the perspective of natural law. As the father of modern international law, Grotius sought to develop a set of principles governing war and peace. In a chapter entitled "The Right of Killing Enemies, in Just War, to be Tempered with Moderation and Humanity," Grotius distinguishes between combatants and noncombatants. He then proceeds to exempt from the "calamities of war" all those who do not bear arms, e.g., children, women, ministers of religion, and those "who devote their lives to the pursuit of letters and other studies beneficial to mankind." In addition, he is willing to exempt those employed in "tilling the ground," merchants and artists (Grotius, 1901:361–363).

Another significant principle Grotius only alludes to is the protection of prisoners of war: "More civilized manners . . . abolished the barbarous practice of putting prisoners to death" (Grotius, 1901:363). This principle was virtually codified during the Civil War when President Lincoln issued General Order 100 providing for the humane treatment of prisoners of war. This order, having been written by Doctor Francis Lieber, eventually became known as the Lieber Code (U.S. Department of the Army, 1985:4). These rules were subsequently expanded and incorporated in other bodies of law, national and international in the nineteenth and twentieth centuries.

The internationalization of the laws and customs of war was significantly advanced with the Declaration of St. Petersburg in 1868. This declaration prohibited the employment of "any projectile of a weight below 400 grams, which is either explosive or charged with fulminating or inflammable substances . . ." on the ground that it is "contrary to the laws of humanity" (Falk, Kolko and Lifton, 1971:32).

The next major development occurred with the promulgation of the Hague Convention in 1907, which sought to codify national practices and customary international laws. Among the salient provisions are that:

- prisoners of war must be "humanely treated;"
- belligerents may not use poison or poisoned weapons nor weapons that cause "unnecessary suffering;"
- undefended towns, villages, dwellings or buildings may not be attacked;
- buildings dedicated to religion, art, science or historic monuments and hospitals must be spared "as far as possible" in sieges and bombardments (Falk, Kolko and Lifton, 1971:36–40).

During World War I, many violations of the laws and customs of war—including the Hague Conventions—occurred. Efforts to prosecute Kaiser Wilhelm II for war crimes, in accordance with the Versailles Peace Treaty of 1919, failed because the Netherlands, which granted him political asylum, refused to extradite him (Bassiouni, vol. III, 1986:26). During World War II, war crimes were committed on an unprecedented scale, so much so that the victorious Allied Powers decided to prosecute the principal surviving political and military leaders of Germany at the Nuremberg trials and the principal military and political leaders of Japan at the Tokyo war crimes trials.

The Nuremberg principles of 1946, summarizing the decisions of the Nuremberg trials, constitute a major advance in international law. Three of the seven principles are as follows:

Principle I

Any person who commits an act which constitutes a crime under international law is responsible therefor and liable to punishment.

Principle III

The fact that a person who committed an act which constitutes a crime under international law acted as Head of State or responsible government official does not relieve him from responsibility under international law.

Principle IV

The fact that a person acted pursuant to order of his Government or of a superior does not relieve him from responsibility under international law, provided a moral choice was in fact possible to him (Falk, Kolko and Lifton, 1971:107).

In addition, in Principle VI, three types of war crimes, under international law, were defined:

a. Crimes against peace:
   (i) Planning, preparation, initiation or waging of a war of aggression or a war in violation of international treaties, agreements or assurances;

   (ii) Participation in a common plan or conspiracy for the accomplishment of any of the acts mentioned under (i).

b. War crimes
   Violation of the laws or customs of war which include, but are not limited to, murder, ill-treatment or deportation to slave labour or for any other purpose of civilian population of or in occupied territory, murder or ill-treatment of prisoners of war or persons on the seas, killing of hostages, plunder of public or private property, wanton destruction of cities, towns, or villages, or devastation not justified by military necessity.

c. Crimes against humanity
   Murder, extermination, enslavement, deportation and other inhuman acts done against any civilian population, or persecutions on political, radical or religious grounds, when such acts are done or such persecutions are carried on in execution of or in connection with any crimes against peace or any war crime (Falk, Kolko and Lifton, 1971:108).

In 1949, a diplomatic conference was convened in Geneva for the purpose of updating and supplementing the Hague Conventions. The four conventions comprising the Geneva Conventions of 1949 deal with the following provisions: 1) wounded and sick in armed forces in the field; 2) sick and shipwrecked members of armed forces at sea; 3) treatment of prisoners of war; and 4) protection of civilians in time of war (International Committee of the Red Cross, 1949:4).

Selected Cases of War Crimes

To illustrate the range and incidence of war crimes, I shall now review selected cases that arose in four wars: World War II, Vietnam War, Persian Gulf War and the War during in Bosnia and Herzegovina. Table 46.1 summarizes the types of war crimes committed and the corresponding laws violated.

World War II

With the invasion of Poland on September 1, 1939, Nazi Germany unleashed World War II. In accordance with the Nazi plan, a "total war" was waged against enemy armies, prisoners of war, and, in occupied territories, against civilian populations in total disregard of virtually all laws and customs of war. In the Nuremberg trial, the

Selected War Crimes Committed in Four Wars

War	War Crimes	International Laws Violated
World War II —Germany	Planning and waging a war of aggression	Crimes against peace Nuremberg Principles[1]
	Deportation to slave labor camps; deportation to extermination camps	War crimes Nuremberg Principles[1]
	Extermination and enslavement	Crimes against humanity Nuremberg Principles[1]
—Japan	Planning and waging a war of aggression	Crimes against peace Nuremberg Principles[2]
	Deportation to slave labor camps; killing prisoners of war	War crimes Nuremberg Principles[2]
Vietnam War	My Lai Massacre	Geneva Convention, 1949 Nuremberg Principles[1]
Persian Gulf War —Iraq	Planning and waging a war against Kuwait	Crimes against peace Nuremberg Principles[1] U.N. Charter Article 39[3]
	Iraqi plunder and pillage of Kuwait; rape of Kuwaiti women; Scud missile attacks on Israeli civilians	War crimes Nuremberg Principles[1] Geneva Conventions, 1949[4]
	Deportation of Kuwaitis; inhumane treatment of Kuwaiti civilians	Crimes against humanity Nuremberg Principles[1]
Bosnian War —Serbia and Bosnian Serbs	Waging a war of aggression	Crimes against peace Nuremberg Principles[1] U.N. Charter Article 39[3]
	Deliberate attacks on non-combatants, hospitals and ambulances	War crimes Nuremberg Principles[1]
	Inhumane treatment of prisoners of war, deportation of civilians, abuse of civilians in detention camps, systematic raping of Muslim women	Geneva Convention, 1949[4]
	Inhumane acts against civilians	Crimes against humanity Nuremberg Principles[1]

[1]International Military Tribunal, *Trial of the Major War Criminals Before the International Military Tribunal, Nuremberg, 14 November 1945–1 October 1946, vol. 22,* Nuremberg, Germany, 1948.

[2]B. V. A. Rölling and C. F. Ruter, eds. *The Tokyo Judgement: The International Military Tribunal for the Far East 29 April 1949–12 November 1948.* University Press Amsterdam, 1977.

[3]Department of Public Information, United Nations, New York. "Charter of United Nations," *Yearbook of the United Nations 1987.* London: Martinus Nijhoff Publishers, 1992, pp. 1321–1324.

[4]International Committee of the Red Cross. "Geneva Convention Relative to the Treatment of Prisoners of War of August 12, 1949; Geneva Convention Relative to the Protection of Civilian Persons in Time of War of August 12, 1949." *The Geneva Convention of August 12 1949.* Geneva: International Committee of the Red Cross, 1949. 77–154, pp. 155–224.

indictment charged the defendants with the following war crimes:

> (a) "murder and ill-treatment of civilian populations of or in occupied territory and on the high seas; (b) deportation for slave labor and for other purposes of the civilian populations of and in occupied territories; (c) murder and ill-treatment of prisoners of war, and of other members of the armed forces of the countries with whom Germany was at war, and of persons on the high seas; (d) killing of hostages; (e) plunder of public and private property; (f) the exaction of collective penalties; (g) wanton destruction of cities, towns and villages and devastation not justified by military necessity; (h) conscription of civilian labor; (i) forcing civilians of occupied territories to swear allegiance to a hostile power;" and (j) "germanization of occupied territories." . . . About 1,500,000 persons were exterminated in Maidenek and about 4,000,000 persons exterminated in Auschwitz, among whom were citizens were gathered of Poland, the U.S.S.R, the United States of America, Great Britain, Czechoslovakia, France, and other countries. . . . Beginning with June 1943, the Germans carried out measures to hide the evidence of their crimes. They exhumed and burned corpses, and they crushed the bones with machines and used them for fertilizer. . . . In the Crimea peaceful citizens were gathered on barges, taken out to sea and drowned, over 144,000 persons being exterminated in this manner (Weston, Falk and D'Amato, 1980:33–34).

In the judgement rendered by the International Military Tribunal, the defendants were indeed found guilty of war crimes:

> The evidence relating to war crimes has been overwhelming in its volume and its detail. It is impossible for this Judgement adequately to review it or to record the mass of documentary and oral evidence that has been presented. The truth remains that war crimes were committed on a vast scale, never before seen in the history of war. They were perpetrated in all the countries occupied by Germany, and on the high seas, and were attended by every conceivable circumstance of cruelty and horror (International Military Tribunal, Trial of the Major War Criminals, 30 September 1946, 469).

The Nazi atrocities of the Holocaust prompted the United Nations to promulgate in 1948 a Convention on the Prevention and Punishment of the Crime of Genocide.

Vietnam War

Of all the war crimes committed during the Vietnam War, the case of Lieutenant William F. Calley, associated with the My Lai massacre on March 16, 1968, is best known (Bilton and Sim, 1992). In a court-martial proceeding in 1972, Lt. Calley was charged with premeditated murder of two separate groups of villagers:

> Private First Class Meadlo was guarding a group of between 30 and 40 unarmed old men, women and children at the trail location. Calley approached Meadlo and told him, "You know what to do," and left. Meadlo continued to stand guard over the villagers. Calley returned and yelled at Meadlo, "Why haven't you wasted them yet?" Meadlo replied that he thought Calley had meant merely to watch the villagers. Calley replied, "No, I mean kill them." First Calley and then Meadlo opened fire on the group, until all but a few children fell. Calley then personally shot the remaining children. . . .
>
> After the killings along the trail at the southern edge of My Lai (4), Calley proceeded to the eastern portion of the hamlet. There along an irrigation ditch, another and larger group of villagers was being held by soldiers. Meadlo estimated the group contained from 75 to 100 persons, consisting of old men, women and children. Calley then ordered Meadlo stating: "We got another job to do, Meadlo." The platoon members with their weapons then began pushing these people into a ditch. They were yelling and crying as they knelt and squatted in the ditch. Calley ordered the start of firing into the people and he with Meadlo and others joined in the killing (Weston, Falk and D'Amato, 1980:196).

For these atrocities, Calley was convicted of the premeditated murder of 22 infants, children, women and old men on March 29, 1971 and given a life sentence. In August 1971, his life sentence was reduced to 20 years. In May 1974, following, a review by the Secretary of the Army and President Nixon, his sentence was further reduced to 10 years. And in April 1976, following a series of habeas corpus proceedings, the United States Army decided to release him. If Calley had been tried in an international tribunal, rather than in a U.S. court-martial, as was the case of the Nazi war criminals, it is unlikely that his punishment would have been so radically abbreviated.

Persian Gulf War

By invading Kuwait on August 2, 1990, Iraq committed an act of aggression and violated U.N. Charter Article 39. In Resolution 660, the Security Council condemned the Iraqi invasion and demanded it withdraw immediately and unconditionally all its forces (Sifry and Cerf, 1991:148). By planning, preparing and prosecuting an aggressive war, Iraq violated the Nuremberg Principle of crimes against peace.

During its occupation of Kuwait, Iraqi forces committed a host of war crimes: torture and murder of civilians, rape of Iraqi women, setting on fire of Kuwait's oil wells and deliberate spilling of oil into the Persian Gulf. In Resolutions 670 and 674, the Security Council explicitly condemned some of these war crimes, e.g., the forced departure of Kuwaitis, the relocation of population in Kuwait and the unlawful destruction and seizure of public and private property in Kuwait, including hospital supplies and equipment.

Amnesty International, in a report issued December 19, 1990, documented Iraqi abuses of human rights and war crimes:

> . . . widespread destruction and looting of public and private property was carried out. Most critical of these has been the looting of medicines, medical equipment and food supplies. The massive scale of destruction and looting which has been reported suggest that such incidents were neither arbitrary nor isolated, but rather reflected a policy adopted by the government of Iraq (Amnesty International Report, 1990).

On August 23, 1990, Amnesty International expressed its concerns to the Iraqi government about "a wide range of human rights violations, including arbitrary arrests, rape, summary executions and extrajudicial killings."

In its repeated Scud missile attacks on Israeli population centers, the Iraqi government also committed a war crime in violation of the Fourth Geneva Convention.

Bosnian War

The war in the former Yugoslavia that began with Serbia's attack on Croatia and Slovenia in 1991 and then spread to Bosnia and Herzegovina in April 1992, is unquestionably the most brutal war since World War II. The major warring partners, Serbs, Croates and Bosnian Muslims have all committed war crimes, although the principal offenders have been the Serbs.

By initiating its war against Croatia and Slovenia, Serbia was guilty of crimes against peace. In prosecuting the war in Bosnia, Bosnian Serbs, with the assistance of Serbia, have committed a great range of war crimes and crimes against humanity. Large scale forcible expulsion of Bosnian Muslims and deliberate killing of Muslim civilians—referred to as "ethnic cleansing"—have taken on a genocidal proportion in violation of the Convention on Genocide.

In a U.S. Department of State report to the Security Council, details of war crimes against Bosnian civilians, in violation of the Geneva Conventions are documented: willful killing, abuses of civilians in detention centers, deliberate attacks on non-combatants, wanton devastation and destruction of property, mass forcible expulsion and deportation of civilians and torture of prisoners of war (U.S. Department of State Dispatch, 1992). News reports of systematic raping of Muslim women and teen-age girls have been reported (Burns, 1992; Kinzer, 1995).

Sarajevo, the capital of Bosnia, has been under siege for over three years, during which time Serbian forces have relentlessly bombarded all areas, including residential dwellings, schools and hospitals. In flagrant violation of Hague and Geneva Conventions, Bosnian Serbs have systematically targeted the civilian population of Sarajevo.

The enormity of the barbarous war crimes committed in Bosnia prompted the Security Council in Resolution 780, in October 1992, to establish a United Nations committee to assemble evidence of war crimes in Bosnia on the basis of which an ad hoc war-crimes tribunal would be established to prosecute alleged war criminals. On May 26, 1993, the Security Council, in Resolution 827, established a U.N. Tribunal for Former Yugoslavia, consisting of a prosecutor and 11 judges. This tribunal held its inaugural session on November 17, 1993: "Massacres, death camps and much publicized atrocities will be remembered as milestones of this Balkan conflict, especially with prolonged and controversial war-crimes trials in prospect . . . " (O'Ballance, 1995:245).

Conclusion: Need for an International Criminal Court

If we start with the truism that no one nation or even two or more nations, even if they be superpowers, are capable of acting as world policemen to prevent the outbreak of wars and the commission of war crimes, it follows that a new global institution is required. Since World War II, the United Nations and its allied organs, notwithstanding their structural defects, have contributed significantly to the maintenance of world peace. One of the new global institutions, the International Court of Justice (ICJ), has fallen far short of expectations. Although the ICJ has the authority, according to its statute, to adjudicate disputes between nations, its docket has been very sparse because of the reluctance of nation-states to submit their disputes. And because ICJ's jurisdiction is confined to international conflicts, war crimes committed by government leaders and individual citizens do not fall within its purview. International lawyers have, therefore, long recognized the need for a new tribunal with a jurisdiction over war crimes and violations of international criminal law and human rights laws. Owing to the limited jurisdiction of ICJ, the only forum for adjudication of war crimes is in national courts and ad hoc international tribunals. Neither of these fora is satisfactory; national bias is likely to intrude in any national trial on war crimes; and international politics is likely to intervene in an ad hoc international war crimes tribunal.

To try Saddam Hussein and other leaders in Iraq as well as individual citizens accused of war crimes in the various Yugoslav wars waged since the spring of 1991, there is a need to establish an International Criminal Court. Fortunately, the International Law Commission of the United Nations has already recommended to the Sixth Committee of the U.N. General Assembly the establishment of an International Criminal Court. Based upon this recommendation, the General Assembly in 1992 authorized the International Law Commission to prepare a Draft Statute for an International Criminal Court. Its work will be greatly expedited thanks to the extensive and thorough scholarly groundwork of M. Cherif Bassiouni and his colleagues over many years (Bassiouni, 1986; 1992; Mueller, 1987).

The creation of such a new institution can have a potentially significant impact in deterring government leaders and members of armed forces from committing war crimes. Better still, if the United Nations succeeds in the twenty-first century in achieving its mission mandated by its Charter of maintaining world peace, it will thereby eliminate the preconditions of war crimes.

References

Amnesty International Report. "Iraq's Occupation of Kuwait," December 19, in Micha L. Sifry and Christopher Cerf, eds., *The Gulf War Reader* (New York: Times Books, 1990).

Barber, James Alden, Jr. "The Social Effects of Military Service" in Stephen E. Ambrose and James Alden Barber, eds., *The Military and American Society* (New York: The Free Press, 1972).

Bassiouni, M. Cherif, ed. *International Criminal Law*, Vols. 1–3. (1986). Dobbs Ferry, (New York: Oceana Publication, 1986).

"The Time has Come for an International Criminal Court." *Indiana International and Comparative Law Review*, Vol. 1:1–43, (1991).

Bilton, Michael and Kevin Sim. *Four Hours in My Lai* (New York: Viking, 1992).

Burns, John F. "150 Muslims say Serbs Raped them in Bosnia." *The New York Times,* October 5, 1992: page 5A.

Falk, Richard A., Gabriel Kolko and Robert Jay Lifton., eds. *Crimes of War* (New York: Vintage Books, A Division of Random House, 1971).

Friedman, Leon. *The Law of War: A Documentary History* (New York: Random House, 1971).

Grotius, Hugo. *The Rights of War and Peace* (New York: M. Walter Dunne, 1901).

Hovland, Carl, Arthur Lumsdaine and Fred Shefield. *Experiments on Mass Communication,* Vol. 3, Sameul A. Stouffer *et al. The American Soldier* (Princeton, NJ: Princeton University Press, 1949).

International Committee of the Red Cross. *The Geneva Conventions of August 12, 1949* (Geneva: International Committee of the Red Cross, 1949).

International Military Tribunal. *Trial of the Major War Criminals Before the International Military Tribunal. Nuremberg. 14 November 1945–1 October 1946,* (1948). Nuremberg, Germany.

Janowitz, Morris. "Basic Education and Youth Socialization in the Armed Forces," in Roger W. Little, ed., *Handbook of Military Institutions* (Beverly Hills CA: Sage Publications 1971).

"Characteristics of the Military Environment," in Stephen E. Ambrose and James Alden Barber, eds., *The Military and American Society* (New York: The Free Press, 1972).

Kinzer, Stephen. "Bosnian Refugees' Accounts Appear to Verify Atrocities" *New York Times,* July 17, 1995.

Mueller, Gerhard O. W. "Four Decades After Nuremberg: The Prospect of an International Criminal Code," *Connectincutt Journal of International Law,* Vol. 2: 499–507, (1987).

O'Balance, Edger. *Civil War to Bosnia 1992–94* (New York: St. Martins Press, 1995).

Rölling, Bert V. A. "The Significance of the Laws of War," in Antonio Cassese, ed., *Current Problems of International Law* (Milano: A. Giuffre Editore Books, 1975).

Sifry, Micah, L. and Christopher Cerf, eds. *The Gulf War Reader: History, Documents, Opinions* (New York: Times Books, 1991).

U.S. Department of the Army. *Instructors Guide: The Law of War Training,* Circular No. 27-10-3, (1985).

U.S. Department of State. "War Crimes in the Former Yugoslavia," *U.S. Department of State Dispatch,* September 28, Vol. 3, No. 30, (1992).

Weston, Burns H., Richard A. Falk and Anthony A. D'Amata. *International Law and World Order* (St. Paul, Minn.: West Publishing Co., 1980).

Legality of the Threat or Use of Nuclear Weapons (Abstract)

8 July 1996

Jurisdiction of the Court to give the advisory opinion requested—Article 65, paragraph 1, of the Statute—Body authorized to request an opinion—Article 96, paragraphs 1 and 2, of the Charter—Activities of the General Assembly—"Legal question"—Political aspects of the question posed—Motives said to have inspired the request and political implications that the opinion might have.

Discretion of the Court as to whether or not it will give an opinion—Article 65, paragraph 1, of the Statute—Compelling reasons—Vague and abstract question—Purposes for which the opinion is sought—Possible effects of the opinion on current negotiations—Duty of the Court not to legislate.

Formulation of the question posed—English and French texts—Clear objective—Burden of proof.

Applicable law—International Covenant on Civil and Political Rights—Arbitrary deprivation of life—Convention on the Prevention and Punishment of the Crime of Genocide—Intent against a group as such—Existing norms relating to the safeguarding and protection of the environment—Environmental considerations as an element to be taken into account in the implementation of the law applicable in armed conflict—Application of most directly relevant law: law of the Charter and law applicable in armed conflict.

Unique characteristics of nuclear weapons.

Provisions of the Charter relating to the threat or use of force—Article 2, paragraph 4—

The Charter neither expressly prohibits, nor permits, the use of any specific weapon—Article 51—Conditions of necessity and proportionality—The notions of "threat" and "use" of force stand together—Possession of nuclear weapons, deterrence and threat.

Specific rules regulating the lawfulness or unlawfulness of the recourse to nuclear weapons as such—Absence of specific prescription authorizing the threat or use of nuclear weapons—Unlawfulness *per se:* treaty law—Instruments prohibiting the use of poisoned weapons—Instruments expressly prohibiting the use of certain weapons of mass destruction—Treaties concluded in order to limit the acquisition, manufacture and possession of nuclear weapons, the deployment and testing of nuclear weapons—Treaty of Tlatelolco—Treaty of Rarotonga—Declarations made by nuclear-weapon States on the occasion of the extension of the Non-Proliferation Treaty—Absence of comprehensive and universal conventional prohibition of the use or the threat of use of nuclear weapons as such—Unlawfulness *per se:* customary law—Consistent practice of non-utilization of nuclear weapons—Policy of deterrence—General Assembly resolutions affirming the illegality of nuclear weapons—Continuing tensions between the nascent *opinio juris* and the still strong adherence to the practice of deterrence.

Principles and rules of international humanitarian law—Prohibition of methods and means of warfare precluding any distinction between civilian and military targets or resulting in unnecessary

295

suffering to combatants—Martens Clause—Principle of neutrality—Applicability of these principles and rules to nuclear weapons—Conclusions.

Right of a State to survival and right to resort to self-defence—Policy of deterrence—Reservations to undertakings given by certain nuclear-weapon States not to resort to such weapons.

Current state of international law and elements of fact available to the Court—Use of nuclear weapons in an extreme circumstance of self-defence in which the very survival of a State is at stake.

Article VI of the Non-Proliferation Treaty—Obligation to negotiate in good faith and to achieve nuclear disarmament in all its aspects.

Advisory Opinion

Present: President BEDJAOUI; *Vice-President* SCHWEBEL; *Judges* ODA, GUILLAUME, SHAHABUDDEEN, WEERAMANTRY, RANJEVA, HERCZEGH, SHI, FLEISCHHAUER, KOROMA, VERESHCHETIN, FERRARI BRAVO, HIGGINS; *Registrar* VALENCIA-OSPINA.

On the legality of the threat or use of nuclear weapons,

THE COURT,

composed as above,

gives the following Advisory Opinion:

1. The question upon which the advisory opinion of the Court has been requested is set forth in resolution 49/75 K adopted by the General Assembly of the United Nations (hereinafter called the "General Assembly") on 15 December 1994. By a letter dated 19 December 1994, received in the Registry by facsimile on 20 December 1994 and filed in the original on 6 January 1995, the Secretary-General of the United Nations officially communicated to the Registrar the decision taken by the General Assembly to submit the question to the Court for an advisory opinion. Resolution 49/75 K, the English text of which was enclosed with the letter, reads as follows:

"*The General Assembly,*

Conscious that the continuing existence and development of nuclear weapons pose serious risks to humanity,

Mindful that States have an obligation under the Charter of the United Nations to refrain from the threat or use of force against the territorial integrity or political independence of any State,

Recalling its resolutions 1653 (XVI) of 24 November 1961, 33/71 B of 14 December 1978, 34/83 G of 11 December 1979, 35/152 D of 12 December 1980, 36/92 1 of 9 December 1981, 45/59 B of 4 December 1990 and 46/37 D of 6 December 1991, in which it declared that the use of nuclear weapons would be a violation of the Charter and a crime against humanity,

Welcoming the progress made on the prohibition and elimination of weapons of mass destruction, including the Convention on the Prohibition of the Development, Production and Stockpiling of Bacteriological (Biological) and Toxin Weapons and on Their Destruction[1] and the Convention on the Prohibition of the Development, Production, Stockpiling and Use of Chemical Weapons and on Their Destruction[2],

Convinced that the complete elimination of nuclear weapons is the only guarantee against the threat of nuclear war,

Noting the concerns expressed in the Fourth Review Conference of the Parties to the Treaty on the Non-Proliferation of Nuclear Weapons that insufficient progress had been made towards the complete elimination of nuclear weapons at the earliest possible time,

Recalling that, convinced of the need to strengthen the rule of law in international relations, it has declared the period 1990–1999 the United Nations Decade of International Law[3],

Noting that Article 96, paragraph 1, of the Charter empowers the General Assembly to request the International Court of Justice to give an advisory opinion on any legal question,

Recalling the recommendation of the Secretary-General, made in his report entitled 'An Agenda for Peace'[4], that United Nations organs that are authorized to take advantage of the advisory competence of the International

Court of Justice turn to the Court more frequently for such opinions,

Welcoming resolution 46/40 of 14 May 1993 of the Assembly of the World Health Organization, in which the organization requested the International Court of Justice to give an advisory opinion on whether the use of nuclear weapons by a State in war or other armed conflict would be a breach of its obligations under international law, including the Constitution of the World Health Organization,

Decides, pursuant to Article 96, paragraph 1, of the Charter of the United Nations, to request the International Court of Justice urgently to render its advisory opinion on the following question: 'Is the threat or use of nuclear weapons in any circumstance permitted under international law?' "

2. Pursuant to Article 65, paragraph 2, of the Statute, the Secretary-General of the United Nations communicated to the Court a dossier of documents likely to throw light upon the question.

3. By letters dated 21 December 1994, the Registrar, pursuant to Article 66, paragraph 1, of the Statute, gave notice of the request for an advisory opinion to all States entitled to appear before the Court.

4. By an Order dated 1 February 1995 the Court decided that the States entitled to appear before it and the United Nations were likely to be able to furnish information on the question, in accordance with Article 66, paragraph 2, of the Statute. By the same Order, the Court fixed, respectively, 20 June 1995 as the time-limit within which written statements might be submitted to it on the question, and 20 September 1995 as the time-limit within which States and organizations having presented written statements might submit written comments on the other written statements in accordance with Article 66, paragraph 4, of the Statute. In the aforesaid Order, it was stated in particular that the General Assembly had requested that the advisory opinion of the Court be rendered "urgently"; reference was also made to the procedural time-limits already fixed for the request for an advisory opinion previously

submitted to the Court by the World Health Organization on the question of the *Legality of the use by a State of nuclear weapons in armed conflict.*

On 8 February 1995, the Registrar addressed to the States entitled to appear before the Court and to the United Nations the special and direct communication provided for in Article 66, paragraph 2, of the Statute.

5. Written statements were filed by the following States: Bosnia and Herzegovina, Burundi, Democratic People's Republic of Korea, Ecuador, Egypt, Finland, France, Germany, India, Ireland, Islamic Republic of Iran, Italy, Japan, Lesotho, Malaysia, Marshall Islands, Mexico, Nauru, Netherlands, New Zealand, Qatar, Russian Federation, Samoa, San Marino, Solomon Islands, Sweden, United Kingdom of Great Britain and Northern Ireland, and United States of America. In addition, written comments on those written statements were submitted by the following States: Egypt, Nauru and Solomon Islands. Upon receipt of those statements and comments, the Registrar communicated the text to all States having taken part in the written proceedings.

6. The Court decided to hold public sittings, opening on 30 October 1995, at which oral statements might be submitted to the Court by any State or organization which had been considered likely to be able to furnish information on the question before the Court. By letters dated 23 June 1995, the Registrar requested the States entitled to appear before the Court and the United Nations to inform him whether they intended to take part in the oral proceedings; it was indicated, in those letters, that the Court had decided to hear, during the same public sittings, oral statements relating to the request for an advisory opinion from the General Assembly as well as oral statements concerning the above-mentioned request for an advisory opinion laid before the Court by the World Health Organization, on the understanding that the United Nations would be entitled to speak only in regard to the request submitted by the General Assembly, and it was further specified therein that the participants in the oral proceedings which had not taken part in the written proceedings would receive the text of the statements and comments produced in the course of the latter. . . .

103. In its resolution 984 (1995) dated 11 April 1995, the Security Council took care to reaffirm "the need for all States Parties to the Treaty on the Non-Proliferation of Nuclear Weapons to comply fully with all their obligations" and urged

> "all States, as provided. for in Article VI of the Treaty on the Non-Proliferation of Nuclear Weapons, to pursue negotiations in good faith on effective measures relating to nuclear disarmament and on a treaty on general and complete disarmament under strict and effective international control which remains a universal goal".

The importance of fulfilling the obligation expressed in Article VI of the Treaty on the Non-Proliferation of Nuclear Weapons was also reaffirmed in the final document of the Review and Extension Conference of the parties to the Treaty on the Non-Proliferation of Nuclear Weapons, held from 17 April to 12 May 1995.

In the view of the Court, it remains without any doubt an objective of vital importance to the whole of the international community today.

104. At the end of the present Opinion, the Court emphasizes that its reply to the question put to it by the General Assembly rests on the totality of the legal grounds set forth by the Court above (paragraphs 20 to 103), each of which is to be read in the light of the others. Some of these grounds are not such as to form the object of formal conclusions in the final paragraph of the Opinion; they nevertheless retain, in the view of the Court, all their importance.

105. For these reasons,

THE COURT,

(1) By thirteen votes to one,

> *Decides* to comply with the request for an advisory opinion;

IN FAVOUR: *President* Bedjaoui; *Vice-President* Schwebel; *Judges* Guillaume, Shahabuddeen, Weeramantry, Ranjeva,

Herczegh, Shi, Fleischhauer, Koroma, Vereshchetin, Ferrari Bravo, Higgins;

AGAINST: *Judge* Oda.

(2) *Replies* in the following manner to the question put by the General Assembly:

A. Unanimously,

> There is in neither customary nor conventional international law any specific authorization of the threat or use of nuclear weapons;

B. By eleven votes to three,

> There is in neither customary nor conventional international law any comprehensive and universal prohibition of the threat or use of nuclear weapons as such;

IN FAVOUR: *President* Bedjaoui; *Vice-President* Schwebel; *Judges* Oda, Guillaume, Ranjeva, Herczegh, Shi, Fleischhauer, Vereshchetin, Ferrari Bravo, Higgins;

AGAINST: *Judges* Shahabuddeen, Weeramantry, Koroma.

C. Unanimously,

> A threat or use of force by means of nuclear weapons that is contrary to Article 2, paragraph 4, of the United Nations Charter and that fails to meet all the requirements of Article 51, is unlawful;

D. Unanimously,

> A threat or use of nuclear weapons should also be compatible with the requirements of the international law applicable in armed conflict, particularly those of the principles and rules of international humanitarian law, as well as with specific obligations under treaties and other undertakings which expressly deal with nuclear weapons;

E. By seven votes to seven, by the President's casting vote,

> It follows from the above-mentioned requirements that the threat or use of nuclear weapons would generally be con-

trary to the rules of international law applicable in armed conflict, and in particular the principles and rules of humanitarian law;

However, in view of the current state of international law, and of the elements of fact at its disposal, the Court cannot conclude definitively whether the threat or use of nuclear weapons would be lawful or unlawful in an extreme circumstance of self-defence, in which the very survival of a State would be at stake;

IN FAVOUR: *President* Bedjaoui; *Judges* Ranjeva, Herczegh, Shi, Fleischhauer, Vereshchetin, Ferrari Bravo;

AGAINST: *Vice-President* Schwebel; *Judges* Oda, Guillaume, Shahabuddeen, Weeramantry, Koroma, Higgins.

F. Unanimously,

There exists an obligation to pursue in good faith and bring to a conclusion negotiations leading to nuclear disarmament in all its aspects under strict and effective international control.

Done in English and in French, the English text being authoritative, at the Peace Palace, The Hague, this eighth day of July, one thousand nine hundred and ninety-six, in two copies, one of which will be placed in the archives of the Court and the other transmitted to the Secretary-General of the United Nations.

(Signed) Mohammed BEDJAOUI,
President.

(Signed) Eduardo VALENCIA-OSPINA,
Registrar.

President BEDJAOUI, Judges HERCZEGH, SHI, VERESHCHETIN and FERRARI BRAVO append declarations to the Advisory Opinion of the Court.

Judges GUILLAUME, RANJEVA and FLEISCHHAUER append separate opinions to the Advisory Opinion of the Court.

Vice-President SCHWEBEL, Judges ODA, SHAHABUDDEEN, WEERAMANTRY, KOROMA and HIGGINS append dissenting opinions to the Advisory Opinion of the Court.

(Initialled) M. B.
(Initialled) E. V. O.

Notes

1. Resolution 2826 (XXVI), Annex.

2. See *Official Records of the 47th Session of the General Assembly, Supplement No. 27* (A/47/27), Appendix I.

3. Resolution 44/23.

4. A/47/277-S/24111.

The Constitution of Japan
(Promulgated November 3, 1946)

Chapter II. Renunciation of War

Article 9.

1. Aspiring sincerely to international peace based on justice and order, the Japanese people forever renounce war as a sovereign right of the nation and the threat or use of force as means of settling international disputes.

2. In order to accomplish the aim of the preceding paragraph, land, sea, and air forces, as well as other war potential, will never be maintained. The right of belligerency of the state will not be recognized.

William M. Evan
Francis A. Boyle

Kashmir: Invoking International Law to Avoid Nuclear War

The military confrontation between India and Pakistan, two nuclear-armed neighbors, has the world in a state of jitters. With each country mobilizing its forces—together totaling about a million troops along their 1800 mile border—there is a high probability that the current face-off may lead to the outbreak of yet another war between these two countries. Although such a war—if it eventuates—is likely to involve a conventional exchange of weapons as happened in the 1947, 1965, and 1972 wars, there is reason to fear that it could escalate into a nuclear war. If such a catastrophe were to occur, American intelligence estimates that about 12 million people would be killed and 7 million would be injured.

What has been the response of the international community to this crisis? President Bush has urged President Musharraf of Pakistan and Prime Minister Vajpayee of India to exercise restraint and stop cross-border attacks. President Jacques Chirac, President Vladimir Putin and other European officials have echoed similar sentiments.

In the meantime, Mr. Vajpayee accuses Pakistan of waging a 20-year campaign of terrorism to dislodge India from the predominantly Muslim state of Kashmir. He also rejects Pakistan's repeated requests for dialogue or negotiation. And the U.N. Secretary-General Kofi Annan reiterates his requests to General Musharraf to crack down on Islamic militants penetrating the Line of Control separating the Pakistani sector of Kashmir from the Indian sector.

Forty-three years ago the U.N. put forth a potentially reasonable solution to the conflict by conducting a plebiscite on the status of Kashmir—whether it should remain part of India, or become part of Pakistan. These two options could be supplemented by (1) outright independence for Kashmir; or (2) shared sovereignty between India and Pakistan over Kashmir. Thus far India has dismissed the idea of holding such a plebiscite.

Clearly missing from all responses so far to the looming nuclear crisis is an argument for using international law to resolve the India–Pakistan conflict over Kashmir. This striking omission underscores, on the one hand, the widespread commitment to power politics and the use of war as a means of resolving international disputes and, on the other hand, a fundamental distrust of international law to resolve international conflicts.

As it happens, both India and Pakistan are parties to the 1899 Hague Convention for the Pacific Settlement of International Disputes. The United States is also a party to this 1899 Convention. Article 8 is the brainchild of the United States. It establishes a procedure for special mediation. The states in conflict would each choose a power to which they would respectively entrust the mission of entering into direct communication with the power chosen by the other side for the purpose of preventing the rupture of pacific relations. For the period of this mandate, which could not exceed thirty days, unless otherwise agreed, the states in conflict would cease all direct communication on the subject of the dispute, leaving it exclusively to the mediating powers. In case of a definite rupture of pacific relations, the mediating powers were charged with the joint task of taking advantage of any opportunity for peace.

The threat of nuclear war between India and Pakistan directly affects the vital national security interests of the United States: The nuclear fallout would poison America and its people as well as the peoples of other countries. So the U.S. government, joined by others, must formally and publicly invoke Hague Article 8 against both India and Pakistan, and demand the required 30-day cooling-off period so that this special mediation procedure could take place.

The U.S. government joined by others must also invoke the requirement of Article 33(1) of the United Nations Charter providing that the two parties to the dispute over Kashmir "shall first of all, seek a solution by negotiation, inquiry, mediation, conciliation, arbitration, judicial settlement, resort to regional agencies or arrangements, or other peaceful means of their own choice." U.N. Charter Article 33 expressly by name requires the pursuit of the "mediation" procedure set forth in Hague Article 8, including the mandatory 30-day cooling off period.

Time is of the essence when it comes to invoking Hague Article 8 and averting a nuclear war!

Questions for Discussion

1. What does Grotius identify as a negative versus a positive stratagem during a war?
2. How can military leaders be given incentives to comply with rules of warfare?
3. Do you think that increased media coverage of modern warfare can help reduce the incidents of war crimes?
4. How does a non-first-use policy correspond to international law on nuclear weapons?
5. Do you think there exists a fundamental distrust of the capability of international law to resolve international conflicts? If so, why?
6. What do you think was the motive behind the Japanese decision to include the war-renouncing provision in Article 9 of the Japanese Constitution?
7. Japan's constitution is unique in the history of the world. Is it feasible to transfer this kind of war-renouncing constitutional provision to any other country that does not enjoy the status of a militarily protected country?
8. Do you think the United States is capable of mediating a negotiation process between India and Pakistan while it sells arms to these countries because of the conflict over Kashmir?

Further Readings

1. Howard, Michael, Andreopoulos, George J., and Shulman, Mark R. *The Laws of War: Constraints on Warfare in the Western World*. New Haven, CT: Yale University Press, 1997.
2. Osiel, Mark J. *Obeying Orders: Atrocity, Military Discipline and the Law of War*. New Brunswick, NJ: Transaction, 2002.
3. Lador-Lederer, J. "A Legal Approach to International Terrorism." *Israel Law Review*, 1974, 9, 2, Apr., 194–220.
4. Buchanan, David. "Gendercide and Human Rights." *Journal of Genocide Research*, 2002, 4, 1, Mar., 95–108.
5. Aggarwal, Lalit K., and Evan, William M. "A Survey on Nuclear Weapons and International Law." *Peace and Change*, 1990, 15, 2, Apr., 195–204.
6. Vogler, Richard. "The Law as a Nuclear-Free Zone: Legality and the Peace Movement." *International Journal of the Sociology of Law*, 1984, 12, 2, May, 195–203.
7. Kauzlarich, David, and Kramer, Ronald C. "The Nuclear Terrorist State." *Peace Review*, 1995, 7, 3–4, Fall–Winter, 333–337.
8. Sugarman, Martin. "The Kashmir Tragedy: A Sociological Portrait of War and Human Rights Abuses." *Dissertation Abstracts International*, 2001, 61, 12, June, 4954-A.
9. Bahadur, Kalim. American Factor in Pakistani Politics. *Man and Development*, 1995, 17, 1, Mar., 176–189.
10. Ganguly, Sumit. "Wars without End: The Indo–Pakistani Conflict." *Annals of the American Academy of Political and Social Science*, 1995, 541, Sept., 167–178.

Minimal Moral Framework

The readings in this section set forth a unique strategy for the prevention of interstate warfare and violence, namely, to institutionalize positive values through the creation of a moral framework and an ethical perspective that restrains hostilities between nations.

In "A Strategy for Peace," Sissela Bok identifies four moral principles that may be used to devise a framework of moral constraints to limit a state's capacity for war. She explains how the principles of nonvio-

lence, veracity, fidelity and publicity may be employed to counter the phenomena responsible for the occurrence of wars, namely, violence, deceit, betrayal and excessive secrecy. The author explores ways in which such a framework may be applied. Bok acknowledges the problems of defining moral parameters with precision.

In "A Global Ethic in World Politics" Hans Küng explains the role of religion in the development of a global code of ethics which may be used to guide the direction of international politics. The author points out the similarities in the ethos preached by various religions of the world and argues that this is why religion could be used as a common ground for creating long-lasting peace by promoting a global culture. Such a culture would include the norms common to all religions. Küng suggests that in order to promote a culture of tolerance and peace, individuals need only adhere to four most basic values: respect for life, honesty, truthfulness and respect for others.

Sissela Bok

A Strategy for Peace

A Framework of Moral Constraints

I have drawn on Kant's essay "Perpetual Peace" and in turn on major moral, religious, and political traditions to propose a set of four moral constraints.[1]

They satisfy the prerequisites for an international morality that can give a strategy for peace the strongest, most focused impact. Of the four, two are the widely acknowledged curbs on violence and deceit and, through them, on the many forms of harm—such as torture and theft—that people can do by means of one or both. To cement agreement about how and to whom these two curbs apply, and to keep them from being ignored or violated at will, a third constraint—on breaches of valid promises, contracts, laws, and treaties—is needed.

Whether expressed in religious or in secular form, these three values are shared by every civilization, past and present. Any community, no matter how small or disorganized, no matter how hostile toward outsiders, no matter how cramped its perception of what constitutes, say, torture, has to impose at least *some* internal curbs on violence, deceit, and betrayal in order to survive.

But because persons acting clandestinely easily bypass or ignore the three constraints, a fourth one is necessary: on excessive secrecy. While its roots are not as ancient as those of the first three, and though it is not as common—least of all in police states, it is as fundamental to the preservation of democratic traditions as the first three are to the survival of communities more generally. It serves two functions: first, to limit practices of secrecy whenever they conceal or facilitate violence, deceit, and breaches of trust, as

was the case in the French assault on the *Rainbow Warrior;* and second, to offer as a test for morally acceptable actions or policies whether its sponsors can defend them publicly.[2]

The four constraints may be experienced to different degrees as personal inhibitions by individuals and expressed through custom and law in societies. International law attempts to codify and enforce them among nations. At all levels, the proportion of trust and distrust present in social relationships reflects the degree to which such constraints are seen as effective.

In considering the four constraints, some might object to the prerequisite suggested above that they should be few in number. Surely cultures require more than these four constraints, such critics might argue, and with good reason. After all, more is clearly needed among family members, friends, and fellow citizens. "Love thy neighbor" has counterparts in many religions, to go along with prohibitions such as those against lying and killing in the Ten Commandments. Thus Confucius spoke of the need for respect and benevolence; Micah enjoined men to observe "only this: to act justly, to love tenderly, and to walk humbly with your God"; and Kant insisted that human beings owe one another both love and respect.[3] Fraternity and support for the weakest and most vulnerable in a society is a related political ideal voiced in many communities. Why not, then, urge nations to abide not only by the four constraints but also by familiar and shared positive injunctions such as those calling for love, sympathy, and mutual benevolence? Surely they, too, serve to build or restore trust.

Certainly, a strategy that stresses the need to restore rather than to erode trust is incomplete so long as it emphasizes only the four constraints I have suggested. They are generally granted priority, however, in law as in morality. Even someone who is incapable of generosity or kindness toward others must refrain from assaulting them. These constraints are only a beginning; but they are indispensable for relationships not only between individuals but also between states.

In addition, the positive values are hard to institutionalize even within nations; between nations, apart from particular alliances and agreements, such values, however desirable, can never serve as requirements. Even if they did, disagreement would be rife as to just what response they might call for in specific cases. Thus, many nations offer support for the victims of earthquakes and famines abroad; but efforts to require such support on an equal basis from all countries would encounter great resistance. The four constraints are different in these respects. It is much clearer what actions they rule out. Most people recognize, at least in principle, that they owe it even to strangers not to injure them, not to lie to them, not to break promises to them, or try to harm them in such ways secretly. . . .

Not only are the four constraints indispensable separately; they must also be seen as linked. All talk of morality that focuses only on one value at the expense of others risks collapsing into moralizing of the most dangerous kind: the trampling on fundamental moral principles in the name of promoting some particular ideal or combating some particular evil. . . . The remedy lies in seeing the four basic moral constraints as *forming a framework* and as thereby both limiting and enhancing one another. In this framework, the constraint on betrayal buttresses those on violence and on deceit, while the limit on excessive secrecy prevents abuses of the first three.

With respect to this framework, another question may arise. Why not see the constraint on violence as foremost in the context of war and peace, with the other three shoring it up? What nations fear most is surely the violence of invasions, of bombardments and the laying waste of cities and countryside. I would agree that the goal of the framework of constraints is indeed to fore-

stall such violence in the first place. The constraint on violence clearly has the most direct bearing on that goal, but it is also needed, along with the other three, to rule out actions that erode trust and increase the threat of war—sabotage or assassination, say, or cheating on arms treaties. The four are then equally important. If you cannot trust a government's pledge or treaty of nonaggression, then you can have no trust that it will refrain from such aggression. . . .

In order to cut back the number of these conflicts, it is indispensable, first of all, to recognize exceptions to the moral constraints selected. They must be seen as strict without being unconditional. Yet how can one allow such a modification, an absolutist like Kant might ask, without compromising the very notion of a framework of moral constraints? Certain acts, even if carried out under duress, are such as to destroy a person's integrity and self-respect; once people allow for even a few exceptions to moral principles they can slip into every form of abuse and misjudgment, the more easily if their judgment is skewed by partisanship. As Kant pointed out, unless we take moral principles to be absolutely binding at all times, we are especially likely to make an exception just for ourselves and "just for this once."

These warnings should carry great weight for anyone who considers violating a moral constraint. But it would be self-defeating for a strategy aimed at reducing the chances of a nuclear catastrophe to insist on hewing to principle even at the cost of making just such a disaster more likely. Less than ever, in the nuclear era, can we afford to hold, with Kant, that one should "do what is right though the world might perish"—refuse to tell a lie, say, even to a band of nuclear terrorists in order to keep them from precipitating a global catastrophe. Kant buttressed his absolutist claim by relying on what he admitted was no more than a hope: that Providence would keep the world from perishing. Yet to gamble on being rescued by Providence in our present circumstances would be far too casual. It is noteworthy, in this respect, that the American Catholic bishops and other religious groups that have contributed so forcefully to the debate about

READING 50   A Strategy for Peace   307

war and peace in recent years have, to the best of my knowledge, consistently steered clear of such an assumption.

"Do what is right though the heavens should fall" still guides some, who regard such a maxim as divinely ordained and are willing to suffer the consequences for the sake of their faith. But they cannot demand that those who disagree with their religious beliefs should nevertheless accept their uncompromising maxim. It cannot serve as a universal precept in the nuclear era and would find few adherents among public officials responsible for choices involving life or death.

The desire for absolute certainty about every issue of right and wrong is tempting in theory but can never be satisfied in practice. Even those who grant no exceptions to certain prohibitions still have to draw lines with respect to what should count as falling within the prohibited category. If they rule out, say, all killing, do they mean to prohibit capital punishment and the killing of animals? Or are they speaking, rather, about the killing of innocent human beings? If so, how do they categorize noncombatants in war? And can they always be sure who is and who is not a noncombatant? Between nations, do they rule out even the killing that takes place in wars of strict self-defense? If not, how do they draw the line, among all the wars that states brazenly claim are strictly in self-defense, between those that are genuinely such and all the other ones? And regardless of how they come out on all these questions, how do they classify policies or acts that, while not directly taking lives, place large numbers of people at risk of near-certain death? Moderate risk? Indeterminate risk? In all such cases, line-drawing will still be needed, no matter how rigidly moral rules may be defined.

Similarly, problems of line-drawing come up for anyone who admits exceptions to moral constraints. It then becomes necessary to weigh marginally different cases and to ask how clear it is that a particular action qualifies as an exception, and on what grounds. If you have concluded, for example, that it is legitimate to lie to deflect a would-be assassin on the trail of an intended victim, what about those borderline cases in which

you are not sure of the pursuer's intention or of his capacity to carry it out? How do you demarcate the kinds of cases where you take lies to be justified from among the many marginally different cases where you are no longer sure?

Line-Drawing

The effort to perceive distinctions and to draw lines between different actions, plans, and characteristics lies at the core of practical choice, whether in legal, religious, or moral contexts. While an area of uncertainty or dispute about difficult cases will always remain, such an effort can reduce it considerably.[4]

To see how questions of line-drawing arise in practice, consider, once again, the French sabotage of the *Rainbow Warrior.* Those who sponsored this venture might agree that it is generally wrong to sink foreign vessels in peacetime and to take human lives in the process. But in this instance, the French officials might argue, the assault, was a clear case of self-defense. In their view, members of the Greenpeace organization threatened France's military preparedness by their insistence on observing its nuclear tests. The government had tried every legal means of stopping such observations, to no avail. And while the action presented serious risks to those on board the vessel, no violence toward any individual had been intended, given the warning blasts meant to frighten all on board into disembarking.

These arguments might well appear less persuasive to the officials who planned the sabotage if environmentalists were to take similar liberties with the property and the lives of French citizens. That question took on practical significance a year later, when Paul Watson, reportedly expelled from Greenpeace in 1977 and the leader of another environmental group, the Shepherds of the Sea, claimed responsibility for sinking two of Iceland's four whaling ships. He argued that his followers had used no explosives and been careful to avoid any loss of life. They had begun opening key valves in the ships only when they had ascertained that the entire crew had left each ship; and they claimed that such destruction of property did not constitute violence. Illegal acts, Mr. Watson is reported to have said, are justified to stop environmental abuse, as long as they defend and do not endanger living things: but "people tend to have more respect for private property than for the sanctity of life."

The Greenpeace organization, though its representatives have long urged an end to whale hunting, denounced such methods of aggression, whether to property or to life. We see, then, three different lines drawn to define what one can rightly do to those regarded as adversaries on a political issue: one line rejects all action meant to injure life or property; a second rejects posing direct risks to life but not destroying property; and a third allows placing lives at risk as well as destroying property. It is possible to envisage any number of additional cases incrementally more or less violent and/or destructive than the attack on the *Rainbow Warrior* . . .

Likewise, one can imagine different degrees of justification for the acts, ranging from self-defense in an imminent national emergency to sheer aggression for its own sake.

Line-drawing, in these cases as in many others, is both unavoidable and open to different forms of error and bias. States, like individuals, define themselves and the integrity they strive for in part through the lines that they draw in principle and the degree to which they honor these lines in practice.

That task is never entirely completed; new cases and new circumstances arise to test boundaries that once seemed clear. To take an analogy from medicine: up to this century, it was usually easy for doctors to state whether a person had died or was still alive. With the advent of modern technology allowing them to keep a patient's heart beating even though the brain may have ceased functioning, physicians and legislatures have had to draw new lines with respect to when death has arrived. . . .

How might policymakers best approach the task of establishing standards and making choices, given these difficulties? It helps to start out with a shared framework of moral constraints and to formulate clear-cut cases to which all

agree that the constraints apply; from such a basis, it is easier to explore remaining differences. For this purpose, one can envisage certain examples of clearly unjustifiable or, on the contrary, clearly justifiable instances of violence, deceit, breaches of faith, or secrecy, as benchmarks.

Terrorism, for instance, is clearly unjustifiable from the point of view of such a framework of constraints. One need not attempt to draw lines with respect to acts of threatening or engaging in violence against civilians, often randomly, so as to spread terror and thereby to further political aims. Such acts are wholly on one side of the line—the side that should be ruled out. Ruling out terrorist practices, however, will call for more than the customary denunciation, the more so as many leaders publicly reject such practices while engaging in them, subsidizing them, or tolerating them in secret. Partisanship leads some to justify terrorist action by those on their own side on the ground that they are freedom fighters while castigating their opponents as terrorists pure and simple. Yet all who place bombs on buses or planes, say, or strafe health clinics or schools, must be seen as terrorists, however dedicated they may be to the cause of freedom. Governments likewise engage in terror if they resort to such methods at home or abroad, no matter how noble the purposes they claim to serve.

Disinformation is another practice that can serve as a benchmark when it comes to violating a fundamental moral constraint. For while one may debate where to draw the line when it comes to different items of deceptive propaganda, depending on how clearly they are intended to deceive and the degree to which they depart from the truth, no such debates need arise over schemes of disinformation; they are planned from the outset to mislead, whether by means of planting false information in the press, forging documents, or inducing officials to give false testimony.

Terrorism and disinformation, and related forms of violence and deceit, not only wreak scatter-shot injury on victims; they also hurt the credibility and the reputation of governments and organizations known to engage in them, damaging the atmosphere in which nations must try to work out responses to the overriding collective threat of war. Once set, such examples of disrespect for law and morality linger long after particular incidents have ceased to dominate newspaper headlines. Such policies invite retaliation and imitation on the part of adversaries and add to public distrust, especially among citizens made complicitous against their will.

With such benchmarks in mind, it becomes easier to separate clear-cut cases from the rest and to determine where, along such different dimensions as that of the degree of violence or the innocence of the victims, uncertainty and disagreement arise. Much of what human beings do—governments as well as private groups and individuals—is perfectly consonant with the four constraints and thus unproblematic from those points of view. Of the types of conduct that do violate the constraints, a small number are within the range of justifiable breaches, while most are clearly illegitimate.

As for cases where there is more disagreement even in principle about how to evaluate them, what might be entailed by deliberating about them? In earlier writings, I have suggested a three-step procedure for weighing an action or a practice fraught with conflict: first, to ask whether there is an alternative course of action that will achieve the aims one takes to be good without breaching moral constraints; second, if one sees no such alternative, to set forth the moral arguments thought to excuse or to justify such breaches, along with possible counterarguments; and third, in weighing them, and as a test of the first two steps, to ask how such arguments would fare if defended in front of an assembly of reasonable critics.

How does this three-step procedure apply in the case of the *Rainbow Warrior* . . .

Those responsible for both actions argued that they chose to act as they did only after having exhausted all lawful means at their disposal. But even if such a claim is accurate, it is not, by itself, sufficient to justify peacetime assaults on civilians or their property. If government officials explained that they had tried every lawful means of raising funds needed to support a friendly regime in distress, and that they had turned to ex-

tortion for this worthy cause only when all else failed, they would not expect to persuade many.

Nor does the moral deliberation called for in the second step justify the French action or that of the Shepherds. France's long-range aim of enhancing national security by preventing observation of her nuclear tests might justify restricting access to the test site but not sinking ships and taking human lives. The Shepherds argued that their assault was called for in defense of innocent lives otherwise at risk—an argument also advanced by those who place explosives in abortion clinics. Among the many groups likewise invoking the defense of innocent lives or national security for their violations of clear-cut moral standards, few go beyond such rationales to examine the impact of their actions on those whom they injure indirectly, on themselves as moral agents, or on their societies. Nor do they consider the moral relevance of inviting, through their conduct, further retaliation by their adversaries and imitation by yet other groups with different agendas, equally passionately held, or the cumulative effect on the climate of distrust within or between communities.

In making such arguments, while shunting aside all but the narrowest considerations, those planning to violate moral constraints often take for granted that these constraints should nonetheless hold for others. Yet the question, What if everybody did that? is in part meant to expose the inadequacy, in the absence of further arguments, of such self-serving exceptions.

The reasons offered in support of violations are especially likely to remain inchoate and partisan so long as they are not open to challenge from the outside. The third step, the test of publicity, is meant to provide such a challenge. It helps counteract biases, errors, and ignorance—and thus the misjudgments they bring about—by asking how justifications and excuses would hold up in open debate and what would happen if, as often occurs, those responsible for planning, authorizing, and carrying out clandestine actions were exposed to public criticism.

When it comes to government policies in a democracy, the test of publicity requires full accountability to the public or to their elected representatives. By making one's arguments explicit and subjecting them to inspection and criticism, the test challenges private biases, errors, and ignorance, and allows the stretching of perspective so crucial to moral choice. Such sensitivity is never more important than when distrust between adversary groups is strong and partisanship risks skewing their judgment.

The three-step procedure may turn out not to be needed in clear-cut cases. And it can rarely bring a fully satisfactory resolution to the most difficult conflicts—least of all to what have come to be known as "tragic conflicts," in which the available alternatives are all dismal from a moral point of view. In *Mortal Questions,* the philosopher Thomas Nagel asks about such a situation: "What if the world itself, or someone else's actions, could face a previously innocent person with a choice between two morally abominable courses of action, and leave him no way to escape with his honor?" An officer may be ordered to torture terrorists to learn where they have concealed the bombs with which they are threatening to blow up a city; a government leader may have to choose between violating a binding treaty and risking full-scale war.

Notes

1. The four moral constraints on violence, deceit, betrayal, and excessive secrecy can be seen as corresponding to four positive moral principles of nonviolence, veracity, fidelity, and publicity, and, in turn, to certain virtues or excellences of character.

2. This fourth constraint is different from the first three in two additional respects. People do not experience secrecy as harming them directly in the way violence, lies, and betrayal do. Indeed, they must often rely on secrecy in order to protect themselves from harm. No one should have the right to demand full openness from others. Nor can citizens properly demand such complete openness from the state. Rather, what is at issue, in this fourth constraint, is excessive secrecy alone.

The constraint on secrecy also differs from the first three in that it has always been much weaker between states than within them. Democratic traditions insist on open government, but this imperative does not apply equally with respect to outsiders. While the French government had no more right to take the life of a foreigner than of a French citizen in the Greenpeace affair, it had every right to try to keep its military secrets from foreign surveillance, so long as it acted in a lawful manner. Yet this second difference is diminishing. Modern technology and communications systems render all efforts at secrecy more vulnerable. And the stress on verification in concluding arms agreements requires far more openness to outside inspection than most governments would formerly have tolerated.

3. Kant specifies that while we owe others both respect and love, the first represents a strict duty, whereas the second leaves us free to choose how best to carry it out and with respect to whom. The injunction to love one's neighbor, he suggests, asks us to wish to further everyone's well-being and happiness; but since doing so at all times in practice is impossible, one has more latitude in what one actually does: "the degree may be very different according to the differences in the persons loved (of whom one may concern me more than another.") Like Confucius, Kant claims that individuals must learn to practice both respect and love in family and community experiences to begin with, in order to be capable of extending them to larger groups. He would have appreciated the view attributed to Confucius, that those who practice respect, good will, and trustworthiness in the family and with close associates can hope, by degrees, to learn to see "all within the Four Seas" as their brothers.

4. Thinkers in the great traditions of practical moral inquiry—among them Confucians, Stoics, and commentators on Christian, Jewish, Buddhist, and Islamic ethics—have developed methods of sorting through moral problems that can illuminate many of the difficulties that still confront us today. They have discussed the ways in which particular choices and ways of leading one's life interact; considered the role played by definitions and different forms of justification; explored the nature of analogies and the relationship between principle and practice; and worked out methods of line-drawing in difficult cases of conflict that distinguish between marginally different definitions, circumstances, and degrees of justification.

Hans Küng

A Global Ethic in World Politics

Let me avoid from the very beginnings all possible misunderstandings concerning the term "global ethic": it is not a new ideology or superstructure; it will not make the specific ethics of different religions and philosophies superfluous; it is therefore no substitute for the Torah, the Sermon on the Mount, the Qur'an, the Bhagavadgita, the Discourses of the Buddha, or the Sayings of Confucius. A global ethic is nothing but the necessary minimum of common values, standards, and attitudes; in other words, a minimally basic consensus relating to binding values, irrevocable standards, and moral attitudes, which can be affirmed by all religions despite their "dogmatic" differences and should also be supported by nonbelievers.

This interreligious and intercultural consensus of values will be a decisive contribution to overcome the crisis of orientation which became a real world problem. And it will also help—which is the topic of this lecture—to build an ethical foundation of global politics. But does global politics really need an ethical foundation? Is it not better to rely on Realpolitik, "real politics"? . . .

Toward a Binding Global Ethic

Certainly all states in the world have an economic and legal order, but in no state will this order function without an ethical consensus, without that ethical concern among its citizens by which the state with a democratic constitution lives. In the parliament of the French Revolution nearly half of those who voted for the Declaration of Human Rights wanted to have human responsibilities (*devoirs*) formulated alongside human rights. This remained an issue of continuing debate.

Now in our century, after two world wars, the international community has already created transnational, transcultural, and transreligious legal structures (without which international treaties would in fact be sheer self-deception). But if a new world order is to exist, it needs a minimum of common values, standards, and basic attitudes, an ethic which, for all its time-conditioned nature, is binding in all senses of the word on the whole of humanity—in short, a global ethic.

And this is of decisive importance precisely in the age of globalization: The globalization of the economy, technology, and the media means also the globalization of problems: from financial and labor markets to the environment and organized crime! What is therefore also needed is the globalization of ethic. Again: not a uniform ethical system ("ethics"), but a necessary minimum of shared ethical values, basic attitudes and standards to which all regions, nations, and interest groups can subscribe—in other words, a shared basic ethic for humankind. Indeed, there can be no new world order without a world ethic, a global ethic.

Is it possible to elaborate and formulate a global ethic? Are the ethical norms of different nations, regions, cultures, and religions not incompatible? Of course they differ in many concrete ways from each other; on the other hand, I discovered that all the great ethical and religious traditions of humanity have very much in common.

I found my conviction confirmed by the fact that my book *Global Responsibility. In Search of a New World Ethic,* published in German in 1990 and in English in 1991, has received widespread international backing in recent years. Two documents are of particular relevance: on 4 September 1993, for the first time in the history of religion, delegates to the Parliament of the World's Religions in Chicago adopted a Declaration Toward a Global

Ethic; on 1 September 1997, again for the first time, the InterAction Council of former presidents and prime ministers called for a global ethic and submitted to the United Nations a proposed Universal Declaration of Human Responsibilities.

These two declarations are not isolated documents. They are responses to the urgent calls of influential international bodies for global ethical standards. An entire chapter is devoted to this issue in the 1995 reports of both the UN Commission on Global Governance and the World Commission on Culture and Development. The same issues have been on the agenda for some time at the World Economic Forum in Davos and also in the new UNESCO Universal Ethics Project. They are also receiving increasing attention in Asia.

The proposed Universal Declaration of Human Responsibilities supports and underpins the Universal Declaration of Human Rights from an ethical angle, as announced in the preamble: "We . . . thus renew and reinforce commitments already proclaimed in the Universal Declaration of Human Rights: namely the full acceptance of the dignity of all people; their inalienable freedom and equality, and their solidarity with one another." If human rights are not being asserted everywhere that they could be, this is usually for want of the necessary political and ethical will. Even the most fervent of human rights activists must acknowledge that "the rule of law and the promotion of human rights depend on the readiness of men and women to act justly."

Of course it would be wrong to suggest that the legal validity of human rights should be dependent on the actual fulfillment of human responsibilities. The idea of human rights as a reward for good behavior is absurd—for this would mean that only those who had shown themselves worthy of the community by fulfilling their responsibilities toward it would be entitled to enjoy such rights. This would clearly conflict with the notion of the unconditional dignity of the individual, which in turn is a precondition for both rights and responsibilities. No one is sug-

gesting that certain human responsibilities must be fulfilled, by the individual or by a community, before any claim can be laid to human rights. The latter are part and parcel of the individual, who is always, however, the bearer of responsibilities as well as rights: All human rights are by definition directly bound up with the duty to respect them.

While rights and responsibilities can be clearly distinguished, they cannot be separated. The relationship between them must be described in differentiated terms. They are not quantities to be superficially added or subtracted, but two interrelated dimensions of humanity in both the individual and the social sphere.

What then are the basic principles of both declarations? I can only quote their very core: first, "every human being must be treated humanely!" And: "What you do not wish done to yourself, do not do to others!" Or in positive terms: "What you wish done to yourself, do to others!"

On this basis four irrevocable directives are developed, extensively in the declarations of the Parliament of the World's Religions, in a more condensed and juridical form in the proposal of the InterAction Council:

1. Commitment to a culture of nonviolence and respect for all life: "You shall not kill!" Or in positive terms: "Have respect for life!"
2. Commitment to a culture of solidarity and a just economic order: "You shall not steal!" Or in positive terms: "Deal honestly and fairly!"
3. Commitment to a culture of tolerance and a life of truthfulness: "You shall not lie!" Or in positive terms: "Speak and act truthfully!"
4. Commitment to a culture of equal rights and partnership between men and women: "You shall not commit sexual immorality!" Or in positive terms: "Respect and love one another!"

I am convinced that the new world order will only be a better order if it will result in a pluralistic world society characterized by a partnership, which encourages peace and is nature-friendly and ecumenical. This is also the conclusion of the declaration of the Parliament of the World's Religions:

> In conclusion, we appeal to all the inhabitants of this planet. Earth cannot be changed for the better unless the consciousness of individuals is changed. We pledge to work for such transformation in individual and collective consciousness, for the awakening of our spiritual powers through reflection, meditation, prayer, or positive thinking, for a conversion of the heart. Together we can move mountains! Without a willingness to take risks and a readiness to sacrifice there can be no fundamental change in our situation! Therefore we commit ourselves to a common global ethic, to better mutual understanding, as well as to socially-beneficial, peace-fostering, and Earth-friendly ways of life.
>
> We invite all men and women, whether religious or not, to do the same.

Questions for Discussion

1. Which of Bok's four moral constraints do you believe to be most important? Why?
2. How do Bok's moral constraints apply to nuclear states?
3. Given that most people around the world identify themselves with some type of religion or belief system, and that all religions preach respect for human life, why do you suppose this sentiment never translates into a reduction in the frequency of warfare?
4. What does Küng mean by the term "global ethic"? What are the principles underlying his global ethic?

Further Readings

1. Adams, Paul. "War, Peace and 'the System': Three Perspectives." *Journal of Sociology and Social Welfare*, 1991, 18, 3, Sept., 75–100.
2. Gasper, Des. "Violence and Suffering Responsibility and Choice: Issues in Ethics and Development." *European Journal of Development Research*, 1999, 11, 2, Dec., 1–22.
3. Brown, Chris. "Theories of International Justice." *British Journal of Political Science*, 1997, 27, 2, Apr., 273–297.
4. Slim, Hugo. "Doing the Right Thing: Relief Agencies, Moral Dilemmas and Moral Responsibility in Political Emergencies and War." *Disasters*, 1997, 21, 3, Sept., 244–257.
5. Martin, E. Cliff, and Dess, T. Karena, "The Truth about Truthfulness: The Proposed Commentary to Rule 4.1 of the Model of Rules of Professional Conduct." *Georgetown Journal of Legal Ethics*, 2002, 15, 4, Summer, 777–793.
6. Furtak, Rick Anthony. "The Virtues of Authenticity: A Kierkegaardian Essay in Moral Psychology." *International Philosophical Quarterly*, 2003, 16, 43, Dec., 423.
7. Cameron III, George D. "Ethics and Equity: Enforcing Ethical Standards in Commercial Relationships." *Journal of Business Ethics,* Jan 15, 2000, 23, 12, 161.
8. Liptak, Adam. "Sometime, a Half-truth Shall Make You Free." *The New York Times*, July 2, 2000.
9. McNamara, Mary. "Looking for Truths about Untruths: Two Writers Put Deception under a Microscope, Attempting to Learn What Society Values and Why." *Los Angeles Times*, September 7, 2001, E-1.
10. Kandel, William L. "Truthfulness and Judgment in Resolving Employment Disputes." *Employee Relations in Law Journal*, 2001, 27, 20, 3, Winter, 49.

Peace Movements

Peace movements and antiwar movements are relatively recent phenomena. Their presence was hardly felt before World War II. All major armed conflicts since then have been marked by a substantial amount of civilian protests, civil disobedience and other tactics employed by peace activists to register their disapproval of warfare.

In "American Peace Activism" Charles DeBendetti identifies two factors that have prevented the American peace activism from achieving its effectiveness: the lack of a political culture to accompany these movements and a tradition deeply embedded in the Cold War ideology. He traces two main trends in American antiwar efforts after World War II: radical pacifism and internationalism. A comparison of their activities during the Cold War explains the difference in their ideology. It was the Vietnam War that precipitated demands for pacifist policies and generated organizational protests. The author recommends that peace activists pursue changes in the U.S. foreign policy as their short-term goal and the institutionalization of "supranational security" in order to achieve international peace as their long-term goal.

In "The Transnational Movement against Nuclear Weapons" Lawrence Wittner outlines the phases in the development of nuclear disarmament movements. The author explains the strength of the American disarmament sentiment by pointing out the fact that the United States was the first to develop and to use nuclear weapons in warfare. This mass protest constituted the first wave of disarmament activism. The second wave, according to the authors, crested during the peak of the Cold War. The third and the most recent phase in this movement occurred during the early 1980s, and it has since lost its strength due to the various nonproliferation measures that have been adopted in the wake of the USSR dismemberment and the end of the Cold War.

The third reading in this section is "Antiwar Movement Morphs from Wild-Eyed to Civil" by Kate Zernike and Dean Murphy. This reading, published at the outbreak of Gulf War II, outlines the evolutionary developments in American peace activism since the Vietnam era. The authors discuss how every aspect of the peace movement has undergone substantial changes due to developments in communications technology and in political thought of the American public. The strategy employed by peace activists is analyzed, and new trends, such as recognition of the importance of diversity of the mobilized population, are also discussed.

Charles DeBenedetti

American Peace Activism

The most remarkable feature of American peace activism in the forty years following World War II has been the disparity between efforts invested and achievements effected. Operating in one of the world's freest and most open societies, citizen peace activists developed ideas, analyses, actions, and organizations that established them as an irrepressible force. Nonetheless, they consistently failed to convert their countless efforts into the kind of political effectiveness that might move them into the main currents of American life. There were two reasons for this failure. The first was the disturbing ambivalence that American peace-seekers felt toward the value and purpose of United States power in the throes of Cold War rivalry. The second was their overriding commitment to the peace of justice, freedom, and liberation within a conservative political culture that attached the highest value to notions of order, security, and stability. Machiavelli once wrote that "the reason for the bad as well as good fortune of men is to be found in the way in which their way of working fits the times." American peace activists experienced more bad than good fortune during these years, mainly because of a disinclination to champion the political values most fitting to their times.

The story of American citizen peace efforts since 1943 is at once heartening and demoralizing. Made up of only a small minority of the population (estimates range from one-half to two percent of the whole population), citizen peace activists initially worked from two wings in their attempts to persuade the American people and their government that the country's principal enemy was international war.

On the one hand, a small band of absolute pacifists struggled for reasons of principle against war and violence. Inspired by figures such as the longtime radical activist A. J. Muste, some of these radicals used their bodies in sustained campaigns of nonviolent direct action against both the war system and domestic injustice. Organized in groups such as the War Resisters League (WRL), these radical pacifists felt a combined commitment to antiwar activism, as shown by their nonviolent attacks on U.S. nuclear test sites or missile installations, and to domestic justice, which they sought to advance by supporting black civil rights and women's liberation movements. Seeing themselves as a saving remnant, radical pacifists like WRL leader David McReynolds and Catholic priest Daniel Berrigan worked to change popular attitudes and national policies, but their first goal was a revolutionary adaptation of human thinking and action to the values of loving nonviolence.

A second thrust came from internationalists who felt the need for a working world political system. They battled with declining influence in Cold War America to advance peace through institutionalized world order. Rallied at first by World Federalists such as Grenville Clark and by atomic scientists like Albert Einstein, internationalists entered the postwar years heady with their success in establishing a new United Nations and eager to extend their achievements into the full-scale realization of a system empowered to achieve global security and national disarmament. Whether or not that aspiration was realistic, they were crushed into irrelevance between the pressures of right-wing nationalists and left-wing supporters of popular liberation movements. It was almost predictable. Having won victory for the United Nations through their support of the Allied cause during World War II, internationalists were unprepared to cope with the collapse of the Allied coalition and the Cold War effort. With the outbreak of war in Korea, most of those in the American Association for the UN and the United World Federalists threw their support behind the United States–United Nations military effort.

Internationalists' support of the war effort in Korea briefly strengthened American popular enthusiasm for the UN, but any real hope of advancing world government fell apart as the war accelerated a resurgence of right-wing hypernationalist politics: McCarthyism. No matter how much public opinion polls indicated sympathy for the UN after 1950, the xenophobic politics of the Cold War overwhelmed designs for real world government and, in fact, effectively wrecked the country's fifty-year-old internationalist movement, which slipped into political sentimentalism and ineffectuality. Although some internationalists joined new single-issue organizations such as the National Committee for a Sane Nuclear Policy, few made any contribution to the domestic opposition to U.S. intervention in Vietnam, and most of them stood apart from the antinuclear and pro-disarmament protests of the late seventies and early eighties. In fact, in a sorry testimonial to the internationalist decline, Thomas L. Hughes, president of the Carnegie Endowment for International Peace, recently wrote that the values and assumptions at the heart of the Endowment and modern internationalism "have pretty well exhausted themselves in mainstream American political life." Even among its supporters, American internationalism is in an enfeebled if not comatose state, with a decidedly bad prognosis.

Gradually, a large and heterogeneous body of concerned liberals, leftists, and moderates emerged in organizations and operations of bewildering diversity. Joined only in common opposition to American Cold War policies, these peace activists first came forward in the midfifties in public protest against atmospheric nuclear testing and against the failure of the UN to extend world order and effective disarmament. These peace-seekers formed new organizations such as SANE and Women Strike for Peace. Although influenced by the New Left, they generally avoided any attempt to define themselves according to any coherent ideology or mode of action. Instead, they prided themselves on their heterogeneity, eclecticism, commitment to action, and common opposition to the prevailing militarized anti-communism and apathy about war in the nuclear age. Lacking a partisan focus, the new activists sought to establish themselves as an extrapartisan domestic opposition to U.S. armed interventionism and a force for multilateral peacekeeping and disarmament.

The war in Vietnam provided, of course, the catalyst for this opposition movement. Generated at first among absolute pacifists, radicals, and liberals, domestic opposition to U.S. intervention in Vietnam proliferated tremendously among a wide array of middle-class Americans between 1965 and 1971. Even when it declined, it left in place both the remembered experience and the functional networks required to rally Cold War critics later. Whether motivated by moral, ideological, or political concerns, the dissatisfied citizens who assembled and sustained organized opposition to Washington's bipartisan war effort made personal sacrifices in order to emphasize their common conviction that the government was terribly wrong and had to be put right. Inevitably, dissidents derived varying lessons from their experiences. In general, however, they shared one conclusion: millions of Americans could be mobilized against national war policy, and their voice would not go unheard among the decision-makers in Washington. The antiwar activists of the Vietnam era found that they could reach those policymakers who placed a particular definition of national interest above the forces of democratic politics. They learned that they could make history work for peace.

In the course of protesting the war in Vietnam, Cold War peace activists proliferated geographically and organizationally throughout the country, to embrace thereafter a variety of causes and concerns. The major international peace organizations, including the Fellowship of Reconciliation and Women's International League for Peace and Freedom, continued to involve tens of thousands of people in their multi-issue activities. In addition, however, groups of people organized according to occupation, such as Physicians for Social Responsibility, concentrated on the nuclear arms race. At the same time, explicitly anti-interventionist organizations, such as the North American Congress on Latin America, emerged in opposition to U.S. intervention in the Third World, while a host of lobbying groups, such as the Council for a Livable World and the Center for Defense Information, developed impressive channels of influence in the media and foreign policy circles. Perhaps most important, the combination of civil rights activism, the opposition to the war in Vietnam and the womens's movement enlisted religious-minded people as everyday activists on the local level, in groups such as Sanctuary, to argue against armed interventionism, the arms race, and economic injustice.

Within the past quarter-century, citizen peace initiatives have proliferated with a breadth and power hitherto unknown in American history. Perversely, however, this burst of peace activism neither gained respectable political power within policymaking circles nor developed substantial lines of transnational contact, communication, and support. In part, this failure of American activists to expand their influence at home and abroad derives from the negative cast that has dogged the U.S. peace movement since World War II.

After failing to build a new world order through the United Nations, peace activists did not reassemble in a visible way until 1955; and then their concerns were defined by opposition to the arms race and the Soviet–American Cold War. Soon afterwards, peace activists provided the core of opposition to the U.S. war in Indochina. Then, after 1975, they lent vital support to domestic opposition to nuclear power and, early in the eighties, to the U.S. arms buildup. Always, it seemed, the peace movement was in op-

position to something, its concerns less international than domestic. Ever it appeared to protest the deployment of American power.

Moreover, the failure of the American peace movement to advance both in U.S. politics and in transnational collaboration had roots in the peculiarly nationalistic bias of the American peace tradition. An America-First reform temperament informed recent peace-seeking in two respects: a traditional ambivalence toward American power, and a priority for justice and liberation over security.

Domestic American reformers historically have felt ambivalent toward the scope and significance of American power. On the one hand, they have taken pride in the growth of American economic and military power as an expression of the rightfulness of the nation's democratic society. Out of this pride, American reformers have enthusiastically backed nearly every major U.S. war effort at the same time as they encouraged national leaders to seek more systematic international cooperation. On the other hand, American reformers have exhibited a healthy skepticism toward American power, partly because of its periodic misuse at home and abroad and partly because of their own discomfort over the very meaning and implications of power. Like all American reformers, the peace-seekers among them have generally assumed that people are basically good, capable of identifying their own self-interests, and prone toward right reasoning in the face of correct evidence. In the world of power relationships, however, these assumptions often are irrelevant if not wrong; and American peace-seekers, like most public figures, never have felt comfortable in confronting realities that contradict their guiding assumptions. . . .

We return to Machiavelli: "since new things disturb the minds of men, you should strive to see that these disturbing changes retain as much of the ancient regime as possible." The prevailing international regime does possess things of value, beginning with various forms of state-maintained order that facilitate the pursuit of peaceable political struggle. American peace advocates must show how they would extend these things of demonstrated value to a supranational world authority that would protect the nations' established values from the threat of war.

In practice, this prescription implies that the American peace movement requires a double strategy. In the short term, American peace-seekers must seize upon all available means to change the foreign policies of the U.S. and its allies in ways that carry the great powers toward the negotiated settlement of the Cold War. In the long term, peace advocates must use political power to enlarge those plans and agencies capable of institutionalizing supranational security which the great powers must establish in the course of extinguishing the Cold War. Peace activists must realize that they cannot be satisfied with standing merely in opposition to U.S. Cold War policies or with questing for distant visions. They must advocate a new world order that is compelling because it is grounded in the wisdom of the past and responsive to the realities of the present. They must advocate a way that not only "fits the times" but also shapes them. They would most effectively proceed with a manifest respect for American power, trying to use it less in search of justice, freedom, and liberation and more for those things that matter to modern, industrial peoples: order, security, stability, and the globally-organized protection of a world of plural values without recourse to war.

Lawrence S. Wittner

The Transnational Movement against Nuclear Weapons

One of the largest, most turbulent movements of modern times has been the transnational crusade against nuclear weapons. For more than four decades, this campaign has mobilized millions of people around the globe. . . . The first wave of nuclear disarmament sentiment was generated by the U.S. atomic bombing of Hiroshima and Nagasaki in August 1945, and continued in strength until approximately 1949.

As the world's first people to develop nuclear weapons and to wage nuclear war, Americans were especially obsessed with them. Even before the bombs fell on Japan, a small group of atomic scientists had sought to prevent their use. Although moved by moral concerns, they emphasized to higher officials the more "practical" consideration of preventing a postwar nuclear arms race. Higher officials, however, remained unimpressed. Nor did many Americans disagree with the use made of the bombs. A poll on 8 August 1945 found that 85 percent of Americans supported the atomic bombing of Japanese cities, while only 10 percent opposed it. The most outspoken critics of the bomb's use were pacifists and Catholic and liberal Protestant church leaders.

American fascination with the bomb was based less upon guilt than upon fear. By September 1945, pollsters contended that 83 percent of Americans believed that, in the event of another world war, there was a genuine danger of the destruction of urban civilization by atomic bombs. Large numbers thought that the way to avoid nuclear catastrophe was to strengthen international authority. The atomic scientists' movement rallied behind the ill-fated Baruch Plan for United Nations control of atomic energy. Many of their leaders, like Albert Einstein, also threw their prestige behind the emerging world government movement.

Naturally, antinuclear sentiment also ran very strong among the first victims of nuclear warfare, the Japanese. The terrible devastation of the war, the postwar exposure of militarist deceptions, and the nightmare of the atomic bombings led the Japanese toward pacifism and, particularly, rejection of nuclear weapons. New rallying cries of "No More Hiroshimas!" and "No More War!" became staples of Japanese life. Article 9 of Japan's new postwar constitution renounced "war . . . and the threat or use of force as a means of settling international disputes." Although this provision appears to have been imposed by the American occupation authorities, it had the solid backing of Japanese public opinion.

In Great Britain, a country indirectly linked to the Hiroshima bombing, the response was less dramatic. As in the United States, overwhelming support for use of the bomb against Japan was accompanied by a brooding sense that survival itself was now at stake. Nevertheless, antinuclear protest was slow to develop. In April 1948, pacifists did manage to stage a public meeting on the question of the new weaponry. And the following year, after the establishment of NATO, a group of prominent Britons published an open letter calling on their governments not to manufacture or borrow atomic bombs and to close American bases that housed them. In 1950, shortly after U.S. President Harry Truman announced his decision to develop a hydrogen bomb, one hundred

READING 53   The Transnational Movement against Nuclear Weapons   **321**

Cambridge University scientists urged the British government to assume world leadership by rejecting the American initiative.

Among nations that had no contact with events at Hiroshima, the reaction was more restrained. In nonaligned Sweden, world government advocacy grew. In France, where grass-roots pacifism was weak and political parties strong, the socialists took an ambiguous stand on nuclear weapons, and the communists condemned nuclear weapons only after it became clear that the U.S. atomic bombs threatened the Soviet Union. Although small in numbers and influence, Australian pacifists focused their energies upon a critique of atomic warfare. Third World nations—generally remote from the nuclear arms race and preoccupied with their own issues of national independence, economic growth, and social and economic equality—remained even more detached from nuclear disarmament concerns.

These and other antinuclear stirrings of 1945–49—never pulled together into a formal nuclear disarmament campaign, but nonetheless substantial in scope—faded rapidly with the intensification of the Cold War. In part, of course, the decline of nuclear concern reflected the passage of time. Alarmed by the bomb after events at Hiroshima, many people gradually became accustomed to it. . . .

The growing commitment to the Cold War had a direct impact upon the critics of nuclear weapons. In Japan, peace groups were thrown on the defensive as the conservative Japanese government, in response to U.S. pressure, flouted the "peace constitution" by developing national armed forces and signed the U.S.-Japan Security Treaty. In Hungary and Czechoslovakia, the advent of communist governments led to the dissolution of pacifist groups. Recognizing the deteriorating international situation, Australian pacifists changed their emphasis to improving Soviet-American relations, but without much effect upon public opinion. In Turkey, the nation's first peace group was suppressed almost immediately.

The impact of the Cold War was particularly severe in the United States. The last stand of the once-feisty atomic scientists' movement came in October 1949, when the General Advisory Committee of the U.S. Atomic Energy Commission unanimously opposed the development of the hydrogen bomb. Thereafter, as the president gave the go-ahead for the H-bomb project and the Cold War lurched forward, the militant wing of the scientists' movement formally dissolved, while the moderate wing continued its existence in a cautious, muted form. The world government movement also crumbled. Membership declined, state legislatures rescinded their supporting resolutions, and self-proclaimed patriots violently denounced "one-worlders."

The decline of the nuclear disarmament movement accelerated when, under pressure from the Soviet Union, the world communist movement seized on the nuclear weapons issue as the focus of its own peace campaign. In August 1948, the Polish government had hosted a World Congress of Intellectuals for Peace, and this led, the following April, to the organization of a World Peace Congress in Paris, directed by French communist leaders. Impressed by the potentialities of this campaign, the Cominform directed all communist parties to make the peace movement the "pivot of [their] entire activity." In March 1950, when the communist-dominated World Peace Committee met in Stockholm to denounce Western military measures, it initiated a mass petition campaign calling for a ban on the atomic bomb. By the end of the year, the organizers of this Stockholm Peace Appeal claimed to have garnered 500 million signatures. Substantial numbers came from Western countries, but the vast majority were drawn from communist nations. . . .

A second and considerably more powerful wave of antinuclear sentiment began developing in the mid-1950s. Generated by the escalation of the nuclear arms race, as symbolized by hydrogen bomb testing and the spread of nuclear weapons to additional nations, it crested between 1957 and 1963.

The most prominent of the nuclear disarmament groups, Britain's Campaign for Nuclear Disarmament (CND), was launched at an exceptionally large, enthusiastic public meeting in February 1958. Unilateralist rather than pacifist, CND called upon Great Britain to renounce possession of the bomb, regardless of what other nations might do. The first CND Easter march began that year, with thousands of demonstrators bearing the nuclear disarmament symbol, designed for the event, from London to the atomic weapons research facility at Aldermaston. These annual Aldermaston marches, with the route reversed in subsequent years, drew large and enthusiastic crowds behind the banners of CND regions, universities, Labour party branches, and church groups. Combined with changes in trade union leadership, the grass-roots nuclear disarmament fervor made a substantial impact upon British politics. Meeting in 1960 for its annual conference, the Labour party adopted a resolution supporting unilateral nuclear disarmament.

In the next few years, however, the British movement suffered some serious reverses. At the insistence of Labour party leader Hugh Gaitskell, the unilateralist resolution was scrapped at the party's 1961 conference. Furthermore, from CND's inception, some activists had been impatient with the legal, electoral route to nuclear disarmament championed by its chair, Canon John Collins. In September 1960, assisted by CND's president, Bertrand Russell, they broke away from CND to form the Committee of 100, which fostered acts of mass civil disobedience. As a result, the British movement not only dissipated much energy in a nasty dispute between the two groups, but also came to be perceived by the general public as a pretty strange bunch. . . .

Whatever its problems in Great Britain, however, the CND model enjoyed considerable popularity elsewhere. CND groups sprang up after 1960 in the Australian cities of Melbourne, Sydney, Brisbane, and Perth, drawing upon an overwhelmingly youthful, middle-class constituency. . . .

In Canada, opposition to nuclear weapons testing crystallized in 1959, when an Edmonton group formed what became the first branch of a national organization, the Canadian Committee for the Control of Radiation Hazards. With the nuclear arms race blossoming as a topic of discussion in Canada, the Committee circulated a petition which urged the Canadian government to reject acquisition of nuclear weapons. At a February 1962 convention, the Committee changed its name to the Canadian Campaign for Nuclear Disarmament and absorbed peace groups in various cities as its branches. Bowing to antinuclear protest, the Conservative Prime Minister, John Diefenbaker, promised not to install nuclear weapons in peacetime. But the powerful Liberal party supported acquisition of nuclear weapons and, after its 1963 election victory, arranged for their installation in Canada.

The antinuclear movement experienced greater success in Scandinavia. Danish participants in Britain's Aldermaston march brought the movement back to their own country, where an antinuclear march and demonstration were first held in October 1960. The following month, Norway's nuclear disarmament movement was launched with a public meeting and an appeal signed by "The 13," a diverse group of Norwegians who protested the inhumanity of the new weapons and sought to prevent their installation in Norway. They staged a number of demonstrations, obtained 225,000 signatures on their petitions, and in April 1961 secured the agreement of the governing Labor party to maintain its earlier decision not to install nuclear weapons on Norwegian territory in peacetime. In neutral Sweden, when the possibility of producing a Swedish atomic bomb was publicly broached in the mid-1950s, the result was the immediate development of an antinuclear weapons movement. Established by about thirty prominent intellectuals, it organized rallies, demonstrations, and debates. Between 1957 and 1961, opposition to the bomb rose to 56 percent of the Swedish population. . . .

The nuclear disarmament movement also made considerable headway in Japan. In March 1954, when a U.S. hydrogen bomb test at Bikini showered a Japanese fishing boat, the *Lucky*

Dragon, with radioactive fallout, a furor erupted in that antinuclear nation. A group of Tokyo housewives began a petition drive against atomic and hydrogen bombs which eventually attracted 32 million signatures. The following year, on August 6, the first World Conference Against Atomic and Hydrogen Bombs convened in Hiroshima, attended by 50,000 people. Sensitive to public opinion, the Japanese government appealed for a global ban on the manufacture and testing of nuclear weapons, a position which polls found to be supported by 89 percent of the population.

Events in West Germany proved considerably less satisfactory to antinuclear activists. In February 1958, General Lauris Norstad, NATO's commander, had declared that it was "absolutely essential" to arm West German military forces with atomic weapons, a position quickly embraced by the ruling Christian Democrats. This inspired the formation of the Campaign Against Atomic Weapons and the Struggle Against Atomic Death, supported by the opposition Social Democrats and the German trade union federation. In July 1958, more than 300,000 people took part in antinuclear demonstrations. The issue set off a passionate debate and near schism within the Protestant Church, although the Catholic Church solidly supported German nuclear armament. But, in 1960, in hopes of entering the government, the Social Democrats and their union allies ended their participation in the antinuclear campaign. . . .

In Greece, another NATO nation, the nuclear disarmament question became caught up in the bitter antagonisms of national politics. Grigoris Lambrakis, an immensely popular former athlete and left-wing member of parliament, had helped to develop a larger nonaligned peace movement in Greece. Returning from the British Aldermaston march in 1963, he planned a similar trek from Marathon to Athens for late April. With that march likely to attract a very large and radical turnout, the rightist government banned the event and arrested about a thousand prospective marchers, beating them up and then releasing them without charges. Lambrakis had parliamentary immunity, however, and made the march himself. About a month later, as he sought to address a political meeting in his home district of Salonika, he was set upon and murdered by right-wing thugs, mobilized for the occasion by top officers of the Greek armed forces. . . .

In these same years, the composition of the peace movement shifted substantially in France. The Cuban missile crisis, the entreaties of independent peace groups, and a revolt against the communist monopoly on "peace" led to the establishment in 1962 of the nonaligned Movement Against Atomic Armament (MCAA). As the conservative government of Charles de Gaulle embarked upon a program to develop French nuclear weapons, the MCAA joined with the communist-controlled MDP to establish a broad umbrella organization, the Committee Against the Force de Frappe. This brought together the major unions, student groups, and left-wing parties, as well as a large number of other organizations, for massive demonstrations against French nuclear weapons and those of other nations.

The nuclear disarmament movement made even greater headway in the United States. Ever since the Bikini bomb tests of 1954, public controversy had swirled over the practice of nuclear testing. With large numbers of scientists warning of the health hazards of radio-active fallout, several dozen prominent pacifists and peace-minded Americans met in 1957 to chart a campaign to end nuclear testing. By the following year their National Committee for a Sane Nuclear Policy (SANE) had 25,000 members. As SANE began its work of education, marches, and lobbying, a more militant group—the Committee for Nonviolent Action (CNVA)—also formed in 1957, sponsored dramatic acts of civil disobedience. Within a short time, SANE and CNVA had catalyzed a very visible campaign, not only against nuclear testing, but against nuclear weapons themselves.

Given their relative remoteness from the nuclear arms race, Third World nations continued to evince considerably less grassroots support for nuclear disarmament. Although remarkable non-violent activism cropped up during the postwar years in Brazil, Nyasaland, South Africa, Namibia, India, Ghana, Algeria, Mozambique, and Zambia, none of these ventures focused upon an international peace issue. By the mid-1960s, the various pacifist internationals claimed branches in only a few Third World nations. Even so, some of their rulers did play very important roles in softening Cold War confrontations and fostering policies of nonalignment and peace. The danger of relying on national leaders without disarmament movements was illustrated in 1962, however, when the Gandhi Peace Foundation held an Anti-Nuclear Arms convention in New Delhi. At the meeting, major Indian leaders supported unilateral disarmament, but only four months later many recanted when a serious border clash developed between India and China. . . .

During the summer of 1959, the French government announced that it would conduct an atomic bomb test in the Sahara desert and began removing local Algerians from the area. In response, prominent activists from the nuclear disarmament campaigns in Great Britain and the United States traveled to Ghana to help organize a nonviolent invasion of the test site. Inside Ghana, the Sahara protest team addressed numerous mass meetings and official gatherings. And beginning in December, the small team—international in composition, but with a Ghanaian majority—commenced the first of three fruitless attempts to reach the test site. Meanwhile, demonstrations or official protests against the tests erupted around the world. Although French West African nations, then negotiating for independence from France, kept their distance from the protest, some 500 African students from French Community nations were arrested in Paris as they sought to present an antitesting petition to the French premier.

The success of Anglo-American nuclear disarmament activists in sparking an international furor over the French bomb tests raised pacifist prestige considerably in Africa. At their suggestion, Kwame Nkrumah called together an All-African Conference on Positive Action for the Peace and Security of Africa in April 1960. Although the Accra conference called for larger-scale measures against French bomb tests and the establishment of African centers for training in nonviolent resistance, no provision was made for funding the nonviolence training centers, and the Sahara team leaders were forced to fall back on Nkrumah for assistance. Distracted by other issues, international and domestic, he seemed to lose interest in the nuclear testing question. Discouraged, the Sahara team decided to disband. . . .

The international nature of the movement in Africa reflected the closer relationships developing among nonaligned nuclear disarmament organizations. In January 1959, in response to an initiative by the British and West German groups, the European Federation Against Nuclear Arms was established at a meeting in London. Although the European Federation brought together groups in Switzerland, Sweden, Holland, West Germany, and Great Britain, it remained a rather weak and ineffectual body. Under pressure from numerous quarters to form a new, nonaligned international, the European Federation organized a meeting for this purpose in January 1963, at Oxford, England. In a final, stormy session, delegates overcame their national, political, and ideological divisions and voted to establish the International Confederation for Disarmament and Peace. By the beginning of the following year, it could point to member groups in nearly thirty countries.

Naturally, relations between the nonaligned nuclear disarmament movement and the communist-led peace movement were strained. When a number of nonaligned nuclear disarmament groups attended the July 1962 World Peace Council meeting in Moscow, they proved a considerable embarrassment to their hosts. Not only did the nonaligned groups from Britain and France issue a minority report, but some nonaligned delegations turned up with leaflets opposing the possession of nuclear weapons by *all* countries. Forbidden to distribute the leaflets outside the conference confines, a nonaligned contingent promptly began handing out thousands of them at a public demonstration they staged in Red Square. This act of *lèse majesté* enraged communist-dominated peace delegations and seriously irked the Soviet government as well. . . .

The second wave of nuclear disarmament activism met with some success. Admittedly, nuclear testing did not end, nuclear weapons proliferated, and the nuclear arms race continued. Nonetheless, popular awareness of nuclear dangers increased substantially. Moreover, government leaders, chastened by the global uproar, did show signs of drawing back from nuclear confrontation, certainly after the Cuban missile crisis of 1962. In this sense, it can be said that the nuclear disarmament movement laid the groundwork for the atmospheric test ban treaty of 1963, the nuclear nonproliferation treaty of 1968, the strategic arms limitation treaty of 1972, and the Soviet–American détente of the 1970s. Under intense popular pressure, a number of governments quite capable of developing nuclear weapons chose not to do so. In December 1967, the Japanese prime minister announced his government's intention not to possess, manufacture, or introduce nuclear weapons into Japan. Other nations, such as Norway and Denmark, banned nuclear weapons from their territory in peacetime. As the 1960s progressed, nuclear war seemed less and less likely.

This perception of dwindling danger contributed to the rapid decline of the antinuclear movement after 1963 and to its virtual disappearance by the end of the decade. With the signing of the partial test ban treaty in 1963, the movement rapidly ebbed in Norway, Sweden, Canada, and Holland. In Great Britain, CND waned quickly after 1963, and, in elections the next year, nuclear disarmament was not a major issue. The test ban treaty also had a substantial impact upon the American peace movement and upon public opinion. Between 1959 and 1964, the percentage of Americans listing nuclear war as the nation's most urgent problem dropped from 64 to 16 percent. Soon, in fact, the issue disappeared from the surveys. In France, the antinuclear positions of

the Socialist and Communist parties had a similarly soothing effect; all the antinuclear forces had to do, it seemed, was to wait for an electoral victory of the Left.

In addition, however, nuclear disarmament activism ebbed because the nuclear danger was preempted by other concerns—in this case, the Vietnam War. In France, Britain, West Germany—indeed, in much of the world—the peace constituency rapidly jettisoned antinuclear efforts in an attempt to bring the brutal Vietnam conflict to an end. Beginning in the mid-1960s, a widespread anti-Vietnam War campaign surged across Japan, drawing upon students, unions, women's groups, citizens' organizations, and the Left parties. The Swedish Peace and Arbitration Society, which had played an important part in the movement against nuclear weapons, organized a Committee for Peace in Vietnam that became a magnet for political parties, the peace movement, and youthful antiwar protestors. In Australia, the government's decision to send combat troops to Vietnam led the peace movement to focus exclusively on the issues of Vietnam and conscription. Similarly, in Canada, local anti-Vietnam War committees replaced CND groups, while the student magazine *Our Generation Against Nuclear War* became simply *Our Generation*. The result was a substantial lull in antinuclear activism. . . .

A third wave of nuclear disarmament sentiment began to develop in the late 1970s, achieved enormous momentum from 1980 to 1983, and declined thereafter. As before, the major stimulus was a surge in the nuclear arms race, symbolized this time by the deterioration of Soviet–American détente; the deployment of Soviet SS-20 missiles in Eastern Europe; the NATO decision (of December 1979) to install cruise and Pershing missiles in Western Europe; and the advent in Washington of the Reagan administration, with its loose talk about fighting and winning a nuclear war. These factors heightened the popular perception of danger and revived the dormant nuclear disarmament movement.

Unlike past surges of nuclear disarmament activism, however, this one began with a strong transnational emphasis. In early 1980, a small group of British CND stalwarts decided to launch a movement to remove all nuclear weapons from Europe. The result was an Appeal for European Nuclear Disarmament (END), drafted by the British historian E. P. Thompson. Issued in April 1980, the Appeal condemned the political leaders of East and West for their "aggressive actions," called upon peace groups to "free Europe from confrontation," and proclaimed an ultimate goal of dissolving "both great power alliances." END urged not great power negotiations, but rather (in Thompson's words) "the regeneration of internationalism," the "resistance of peoples inside each bloc." Consequently, END sought to develop a transnational alliance of peoples that would take unilateral initiatives toward multilateral disarmament. With the upsurge of nuclear disarmament activism in the following years, END's goals began to appear a real possibility. Annual END conventions brought together most of the nonaligned peace groups and sympathetic forces in Europe—part of what an END pamphlet enthusiastically called "the biggest mass movement in modern history."

The revival of the British movement was particularly dramatic. Between 1979 and 1984, CND's national membership jumped from 4,267 to 90,000, while local membership soared to 250,000. CND rallies attracted unprecedented numbers of people, including an estimated 400,000 in 1983. As before, CND drew very heavily upon the educated middle class and, once again with the assistance of the unions, prevailed upon the Labour party (in opposition) to support unilateral nuclear disarmament. Polls never found more than 31 percent of the population in favor of unilateral nuclear disarmament, but they did report that most Britons opposed the installation of cruise missiles. This provided support for the daring (and controversial) women's actions at the U.S. air force base at Greenham Common, a site for missile installation.

Although the Dutch movement had different origins than the British, it was soon heading in a similar direction. In 1966, the major Protestant and Catholic churches in the Netherlands had founded the Inter-Church Peace Council (IKV) to foster reflection on problems of war and peace. A decade later, appalled by the lack of progress in halting the nuclear arms race, IKV embarked upon a campaign to "help rid the world of nuclear weapons, starting in the Netherlands." IKV led the battle against deployment of cruise missiles, sparked unprecedented demonstrations, and hoped to pull together a parliamentary majority. But although the social democrats and the small Left parties voted solidly against deployment, the Christian Democrats proved more hawkish than expected. . . .

A somewhat different pattern emerged in Italy, where the communists for some time had been behaving like cautious social democrats and the tiny Radical party had taken the lead in pacifist ventures. Although Catholic antimilitarism had been growing ever since the 1960s, the Catholic Church formally supported nuclear deterrence, as did its major political expression, the ruling Christian Democratic party. In 1979, when the NATO missile announcement was made, the Radicals were in the vanguard of the opposition, along with other prominent figures of the independent Left. Initially vague, the position of the small Socialist party hardened in 1981 in favor of the missiles. That August, when the Italian government declared that cruise missiles would be installed at Comiso, Sicily, there was an upsurge of protest. A march of half a million people several months later in Rome owed much to demonstrations elsewhere and to the organizing efforts of the Communist party, which was determined not to lose ground to the mushrooming forces on its Left.

In other Mediterranean nations, antinuclear activism was also on the ascendant. Freed at last of Franco's right-wing dictatorship, a large Spanish peace movement developed, pressing both for the rejection of NATO membership and a nuclear-free Spain. In Greece, the 1981 electoral victory of Andreas Papandreou's Pan-Hellenic Socialist Movement also opened up antinuclear prospects. And, in fact, Papandreou promptly opposed missile deployment and supported the creation of a nuclear-free zone in the Balkans—both stands favored by Greek public opinion. Perhaps the most surprising development in the region was the formation, in 1977, of the Turkish Peace Association. Founded during a period of the democratization of Turkish public life, the Peace Association campaigned for nuclear disarmament and against proposals to site the neutron bomb, cruise, and Pershing missiles in Turkey. . . .

Only in France did the growing alliance between the social democratic Left and the nuclear disarmament movement become unhinged. Ironically, the 1981 election victory of the socialist–communist coalition provided the occasion. Like much of the public, both left-wing parties had come to accept French nuclear weapons as a guarantor of foreign policy independence. Nevertheless, nuclear disarmament activism grew at the grassroots. The communist-led MDP and a somewhat more independent Appeal of the 100 staged massive demonstrations behind vaguely worded peace declarations. At the same time, representatives of twenty-seven nonaligned peace, women's, and ecological organizations met in late 1981 and formed the Committee for Nuclear Disarmament in Europe (CODENE). Taking a moderate approach, CODENE called for a freeze on all French nuclear weapons systems and testing and for international action toward creating a nuclear-free Europe—a position quite in line with public sentiment.

As before, the nuclear disarmament movement showed particular strength in the Nordic countries. Launched as a spontaneous protest in October 1979, the Norwegian No to Nuclear Weapons campaign sharply assailed plans for cruise and Pershing missiles and the deployment of Soviet SS-20s. A Danish No to Nuclear Weapons campaign, with a similar orientation, followed in January 1980. The idea of a nuclear weapon-free zone, suggested by government leaders in Sweden and Finland in the early 1960s, became exceptionally popular in 1981 and 1982,

when more than 2.5 million citizens of Finland, Sweden, Norway, and Denmark signed petitions calling upon their governments to implement it and vast demonstrations around the issue erupted in Sweden and Finland. Such campaigns drew the enthusiastic support of the major nonaligned peace movements in the region.

Japan, too, resumed antinuclear efforts on a remarkable scale. The immediate occasion was the United Nations' second Special Session on Disarmament, which inspired a coalition effort that brought together not only Gensuikyo and Gensuikin but also national labor federations, women's groups, youth associations, and religious groups. By 1982, 28.8 million signatures had been gathered on a petition urging the United Nations and the Japanese government to publicize the effects of nuclear weapons, adopt an international convention outlawing their use, expand nuclear-free zones, and draft an overall treaty for disarmament. Furthermore, numerous municipalities passed resolutions declaring themselves nuclear-free zones, vast antinuclear rallies occurred in Hiroshima and Tokyo, and polls found that 76 percent of the population reacted favorably to antinuclear movements. . . .

Elsewhere in the Pacific, antinuclear sentiment attained unprecedented dimensions. In Australia, nuclear disarmament activism began to resume in the late 1970s, in large part as a response to that country's mining of uranium for nuclear power and weapons. Thereafter, the revival of the Cold War and of the nuclear disarmament movement elsewhere led to enormous antinuclear rallies, as well as to heightened protests by church groups, doctors, scientists, and academics. In New Zealand, antinuclear sentiment intensified in the late 1970s, as doubts grew about the rationality of U.S. foreign policy and as the conservative government began to welcome visits by U.S. nuclear-powered and -armed warships to New Zealand ports. With anxiety spreading that New Zealand would become a nuclear target, the very fragmented peace groups banded together in 1981 into Peace Movement New Zealand.

Indeed, support grew rapidly for a nuclear-free Pacific. When the Pacific Conference of Churches organized a 1975 conference in Fiji to discuss French nuclear testing in the area, Pacific islanders established the Nuclear Free and Independent Pacific movement. A decade later, it was comprised of 185 organizations and could point to some impressive achievements: stopping the Japanese government from dumping nuclear waste in the Pacific, mobilizing Pacific nations against French nuclear testing, and securing agreement of nine out of ten South Pacific countries to a treaty for a nuclear-free zone. A number of small nations—including Vanuatu, Papua New Guinea, the Solomon Islands, and Belau—adopted nuclear-free constitutions.

Antinuclear sentiment also reached unprecedented levels in the United States. In the late 1970s and early 1980s, groups such as Mobilization for Survival and Physicians for Social Responsibility publicized the effects of nuclear war, while radical Christians carried out acts of civil disobedience at weapons sites. These stirrings turned into a mass movement with the advent, in 1980, of the campaign for a Nuclear Freeze—a bilateral agreement to halt nuclear testing, production, and deployment of nuclear weapons. More than 70 percent of the public supported a Freeze, all polls indicated. In June 1982, nearly a million Americans participated in an antinuclear rally in New York City—the largest demonstration in U.S. history. That fall, a majority of voters backed the Freeze in nine of the ten states where it appeared on the ballot. Older peace groups like SANE and the Council for a Livable World grew substantially, and were joined in their critique of the nuclear arms race by mainline Protestant and Catholic churches and, for the first time, by major unions.

The newest and most courageous antinuclear activism appeared in the nations of Eastern Europe. Deeply suspicious of autonomous ventures, and particularly of those raising questions about official policy, the authorities viewed these independent peace efforts with considerable apprehension. Furthermore, it was easy enough for the population to focus on other problems—such as shortages of housing and consumer goods—which were both more immediate and more acceptable as topics of conversation. . . .

The independent antinuclear movement was particularly vigorous in East Germany. Here, the growing fear of nuclear war (with Germany as the battleground), the high level of militarization, the example of Western peace demonstrations, and the sanction afforded by the powerful Evangelical Church combined to stir unprecedented demands. Official church bodies initiated proposals in the early 1980s for the creation of a "peace service" as an alternative to conscription, for "peace studies" courses in the schools, and for the renunciation of nuclear deterrence and nuclear war. In November 1980, the Evangelical Church began its first Peace Week under the slogan "Make Peace Without Weapons." As enthusiasm grew, the churches repeated their peace sermons and discussions the following year, adding "peace festivals" of poetry, music, and song. Young people, particularly, flocked to these events. . . .

In Hungary, a somewhat more tolerant government and official Peace Council helped compensate for the absence of a peace-oriented church hierarchy. One key constituency of the new peace movement consisted of 300 religious "base communities," organized in Hungary during the 1960s. Formed around the radical Catholic Eucharist movement of Father Gyorgy Bulanyi, these communities campaigned for nonviolence and the right to conscientious objection. In January 1982, their Committee for Human Dignity issued a statement opposing nuclear weapons in either bloc. Meanwhile, in late 1981, students at Budapest University proposed a peace march condemning American and Soviet nuclear weapons. Although authorities frustrated this plan, the following spring, high school students revived the idea and established a Hungarian Anti-Nuclear Campaign. Student antinuclear activism spread rapidly in secondary and trade schools, with leaflets, posters and buttons. University activism, largely confined to a few arts universities, crystallized around the Peace Group for Dialogue.

Nonaligned peace activism also flared up in other Warsaw Pact nations. Despite the imposition of martial law in Poland, underground periodicals debated missile deployment and the impact of military spending on the economy, while the Committee for Social Resistance issued statements calling for opposition to the deployment of U.S. and Soviet missiles. In Czechoslovakia, the human rights group Charter 77 published a letter of solidarity with the East German peace movement, carried on a friendly dialogue with the Western peace movement, and distributed leaflets protesting deployment of nuclear missiles in its own country. The Protestant Church in Czechoslovakia spoke out strongly against missile installation, student antinuclear protests erupted, and petitions against missile deployment were circulated successfully in a number of large industrial plants. . . .

Despite the enormous upsurge from 1980 to 1983, the world antinuclear movement usually proved unable to translate popular support for its positions into public policy. Euromissile deployment, opposed by majority sentiment in each of the five countries scheduled for it, eventually secured parliamentary majorities and was implemented in all of them. In the United States, the federal government rejected a Freeze, scrapped the SALT II treaty, and moved forward with plans to militarize space. Social democratic parties opposing missile deployment lost elections in the Netherlands (1982 and 1986), West Germany (1983), and Great Britain (1983), while the pro-Freeze Democrats suffered an electoral debacle in the United States in 1984. Elsewhere, too, antinuclear parties proved unable to win the majorities necessary to govern (as in Japan and Italy). In large part, this reflected the difficulty of diverting governments from their Cold War fixations and of mobilizing most voters around the antinuclear issue, particularly when other matters seemed of more immediate relevance to them. Even peace activists were often distracted from the nuclear question by other foreign policy

crises: repression in Poland, the Falklands war, the struggle in South Africa, conflict in the Middle East, the war in Afghanistan, and U.S. intervention in Central America. Once again, there arose the difficulty of isolating the nuclear issue from other elements of public and governmental concern.

This was all the more true where governments, obsessed with the Cold War, also had a limited tolerance for dissent. In Turkey, a right-wing military coup in 1980 led to the silencing of the Turkish Peace Association and the imprisonment of eighteen of its leaders by military tribunals. In Czechoslovakia and Poland, frightened governments also clapped peace activists into prison. In East Germany, during 1983, the authorities expelled twenty young peace activists, charged two leaders of Women for Peace with "treason" for providing news of their activities to a British peace worker, and arrested young activists in Weimar for their graffiti campaign ("SS-20—No thanks!"). As harassment, detention, and fines accelerated in Hungary, the Dialogue group voted to dissolve; one fragment turned to closer work with the official Peace Council and the other chose the risks of illegal autonomy. . . .

As an organ of Soviet diplomacy, the World Peace Council also remained a prisoner of the Cold War. Although it could claim affiliates in 141 nations by the mid-1980s, only a few of these had any influence in the West. Publications of the WPC sharply contrasted Moscow's work "towards promoting peace and security in the world" with Washington's "maniacal space militarization program," "global war plans," and "drive towards a global apocalypse." Unable to control or even influence the nonaligned nuclear disarmament movement, the WPC eventually turned savagely against it. Yuri Zhukov, president of the Soviet Peace Committee, claimed that the "true objective" of nonaligned groups like END was to "split the anti-war movement," "infiltrate cold war elements into it," and "conceal and justify an aggressive militarist polity of the USA and NATO." Naturally, nonaligned peace groups found it very difficult to deal with the WPC and its affiliates.

Despite these problems, the third round of nuclear disarmament activism did produce some victories. In Spain, voters approved a referendum that, while providing for continued membership in NATO, banned nuclear weapons from Spanish soil. In India, now nuclear-capable, no nuclear arsenal was constructed. In New Zealand, where the Labour Party campaigned vigorously against admitting nuclear-powered or -armed ships, it swept to victory in 1984, ousted the ruling conservatives, mobilized other nations behind a nuclear-free Pacific, and bravely defied the U.S. government. Furthermore, having won the support of most social democratic parties, antinuclear forces looked forward to policy changes in numerous Western countries where they were serious contenders for power. At the same time, nonaligned peace movements in Eastern bloc countries seemed to have taken root, even though they remained beleaguered. Nor, despite a lull in mass demonstrations, was the nuclear issue dead. In January 1985, the leaders of Argentina, Greece, India, Mexico, Sweden, and Tanzania called for a halt to the testing, production, and deployment of nuclear weapons, followed by substantial reductions in nuclear arsenals. The following October, they renewed this "five continents' peace initiative."

Not least among the antinuclear movement's accomplishments was the creation of a new and broader peace movement international. The International Confederation for Disarmament and Peace had failed to flourish, in part for financial reasons, while END and the International Peace Communication and Coordination Center (organized by IKV in 1981) remained oriented toward Europe and opposed to building "bureaucratic" organizations. In order to accommodate the new array of nonaligned nuclear disarmament groups, leaders of the International Confederation and of the International Peace Bureau (founded in 1892) met at Gothenburg, Sweden, in September 1983, voted to merge, and adopted the name of the latter. Although the International

Peace Bureau remained considerably weaker than many of its constituent organizations, by 1986 it had drawn together 41 of the major nonaligned groups from Europe, North America, and Asia. . . .

What are we to conclude from this survey of the forty-one-year history of the world antinuclear movement? First, the movement has ebbed and flowed in response to the perceived dangers of nuclear war. Divisions on national, political, and bloc interest lines have been overcome to some degree in proportion to the apparent likelihood of nuclear destruction. Second, the movement, in turn, has heightened public consciousness about the implications of nuclear weapons and brought significant pressure to bear upon political leaders. In this fashion, it has served as a brake on the nuclear arms race. Without the eruption of a mass antinuclear movement, nuclear testing would almost certainly have been more common, nuclear proliferation greater, and nuclear war more likely. Third, despite the popularity of unilateral nuclear disarmament among a substantial minority and of proposals to block new missile deployment or freeze the arms race (i.e. to maintain the status quo) among a majority, the antinuclear movement has failed to stop the nuclear arms race—much less secure nuclear *dis*armament. . . .

How should one account for this? It appears that both the strength and the weakness of the nuclear disarmament movement are inherent in its emphasis on weapons. The strength of the movement lies in the fact that it focuses narrowly upon eliminating a weapon which most people consider odious, even suicidal. Therefore, the nuclear disarmament movement has the potential for overcoming political, national, and ideological divisions and for mobilizing considerably larger numbers of people than does traditional pacifism, with its more fundamental critique of violence, nationalism, and warfare. On the other hand, weapons are a symptom—and not the cause—of the problem: the problem of violent competition among nations. Thus, as Einstein wrote in 1949, "so long as security is sought through national armament, no country is likely to renounce any weapon that seems to promise it victory in war." Weapons, in short, cannot be divorced from the international conflicts that inspire their development and use. Certainly this is the tragic backdrop to the relentless nature of the nuclear arms race. It explains why so many national leaders are not serious about nuclear arms negotiations and why average citizens are so easily sidetracked from the cause of nuclear disarmament.

To confront the problem (and not merely the symptom) does not require accepting the existence of nuclear weapons and the prospect of nuclear holocaust. But this study suggests that it does require a recognition that the bomb proba-bly cannot be banned if nations remain free to go about their traditional business of waging war. If this is correct, avoiding nuclear catastrophe may mean—as some peace leaders have recently argued—that peace movements around the world must tunnel under the nation-state to secure "détente from below." Or it may mean—as many internationalists have argued—that transnational authority at the top should be strengthened to the point that nations lose the ability to opt for war. Perhaps it means some combination of the two. In any case, nuclear disarmament seems unlikely without constraints upon the right to violence of the nation state. The real lesson of Hiroshima is that there must be no more war.

Kate Zernike
Dean E. Murphy

Antiwar Movement Morphs from Wild-Eyed to Civil

With the war against Iraq in its second week, the most influential antiwar coalitions have shifted away from large-scale disruptive tactics and stepped up efforts to appeal to mainstream Americans.

One of the largest groups, Win Without War, is encouraging the two million people on its e-mail list to send supportive letters to soldiers. Other groups have redoubled their fund-raising for billboards that declare "Peace is Patriotic" and include the giant image of an unfurling American flag.

The changed tone comes after a week of street protests marking the start of the war that reduced San Francisco to anarchy, turned Chicago's Lakeshore Drive into a parking lot and paralyzed major roads in Atlanta, Boston and other cities.

This week, the nation's largest antiwar coalitions said that they were abandoning their plan to disrupt everyday life.

Instead, they said, they would direct protests at federal institutions, corporations and media conglomerates that "profit from war" in an effort to attract attention but not offend most Americans.

The shift reflects a tension that has existed within the nation's antiwar movement for months.

Radical groups like those weaned on the antiglobalization protests that disrupted Seattle four years ago sought more civil disobedience.

More mainstream antiwar groups like the National Council of Churches were afraid that confrontational tactics would only alienate the American public.

At least for now, the more mainstream groups have gained the upper hand.

They have sought to cast their movement as the loyal opposition, embracing the troops but condemning the war. Within the movement, which includes everything from small groups in small towns to a large alliance of more than 200 organizations, radical elements still exist.

But the larger and more influential groups have sought over time to sideline them, deliberately excluding certain speakers, dismissing certain tactics, marginalizing certain protests, in a determined effort to avoid being dismissed as career malcontents.

The week before the war began, another major coalition, United for Peace and Justice, declined to join in sponsoring a rally put on by International Answer, a group whose names stands for Act Now to Stop War and End Racism, saying its message was too left-wing and alienating.

And even the umbrella organization that helped shut down San Francisco's financial district last week began its more mundane protests this week with an announcement that demonstrators interested in thuggery should keep their distance.

"If we're going to be a force that needs to be listened to by our elected officials, by the media, by power, our movement needs to reflect the population," said Leslie Cagan, co-chairwoman of United for Peace and Justice, and a career political organizer.

"It needs to be diverse," Ms. Cagan went on, "it needs to be large, it needs to include the people who could be described as mainstream—but that doesn't exclude the people who are sometimes thought of as the fringes."

Even the more mainstream groups are full of people who have spent large stretches of their lives on the front lines of various protest movements, from the civil rights struggles to antiglobalization campaigns. But they say they have learned from their own mistakes. So while attacking corporate America for driving this war, antiwar groups have co-opted corporate strategies, rolling out media campaigns as if opposition to war were a new kind of cola.

For weeks, public relations firms have sent news organizations daily suggestions for interviews and "great visuals" that feature protesters. Groups practicing civil disobedience make sure their designated publicity person avoids arrest, to remain available to television cameras. One organization even "embedded" reporters among protesters the way the Pentagon did with its troops.

"The great lesson from Madison Avenue is repetition," Ms. Cagan said. "If you get the same message out in different ways, you begin to break into people's consciousness."

The New Era: Rallying Round the E-Mail Lists

The last time a vast antiwar movement took American streets was during the Vietnam War, so comparisons between this movement and that one are inevitable.

The new antiwar groups take pride in the size of the crowds they have been able to mobilize. They have grown a protest movement the size of which it took Vietnam-era organizers four years to build—this time, without a draft and

even before the first body bags might shock people into the streets.

United for Peace and Justice, for example, says it took only six weeks to get 350,000 people to a rally in New York in February, and Win Without War says it took four days to set up 6,800 candlelight vigils the week the war began.

"I am rather pleased with the way things have gone," said Michael N. Nagler, the founder and former chairman of the Peace and Conflict Studies Department at the University of California at Berkeley. "I have been monitoring the peace movement for almost four decades, and often wringing my hands in despair for its lack of savvy and lack of organization."

Still, it is a different era now.

Protest has become routine, no longer seen as an assault on the country's values and culture the way it was when demonstrators descended on Washington in the 1960's.

The Internet makes it far easier to organize swiftly and draw out crowds.

In fact, some might say this movement—which unlike the one during Vietnam began before the start of the Iraq conflict—failed in its most important goal: to stop the war before it commenced. Certainly the protesters say they have learned that they need a long-term strategy.

"It's tremendously saddening," said Eli Pariser, international campaigns director of MoveOn.org, a member of the Win Without War coalition, said of the start of the war.

"At the same time, there still is optimism that in terms of our larger goal, which is to end this foreign policy that is so dangerous, there's still hope, and quite a lot of it."

The Mobilization: In Diversity There Is Strength

The antiwar movement is a set of diverse groups that often overlap, swapping staff, money, and office space, acting in concert and alone.

Some are offshoots of well-known national groups with multimillion-dollar budgets, large paid staffs and other agendas: The Sierra Club and the National Council of Churches, the National Organization for Women and the N.A.A.C.P.

Others are more obscure or formed explicitly in the context of the war: Code Pink, September 11 Families For Peaceful Tomorrows, People for a Gasoline-Free Day. And many cities have their own organizations with their own distinct local flavor.

Direct Action to Stop the War, with no paid staff, no offices and no formal fundraising efforts, dominates the protest scene in San Francisco.

One of its leaders, Patrick Reinsborough, had led an effort to pressure Home Depot to discontinue the sale of products made with old-growth trees. Another, Mary Bull, is the coordinator of the Save the Redwoods/Boycott the Gap Campaign. She was once arrested, dressed as a tree, outside the World Bank and International Monetary Fund in Washington.

The coalitions against the war have drawn on the budgets and staffs of the larger national groups that have joined in.

Many of the newer organizations are too fresh to have reported finances to government regulators. But they say they have also gotten money from various other sources, including the Barbra Streisand Foundation; Ben Cohen of Ben and Jerry's; and Paulette Cole of ABC Carpet and Home in New York City.

They say they have also raised significant amounts of money in smaller increments online. Win Without War says it raised $400,000 online in 48 hours, with an average donation of $35.

The Mainstream Shift: Opposing the War, but Still Patriotic

When the antiwar protests began to gather steam in the fall, the large-scale rallies were being run by International Answer.

Answer brought together an amalgam of demonstrators, including antiglobalization protesters and long-time Socialists. Some of its chief organizers were members of the Workers World Party, a radical Socialist group that has defended Slobodan Milosevic and the North Korean and Iraqi governments.

In the protest community, the group was especially known for good organization: in some cities, Answer would go early in the year and snap up protest permits for the largest public places on the best dates. Last fall, many smaller groups opposed to the war were planning to attend the rally Answer had organized for Oct. 26 in Washington.

But the afternoon before the event, representatives of about 50 groups gathered at the Washington office of People for the American Way, a liberal group that is known for causes like opposition to conservative judges.

It was a diverse set, including Black Voices for Peace; the Institute for Policy Studies, which is a left-leaning research center; and the American Friends Service Committee, a Quaker group. Many in attendance knew each other from past protests.

For nearly a month in private conversations, they say they had been sharing their concerns that Answer's oratory was too anti-Israel, too angry. They worried that its rallies were not focused enough on the war: banners in the crowd were as much about "Free Palestine" and "Free Mumia"—a reference to Mumia Abu-Jamal, imprisoned for killing a Philadelphia police officer—as they were "No Blood For Oil."

"Answer is a radical left group and not very mainstream in terms of its image," said David Cortright, a veteran of the Vietnam War and the protests against it, who attended the meeting as head of the Fourth Freedom Forum, a research center promoting peaceful resolution of international conflicts. "It was not the kind of movement I thought would be able to attract the kind of mainstream support I thought was out there."

They decided that afternoon to form a new coalition that would operate apart from Answer. They named it United for Peace and Justice. It immediately began planning small actions for December and January in various cities, and a large rally in New York City on Feb. 15, where speakers would be told that their remarks had to be about the war and nothing else.

Later that same October day, eight people from the meeting went out for dinner, worried, some of them say, that even their new alternative to Answer would not get the support of important mass constituency groups like labor, veterans and churches.

Over Chinese food, those eight agreed to create another group, calling this one Win Without War. To join, said Mr. Pariser of MoveOn, one of those attending, organizations had to explicitly sign on to the notion of being patriotic and taking a "reasonable" stance toward a conflict with Iraq, which at that time meant the continuation of weapons inspections.

"Right from the beginning we tried to frame it as a message that would go down well in broader communities than just the antiwar crowd," said Mr. Cortright, another of the eight. "The average labor guy out there wants to be seen in that mainstream, patriotic light."

Win Without War announced itself in December with a news conference and a Web site identifying itself as the "mainstream" voice against the war. Doing so allowed it to win members like the N.A.A.C.P., the National Organization for Women, the Sierra Club and the National Council of Churches and gain access to their mailing lists and memberships.

"Affiliating with other organizations that don't normally get involved in peace movements gave us a way to appeal to middle America," said Bob Edgar, general secretary of the council of churches.

Answer itself continued to organize rallies. Mara Verheyden-Hilliard, a steering committee member, said her group took the "most progressive stand." She said the other coalitions included elements "far more to the right."

And other smaller groups would spawn, local groups in various cities and towns, national groups like Code Pink, which appealed to women, and the Iraq Pledge of Resistance, which signed people up in advance to commit nonviolent civil disobedience the day the war began.

But most of those groups affiliated in some way with one of the two large national groups—if only to list their events on the national Web site.

As time went on, United for Peace and Justice took on the job of organizing rallies. Win Without War's task focused on the news media. It took as its national director a former Democratic congressman from Maine, Tom Andrews, who had been working with a public relations firm hired by the coalition.

The Internet would prove crucial to both organizing and media. United for Peace and Justice said 40,000 people signed up for e-mail bulletins about actions against the war. Win Without War says its e-mail list includes more than two million addresses. Earlier this month, Win Without War created a worldwide candlelight vigil online, allowing people to enter their ZIP codes to find the nearest one.

A crucial player in Win Without War's campaigns has been MoveOn, an organization originally started by two Silicon Valley entrepreneurs to provide a way for voters to go online to express their opposition to the impeachment of President Bill Clinton.

In January, Mr. Pariser sent out an e-mail message saying that the organization wanted to buy a newspaper advertisement, and could raise $27,000 privately if it could raise the same amount online.

The Debate: Civil Disobedience Is Toned Down

Within two days, Mr. Pariser said, online donors pledged $400,000, and the group bought several newspaper advertisements, a radio commercial, and ultimately, several television spots. One, in which a scene of a small girl plucking daisy petals morphs into military images and a mushroom cloud, borrowed heavily from the "daisy" commercial that Lyndon B. Johnson's campaign used against Barry Goldwater in 1964 to stir fears about nuclear Armageddon.

When the war started last week, United for Peace and Justice and Win Without War were split over civil disobedience, the tool that many in the antiwar movement had been saving for the start of hostilities.

United for Peace said it supported nonviolent civil disobedience, while Win Without War said it did not. But as the general shift in strategy swept the peace movement over last weekend, United for Peace and Justice scaled back its advocacy of civil disobedience. Its Web site now encourages those against the war to light a candle for peace, to wear a black armband, to display a yellow ribbon.

Smaller regional groups seemed to take the cue, trading sit-ins for bike rides for peace. In New York, antiwar groups called for mass civil disobedience on Thursday. There were more than 200 arrests but most protesters remained orderly. They specifically fixed on Rockefeller Center, because it is the home of General Electric, its NBC subsidiary and The Associated Press. Organizers say news media companies and companies like G.E. will profit from the war, whether from high ratings, newspaper sales, military contracts or payments to rebuild Iraq after the war.

The most notable example of the new tone came in San Francisco, which had emerged early on as a hotbed of the antiwar movement.

Last week, the goal of the San Francisco umbrella organization, Direct Action to Stop the War, had been to disrupt the city's everyday life. Twenty intersections and thoroughfares were picked as places to stop traffic, with demonstrators sitting on the asphalt and refusing to budge.

More than 2,300 people were arrested in three days, the largest number of arrests in such a short time period in decades, the police said.

The civil disobedience achieved its main goal of attracting attention around the world. But it also annoyed a good number of San Francis-cans, most notably Mayor Willie L. Brown Jr., a Democrat who is sympathetic to the antiwar cause. At one point he urged the demonstrators to leave San Francisco and converge on Crawford, Tex., where President Bush has a ranch.

So at a meeting Sunday night at San Francisco's St. Boniface Church, some of Direct Action's most active supporters, joined by members from many other groups, including United For Peace and Justice, decided to accommodate the mood of a city—and country—at war.

"We agreed to a change in tactics," said Renee Sharp, who when not protesting the war works as an analyst for an environmental advocacy group in Oakland. "We no longer need to disrupt business as usual; we've made that point. Our goal isn't to make life difficult for everybody living here."

The shift was swift. At a training session for protesters early Monday morning near the San Francisco waterfront, a young woman in a knit cap took the microphone. As had been the routine at other gatherings, she led the crowd of 300 or so in a recitation. "Repeat after me," she said. "I do not want to answer questions. I want to talk with my lawyer."

But the script then deviated markedly from that of the weeks before. After people pored over a poster board map and got their assignments—most were told to block entrances to the Transamerica Pyramid building—they were sent marching in a fairly obedient form of disobedience.

They headed down the sidewalk alongside the streets that last week they had mobbed. This time they were in neat double file led by a Franciscan priest holding two church candles. The procession was so orderly, a large group of police officers having breakfast outside a nearby bagel shop did not even budge as it passed.

■ FIGURE 54.1.

SORTING IT OUT

Parsing the Antiwar Movement

Three national coalitions have helped to organize many recent protests.

	International Answer (Act Now to Stop War and End Racism)	United for Peace and Justice	Win Without War
DATE FOUNDED	Sept. 14, 2001	Oct. 25, 2002	Dec. 10, 2002
SOME GROUPS INVOLVED	Free Palestine Alliance, U.S.	Code Pink	MoveOn.org
	Mexico Solidarity Network	Greenpeace	N.A.A.C.P.
	Middle East Children's Alliance	Iraq Pledge of Resistance	National Council of Churches
	Muslim Student Association of the U.S. and Canada	Not In Our Name	National Organization for Women
		September 11 Families for Peaceful Tomorrows	Physicians for Social Responsibility
		Socialist Party U.S.A.	Veterans for Peace

More than 2,400 cities have registered antiwar demonstrations with United for Peace and Justice and MoveOn.org
From Nov. 1, 2002 to March 22, 2003

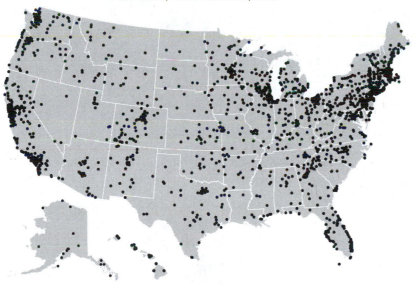

Sources: Individual groups; WarTimes; Moveon.org. Copyright © 2003 by The New York Times Co. Reprinted with permission.

Questions for Discussion

1. Do you agree with DeBenedetti that U.S. peace activists experienced more bad than good fortune during the forty years following World War II? Why or why not?
2. What lessons were learned from peace activism in the United States during the Vietnam War?
3. What is the most effective way to protest against the development of nuclear arsenals by both developed and developing countries?
4. Do you agree with Wittner that "weapons are a symptom not the cause of the problem: the problem of violent competition among nations?"
5. What, if anything, can be achieved by the civil disobedience movements?
6. Considering the thesis of Zernike and Murphy, do you think that more "civil" antiwar movements in the future will be more effective than the "wild-eyed" movements? Why or why not?

Further Readings

1. Grundy, John, and Howell, Alison. "Negotiating the Culture of Resistance: A Critical Assessment of Protest Politics." *Studies in Political Economy*, 2001, 66, Autumn, 121–132.
2. Galtung, Johan. "The Peace Movement: An Exercise in Micro-Macro Linkages," *International Social Science Journal*, 1998, September, 401–405.
3. Kriesberg, Louis, "Social Movements and Global Transformation," in Jackie Smith, Charles Chatfield, and Ron Pagnucco, eds., *Transnational Social Movements and Global Politics*. New York: Syracuse University Press, 3–18.
4. Rucht, Dieter, ed. *Research on Social Movements: The State of Art in Western Europe and the USA*. Boulder, CO: Westview Press, 1991.
5. Ekins, Paul. *A New World Order: Grassroots Movements for Global Change*. London/New York: Routledge, 1992.
6. Kim, Quee-Young. "Minutes to Midnight: Nuclear Weapons Protest in America." *Contemporary Sociology*, 1991, 20, 1, Jan., 40–41.
7. McCrea, Frances B., and Markle, Gerald E. "Atomic Scientists and Protest: The Bulletin as a Social Movement Organization." *Research in Social Movements, Conflicts and Change,* 1989, 11, 219–233.
8. Moore, Kelly. "Political Protest and Institutional Change: The Anti-Vietnam War Movement and American Science" in Marco Giugni, Doug McAdam, and Charles Tilly, eds., *How Social Movements Matter*. Minneapolis: University of Minnesota Press, 1999, 97–115.

Democracy, Democratization and Peace

The relationship between democracy and peace is one that has been extensively researched by political scientists. The major empirical finding that democracies do not wage war against each other is explored at length in this section.

In "Grasping the Democratic Peace: Principles For a Post–Cold War World" Bruce Russett explains the meaning of the concept of democratic peace by meticulously defining the terms *democracy* and *peace*. He uses history to demonstrate that two democratic countries have never fought each other. The author refutes all examples that are cited as being contrary to this claim. The Spanish–American War and the Franco–Prussian War are disqualified by the author on the basis of his definition of democracy and peace.

Edward Mansfield and Jack Snyder, in "Democratization and War," explain that the issue is not as simple as implied by some theorists. Although it may be true that well-established democracies do not engage each other in violent conflict, nascent democracies and ones that are still in the process of democratization are more vulnerable to warfare. The authors identify a breakdown of central authority, reformation of state institutions, and the phenomenon of nationalism, as possible causes of the interstate wars. The statistics provided in this reading, relevant to the probability of states engaging in warfare, are based on the "kind" of transition they have undergone, and the rapidity of their transition from autocracy to democracy. The authors also criticize the U.S. policy of supporting "overnight" democratic change in other states. This reading presents arguments as to why the United States should pay close attention to the process through which democracy is established in different countries.

In "Fanatical Terrorism versus Disciplines of Constitutional Democracy" Chester A. Newland argues that the terrorist attacks on the World Trade Center and the Pentagon were also attacks on civilization. For over two decades, fanatical terrorists have waged a global war. Although conventional warfare opponents are symmetrically matched, the war on terror employs methods of asymmetrical strategies of violence that pose asymmetric threats. Will an international terrorist network inaugurate World War III? How should civilization respond to this pervasive threat? Newland proposes that we employ the disciplines of constitutional democracy, the rule of law, and human caring with duty and public service.

In "Promoting Democracy and Fighting Terror" Thomas Carothers examines U.S. foreign policy regarding the promotion of democracy abroad. The author points out the liaisons the U.S. has been forging with different autocracies and semidemocracies around the world to garner support for its antiterrorism campaign. A detailed analysis of U.S. efforts to promote democracy in the Middle East is also presented in this reading. The various intervention campaigns that the United States has undertaken in the past, to "install" democracies in Latin American countries are compared with the recent efforts to democratize Afghanistan and Iraq. The potential disadvantages of such ambitious operations are discussed.

Bruce Russett

Grasping the Democratic Peace: Principles for a Post–Cold War World

Scholars and leaders now commonly say "Democracies almost never fight each other." What does that mean? Is it true? If so, what does it imply for the future of international politics? Would the continued advance of democracy introduce an era of relative world peace? Can policymakers act so as to make that kind of peaceful world more likely, and, if so, how? Does the post–Cold War era represent merely the passing of a particular adversarial relationship, or does it offer a chance for fundamentally changed relations among nations?

During the Cold War, Soviet-American hostility was overdetermined. The very different political systems of the two superpowers, with their built-in ideological conflict, ensured a deadly political and military rivalry. So too did the systemic stresses of two great powers, each leading a big alliance in a bipolar confrontation, which ensured that each would resist any enhancement of the other's strength as a threat to its own security. But the end of the Cold War destroyed both those sources of hostility. The ideological conflict dissolved with the end of communism, and the bipolar confrontation collapsed with that of the Soviet alliance system and of the Soviet Union itself. Given the revolutionary changes both in the global system and in the states that comprise it, the old bases for evaluating the character of international relations have also collapsed.

The end of ideological hostility matters doubly because it represents a surrender to the force of Western values of economic and especially political freedom. To the degree that countries once ruled by autocratic systems become democratic,

a striking fact about the world comes to bear on any discussion of the future of international relations: in the modern international system, democracies have almost never fought each other. This statement represents a complex phenomenon: (a) Democracies rarely fight each other (an empirical statement) because (b) they have other means of resolving conflicts between them and therefore do not need to fight each other (a prudential statement), and (c) they perceive that democracies should not fight each other (a normative statement about principles of right behavior), which reinforces the empirical statement. By this reasoning, the more democracies there are in the world, the fewer potential adversaries we and other democracies will have and the wider the zone of peace. . . .

The vision of a peace among democratically governed states has long been invoked as part of a larger structure of institutions and practices to promote peace among nation-states. Immanuel Kant (1970) spoke of perpetual peace based partially upon states sharing "republican constitutions." His meaning was compatible with basic contemporary understandings of democracy. As the elements of such a constitution he identified freedom (with legal equality of subjects), representative government, and separation of powers. The other key elements of his perpetual peace were "cosmopolitan law" embodying ties of international commerce and free trade, and a "pacific union" established by treaty in international law among republics.

Woodrow Wilson expressed the same vision for the twentieth century. This normative political basis of Wilson's vision of world order, evident as early as 1894, grew naturally from his progressive inclinations in domestic politics (Knock 1992, 9ff.); and his Fourteen Points sound almost as though Kant were guiding Wilson's writing hand. They included Kant's cosmopolitan law and pacific union. The third point demanded "the removal, so far as possible, of all economic barriers and the establishment of an equality of trade conditions among all the nations consenting to the peace and associating themselves for its maintenance"; and the fourteenth point called for "a general association of nations . . . formed under specific covenants for the purpose of affording mutual guarantees of political dependence and territorial integrity to great and small states alike." He did not so clearly invoke the need for universal democracy, since at that time not all of America's war allies were democracies. But the suggestion of this principle is clear enough if one thinks about the domestic political conditions necessary for his first point: "Open covenants of peace, openly arrived at, after which there shall be no private international understandings of any kind but diplomacy shall proceed always frankly and in the public view." Moreover, his 1917 war message openly asserted that "a steadfast concert of peace can never be maintained except by a partnership of democratic nations.". . .

The Spread of Democratic Peace

At the time of Kant, and even of Wilson, the hope for a world of democratic nation states was merely that: a hope, a theory perhaps, but without much empirical referent. Certainly in Kant's time, Europe was hardly an area in which republics flourished. By the time of Wilson's Fourteen Points there were more, in the New World as well as the Old, but the dozen or so democracies of that time still were substantially in a minority.

Wilsonian "idealism" was widely regarded as discredited by the outbreak of World War II. True, the principles of collective security, as embodied in the League of Nations, failed to contain aggression by the Axis powers. In that sense,

the element of international law in the Kantian and Wilsonian vision failed. But the elements of trade and democracy were never given a fair chance. International trade was damaged first by the imposition of war reparations on defeated Germany—with some of the effects forecast by Keynes—and then by the round of "beggar my neighbor" trade restraints imposed with the collapse of the world economy in the Great Depression. Not coincidentally, democracy also was lost in many countries; first in Russia, then Italy, Germany, Central Europe, Japan, and elsewhere. Thus the Kantian prescription once again had little basis on which to work.

Largely unnoticed, however, was the empirical fact that democracies had rarely if ever gone to war with each other during this period. Since there were few democracies, often at a distance from each other, it is hardly surprising that their failure to fight each other was little noticed. States need both an opportunity and a willingness (Most and Starr 1989) to go to war with each other. Noncontiguous democracies, unless one or both were great powers, had little opportunity to fight each other. States cannot fight unless they can exert substantial military power against each others' vital territory. Most states, if not great powers with "global reach" . . . could exert such power only against contiguous states or at least near neighbors. Furthermore, the willingness of states to fight depends in large part on issues over which they have conflicts of interest. Territorial disputes (over borders, or rights of ethnic groups whose presence is common to both) are rare in the absence of proximity (Diehl and Goertz 1992). Since relatively few of the democracies bordered each other in the 1920s and 1930s, it is not surprising that they generally avoided war with each other. Thus the empirical fact of little or no war between democracies up to this time could be obscured by the predominance of authoritarian states in the international system, and the frequent wars involving one or more such authoritarian states. One could still see the international system as not only anarchic, but in principle threatening the "war of all against all."

Following World War II the situation changed, again, ironically, with a vision of war prevention geared primarily to the last war. The post–World War II era began with the founding of the United Nations, dedicated—as was the League—to the general principle of collective security as carried out by Franklin Roosevelt's "four (ultimately five) policemen" with the power of permanent representatives on the Security Council. But with the Cold War and Soviet-American deadlock in the Security Council arising almost immediately, attention shifted to the more traditional means of collective security through alliance. Despite rhetorical statements like the Universal Declaration of Human Rights and the fact that most—but not all—members of the newly formed North Atlantic Treaty Organization were democracies, democracy was seen more as a binding principle of the Cold War coalition against communism than as a force actively promoting peace among democracies themselves. Moreover, many members of the wider Western alliance system (in Latin America, the Middle East, and Asia) certainly were not democratic.

But by the 1970s, with the increasing numbers of democracies in the international system, the empirical fact of peace among democracies became harder to ignore. There were at one time by various counts thirty-five or so democratic states, and more of them were proximate to one another. Still there was little war, or even serious threats of war, to be found in relationships among those democracies. And more clearly than before, the phenomenon of democratic peace extended beyond the North Atlantic area, and beyond merely the rich industrialized countries belonging to the OECD. The phenomenon began then to be more widely recognized, and by the end of the 1980s it had been widely accepted in the international relations literature, though not so easily explained. This research result is extremely robust, in that by various criteria of war and militarized diplomatic disputes, and various measures of democracy, the relative rarity of violent conflict between democracies still holds up.

By early 1992 it even had passed into popular political rhetoric, with the international zone of "democratic peace" invoked in speeches by then Secretary of State James Baker and President George Bush, and by Bill Clinton during his presidential campaign.

Wide recognition is not, however, synonymous with universal acceptance. It became confused with a claim that democracies are *in general,* in dealing with all kinds of states, more peaceful than are authoritarian or other nondemocratically constituted states. This is a much more controversial proposition than "merely" that democracies are peaceful in their dealings with each other, and one for which there is little systematic evidence. Especially in the Vietnam era of U.S. "imperial overreach," it was a politically charged and widely disbelieved proposition. In that light, both academic observers and policymakers refused to accept even the statement that democracies are peaceful toward each other as a meaningful empirical generalization without some kind of theoretical explanation indicating that it was not merely a coincidence or accident.

Furthermore, some variants of the proposition took the form of statements like "democracies never go to war with each other," or even "democracies never fight each other." The latter statement, applied to relatively low-level lethal violence, is demonstrably wrong as a law-like "never" statement even for the modern international system. The former, limiting the statement to the large-scale and typically sustained form of organized international violence commonly designated as war, nonetheless tempts the historically minded reader to come up with counterexamples. And, especially with the key terms still largely undefined, it is not hard to identify candidate counterexamples.

Democracy, War, and Other Ambiguous Terms

. . . First, democratically organized political systems in general operate under restraints that make them more peaceful in their relations with other democracies. Democracies are not necessarily peaceful, however, in their relations with other kinds of political systems. Second, in the modern international system, democracies are less likely to use lethal violence toward other democracies than toward autocratically governed states or than autocratically governed states are toward each other. Furthermore, there are no clearcut cases of sovereign stable democracies waging war with each other in the modern international system. Third, the relationship of relative peace among democracies is importantly a result of some features of democracy, rather than being caused exclusively by economic or geopolitical characteristics correlated with democracy. Exactly what those features are is a matter of theoretical debate, which we shall explore.

At the risk of boring the reader, further discussion requires some conceptual precision. Without it everyone can—and often does—endlessly debate counter-examples while by-passing the phenomenon itself. We need to define what we mean by democracy and war, so as to be able to say just how rare an occasion it is for two democracies to go to war with each other. When we do so it will be evident that those occasions virtually never arise. . . .

Interstate War

War here means large-scale institutionally organized lethal violence, and to define "large-scale" we shall use the threshold commonly used in the social scientific literature on war: one thousand battle fatalities (Small and Singer 1982). The figure of one thousand deaths is arbitrary but reasonable. It is meant to eliminate from the category of wars those violent events that might plausibly be ascribed to:

1. "Accident" (e.g., planes that may have strayed across a national boundary by mistake, and been downed).
2. Deliberate actions by local commanders, but not properly authorized by central authorities, as in many border incidents.

3. Limited, local authorized military actions not necessarily intended to progress to large-scale violent conflict but undertaken more as bargaining moves in a crisis, such as military probes intended to demonstrate one's own commitment and to test the resolve of the adversary.
4. Deliberate military actions larger than mere probes, but not substantially resisted by a usually much weaker adversary. The Soviet invasion of Czechoslovakia in 1968, which was met with substantial nonviolent resistance but not force of arms and resulted in less than a score of immediate deaths, is such an example, and contrasts with the Soviet invasion of Hungary in 1956 which produced roughly seventeen thousand Hungarian and Soviet dead.

A threshold of one thousand battle deaths rather neatly cuts off the above kinds of events while leaving largely intact the category of most conflicts that intuitively satisfy the commonsense meaning of war. (Not, of course such rhetorical examples as the "war on poverty" . . . [or] between Britain and Iceland in the 1975 "Cod War" over fishing rights.) It is also convenient that the one thousand-battle-death threshold provides a neat empirical break, with few conflicts between nation states very near it on either side. The most questionable case is probably that between Britain and the Argentine military dictatorship in 1982, over the Falkland Islands/Islas Malvinas. . . . It was deliberate, authorized, and involved some fierce land, naval, and air engagements and two invasions (first by Argentina, and then when the British returned to expel the Argentine invaders). It should count as a war, without apology.

The U.K.-Argentine war was unusual in that it inflicted very few civilian casualties. Most wars are not so limited, with civilian deaths frequently far outnumbering those of combatants. Deaths from hunger and disease may also far outnumber battle-inflicted casualties, as surely happened in many nineteenth-century wars and may well have been the case with the Iraqis after Operation

Desert Storm. But the number of such deaths may be difficult or impossible to estimate reliably and may be as much a consequence of inadequate medical and public-health capabilities as of military actions. Without minimizing the human consequences of such civilian deaths, it is simply less ambiguous to limit the definition to battle deaths. Similarly, the definition omits wounded and military personnel missing in action, figures commonly included in "casualty" totals but of lower reliability.

A related problem is that of deciding which political units are to be listed as fighting in a war. Sometimes in coalition warfare most or all of the deaths in a particular coalition will be borne by one or a few members with other members formally but not practically engaged in combat. For the latter, especially in circumstances where a nominal combatant suffers few or *no* identifiable deaths, it seems forced to include it among war participants. Small and Singer (1982, chap. 4) use a criterion requiring a state either to commit at least one thousand troops to battle, or to suffer at least one hundred battle fatalities, in order to count as a participant.

This definition also excludes, on theoretical grounds, covert actions in which one government secretly undertakes activities, including the use of lethal violence and the support of violent actors within the other government's territory, either to coerce or to overthrow that government. Such activities may not involve deaths on the scale of "wars," and when they do the foreign intervention is by its very covert nature hard to document (though one can often, if perhaps belatedly, discover the metaphoric "smoking gun"). But these activities, precisely because they are denied at the time by the government that undertakes them, imply very different political processes than does a war publicly and officially undertaken. . . .

For purposes of theoretical precision in argument yet another qualification is required, and that is a definition of "interstate" war. Here that term means war between sovereign "states" internationally recognized as such by other states,

including by major powers whose recognition of a government typically confers de facto statehood. Some such definition focusing on organized independent states is common in the social science literature, and is important for the analysis. . . . It is meant to exclude those "colonial" wars fought for the acquisition of territory inhabited by "primitive" people without recognized states, as practiced by nineteenth-century imperialism, or for the twentieth-century liberation of those people. War it may certainly be, but interstate it is not unless or until both sides are generally recognized as having the attributes of statehood. Applying this definition may well display a Western cultural bias, but it is appropriate to the behavior of states which, in the period, also are defined as "democratic" by the admittedly Western standards spelled out below. Nonstate participants would not meet those standards.

Wars of liberation—with one or both parties not yet recognized as a state—are in this respect similar to those civil wars in which one or both parties to the conflict fights precisely so as to be free of sharing statehood with the other. Such wars are fought to escape from the coercive institutions of a common state, and to include them would confuse rather than clarify the generalization that democracies rarely go to war with each other. . . .

Democracy

For modern states, democracy (or polyarchy, following Dahl 1971) is usually identified with a voting franchise for a substantial fraction of citizens, a government brought to power in contested elections, and an executive either popularly elected or responsible to an elected legislature, often also with requirements for civil liberties such as free speech. Huntington uses very similar criteria of "a twentieth-century political system as democratic to the extent that its most powerful collective decision makers are selected through fair, honest, and periodic elections in which candidates freely compete for votes and in which virtually all the adult population is eligible to vote."

In addition, he identifies a free election for transfer of power from a nondemocratic government as "the critical point in the process of democratization." Ray similarly requires that the possibility for the leaders of the government to be defeated in an election and replaced has been demonstrated by historical precedent.

A simple dichotomy between democracy and autocracy of course hides real shades of difference, and mixed systems that share features of both. Moreover, the precise application of these terms is to some degree culturally and temporally dependent. As we shall see, democracy did not mean quite the same to the ancient Greeks as it does to people of the late twentieth century. Even in the modern era the yardstick has been rubbery. Nineteenth century democracies often had property qualifications for the vote and typically excluded women, while the United States—democratic by virtually any standard of the day—disenfranchised blacks. Britain, with its royal prerogatives, rotten boroughs, and very restricted franchise before the Reform Act of 1832, hardly could be counted as a democracy. Even that reform brought voting rights to less than one-fifth of adult males, so one might reasonably withhold the "democracy" designation until after the Second Reform Act of 1867, or even until the secret ballot was introduced in 1872. By then, at the latest, Britain took its place with the relatively few other states commonly characterized as democratic in the parlance of the era. But if, before the late nineteenth century, we admit countries with as few as 10 per cent of all adults eligible to vote as democratic (a criterion used by Small and Singer; Doyle uses a cutoff of 30 percent of all males), by the middle to late twentieth century nothing less than a substantially universal franchise will suffice.

The term "contested elections" admits similar ambiguities, but in practice it has come to require two or more legally recognized parties. States with significant prerogatives in military and foreign affairs for nonelected agents (e.g., monarchs) should be excluded as having nonresponsible executives, even in the nineteenth century.

By the middle to late twentieth century the matter of guaranteed and respected civil rights, including rights to political organization and political expression, also become a key element in any commonsense definition of democracy (Dahl 1989). The exercise of such civil rights tends to be highly correlated with the existence of democratic institutions as just elaborated, but not perfectly so. The institutions may be found without the regular widespread exercise of the rights; the opposite (civil liberties assured, but not democratic institutions) is rarer. For purposes of the discussion here we will nevertheless not use civil liberties per se as a defining quality, and we shall also ignore the matter of free-market economic liberties. While there is very likely a causal nexus between economic liberties and secure political freedom, the relationship is complex and, unlike some authors (Rummel 1983, Doyle 1983) I will not build it into the definition.

In not including civil rights and economic liberty as defining qualities of democracy we are lowering the standards by which a country can be labeled a democracy. That is highly relevant to our text topic, an examination of conflicts alleged by some scholars to be wars between democracies. By lowering the standards we are making it more likely that some events will be labeled wars between democracies—events that I and many other writers contend are, at most, exceedingly rare.

Theoretical precision, however, requires one further qualification: some rather minimal stability or longevity. Huntington (1991) emphasizes stability or institutionalization as "a central dimension in the analysis of any political system." To count a war as one waged by a democracy Doyle (1983) requires that representative government be in existence for at least three years prior to the war. Perhaps that is a bit too long, yet some period must have elapsed during which democratic processes and institutions could become established, so that both the citizens of the "democratic" state and its adversary could regard it as one governed by democratic principles. Most of the doubtful cases arise within a single year of the establishment of democratic government.

By application of these criteria it is impossible to identify unambiguously *any* wars between democratic states in the period since 1815. A few close calls exist, in which some relaxation of the criteria could produce such a case. But to have no clearcut cases, out of approximately 71 interstate wars involving a total of nearly 270 participants, is impressive. Even these numbers are deceptively low as representing total possibilities. For example, as listed by Small and Singer (1982), 21 states count as participating on the Allied side in World War II, with 8 on the Axis side. Thus in that war alone there were 168 pairs of warring states. Allowing for other multilateral wars, approximately 500 pairs of states went to war against each other in the period. Of these, fewer than a handful can with any plausibility at all be considered candidates for exceptions to a generalization that democracies do not fight each other.

Some Alleged Wars between Democracies

To see what these criteria produce, consider the list in Table 55.1 of wars that have sometimes been suggested as exceptions to the generalization that democracies do not go to war with each other.

Four should be dismissed because they fall outside the criteria established even for any kind of interstate war in the period. The first, the War of 1812, is easy to dismiss simply because it precedes the beginning date—1815—of the best-known compilation of all wars (Small and Singer 1982). That may seem like a cheap and arbitrary escape, but it is not. There simply were very few democracies in the international system before that date, and as we discussed with the British case above, though Britain had moved quite far from royal absolutism it just did not fit the criteria either of suffrage or of fully responsible executive.

The American Civil War and the Second Philippine War are also readily eliminated as plausible candidates by straightforward use of the definitions. Whatever it may be called below the Mason-Dixon line, the Civil War is rightly

■ **TABLE 55.1**
Some "Candidate" Wars between Democracies

War of 1812, U.S. and Great Britain

Roman Republic (Papal States) vs. France, 1849

American Civil War, 1861

Ecuador-Colombia, 1863

Franco-Prussian War, 1870

Boer War, 1899

Spanish-American War, 1898

Second Philippine War, 1899

World War I, Imperial Germany vs. western democracies 1914 / 17

World War II, Finland vs. western democracies 1941

Lebanon vs. Israel, 1948

Lebanon vs. Israel, 1967

named, in that the Confederacy never gained international recognition of its sovereignty; as a war for separation or to prevent separation it comes under our rubric of wars induced by the frictions of sharing common statehood. The Philippine War of 1899 was a colonial war, in which the United States was trying to solidify control of a former Spanish colony it had acquired. The Philippine resistance constituted an authentic war of resistance against colonialism, but not on the part of an elected democratic government. . . .

The Boer War, begun in 1899, also fails to fit the requirements for an interstate war. Small and Singer (1982) identify it as an extrasystemic war because the South African Republic—by far the larger of the two Boer combatants, the other being the Orange Free State—was not generally recognized as an independent state. Britain recognized only its internal sovereignty, retaining suzerainty and requiring it to submit all treaties to the British government for approval. This, too, is properly an unsuccessful war for independence. Moreover, the two Boer republics strained the definition of democracy, then as for almost a century subsequently. Not only was suffrage restricted to the white male minority (roughly 10 percent of the adult population) in the South African Republic, but the electorate was further reduced, perhaps by half, by a property qualification and long-term residence requirements (Lacour-Gayet 1978). . . .

Two other conflicts can be dismissed because they fall short of the casualty levels required for a "war." These are Finland's participation in World War II on the "wrong" side and Lebanon's involvement in the Six-Day War of 1967. Finland was actively at war only with the Soviet Union, in an attempt to wrest back the territory taken from it in the Winter War of 1939–40. Although it was nominally at war with the Western allies, there is no record of combat or casualties between Finland and democratic states that would even approach the rather low threshold specified above. In the Six-Day War of 1967 Lebanon (then still an at least marginally democratic state, as it was not when invaded by Israel in 1982) participated in "combat" only by sending a few aircraft into Israeli airspace; the planes were driven back with, apparently, no casualties at all.

In the remaining six cases one or both of the participants fails the test for democracy. Lebanon's participation in the 1948 war was well above the criterion used for a belligerent. Israel, however, had not previously been independent, and had not yet held a national election. While the authenticity of Israel's national leadership was hardly in question, Lebanon—itself not fully democratic—could not have been expected to accredit it as a democratic state.

The 1863 war between Ecuador and Colombia also fits the criteria for war, but neither regime meets any reasonable requirement for democratic stability. Both governments came to power through revolution. Colombia's president governed with a new federal constitution promulgated only in May 1863; Ecuador's Gabriel García Moreno became president two years earlier, but is described as heading an "autocratic regime" (Kohn 1986, 150) and governing "with absolute authority" (Langer 1972, 852). As for France against the Roman Republic, both parties were but ephemerally democratic. Following the revolution of early 1848, presidential elections took place under the new French constitution only in December of that year. The notion of a democratic Papal States sounds oxymoronic. The pope introduced a constitution with an elective council of deputies in 1848, but reserved veto power to himself and the College of Cardinals. After an insurrection in November, he fled and the Roman Republic was proclaimed in February 1849. Within two months the republic was at war with France.

The Franco-Prussian War can be eliminated simply by looking at France. Reforms ratified in the plebiscite of May 1870 could be interpreted as making the empire into a constitutional monarchy, but war began a mere two months later. In Prussia/Germany the emperor appointed and could dismiss the chancellor, a defeat in the

Reichstag did not remove the chancellor from office. The emperor's direct authority over the army and foreign policy deprives the state of the democratic criterion of "responsible executive" on war and peace matters; Berghahn (1973, 9) calls the constitutional position of the monarchy "almost absolutist." Doyle (1983) rightly excludes Imperial Germany from his list of liberal states. Such a decision removes World War I from the candidate list.

The most difficult case is the Spanish-American War of 1898. Spain after 1890 had universal male suffrage, and a bicameral legislature with an executive nominally responsible to it. But the reality was more complex. The ministry was selected by the king, who thus remained the effective ruler of the state. Nominally competitive elections were really manipulated by a process known as *caciquismo.* By mutual agreement, the Liberal and Conservative parties rotated in office; governmental changes preceded rather than followed elections. Through extensive corruption and administrative procedures the king and politicians in Madrid controlled the selection of parliamentary candidates and their election. Election results were often published in the press before polling day. The meaningless elections were thus manipulated by the king and his close advisers; the system lacked the democratic quality of a responsible executive (Carr 1980). May (1961) describes the system as "preserving the appearance of a parliamentary democracy with none of its suspected dangers." None of the published large-scale analyses of the question of democracies fighting each other puts Spain among the democratic countries (Small and Singer 1976, Doyle 1983, b; Chan 1984; Maoz and Abdolali 1989; Bremer 1992a), nor do most major long-term political surveys. (Vanhanen 1984; Banks 1971; Gurr et al. 1989 code it as sharing democratic and autocratic characteristics.)

It seems, therefore, best to treat it as a close call but probably not a refutation even of the strong statement that democracies *never* make war on each other. Equally important . . . is the matter of perceptions. The Spanish political situation was at best marginal enough that key United States decisionmakers could readily persuade themselves and their audiences that it was not democratic. Consider, for example, the remarks of the two Republican senators from Massachusetts. Senator Henry Cabot Lodge: "We are there because we represent the spirit of liberty and the spirit of the new time, and Spain is over against us because she is mediaeval, cruel, dying." Senator George Hoar: "The results of a great war [on which the U.S. was embarking] are due to the policy of the king and the noble and the tyrant, not the policy of the people" (*Congressional Record,* April 13, 1898, p. 3783 and April 14, 1898, p. 3831).

Subsequent to my writing the above, Ray (1993) has presented a thorough review of these and other alleged cases of wars between democracies, and concludes that the generalization of no wars between democracies remains true. Whether or not one holds to the lawlike "never" statement may not really be very important. Almost all of the few near misses are in the nineteenth century. Since that was an era of generally very imperfect democracy by modern criteria, it is no surprise to find most of the near misses then.

Depending on the precise criteria, only twelve to fifteen states qualified as democracies at the end of the nineteenth century. The empirical significance of the rarity of war between democracies emerges only in the first half of the twentieth century, with at least twice the number of democracies as earlier, and especially with the existence of perhaps sixty democracies by the mid-1980s. Since the statistical likelihood of war between democracies is related to the number of pairs of democracies, the contrast between the two centuries is striking: by a very loose definition, possibly three or four wars out of roughly sixty pairs before 1900, and at most one or two out of about eighteen hundred pairs thereafter. As twentieth-century politics unfold, the phenomenon of war between democracies becomes impossible or almost impossible to find.

Even with the differing definitions of democracy and of war, this generalization is exceedingly robust. Long-term rival states, with many conflicts of interest between them, have gone to war or had substantial fatal clashes only when one or both of them was not governed democratically. For example, in the case of the Greek-Turkish dispute over Cyprus, by far the worst violence erupted in 1974 under the most dictatorial government either country experienced since 1945, when the Greek colonels over-threw the elected Cypriot government of Archbishop Makarios. Faced with the prospect of forcible *enosis* between Greece and Cyprus, Turkey replied by invading the island and occupying nearly a third of its territory. By contrast, the 1963–64 clashes—when democratic Greek and Turkish governments supported their protégés during outbreaks on the islands—were much more easily contained, largely by an American warning and UN peacekeeping action. And confrontations later in the 1970s, between democratic governments, were restrained short of any fatalities (Markides 1977; Rustow 1987; Stearns, ed., 1992). India and Pakistan have of course fought repeatedly and sometimes bloodily during their history as independent states. Yet no fatalities are recorded in disputes between them during Pakistan's most democratic periods of 1962–64 and 1988–92 (Burke 1973; Thomas 1986; Tillema 1991). . . .

It is tempting to believe that a norm against the use of force between democracies, and even the threat of use of force, has emerged and strengthened over time. To pursue the matter of norms, however, becomes a subject for much further analysis. The emergence of norms against democracies fighting each other is traceable, and by many theories it did indeed become a powerful restraint. Other theories, however, attribute the relative absence of lethal violence between democracies to many other influences. . . .

The emergence of new democracies with the end of the Cold War presents an opening for change in the international system more fundamental even than at the end of other big wars—World Wars I and II and the Napoleonic Wars. For the first time ever, in 1992 a virtual majority of states (91 of 183; McColm et al., 1992, 47) approximated the standards we have employed for democracy. Another 35 were in some form of transition to democracy. Democracy in many of these states may not prove stable. This global democratic wave may crest and fall back, as earlier ones have done. But if the chance for wide democratization can be grasped and consolidated, international politics might be transformed.

A system composed substantially of democratic states might reflect very different behavior than did the previous one composed predominantly of autocracies. If, after winning the Cold War at immense cost, the alliance of industrial democracies should now let slip a chance to solidify basic change in the principles of international order at much lower cost, our children will wonder. If history is imagined to be the history of wars and conquest, then a democratic world might in that sense represent "the end of history." Some autocratically governed states will surely remain in the system. But if enough states become stably democratic in the 1990s, then there emerges a chance to reconstruct the norms and rules of the international order to reflect those of democracies in a majority of interactions. A system created by autocracies centuries ago might now be recreated by a critical mass of democratic states.

Edward D. Mansfield
Jack Snyder

Democratization and War

Dangers of Transition

The idea that democracies never fight wars against each other has become an axiom for many scholars. It is, as one scholar puts it, "as close as anything we have to an empirical law in international relations." This "law" is invoked by American statesmen to justify a foreign policy that encourages democratization abroad. In his 1994 State of the Union address, President Clinton asserted that no two democracies had ever gone to war with each other, thus explaining why promoting democracy abroad was a pillar of his foreign policy.

It is probably true that a world in which more countries were mature, stable democracies would be safer and preferable for the United States. But countries do not become mature democracies overnight. They usually go through a rocky transition, where mass politics mixes with authoritarian elite politics in a volatile way. Statistical evidence covering the past two centuries shows that in this transitional phase of democratization, countries become more aggressive and war-prone, not less, and they do fight wars with democratic states. In fact, formerly authoritarian states where democratic participation is on the rise are more likely to fight wars than are stable democracies or autocracies. States that make the biggest leap, from total autocracy to extensive mass democracy—like contemporary Russia—are about twice as likely to fight wars in the decade after democratization as are states that remain autocracies.

This historical pattern of democratization, belligerent nationalism, and war is already emerging in some of today's new or partial democracies, especially some formerly communist states. Two pairs of states—Serbia and Croatia, and Armenia and Azerbaijan—have found themselves at war while experimenting with varying degrees of electoral democracy. The electorate of Russia's partial democracy cast nearly a quarter of its votes for the party of radical nationalist Vladimir Zhirinovsky. Even mainstream Russian politicians have adopted an imperial tone in their dealings with neighboring former Soviet republics, and military force has been used ruthlessly in Chechnya.

The following evidence should raise questions about the Clinton administration's policy of promoting peace by promoting democratization. The expectation that the spread of democracy will probably contribute to peace in the long run, once new democracies mature, provides little comfort to those who might face a heightened risk of war in the short run. Pushing nuclear-armed great powers like Russia or China toward democratization is like spinning a roulette wheel: many of the outcomes are undesirable. Of course, in most cases the initial steps on the road to democratization will not be produced by any conscious policy of the United States. The roulette wheel is already spinning for Russia and perhaps will be soon for China. Washington and the international community need to think not so much about encouraging or discouraging democratization as about helping to smooth the transition in ways that minimize its risks.

The Evidence

Our statistical analysis relies on the classifications of regimes and wars from 1811 to 1980 used by most scholars studying the peace among democracies. Starting with these standard data, we classify each state as a democracy, an autocracy, or a mixed regime—that is, a state with features of both democracies and autocracies. This classification is based on several criteria, including the constitutional constraints on the chief executive, the competitiveness of domestic politics, the openness of the process for selecting the chief executive, and the strength of the rules governing participation in politics. Democratizing states are those that made any regime change in a democratic direction—that is, from autocracy to democracy, from a mixed regime to democracy, or from autocracy to a mixed regime. We analyze wars between states as well as wars between a state and a non-state group, such as liberation movements in colonies, but we do not include civil wars.[1]

Because we view democratization as a gradual process, rather than a sudden change, we test whether a transition toward democracy occurring over one, five, and ten years is associated with the subsequent onset of war. To assess the strength of the relationship between democratization and war, we construct a series of contingency tables. Based on those tables, we compare the probability that a democratizing state subsequently goes to war with the probabilities of war for states in transition toward autocracy and for states undergoing no regime change. The results of all of these tests show that *democratizing states were more likely to fight wars than were states that had undergone no change in regime.* This relationship is weakest one year into democratization and strongest at ten years. During any given ten-year period, a state experiencing no regime change had about one chance in six of fighting a war in the following decade. In the decade following democratization, a state's chance of fighting a war was about one in four. When we analyze the components of our measure of democratization separately, the results are similar. On average, an increase in the openness of the selection process for the chief executive doubled the likelihood of war. Increasing the competitiveness of political participation or increasing the constraints on a country's chief executive (both aspects of democratization) also made war more likely. On average, these changes increased the likelihood of war by about 90 percent and 35 percent respectively.

■ **FIGURE 56.1**
Regime Change (Composite Index)

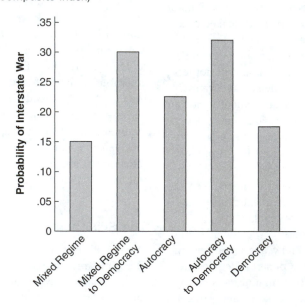

■ **FIGURE 56.2**
Openness of Selection of Chief Executive

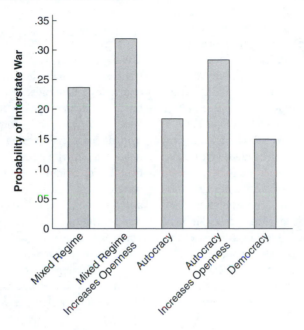

FIGURE 56.3
Competitiveness of Political Participation

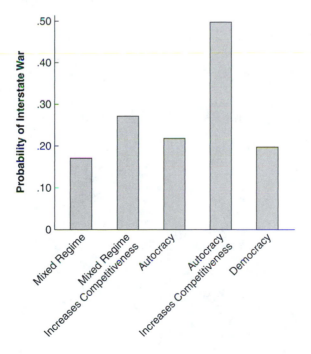

The statistical results are even more dramatic when we analyze cases in which the process of democratization culminated in very high levels of mass participation in politics. States changing from a mixed regime to democracy were on average about 50 percent more likely to become engaged in war (and about two-thirds more likely to go to war with another nation-state) than states that remained mixed regimes.

The effect was greater still for those states making the largest leap, from full autocracy to high levels of democracy. Such states were on average about two-thirds more likely to become involved in any type of war (and about twice as likely to become involved in an interstate war) than states that remained autocracies. Though this evidence shows that democratization is dangerous, its reversal offers no easy solutions. On average, changes toward autocracy also yielded an increase in the probability of war, though a smaller one than changes toward democracy,

compared to states experiencing no regime change.

Nationalism and Democratization

The connection between democratization and nationalism is striking in both the historical record and today's headlines. We did not measure nationalism directly in our statistical tests. Nonetheless, historical and contemporary evidence strongly suggests that rising nationalism often goes hand in hand with rising democracy. It is no accident that the end of the Cold War brought both a wave of democratization and a revival of nationalist sentiment in the former communist states.

In eighteenth-century Britain and France, when nationalism first emerged as an explicit political doctrine, it meant self-rule by the people. It was the rallying cry of commoners and rising commercial classes against rule by aristocratic elites, who were charged with the sin of ruling in

■ **FIGURE 56.4**
Constraints on the Chief Executive

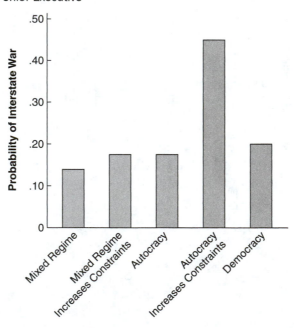

■ FIGURE 56.5

Change in the Probability of Interstate War for a State Undergoing Democratization
(Based on the Results in Previous Graphs)

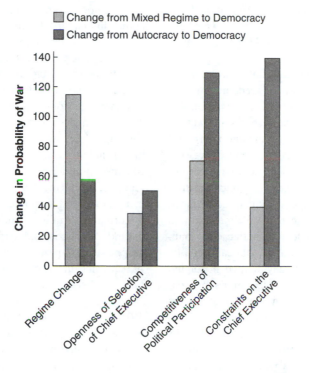

□ Change from Mixed Regime to Democracy
■ Change from Autocracy to Democracy

their own interests, rather than those of the nation. Indeed, dynastic rulers and imperial courts had hardly been interested in promoting nationalism as a banner of solidarity in their realms. They typically ruled over a linguistically and culturally diverse conglomeration of subjects and claimed to govern by divine right, not in the interest of the nation. Often, these rulers were more closely tied by kinship, language, or culture to elites in other states than to their own subjects. The position of the communist ruling class was strikingly similar: a transnational elite that ruled over an amalgamation of peoples and claimed legitimacy from the communist party's role as the vanguard of history, not from the consent of the governed. Popular forces challenging either traditional dynastic rulers or communist elites naturally tended to combine demands for national self-determination and democratic rule.

This concoction of nationalism and incipient democratization has been an intoxicating brew, leading in case after case to ill-conceived wars of expansion. The earliest instance remains one of the most dramatic. In the French Revolution, the radical Brissotin parliamentary faction polarized politics by harping on the king's slow response to the threat of war with other dynastic states. In the ensuing wars of the French Revolution, citizens flocked to join the revolutionary armies to defend popular self-rule and the French nation. Even after the revolution turned profoundly antidemocratic, Napoleon was able to harness this popular nationalism to the task of conquering Europe, substituting the popularity of empire for the substance of democratic rule.

After this experience, Europe's ruling elites decided to band together in 1815 in the Concert of Europe to contain the twin evils of nationalism and democratization. In this scheme, Europe's crowned heads tried to unite in squelching demands for constitutions, electoral and social democracy, and national self-determination. For a time nationalism and democratization were both held back, and Europe enjoyed a period of relative peace.

But in the long run, the strategy failed in the face of the economic changes strengthening popular forces in Western and Central Europe. British and French politicians soon saw that they would have to rule by co-opting nationalist and democratic demands, rather than suppressing them. Once the specter of revolution returned to Europe in 1848, this reversal of political tactics was complete, and it led quickly to the Crimean War. British Foreign Secretary Palmerston and French Emperor Napoleon III both tried to manage the clamor for a broader political arena by giving democrats what they wanted in foreign affairs—a "liberal" war to free imprisoned nations from autocratic rule and, incidentally, to expand commerce.

But this was just the dress rehearsal for history's most potent combination of mass politics and rising nationalism, which occurred in Germany around the turn of the twentieth century. Chancellor Otto von Bismarck, counting on the conservative votes of a docile peasantry, granted universal suffrage in the newly unified Reich after 1870, but in foreign and military affairs, he kept the elected Reichstag subordinate to the cabinet appointed by the kaiser. Like the sorcerer's apprentice, however, Bismarck underestimated the forces he was unleashing. With the rise of an industrial society, Bismarck's successors could not control this truncated democracy, where over 90 percent of the population voted. Everyone was highly politicized, yet nobody could achieve their aims through the limited powers of the Reichstag. As a result, people organized direct pressure groups outside of electoral party politics. Some of these clamored for economic benefits, but many of them found it tactically useful to cloak their narrow interests in a broader vision of the nation's interests. This mass nationalist sentiment

exerted constant pressure on German diplomacy in the Wilhelmine years before 1914 and pushed its vacillating elites toward war.

Democratization and nationalism also became linked in Japan on the eve of the Manchurian invasion in 1931. During the 1920s Japan expanded its suffrage and experimented with two-party electoral competition, though a council of military elder statesmen still made the ultimate decisions about who would govern. These semi-elected governments of the 1920s supported free trade, favored naval arms control, and usually tried to rein in the Japanese army's schemes to undermine the Open Door policy in China. During the 1920s, Young Turks in the army developed a populist, nationalist doctrine featuring a centrally planned economy within an autarkic, industrialized, expanded empire, while scapegoating Japan's alleged internal and external enemies, including leftist workers, rich capitalists, liberals, democrats, Americans, and Russians. After the economic crash of the late 1920s, this nationalist formula became persuasive, and the Japanese military had little trouble gaining popular support for imperial expansion and the emasculation of democracy. As in so many previous cases, nationalism proved to be a way for militarist elite groups to appear populist in a democratizing society while obstructing the advance to full democracy.

The interconnection among nationalism, democratization, and war is even clearer in new states. In today's "Weimar Russia," voters disgruntled by economic distress backed belligerent nationalists like Zhirinovsky, put ostensible liberals like President Boris Yeltsin and Foreign Minister Andrei Kozyrev on the defensive on ethnic and foreign policy issues, and contributed to the climate that led to war in Chechnya. In "Wilhelmine Serbia," the political and military elites of the old regime, facing inexorable pressure for democratization, cynically but successfully created a new basis for legitimacy through nationalist propaganda and military action, and they recently won elections that were only partially manipulated. Until its recent decree suspending the activities of the main opposition party, Armenia had moved quite far toward full democracy while at the same time supporting an invasion of its ethnic foes in Azerbaijan. The Azeris have been less successful in sustaining momentum toward democracy. However, in Azerbaijan's one relatively free and fair presidential election, the winner, Abulfaz Ali Elchibey, attacked the incumbent for being insufficiently nationalist and populist. Elchibey's platform emphasized Turkic identity and the strengthening of the Azeri nation-state to try to mount a counteroffensive against the Armenians. In other ethnically divided societies, where holding an election is like taking a census, democratization has often become an opportunity to exercise the tyranny of the majority.

The Sorcerer's Apprentice

Although democratization in many cases leads to war, that does not mean that the average voter wants war. Public opinion in democratizing states often starts off highly averse to the costs and risks of war. In that sense, the public opinion polls taken in Russia in early 1994 were typical. Respondents said, for example, that Russian policy should make sure the rights of Russians in neighboring states were not infringed, but not at the cost of military intervention. Public opinion often becomes more belligerent, however, as a result of propaganda and military action presented as faits accomplis by elites. This mass opinion, once aroused, may no longer be controllable.

For example, Napoleon III successfully exploited the domestic prestige from France's share of the victory in the Crimean War to consolidate his rule, despite the popular reluctance and war-weariness that had accompanied the war. Having learned this lesson well, Napoleon tried this tactic again in 1859. On the eve of his military intervention in the Italian struggle with Austria, he admitted to his ministers that "on the domestic front, the war will at first awaken great fears; traders and speculators of every stripe will shriek, but national sentiment will [banish] this domestic fright; the nation will be put to the test once more in a struggle

that will stir many a heart, recall the memory of heroic times, and bring together under the mantle of glory the parties that are steadily drifting away from one another day after day."[2] Napoleon was trying not just to follow opinion but to make public opinion bellicose, in order to stir a national feeling that would enhance the state's ability to govern a split and stalemated political arena.

Much the same has happened in contemporary Serbia. Despite the memories of Ustashe atrocities in World War II, intermarriage rates between Croats and Serbs living in Croatia were as high as one in three during the 1980s. Opinion has been bellicized by propaganda campaigns in state-controlled media that, for example, carried purely invented reports of rapes of Serbian women in Kosovo, and even more so by the fait accompli of launching the war itself.

In short, democratizing states are war-prone not because war is popular with the mass public, but because domestic pressures create incentives for elites to drum up nationalist sentiment.

The Causes of Democratic Wars

Democratization typically creates a syndrome of weak central authority, unstable domestic coalitions, and high-energy mass politics. It brings new social groups and classes onto the political stage. Political leaders, finding no way to reconcile incompatible interests, resort to shortsighted bargains or reckless gambles in order to maintain their governing coalitions. Elites need to gain mass allies to defend their weakened positions. Both the newly ambitious elites and the embattled old ruling groups often use appeals to nationalism to stay astride their unmanageable political coalitions.

Needing public support, they rouse the masses with nationalist propaganda but find that their mass allies, once mobilized by passionate appeals, are difficult to control. So are the powerful remnants of the old order—the military, for example—which promote militarism because it strengthens them institutionally. This is particularly true because democratization weakens the central government's ability to keep policy coherent and consistent. Governing a society that is democratizing is like driving a car while throwing away the steering wheel, stepping on the gas, and fighting over which passenger will be in the driver's seat. The result, often, is war.

Political Stalemate and Imperialist Coalitions

Democratization creates a wider spectrum of politically significant groups with diverse and incompatible interests. In the period when the great powers were first democratizing, kings, aristocrats, peasants, and artisans shared the historical stage with industrialists, an urban working class, and a middle-class intelligentsia. Similarly, in the post-communist world, former party apparatchiks, atavistic heavy industrialists, and downwardly mobile military officers share the stage with populist demagogues, free-market entrepreneurs, disgruntled workers, and newly mobilized ethnic groups. In principle, mature democratic institutions can integrate even the widest spectrum of interests through competition for the favor of the average voter. But where political parties and representative institutions are still in their infancy, the diversity of interests may make political coalitions difficult to maintain. Often the solution is a belligerent nationalist coalition.

In Britain during the period leading up to the Crimean War, neither the Whigs nor Tories could form a lasting governing coalition because so many groups refused to enter stable political alliances. None of the old elites would coalesce with the parliamentary bloc of radicals elected by urban middle-class and Irish voters. Moreover, protectionist Tories would not unite with free-trading Whigs and Peelite Tories. The social and political mid-Victorian equipoise between traditional and modern Britain created a temporary political stalemate. Lord Palmerston's pseudo-liberal imperialism turned out to be the only successful formula for creating a durable ruling coalition during this transitional period of democratization.

The stalemate in Wilhelmine-era electoral politics was even more serious. In principle, coalitions of the left and right might have formed a two-party system to vie for the favor of the average voter, thus moderating policy. In fact, both left and right were too internally divided to mount effective coalitions with internally consistent policies. Progressives dreamed of a bloc extending "from Bassermann to Bebel," from the liberal-democratic middle classes through the Marxist working classes, but the differences between labor and capital chronically barred this development. Conservatives had more success in forging a "marriage of iron and rye," but fundamental differences between military-feudal Junkers and Ruhr industrialists over issues ranging from the distribution of tax burdens to military strategy made their policies incoherent. Germany wound up with plans for a big army and a costly navy, and nobody willing to pay for it.

In more recent times, incipient democratization has likewise caused political impasses by widening the political spectrum to include too many irreconcilable political forces. In the final days of Yugoslavia, efforts by moderates like former Prime Minister Ante Marković to promote a federalist, democratic, economic reformist platform were hindered not only by ethnic divisions but also by the cleavage between market-oriented business interests on the one hand and party bosses and military officers on the other. Similarly, in Russia, the difficulty of reconciling liberal, neo-communist, and nationalist political platforms and the social interests behind them has led to parliamentary stalemate, attempts to break the stalemate by presidential decree, tanks in the streets, and the resort to freelancing by breakaway regions, the military, and spontaneous privatizers of state property. One interpretation of Yeltsin's decision to use force in Chechnya is that he felt it necessary to show that he could act decisively to prevent the unraveling of central authority, with respect not only to ethnic separatists but also to other ungovernable groups in a democratizing society. Chechnya, it was hoped, would allow Yeltsin to demonstrate his ability to coerce Russian society while at the same time exploiting a potentially popular nationalist issue.

Inflexible Interests and Short Time Horizons

Groups threatened by social change and democratization, including still-powerful elites, are often compelled to take an inflexible view of their interests, especially when their assets cannot be readily adapted to changing political and economic conditions. In extreme cases, there may be only one solution that will maintain the social position of the group. For Prussian landowners, it was agricultural protection in a nondemocratic state; for the Japanese military, it was organizational autonomy in an autarkic empire; for the Serbian military and party elites, it was a Serbian nationalist state. Since military bureaucracies and imperial interest groups occupied key positions in many authoritarian great powers, whether monarchal or communist, most interests threatened by democratization have been bound up with military programs and the state's international mission. Compromises that may lead down the slippery slope to social extinction or irrelevance have little appeal to such groups. This adds to the difficulty of finding an exit from the domestic political impasse and may make powerful domestic groups impervious to the international risks of their strategies.

Competing for Popular Support

The trouble intensifies when elites in a democratizing society try to recruit mass allies to their cause. Threatened elite groups have an overwhelming incentive to mobilize mass backers on the elites' terms, using whatever special resources they might retain. These resources have included monopolies of information (the Wilhelmine navy's unique "expertise" in making strategic assessments), propaganda assets (the Japanese army's public relations blitz justifying the invasion of Manchuria), patronage (Lord Palmerston's gifts of foreign service postings to the sons of cooperative journalists), wealth (the Krupp steel company's bankrolling of mass nationalist and militarist leagues), organizational skills and networks (the Japanese army's exploitation of rural reservist organizations to build a social base), and

the ability to use the control of traditional political institutions to shape the political agenda and structure the terms of political bargains (the Wilhelmine ruling elite's agreement to eliminate anti-Catholic legislation in exchange for Catholic support in the Reichstag on the naval budget).

This elite mobilization of mass groups takes place in a highly competitive setting. Elite groups mobilize mass support to neutralize mass threats (for instance, creating patriotic leagues to counter workers' movements) and counter other elite groups' successful efforts at mass mobilization (such as the German Navy League, a political counterweight to the Junker-backed Agrarian League). The elites' resources allow them to influence the direction of mass political participation, but the imperative to compete for mass favor makes it difficult for a single elite group to control the outcome of this process. For example, mass groups that gain access to politics through elite-supported nationalist organizations often try to outbid their erstwhile sponsors. By 1911, German popular nationalist lobbies were in a position to claim that if Germany's foreign foes were really as threatening as the ruling elites had portrayed them, then the government had sold out German interests in reaching a compromise with France over the Moroccan dispute. In this way, elite mobilization of the masses adds to the ungovernability and political impasse of democratizing states.

Ideology takes on particular significance in the competition for mass support. New entrants to the political process, lacking established habits and good information, may be uncertain where their political interests lie. Ideology can yield big payoffs, particularly when there is no efficient free marketplace of ideas to counter false claims with reliable facts. Elites try out all sorts of ideological appeals depending on the social position they are defending, the nature of the mass group they want to recruit, and the kinds of appeals that seem politically plausible. A nearly universal element of these ideological appeals, however, is nationalism, which has the advantage of positing a community of interest uniting elites and masses. This distracts attention from class cleavages that divide elites from the masses they are trying to recruit.

The Weakening of Central Authority

The political impasse and recklessness of democratizing states is deepened by the weakening of the state's authority. The autocrat can no longer dictate to elite interest groups or mass groups. Meanwhile, democratic institutions lack the strength to integrate these contending interests and views. Parties are weak and lack mass loyalty. Elections are rigged or intermittent. Institutions of public political participation are distrusted because they are subject to manipulation by elites and arbitrary constraints imposed by the state, which fears the outcome of unfettered competition.

Among the great powers, the problem was not excessive authoritarian power at the center, but the opposite. The Aberdeen coalition that brought Britain into the Crimean War was a makeshift cabinet headed by a weak leader with no substantial constituency. Likewise, on the eve of the Franco-Prussian War, Napoleon III's regime was in the process of caving in to its liberal opponents, who dominated the parliament elected in 1869. As Europe's armies prepared to hurtle from their starting gates in July 1914, Austrian leaders, perplexed by the contradictions between the German chancellor's policy and that of the German military, asked, "Who rules in Berlin?" Similarly, the 1931 Manchurian incident was a fait accompli by the local Japanese military; Tokyo was not even informed. The return to imperial thinking in Moscow today is the result of Yeltsin's weakness, not his strength. As the well-informed Moscow analyst Sergei Karaganov recently argued, the breakdown of the Leninist state "has created an environment where elite interests influence [foreign] policy directly."[3]

In each of these cases, the weak central leadership resorts to the same strategies as do the more parochial elite interests, using nationalist ideological appeals and special-interest payoffs to maintain their short-run viability, despite the long-run risks that these strategies may unleash.

Prestige Strategies

One of the simplest but riskiest strategies for a hard-pressed regime in a democratizing country is to shore up its prestige at home by seeking victories abroad. During the Chechen intervention, newspaper commentators in Moscow and the West were reminded of Russian Interior Minister Viacheslav Plehve's fateful remark in 1904, on the eve of the disastrous Russo-Japanese War, that what the tsar needed was "a short, victorious war" to boost his prestige. Though this strategy often backfires, it is a perennial temptation as a means for coping with the political strains of democratization. German Chancellor Johannes Miquel, who revitalized the imperialist-protectionist "coalition of iron and rye" at the turn of the century, told his colleagues that "successes in foreign policy would make a good impression in the Reichstag debates, and political divisions would thus be moderated."[4] The targets of such strategies often share this analysis. Richard Cobden, for example, argued that military victories abroad would confer enough prestige on the military-feudal landed elite to allow them to raise food tariffs and snuff out democracy: "Let John Bull have a great military triumph, and we shall have to take off our hats as we pass the Horse Guards for the rest of our lives."[5]

Prestige strategies make the country vulnerable to slights to its reputation. Napoleon III, for example, was easily goaded into a fateful declaration of war in 1870 by Bismarck's insulting editorial work on a leaked telegram from the kaiser. For those who want to avoid such diplomatic provocations, the lesson is to make sure that compromises forced on the leaders of democratizing states do not take away the fig leaves needed to sustain their domestic prestige.

Managing the Dangers

Though mature democratic states have virtually never fought wars against each other, promoting democracy may not promote peace because states are especially war-prone during the transition toward democracy. This does not mean, however, that democratization should be squelched in the interests of peace. Many states are now democratizing or on the verge of it, and stemming that turbulent tide, even if it were desirable, may not be possible. Our statistical tests show that movements toward autocracy, including reversals of democratization, are only somewhat less likely to result in war than democratization itself. Consequently, the task is to draw on an understanding of the process of democratization to keep its unwanted side effects to a minimum.

Of course, democratization does not always lead to extreme forms of aggressive nationalism, just as it does not always lead to war. But it makes those outcomes more likely. Cases where states democratized without triggering a nationalist mobilization are particularly interesting, since they may hold clues about how to prevent such unwanted side effects. Among the great powers, the obvious successes were the democratization of Germany and Japan after 1945, due to occupation by liberal democracies and the favorable international setting provided by the Marshall Plan, the Bretton Woods economic system, and the democratic military alliance against the Soviet threat. More recently, numerous Latin American states have democratized without nationalism or war. The recent border skirmishes between Peru and Ecuador, however, coincide with democratizing trends in both states and a nationalist turn in Ecuadorian political discourse. Moreover, all three previous wars between that pair over the past two centuries occurred in periods of partial democratization.

In such cases, however, the cure is probably more democracy, not less. In "Wilhelmine Argentina," the Falkland Islands/Malvinas War came when the military junta needed a nationalist victory to stave off pressure for the return of democracy; the arrival of full democracy has produced more pacific policies. Among the East European states, nationalist politics has been unsuccessful in the most fully democratic ones— Poland, the Czech Republic, and Hungary—as protest votes have gone to former communists. Nationalism has figured more prominently in the politics of the less democratic formerly communist states that are nonetheless partially democratizing. States like Turkmenistan that remain outright autocracies have no nationalist mobilization— indeed no political mobilization of any kind. In those recent cases, in contrast to some of our statistical results, the rule seems to be: go fully democratic, or don't go at all.

In any given case, other factors may override the relative bellicosity of democratizing states. These might include the power of the democratizing state, the strength of the potential deterrent coalition of states constraining it, the attractiveness of more peaceful options available to the democratizing state, and the nature of the groups making up its ruling coalition. What is needed is to identify the conditions that lead to relatively peaceful democratization and try to create those circumstances.

One of the major findings of scholarship on democratization in Latin America is that the process goes most smoothly when elites threatened by the transition—especially the military— are given a golden parachute. Above all, they need a guarantee that they will not wind up in jail if they relinquish power. The history of the democratizing great powers broadens this insight. Democratization was least likely to lead to war when the old elites saw a reasonably bright future for themselves in the new social order. British aristocrats, for example, had more of their wealth invested in commerce and industry than in agriculture, so they had many interests in common with the rising middle classes. They could face democratization with relative equanimity. In contrast, Prussia's capital-starved, small-scale Junker landholders had no choice but to rely on agricultural protection and military careers.

In today's context, finding benign, productive employment for the erstwhile communist nomenklatura, military officer corps, nuclear scientists, and smokestack industrialists ought to rank high on the list of priorities. Policies aimed at giving them a stake in the privatization process and subsidizing the conversion of their skills to new, peaceful tasks in a market economy seem like a step in the right direction. According to some interpretations, Russian Defense Minister Pavel Grachev was eager to use force to solve the Chechen confrontation in order to show that Russian military power was still useful and that increased investment in the Russian army would pay big dividends. Instead of pursuing this reckless path, the Russian military elite needs to be convinced that its prestige, housing, pensions, and technical competence will improve if and only if it transforms itself into a Western-style military, subordinate to civilian authority and resorting to force only in accordance with prevailing international norms. Not only do old elites need to be kept happy, they also need to be kept weak. Pacts should not prop up the remnants of the authoritarian system, but rather create a niche for them in the new system.

Another top priority must be creating a free, competitive, and responsible marketplace of ideas in the newly democratizing states. Most of the war-prone democratizing great powers had pluralistic public debates, but the debates were skewed to favor groups with money, privileged access to the media, and proprietary control over information ranging from archives to intelligence about the military balance. Pluralism is not enough. Without a level playing field, pluralism simply creates the incentive and opportunity for privileged groups to propound self-serving myths, which historically have often taken a nationalist turn. One of the rays of hope in the Chechen affair was the alacrity with which Russian journalists exposed the costs of the fighting and the lies of the government and the military. Though elites should get a golden parachute regarding their pecuniary interests, they should be given no quarter on the battlefield of ideas. Mythmaking should be held up to the utmost scrutiny by aggressive journalists who maintain their credibility by scrupulously distinguishing fact from opinion and tirelessly verifyng their sources. Promoting this kind of journalistic infrastructure is probably

the most highly leveraged investment the West can make in a peaceful democratic transition.

Finally, the kind of ruling coalition that emerges in the course of democratization depends a great deal on the incentives created by the international environment. Both Germany and Japan started on the path toward liberal, stable democratization in the mid-1920s, encouraged by abundant opportunities for trade with and investment by the advanced democracies and by credible security treaties that defused nationalist scaremongering in domestic politics. When the international supports for free trade and democracy were yanked out in the late 1920s, their liberal coalitions collapsed. For China, whose democratization may occur in the context of expanding economic ties with the West, a steady Western commercial partnership and security presence is likely to play a major role in shaping the incentives of proto-democratic coalition politics.

In the long run, the enlargement of the zone of stable democracy will probably enhance prospects for peace. In the short run, much work remains to be done to minimize the dangers of the turbulent transition.

Notes

1. On the definition of war and the data on war used in this analysis, see Melvin Small and J. David Singer, *Resort to Arms: International and Civil Wars, 1816–1980,* Beverly Hills: Sage, 1982.

2. Alain Plessis, *The Rise and Fall of the Second Empire, 1852–1871,* Cambridge: Cambridge University Press, 1985, pp. 146–47.

3. Karaganov, "Russia's Elites," in Robert Blackwill and Sergei Karaganov, *Damage Limitation,* Washington: Brassey's, 1994, p. 42.

4. J. C. G. Rohl, *Germany without Bismarck,* Berkeley: University of California Press, 1967, p. 250.

5. Letter to John Bright, October 1, 1854, quoted in John Morley, *The Life of Richard Cobden,* abridged ed., London: Thomas Nelson, pp. 311–12.

Chester A. Newland

Fanatical Terrorism versus Disciplines of Constitutional Democracy

Fanatical terrorism of 11 September 2001 wiped out already-shaken illusions of American invulnerability. Far more, this epochal attack made it clear that asymmetrical threats beyond conventional understanding are now powerful challenges to enlightened civilization globally. That is, the enemy differs enormously in organization, methods of attack, and defense from nation-state opponents in past warfare, in which opposing forces were more-or-less matched symmetrically. The assaults on the World Trade Center and the Pentagon were atrocities that were deliberately visited upon internationally best-known symbols. In short, these horrific attacks targeted not simply American buildings and people; they struck hard at world civilization, challenging social, economic, and political frameworks designed to facilitate human dignity and justice under disciplined standards of reasonableness.

This was one day of actions in an ongoing war that has been waged internationally for over two decades already by fanatical terrorists. It was not a new declaration of war, except in the magnitude of the devastating abandon in this targeting of the American homeland. . . . Clearly now, if it was not previously understood, this war is not between alternative civilizations. It is between civilization and its antithesis. Unconventional in key respects, should it earn the title of World War III? . . . How can an antiterrorist war be fought and won on behalf of enduring *facilitation of civilization* of valued diversity and constructively connected humanity?

Grief and Sanctification of Civilization's Moral Foundations

By many measures, a globally historic one-day high was scored on 11 September by dogmatic ideology and wickedly inflamed hate. This terrorism was a proclamation against the shared respect for the higher authority of civilization that inspires self-confidence balanced by respectful humility in being human. It contradicted what people of many faiths and humane persuasions embrace together as ennobling higher law and enduring responsibility for civilization building among humankind—what constitutional democracy practices as a search, through a rule of law, for reasonableness and human dignity. All but the most bitterly hard-hearted and fanatically indoctrinated must weep through eternity not simply from private and shared human feelings experienced but because of the compelling dark thought and meanings of such fanatical terrorism.

Disciplines of humble and confident faith and of constitutional democracy—human caring, civic duty, and public service, most particularly—scored much higher than terrorism in September. They did so locally, nationally, and, in some important respects, globally. A broadly shared search for human dignity in the presence of the unimaginable assault upon it quickly connected diverse individuals, groups, communities, and many nations.

Although the disciplined search for shared reasonableness in self-governance and government overwhelmingly dominated in the United States and *in and among* other constitutional democracies, responsible self-governance was marred in America by some unorganized acts of opportunistic revenge against innocent Muslims and others. During the first two weeks following the attacks on the World Trade Center and the Pentagon, local police made arrests and the FBI investigated in some 90 incidents of vengeful retaliation, including two killings of the innocent. . . .

Civic Duty and Public Service: Symbiosis in Democracy

Responsible self-governance and its facilitation by two inseparable values of constitutionally democratic culture, civic duty and public service, were the sustaining hallmarks of September 2001. The enormous numbers of recorded examples are beyond review in this brief account. Reconsider the following . . . among others, as demonstrations of the *practice of precepts for ages to come.*

United Airlines Flight 93, a Boeing 757 with a flight crew of seven, departed Newark at 8:01 a.m. on 11 September, bound for San Francisco with 38 passengers, including four now-known, self-glorifying terrorists in their twenties. Following the hijacking, some victim passengers learned by phone that other hijacked planes had been deliberately crashed in destructive attacks. When what had been unimaginable became known to them, civically responsible, self-sacrificing passengers successfully terminated their captors' evil scheme, as UA 93 crashed nose first at an estimated 450 mph at 10:37 a.m. in a rural area near Shanksville, Pennsylvania. A deep hole in the countryside, scattered wreckage, and national gratitude instantly memorialized these passengers' exercise of civic duty. Their disciplined actions of self-governance attest to the faith and social capital of constitutional democracy. People acting dutifully on their own—sacrificing their being in this example—is liberty's fundamental strength. Such activated popular sovereignty facilitates reliance by constitutional

government on limited numbers of professionally expert employees, in turn enabling these relatively few public servants and officials to perform their many valued, specialized responsibilities in relative openness and within other limits of constitutionally democratic culture. A challenge now is to preserve and nourish, with sustained devotion to reasonableness, that balance of self-governance and limited but robust government that the terrorists had hoped to destroy.

Consider this second example: Among the most visible public servants in the rescue efforts following the attack on the first of the Twin Towers and for days thereafter were firefighters, police, and other emergency-services personnel. Remember them! Loaded with equipment, many firefighters were seen climbing up stairs, all the while facilitating movement down by fleeing people who sought to escape what became the fate of some 300 of these government employees, along with . . . other people. These personnel demonstrated for all the world to see that such public service is not most essentially an economic employment transaction; it requires a principled culture of professional responsibility and specialized expertise that merits trusted exercise of the awesome authority of constitutional democracy. Can any careful observer ever again discount such governmental servants of the people as chiefly burdensome economic calculators of self-interests? . . .

Fanatical Terrorism versus Civilization: World War III?

Make no mistake: The intertwined terrorist networks that attacked the American homeland on 11 September have been engaged in global warfare for over two decades. Fanatical terrorists finally got America to understand that in September 2001.

This war is not a conventional one between blocs of nations. It is a war against civilization by more-and-less linked networks of fanatical terrorists. It is asymmetrical. It is waged against all advanced nation-states, their instrumentalities, and their social, market, and political institutions.

Although this war by international fanatical terrorists differs enormously from America's earlier exposures to domestic and international terrorism, including enduring street-gang wars, struggles against narcoterrorists, and most attacks on information-based infrastructures, lessons from those experiences are relevant to the present struggle to preserve advanced human civilization. Therefore, some of those are woven into the following analysis.

Fanatical terrorism since the early 1980s includes a long list of horrendous acts, many in the same war on civilization as the September 2001 attacks. In the aftermath of the most recent terrors, especially remember these earlier acts and the relatively limited, unsustained responses to them: *63 people died* in the bombing of the U.S. Embassy in Beirut in April 1983; *299 people died* in the U.S. Marine Barracks in Beirut in October 1983; *329 people died* in the Air India flight over the Irish Sea in June 1985; *150 people died* in the Sri Lanka bus attack in April 1987; *270 people died* in the Pan Am explosion over Lockerbie in December 1988; *170 people died* in the UTA flight over Chad in September 1989; *6 people died* in the attack on the World Trade Center in February 1993; *96 people died* in the attack on the Jewish Center in Buenos Aires in July 1994; *23 people died* in the suicide bus bombing in Tel Aviv in October 1994; *19 people died* in the bombed U.S. military complex in Saudi Arabia in June 1996; *62 people died* in Luxor, cut down in November 1997; *224 people died* in the U.S. Embassy bombings in Kenya and Tanzania in August 1998; *29 people died* in the Omagh Town Center bombing in August 1998; *118 people died* in the bombings of Moscow apartments in September 1999; *17 people died* in the attack on the USS Cole in Aden in October 2000; and *15 people died* in the Sbarro Restaurant bombing in Israel in August 2001. . . .

Terrorism generates terrorism. Actions warrant that term, whether a friend's child or one's own is killed alone or among a multitude by terrorism, whether by an Irish bomb at a busy London site, gunshots into a Boyle Heights residence, an adult taunter's shooting in Khan Younis in Gaza, or a suicide-bomb attack on a crowded pizza parlor in Israel. Connected horror, sorrow, and, too often, hate-filled divisiveness among humankind follow.

Fanatical terrorists' war against civilization has now struck America's homeland hard. Many have died horribly. Sorrow and grief remain. It now seems clear that the September attack was not only on innocent people and the buildings that housed them. It was present in financial-market manipulations designed to serve greed as well as fanatical ideology by profiting in and disrupting economies. Osama bin Laden and his base group, *al-Qaeda,* were identified quickly as leaders among the perpetrators of September's terror and, thus, as the principal targets of a war on terrorism. Personalization of an enemy leader and forces has been both a reality and an effective method in conventional warfare (Hitler and Nazism). It clearly has continued value in the current situation, but with a big *however.* The terrorist network of which al-Qaeda is the base consists of some two dozen, more-or-less separate groupings centered from Indonesia and the Philippines through the Middle East and Africa. Hundreds of invisible cells are thought to exist worldwide, including key ones in Western Europe and North America. This network is global, and it is engaged in world war against civilization. But it is not a nation-state enemy, although dictatorial political regimes of such nation-states as Afghanistan and Iraq support the network. Therefore, among many other clear reasons, this war cannot be *won* through dominant reliance on conventional warfare, although robust traditional methods remain useful.

As noted above, destruction of fanatical terrorism's networks cannot succeed without correcting long-festering conditions of Iraq, Israel, and Palestine, as well as those in Afghanistan. It is necessary to deal with such terrorist networks as Hamas, Islamic Jihad, and, if it has not moved into a nonterrorist mainstream, Lebanon's Shia militia, Hizbullah. However, a practical question is: Can a workable coalition against fanatical international terrorism be formed and sustained that does not make distinctions between varied terrorists and acts of terrorism? Because the present terrorism is in essence at war with civilization, how can such distinctions be made? If oneness of horror characterizes terror, how can effective counterterrorism against al-Qaeda and/or others be conducted so as to avoid the terrorists' purpose of generating self-destruction of fundamentally moral institutions of constitutionally democratic civilization? . . .

Interdependent Facilitative-State Ideals and Antiterrorist Garrison-State Realities

As the present century approached, advanced nation-states and international instrumentalities became transformed from many ideals and practices of the Administrative State era of the middle years of the twentieth century, when nation-state socialism and Garrison State requirements of World War II, the Korean War, and the Cold War resulted in heavy reliance on governmental controls and regimented, big bureaucracies. In recent years, by contrast, facilitative governance concepts and practices have constituted much of the framework of interdependent nation states and of public administration. These widely applied ideas deal broadly with social self-governance, responsible economic markets, constitutionally limited and empowered political/governmental affairs, and collaborative international activities. Government is valued, not dismissed as minimally important or as *the problem,* as in the 1980s. But government and tightly wound, all-controlling bureaucracies are not elevated as the be all and end all. *Facilitation of social self-governance, responsible markets, and security and opportunity within constitutionally democratic frameworks is now understood to be the essential role of responsible government.*

Antiterrorist Garrison-State realities to deal with today's asymmetrical threats constitute an enormous challenge to these ideals and practices. Successful conventional warfare of the past century, even when fought far from America's home-

land, resulted in extreme difficulties in reconciling democracy and bureaucracy, as in Japanese relocation during World War II. . . . Considering that historic record and complicated challenges of defense against *who-knows-what-or-when terrorism,* how may America go about antiterrorist warfare policies and their implementation?

War is hell may apply more to today's fight to control fanatical international terrorism than it did in America's past wars. In Lower Manhattan and at the Pentagon, that characterization has already applied far more than ever imagined by most Americans. This reality, dealing with asymmetric threats that stretch beyond conventional experience and even some boundaries of today's *Advanced Knowledge Society,* presents a major challenge for public administration. How can war be waged successfully on fanatical terrorism while also advancing constructive frameworks of the field?

Constitutional democracy's disciplines are principal answers to that question, as they were in earlier conflicts in defense of civilization. Facilitative governance, consistent with constitutional democracy's values of an enduring search for human dignity and reasonableness, through a rule of law, is splendidly equipped in key respects for this war against terrorism. As demonstrated in numerous examples on 11 September and in its wake, when push comes to shove, civic duty and public service are strongly held and practiced disciplines of democracy in America. Social capital and government's civil institutions and military services are strong. Self-direction and spontaneity work. While many security measures are necessarily classified, it is understood that America has invested heavily in varied capacities to cope with cyberterrorism and several other unconventional threats. Economic markets remain reasonably resilient, despite a global downturn that preceded the attack on the financial center in New York. America is a nation with strength to be patient, vigorous, and unrelenting in support of effective war on fanatical terrorist leaders and their destructive networks.

Despite America's strengths, however, a sustained multilateral coalition is crucial to bring terrorism under control. Examples of fruitful collaboration include swift actions by police and financial institutions in Germany and elsewhere to identify and deal with terrorists' sponsors and funds. The European Central Bank in Frankfurt and the central banks of European Monetary Union nations and key commercial financial institutions have exercised initiatives and worked collaboratively with U.S. Treasury and U.S. Federal Reserve efforts. On other current war fronts . . . developing and sustaining collaboration for war on asymmetrical threats of fanatical terrorism are enormously challenging. Some regimes are threatened by their own people as well as by terrorist networks. In current and ongoing engagements, coalition actions are promised against top leaders, their networks, and their financial and political sponsors, and reason-

able care is promised to protect innocents in these difficult processes. However, protection of coalition members raises the ante; through direct experience, most know well some meanings of asymmetrical threats, as Americans now do.

Will this struggle against enemies of diverse human civilization be recorded in history as World War III? However the future may answer that, American leadership with others in this enterprise on behalf of civilized humanity is certain to test severely the disciplines of constitutional democracy. Those are deeply rooted in enduring faith in ennobling higher law and knowing embrace of popular responsibility for human dignity. By example, those disciplines and their roots are precepts to be advanced locally and globally to win this war against fanatical terrorists.

Thomas Carothers

Promoting Democracy and Fighting Terror

The tensions posed by the war on terrorism for U.S. support of democracy abroad have quickly spread out beyond the immediate front lines. Southeast Asia is one affected region. Indonesia has become an important theater in the U.S. anti-terrorist campaign, because of U.S. fears that al-Qaeda leaders are taking refuge there and that the country's numerous Islamist groups are connecting with extremist networks. The White House continues to support Indonesia's shaky, somewhat democratic government. But in a setback on human rights policy, the administration has proposed restarting aid to the Indonesian military. That aid was progressively reduced during the 1990s in response to the Indonesian forces' atrocious human rights record and was finally terminated in 1999, when Indonesian troops participated in massacres in East Timor. Administration officials have downplayed this decision to renew military aid, stressing that most of the proposed $50 million package is directed at the police rather than the military. But the willingness of the U.S. government to enter into a partnership with a security force that just a few years ago was involved in a horrendous campaign of slaughter and destruction against civilians sends a powerful negative message throughout the region and beyond. Some officials argue that the new training programs will give U.S. military personnel a chance to instruct their Indonesian counterparts in human rights. But U.S. officials repeatedly made the same argument in defense of these programs in previous decades, right up to when the Indonesian military committed the human rights abuses that sank the relationship.

Malaysia's leader, Prime Minister Mahathir Mohamad, is another beneficiary of a changed U.S. foreign policy. Mahathir has made himself useful to Washington by arresting Islamic militants, sharing intelligence, and cooperating in other ways with an antiterrorist campaign that neatly dovetails with his authoritarian domestic agenda. And in response, Washington's previous critical stance toward the Malaysian leader—highlighted in Vice President Al Gore's much-publicized call for reforms during his visit to Kuala Lumpur in 1998—has been reversed. Top U.S. officials now laud Mahathir as "a force for regional stability" and "a model of economic development that has demonstrated tolerance," and President Bush praised him at an amicable joint press conference after Mahathir's visit to the White House in May 2002.

An emphasis on democracy and human rights is also in question in U.S. policy toward Russia and China. Russia's new role as a U.S. ally in the war on terrorism has progressed less smoothly than some initially hoped, with significant continuing differences over Iraq, Iran, Georgia, and other places. Nevertheless, President Bush regards President Vladimir Putin very favorably and has not pressed the Russian leader about his shortcomings on democracy and human rights, such as in Chechnya or with regard to maintaining a free press. Somewhat similarly, the Chinese government has been able to leverage the new security context to solidify a much friendlier U.S.-China relationship than seemed likely in the early months of 2001, when the Bush administration appeared to view China as threat number one.

In both cases, however, the change is more of degree than kind. Bush's surprisingly personal and warm embrace of Putin started before September 11, with Bush getting "a sense of [Putin's] soul" during their meeting in Slovenia in June 2001. And at no time prior to September 11, whether under Bush or Clinton before him, was the Russian government subjected to any significant U.S. government criticism for Chechnya or any of its other democratic flaws. With respect to China, it is true that September 11 did block movement toward a new hard-line policy from Washington that some administration hawks may have wanted. But the current relatively positive state of relations, with mild U.S. pressure on human rights greatly outweighed by an ample, mutually beneficial economic relationship, is not especially different from the overall pattern of the past decade or more.

One can look even further afield and identify possible slippage in U.S. democracy policies resulting from the war on terrorism, such as insufficient attention to the growing crisis of democracy in South America or inadequate pressure on oil-rich Nigeria's flailing president, Olusegun Obasanjo, to turn around his increasingly poor governance of Africa's most populous nation. Ironically, and also sadly, however, the greatest source of negative ripple effects has come from the administration's pursuit of the war on terrorism at home. The heightened terrorist threat has inevitably put pressure on U.S. civil liberties. But the administration failed to strike the right balance early on, unnecessarily abridging or abusing rights through the large-scale detention of immigrants, closed deportation hearings, and the declaration of some U.S. citizens as "enemy combatants" with no right to counsel or even to contest the designation. The Justice Department's harsh approach sent a powerful negative signal around the world, emboldening governments as diverse as those of Belarus, Cuba, and India to curtail domestic liberties, supposedly in aid of their own struggles against terrorism. In the United States, an independent judiciary and powerful Congress ensure that the appropriate balance between security and rights is gradually being achieved. In many countries, however, the rule of law is weak and copycat restrictions on rights resound much more harmfully.

Reagan Reborn?

Whereas "Bush the realist" holds sway on most fronts in the war on terrorism, a neo-Reaganite Bush may be emerging in the Middle East. In the initial period after September 11, the administration turned to its traditional autocratic allies in the Arab world, especially Egypt and Saudi Arabia, for help against al-Qaeda. This move did not sacrifice any U.S. commitment to democracy; for decades, the United States had already suppressed any such concerns in the region, valuing autocratic stability for the sake of various economic and security interests. Over the course of the last year, however, a growing chorus of voices within and around the administration has begun questioning the value of America's "friendly tyrants" in the Middle East. These individuals highlight the fact that whereas the autocratic allies once seemed to be effective bulwarks against Islamic extremism, the national origins of the September 11 attackers make clear that these nations are in fact breeders, and in the case of Saudi Arabia, financiers, of extremism. Invoking what they believe to be the true spirit of President Ronald Reagan's foreign policy, they call for a change toward promoting freedom in U.S. Middle East policy. The core idea of the new approach is to undercut the roots of Islamic extremism by getting serious about promoting democracy in the Arab world, not just in a slow, gradual way, but with fervor and force. President Bush is clearly attracted by this idea. Last summer his declarations on the Middle East shifted noticeably in tone and content, setting out a vision of democratic change there. According to this vision, the United States will first promote democracy in the Palestinian territories by linking U.S. support for a Palestinian state with the achievement of new, more democratic Palestinian leadership. Second, the United States will effect regime change in Iraq and help transform that country into a democracy. The establishment of two successful models of Arab democracy will have a powerful demonstration effect, "inspiring reforms throughout the Muslim world," as Bush declared at the United Nations in September. As the policies toward Iraq and Palestine unfold, the administration may also step up pressure on recalcitrant autocratic allies and give greater support to those Arab states undertaking at least some political reforms, such as some of the smaller Persian Gulf states. The decision last August to postpone a possible aid increase to Egypt as a response to the Egyptian government's continued persecution of human rights activist Saad Eddin Ibrahim was a small step in this direction.

It is not yet clear how sharply Bush will shift U.S. Middle East policy toward promoting democracy. Certainly it is time to change the longstanding practice of reflexively relying on and actually bolstering autocracy in the Arab world. But the expansive vision of a sudden, U.S.-led democratization of the Middle East rests on questionable assumptions. To start with, the appealing idea that by toppling Saddam Hussein the United States can transform Iraq into a democratic model for the region is dangerously misleading. The United States can certainly oust the Iraqi leader and install a less repressive and more pro-Western regime. This would not be the same, however, as creating democracy in Iraq. The experience of other countries where in recent decades the United States has forcibly removed dictatorial regimes—Grenada, Panama, Haiti, and most recently Afghanistan—indicates that post-invasion political life usually takes on the approximate character of the political life that existed in the country before the ousted regime came to power. After the 1982 U.S. military intervention in Grenada, for example, that country was able to recover the tradition of moderate pluralism it had enjoyed before the 1979 takeover by Maurice Bishop and his gang. Haiti, after the 1994 U.S. invasion, has unfortunately slipped back into many of the pathologies that marked its political life before the military junta took over in 1991. Iraqi politics prior to Saddam Hussein were violent, divisive, and oppressive. And the underlying conditions in Iraq—not just the lack of significant previous experience with pluralism but also sharp ethnic and religious differences and an oil-dependent economy—will inevitably make democratization there very slow and difficult. Even

under the most optimistic scenarios, the United States would have to commit itself to a massive, expensive, demanding, and long-lasting reconstruction effort. The administration's inadequate commitment to Afghanistan's reconstruction undercuts assurances by administration officials that they will stay the course in a post-Saddam Iraq.

Furthermore, the notion that regime change in Iraq, combined with democratic progress in the Palestinian territories, would produce domino democratization around the region is far-fetched. A U.S. invasion of Iraq would likely trigger a surge in the already prevalent anti-Americanism in the Middle East, strengthening the hand of hard-line Islamist groups and provoking many Arab governments to tighten their grip, rather than experiment more boldly with political liberalization. Throughout the region, the underlying economic, political, and social conditions are unfavorable for a wave of democratic breakthroughs. This does not mean the Arab world will never democratize. But it does mean that democracy will be decades in the making and entail a great deal of uncertainty, reversal, and turmoil. The United States can and should actively support such democratic change through an expanded, sharpened set of democracy aid programs and real pressure and support for reforms. But as experience in other parts of the world has repeatedly demonstrated, the future of the region will be determined primarily by its own inhabitants.

Aggressive democracy promotion in the Arab world is a new article of faith among neoconservatives inside and outside the administration. However, it combines both the strengths and the dangers typical of neo-Reaganite policy as applied to any region. Perhaps the most important strength is the high importance attached to the president's using his bully pulpit to articulate a democratic vision and to attach his personal prestige to the democracy-building endeavor. But two dangers are also manifest. One is the instrumentalization of prodemocracy policies—wrapping security goals in the language of democracy promotion and then confusing democracy promotion with the search for particular political outcomes that enhance those security goals. This was often a problem with the Reagan administration's attempts to spread democracy in the 1980s. To take just one example, for the presidential elections in El Salvador in 1984, the Reagan administration labored mightily to establish the technical structures necessary for a credible election. The administration then covertly funneled large amounts of money to the campaign of its preferred candidate, Jose Napoleon Duarte, to make sure he won the race. This same tension between democracy as an end versus a means has surfaced in the administration's press for democracy in the Palestinian territories. Bush has urged Palestinians to reform, especially through elections, yet at the same time administration officials have made clear that certain outcomes, such as the reelection of Yasir Arafat, are unacceptable to the United States. A postinvasion process of installing a new "democratic" regime in Iraq would likely exhibit similar contradictions between stated principle and political reality. The administration demonstrated worrisome signs of the same tendency last April during the short-lived coup against Venezuela's problematic populist president, Hugo Chavez. Washington appeared willing or even eager to accept a coup against the leader of an oil-rich state who is despised by many in the U.S. government for his anti-American posturing and dubious economic and political policies. But given that it came in a region that has started to work together to oppose coups, and that other regional governments condemned Chavez's ouster, the administration's approach undermined the United States' credibility as a supporter of democracy. If democracy promotion is reduced to an instrumental strategy for producing political outcomes favorable to U.S. interests, the value and legitimacy of the concept will be lost.

The second danger is overestimating America's ability to export democracy. U.S. neoconservatives habitually overstate the effect of America's role in the global wave of democratic openings that occurred in the 1980s and early 1990s. For example, they often argue that the Reagan administration brought democracy to Latin America through its forceful anticommunism in the 1980s. Yet the most significant democratization that occurred in Argentina, Brazil, and various other parts of South America took place in the early 1980s, when Reagan was still trying to embrace the fading right-wing dictators that Jimmy Carter had shunned on human rights grounds. Excessive optimism about U.S. ability to remake the Middle East, a region far from ripe for a wave of democratization, is therefore a recipe for trouble—especially given the administration's proven disinclination to commit itself deeply to the nation building that inevitably follows serious political disruption.

A Fine Balance

The clashing imperatives of the war on terrorism with respect to U.S. democracy promotion have led to a split presidential personality and contradictory policies—decreasing interest in democracy in some countries and suddenly increasing interest in one region, the Middle East. The decreases are widespread and probably still multiplying, given the expanding character of the antiterrorism campaign. Yet they are not fatal to the overall role of the United States as a force for democracy in the world. Some of them are relatively minor modifications of policies that for years imperfectly fused already conflicting security and political concerns. And in at least some countries where it has decided warmer relations with autocrats are necessary, the Bush administration is trying to balance new security ties with proreform pressures.

More broadly, in many countries outside the direct ambit of the war on terrorism, the Bush administration is trying to bolster fledgling democratic governments and pressure nondemocratic leaders for change, as have the past several U.S. administrations. Sometimes diplomatic pressure is used, as with Belarus, Zimbabwe, and Burma. In other cases, Washington relies on less visible means such as economic and political support as well as extensive democracy aid programs, as with many countries in sub-Saharan Africa, southeastern Europe, the former Soviet Union, Central America, and elsewhere. Quietly and steadily during the last 20 years, democracy promotion has become institutionalized in the U.S. foreign policy and foreign aid bureaucracies. Although not an automatically overriding priority, it is almost always one part of the foreign policy picture. Partly to address "the roots of terrorism," moreover, the administration has also proposed a very large new aid fund, the $5 billion Millennium Challenge Account. By signaling that good governance should be a core criterion for disbursing aid from this fund, President Bush has positioned it as a potentially major tool for bolstering democracies in the developing world.

Although the new tradeoffs prompted by the war on terrorism are unfortunate, and in some cases overdone, the fact that U.S. democracy concerns are limited by security needs is hardly a shocking new problem. Democracy promotion has indeed become gradually entrenched in U.S. policy, but both during and after the Cold War it has been limited and often greatly weakened by other U.S. interests. President Clinton made liberal use of pro-democracy rhetoric and did support democracy in many places, but throughout his presidency, U.S. security and economic interests—whether in China, Egypt, Jordan, Kazakhstan, Saudi Arabia, Vietnam, or various other countries—frequently trumped an interest in democracy. The same was true in the George H. W. Bush administration and certainly also under Ronald Reagan, whose outspoken support for freedom in the communist world was accompanied by close U.S. relations with various authoritarian regimes useful to the United States, such as those led by Suharto in Indonesia, Mobutu Sese Seko in Zaire, the generals of Nigeria, and the Institutional Revolutionary Party of Mexico.

George W. Bush is thus scarcely the first U.S. president to evidence a split personality on democracy promotion. But the suddenness and prominence of his condition, as a result of the war on terrorism, makes it especially costly. It is simply hard for most Arabs, or many other people around the world, to take seriously the president's eloquent vision of a democratic Middle East when he or his top aides casually brush away the authoritarian maneuverings of Musharraf in Pakistan, offer warm words of support for Nazarbayev in Kazakhstan, or praise Mahathir in Malaysia. The war on terrorism has laid bare the deeper fault line that has lurked below the surface of George W.

Bush's foreign policy from the day he took office—the struggle between the realist philosophy of his father and the competing pull of neo-Reaganism.

There is no magic solution to this division, which is rooted in a decades-old struggle for the foreign policy soul of the Republican Party and will undoubtedly persist in various forms throughout this administration and beyond. For an effective democracy-promotion strategy, however, the Bush team must labor harder to limit the tradeoffs caused by the new security imperatives and also not go overboard with the grandiose idea of trying to unleash a democratic tsunami in the Middle East. This means, for example, engaging more deeply in Pakistan to urge military leaders and civilian politicians to work toward a common vision of democratic renovation, adding teeth to the reform messages being delivered to Central Asia's autocrats, ensuring that the Pentagon reinforces proreform messages to new U.S. security partners, not cutting Putin slack on his democratic deficits, going easy on the praise for newly friendly tyrants, more effectively balancing civil rights and security at home, and openly criticizing other governments that abuse the U.S. example. In the Middle East, it means developing a serious, well-funded effort to promote democracy that reflects the difficult political realities of the region but does not fall back on an underlying acceptance of only cosmetic changes. This will entail exerting sustained pressure on autocratic Arab allies to take concrete steps to open up political space and undertake real institutional reforms, bolstering democracy aid programs in the region, and finding ways to engage moderate Islamist groups and encourage Arab states to bring them into political reform processes. Such an approach is defined by incremental gains, long-term commitment, and willingness to keep the post-September 11 security imperatives in perspective. As such it has neither the hard-edged appeal of old-style realism nor the tantalizing promise of the neoconservative visions. Yet in the long run it is the best way to ensure that the war on terrorism complements rather than contradicts worldwide democracy and that the strengthening of democracy abroad is a fundamental element of U.S. foreign policy in the years ahead.

Questions for Discussion

1. Why does Russet assert that democracies do not wage war against each other?
2. With the creation of a unipolar world order after the end of the Cold War and the collapse of the USSR, what can be done to create a more stable and democratized world?
3. While it may be proven that democracies do not tend to fight each other, what can be done to reduce internal conflicts that occur in democratic countries?
4. What does Newland mean by asymmetric threats?
5. What does Newland mean by "disciplines of constitutional democracy"?
6. Do you think Newland's concept will be helpful in combating terror in the United States and elsewhere?
7. Do you think that democratic political cultures and political structures alone account for the behavior of democracies? Why or why not?

Further Readings

1. Barber, Benjamin R. *Fear's Empire: War, Terrorism and Democracy.* New York; W. W. Norton and Company, 2003.
2. Oberschall, Anthony. "Social Movements and the Transition to Democracy." *Democratization,* 2000, 7, 3, Autumn, 25–45.
3. Conway, Martin. "Democracy in Postwar Western Europe: The Triumph of a Political Model." *European History Quarterly,* 2002, 32, 1, Jan., 59–84.
4. Gills, Barry K. "Democratizing Globalization and Globalizing Democracy." *Annals of the American Academy of Political and Social Science,* 2002, 581, May, 158–171.
5. Burkhart, Ross E. "Economic Freedom and Democracy: Post-Cold War Tests." *European Journal of Political Research,* 2000, 37, 2, Mar., 237–253.
6. Chomsky, Noam. *Hegemony or Survival: America's Quest for Global Dominance.* New York: Metropolitan Books, 2003.
7. Montiel, Cristina Jayme, and Wessells, Michael. "Democratization, Psychology, and the Construction of Cultures of Peace." *Peace and Conflict: Journal of Peace Psychology,* 2001, 7, 2, 119–129.
8. Jonas, Susanne. "Democratization through Peace" in Christopher Chase-Dunn, Susanne Jonas, and Nelson Amaro, eds., *Globalization on the Ground: Postbellum Quatemalan Democracy and Development.* Lanham, MD: Rowman and Littlefield, 2001, 49–81.
9. Barkavi, Tarak. "Democratic States and Societies at War: The Global Context." *Comparative Social Research,* 2002, 20, 361–376.
10. Gross, Emmanuel. "Democracy's Struggle Against Terrorism." *Georgia Journal of International and Comparative Law,* 2002, 30, 165–208.
11. Lewis, Anthony. "Fear Terrorism, and the Constitution." *Public Administration Review,* 2002, 62, special issue, September, 61–62.
12. Archibugi, Daniele. "So What If Democracies Don't Fight Each Other?" *Peace Review,* 1997, 9, 3, Sept., 379–384.
13. Hermann, Margaret G. and Kegley, Charles W., Jr. "Ballots, a Barrier against the Use of Bullets and Bombs: Democratization and Military Intervention." *Journal of Conflict Resolution,* 1996, 40, 3, Sept., 436–460.
14. Gowa, Joanne. "Democratic States and International Disputes." *International Organization,* 1995, 49, 3, Summer, 511–522.
15. Gleditsch, Nils Petter, "Democracy and Peace." *Journal of Peace Research,* 1992, 29, 4, 369–376.

16. Dixon, William J., and Senese, Paul D., "Democracy, Disputes, and Negotiated Settlements" *Journal of Conflict Resolution,* 2002, 46, 4, Aug., 547–571.

17. Mansfield, Edward D., and Snyder, Jack. "Incomplete Democratization and the Outbreak of Military Disputes." *International Studies Quarterly,* 2002, 26, 529–549.

18. Mansfield, Edward D., and Snyder, Jack, "Democratic Transitions, Institutional Strength, and War." *International Organization,* 2002, 56, 2, Spring, 297–337.

19. Moore, John Norton. "Beyond the Democratic Peace: Solving the War Puzzle." *Virginia Journal of International Law,* 2004, 341, Winter.

Appendices

To illuminate the readings in this book, three appendices have been compiled. The first one is included to help the reader understand the recurrent armed conflicts, both civil and international. Undergirding these conflicts are immense military expenditures.

The second appendix provides statistical information on the extensive investments made by governments in importing and exporting arms, along with expenditures to support military personnel.

We conclude the appendices with a list of Nobel Peace Prize laureates from 1901 to 2003. We hope the list of laureates will inspire readers to find out more about these exemplary individuals who have made outstanding efforts to reduce the frequency of armed conflicts.

Civil Wars and International Wars, 1945–1995

001. China
Civil war, communist revolution; the Chinese civil war (1945–1949)

002. Greece
Antimonarchist communist insurgency; the Greek civil war (1945–1949)

003. India
Civil war; partition and independence (1945–1948)

004. France–Levant (Syria and Lebanon)
Independence crisis (1945–December 1946)

005. USSR–Iran
Procommunist campaign of secession; the Azerbaijan crisis (August 1945–October 1947)

006. The Netherlands–Dutch East Indies (Indonesia)
Indonesian nationalism; war of independence (late 1945–November 1949)

007. France–French Indochina (Cambodia, Laos, and Vietnam)
War of independence; the French-Indochina war (December 1945–July 1954)

008. United States–Yugoslavia
Cold war air incidents (August 1946)

009. France–Madagascar
Nationalist rebellion (March–August 1947)

010. India–Pakistan
Postpartition separatism; the first Kashmir war, the India-Pakistan wars (October 1947–January 1949)

011. Costa Rica
Anticorruption military insurgency, civil war; the Costa Rican civil war (March–April 1948)

012. Israel
British decolonization, Arab-Israeli territorial dispute; war of independence (May 1948–January 1949)

013. Western Powers–USSR; Berlin
Cold war conflict; the Berlin airlift crisis (June 1948–May 1949)

014. United Kingdom–Malaya (Malaysia and Singapore)
Anti-British communist insurgency; the Malayan emergency (June 1948–July 1960)

015. India
Postpartition separatist violence (July–September 1948)

016. Burma–China
KMT-PLA cross-border conflict (August 1948–1954)

017. Costa Rica–Nicaragua
Antigovernment rebel activity; border incidents (December 1948–February 1949)

018. Burma
Civil war, Karen separatist insurgency (January 1949–)

019. Eritrea–Ethiopia
Eritrean nationalism, agitation for independence (July 1949–December 1950)

020. Pakistan–Afghanistan
Postindependence territorial dispute (August 1949)

021. China–Taiwan
KMT-CCP territorial dispute; amphibious assaults in the Taiwan Strait (October 1949–June 1953)

022. United States–USSR
Cold war air incidents (April–October 1950)

023. Afghanistan–Pakistan
Territorial dispute; the Pathan conflict
(June–October 1950)

024. United States–North Korea
Cold war territorial dispute; the Korean War
(June 1950–July 1953)

025. China–Tibet
Military occupation, reincorporation (October
1950–May 1951)

026. Syria–Israel
Arab-Israeli territorial/resource dispute; Lake
Tiberias (April–May 1951)

027. Oman–Saudi Arabia
Territorial/resource dispute; the Buraīmi crisis
(1952–October 1955)

028. Tunisia
African nationalism; war of independence
(January 1952–March 1956)

029. Egypt–United Kingdom
Sovereignty dispute; the Canal Zone dispute
(January 1952–January 1956)

030. Italy–Yugoslavia
Cold war territorial dispute; the Trieste crisis
(March 1952–October 1954)

031. China–Portugal
Territorial dispute; the Macao conflict
(July–August 1952)

032. Argentina–Chile
Border conflict; the Beagle Channel dispute
(July 1952–1968)

033. Kenya–United Kingdom
Anticolonial tribal uprising; the Mau Mau revolt (August 1952–December 1963)

034. United States–USSR
Cold war air incidents (October 1952–July 1956)

035. Israel–Jordan
Arab-Israeli hostilities; PLO incursions, West
Bank border incidents (January 1953–December
1954)

036. Taiwan–China
KMT-CCP territorial dispute; bombardment of
Quemoy (April 1954–April 1955)

037. Guatemala
Left-wing insurgency; the Guatemalan civil war
(June 1954–1995)

038. Algeria
African nationalism; war of independence
(November 1954–March 1962)

039. Nicaragua–Costa Rica
Attempted invasion by exiled rebels (January
1955)

040. Turkey–Syria
Cold war tensions, border incidents (March
1955–1957)

041. Cyprus
Intercommunal violence; the *enosis* movement
(September 1955–February 1959)

042. Syria–Israel
Arab-Israeli hostilities; cross-border raids; Lake
Tiberias (October–December 1955)

043. Yemen–United Kingdom
Anti-British autonomy campaign; the Aden
conflict (1956–1960)

044. Tibet–China
Anti-Chinese guerrilla war; incorporation struggle (March 1956–September 1965)

045. Taiwan–South Vietnam
Territorial dispute; Paracel Islands (June–August
1956)

046. Israel–Jordan
Arab-Israeli territorial dispute; the Mt. Scopus
conflict (July 1956–January 1958)

047. Egypt–United Kingdom, France
Sovereignty dispute; the Suez crisis
(October–November 1956)

048. Hungary–USSR
Anticommunist revolt, Soviet invasion; the Hungarian uprising of 1956 (October–December
1956)

049. Cuba
Civil war, communist revolution; the Cuban civil war (December 1956–January 1959)

050. Honduras–Nicaragua
Boundary dispute; Mocoran seizure (April–June 1957)

051. Israel–Syria
Arab-Israeli territorial dispute; Golan Heights conflict (June 1957–February 1958)

052. Spain–Morocco
Postindependence autonomy dispute; the Sahara conflict (November 1957–April 1958)

053. Panama
Cuban-backed invasion; the Panama revolutionaries conflict (1958–May 1959)

054. Egypt–Sudan
Postindependence territorial dispute (February 1958)

055. France–Tunisia
Post independence autonomy dispute; the military bases conflict (February–May 1958)

056. India–East Pakistan
Postpartition border tensions; the Surma River incidents (March 1958–September 1959)

057. Lebanon
Internal strife; the first Lebanese civil war (May 1958–June 1959)

058. United States–China; Taiwan
KMT-CCP territorial dispute; bombardment of Quemoy (July–December 1958)

059. Cambodia–Siam (Thailand)
Regional rivalry, communist insurgency fears; border conflict (November 1958–February 1959)

060. Laos
Political anarchy, civil war; the first Laotian civil war (December 1958–1962)

061. France–Tunisia
French-Algerian war; border incidents (February–August 1959)

062. Syria–Iraq
Syrian-backed putsch, government suppression; the Mosul revolt (March–April 1959)

063. Dominican Republic
Cuban-sponsored military invasion; the exiles conflict (June–July 1959)

064. China–Nepal
Boundary dispute (June 1959–July 1960)

065. Haiti
Cuban-sponsored military invasion; the Haitian exiles conflict (August 1959)

066. China–India
McMahon Line boundary dispute; Sino-Indian wars (August 1959–February 1960)

067. The Belgian Congo (Congo, Zaire)
Secession, anarchy, civil war; the Congo crisis (July 1960–mid-1964)

068. Pakistan–Afghanistan
Boundary dispute; the Pathan conflict (September 1960–May 1963)

069. United States–Vietnam
Civil war, anticommunist U.S. military intervention; the Vietnam War (December 1960–May 1975)

070. African Territories–Portugal
African nationalism; struggle for independence (1961–July 1975)

071. The Kurds–Iraq
Attempted secession (March 1961–1966)

072. United States–Cuba
Anti-Castro military invasion; the Bay of Pigs (April–May 1961)

073. Iraq–Kuwait
Territorial dispute; the Kuwaiti independence crisis (June 1961–February 1962)

074. United States–USSR
Cold war dispute; the Berlin Wall (July–November 1961)

075. France–Tunisia
Postindependence autonomy dispute; the Bizerte conflict (July–September 1961)

076. India–Portugal
Anti-Portuguese territorial dispute; the Goa conflict (December 1961)

077. Indonesia–Malaysia
Separatist civil disturbances; the Borneo conflict (1962–November 1965)

078. The Netherlands–Indonesia; West Irian
(Irian Jaya)
Separatist insurgency; the West Irian conflict
(January–August 1962)

079. China–Taiwan
KMT-CCP territorial dispute; invasion threat
(March–December 1962)

080. Nepal–India
Prodemocratic rebellion; border incidents
(April–November 1962)

081. Syria–Israel
Arab-Israeli territorial dispute; Lake Tiberias
(June 1962–August 1963)

082. United States–USSR
Cold war confrontation; the Cuban Missile Crisis (September–November 1962)

083. North Yemen
Civil war; the royalist rebellion (September 1962–October 1967)

084. India–China
McMahon Line border dispute; Sino-Indian wars (October–November 1962)

085. Somalia–Kenya; Ethiopia
Somali expansionism; separatist insurgency
(November 1962–September 1967)

086. China–USSR
Territorial dispute; the Ussuri River conflict
(March 1963–September 1969)

087. Sudan
Southern separatism, Anya-Nya terrorism; the first Sudan civil war (September 1963–March 1972)

088. Algeria–Morocco
Territorial dispute; the Tindouf war (October 1963–February 1964)

089. Cyprus
Intercommunal violence; the Cypriot civil war
(December 1963–November 1967)

090. Somalia–Ethiopia
Somali expansionism, separatist guerrilla fighting; the first Ogaden war (January–March 1964)

091. United States–Panama
Sovereignty dispute; the flag riots
(January–April 1964)

092. Rwanda–Burundi
Postindependence ethnic violence (January 1964–January 1965)

093. France–Gabon
Military putsch; French military intervention;
Aubame's coup (February 1964)

094. South Vietnam–Cambodia
Anti-Vietminh cross-border raids (March–December 1964)

095. Laos–North Vietnam
Political anarchy; the second Laotian civil war
(April 1964–May 1975)

096. Syria–Israel
Arab-Israeli dispute; border incidents (June 1964–July 1966)

097. Israel–Jordan
Arab-Israeli dispute; border incidents (December 1964–April 1966)

098. India–Pakistan
Regional rivalry, territorial dispute; the India-Pakistan wars (1965–1970)

099. Eritrea–Ethiopia
Eritrean nationalism; war of secession
(1965–May 1993)

100. Irian Jaya–Indonesia
Territorial dispute; secessionist insurgency
(1965–)

101. Colombia
Banditry, leftist guerrilla insurgency (1965–)

102. Ghana–Togo
Ghanaian expansionism, border incidents
(January–May 1965)

103. Congo (Zaire)–Uganda
Rebel activity, border incidents
(February–March 1965)

104. United States–Dominican Republic
Civil war, U.S. intervention; the constitutionalist rebellion (April 1965–September 1966)

105. North Korea–South Korea
Cold war border incidents (mid-1965–March 1968)

106. India–Pakistan
Territorial dispute; the second Kashmir war, the India-Pakistan wars (August–September 1965)

107. China–India
McMahon Line border incidents; the Sino-Indian wars (September 1965)

108. Lebanon–Israel
Arab-Israeli dispute (PLO sorties, IDF counter-attacks); the Hoûla raids (October 1965)

109. Chad–Sudan
Internal strife, Sudanese intervention; the first Chad civil war (November 1965–1972)

110. South West Africa (Namibia)
Violent insurrection, war; independence (1966–March 1990)

111. Guinea–Ivory Coast
Coup plot (March–April 1966)

112. Ghana–Guinea
Postcoup tensions (October–November 1966)

113. Bolivia
Cuban-assisted guerrilla insurgency (November 1966–July 1970)

114. Rhodesia (Zimbabwe)
African nationalism, guerrilla warfare; war of independence (1967–January 1980)

115. Guinea–Ivory Coast
Regional rivalry; hostage crisis (February–September 1967)

116. Cuba–Venezuela
Cuban-assisted invasion (April–May 1967)

117. Israel–Arab States
The Six-Day war, the Arab-Israeli wars (June 1967)

118. Nigeria–Biafra
Ethnic and regional rivalries; attempted secession; the Biafran civil war (July 1967–January 1970)

119. Congo (Zaire)–Rwanda
Regional instability; the mercenaries dispute (August 1967–April 1968)

120. USSR–Czechoslovakia
Liberalization movement (the "Prague Spring"), Soviet military invasion (August 1968)

121. Iraq–the Kurds
Struggle for autonomy (October 1968–March 1970)

122. China–Burma
Tribal conflict; border incidents (January–November 1969)

123. El Salvador–Honduras
Border dispute; the football war (July 1969)

124. Guyana–Suriname
New River Triangle border dispute (August 1969–November 1970)

125. North Yemen–Saudi Arabia
Post–civil war tensions; border conflict (November 1969–January 1970)

126. Cambodia–South Vietnam; United States
U.S. bombing campaign; the Vietnam War (January 1970–April 1975)

127. Mindanao–the Philippines
Communal violence, land disputes; Muslim secessionist insurgency (January 1970–1995)

128. PLO–Jordan; Syria
Attempted coup (February 1970–August 1971)

129. Guinea–Portugal
PAIGC guerrilla warfare; the Conakry raids (November 1970)

130. Iraq–Iran
Territorial dispute, border tensions (1971)

131. Uganda–Tanzania
Postcoup tensions; border clashes (1971–October 1972)

132. Pakistan–Bangladesh
Secessionist warfare; the Bangladesh war of independence (March 1971–February 1974)

133. North Yemen–South Yemen
Anticommunist insurgency; border conflict (October 1971–October 1972)

134. Iran–United Arab Emirates
Territorial dispute; the Tunb islands dispute (November 1971)

135. Oman–South Yemen
Antigovernment insurgency; the Dhofar rebellion (1972–August 1974)

136. Iran–Iraq
Territorial dispute; border war (January 1972–February 1975)

137. Syria–Israel; PLO
PLO raids, retaliatory air strikes; the Golan Heights conflict (March 1972–January 1973)

138. Equatorial Guinea–Gabon
Territorial dispute; the Corisco Bay islands dispute (June–November 1972)

139. Ethiopia–Somalia
Somali expansionism, territorial dispute; the second Ogaden war (June 1972–March 1978)

140. Iraq–Kuwait
Territorial dispute, border incidents (March 1973–July 1975)

141. Israel–Egypt
Arab-Israeli territorial dispute; the Yom Kippur war, the Arab-Israeli wars (October 1973)

142. South Vietnam–China
Territorial dispute; the Paracel Islands (January 1974–June 1978)

143. Cyprus
Communal violence, Turkish-Greek invasions; partition (January 1974–June 1978)

144. The Kurds–Iraq
Attempted secession; the Kurdish rebellion (March 1974–July 1975)

145. Israel–Lebanon
Arab-Israeli dispute; cross-border attacks (April 1974–July 1975)

146. Morocco–Mauritania; Western Sahara
Saharan nationalism, territorial dispute; the Western Saharan conflict (October 1974–)

147. Mali–Upper Volta (Burkina Faso)
Territorial/resource dispute (December 1974–June 1975)

148. Angola–South Africa
Guerrilla warfare in Namibia; intervention and civil war (1975–1995)

149. Bangladesh
Postindependence territorial dispute; the Chittagong Hill Tracts conflict (1975–)

150. North Korea–South Korea
Cold war border crisis (February–July 1975)

151. Lebanon
Internal strife, communal violence; the second Lebanese civil war (February 1975–1976)

152. Syria–Iraq
Resource dispute; the Euphrates dispute (April–late 1975)

153. United States–Cambodia
Post–Vietnam War tensions; the *Mayaguez* incident (May 1975)

154. Laos–Thailand
Postrevolution exodus; border incidents (June 1975–January 1976)

155. China–India
McMahon Line territorial dispute; border incidents (October 1975)

156. East Timor–Indonesia
Independence struggle (October 1975–)

157. Zaire–Angola
Rebel activity; border war (November 1975–February 1976)

158. Cambodia–Thailand
Refugee influx, regional tensions; border skirmishes (December 1975–February 1976)

159. Iran
Internal strife, orthodox Muslim backlash; the Iranian civil war and revolution (1976–1980)

160. Mozambique–South Africa
African nationalism; intervention and civil war (1976–October 1992)

161. Uganda–Kenya
Amin provocations; border incidents (February–August 1976)

162. Bangladesh–India
Postcoup tensions; border incidents (April 1976)

163. Iraq–the Kurds
Kurdish separatist insurgency (May 1976–)

164. Chad–Libya
Guerrilla warfare, factional fighting, Libyan annexation of the Aozou strip (June 1976–November 1979)

165. El Salvador–Honduras
Territorial dispute, border incidents (July 1976–October 1980)

166. Thailand–Cambodia
Refugee influx, regional instability, Khmer Rouge border incidents (November–December 1976)

167. El Salvador
Civil conflict; the Salvadoran civil war (January 1977–end of 1992)

168. Cambodia–Thailand
Refugee influx, regional instability; Khmer Rouge border incidents (January 1977–October 1978)

169. Zaire–Angola
Regional instability; the first invasion of Shaba (March–May 1977)

170. Israel–Lebanon
Arab-Israeli dispute, Christian-Muslim factional fighting; border incidents (mid–late 1977)

171. Ecuador–Peru
Regional rivalry, territorial dispute; border incidents (June 1977–January 1978)

172. Egypt–Libya
Regional tensions; border war (July–September 1977)

173. Argentina–Chile
Regional rivalry, territorial dispute; the Beagle Channel dispute (July 1977–November 1984)

174. Nicaragua–Costa Rica
Regional rivalry, border incidents (October 1977)

175. Chad
Internal strife, foreign intervention; the second Chad civil war (January 1978–June 1982)

176. Israel–Lebanon; PLO
Arab-Israeli tensions, PLO incursions; Israeli invasion of southern Lebanon (March–June 1978)

177. Zaire–Angola
Regional instability, Congolese dissension; the second invasion of Shaba (May 1978)

178. Nicaragua–Costa Rica
Regional rivalry, cross-border raids; border incidents (September–December 1978)

179. Tanzania–Uganda
Cross-border raids, invasion; Amin ouster (October 1978–May 1979)

180. USSR–Afghanistan
Civil war, Soviet invasion; the Afghanistan civil war (1979–)

181. Cambodia–Vietnam
Border fighting, Vietnamese invasion; the Cambodian civil war (January 1979–)

182. China–Vietnam
Regional rivalry; border war (February 1979–June 1982)

183. North Yemen–South Yemen
Border war (February 1979–February 1980)

184. Afghanistan–Pakistan
Promonarchist revolt; the Peshawar rebellion (March–July 1979)

185. Algeria–Morocco; Western Sahara
Western Sahara nationalism; border conflict (June–October 1979)

186. Israel–Syria
Arab-Israeli tensions; air incidents (June 1979–February 1980)

187. India–Bangladesh
Boundary dispute; border incidents (November 1979)

188. United States–Iran
Anti-U.S. sentiment, Islamic revolution; the hostage crisis (November 1979–January 1981)

189. Cambodia–Thailand
Khmer Rouge insurgency; border conflict (December 1979–October 1980)

190. Honduras–Nicaragua
Right-wing insurgency; the contra war (January 1980–February 1994)

191. Iran–Iraq
Regional rivalry, territorial dispute; the Iran-Iraq War (February 1980–1989)

192. Vanuatu–Espiritu Santo
Secessionist fighting (May–September 1980)

193. Ecuador–Peru
Territorial dispute; border war (January–April 1981)

194. Cameroon–Nigeria
Territorial dispute; border incident (May–July 1981)

195. Pakistan–India
Regional rivalry; border incidents, the India-Pakistan wars (July 1981–August 1982)

196. United States–Libya
Regional instability, air incidents (August 1981)

197. Poland
Labor turmoil, martial law (December 1981–February 1982)

198. Uganda
Post-Amin civil war (December 1981–1995)

199. Israel–Lebanon
Arab-Israeli conflict; Israeli military invasion
(early 1982–mid-1983)

200. Zaire–Zambia
Lake Mweru border dispute (February–September 1982)

201. United Kingdom–Argentina
Sovereignty dispute; the Falklands war
(April–June 1982)

202. Indonesia–Papua New Guinea; Irian Jaya
Secessionist warfare; border incidents (May
1982–October 1985)

203. Chad–Libya
Political instability, rebel fighting, foreign intervention; the third Chad civil war (mid-1982–)

204. Laos–Thailand
Territorial dispute; border incidents (June 1982)

205. Sri Lanka; Tamils vs. Sinhalese
Communal violence, separatist fighting; the
Tamil conflict (July 1982–)

206. Ghana–Togo
Territorial dispute; border incidents
(August–October 1982)

207. Guatemala–Mexico
Regional instability, Guatemalan civil war; border incidents (September 1982–January 1983)

208. South Africa–Lesotho
Guerrilla insurgency fears; anti-ANC raid (December 1982)

209. Sudan
Secessionist fighting, civil war; the second
Sudan civil war (January 1983–)

210. Liberia–Sierra Leone
Doe regime tensions (February–March 1983)

211. China–Vietnam
Regional rivalry; border conflict (April 1983)

212. Chad–Nigeria
Boundary/resources dispute; the Lake Chad
conflict (April–July 1983)

213. Israel–Lebanon
Arab-Israeli hostilities, Muslim-Christian factional fighting; the security zone (mid-1983–)

214. Zaire–Zambia
Regional tensions, deportations; border dispute
(September 1983–July 1984)

215. United States–Grenada
Anticommunist U.S. military invasion
(October–December 1983)

216. India–Bangladesh
Boundary dispute; border conflict (December
1983–June 1984)

217. Ecuador–Peru
Regional rivalry, territorial dispute; border conflict (January 1984)

218. Vietnam–China
Regional rivalry; border conflict (January
1984–March 1987)

219. India–Pakistan
Territorial dispute; the Siachen Glacier dispute,
the India-Pakistan wars (April 1984–September
1985)

220. Burma–Thailand; the Karens
Karen separatist insurgency, counterinsurgency
raids; border incidents (March 1984)

221. Turkey–Greece
Regional rivalry; naval incidents (March
1984–January 1988)

222. Guatemala–Mexico
Regional instability; Guatemalan civil war, border incident (April 1984)

223. Thailand–Laos
Boundary dispute; border war (June 1984–
December 1988)

224. The Kurds–Turkey
Kurdish separatist insurgency (August 1984–)

225. South Africa–Botswana
African nationalism; anti-ANC raids (October
1984–May 1986)

226. Zaire
Internal dissent; the third invasion of Shaba
(November 1984)

227. North Korea–South Korea
Cold war border incidents (November 1984)

228. Nicaragua–Costa Rica
Regional rivalry; border incidents (May–June 1985)

229. Zaire
Internal strife; the fourth invasion of Shaba (June 1985)

230. Mali–Burkina Faso
Territorial/resource dispute; border war (December 1985–January 1986)

231. India–Pakistan
Territorial dispute; the Siachen Glacier/Kashmir conflict, India-Pakistan wars (1986–)

232. United States–Libya
International terrorism fears; naval incidents (January–April 1986)

233. India–Bangladesh
Boundary dispute; the Muhuri River incidents (February–April 1986)

234. Qatar–Bahrain
Sovereignty dispute; the Hawar Islands (April 1986)

235. Nicaragua–Costa Rica
Regional rivalry; border incidents (April 1986)

236. Suriname
Guerrilla insurgency (July 1986–December 1992)

237. Togo–Ghana
Regional rivalry; attempted coup (September 1986)

238. Zaire–People's Republic of the Congo
Regional instability; border incident (January 1987)

239. Ethiopia–Somalia
Somali expansionism; the third Ogaden war (February 1987–April 1988)

240. South Africa–Zambia
African nationalism, insurgency fears; anti-ANC raid (April 1987)

241. People's Republic of the Congo
Civil unrest; army rebellion (September 1987–July 1988)

242. Uganda–Kenya
Ugandan civil war, refugee influx; border conflict (December 1987)

243. Vietnam–China
Regional rivalry, sovereignty dispute; the Spratlys dispute (March 1988)

244. Somalia
Clan-based violence; the Somalian civil war (May 1988–)

245. Burundi
Tribal-based communal violence; the Hutu conflict (August 1988–)

246. Bougainville–Papua New Guinea
Separatist insurgency (October 1988–)

247. Maldives
Attempted coup; invasion (November 1988)

248. United States–Libya
Rabat chemical plant tensions; air incident (January 1989)

249. Uganda–Kenya
Political turmoil; border conflict (March 1989)

250. Georgia–South Ossetia, Abkhazia
Post-Soviet political instability; separatist warfare (March 1989–)

251. Mauritania–Senegal
Ethnic violence (April 1989–January 1990)

252. Bosnia
Ethnic, religious warfare; the Balkans conflict (mid-1989–)

253. United States–Panama
Anti-Noriega U.S. military invasion (December 1989)

254. Liberia
Civil war (December 1989–)

255. USSR–Lithuania
Post-Soviet independence crisis (March 1990–late 1991)

256. Guinea-Bissau–Senegal
Border conflict (April–May 1990)

257. Niger–Tuaregs
Sahel pastoralist separatism (May 1990–October 1994)

258. Kyrgyzstan
Post-Soviet ethnic strife (June 1990)

259. Mali–Tuaregs
Sahel pastoralist rebellion, military coup (June 1990–)

260. Senegal
Secessionist armed insurrection; the Casamance rebellion (mid-1990–)

261. Iraq–Coalition Forces
Territorial dispute, Iraqi expansionism, the Gulf war (August 1990–March 1991)

262. Azerbaijan–Armenia; Nagorno–Karabakh
Post-Soviet strife, ethnic violence; the Nagorno-Karabakh conflict (August 1990–)

263. Rwanda
Tribal conflict, genocide, rebel invasion (September 1990–)

264. Moldova
Post-Soviet strife; Gagauz struggle for autonomy (October 1990–July 1992)

265. USSR–Latvia
Post-Soviet independence crisis (January 1991)

266. Liberia–Sierra Leone
Intervention, destabilization; Sierra Leone civil war (March 1991–)

267. Djibouti
Ethnic-based violence; civil war (November 1991–July 1993)

268. Burma–Bangladesh
Rohingya Muslim rebellion; border incidents (December 1991)

269. Iran–United Arab Emirates
Territorial dispute; the Tunb Islands dispute (April 1992)

270. North Korea–South Korea
Historical enmity; border incident (May 1992)

271. Tajikistan
Post-Soviet strife; ethnic-based civil war (May 1992–)

272. Saudi Arabia–Qatar
Post–Gulf war tensions; border incidents (September–October 1992)

273. Russia–Chechnya; the Caucasus
Post-Soviet lawlessness, separatist fighting; the Chechen war, the Caucasus conflict (October 1992–)

274. Egypt–Sudan
Territorial/resource dispute; the Halaib dispute (December 1992)

275. Iraq–the Coalition
Post–Gulf war incidents (December 1992–July 1993)

276. Burma–Bangladesh
Border incidents (March–September 1993)

277. Cyprus
Ethnic-based tensions (April 1993)

278. Yemen
Unification difficulties; civil war (November 1993–July 1994)

279. Nigeria–Cameroon
Border dispute; the Diamond Islands (December 1993–March 1994)

280. Ghana–Togo
Border incidents (January–February 1994)

281. Greece–Albania
Border tensions (April 1994)

282. Burma–Bangladesh
Border incidents (May–August 1994)

283. United States–Haiti
U.S. military invasion, reinstallation of Aristide (September 1994)

284. Iraq–the Coalition
Post–Gulf war border tensions (October 1994)

285. Taiwan–China
Communist-Nationalist dispute; shelling incident (November 1994)

286. Saudi Arabia–Yemen
Post–Gulf war border conflict (December 1994)

287. Ecuador–Peru
Regional rivalry; border conflict (January–March 1995)

288. China–the Philippines
Territorial dispute; the Paracel and Spratly islands (January–February 1995)

289. Taiwan–Vietnam
Territorial dispute; the Spratlys clash (March 1995)

290. Belize–Guatemala
Postindependence territorial dispute; border incidents (August 1995)

291. Comoros
Attempted coup (September–October 1995)

292. Eritrea–Yemen
Invasion of the Hanish Islands (November–December 1995)

Country Rankings (1999)

Country Rank in 1999 by Indicator

Military Expenditures (ME) / GNP (percent)

Rank	Country	Value	Rank	Country	Value
1	Eritrea	27.4	85	Brazil	1.9
2	Angola	21.2	86	Kenya	1.9
3	North Korea	18.8	87	Cuba	1.9
4	Oman	15.3	88	Togo	1.8
5	Saudi Arabia	14.9	89	Bolivia	1.8
6	Congo (Kinshasa)	14.4	90	Australia	1.8
7	Qatar	10.0	91	Slovakia	1.8
8	Jordan	9.2	92	Suriname	1.8
9	Ethiopia	8.8	93	Tunisia	1.8
10	Israel	8.8	94	Cameroon	1.8
11	Bahrain	8.1	95	Netherlands	1.8
12	Burma	7.8	96	Senegal	1.7
13	Kuwait	7.7	97	Uzbekistan	1.7
14	Burundi	7.0	98	Hungary	1.7
15	Syria	7.0	99	Thailand	1.7
16	Azerbaijan	6.6	100	Nigeria	1.6
17	Croatia	6.4	101	Belize	1.6
18	Yemen	6.1	102	Romania	1.6
19	Libya	NA	103	Burkina Faso	1.6
20	Pakistan	5.9	104	Denmark	1.6
21	Armenia	5.8	105	Guinea	1.6
22	Russia	5.6	106	Argentina	1.6
23	Iraq	5.5	107	Germany	1.6
24	Turkey	5.3	108	Swaziland	1.5
25	China - Taiwan	5.2	109	South Africa	1.5
26	Zimbabwe	5.0	110	Somalia	NA
27	Serbia and Montenegro	5.0	111	Estonia	1.5
28	Singapore	4.8	112	Belgium	1.4
29	Sudan	4.8	113	Benin	1.4
30	Greece	4.7	114	Trinidad and Tobago	1.4
31	Sri Lanka	4.7	115	Venezuela	1.4
32	Botswana	4.7	116	Tanzania	1.4
33	Rwanda	4.5	117	Panama	1.4
34	Bosnia and Herzegovina	4.5	118	Finland	1.4
35	Djibouti	4.3	119	Philippines	1.4
36	Morocco	4.3	120	Slovenia	1.4
37	United Arab Emirates	4.1	121	Canada	1.4
38	Cambodia	4.0	122	Bangladesh	1.3
39	Brunei	4.0	123	Belarus	1.3
40	Mauritania	4.0	124	Uruguay	1.3
41	Algeria	4.0	125	The Gambia	1.3
42	Lebanon	4.0	126	Lithuania	1.3
43	Ecuador	3.7	127	Tajikistan	1.3
44	Congo (Brazzaville)	3.5	128	Spain	1.3
45	Afghanistan	NA	129	Albania	1.3
46	Cyprus	3.4	130	Liberia	1.2
47	Turkmenistan	3.4	131	Switzerland	1.2
48	Equatorial Guinea	3.2	132	Madagascar	1.2
49	Colombia	3.2	133	Georgia	1.2
50	Sierra Leone	3.0	134	Niger	1.2
51	Ukraine	3.0	135	Nicaragua	1.2
52	United States	3.0	136	Haiti	NA
53	Chile	3.0	137	New Zealand	1.2
54	Bulgaria	3.0	138	Indonesia	1.1
55	Namibia	2.9	139	Paraguay	1.1
56	Iran	2.9	140	Papua New Guinea	1.1
57	South Korea	2.9	141	Zambia	1.0
58	Central African Republic	2.8	142	Sao Tome and Principe	1.0
59	Guinea-Bissau	2.7	143	Japan	1.0
60	France	2.7	144	Bhutan	NA
61	Egypt	2.7	145	Ireland	1.0
62	Lesotho	2.6	146	Latvia	0.9
63	India	2.5	147	Kazakhstan	0.9
64	Mozambique	2.5	148	El Salvador	0.9
65	United Kingdom	2.5	149	Cape Verde	0.9
66	Macedonia	2.5	150	Nepal	0.8
67	Chad	2.4	151	Austria	0.8
68	Gabon	2.4	152	Ghana	0.8
69	Kyrgyzstan	2.4	153	Guyana	0.8
70	Peru	2.4	154	Malta	0.8
71	Uganda	2.3	155	Ivory Coast	0.8
72	Mali	2.3	156	Jamaica	0.8
73	Vietnam	NA	157	Luxembourg	0.8
74	Sweden	2.3	158	Dominican Republic	0.7
75	Czech Republic	2.3	159	Guatemala	0.7
76	China - Mainland	2.3	160	Honduras	0.7
77	Malaysia	2.3	161	Mexico	0.6
78	Norway	2.2	162	Malawi	0.6
79	Portugal	2.1	163	Costa Rica	0.5
80	Mongolia	2.1	164	Barbados	0.5
81	Poland	2.1	165	Moldova	0.5
82	Italy	2.0	166	Mauritius	0.2
83	Laos	2.0	167	Iceland	0.0
84	Fiji	2.0			

ME per Capita (dollars)

Rank	Country	Value	Rank	Country	Value
1	Israel	1,510	85	Belize	47
2	Qatar	1,470	86	South Africa	45
3	Kuwait	1,410	87	Peru	45
4	Singapore	1,100	88	Panama	45
5	United States	1,030	89	Barbados	44
6	Saudi Arabia	996	90	Vietnam	NA
7	United Arab Emirates	935	91	Fiji	42
8	Brunei	897	92	Equatorial Guinea	40
9	Norway	742	93	Kazakhstan	40
10	Oman	726	94	Uzbekistan	38
11	China - Taiwan	690	95	Sri Lanka	38
12	Bahrain	666	96	Ecuador	38
13	France	658	97	Tunisia	38
14	United Kingdom	615	98	Egypt	36
15	Sweden	601	99	Thailand	34
16	Greece	573	100	Suriname	33
17	Denmark	524	101	Georgia	33
18	Croatia	491	102	Afghanistan	NA
19	Switzerland	469	103	Cambodia	28
20	Netherlands	445	104	Mexico	27
21	Italy	412	105	Pakistan	25
22	Cyprus	411	106	Zimbabwe	23
23	Libya	NA	107	Yemen	22
24	Germany	395	108	Congo (Brazzaville)	21
25	Australia	372	109	Albania	21
26	Belgium	352	110	Swaziland	20
27	Finland	344	111	Jamaica	19
28	Japan	342	112	Costa Rica	19
29	Luxembourg	326	113	Bolivia	18
30	Czech Republic	292	114	El Salvador	18
31	Syria	280	115	Paraguay	15
32	Canada	269	116	Dominican Republic	15
33	Angola	248	117	Mauritania	14
34	South Korea	246	118	Philippines	14
35	Portugal	240	119	Lesotho	14
36	Russia	239	120	Nigeria	13
37	Slovenia	227	121	Cape Verde	13
38	Austria	208	122	Tajikistan	13
39	Ireland	208	123	Sudan	12
40	North Korea	199	124	Rwanda	12
41	Spain	192	125	India	11
42	Slovakia	187	126	Cameroon	10
43	Lebanon	185	127	Guatemala	10
44	Hungary	185	128	Moldova	10
45	Poland	173	129	Ethiopia	9
46	Armenia	170	130	Central African Republic	8
47	Bulgaria	158	131	Burundi	8
48	New Zealand	156	132	Senegal	8
49	Turkey	154	133	Papua New Guinea	7
50	Jordan	150	134	Haiti	NA
51	Botswana	142	135	Mauritius	7
52	Chile	133	136	Guinea	7
53	Turkmenistan	122	137	Guyana	7
54	Estonia	120	138	Kenya	7
55	Azerbaijan	120	139	Indonesia	7
56	Argentina	118	140	Uganda	6
57	Macedonia	112	141	Mali	6
58	Burma	112	142	Honduras	6
59	Iran	106	143	Benin	5
60	Ukraine	103	144	Somalia	NA
61	Serbia and Montenegro	103	145	Ivory Coast	5
62	Congo (Kinshasa)	102	146	Laos	5
63	Romania	97	147	Togo	5
64	Belarus	89	148	Nicaragua	5
65	Lithuania	87	149	Mongolia	5
66	Uruguay	83	150	Mozambique	5
67	Trinidad and Tobago	78	151	Bangladesh	5
68	Malaysia	78	152	Chad	5
69	Gabon	78	153	Guinea-Bissau	4
70	Bosnia and Herzegovina	75	154	Sierra Leone	4
71	Malta	73	155	The Gambia	4
72	China - Mainland	71	156	Burkina Faso	4
73	Colombia	68	157	Tanzania	4
74	Kyrgyzstan	62	158	Zambia	3
75	Venezuela	61	159	Ghana	3
76	Algeria	60	160	Madagascar	3
77	Latvia	59	161	Sao Tome and Principe	3
78	Brazil	58	162	Niger	2
79	Cuba	57	163	Bhutan	NA
80	Iraq	57	164	Liberia	2
81	Namibia	53	165	Nepal	2
82	Eritrea	52	166	Malawi	1
83	Djibouti	51	167	Iceland	0
84	Morocco	49			

Country Rank in 1999 by Indicator — continued

ME per Soldier (dollars)

#	Country	Value	#	Country	Value
1	United States	189,000	85	Uruguay	11,400
2	Japan	180,000	86	Belize	11,400
3	United Kingdom	167,000	87	Tajikistan	11,400
4	Luxembourg	141,000	88	Armenia	11,400
5	Canada	139,000	89	Lebanon	11,300
6	Netherlands	130,000	90	Mexico	10,600
7	Australia	128,000	91	Peru	10,400
8	Kuwait	128,000	92	Philippines	10,300
9	Saudi Arabia	112,000	93	Tunisia	10,200
10	Denmark	103,000	94	Fiji	9,860
11	Sweden	103,000	95	Cameroon	9,840
12	Norway	100,000	96	Serbia and Montenegro	9,780
13	Germany	98,500	97	Central African Republic	9,710
14	Congo (Kinshasa)	93,700	98	Panama	9,540
15	France	92,400	99	Bosnia and Herzegovina	9,210
16	Qatar	88,400	100	Papua New Guinea	8,920
17	Switzerland	87,100	101	Ghana	8,890
18	Belgium	85,700	102	India	8,670
19	Singapore	73,300	103	Kenya	8,330
20	Italy	60,600	104	Ecuador	8,260
21	Brunei	59,000	105	Morocco	7,440
22	Argentina	58,900	106	El Salvador	7,330
23	New Zealand	58,700	107	Jordan	7,110
24	Ireland	55,700	108	Suriname	7,030
25	Czech Republic	55,600	109	Costa Rica	6,930
26	Finland	50,600	110	Swaziland	6,930
27	Israel	50,300	111	Vietnam	NA
28	Spain	48,700	112	Thailand	6,790
29	Oman	46,800	113	Sri Lanka	6,620
30	Bahrain	46,100	114	Sierra Leone	6,620
31	Trinidad and Tobago	46,000	115	Zimbabwe	6,570
32	Slovenia	43,600	116	Senegal	6,250
33	China - Taiwan	41,000	117	Pakistan	5,970
34	Russia	38,900	118	Mali	5,840
35	China - Mainland	37,000	119	Congo (Brazzaville)	5,840
36	Hungary	36,900	120	Mauritius	5,740
37	Turkmenistan	36,100	121	Bangladesh	5,670
38	Poland	35,700	122	Egypt	5,550
39	Croatia	34,800	123	Cambodia	5,530
40	Austria	34,400	124	Ivory Coast	5,480
41	Portugal	33,900	125	Yemen	5,430
42	United Arab Emirates	33,500	126	The Gambia	5,060
43	Brazil	33,100	127	Cape Verde	5,040
44	Namibia	30,500	128	Paraguay	4,940
45	Barbados	30,000	129	Indonesia	4,900
46	Greece	29,700	130	Burkina Faso	4,640
47	Botswana	29,600	131	Guinea	4,500
48	South Africa	28,900	132	Benin	4,490
49	Latvia	28,700	133	Bolivia	4,470
50	Slovakia	28,100	134	Honduras	4,270
51	Lithuania	26,200	135	North Korea	4,260
52	Estonia	24,700	136	Dominican Republic	4,100
53	Angola	24,600	137	Sudan	4,040
54	Kyrgyzstan	23,800	138	Guatemala	4,020
55	Libya	NA	139	Albania	3,980
56	Chile	22,600	140	Niger	3,930
57	Cyprus	22,100	141	Moldova	3,900
58	Kazakhstan	20,300	142	Tanzania	3,490
59	Nigeria	20,200	143	Mauritania	3,360
60	Venezuela	18,900	144	Iraq	2,980
61	Bulgaria	17,800	145	Djibouti	2,810
62	Malaysia	17,500	146	Uganda	2,800
63	South Korea	17,400	147	Guyana	2,530
64	Colombia	17,200	148	Togo	2,300
65	Jamaica	17,100	149	Madagascar	2,250
66	Afghanistan	NA	150	Rwanda	2,170
67	Uzbekistan	15,500	151	Malawi	1,990
68	Algeria	15,200	152	Nicaragua	1,990
69	Ukraine	15,000	153	Zambia	1,820
70	Iran	15,000	154	Ethiopia	1,780
71	Lesotho	14,500	155	Somalia	NA
72	Equatorial Guinea	14,400	156	Nepal	1,250
73	Syria	14,300	157	Chad	1,230
74	Macedonia	14,200	158	Burundi	1,230
75	Belarus	14,200	159	Liberia	NA
76	Malta	14,200	160	Eritrea	966
77	Burma	13,500	161	Mongolia	901
78	Gabon	13,300	162	Guinea-Bissau	800
79	Romania	12,900	163	Laos	563
80	Turkey	12,600	164	Bhutan	NA
81	Cuba	12,600	165	Sao Tome and Principe	422
82	Azerbaijan	12,400	166	Haiti	NA
83	Georgia	11,800	167	Iceland	0
84	Mozambique	11,700			

Armed Forces (AF) per 1000 Persons (soldiers)

#	Country	Value	#	Country	Value
1	Eritrea	54.0	85	Bhutan	4.1
2	North Korea	46.8	86	Germany	4.0
3	Israel	30.1	87	Colombia	4.0
4	United Arab Emirates	27.9	88	Spain	3.9
5	Jordan	21.1	89	Algeria	3.9
6	Syria	19.5	90	Ireland	3.7
7	Greece	19.3	91	Tunisia	3.7
8	Iraq	19.1	92	Chad	3.7
9	Cyprus	18.6	93	United Kingdom	3.7
10	Djibouti	18.0	94	Congo (Brazzaville)	3.6
11	Libya	17.0	95	Dominican Republic	3.6
12	China - Taiwan	16.8	96	Zimbabwe	3.5
13	Qatar	16.7	97	Netherlands	3.4
14	Lebanon	16.4	98	Turkmenistan	3.4
15	Oman	15.5	99	Lithuania	3.3
16	Brunei	15.2	100	Somalia	NA
17	Singapore	15.0	101	Venezuela	3.2
18	Armenia	14.9	102	Paraguay	3.1
19	Bahrain	14.5	103	Sudan	3.1
20	South Korea	14.1	104	Australia	2.9
21	Croatia	14.1	105	Guyana	2.9
22	Turkey	12.2	106	Swaziland	2.8
23	Kuwait	11.0	107	Equatorial Guinea	2.8
24	Serbia and Montenegro	10.5	108	Georgia	2.8
25	Angola	10.1	109	Costa Rica	2.7
26	Azerbaijan	9.7	110	New Zealand	2.6
27	Laos	9.3	111	Kyrgyzstan	2.6
28	Saudi Arabia	8.9	112	Mexico	2.6
29	Bulgaria	8.9	113	Nicaragua	2.5
30	Burma	8.3	114	Cape Verde	2.5
31	Bosnia and Herzegovina	8.1	115	El Salvador	2.5
32	Macedonia	7.9	116	Moldova	2.5
33	Romania	7.6	117	Uzbekistan	2.5
34	Norway	7.4	118	Guatemala	2.4
35	Uruguay	7.3	119	Luxembourg	2.3
36	France	7.1	120	Togo	2.3
37	Portugal	7.1	121	Uganda	2.2
38	Iran	7.1	122	Latvia	2.1
39	Ukraine	6.9	123	Argentina	2.0
40	Burundi	6.8	124	Kazakhstan	2.0
41	Italy	6.8	125	Canada	1.9
42	Finland	6.8	126	China - Mainland	1.9
43	Slovakia	6.7	127	Japan	1.9
44	Morocco	6.6	128	Zambia	1.8
45	Sao Tome and Principe	6.5	129	Afghanistan	NA
46	Egypt	6.4	130	Brazil	1.8
47	Belarus	6.3	131	Namibia	1.7
48	Vietnam	6.2	132	Trinidad and Tobago	1.7
49	Russia	6.1	133	Liberia	NA
50	Austria	6.0	134	Guinea	1.6
51	Chile	5.9	135	South Africa	1.6
52	Sweden	5.9	136	Barbados	1.5
53	Gabon	5.9	137	Nepal	1.5
54	Sri Lanka	5.8	138	Philippines	1.3
55	Rwanda	5.6	139	Senegal	1.3
56	Mongolia	5.6	140	Indonesia	1.3
57	Guinea-Bissau	5.6	141	Madagascar	1.3
58	United States	5.4	142	Honduras	1.3
59	Switzerland	5.4	143	India	1.3
60	Czech Republic	5.3	144	Mauritius	1.3
61	Albania	5.2	145	Benin	1.2
62	Slovenia	5.2	146	Jamaica	1.1
63	Malta	5.1	147	Tajikistan	1.1
64	Denmark	5.1	148	Congo (Kinshasa)	1.1
65	Cambodia	5.0	149	Tanzania	1.0
66	Hungary	5.0	150	Cameroon	1.0
67	Thailand	4.9	151	Mali	1.0
68	Estonia	4.9	152	Ivory Coast	1.0
69	Poland	4.8	153	Lesotho	0.9
70	Ethiopia	4.8	154	Central African Republic	0.9
71	Botswana	4.8	155	Bangladesh	0.9
72	Panama	4.7	156	Papua New Guinea	0.8
73	Suriname	4.7	157	Kenya	0.8
74	Ecuador	4.6	158	Burkina Faso	0.8
75	Cuba	4.5	159	The Gambia	0.8
76	Malaysia	4.4	160	Nigeria	0.6
77	Peru	4.3	161	Niger	0.6
78	Fiji	4.3	162	Sierra Leone	0.6
79	Pakistan	4.3	163	Malawi	0.5
80	Mauritania	4.2	164	Mozambique	0.4
81	Belize	4.1	165	Ghana	0.4
82	Bolivia	4.1	166	Haiti	0
83	Belgium	4.1	167	Iceland	0
84	Yemen	4.1			

Country Rank in 1999 by Indicator — continued

Arms Exports (AE) (millions of dollars)

Rank	Country	Value	Rank	Country	Value
1	United States	33,000	85	Ecuador	0
2	United Kingdom	5,200	86	Egypt	0
3	Russia	3,100	87	El Salvador	0
4	France	2,900	88	Equatorial Guinea	0
5	Germany	1,900	89	Estonia	0
6	Sweden	675	90	Ethiopia	0
7	Israel	600	91	Fiji	0
8	Australia	550	92	Gabon	0
9	Canada	550	93	The Gambia	0
10	Ukraine	550	94	Ghana	0
11	Italy	380	95	Guatemala	0
12	China - Mainland	320	96	Guinea	0
13	Belarus	310	97	Guinea-Bissau	0
14	Bulgaria	200	98	Guyana	0
15	North Korea	140	99	Haiti	0
16	Netherlands	140	100	Honduras	0
17	Indonesia	100	101	Iceland	0
18	Greece	90	102	Iraq	0
19	Czech Republic	80	103	Ireland	0
20	Spain	70	104	Ivory Coast	0
21	Turkey	70	105	Jamaica	0
22	Finland	50	106	Jordan	0
23	Switzerland	50	107	Kenya	0
24	Romania	40	108	Kuwait	0
25	Austria	30	109	Kyrgyzstan	0
26	Belgium	30	110	Laos	0
27	Georgia	30	111	Latvia	0
28	Libya	30	112	Lebanon	0
29	Mexico	30	113	Lesotho	0
30	Poland	30	114	Liberia	0
31	South Africa	30	115	Lithuania	0
32	Brazil	20	116	Luxembourg	0
33	China - Taiwan	20	117	Macedonia	0
34	Eritrea	20	118	Madagascar	0
35	Japan	20	119	Malawi	0
36	South Korea	20	120	Malaysia	0
37	Moldova	20	121	Mali	0
38	Norway	20	122	Malta	0
39	Serbia and Montenegro	20	123	Mauritania	0
40	Singapore	20	124	Mauritius	0
41	Chile	10	125	Mongolia	0
42	Croatia	10	126	Morocco	0
43	Denmark	10	127	Mozambique	0
44	Hungary	10	128	Namibia	0
45	India	10	129	Nepal	0
46	Iran	10	130	New Zealand	0
47	Kazakhstan	10	131	Nicaragua	0
48	Pakistan	10	132	Niger	0
49	Slovakia	10	133	Nigeria	0
50	Uzbekistan	10	134	Oman	0
51	Philippines	5	135	Panama	0
52	Afghanistan	0	136	Papua New Guinea	0
53	Albania	0	137	Paraguay	0
54	Algeria	0	138	Peru	0
55	Angola	0	139	Portugal	0
56	Argentina	0	140	Qatar	0
57	Armenia	0	141	Rwanda	0
58	Azerbaijan	0	142	Sao Tome and Principe	0
59	Bahrain	0	143	Saudi Arabia	0
60	Bangladesh	0	144	Senegal	0
61	Barbados	0	145	Sierra Leone	0
62	Belize	0	146	Slovenia	0
63	Benin	0	147	Somalia	0
64	Bhutan	0	148	Sri Lanka	0
65	Bolivia	0	149	Sudan	0
66	Bosnia and Herzegovina	0	150	Suriname	0
67	Botswana	0	151	Swaziland	0
68	Brunei	0	152	Syria	0
69	Burkina Faso	0	153	Tajikistan	0
70	Burma	0	154	Tanzania	0
71	Burundi	0	155	Thailand	0
72	Cambodia	0	156	Togo	0
73	Cameroon	0	157	Trinidad and Tobago	0
74	Cape Verde	0	158	Tunisia	0
75	Central African Republic	0	159	Turkmenistan	0
76	Chad	0	160	Uganda	0
77	Colombia	0	161	United Arab Emirates	0
78	Congo (Kinshasa)	0	162	Uruguay	0
79	Congo (Brazzaville)	0	163	Venezuela	0
80	Costa Rica	0	164	Vietnam	0
81	Cuba	0	165	Yemen	0
82	Cyprus	0	166	Zambia	0
83	Djibouti	0	167	Zimbabwe	0
84	Dominican Republic	0			

Arms Imports (AI) (millions of dollars)

Rank	Country	Value	Rank	Country	Value
1	Saudi Arabia	7,700	85	Somalia	20
2	Turkey	3,200	86	Armenia	10
3	Japan	3,000	87	Azerbaijan	10
4	China - Taiwan	2,600	88	Bolivia	10
5	United Kingdom	2,600	89	Bulgaria	10
6	Israel	2,400	90	Chad	10
7	South Korea	2,200	91	Croatia	10
8	Greece	1,900	92	El Salvador	10
9	United States	1,600	93	Estonia	10
10	Germany	1,300	94	Georgia	10
11	Australia	1,100	95	Honduras	10
12	Switzerland	1,100	96	Iceland	10
13	Canada	1,000	97	Jamaica	10
14	Pakistan	1,000	98	Lebanon	10
15	Singapore	950	99	Paraguay	10
16	United Arab Emirates	950	100	Sierra Leone	10
17	Malaysia	925	101	Slovenia	10
18	France	800	102	Sudan	10
19	Netherlands	775	103	Suriname	10
20	Spain	750	104	Tunisia	10
21	Kuwait	725	105	Turkmenistan	10
22	Egypt	700	106	Ukraine	10
23	India	700	107	Uruguay	10
24	Italy	700	108	Zimbabwe	10
25	China - Mainland	675	109	Benin	5
26	New Zealand	575	110	Cambodia	5
27	Algeria	550	111	Cameroon	5
28	Norway	480	112	Cape Verde	5
29	Russia	470	113	Iraq	5
30	Indonesia	450	114	Kenya	5
31	Finland	400	115	Latvia	5
32	Angola	350	116	Mozambique	5
33	Belgium	350	117	Panama	5
34	Cyprus	340	118	Tanzania	5
35	Thailand	330	119	Afghanistan	0
36	Venezuela	310	120	Barbados	0
37	Denmark	290	121	Belarus	0
38	Ethiopia	270	122	Belize	0
39	Sweden	230	123	Bhutan	0
40	Czech Republic	220	124	Burkina Faso	0
41	Syria	210	125	Burundi	0
42	Romania	200	126	Central African Republic	0
43	Brazil	180	127	Congo, Rep. of (Brazzaville)	0
44	Eritrea	170	128	Costa Rica	0
45	Kazakhstan	160	129	Cuba	0
46	Mexico	160	130	Djibouti	0
47	Iran	150	131	Equatorial Guinea	0
48	Morocco	130	132	Fiji	0
49	Qatar	120	133	Gabon	0
50	Congo (Kinshasa)	110	134	The Gambia	0
51	Philippines	110	135	Ghana	0
52	Chile	100	136	Guatemala	0
53	Argentina	90	137	Guinea	0
54	Bangladesh	80	138	Guinea-Bissau	0
55	Hungary	80	139	Guyana	0
56	Bahrain	70	140	Haiti	0
57	Jordan	70	141	Ivory Coast	0
58	Vietnam	70	142	Kyrgyzstan	0
59	Burma	60	143	Laos	0
60	Colombia	60	144	Lesotho	0
61	Portugal	60	145	Liberia	0
62	Luxembourg	50	146	Madagascar	0
63	South Africa	50	147	Malawi	0
64	Bosnia and Herzegovina	40	148	Mali	0
65	Botswana	40	149	Malta	0
66	Ireland	40	150	Mauritania	0
67	Poland	40	151	Mauritius	0
68	Sri Lanka	40	152	Moldova	0
69	Albania	30	153	Mongolia	0
70	Austria	30	154	Nepal	0
71	North Korea	30	155	Nicaragua	0
72	Oman	30	156	Niger	0
73	Peru	30	157	Nigeria	0
74	Rwanda	30	158	Papua New Guinea	0
75	Uganda	30	159	Sao Tome and Principe	0
76	Yemen	30	160	Senegal	0
77	Brunei	20	161	Serbia and Montenegro	0
78	Dominican Republic	20	162	Swaziland	0
79	Ecuador	20	163	Tajikistan	0
80	Libya	20	164	Togo	0
81	Lithuania	20	165	Trinidad and Tobago	0
82	Macedonia	20	166	Uzbekistan	0
83	Namibia	20	167	Zambia	0
84	Slovakia	20			

Nobel Peace Prize Winners 2003–1901

2003	*Shirin Ebadi*, Iranian lawyer, for her efforts for democracy and human rights
2002	*Jimmy Carter, Jr.*, former President of the United States, for his decades of untiring effort to find peaceful solutions to international conflicts, to advance democracy and human rights, and to promote economic and social development
2001	*United Nations,* New York, NY, United States *Kofi Aannan,* United Nations Secretary General
2000	*Kim Dae Jung,* for his work for democracy and human rights in South Korea and in East Asia in general, and for peace and reconciliation with North Korea in particular
1999	*Doctors without Borders (Médecins sans Frontières),* Brussels, Belgium
1998	*John Hume* and *David Trimble,* for their efforts to find a peaceful solution to the conflict in Northern Ireland (awarded jointly)
1997	*International Campaign to Ban Landmines (ICBL)* and *Jody Williams,* for their work for the banning and clearing of anti-personnel mines (awarded jointly)
1996	*Carlos Felipe Ximenes Belo* and *Jose Ramos-Horta,* for their work toward a just and peaceful solution to the conflict in East Timor (awarded jointly)
1995	*Joseph Rotblat* and the *Pugwash Conferences on Science and World Affairs,* for their efforts to diminish the part played by nuclear arms in international politics and in the longer run to eliminate such arms (awarded jointly)
1994	*Yasser Arafat,* Chairman of the Executive Committee of the PLO, President of the Palestinian National Authority; *Shimon Peres,* Foreign Minister of Israel; and *Yitzhak Rabin,* Prime Minister of Israel; for their efforts to create peace in the Middle East (awarded jointly)
1993	*Nelson Mandela,* leader of the ANC, and *Fredrik Willem De Klerk,* President of the Republic of South Africa (awarded jointly)
1992	*Rigoberta Menchu Tum,* Guatemala, campaigner for human rights, especially for indigenous peoples
1991	*Aung San Suu Kyi,* Burma, oppositional leader, human rights advocate
1990	*Mikhail Sergeyevich Gorbachev,* President of the USSR, for helping bring the Cold War to an end
1989	*The 14th Dalai Lama (Tenzin Gyatso),* Tibet, religious and political leader of the Tibetan people
1988	*The United Nations Peace-Keeping Forces,* New York, NY, United States
1987	*Oscar Arias Sanchez,* Costa Rica, President of Costa Rica, initiator of peace negotiations in Central America
1986	*Elie Wiesel,* United States, Chairman of "The President's Commission on the Holocaust," author, humanitarian

1985   *International Physicians for the Prevention of Nuclear War,* Boston, MA, United States

1984   *Desmond Mpilo Tutu,* South Africa, Bishop of Johannesburg and former Secretary General of the South African Council of Churches (SACC), for his work against apartheid

1983   *Lech Walesa,* Poland, founder of Solidarity, campaigner for human rights

1982   *Alva Myrdal,* former Cabinet Minister, diplomat, delegate to United Nations General Assembly on Disarmament, writer; and *Alfonso García Robles,* diplomat, delegate to the United Nations General Assembly on Disarmament, former Secretary for Foreign Affairs (awarded jointly)

1981   *Office of the United Nations High Commissioner for Refugees,* Geneva, Switzerland

1980   *Adolfo Perez Esquivel,* Argentina, architect, sculptor and human rights leader

1979   *Mother Teresa,* India, leader of the Order of the Missionaries of Charity

1978   *Mohamed Anwar Al-Sadat,* President of the Arab Republic of Egypt, and *Menachem Begin,* Prime Minister of Israel, for jointly negotiating peace between Egypt and Israel (divided equally)

1977   *Amnesty International,* London, Great Britain, a worldwide organization for the protection of the rights of prisoners of conscience

1976   *Betty Williams* and *Mairead Corrigan,* founders of the Northern Ireland Peace Movement (later renamed Community of Peace People)

1975   *Andrei Dmitrievich Sakharov,* Soviet nuclear physicist, campaigner for human rights

1974   *Seán Mac Bride,* President of the International Peace Bureau, Geneva, and the Commission of Namibia, United Nations, New York; and *Eisaku Sato,* Prime Minister of Japan (divided equally)

1973   *Henry A. Kissinger,* Secretary of State, State Department, Washington, DC; and *Le Duc Tho,* Democratic Republic of Viet Nam (who declined the prize) for jointly negotiating the Vietnam peace accord in 1973 (awarded jointly)

1972   The prize money for 1972 was allocated to the Main Fund.

1971   *Willy Brandt,* Federal Republic of Germany, Chancellor of the Federal Republic of Germany, initiator of West Germany's *Ostpolitik,* embodying a new attitude towards Eastern Europe and East Germany

1970   *Norman Borlaug,* led research at the International Maize and Wheat Improvement Center, Mexico City

1969   *International Labour Organization (ILO),* Geneva

1968   *René Cassin,* President of the European Court for Human Rights

1967–1966   The prize money was allocated to the Main Fund ($\frac{1}{3}$) and to the Special Fund ($\frac{2}{3}$) of this prize section.

1965   *United Nations Children's Fund (UNICEF),* New York, founded by the UN in 1946, an international aid organization

1964   *Martin Luther King Jr.,* leader of the Southern Christian Leadership Conference, campaigner for civil rights

1963   *Comité International de la Croix-Rouge (International Committee of the Red Cross),* Geneva, founded 1863; and *Ligue des Sociétés de la Croix-Rouge (League of Red Cross Societies),* Geneva (divided equally)

1962   *Linus Carl Pauling,* California Institute of Technology, Pasadena, campaigner especially for an end to nuclear weapons tests

1961   *Dag Hjalmar Agne Carl Hammarskjöld,* Secretary General of the United Nations (awarded the prize posthumously)

1960   *Albert John Lutuli,* President of the South African liberation movement, the African National Congress

1959   *Philip J. Noel-Baker,* Great Britain, Member of Parliament, lifelong ardent worker for international peace and cooperation

1958   *Georges Henri Pire,* Belgium, Father of the Dominican Order, leader of the relief organization for refugees, l'Europe du Coeur au Service du Monde

1957   Lester Bowles Pearson, former Secretary of State for External Affairs of Canada, President, 7th Session of the United Nations General Assembly

1956–1955   The prize money was allocated to the Main Fund ($\frac{1}{3}$) and to the Special Fund ($\frac{2}{3}$) of this prize section.

1954   *Office of the United Nations High Commissioner for Refugees,* Geneva, an international relief organization founded by the UN in 1951

1953   *George Catlett Marshall,* General, President of the American Red Cross, former Secretary of State and of Defense, Delegate to the UN, originator of the *Marshall Plan*

1952   *Albert Schweitzer,* missionary surgeon, founder of Lambaréné Hospital in République du Gabon

1951   *Léon Jouhaux,* France, President of the trade union CGT Force Ouvrière, President of the International Committee of the European Council, Vice President of the International Confederation of Free Trade Unions, Vice President of the World Federation of Trade Unions, member of the ILO Council, delegate to the UN

1950   *Ralph Bunche,* professor at Harvard University, Cambridge, MA, Director of the UN Division of Trusteeship, Acting Mediator in Palestine, 1948

1949   *Lord John Boyd Orr of Brechin,* physician, alimentary politician, prominent organizer and Director General of the Food and Agricultural Organization, President of the National Peace Council and World Union of Peace Organizations

1948   The prize money was allocated to the Main Fund ($\frac{1}{3}$) and to the Special Fund ($\frac{2}{3}$) of this prize section.

1947   *The Friends Service Council (The Quakers),* London, founded in 1647; and *The American Friends Service Committee (The Quakers),* Washington, first official meeting held in 1672 (awarded jointly)

1946   *Emily Greene Balch,* former Professor of History and Sociology, Honorary International President Women's International League for Peace and Freedom; and *John Raleigh Mott,* Chairman of the First International Missionary Council, President of the World Alliance of Young Men's Christian Associations (divided equally)

1945   *Cordell Hull,* former Secretary of State, one of the initiators of the United Nations

1944   *Comité International de la Croix-Rouge (International Committee of the Red Cross)*

1943–1939   The prize money was allocated to the Main Fund ($\frac{1}{3}$) and to the Special Fund ($\frac{2}{3}$) of this prize section.

1938   *Office International Nansen Pour les Réfugiés (Nansen International Office for Refugees),* an international relief organization in Geneva started by Fridtjof Nansen in 1921

1937   *Cecil of Chelwood, Viscount (Lord Edgar Algernon Robert Gascoyne Cecil),* writer, former Lord Privy Seal, founder and President of the International Peace Campaign

1936   *Carlos Saavedra Lamas,* foreign minister, President of the Société des Nations (League of Nations), meditator in a conflict between Paraguay and Bolivia in 1935

1935   *Carl Von Ossietzky,* journalist (with *Die Weltbühne,* among others), pacifist

1934   *Arthur Henderson,* former Foreign Secretary, Chairman of the League of Nations Disarmament Conference, 1932–1934.

1933   *Sir Norman Angell (Ralph Lane),* writer, member of the Commission Exécutive de la Société des Nations (Executive Committee of the League of Nations) and the National Peace Council, author of the book *The Great Illusion,* among others

1932   The prize money for 1932 was allocated to the Special Fund of this prize section.

1931   *Jane Addams,* sociologist, International President of the Women's International League for Peace and Freedom; and *Nicholas Murray Butler,* President of Columbia University, promoter of the Briand-Kellogg Pact (divided equally)

1930   *Lars Olof Nathan (Jonathan) Söderblom,* Archbishop, leader of the ecumenical movement

1929   *Frank Billings Kellogg,* former Secretary of State, negotiated the Briand-Kellogg Pact

1928   The prize money for 1928 was allocated to the Special Fund of this prize section.

1927   *Ferdinand Buisson,* former Professor at the Sorbonne University, Paris, founder and President of the Ligue des Droits de l'Homme (League for Human Rights); and *Ludwig Quidde,* historian, professor at Berlin University, Member of Germany's constituent assembly 1919, delegate to numerous peace conferences (divided equally)

1926   *Aristide Briand,* Foreign Minister, negotiator of the Locarno Treaty and the Briand-Kellogg Pact; and *Gustav Stresemann,* former Lord High Chancellor (Reichs-kanzler), Foreign Minister, negotiator of the Locarno Treaty (awarded jointly)

1925   *Sir Austen Chamberlain,* Foreign Minister, negotiator of the Locarno Treaty; and *Charles Gates Dawes,* Vice President of the United States of America, Chairman of the Allied Reparation Commission, originator of the *Dawes Plan* (awarded jointly)

1924–1923   The prize money for 1924–1923 was allocated to the Special Fund of this prize section.

1922   *Fridtjof Nansen,* Norway, scientist, explorer, Norwegian delegate to Société des Nations (League of Nations), originator of the Nansen passports (for refugees)

1921   *Karl Hjalmar Branting,* Prime Minister, Swedish delegate to the Conseil de la Société des Nations (Council of the League of Nations); and *Christian Lous Lange,* Secretary General of the Inter-Parliamentary Union, Brussels (divided equally)

1920   *Léon Victor Auguste Bourgeois,* France, former Secretary of State, President of the Parliament (Sénat), President of the Conseil de la Société des Nations (Council of the League of Nations)

1919   *Thomas Woodrow Wilson,* President of the United States, founder of the Société des Nations (League of Nations)

1918   The prize money for 1918 was allocated to the Special Fund of this prize section.

1917   *Comité International de la Croix Rouge (International Committee of the Red Cross),* Geneva

1916–1914   The prize money for 1916–1914 was allocated to the Special Fund of this prize section.

1913   *Henri La Fontaine,* Belgium, member of the Belgian Parliament (Sénateur), President of the Permanent International Peace Bureau, Berne

1912   *Elihu Root,* former Secretary of State, initiator of several arbitration agreements

1911   *Tobias Michael Carel Asser,* the Netherlands, Cabinet Minister, member of the Privy Council, initiator of the International Conferences of Private Law at the Hague; and *Alfred Hermann Fried,* Austria, journalist, founder of the peace journal *Die Waffen Nieder* (later renamed *Die Friedenswarte*) (divided equally)

1910   *Bureau International Permanent de la Paix (Permanent International Peace Bureau),* Bern

1909   *Auguste Marie François Beernaert,* Belgium, former Prime Minister, member of the Belgian Parliament, member of the Cour Internationale d'Arbitrage (International Court of Arbitration) at the Hague; and *Paul Henribenjamin Balluet D'estournelles de Constant, Baron de Constant de Rebecque,* France, member of the French Parliament (Sénateur), founder and President of the French parliamentary group for international arbitration (groupe parlementaire de l'arbitrage international), founder of the Comité de Défense des Intérêtsnationaux et de Conciliation Internationale (Committee for the Defense of National Interests and International Conciliation) (divided equally)

1908   *Klas Pontus Arnoldson,* Sweden, writer, former member of the Swedish Parliament, founder of the Swedish Peace and Arbitration League; and *Fredrik Bajer,* Denmark, member of the Danish Parliament, Honorary President of the Permanent International Peace Bureau, Berne (divided equally)

1907   *Ernesto Teodoro Moneta,* Italy, President of the Lombard League of Peace; and *Louis Renault,* France, professor of International Law, Sorbonne University, Paris (divided equally)

1906   *Theodore Roosevelt,* President of the United States, drew up the 1905 peace treaty between Russia and Japan

1905   *Baroness Bertha Sophie Felicita von Suttner* née *Countess Kinsky von Chinic und Tettau,* Austria, writer, Honorary President of the Permanent International Peace Bureau, Berne, author of *Die Waffen Nieder* (Lay Down Your Arms)

1904   *Institut de Droit International (Institute of International Law),* Gent, Belgium, a scientific society

1903   *Sir William Randal Cremer,* Great Britain, member of the British Parliament, Secretary of the International Arbitration League

1902   *Élie Ducommun,* Switzerland, Honorary Secretary of the Permanent International Peace Bureau, Berne; and *Charles Albert Gobat,* Switzerland, Secretary General of the Inter-Parliamentary Union, Berne; Honorary Secretary of the Permanent International Peace Bureau, Berne (divided equally)

1901   *Jean Henri Dunant,* Switzerland, founder of the International Committee of the Red Cross, Geneva, initiator of the Geneva Convention (Convention de Genève); and *Frédéric Passy,* France, founder and President of the first French peace society (since 1889 it has been called the Société Francaise pour l'arbitrage entre nations) (divided equally)